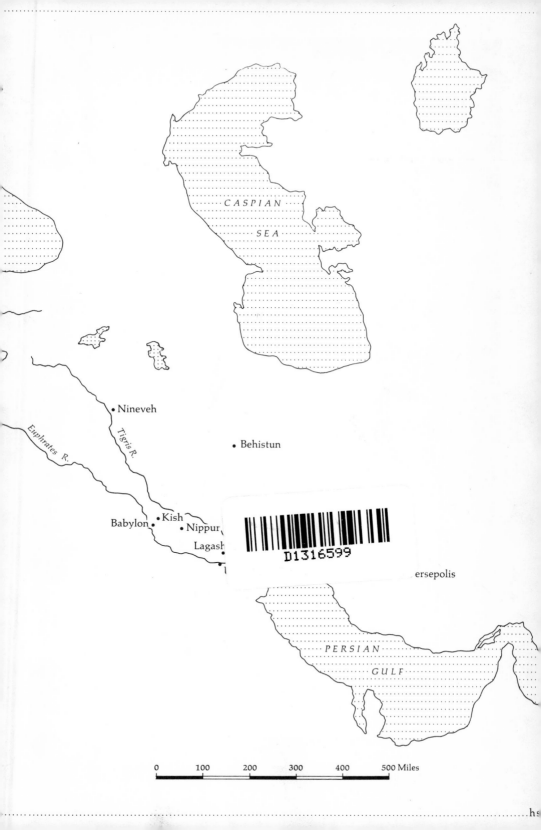

CASPIAN

SEA

• Nineveh

• Behistun

Euphrates R.

Tigris R.

Babylon • • Kish
        • Nippur
      Lagash

ersepolis

PERSIAN

GULF

0   100   200   300   400   500 Miles

LIBRARIES AND
LIBRARIANSHIP IN THE WEST

McGRAW-HILL SERIES IN LIBRARY EDUCATION

Jean Key Gates, Consulting Editor
University of South Florida

LIBRARIES AND LIBRARIANSHIP IN THE WEST
A Brief History

Sidney L. Jackson

Professor of Library Science
Kent State University

McGraw-Hill Book Company

New York   St. Louis   San Francisco   Düsseldorf
Johannesburg   Kuala Lumpur   London   Mexico   Montreal
New Delhi   Panama   Paris   São Paulo   Singapore   Sydney   Tokyo   Toronto

LIBRARIES AND LIBRARIANSHIP IN THE WEST: A BRIEF HISTORY

1 2 3 4 5 6 7 8 9 0   KPKP   7 9 8 7 6 5 4 3

Library of Congress Cataloging in Publication Data
Jackson, Sidney Louis, date
Libraries and librarianship in the West.

(McGraw-Hill series in library education)
Bibliography: p.
1. Libraries—History.   2. Library science—
History.   I.   Title.
Z721.J245   021'.009   73-13619
ISBN 0-07-032118-3

This book was set in Elegante by Rocappi, Inc.
The editors were Janis Yates and James R. Belser;
the designer was J. E. O'Connor;
and the production supervisor was Leroy A. Young.
Kingsport Press, Inc., was printer and binder.

ACKNOWLEDGMENTS

Permission   is gratefully acknowledged to use here material already published elsewhere in slightly altered form, as follows: Academic Press, Inc. (London) Ltd., for *International Library Review,* 3:67–76, 1971; American Library Association, for *Library Resources and Technical Services,* Fall 1970, pp. 579–581; Association of American Library Schools, for *Journal of Education for Librarianship,* 11:-344–350, 1970–1971; *Journal of Library History,* for *Journal of Library History,* 1:89–100, 1966, 3:185–200, 1967, *Proceedings* of Library History Seminar No. 3, pp. 17–25, 1968, and *Proceedings* of Library History Seminar No. 4, pp. 109–114, 1971; The Library Association, for *Library Association Record,* 72:95–96, 1970; *Libri,* for *Libri,* 18:35–50, 1968; Marcel Dekker, Inc., for *The Encyclopedia of Library and Information Science* (© 1970, All Rights Reserved), 4:434–437; Stechert-Hafner, Inc. for *Stechert-Hafner Book News,* 22:37–38, 1967, 23:65–67, 1968, 24:65–66, 133–134, 1970, 25:1–3, 1970; The University of Chicago Press, for *Library Quarterly* (© 1969, All Rights Reserved), 39:253–270. Also much appreciated is the permission to use illustrations, granted by the Bettmann Archive, the Cambridge University Press, and Macmillan & Co., Ltd.

To my wife
and our children

"The most responsible person . . . among you, and also the most careful, will be he who may be entrusted by the emperor with the custody of his library, . . . a person of proved knowledge, . . . grave and adapted to great affairs, and ready to reply to all applications for information . . ."

—from a letter (in Greek) of A.D. 300, offering advice to the Chief Chamberlain of the imperial Roman court.

". . . vita omnium spiritualium hominum sine libris nichil est."
("for men of spiritual bent, life without books is nothing.")

—from a twelfth-century catalog listing the 143 codexes in a German monastery library.

"La Magesté Imperialle a souvent taché de resister aux susdictz abuz, et par les edictz, tant que en elle a esté, a souvent faict oster hors des mains des simples gens les susdictz pernicieux livres . . . Mais que proufittent les loix souvent publiees et jamais observees?"

("The Throne has often tried to resist the above-mentioned abuses, and by a few edicts to keep the cited pernicious books out of the hand of the common people. . . . But what use are laws often published and never observed?")

—from the preface to the 1558 Index of Prohibited Books issued at the University of Louvain.

CONTENTS

LIST OF ILLUSTRATIONS

PREFACE

This book was written in an attempt to fill a gap. If one ignored the major historical resources in other languages (which few United States students read), notably the *Handbuch der Bibliothekswissenschaft,* edited by Fritz Milkau and others (2d ed., Leipzig: Harrassowitz, 1952–1957; *Registerband,* 1965), it was plain that the goodly company of works available did not meet all fundamental needs. The most nearly comprehensive treatment was Elmer C. Johnson's *A History of Libraries in the Western World* (Scarecrow, 1965), which remains in its second edition (Scarecrow, 1970) solid and attractive reading but continues as announced to cover only libraries. Its attention to librarianship is very limited; numerous important theorists are not even mentioned. Furthermore, the predominant organization by type of library hampers the analysis of crosscurrents between libraries and life and thought, particularly the development of the image of the library and librarian. The aim here has been to tie it all together.

In the present offering, "the West" is used conventionally: European civilization, with its Near Eastern ancestors and its Western Hemisphere progeny. The limitation is practical. To try to "cover" even the West may prove to be too much for one person; to go beyond would be rash. Yet an understanding of those lands "beyond" would be most valuable to us all. Let us hope that someone will soon try to provide it.

The phrase "libraries and librarianship" has been fashioned deliberately. "Libraries" is a term covering book collections of every breed. The focus here is upon those utilized not only by their owners but by other persons. This social aspect of the institution is largely responsible for the emergence of some of the skills incorporated in "librarianship," and for some aspects of the professional spirit and artistry which are sustained by and spur advance in the skills. To bring out such relationships between libraries and society is one of the hopes behind this effort.

Since no more is intended than a general introduction, and the pertinent literature is substantial, documentation within has been confined to quotations from original sources or very close equivalents thereof.

Like all serious studies, this one rests very largely on the fruit of past labor, selected and treated according to the author's judgment. The outstanding single resource, seldom acknowledged within, is the above-mentioned *Handbuch der Bibliothekswissenschaft*. Also drawn upon freely, though without explicit credit, were the useful outline histories by Alfred Hessel (*A History of Libraries*, translated by R. Peiss, New Brunswick, N.J.: Scarecrow, 1955) and Joris Vorstius (*Grundzüge der Bibliotheksgeschichte*, 5th ed., 1954, and 6th ed., revised by S. Joost, 1969, Leipzig: Harrassowitz), Arnim Graesel's *Handbuch der Bibliothekslehre* (2d ed., Leipzig: Weber, 1902), and the numerous essays by Vleeschauwer in his unique organ, *Mousaion*. Often convenient for facts were Elmer D. Johnson's *Libraries in the Western World* (New York: Scarecrow, 1965), Josephine M. Smith's *Chronology of Librarianship* (Metuchen, N.J.: Scarecrow, 1968), and the standard reference tools.

One does not close the preliminaries decently without thanking those whose services made the task easier. The book would never have been written without the time authorized and protected by Library School Dean Guy A. Marco, and the cooperation of the Kent State University administration. It owes a great deal to several graduate assistants—in particular Luciana Marulli, who laid the basis for the index, and Susan Masirovits, who gave indispensable help with materials on Spanish America. An asset beyond measure was the "advance feedback" on what was then available volunteered by 1968–1969 students Robert Gutzke, Nancy Huffman, James Lehman, and Jayne McQuade. Professors Walter DeVolld and Henry Tapp of Kent's Department of Germanic and Slavic Languages rendered sturdy aid on the glories of German, Professor John Parks of the Romance Languages and Classics Department on the lures of Latin, and Professor Coburn Graves of the History Department on matters medieval. Obvious perhaps, but vital, are the debts to the Kent State University Libraries staff, and to their colleagues who answered questions by correspondence and furnished material, at the Bodleian, Harvard, the Library of Congress, the Newberry Library, and the National Union Catalog, and the interlibrary loan services at a score of libraries.

A work of this scope is bound to have some errors of fact and some judgments open to challenge. Library architecture has been chronicled very meagerly; data about daily routines have been alluded to only illustratively. Certainly, as will be plain in particular from the selectivity of coverage in Chapter Nine, there is much yet to be done. May the next try be a better one.

Sidney L. Jackson

Note: "Germanica" is used in this work to name briefly the entire area where the German language and academic style were strong: not only Germany and Austria but western Czechoslovakia and northern Switzerland.

LIBRARIES AND
LIBRARIANSHIP IN THE WEST

Chapter One

ANTIQUITY

The roots of Western civilization lie in ancient societies relying principally upon the hard labor of thousands of peasants. Productivity was very low. Unproductive groups like warriors and courtiers could be supported only because bare subsistence was the lot of the majority. Writing other than essential record keeping was accordingly an activity long confined to very limited circles.

Before Alexandria

In ancient Egypt and the Near East these circles comprised mainly temple and court scribes. The little evidence we find for libraries in those cultures tends to concern the scribes, the men they served, and the schooling associated with their respective functions. Ancient Greece was different; there the written word matched the oral in acceptance long after that point had been reached in the preceding cultures, but the proportion of the population involved was far greater. Circumstances were such, however, that few clear traces of Greek library life have come down to us.

Egypt   The Old Kingdom flourished about 2500 B.C. From those days of power and glory expressed partly in pyramid building we have no data for either libraries or archives. The next stable society, the Middle Kingdom based on Thebes, roughly 2100 to 1800 B.C., generated considerable writing of various kinds. There are plain indications that to be a scribe had decided advantages over many other occupations; in fact, the scribes were at times an important factor in Middle Kingdom politics. The archives they produced were apparently housed in a number of temples. One of these "houses of rolls" has been identified among the ruins of the sun god temple at Heliopolis, 6 miles northeast of modern Cairo; it is dated about 1800 B.C., just before the Hyksos invasion. Many similar institutions are referred to in subsequent Egyptian records. Initially, the person in charge was a very high official with many other responsibilities.

The horsemen-led Hyksos held Egypt in subjection for more than 300 years, leaving no known cultural imprint. They were ejected about the year 1570 B.C., and a New Kingdom was founded, which soon developed crises of its own. In connection with the struggles over religious reform, Amenophis IV (Ikhnaton) left the then capital of Thebes for a fresh start at Amarna. There, within the present century, Egyptologists uncovered some 400—more originally?—tablets inscribed in Babylonian cuneiform, given largely to commercial and diplomatic correspondence with other Near Eastern governments. Some bore a sort of "ex libris" denoting the property of the reformer's father, Amenophis III.

Was this a library? Among the pieces of quartz-based material excavated, suitable to cover a box of papyri or the sheets of papyri constituting a book, at least one was marked with the title of a book and the names of the owners, the king and queen. The same diggings yielded a handful of tablets devoted not to commerce or diplomacy but to Babylonian myths—gifts to a negotiator or the king, perhaps? On this discovery of the possible presence of both papyri and tablets at the same location and apparently from the same period rests the hypothesis that the repository was a library rather than mere archives.

A few hundred years later, the celebrated pharaoh Ramses II (1304–1237 B.C.) had several buildings erected, partly in self-advertisement. In one of those at Thebes, the imperial capital, was a room which became known to venerable tradition as a "sacred library." By the time of Caesar these places were a tourist attraction, and when the Greco-Roman historian Diodorus Siculus visited them in those days or soon afterward, he had already read about the "sacred library" and its supposed entrance inscription, "Healer of the Soul." In his Library of History (1:49), largely a set of paraphrases of earlier works, Diodorus spoke of this inscription and also the flanking statues of Thoth, ibis-headed god of knowledge and patron of scribes, and his wife Safekht, goddess of writing. Numerous scholars long sought these items in surviving ruins; they located indications of a book collection in a nearby building, but no inscription. Diodorus may have been too friendly to the rather fanciful reports of his stated source of the third century B.C. The temptation was strong: by the time a fifteenth-century Latin version of Diodorus was "Englished" by John Skelton in the sixteenth, the library had become "huge."

Still, one must concede the possible significance of the graves of two librarians, father and son, identified in 1849 near the pharaoh's sepulcher.

Clearer evidence of a library turns up in the days of the last Egyptian rulers of Egypt. Far up the Nile near the first cataract, on the island of Philae,

which had been settled as a frontier post in the epoch of the pyramid builders, a group of edifices were erected in the middle of the fourth century B.C.
Among them was a temple of Isis with the inscriptions and wall recesses
accepted by modern authorities as proof of a collection of papyrus-roll
"books." The papyri themselves were not on hand; the oldest ones found so
far date from the next century, the third.

Not until the Ptolemies, the alien rulers installed after the death of
Alexander the Great, do we encounter remains whose origins as a library are
beyond doubt. At Edfu, a southern provincial town somewhat north of
Philae, they built a Horus temple and other structures in the manner of the
old kings, one of many moves to ingratiate themselves with the priesthood.
The first large room in the temple had two smaller rooms within it, leading
off the sides of the main entrance. One was devotional, Horus and Thoth
being depicted spraying water on the king. The other was a library. Over the
door was a palette, one of the symbols of Thoth, who weighed each man's
heart against the feather of truth before he entered the afterworld. Inscribed
on the stone walls within were thirty-seven titles, the catalog of a collection
whose existence has been verified, a unique phenomenon. Intended presumably for the priests, it included works on wall painting, the proportions of
limbs, and a "Guide to inhabited places and what is known about them."
These titles were preceded by a grandiloquent dedication to Horus from the
king, who refers to "many boxes of books and great rolls of consecrated
leather." Whether all the books reposed in the two wall niches or additional
rolls were housed in other containers remains unclear.

Unclear also are many other matters. Some of the Amarna pieces of
quartz-based material usable as covers had holes at the edges, as though for
binding; others did not. Some of the papyri were kept in boxes, whether
lying down or standing up is unknown. Thanks to the absence of perspective in Egyptian art it is unresolved whether the "handles" apparently depicted on the boxes were really handles; if their mystifying location at one
end is what it seems to be, they probably were not. Papyri have been discovered in both wooden boxes and earthen jars. Was the type of container
chosen according to the ownership of the book, or its contents, or on some
other basis? Worse than the uncertainties of the extant evidence, we have
every reason to suppose that much other material has disappeared. We have
very little idea of how much or what sort.

In a word, reliable information about libraries in ancient Egypt is very
nearly a will o' the wisp. If the meager survivals represent a larger number
of "book" collections, one may hesitantly conclude that the temples used
some of their revenues to keep records and some other reading matter in
rooms designated as libraries. That anyone but priests used them is extremely doubtful; the scribes and some of their clients were capable of it but
would have had little or no reason to do so, even if permitted.

The Near East　In the case of Egypt it may be supposed, reasonably, that the
arts of cutting inscriptions in stone and writing them on papyrus, wood, or
leather were taught in an organized fashion. Perhaps there were training
schools, with materials centers. But that is only supposition.

From the excavations at Ur "of the Chaldees," on the other hand, 400 tablets and about 1,000 fragments were recovered which are regarded by the experts as precisely that—the library of a temple school for scribes, whose number may have included women. (Ur was then about 75 miles from the mouth of the Euphrates; further now.) Represented in the collection were economics, law, religion, textbooks, and correspondence; apparently, as in Egypt, the scribes-in-training were taken seriously. The containers of the economic material were arranged by subject and chronology; they had identification labels, and tags with contents notes. Whether other types of writing were also organized is not known. Nor is there any certainty about the period: it is thought to have been the third millennium B.C.

Additional tablets, in large numbers, were unearthed at Nippur, especially at "Tablet Hill," leading some archaeologists to the conclusion that Old Babylon maintained in the third millennium an impressive library. Indeed two different establishments at two separate periods have been suggested because evidence was found at two different levels of digging. Unfortunately, clear information was obtained only about the contents of the tablets.

Subject organization did prove identifiable at Kish. The sand surrendered a collection of Old Babylonian tablets from approximately the days of Hammurabi, early in the second millennium, separated subject by subject in different rooms. In this instance, however, as in numerous others in antiquity, doubts persist among the scholars as to whether this was a library or "merely" archives. The uncertainty derives partly from the fact that these particular tablets were found in damaged jars, unbaked and badly soiled by the surrounding dirt; they were hard to clean and read. It also testifies to the continuing controversy between those who try to distinguish libraries from archives and those who say that a satisfactory distinction cannot be made for lack of evidence or that it need not concern us inasmuch as it apparently did not concern the ancients.

Descriptive cataloging and the ownership stamp may date likewise from oldest Babylon. This hypothesis rests principally on the generally accepted view that the later Hittite civilization, at peak about 1500 B.C., was influenced powerfully by Babylonian culture. Thanks to the labors of many investigators, there have been isolated among the Hittite remains tablets which constituted a state library. Each tablet (at the site of today's Boghaz-Köi, Turkey, some 90 miles east of Ankara) had a descriptive element comparable to the modern colophon, including a title composed of the opening words of the text. When appropriate, a series number was provided, and data as to whether a given tablet was the last one in the series. Some bore an author's name and address, and the name of the copyist. References were made to damaged or lost originals. An author catalog was furnished.

Such sophistication may be presumed to have developed over a rather long period. If the presumption is correct, either the Old Babylonians or the Hittites or both had at least one library of consequence and enough librarians to bequeath a tradition.

Whether related or not, similar practices flowered in the Assyrian Empire of the eighth and seventh centuries B.C., also a conscious heir to the Babylonian culture. The Assyrologists are satisfied that when King Assurbanipal kept a very sympathetic eye on the royal library at Nineveh, he was probably continuing deliberately what his immediate predecessors had undertaken.

In this library, the earliest verified discovery of its kind (A. Henry Layard, 1848), the tablets incorporated the descriptive elements mentioned above, and were arranged in subject series with links marked. Furthermore, the titles and series were listed in registers having apparently something of the character of a modern calendar of documents. This "catalog" did not list locations, however, although some tablets bore little clay markers evidently designed to ease locating and shelving them. The markers, *girginakku,* gave their name to the man in charge of them, *rab girginakku,* "keeper of the books." We are not told whether these gentlemen were trained, although the indications of an hereditary occupation seem to imply something of the sort. Nor can much be surmised of their daily work, because the recovered tablets were so scattered that the library cannot be reconstructed.

Certain features recur in several of the excavation sites. There were often literary texts as well as administrative and religious documents: this is the principal basis for calling them "libraries." Tablets were protected in earthen jars or troughs, sometimes bound up in packets. Wall sockets, for the jars or perhaps for wooden frames to support them, occasionally had an asphalt lining; whether this was a means of anchoring the legs of a frame, or direct protection for jars, or utilized for some other purpose, is not known. Tables and benches seem to have been provided too. Their supposed presence has been interpreted (Milkau, III-1:50) as an indication of insufficient wall space for all the tablets. Were they on the contrary intended for the reader's convenience?

It would be fascinating to learn, moreover, whether the frequent appearance of economic, scientific, legal, and literary items, and polyglot dictionaries, reflects a clientele beyond the priests and government scribes. One thinks particularly of the lost "library" at Ras-Shamra, on the present-day Syrian coast, part of the remains of the Ugaritic civilization of the early second millennium. Did the merchants of that once-flourishing entrepôt use it? Did they go in person, or send clerks? Did they themselves read or were they dependent upon the library's own staff? Were there any literate individuals not associated with state or church? We do not know.

Other important questions also remain. For all the ingenuity displayed in some of these "libraries," it is still a mystery how a particular tablet was located when wanted; after all, the collections ran into the tens of thousands.

Furthermore, doubt continues to throw a long shadow over many tablet finds. That hundreds lay in close proximity when unearthed does not necessarily prove that they once constituted a book or records collection. It has been hypothesized that, in some instances at least, they were stored out of respect rather than for use, or even that they were indeed assembled for use—as building materials! The occasional discovery of tablets in ash heaps is a warning that they were not always treated as repositories of writing.

The uncertainties are underlined by the apparent fact that, at this writing, no general reference work or standard history offers a list of the sites yielding evidence suggestive of libraries.

Greece The story of Greek books and libraries rests on quite different testimony. Inscriptions on portable tablets played no role of consequence in the writings of classical Hellas. Papyrus rolls were depicted on vases, for instance, as early as the sixth century B.C. And in the fifth century B.C., those reached by the words of historian Herodotus, recited far and wide, could have known that the Egyptians used the reed to make food, sails for Nile boats, and "for some other purpose" (Herodotus, *Histories,* Penguin ed., p. 135). In any event the Greeks were at home with papyrus by the time their public communications habits had shifted—in the dissension-torn fourth century B.C.—from the oral to the written; indeed the availability of papyrus via trade with Egypt and the change in the attitude toward the written word may well have encouraged each other. Yet in the physical conditions characteristic of Greece, very much rock and very little sand, papyrus rarely survived. For precise knowledge of what those great minds contributed, posterity is dependent upon a chain of many links.

The thoughts and words of classical Greece were recorded later, in Hellenistic days, with varying degrees of accuracy; some documents lived on and others perished. This process was repeated for century after century, its scope broadening as each new language entered the stream of international culture: Syriac, Persian, Arabic, Hebrew, Latin. Translations, and translations of translations, assumed great importance. As one of the earliest major practitioners, St. Jerome, put it, late in the fourth century (in his *Apology . . . against . . . Rufinus,* I. 20), "a plentiful crop of uncertainties" had to be dealt with. A few years later, like-minded St. Augustine complained *(On Christian Doctrine,* II. XII. 16) that everyone who thought he knew any Greek at all had felt called upon to try translating some of it into Latin—with wretched results. Attempts to establish authentic texts were already being made, reportedly, as early as the third century B.C. If Diogenes Laërtius, a Greek writer of the third century, can be trusted (*Lives of the Eminent Philosophers,* III. 66), written versions of Plato had been edited long since, with such critical symbols as the hyphen to designate a spurious passage. He probably drew that information from the third-century-B.C. figure whom he explicitly credited with the statement that the owners of an editorially marked manuscript would charge a fee for the privilege of consulting it. However reliable these details may be, it is known that many more such efforts followed, often at organized centers of scholarship. Even in the early 1970s, by no means all the output of the Greek thinkers—Plato possibly excepted—is available in editions of unquestionable accuracy and fullness.

One must therefore handle with great care such accounts as that of Strabo, a geopolitician of the time of Emperor Augustus (27 B.C.–A.D. 14), about the fate of Aristotle's personal library. Strabo reported confidently, for example (*Geography,* XIII. 1. 54), that the books had been bequeathed to a pupil of Aristotle's leading disciple, that they had at one stage been hidden in the cellar of a legatee's provincial home and damaged by moisture and moths, and that a subsequent owner had made new copies, filling in the gaps incorrectly. Strabo was not a scholar in the modern sense; he seldom cited sources. It was only through considerable labor that his account was eventually confirmed on the first point, accorded high probability on the second, and taken with some seriousness on the third. A still later writer, Athenaeus, remarks about A.D. 225 (*Deipnosophistae,* I. 3) that among those celebrated for their "large libraries" were the Athenian tyrant Peisistratus, the kings of Pergamum, and Aristotle. Since these figures go back as far as the sixth century B.C. (Peisistratus), it is certain only that a number of traditions were in circulation around the eastern Mediterranean for more than 800 years. Behind them, no doubt, are some facts—but do they outweigh the fiction?

It is inferred, from allusions in contemporary drama and other sources, that books were fairly common and cheap, perhaps in Socrates' time (second half of the fifth century B.C.) and surely afterward. The level of discussion at Plato's Academy implies that the students had already learned much before they arrived, perhaps by means of reading. Aristotle told the fourth-century-B.C. audience for his *Politics* (McKeon ed., I. 11) that he would not go into detail about husbandry or household economy because the literature was ample; he seemed to imply that it was readily available. He may have been referring to cheap books, or a library at his school. Archaeology suggests that there was space for a large book collection at the site, but one cannot be sure.

The acceptance of the book in Greece was favored from the outset by the absence of two social phenomena well established in Egypt and the Near East: there was neither a priestly caste nor an aura of sacred mystery about written characters.

Greek philosophy and pedagogy initially affected book use rather negatively. Socrates is said to have regarded the written word as a mere copy of what is truly "living and possessed of soul," the oral (Plato's *Phaedrus,* 276A). Plato was characteristically more flexible, as well as a generation later and thereby nearer the age of writing. Yet the Platonic conception of philosophy and education required dialogue, proceedings which could not properly submit to the rigidity of what was written; and from that point of view Plato was apparently never comfortable about books. On the other hand, while Aristotle's teaching method also relegated reading to a subordinate level, student "feedback" was not the vital center: he lectured. Lectures tend to become books. Furthermore, his anti-Platonic respect for poetry, his attention to the art of persuasion ("rhetoric"), and his emphasis on systematic study of concrete particulars in nature and politics are all consistent with not only a passive audience but written communication and records.

How much the higher educators wrote for immediate exposure to those beyond the fee-paying students, precisely what institutional or commercial means were at hand for book distribution, who read these works and how they obtained them—all this remains largely conjectural, so far as Golden Age Athens is concerned. It is likely that cheap books were secondhand books, inasmuch as a roll of papyrus was reportedly rather expensive. Acquiring books was an affair limited mainly to persons owning literate slaves, who could be assigned individually to produce single copies or given dictation as a group to produce multiple copies simultaneously; there were probably also free persons willing and able to do their own copying. Books were indeed bought and sold, without much consideration of or pecuniary benefit to authors; but the tradesmen involved were apparently dealers in general merchandise, as a rule. The birth of the book trade proper awaited conditions which had not yet matured.

Greek culture was first imported northward into Macedonia at the end of the fifth century B.C., by King Archelaos, in the persons of numerous literary figures. It is supposed that he had some familiarity with their writings and maintained a book collection for their benefit at or near his palace. Similar in this respect were his successors, the better known Philip II and Alexander. The latter assembled a personal library whose catholicity probably owed something to his celebrated tutor, Aristotle. Alexander used to have parts of his collection carried into the field for his leisure hours; after his death it was reunited at the capital, Pella (near modern Salonika).

These books may have served as the nucleus for a later library, thought to have been established by a man who fought his way to the Macedonian throne in 276 B.C. The new king, Antigonos Gonatas, we hear, invited Zeno, the leader of the Stoa school, to his court and was turned down only because of the philosopher's advanced age. The monarch did however attract several writers and thinkers of the Stoic outlook: the library may have been intended for their use. It is believed, accordingly, to have included philosophy, history, and poetry, but not the scientific type of material Alexander would have favored. The institution emerges from the mists into the light of historical records only a century afterward. The victor at the battle of Pydna (168 B.C.), Aemilius Paulus, confiscated it as war booty and shipped it to Rome, in perhaps the first act of that kind by a Roman general.

Similarly, Lucullus is alleged to have carried off home the library of the famed Mithridates of Pontus, after his defeat in 70 B.C. That was quite a journey, all the way from conquered Sinope, on the south shore of the Black Sea, about halfway between the Dardanelles and the Caucasus. A report so colorful was understandably welcomed into the seventh-century encyclopedia of Isidor of Seville, by way of an unknown number of intermediate hands. That there are apparently no firsthand accounts is unfortunately characteristic of the literature concerning possible other court libraries in the capital cities of the Hellenistic culture area. Although it has been contended (for example, Milkau, III-1:89) that a potentate who collected writers and philosophers must have collected books for their use, this theory has never been substantiated.

Happily, the record is more encouraging with regard to libraries at the gymnasia, thanks to archaeology. More convincingly than the literary evidence just discussed, inscriptions and other items found at numerous sites testify to the existence of such libraries all over the Greek world in the last two centuries before Christ. Remains at the island of Cos (near the southwestern Turkish coast), for example, strongly suggest that a gymnasium library was supported by the semivoluntary donations of the upper strata of the citizenry—a custom then characteristic of many public endeavors. There survives also a badly mutilated "catalog," actually just a list, of the books in the library of an Athens gymnasium.

The gymnasia were intended originally for the development of the body. Some time early in the third century B.C., however, educational reforms brought the intellectual instruction of the young men in many instances into the gymnasia. With that transfer, it has been suggested, went also the books the young men had often used in the homes of tutors. If so, these books would account for some gymnasium libraries. Futhermore, if a gymnasium so favored also continued to be a center for grown men, the books may have assumed the quality of a public library as well as a school library.

The first professional schools also appeared in this epoch. Between Hippocrates and his associates at Cos early in the fourth century B.C., and Galen in Rome late in the second century, several centers of medical instruction graced major cities. The tradition of learning medicine from books was strong and obstacles to the examination of dead human bodies even stronger. It would seem very likely that book collections were maintained at those schools, but no clear proof has survived.

Alexandria and Pergamum

Certain elements of Greek culture were carried on the spears of Alexander the Great through a vast area. They fared variously according to local circumstances. After the thirty-three-year-old conqueror's death in 323 B.C., his dominions were divided among his leading generals. The regime established in Egypt proved able to create a center of civilization, Hellenistic Alexandria, which dominated Western antiquity for approximately a century and a half (ca. 300–ca. 150 B.C.) and remained important until the Mohammedan occupation in A.D. 640; indeed, its effects are with us still. Several of them are partly or entirely the legacy of the great Alexandrian Library. Since the "father" of the history of science, the notable cultural historian George Sarton (1884–1956), portrayed the library about as clearly and engagingly as anyone could, the balance of the present discussion will be drawn directly (with omissions indicated) from the text, minus the footnotes, of his *History of Science* (vol. II, 1959, pp. 142-145, 147-157 passim, by permission of the Harvard University Press; the occasional bracketed interpolations are SLJ's).

[**Pharaohs and Librarians**] The nucleus of the Library was collected in Greece by Demetrios of Phaleron. He may be called the founder of the Library, though this honor might be ascribed with equal or greater justice to the first and second kings. The Library was organized by the will and at the expense of Ptolemaios Soter; the organization was completed by his successor Ptolemaios Philadelphos. Hence the fairest way of summarizing the matter would be to say that the Library was founded by Soter, Philadelphos, and Demetrios. Was Demetrios the first librarian? If you please; but it would perhaps be more correct to call Zenodotos of Ephesos the first one.

An elaborate study of the Alexandrian library was published by Edward Alexander Parsons (*The Alexandrian Library,* Amsterdam: Elsevier, 1952), and according to him the list of librarians [leaving open the question of a formally acknowledged "chief" or "head"] is:

	Tentative Dates
Demetrios of Phaleron	c. 284 [B.C.]
Zenodotos of Ephesos	284–260
Callimachos of Cyrene	260–240
Apollonios of Rhodos	240–235
Eratosthenes of Cyrene	235–195
Aristophanes of Byzantion	195–180
Apollonios Eidographos	180–160
Aristarchos of Samothrace	160–145

All these men will reappear in our story later on, except Apollonios Eidographos, a grammarian of undetermined time who occupied himself in the Library with the arrangement of Pindaros' odes.

The list is uncertain in other respects. The only names about which every scholar would probably agree are Zenodotos, Apollonios of Rhodos, Eratosthenes, Aristophanes, another Apollonios, Aristarchos. Such as it is, the list calls for two obvious remarks. First, it well illustrates Alexandrian cosmopolitanism. Second, it ends in the middle of the second century B.C. No librarian posterior to that time has ever been mentioned by anybody. We shall come back to that ominous fact presently. As far as its librarians are known (and what is a library without librarians?) the golden age of the library lasted less than one century and a half.

Growth [and Role] of the Library   Thanks to the enthusiasm of its royal patrons and the ability of their first advisers, Demetrios and Zenodotos, the Library grew very rapidly. The original building was already too small by the middle of the third century, and it was necessary to create a secondary library in the Sarapeion (or Serapeum). Some 42,800 rolls were given or lent to the Serapeum library by the main one; this was perhaps a way of finding more room in the latter by the rejection of imperfect copies or duplicates.

The kings of Egypt were so eager to enrich their library that they employed highhanded methods for that purpose. Ptolemaios III Evergetes (ruled 247–222 [B.C.]) ordered that all travelers reaching Alexandria from abroad should surrender their books. If these books were not in the library, they were kept, while copies on cheap papyrus were given to the owners. He asked the librarian of Athens to lend him the state copies of Aischylos, Sophocles, and Euripides, in order to have transcripts made of them, paying as a guarantee of return the sum of fifteen talents; then he decided to keep them, considering that they were worth more than the money he had deposited and he returned copies instead of the originals. [This recital seems to have started with Galen, celebrated physician-philosopher of the second century (Milkau, III-1:66); his sources are not mentioned.]

The Library was the memory of the scientific departments of the Museum. The physicians needed the works of Hippocrates and other predecessors; the astronomers needed the records of early observations and theories. One would like to know whether Babylonian and Egyptian observations were available there. How many of the earlier astronomical and astrological papyri did they have? The scientists of the Museum must know what had been done before them. It does not follow, however, that the early records were in the Library proper. The mass of those early scientific writings was not considerable and it was handier for men of science to keep them on their own bookshelves, either at home or in their laboratories. We may be sure that one of the nightmares of modern university librarians was already experienced in Alexandria, to wit, how can one reconcile the needs of the general readers with those of the special ones, and divide the books between the main library and the departmental ones?

When one passes from science to the humanities, however, the importance of the library increases immeasurably. For in the case of the humanities the library does not simply provide information, it contains the very masterpieces. The anatomist might find books in the library, but not bodies; the astronomer might find books, but not the stars, not the glory of heaven. On the other hand, if the humanist wanted to read the *Iliad* or the *Odyssey*, the songs of Anacreon or the odes of Simonides, those very treasures would be available to him in the Library and perhaps nowhere else. The Library might be called the brains or the memory of the Museum; it was the very heart of the humanities.

[Scholar-Librarians] The Library of Alexandria was really a new start, as much of the Museum was. As much work had been done before in the field of the humanities as in the field of science, and we are fully aware, as far as the Greek world is concerned, that many books were published, sold, collected, criticized at least from the fifth century [B.C.] on. There had been also many libraries, large and small, private and public, but now for the first time a large number of scholars were assigned to library service.

That service was enormously more complex and difficult than that of modern librarians. To keep printed books in good order is relatively easy, for each of those books is a definite and recognizable unit. The Alexandrian librarians had to struggle with an enormous number of papyrus rolls, each of which had to be identified first, then classified, catalogued, edited. The last word is the key to the main difficulties. The majority of the texts represented in the rolls were not standardized in any way, and their clear definition would remain almost impossible as long as they had not been thoroughly investigated, edited, and reduced to a canonic form.

To put it otherwise, the librarians of Alexandria were not simply custodians and cataloguers like those of today; they had to be, and were, full-fledged philologists. Indeed, the Alexandria Library was the nursery of philologists and humanists, even as the Museum was a nursery of anatomists and astronomers. This will be shown in some detail when we describe the activities of individual scholars.

[Character of the Collection] The Library and its elaborate catalogue being lost, we have no idea of its contents, except that it was exceedingly rich and included many works that are no longer extant. The many thousands of papyri that have been discovered in Egypt [not necessarily from the Alexandrian Library] and investigated in our century have revealed that the Greek population of Egypt (and the Greek-speaking Orientals) were fairly well acquainted with Greek literature. Homer was obviously the most popular author; Homeric papyri are more abundant than all the other literary papyri put together; then follow, in order of decreasing frequency, Demosthenes, Euripides, Menandros, Plato, Thucydides, Hesiodos, Isocrates, Aristophanes, Xenophon, Sophocles, Pindaros, Sappho. There are very few fragments of Aristotle, but that is compensated by the discovery of a whole work of his, the *Constitution of Athens,* in a British Museum papyrus. Strangely enough, Herodotos, who should have been of special interest to the Greeks of Egypt, was hardly represented. Not only did the papyri give us many fragments of known works but they revealed lost works like . . . the medical papyrus of London, and they increased considerably our knowledge of other authors. . . . "Toutes proportions gardées," the Greeks of Egypt were more literate than our American contemporaries.

Rolls of Papyrus How were the rolls arranged on the shelves of the Library, or what corresponded to our shelving of books? It is impossible to say. Obviously the rolls could not be placed vertically on the shelves, as books are, but they might be placed horizontally. Even when the rolls were finally replaced by codices, it is probable that the latter were laid flat on the shelves, as is often done to this day in Oriental countries in the case of Arabic, Persian, or Chinese books. Codices did not appear, however, until considerably later and were not predominant before the fifth century of our era. . . .

But we must not anticipate too much. How were the rolls arranged? As they were classified, it was necessary to group them in separate bunches. This could be done when they were placed flat on shelves, provided that they could not roll away from their companions; their rolling off could be easily avoided by adding enough vertical partitions and dividing the shelves into as many compartments or pigeonholes as might be desired.

It is probable that the more precious rolls were dealt with as the Japanese do. . . . That is, the ends were reinforced, maybe, with a piece of wood which emerged on both sides and facilitated the folding in or out. A protruding label *(sillybos)* might be attached to the roller. In Roman times a number of rolls were placed in a bucket *(capsa),* which might bear a title of its own. The bucket or the pigeonhole were two equivalent solutions of the same problem and we may be sure that the one or the other was used in any large library. . . .

As the librarians were anxious to increase their collections, a good many rolls were copied if they could not be obtained otherwise. Certain halls of the library must have looked like a medieval scriptorium. It is possible that certain scribes supervised and corrected the work of the others, but it does not appear that a method or style of copying was developed, as happened later in medieval scriptoria such as those of Tours or Corbie, St. Albans or Bury St. Edmunds, which enables the trained paleographer not only to date a manuscript but also to say that it was written at one particular place. It is possible to distinguish Ptolemaic rolls from later ones but the specification cannot be carried further (on paleographic grounds).

The Hellenistic copyists were generally faithful, the main cause of error being the same as for modern typists, the omission of one or more lines, because the eye confuses two identical words at the beginning of two lines or the end of them. . . . Their faithfulness did not begin to compare, however, with that of the Hebrew scribes, whose duties were religious.

Size of the Library   The Library was very large, but it is impossible to know how many rolls it included. The numbers mentioned by various authors vary considerably. As the Library was steadily growing, the numbers were increasing; according to one account, there were already 200,000 rolls at the end of Soter's rule; according to another, there were only 100,000 at the end of his son's rule; other accounts speak of 500,000 rolls or even 700,000 in Caesar's time. Never mind those conflicting dates. The numbers relative to definite dates may have different meanings; they may refer to works or to rolls, and there were sometimes many works to a roll or many rolls to a single work. Even today, it is difficult to answer this apparently single question, "How many books does your library contain," exactly and without ambiguities. After all, the number of books does not matter so much; the books might be very important or else trivial and worthless; they might be in perfect condition or not, there might be many imperfect or duplicate copies, or there might be few. The true richness and greatness of a library does not depend so much on the number of its books as on their quality.

Artist's conception of a scene in the Alexandrian Library. (Courtesy of The Bettmann Archive, Inc.)

It is a pity that we cannot visualize the Library. No doubt it was a fine building with elegant halls and colonnades. One would like to see the "stacks" of papyri, the desk or office where readers applied for them, the place where they were permitted to study. The halls were probably adorned with statues, bas-reliefs, or wall paintings. The most important features of a scientific institute are not the walls and fixtures, however, but the men using them; the pride of a great library is not so much its books as the distinguished scholars who are studying them, for without the latter the former are worthless.

Let us speak first of the few scholars who are named as directors of the Library or as scientific investigators charged with the organization of its contents.

[Literary Librarians] It would seem that some scholars combined the duties of librarians and of tutors to the royal princes. This would not be surprising, for everything in Ptolemaic Egypt gravitated around the king. The latter was not king by divine grace; he was himself divine. Straton was tutor to Philadelphos and when he was called to Athens to head the Lyceum, c. 288, he was replaced as tutor by the poet Philetas of Cos. The first head of the Library, Zenodotos of Ephesos . . . was a pupil of Philetas; his scholarly activities were so considerable that he probably devoted to them the whole of his time that was not eaten up by the library administration. It is highly probable, however, that the administration was still rudimentary; this was an age of administrative innocence, truly a golden age. All the chores were shared or divided amicably, without red tape, and done informally and wholeheartedly. The work was immense, for it did not suffice to put the rolls in order; each of them needed a special investigation, and not only that but the texts themselves required editing.

Zenodotos discussed the matter with his assistants, Alexander of Pleuron (in Aitolia) and Lycophron of Chalcis (in Euboia), both Greeks of Greece proper, and they divided between them one great task, the collection and revision of the Greek poets. Zenodotos took for himself the lion's share, Homer and other poets. He produced the first revision . . . of the *Iliad* and the *Odyssey*. . . . He was probably responsible for the division of each epic into 24 books. His study of the text implied grammatical analysis and thus led to grammatical improvements. . . .

Callimachos of Cyrene was probably born c. 310 [B.C.]. He . . . was for a time teacher of grammar at Eleusis, near Alexandria. He was introduced to the king Ptolemaios II and appointed librarian, c. 260; he held that office until his death, c. 240. By that time the Library was already so rich that it had become impossible to use it without a catalogue. Callimachos compiled one entitled *Pinaces* . . . ([or] *Tables of the outstanding works in the whole of Greek culture and of their authors),* which was so elaborate that it filled 120 rolls. [That it was actually a Library "catalog" is a pleasing hypothesis but not yet proven.] The books were divided into eight classes: (1) dramatists, (2) epic and lyric poets, (3) legislators, (4) philosophers, (5) historians, (6) orators, (7) rhetoricians, (8) miscellaneous writers. This classification is very interesting, because it reveals that the Library was essentially a literary institution. In which class were the scientific books placed? Perhaps in the fourth, or in the eighth, which was the "varia," the "glory-hole," which is necessary to complete any scheme of classification. In some of the classes the arrangement was chronological, in others by subject or alphabetical. For each book the title was given, the author's name (with discussion of author-ship if necessary), the incipit [the first word or two], and the number of lines. Some of those indications were probably repeated on the label *(sillybos)* attached to each roll, for the classification of a large number of items re-quires some marks of identification and some labeling for each of them.

The *Pinaces* was far more than a single list, for it included historical and critical remarks; thus it was a kind of *catalogue raisonné,* or it might even be called a history of Greek literature. Would that we had it, for a majority of the books that were available to Alexandrian scholars are completely lost, and many others are known only by the quotations made from them by compilers. . . .

The composition of the *Pinaces* was an immense undertaking; on the strength of it Callimachos could be called the first cataloguer (though his labor was incomparably more difficult and more original than that of mod-ern cataloguers). It has been argued that he was not the librarian or director of the Library but its cataloguer. In the total absence of definitions of those offices, the matter cannot be profitably discussed. We must remember once for all that those early librarians were not simply librarians as with us, but men of letters, philologists, editors, lexicographers, historians, philosophers, poets. They might be each of these things, some, or all of them. . . .

[Scientist Eratosthenes]   The first librarians . . . were all men of letters. Was it finally realized that the classification and investigation of scientific books required the care of a man of science? At any rate, the next librarian, Eratos-thenes of Cyrene [235–195 B.C.], was one of the greatest men of science of antiquity. He was not only a mathematician, astronomer, and geographer, but also a chronologist and even a philologist. One might even say that he was the first conscious philologist, for he was the first to assume the name *philologos.* That would be all wrong, however, for many men have deserved that name before him, and more than he, not only in Greece but also in Pharaonic Egypt, in Mesopotamia, and in India.

He completed his education in Athens but was called to Alexandria by Ptolemaios III Evergetes (ruled 247–222 [B.C.]) and appointed librarian c. 235; he probably remained in office until his death c. 192, at the age of 80. Two of his abundant writings were the by-products of his librarianship. One was his elaborate study of the Old Attic Comedy . . . and the other his *Chrono-graphia,* an attempt to establish the chronology of ancient Greece on a scien-tific basis. Callimachos and his successors were often puzzled by chronologi-cal difficulties. These difficulties were immense in antiquity because the local chronologies were independent of each other and often discordant. It was thus natural enough for a scientific librarian like Eratosthenes to try to put some order in that chronological chaos even as he did in geodesy and the history of geography. . . .

[Philologist Librarians]   Eratosthenes died in c. 195 and was succeeded by Aristophanes of Byzantion (c. 257–c. 180 [B.C.]), who was primarily a grammarian and lexicographer and perhaps the greatest philologist of classical antiquity. He improved the technique of textual criticism and prepared better editions of Homer, Hesiod's *Theogony,* Alcaios, Anacreon, Pindaros, Euripedes, Aristophanes. He made a study of grammatical analogies or regularities; that is, he helped to organize Greek grammar and compiled a Greek dictionary *(lexeis).* Eumenes II (197–159 B.C.) tried to steal Aristophanes from Ptolemy Epiphanes (205–182 B.C.) for his own library in Pergamum, whereupon Ptolemy put Aristophanes in prison.

His greatest contribution to grammar was the invention or systematization of punctuation. We are so used to reading texts which are fully punctuated that we take punctuation for granted, as we take the whole of grammar or writing itself. It is clear that punctuation is not absolutely necessary but when one has been obliged to read texts without punctuation and without capitals (like Arabic) one appreciates these aids very much. It is much easier to read a text that has been carefully written, of which the words are separated, the proper words emphasized by capitals, and the sentences articulated by means of punctuation marks; it may even happen that punctuation removes ambiguities and misunderstandings. Aristophanes was the first to understand all that clearly, but he was so much ahead of his time that those grammatical reforms were not adopted by the copyists until a long time afterward; they were still disregarded by the early printers and were not generally adopted before the middle of the sixteenth century.

The case of Aristophanes illustrates the complexity of the services performed by the Alexandrian librarians. Librarianship in the modern sense was only a part of their job; their primary duties were philological. It was not enough to classify the books; they had to edit and rewrite them, or at least to make possible the necessary rewriting. Aristophanes invented not simply the ordinary marks of punctuation (similar to those that we use), but also various symbols needed in textual criticism, such as those to indicate a spurious line, missing words, metrical changes, tautology. . . .

One of the works ascribed to him was a commentary on the *Pinaces* of Callimachos, and this confirms our belief that the *Pinaces* was far more than a catalogue and came close to being a history of Greek literature. . . .

Later History of the Library   Readers may be curious to know right now what happened to the Library after the middle of the second century B.C. The fact that one cannot name any librarians after Aristarchos of Samothrace [d. ca. 140 B.C.] is already sufficient proof of the decadence of the Library, which was but one aspect of the decadence of Hellenistic Egypt.

At the time of Caesar's siege of Alexandria, in 48 B.C., the Library was still exceedingly rich. As he could not man the Egyptian fleet riding in the harbor, which might be taken by the Egyptian commander Achillas and used against him, Caesar set fire to it. The conflagration extended to the wharves and is said to have destroyed part of the Library. This is difficult to believe, because the main library was sufficiently distant from the harbor and docks, and the Serapeum was very far away on a hill. It is possible, however, that a quantity of books had been taken to the waterside to be shipped to Rome, and that it was those books that were destroyed.

This may explain why Marcus Antonius, the triumvir, gave to Cleopatra in 41 B.C. some 200,000 volumes taken from the Library of Pergamum. That story is far from certain, but it is plausible. If the Library had been diminished by Caesar's action, it would have been natural enough for the queen to complain and for Marcus Antonius to give her a rich compensation at the expense of his enemies.

The Library was still very important at the beginning of the Roman rule, when the Romans thought of themselves as liberators of Egypt. This is not proved, however, by the account of Josephus Flavius [late first century], who does not speak of the library as it was in his own time. During the rule of Aurelian (emperor, 270-275) the greater part of the Bruchion was destroyed. Did that involve the destruction of the main Library [housed in it]? At any rate, the Serapeum [supplementary library] continued to exist.

It is possible also that books of either library or of both had been sequestered by the Roman authorities and taken to the capital. Conquerors have perpetrated such dilapidations in our own century; it was much easier to get away with them at the beginning of our era. The main enemies of the Library, however, were not the Romans but the Christians. Its decline was accelerated in proportion as Alexandria was more effectively controlled by bishops, whether Orthodox or Arian. By the end of the fourth century, paganism was ebbing out of Alexandria; the Museum (if it still existed) and the Serapeum were its last refuges. The old Christians and the proselytes hated the Library, because it was in their eyes a citadel of disbelief and immorality; it was gradually undermined and brought into decay.

The Library was now concentrated in the Serapeum and the latter was finally destroyed [many scholars disagree] under Theodosios the Great (emperor, 379-395), by order of Theophilos (bishop of Alexandria, 385-412), whose antipagan fanaticism was extreme. Many of the books may have been salvaged but, according to Orosius [416 or 417], the Library was virtually nonexistent in 416.

The story has often been told that when the Muslims took Alexandria in 640, then again in 645 and sacked it, they destroyed the Library. The *khalifa* 'Umar is supposed to have said: "The text of those books is contained in the Qur'an or not: If it is, we do not need them; if it is not, they are pernicious." That story is unproved. There was not much if anything left of the original library to be destroyed. The Christian fanatics had argued in the same vein as their Muslim emulators. Moreover, the pagan books were far more dangerous to the Christians, who could easily read them, than to the Muslims, who could not read them at all. [Here ends our borrowing from George Sarton.]

The Pergamene Library Second only to the collections in Alexandria were those of the briefly resplendent court of Pergamum (opposite Lesbos, a few miles inland in northwest Turkey). Born in revolt against Macedonia in 282 B.C., it flourished for about a century and a half, like Ptolemaic Egypt, on the proceeds of taxes on the peasants and traders and textile production, to be absorbed in the 120s B.C. as a part of the Roman province of "Asia." Attalus I (241-197 B.C.) assembled a respectable library; Eumenes II (197-159 B.C.) gave it a new building and other improvements. Thanks to the physical remains not vouchsafed us in the case of Alexandria, the Pergamene Library may reasonably be credited with a colonnade area of some 70 by 10 yards housing possibly 160,000 rolls. From scattered additional evidence scholars estimate that the acquisitions style was as rough and ready as at Alexandria and that the cataloging was very much like that reflected in the *Pinaces* of Callimachos. The library's achievements and architectural attractions seem to have reached Rome, thanks partly to the arrival there in 170 B.C. of Crates of Mallos as Eumenes' ambassador: Crates was a scientist and recognized Homer scholar, presumably familiar with the library, and may have served on its staff.

The Roman Empire

Many years ago, Emil Ludwig wrote of "the grandeur that was Rome." There seems to be no doubt that books were part of that grandeur. Not only did the importation of Greek culture in the days of the Republic stimulate the book trade and the assembling of private libraries of note, but the idea of a physically magnificent cultural center appealed to the builders of empire as a molder of favorable public opinion.

Library Founders   Julius Caesar was probably the first to try to found a library. From his biography written about A.D. 120 by Suetonius, who had access to archives long since lost, and other evidence, it is believable that Caesar's agenda included establishing a library of public character. Charged with this task was the veteran scholar and teacher, land magnate, and retired public servant, Marcus Terentius Varro (116–27 B.C.), credited by Roman chroniclers with—among other writings—a work on libraries. The Ides of March, 44 B.C., however, brought an end to any such plans. Some five years later, C. Asinius Pollio, an intimate of the murdered leader's, tried to carry forward the interrupted project with the help of war booty from Illyria (roughly present-day Albania). He installed in the Atrium Libertatis, near the Forum, Latin and Greek sister libraries, decorated with the likenesses of the renowned; the aged Varro was the only living author thus honored. Nothing more has been learned.

Many efforts thereafter also revealed the influence of the Alexandrian (and Pergamene?) model. From the Emperor Augustus on, a tradition was cultivated of establishing libraries in temple complexes, even sometimes in buildings of their own, in Rome, in Alexandria itself, and elsewhere. At the end of the first century, indeed, after numerous losses of public library collections by fire, replacement copies were obtained from Alexandria by order of him usually labeled a monster, Emperor Domitian. The Museum too was imitated, when the energetic Emperor Hadrian sponsored a university at Athens and then, in A.D. 134, inaugurated the Athenaeum at Rome. This institution, whose location has never been settled, was a prime seat of learning in the sixth century and is thought likely to have incorporated a library from its birth.

Besides the libraries begun with the aid of rulers, others were made possible by the gifts of successful men to their native towns, some donors like Pliny the Younger known to posterity, some long since forgotten. In the latter category is the gentleman acknowledged in an inscription at the site for having presented 400,000 sesterces to Thamugadi (modern Timgad, about 25 miles south of Constantine, Algeria) for a library; founded in A.D. 100 by Trajan as a veterans' colony, the community had by the late third century grown enough to make such an act appropriate. Still other "public" libraries enjoyed a support whose nature remains unknown.

Conceivably unique is the case of a second-century library endowed for the use of the Musicians and Actors Association in Rome. The contributor was a wealthy out-of-towner whose citation of honor by the emperor (Milkau, III-1:125) is the source of our information.

The status of the library in Hadrian's time, the early second century, is suggested by the contemporary reporting of Suetonius. In his life of Julius Caesar (*Lives of the Twelve Caesars,* Book I; London: Heinemann, 1924–1927), he speaks of the proposed library in a paragraph (XLIV) on Caesar's projects "for the adornment and convenience of the city, also for the protection and extension of the Empire." The library is in the middle of Suetonius' list, following the consolidation of the statutes and preceding the draining of the Pontine marshes. The verb employed to describe Varro's assignment is *publicare,* whose varied meanings range from "publish officially" to simply "make available to the public."

The Spread of Libraries Library service was indeed available to a public of sorts in numerous communities throughout the Roman Empire and neighboring jurisdictions. The first-century educator Quintilian once remarked (*Oratory,* X. I. 57) that he was not obliged to talk about every last poet known because anyone "could . . . if he chose, copy a catalogue of such poets from some library." An inscription of A.D. 100 records the hours of service at a library in Athens. Aulus Gellius, a Roman writer a little later in the second century, described how an argument over the drinkability of snow water moved a follower of Aristotle to produce the master's text opposing its consumption by humans. The volume "he drew out . . . and brought . . . to us" had been obtained from the library at Tibur (today's Tivoli, a suburb of Rome since the first century B.C.), which according to Gellius (*Attic Nights,* XIX. V) was "at that time in the temple of Hercules" and "well supplied with books." Libraries are known to have been in operation in the second century in central Italy, and in the Roman centers in what are now France and Germany. By A.D. 107 there was a library at Ephesus (near ancient Smyrna, in the middle of the Aegean coast of Turkey), celebrated for scholarship, especially in medicine, and by midcentury another at Carthage (near modern Tunis).

On at least one occasion, Apuleius, the second-century satirist of *Golden Ass* fame, told an audience in Carthage, his home town, that they were meeting in "the very senate-house, the very library of Carthage itself," and asked them therefore to treat his words as scholarly (*Florida,* pp. 397–398 in his *Works,* London: Bell, 1910). Also, in a lengthy denial that he had contracted an advantageous marriage by practicing magic, he spoke of reading the names of many magicians "in public libraries, in the works of authors of the highest reputation" (*Defence,* p. 337, ibid.); unfortunately, the well-traveled Apuleius did not name either libraries or authors, although he did name the "magicians"—Moses included—in standard pagan fashion.

Libraries and Users The relative ease of travel and communication, the systematic foundation of permanent population centers which often became cities, and the stability and cross-fertilization they nourished, were products of deliberate Roman policy. Highly probable is the establishment and supplying of more libraries than we can be sure about. Yet the archaeological and literary evidence from imperial times is sufficient to indicate a number of widespread features: location in the middle of a city, close proximity to a temple, a hall of columns—often with statuary, marble floors, a central reading area with some rolls shelved in the niches in the enclosing walls, and the storage of most of the rolls in adjacent areas. Maintaining a collection of reading matter at the public baths, Caracalla's for instance, was evidently popular among the Romans but left no imprint on subsequent library practice.

Those coming to use the library resources were clearly scholars, students, and persons in touch with the recorded word. According to Pliny the Elder, writing in A.D. 77 (*Natural History,* preface), that included "the common herd, the mob of farmers and artisans." It is very doubtful, however, that many plebeians could read easily enough to become library users. In any case, the animosity of the peasants and urban poor toward the urban privileged classes can hardly have advanced friendly feeling for one of "their" institutions. Such sentiments were to remain in the picture for many centuries to come, modified somewhat by the social mobility of the church.

The known clientele presumably had specialized interests, but did not necessarily pursue them at a library. Despite the influence of Roman law, for example, notably greater than the influence of Roman libraries, little trace of Roman law can be found in the libraries because instruction was for so long oral, by such means as attendance at the law courts. Even the conflicts between Roman law and others like Syrian customary law generated large-scale action for accommodation and codification only in the fourth century; law schools appeared a century later. It has been contended (Milkau, III-1:103) that the codes could hardly have been composed or subsequently taught without libraries; but no proof has yet been adduced that the materials presumably collected were ever treated as a library, except at Caesarea (see below).

Inasmuch as "literature" then included philosophy, medicine, and engineering, those wanting reading matter for whatever purpose evidently accepted the Roman-style "public" library. The library user normally asked at the desk for his book, direct access being forbidden. Unable to browse, Aulus Gellius nevertheless testified that he learned the unexpected at times by studying the catalog carefully or by receiving a book he had not requested. Not every book was circulated: under Emperor Augustus for instance certain works of the youthful Caesar were reportedly locked up. Reading had to be done on the premises, except when the reader was a person able to enforce other desires. If a surviving inscription indicates a pattern, some libraries obliged the borrower to swear that he would not remove the roll from the building. From the same source, an Athenian library document, it may be inferred that at least in some such institutions in Greece the hours of service were six daily, beginning at sunrise.

Book Collections Book selection, then as later, was difficult to separate from censorship. Ever since books were accepted as a medium of communication, certain types of controversial works had attracted hostile attention. The Roman Senate of Punic War days, Emperor Augustus, and many authorities after him, proscribed and when possible destroyed books of prophecy and soothsaying; such items were evidently feared as effective channels of opposition, an early form as it were of psychological warfare. Christian dependence upon the reading of the Scriptures and related liturgical materials was often exploited by pagan persecutors, notably Diocletian. That same thoroughgoing ruler (of the Roman Empire, 284–305) also banned alchemical works and any others concerning gold and silver—an effort to protect the imperial currency. After the Christians' victory libraries often excluded three bodies of writings: the pagans', those of Christian claimants to authoritative standing as theoreticians who were not accepted as such by the church, and the works of outright heretics.

By the third century fire was familiar not only as an accidental remover of books but as an instrument deliberately chosen. The story long circulated that the Athenians had in 411 B.C. burned all the copies they could find of the writings of the philosopher Protagoras, charged with public expression of doubts as to the existence of the gods. The episode has a doubtful ring, in particulars which need not detain us here. Whatever their truth or falsity, the point is that the tale did seem plausible when related by the third-century Greek biographer Diogenes Laërtius (*Lives of Eminent Philosophers,* IX. 51–52).

Classical literature was a staple in the secular libraries of Empire times, as one might expect. Nor was such reading matter so far considered a menace in church collections. Certainly the great names of Greek and Latin prose and poetry were intimately known to the Fathers, however little the rank and file may have heard of them. The heritage also included anthologies, digests, and handbooks, which, as in later generations, may have found more use among some readers than the full originals. Thus Pliny's assurances to the emperor in presenting his *Natural History,* the oldest (A.D. 77) encyclopedia-type item in the Western tradition which has survived complete: Livy's lengthy history points up our far greater need for summary reference works (*thesauros*); I have culled from about 2,000 titles by 100 authors 20,000 noteworthy facts, and unlike my predecessors credited the original writers; further:

> As it was my duty in the public interest to have consideration for the claims upon your time, I have appended to this letter a table of contents of the several books, and have taken very careful precautions to prevent your having to read them. You by these means will secure for others that they will not need to read right through them either, but only look for the particular point that each of them wants, and will know where to find it. (*Natural History,* preface.)

Scriptorium and Bookdealer   Indispensable to the acquiring and maintaining of those library collections was the copying shop, or "scriptorium." Papyrus rolls once exposed to the air had at most a life of about 200 years, and handling rapidly shortened it. Nor did the papyrus codex, composed of folded sheets, solve the problem. The ravages of the "black bookworm" were familiar enough, some time between 50 B.C. and A.D. 50, to inspire an epigram by a hardly known Greek teacher.

Replacements, and titles new to the collection, were available to some extent from itinerant merchants, book shops in the larger towns of the empire, auctions, and the establishments in the key cities (Rome above all) which not only sold books but produced them. Publishing copies of titles by authors no longer living was often a matter of obtaining a version from a large library and putting scribes to work. Errors were frequent enough to evoke wails and jibes; now and then, a particularly scholarly or conscientious or shrewd bookdealer assembled varying versions of a book thought important, and employed savants to supervise the scribes turning out a new recension. To a degree still undetermined, dealers' master copies were loaned by their owners to whoever was ready to pay for the privilege of copying them; also, hard-to-get books were accessible, for a fee, to persons wishing to borrow them briefly simply to read them.

Acquiring new writings by living authors also presented problems. Publishers reportedly favored such works, especially if sales looked promising. Errors in copying were corrected in many instances by the author himself. But there was no copyright, and authors did not always submit a composition for public issue. To obtain a complete set of a popular writer's output might be very difficult for those interested: readers, booksellers, and libraries. Furthermore, since the dealer was vulnerable to harassment by the agents of an angry emperor, it is not surprising that some controversial manuscripts found publishers only with exceptional effort and others presumably never.

Although the numerous book outlets of early Empire days may be supposed to have furnished their proprietors a living, principally from sales to private parties, we know very little of booksellers' relations with "public" libraries, cash or otherwise. The record shows twenty-eight of the latter in Rome by the fourth century and quite a few more in other cities; it does not show how many books they bought or at what price.

Gifts   While "public" libraries were frequently launched with a gift from a wealthy individual, most such donations, unlike the modern endowment, produced neither interest nor any other continuing means of purchase of library materials. And they paid no operating bills. Enlarging the collections therefore depended somewhat on presentation copies from authors. Many were glad to win some prestige in that manner, partly perhaps with the hope that the emperor would take notice: if he did, a statue of that writer might be commissioned and placed in the library.

Arrangement and Control   These decorations served also on occasion as part of the apparatus of bibliographical control. Either busts near the books, or likenesses painted on the walls whose niches supported the roll-*armaria* (closets), may have eased locating materials. Sometimes quotations from the books within were inscribed on the closet door; these doors were usually closed to protect the contents from light. The contents of each closet or room were listed on tablets.

That rolls were assigned to closets by subject, and arranged within alphabetically by author, seems indicated by the catalogs. Each roll was likely to have a *titulus* inserted with the identification end projecting. Among the remains of the library of the Rhodes gymnasium were found evidences of small marble slab *tituli;* it is conjectured that most libraries probably used whitened wood instead. Nowhere has any trace been found of the use of location numbers or equivalent symbols.

The combination of arrangement by subject, corresponding listing in catalogs, and supporting(?) art work, seems to have been maintained in libraries at least to the early-seventh-century days of Isidor of Seville. Surviving evidence does not tell us whether or not it was characteristic. For quite a while, Greek and Latin collections were housed separately at several leading libraries in Rome itself; but that seems to have been unique, inasmuch as other Western libraries had few Greek books and Eastern libraries few in Latin.

During the Roman epoch and for several centuries thereafter, book control and biobibliography were apparently not combined. Callimachos of the Alexandrian Library and his *pinaces* had no imitators so far discovered. While book control was exercised through *tituli* and the other devices mentioned, biobibliography was left to writers of varied capacity and purpose. Among the surviving examples are the above-mentioned early-third-century work by Diogenes Laërtius, most chapters of which include a list of the writings of the biographee; and Eusebius' *Ecclesiastical History* (early fourth century), in which bibliography is woven into the narrative and often accompanied by comment.

More important was an event in the study of "rhetoric." About A.D. 400, Servius, a pagan Latin teacher who adored Virgil, began his long-admired remarks on the *Aeneid* with the following list of items for discussion: (1) author's life, (2) title of the work, (3) poetic genre, (4) author's intention, (5) number of books, (6) order of the books, (7) explanation. Obviously, items 2, 5, and 6 pertain to descriptive cataloging, items 3 and 4 to classification; item 7 might have a bearing on subject analysis. This approach, especially the explanations which rendered pagan literature acceptable to Christendom by treating it allegorically, contributed heavily to medieval book selection. But Servius was not organizing a library catalog, and his readers could benefit from his analytical technique without considering libraries. The two would be brought closer when conditions again existed comparable to those under which Callimachos had worked. The collation of texts requiring a library and good bibliographical control was not to appear in the Christian West for approximately another 600 years.

Library Functions and Personnel   Among the tasks to be performed in libraries were recognized acquisition of manuscripts, completing incomplete copies, replacing poor copies with better ones, indicating contents, and arranging manuscripts. In the establishing of large libraries the scholars were expected either to do the whole job of organizing and assembling or to execute the specific duties of acquisitions, arranging, and making the materials available. While acquisitions and cataloging were thus the responsibility of the scholars, their assistants took care of copying and repairing manuscripts, placing labels, and presumably waiting on patrons.

The clerical staff needed to be able to read and, for some tasks, to be familiar with the library. In the first century, indeed, slaves' names were sometimes listed with the assignment suffixed thus: *a bybliotheca;* one inscription reads even *medicus a bybliotheca* (staff physician?). For the most part, though, the slave force, like modern library clerks, remained in general nameless, if not always unsung. About the time of Hadrian, records associating slaves with libraries cease. The emperor's civil service reorganization may have led to classifying clerks by level of work, without regard to where they worked; if so, that would help account for the change.

Library personnel do not seem to have been organized in any fashion. Although tradesmen and craftsmen of many types had their respective *collegii* (ancestors of both the trade association and the labor union), no *collegium* so far identified was related even distantly to a library function.

The library director in the Greek tradition was normally a scholar, or at any rate one reputed to be a scholar. Such individuals were apparently the librarians in Rome too, albeit sometimes legally slaves. In the mid-first century, together with numerous other governmental reforms, Emperor Claudius formalized library administration under an official of the imperial civil service. These career men were of the equestrian class, the "knights," drawn from the municipal aristocracy of Italy and the provincial towns, and had normally performed military service. For the next hundred years or so the scholars operated the libraries under the control of these frequently able administrators. Not surprisingly, financial affairs seem to have occupied the library directors more and more. In the course of the second century those functions apparently crowded out the others, and the professional part of librarianship was left to the scholars, book buying included. By the third century the library manager was a finance officer; and in the fourth, his functions became part of the responsibilities of the city prefect. The crisis of the empire had by then overwhelmed the old aristocracy with new privileges for the soldiery; the equestrian class was no more; and city officials were rarely more than pliant tools of the emperor. Whatever effect these developments may have had upon those who operated libraries, none were dramatic enough to have achieved notice in our histories.

Library Literature Nor, despite all the experience and recorded rules of operation, has any work on librarianship survived from classical antiquity. According to some empire writers, and the medieval figures who often copied them more or less faithfully, Varro penned a three-volume treatise. Whatever the irretrievable facts may have been, we have today only this meager evidence. Pliny the Elder, famous for his encyclopedic *Natural History* of the late first century, apparently wrote a grammar. From that grammar survive two passages which Pliny allegedly credited to *Varro de bibliothecis libri III.* (Nos. 53 and 54, pp. 208-209, in G. Funaioli, *Grammaticae Romanae Fragmenta,* Leipzig: Teubner, 1907.) The second refers to book repair. The first speaks of *vectigaliorum* (genitive case), which may mean taxes, honoraria, or contributions. Perhaps Varro took note of the widespread Hellenistic custom of supporting libraries and other public institutions by means of levies sometimes voluntary sometimes not. The idea might have appeared in some work circulating then but since lost. The Greeks, after all, had been writing handbooks in the various applied arts and sciences for about three hundred years, such as those on "argument" mentioned in Aristotle's *Topics* (I. 14); few have survived, and a library handbook may be among the missing. Or Varro may have developed his views on the basis of his observations of the private collections familiar to him; or perhaps his main sources were Romans who had been abroad and seen libraries there. It must be remembered, meanwhile, that we have no other details about his "work on libraries," and the two passages on record remain to be verified.

The nearest surviving equivalent, apparently, is the paragraph about the duties of the emperor's own librarian, included in a most revealing document of about A.D. 300, a translation of which is rather easily accessible in the *Ante-Nicene Fathers* (VI. 158-161). The writer, believed to have been Bishop Theonas of Alexandria, Egypt, addresses a fellow Christian who is chief chamberlain at the emperor's court, advising him on the performance of his duties and behavior in general, primarily in the interest of his becoming influential enough to draw more pagans into the Christian fold. Of all the personnel the chief chamberlain will supervise, he affirms (sec. VII), "the most responsible . . . and also the most careful," in the emperor's view, will be the librarian. In fact the emperor "will himself select" that functionary, because he wants "a person of proved knowledge, a man grave and adapted to great affairs, and ready to reply to applications for information." Were a Christian to be tapped for the honor, he "should not despise that secular literature and those Gentile intellects which please the emperor." Well may the collection include poets, orators, philosophers, historians. "On occasion" this Christian librarian will "also . . . endeavor to laud the divine Scriptures"; "little by little" the "exclusive Divinity" of Christ will be explained.

To this end, he should know "all the books which the emperor possesses" and arrange them "neatly" in their order "by catalog." He will have copying done by "the most accurate" scribes obtainable and if necessary employ as revisers "learned men" paid "justly"; he ought not concern himself with ornate paper or lettering. He should be "agreeable to Caesar," recommending books "as he is able"; and to avoid any appearance of relying upon "his own understanding only," had better cite supporting opinions of others.

How many of those functions would have been familiar to librarians in the public libraries of the Empire? We know neither that nor how often Christians sought library jobs to try to promote Christianity.

Words and Thoughts

Paralleling these achievements of Greco-Roman civilization were developments in terminology and thought destined to exert great influence long after many libraries and books disappeared.

Bibliotheca The original Greek term *bibliotheke* apparently denoted at first any *theke* or *theca* (container or receptacle) suitable to hold a *biblion:* i.e., initially, papyrus with writing on it. Latin adopted it for the same meaning, then for a building which housed such writings, and still later, for the collection thus housed. The transit did not carry along the additional Greek meaning of "archives," a welcome small blessing for those who search the sources. But the developments in usage did present problems: Roman jurists of the early third century debated whether the bequest of a *bibliotheca* included the books or simply the *armaria* which contained them. At some point in antiquity, the use of *bibliotheke* took an additional twist. It was used in titles by anthologists and digesters to suggest that their compilations were so near being whole "libraries" that one scarcely needed any other reading matter. Possibly the earliest was the *Bibliotheke* of one Apollodorus, a systematic handbook of Greek mythology, compiled most likely in the first century. Medieval Christians often used the word as a synonym for the Bible. While the broader assumption was to be found serviceable at least to the twentieth century, it was also to be elbowed aside by a product of educational philosophy, the concept "encyclopedia."

The Classification of Knowledge Inevitably affecting not just encyclopedias but nearly every aspect of thought and study was the very classification of knowledge, beginning with the earliest known Greek philosophers. Whether or not their schemes had any influence upon contemporary book arrangement is not known; but they are important nonetheless as evidence of the state of agreement or disagreement over what a given subject covered and its relationships to other subjects.

Mathematics apparently meant roughly the same thing to all who used it, although views of its importance differed; likewise such lesser subjects as Military Science, and the Productive Arts concerned with goods.

There was more limited consensus with respect to Politics. It was taken, by and large, to embrace not only the political but economics and education. To the Stoics, however, absorbed above all with what was right, it was a branch of Ethics; whereas in the Aristotelian scheme, more pragmatic, it was coequal with Ethics, and both Military Science and Rhetoric (persuasion) were regarded as arms of political action.

For the Stoics, Rhetoric was expression in the service of truth, paired with Dialectic as a subdivision of Logic. In the same ethical-purposeful spirit, Plato treated poetry from several points of view, but not that of the aesthetic. Aristotle did, using the word "poetry" at times to mean the production of beauty in various forms.

Even greater was the divergence of views about fundamentals. In Plato the Dialectic was the essence of existence, intellectual give-and-take rising through many stages to comprehension (?) of the Ultimate. In Aristotelian thinking the Ultimate was uncertain at key points, sometimes explicitly: there was little supernatural in what Aristotle called variously Metaphysics, First Principles, or Theology. The Dialectic was to him but one mode of logical reasoning, and the several modes were jointly a tool for understanding "subjects." The Stoics treated the Dialectic as a branch of Logic, but provided for Theology separately, as a branch of Natural Science, in conformity with their idea of God as omnipresent.

All these concepts were objectified and many of them abstract, characteristic products of Greek civilization. A pattern centered rather on man and his behavior was fashioned a little later, in the Rome of the first century B.C. As the waxing of Roman power nourished a strong business class and contributed to strife among merchant, city plebeian, landowner, and farmer, Julius Caesar's leadership betokened the end of the republic. Partly to win mass acceptance of the strong-man "patriot," Varro prepared a large work on "antiquities"; it presumably helped him make a favorable impression on Caesar. Thanks principally to St. Augustine, who 400 years later attacked it in the *City of God* (VI. 3), we know that it consisted of twenty-five "books" on "human affairs" and sixteen on "the divine." Four main divisions appeared in each group: men, places ("where they perform"), times ("when . . ."), and things ("what . . ."); the divine related each of these to the obeisance of men to the gods, and added a "book" on the gods themselves. Augustine considered Varro's achievement one of "most subtle distinction." Its loss is painful to contemplate.

Varro's treatment of the "gods," as reported by Augustine—with what appear to be quotations from the original—is remarkable both semantically and politically. He spoke, it seems (*City of God,* VI. 5. 1), of three kinds of "theology." The first was the "mythical," which included theatrical spectacles and "fictions" and was used chiefly by the poets. The "physical" was next. In the "many books" left by the "'philosophers'" were such questions as whether "gods" were "'of fire, as Heraclitus believes, or of number, as Pythagoras, or of atoms, as Epicurus says.'" This theology was kept by the philosophers in schools, away from the populace "in the Forum." Indeed Varro thought, says Augustine (VI. 6. 3), that because the philosophers' offerings were "more than it is expedient for the people to pry into," and the poets' writings provided insufficient guidance for the Romans, a middle way was necessary. Varro, therefore, devised a third, "civic" theology focused on which gods it was suitable to worship and with what ceremonies. So shrewd a balance nearly drove moralist Augustine to distraction just reading it long after the event. For contemporary power builder Julius Caesar to have liked it seems logical.

Another important contribution from Varro, in the tradition of the seven liberal arts, is more conveniently considered in the next chapter.

Philonic-Christian Revelation   The association of worship with drama and the imaginative, the association of natural and supernatural, had arrived at Rome from many sources and would continue in men's thinking for several centuries to come. How much Varro's writings contributed to that stream directly is not known. Well established, on the contrary, is the new conception of Theology projected by Philo of Alexandria, renowned Jewish philosopher of the first century. The meaning of the term made familiar by usage in Greek philosophy had been the study of a rather remote and abstract Divine from books no more important in themselves than those on any other subject. Aristotle had reasoned that top importance belonged to Theology only "if there is an immovable substance," otherwise, to Natural Science (*Metaphysics,* VI. 1). The issue was not cleared up either by the Stoics or by Philo, who, accepting their general model, transferred the Stoic Theology from Natural Science to Ethics.

But Philo also regarded Jewish law as revealed by God, the Old Testament as a book apart from and above all others. The "wisdom" represented therein was the apex of what men strove to achieve in their studies and other activities: all the latter were subordinate to it. The hierarchy of subjects thus added a new and higher level. The Greeks had long spoken of ordinary school courses like geometry and grammar as handmaidens to Philosophy (Logic, Ethics, and Natural Science taken together). Philo pronounced Philosophy and all its individual components in turn handmaidens to the revealed "wisdom" of the Old Testament (*Preliminary Studies,* XIV). The early Christian Fathers followed suit, adding the New Testament to the "wisdom" literature.

Thanks, therefore, to successive Hellenistic, Jewish, and patristic contributions, "theology" was established as a word with two different meanings, representing subjects with entirely different positions in the classification of knowledge: (1) the supreme subject, Revelation, comparatively well defined; (2) an ill-defined array of subjects ranging from Greek metaphysics (problems of being, becoming, etc.) to rituals both dignified and orgiastic in honor of Aphrodite-Venus. Group (2) subjects were often considered a branch of Philosophy, in turn normally subordinate to Revelation-Theology. This dualism would be felt throughout Christendom, affecting bibliographies and catalogs demonstrably, although its impact on book shelving remains obscure.

Christianity

Christendom, indeed, was stirring noticeably in the womb of the Roman Empire. By the fourth century it was a major influence.

Urban Beginnings   Often quoted is the lament late in the fourth century by the historian Ammianus Marcellinus. The grand old city was going to the dogs, he complained; high living and indolence were conspicuous and "the libraries are shut up forever like tombs." The paragraph in question, however (*History,* XIV. 6. 18), is a diatribe against the triumph of idle luxury "in the few houses that were formerly famed for devotion to serious pursuits." One must bear in mind, moreover, that the author was a Syrian Greek, a veteran of the empire's wars against Persia, anxious to play the Roman patriot and to show the literary lions at Rome that he could most worthily continue the history composed by their hero, Livy. Ammianus Marcellinus had utilized the library at his native Antioch and very likely others in the Near East as well; he records unhappily the destruction of books occasionally incident to political and religious strife. If his tones about Roman libraries seem especially sad, he may have wished to point up the lag of the metropolis behind the provinces. Perhaps he had suffered some of the ill-treatment meted out to noncitizens at that time in Rome, or had been denied access to some libraries there.

Of course that does not signify that our observer had no reason for his lamentations or that he was the only person in that frame of mind. Ever since the days of Christ, indeed, there had been a growing movement of those rejecting Roman principles of behavior. The early Christians began with the Holy Scriptures as well as polemics against both the pagans and each other. Their churches also accumulated records, service books, and the like. How much of this reading matter was simply in private possession and how much in church libraries has not been established. Painfully clear is Diocletian's last-ditch effort in 303 to wipe out Christianity partly by burning all the books within the reach of his agents. Some books escaped because a church official here and there surrendered heretical works, medical works, etc., while hiding approved doctrinal material, but the surviving items were probably too few to contribute significantly to a library tradition.

Whatever may have been the precise fate of the Christian community's books in Rome, the achievements associated with certain other communities are better documented. By the testimony of Eusebius, and other sources, it is known that his great ecclesiastical history was composed largely from the collections in two libraries. One was founded in Jerusalem in 212 and somehow spared the end decreed by Diocletian. Inasmuch as the founder of this library had earlier studied under the scholarly Clemens and Origen, at a school in Alexandria, a library may be supposed to have flourished there too. The second one utilized by Eusebius was the library at ancient Caesarea (near Jerusalem), which appears in the records from 231 to 386. It was admired not only for Greek and Latin theology, philosophy, and science titles but for literature of the law.

The attainment by Christianity of the same status enjoyed by other religions, formalized by Emperor Galerius in 311 and Constantine in 313, was soon evident in the realm of books and libraries as well as in other ways. By order of the imperial government much energy was applied to the restoration of lost religious writings and the production of numerous copies for wide distribution. Several church libraries were founded in Rome in the fourth century, at least one of which separated Greek and Latin materials in the Roman secular style. Possibly representative of those elsewhere in the west, gone so often without a trace, was the church library at Nola (a few miles east of Naples), of which an inscription survives directing the devout to the theological collections.

Rural Solitude Another element was being added. Even in the third century, and more in the fourth, the imperial pressure upon the urban middle class and the frequent misery of the peasants produced considerable flight from urban centers and in many areas from the cultivated land as well; more stringent controls over tax collection and mobility were attempted, with limited and spotty success. In some minds these forces and events took shape as religious impulses. Out to the caves and deserts of Egypt and Syria they trudged, to meditate in solitude.

The anchorites and ascetics, some of them scholars, devoted part of their isolation to the reading of books, either personal copies carried with them or library copies borrowed from area centers like Jerusalem. When monasteries arose in the fourth century, copying and reading were fre-

quently prominent in their routines. The oft-cited regulations of St. Pachomius (d. 346) required among other things manual labor and daily reading;
each monk was to borrow his book in the morning and return it at night to
the wall closet; a book should never be left open in the cell if the reader
stepped out. The original Rule is not extant and the reliability of details in
surviving later versions remains in some doubt. Yet Pachomius was reportedly the first to organize an economically viable community life, with 1,400
monks in his own *coenobium* and 7,000 in the group of units under his
direction. The influence of his example presumably extended more or less to
all his prescriptions. Less than two generations later Augustine composed
similar rules for monks and nuns: among other things the librarian was
obliged to furnish codexes at stipulated hours and refuse them outside those
hours. That and other Augustinian customs traveled widely when the
monks fled before the Vandals to southern Europe and France. The status of
these ideas may be judged from the conviction of the biobibliographer Gennadius, writing at the end of the fifth century a supplement to Jerome's *Lives
of Illustrious Men* (*A Select Library of Nicene and Post-Nicene Fathers*, 2d
ser., vol. III, pp. 385-402), that the holy Pachomius had received his rule "by
angelic dictation" (chap. VII).

In the church libraries books were usually in the care of clericals; the
inventory was the deacon's responsibility. It seems reasonable to suppose
that the larger churches had library staffs, but we have no proof of it. That
some monasteries of the fourth century were already conducting their libraries in an organized manner is evident from the rules referred to. In the
system of St. Pachomius the *secundus* (deputy abbot?) was responsible for
the library. Accessibility of the monastery collections to outsiders seems
unlikely, except for the numerous church scholars who profited widely from
a sort of interlibrary loan. Church libraries, more often urban installations,
may have been administered more freely, but we do not know.

Some basis for an optimistic view is afforded by a remark of St. Jerome's. In his late-fourth-century *Apology* alluded to above (p. 6), in good
part a defense of bishop-historian Eusebius (260-340), he quotes Eusebius'
tribute to one Pamphilus. Founder of a theological school in Caesarea, he
had promptly won the admiration of the young Eusebius when the latter
settled there. One of the specific services for which Eusebius praised
Pamphilus—in Jerome's reporting (*Apology*, I. 9)—was his readiness to loan
copies of the Holy Scriptures "'not only to men, but to women also, if he
saw that they were given to reading.'" This passage does not tell us whether
the borrowers were members of the seminary community or townspeople or
the frequency and conditions of borrowing or what if anything was issued
aside from the Holy Scriptures. Nor have we, apparently, independent assurance that such quasi-library service actually existed. It is striking testimony to a state of mind, nonetheless, that Jerome thought the story worth
relating.

How many officials of church or monastery read these works of St.
Jerome's no one can tell; still less, what influence they exerted. But it is a fact
that the written word, even an education, was to assume in medieval Christendom a status substantially new in the West. In time it would become an
opportunity within reach of the commoner, male or female.

Chapter Two

THE MIDDLE AGES TO 1225

Ancient times in Western civilization may be said to have given way to the Middle Ages at various dates, depending upon what seems most significant for the purpose in hand. One may start as early as 212, with Emperor Caracalla's decree that businessmen accept Roman citizenship, for that status was by then tax-burdensome, and the decree exposed the fatal gulf between those businessmen and the imperial government. Or one may take it politically, with Constantine's founding of the Byzantine Empire in the early fourth century; or organizationally, in the mid-fourth century, with the first known "rules" of monastic life composed in the sandy wastes of the Near East. From the point of view of book selection one might prefer as a bench mark the illegalization of pagan cults in the Western empire at the end of the fourth century, the closing of pagan temples and the libraries in them; these acts ostentatiously reversed previous Roman custom and began formally a succession of strong pressures against classical literature in the West. Or perhaps the key shift was the technical advance in the fifth century, when the codex—the handwritten book, in use at least since the early third century—achieved enough acceptance to supersede the *volumen* ("roll"), making easier the physical handling of reading matter, especially the longer works.

Books and Libraries, ca. 400–1225

Whichever event or combination of events one regards as the boundary line or transition period, certain facts of the library life of antiquity probably suffered little change before the Renaissance.

The Limits of Literacy Those able to read included laymen favored by occupation or status. This was notably the condition in Italy, unique for the prominence of laymen in the professions almost uninterruptedly right through to the Renaissance. North of the Alps, the fading of the Roman public schools gravely undermined literacy in Latin among laymen, but it survived among the ecclesiastics; by the twelfth century literacy in the vernaculars was rising in both sectors. As for the peasant masses, the slim chance for improvement through the army was now joined by a similarly slim chance through the church; not until the eleventh century did such opportunity for education and advancement on merit become significant. In any case, the bulk of the peasants who continued tilling the soil enjoyed little beyond the barest of literacy; few could have had either motive or permission to use a library.

Books, Libraries, and the Christian Church Books and writing had by Hellenistic times been assured the respect of least the educated. Whereas the illustrious tragedy writer Aeschylus had in the mid-fifth century B.C. composed an epitaph speaking not of his drama but of his share in the Battle of Marathon, a hero of the repulse of Germanic invaders from Athens in A.D. 269 said nothing of that in his epitaph, alluding only to his quality as a rhetor and writer. This high status of the book was to be sustained.

It was assured in the first place by the indispensability of the Bible to Christians, a phenomenon new to the West, surpassing even the veneration of the Greek Neoplatonists for Homer. Besides, other writings soon became important. When Christianity appeared on the scene, its followers were in general poor, persecuted, and literate barely or not at all. Little by little, however, churches were established and service literature produced. As competing ideas and practices emerged, and polemics were hurled by rival factions at each other, and at non-Christian religious forces, collections of these bodies of thought were assembled, organized, and cared for. The cumulative investment in books as community property by ecclesiastical organizations proved far more favorable to respect for books than the transitory performances of private collectors, whatever their wealth, power, or talents. Outstanding as a symbol of the church commitment was the initiation of a papal (forerunner of the Vatican) library in Rome, in 384, shortly after Ammianus Marcellinus published his complaints.

Others Interested in Books and Libraries From the fourth century to the fifteenth, library life in the West was very largely in the hands of organized Christianity. Significant exceptions were the installations of Moslem Spain (711-1031), Norman South Italy (1016-1189), many North European towns in the days of the Hanseatic League, and some provincial courts all over Europe. During the same epoch library life in the Roman East was also primarily an organized Christian endeavor; but the secular tradition remained alive in Constantinople despite severe trials, and the influence of Islam from the eighth century on contributed both positively and negatively to all the culture of Christendom.

Unchanging Library Features   Owing to these social circumstances, and the technical limitations on book production by hand, book selection before the invention of printing consisted not of choices from myriad publication lists but of decisions as to what was worth assigning man-hours to copy. Copying was indispensable. Library collections and library quarters were developed, or not developed, according to the outcome of struggles beyond the walls. The space between *armarium* shelves having been increased enough to allow codexes to be stored standing up, the closet with shelves ("book press" in the terminology of the many writers of English English) remained the principal furniture. (A striking exception, evident from ninth-century miniatures, was the resort of the age of uncertainty often called "Dark" to chests easily transported as well as locked.) Fire was probably the most redoubtable foe, although injunctions to handle books carefully were common, even rules about how to hold a book. There were individuals who spent their adult years in library work, traditions associated with those labors, and libraries which earned international fame; there were dozens of handwriting texts and scores of loan-and-recover regulations, but neither literature nor schools of librarianship.

The Empire and Libraries, in the Fifth and Sixth Centuries

The Provinces and Libraries   In nearly all the provinces of the empire, about 400, there were church libraries and also private collections of the numerous senators who shrewdly left the declining capital for the greater ease and personal security of their estates. Gaul was for the moment particularly favored by circumstances. The Franks and the Romans produced a Gallo-Roman aristocracy agreeable to education; the balance was not upset when the Frankish kingdom was formed and Clovis, its ruler, became a Roman Catholic at the end of the fifth century. Yet the weakening of the empire meant in daily life injuries to commerce, the growth of isolation, and the dilution of culture. The brothers at the monasteries founded at that time by St. Martin of Tours (about 130 miles southwest of Paris) copied orthodox Christian writings but nothing else. The sisters living according to the Augustinian Rule as adapted early in the sixth century by Caesar of Arles were assigned primarily to the copying of holy writings, and the abbess kept a record of all these books. When Bishop Gregory of Tours wrote his *History of the Franks,* late in the sixth century, there were few words about books and none about libraries.

The Romans in Spain, established for some time in a rather similar fashion, accommodated themselves in the fifth century to the successive waves of Germanic invasion, notably those of the Vandals and the Visigoths. However low the general state of affairs may have sunk, something must have survived at higher levels. In some cities of the Iberian peninsula, in subsequent decades, there were families enjoying comfort and culture. From one, in the late sixth century, came Bishop Isidor of Seville, who prepared an encyclopedic work on the basis of passable book resources and the impulse to use them.

North Africa, granary of the empire, presents a different scene. The Vandals were invited there from Spain in 430 by the rebellious Roman governor of the province. The combined forces' second, successful siege of Hippo (near modern Tunis) was the backdrop for the death in 431 of its great bishop, St. Augustine. The destruction wreaked there, and afterward in Rome also, gave the English language "vandalism." But church schools were not interrupted in their work; and at the very court of the Vandal warrior-king the compiler Martianus Capella completed his influential encyclopedia. The next hundred years, however, witnessed many revolts of the local Berbers, and the defeat of the Vandals in the 540s by the Eastern (Byzantine) Empire. One hears less of libraries in churches. The rural monastic foundation, testimony to urban decay, rapidly assumes greater prominence.

Productivity in Eastern monasteries was doubtless increased in the late fourth century with the adoption rather widely of the Rule of St. Basil, emphasizing supervision where individual decision had been dominant. That manuscript copying benefited therefrom is highly probable; but the precise effects on library service remain obscure.

Egypt's Alexandria in the first place, and the Eastern provinces generally, were more involved than the Western provinces in church ideological struggle. To mention only the best known clash, the dogma that Christ was created on a particular occasion and only similar to God was voted down at the Council of Nicaea in 325; official favor went to the opposing dogma that Christ is coequal to and coeternal with God. The rejected view, known as the Arian heresy, remained popular among the masses of the East and many of the Germanic tribes which gradually came to dominate the Western provinces. Propagandizing against that heresy and several others accordingly became one of the principal occupations of the majority leaders of the church—with success considerable but never complete. Feeling sometimes ran high: early in the fifth century a Christian mob in Alexandria lynched Hypatia, a teacher of philosophy known for her appreciation of the pagan masters. Early in the sixth, more decorously, the imperial government closed the academy founded by Plato at Athens—hardly more than one generation after Boëthius, the last important Roman votary of pagan culture, had learned his classics there.

The collections may have suffered from the unwelcome attention given them in Alexandria and Athens, but in general libraries East and West were apparently touched little by daily events. More often, libraries fell victim to flames, accidentally as a rule, or, in the East, to earthquakes. In many such instances rehabilitation or reconstruction was undertaken. How many disappeared, how many were restored, how great was the lag, are questions not yet answered.

That major libraries were held important and that their insulation from political or other controversy was taken for granted seem indicated by evidence from the fourth-century capital of the Eastern Empire.

The Imperial Library in Constantinople   In 330 Emperor Constantine built a new capital on the western shore of the Bosphorus, near ancient Byzantium, and soon called the entire urban area Constantinople (330). A large (royal or university or both?) library was erected under his son, Emperor Constantius, in 353. What the twenty-year interval signifies is not clear. Did the administrators and scholars rely on the already existing monastery and other collections in the older parts of the city?

Similarly tantalizing is the apparently unique decree of 372, the second of three incorporated in the *Theodosian Code* ("Pursuit of Liberal Studies in Rome and Constantinople," Book XIV, Title 9 in Pharr's translation, Princeton University Press, 1952). It is worth full quotation:

> The same Augustuses to Clearchus, Prefect of the City [Constantinople] We command that four Greek and three Latin copyists, skilled in writing, shall be selected for copying the manuscripts of the library and for repairing them on account of their age. To them the appropriate subsistence allowances shall be issued from the caducous supplies of the people, for the copyists themselves also appear to be from the people. For the custody of the aforesaid library, men of ignoble status shall be sought out and immediately assigned to that duty.

At least three points deserve attention: the meaning of "copyists," the nature of the compensation stipulated, and the role and status of the library. First, "copyists" is the standard rendering of *antiquarii*, but "copying" may be an inadequate translation of *componere*, for (as indicated by the translator himself) it also means "collect" or "arrange." That is, the copyists may have performed more functions than merely copying correctly. One ground for thinking so is that they were almost surely hired to clear away known errors and confusion, and for that task they needed more than the ability to read and write. Another is that "men of ignoble status" were specified for the "custody" of the library but for no other function listed in the decree. Finally, that "immediately assigned" sounds as though the library had lately been given hardly any care at all.

Secondly, the copyists, skilled men, were apparently to be paid in goods rather than cash. "From the people," cited as the justification for assigning shares from "the caducous supplies of people," is manifestly a designation of social-legal standing, and "men of ignoble status" may be the label of a lower level. *Caduca* was that class of property which, in the absence of children or certain other legal heirs, went to the state. Did this mode of compensation apply only to temporary (?) employees of the imperial library in Constantinople or to others as well? Was it in fact a further application of imperial beneficence toward professors of letters, on behalf of the highly valued liberal education—of a piece with Constantine's decree that they should have salaries from the state and the municipalities?

Third, if this order was carried out it surely benefited "the library" and its users. Had the order any other purpose or significance? The empire was then under the joint control of *augusti* elected by the soldiers, and menaced by unrest in the major cities on the frontiers. The Eastern *augustus* was Valens, reportedly an intolerant Arian, and the Western *augustus* was Valentinian, said to have been a tolerant orthodox Trinitarian and known to have been neutral in a number of key contests. The decree, addressed to the prefect of Constantinople, was signed by both *augusti*. If that act was just a formality—most decrees were signed thus—the neutral, service character of library operation would seem to be underlined.

Yet the influence of political life was not altogether absent. The late fourth century saw much effort by the Romans to improve and extend schooling, largely because provincial talent was vital to help administer the empire. The three edicts referred to were a part of that effort. Furthermore, it is perhaps not accidental that the copyist assignment favored Greek, if only slightly. The use of Latin had been brought to Byzantium by Constantine, together with the seat of central government. But the local civil servants were more at home in Greek; by 600, in fact, Latin was to be very little known there. The decree of 372 may reflect accurately the condition at an early stage in this development.

Organization for Preservation in Sixth-Century Italy

The formal end of the "Western" Empire in 476 was of course a single incident in a long decline. Ever since the third century it had been increasingly evident that there were not enough Romans to run the enterprise, and the emperors' resort to infiltrating "barbarians" brought the provincial peasant population onto the scene in a fashion new in Western history. The emperors also squeezed the urban middle class into impotence without eliminating the envy of urban privilege often endemic among the soldiery. In the heaving and spasms of a dying system, libraries and reading were thus profoundly, if indirectly, affected by peasant masses who could not read and probably gave books little thought.

Rome was sacked in 410 and again later by invading Germanic tribes, which before long converted northern and central Italy into one of their own kingdoms. These Ostrogoths were pleased enough with Roman culture to allow in the sixth century the generously oriented labors of Boëthius, whose writings on music and philosophy are only the best known of a large bibliography. The new rulers were also glad to utilize the services at court of the Roman patrician Cassiodorus. But social and cultural conditions were being altered enough so that the atmosphere would have seemed very strange to Marcus Aurelius, the second-century philosopher-king. At the end of the fifth century some of the Italian nobles were engaged in copying manuscripts, it is said, because there were not enough slaves capable of it. At the end of the sixth, Pope Gregory the Great was ignorant of Greek, contemptuous of classical Latin, and militantly opposed to pagan literature. That the Pope was an able man who reportedly made interlibrary loan agreements with church officials in Spain and Constantinople underscores the fact that Christian theology had by then enough standardization of technical terminology in Latin to be able to dispense with classical models.

From these changes, at once retrogressive and progressive, emerged one of those zigzag advances so familiar to the student of history. The Italian nobles who were willing to copy classical manuscripts were in part expressing late-fifth-century pagan resistance to rising Christianity. From such motives did they pick up the slack left by declining Roman public libraries apparently no longer able to meet all the copying necessities. Yet, in just a few more generations, pagan resistance would matter much less, while the full-time servants of Christendom would be preserving not only the Bible and liturgy but some of the classical writings initially ignored or even condemned.

Benedict   About the year 500, a twenty-year-old aristocrat, Benedict of Nursia, saw decrepit Rome, and rejected it for religious contemplation. In 529, after several unsatisfactory experiences with individuals and groups following various rules, he established a monastery on a famous hill some 90 miles southeast of Rome (halfway to Naples), Monte Cassino; and there he lived until his death some fifteen years afterward. Firmly in the monastic tradition, Benedict considered reading and meditation virtually one. So it seemed also to many before and since. But in this framework, the "profane" titles were not in the picture: only "divine" reading counted. Reading indeed was not projected as an aspect of individual self-fulfilment, of self-directed study or pleasure. It was a duty, the duty of a sinful insignificant member of a community seeking to know its God. Edifying passages were daily read to a strictly silent assemblage of brethren at meals and in the evening. Individual reading was required on Sundays, discretionary at some other times; certain portions of the Bible were not to be read at night, lest they overstimulate. At the outset of Lent, books were distributed to the brothers from the "library" (a book closet?) and each was obliged to read his through, alone in his cell. Senior monks patrolled the corridors to make sure that the expected zeal was in evidence and to report laggards for punishment. These regulations were spelled out in the chapter of the Rule (48) concerning the "daily manual labor" and the "sacred reading" alternating with it.

Necessary accordingly was the maintenance of a "library," or perhaps more accurately, reserve shelves; nothing was said of a "librarian." Furthermore, because a small number of titles had to be kept accessible to a large number of readers, who were forbidden to own anything except by permission of the abbot, much copying was implied. Whether the contemporary book trade was incapable of meeting the need, or Benedict wanted no part of the urban-commercial world, the copying was organized on the premises, presumably as part of the manual labor which his Rule nowhere particularizes. Actually, explicit reference to copyist labor was hardly necessary, having become long since a familiar feature of the preceding rules.

The Benedictine way came closer to scholarship when the lives of the monks were completely upset and reorganized. In 589, some forty years after the founder's death, the Monte Cassino community was destroyed by the most recent Germanic arrivals, the Lombards, and the brothers fled to Rome. Since their normal stint of manual labor, country-style, was not practicable there, much more time went henceforth into study, as Pope Gregory suggested. Thus were shaped some of the practices favorable to learning which the adoption of Benedictinism carried far and wide, for a few centuries. The Lenten ceremony, for example, was to become familiar in monasteries all over Europe—by the ninth century a sort of "Library Day" when each brother's borrowing and presumed reading for the year was announced and inventory taken.

For this good fortune book culture is indebted first, of course, to political and social circumstances. Hundreds of young men were then faced with the choice of hard work on the land, with both normal insecurity and the distress of intermittent war, or hard work as a monk, without family life but with a large measure of security. Not all monastic communities solved the problems of celibacy. But those following the Benedictine Rule did succeed, thanks to the twin principles of specific regulations and a strong abbot with broad executive discretion. Book culture is thus indebted, secondly, to a vital advance at that point in the art of personnel management.

It must be noted, on the other hand, that studying and copying under Benedictine auspices were seldom aided by specific provision of or directions for a librarian. Such help did appear in the more tightly organized Augustinian pattern: the *armarius* is alluded to quite regularly in extant regulations. It is not surprising that when Benedictine decentralization proved unable to avert decline—witness the Cluniac reform in the tenth century—several new monastic orders adhered to the Rule of Augustine. The comparative effectiveness of the two approaches under varying circumstances, particularly with reference to library life, has never been thoroughly investigated.

Cassiodorus and Vivarium A tradition focused less on monastic administration and more on books was being planted meanwhile by the slightly younger and longer-lived Cassiodorus. Like Boëthius he valued the classical heritage. Unlike Boëthius he respected the Ostrogoths and found it desirable to serve their king: he worked for years for reconciliation among the Romans, the Ostrogoths, and the Eastern Empire. Soon after the death in 526 of his master, Theodoric, Cassiodorus tried to found a Christian university at Rome. That failed, because Eastern Empire forces had moved up from reconquering North Africa and Sicily to engage the Ostrogoths for control of Italy, and war raged over the Eternal City for ten years. In 540, moreover, Eastern Emperor Justinian won Ravenna itself (on the Adriatic, 70 miles south of Venice), capital of the Ostrogothic kingdom. Many prominent individuals went to Constantinople. Among them in all likelihood was Cassiodorus, trying to promote peace by every means, even the exclusion from his writings of anything unfriendly to Justinian. By 554, probably, he was back in Italy, perhaps expecting the best of the emperor.

Unfortunately, Justinian chose on the contrary to try to exterminate the Goths. At this point, apparently despairing of anything constructive in northern and central Italy, Cassiodorus made his way far south to his estate at Squillace (on "the ball of the foot," near present-day Catanzaro). There, in his sixties, he inaugurated a monastery, named Vivarium, the story goes, after the nearby fishpond. What he may have known of Benedict does not appear in the records, but he reckoned that the monastery was by far the best available means of preserving the endangered heritage of antiquity, both Christian and pagan, both Latin and Greek.

Life was not controlled there by Benedict's rule or any other, although Cassiodorus commended one of them to the monks' attention. Indeed, fully conscious of the Fathers' preoccupation with prayer, the reading of the Holy Scriptures, and physical work, and the very minor role in the traditional monastic routine of even Christian scholarship, Cassiodorus took particular pains to raise the status of the latter. The Scriptures remained the center of concern, but they were regarded now not only as a means of indoctrination and salvation but as a subject for philological and other critical research. The profane branches of learning, the *artes,* were promoted on the grounds that they were all present in germ in the Old Testament, and had to be studied if the Holy Scriptures' value was to be appreciated in full.

For this, obviously, books were indispensable. It is unlikely that Cassiodorus shared the apparently dim view of the book trade noticed in the case of Benedict. He acquired codexes from all over Italy, from North Africa, already well established as the vital center of Latinized Christianity, and from anywhere else that his contacts and unusual private funds could reach. Whatever the book trade might furnish a library near a large city like Rome, however, it probably contributed little to these efforts of Cassiodorus. In any event, the building of the collections required much copying, either of items borrowed or for other reasons.

Copying had been assigned by St. Martin of Tours only to the younger, less experienced monks. And one of Cassiodorus' contemporaries thought it appropriate only for older monks incapable of physical labor. Cassiodorus himself disagreed vigorously. Summarizing earlier writings on theology and the seven liberal arts in the *Institutes,* his text for the monks, he deliberately incorporated in Book I, "On Divine Letters," glowing praise of the art of copying, and set an example by doing some himself. Certain phases of copying, indeed, the deciphering of text and correction of palpable errors, called for professional judgment based on a solid knowledge of grammar.

Nor was the aesthetic neglected. It had enjoyed honorable standing in Aristotle's works, and although the key items were lost for many centuries, later figures like the Roman poet Horace (65–8 B.C.) gave it renewed respectability. True, the early Christian Fathers were cool, if not hostile, to "outward" beauty. Yet many of them were also impressed by the neo-Platonic concept of spiritual light streaming from a divine source to souls everywhere. The third-century pagan philosopher Plotinus, credited by Augustine with "the reputation of having understood Plato better than any other of his disciples" (*City of God,* IX. 10), resolved those streams into imaginative intuitions. The association of the divine with beauty was apparently new to his audience, and agreeable, and his writings were enormously influential. It is therefore not surprising that the master of Vivarium expected the scribe's handwriting to match the spiritual beauty of what he penned. Bindings were likewise to enhance the appeal of the contents: Cassiodorus called the monks' attention to a pattern book and stated that local craftsmen were available to do the work. Many books, moreover, were carefully illustrated, contributing no little to the subsequent renown of Vivarium.

According to his own statements, Cassiodorus facilitated these efforts by providing a sundial, a water clock, and self-filling oil lamps.

Cassiodorus' Institutes The library materials were apparently arranged by subject. The founder discussed books in that fashion in his *Institutes,* and called attention to symbols marked on codexes, which related a given commentary to the item commented on. There may have been an exception to subject arrangement. In Book I, "On Divine Letters," he refers (VIII. 15) to the "Greek codexes" in the eighth *armarium;* also (XIV. 4) to the "various short works by Greeks" in that same *armarium*. Apparently, a single closet sufficed for all the Greek "divine" works; what would have been done had there been too many for it we do not know. Nor is it entirely settled that there were no Greek works on secular subjects. It is striking, however, and possibly significant, that these two are the only references in the *Institutes* to *armaria*.

The size of the collection is not very clear. Some observers have reckoned that nine *armaria* were assigned to the Holy Scriptures and works pertinent to their study; no estimates seem to have been ventured regarding the profane works. Since, however, the word *armarium* appears only twice in the *Institutes,* and on both occasions with reference to Greek books, the number of *armaria* must remain undetermined. Analysis of text passages concerning particular books, and other data, have yielded the hypothesis that some 120 codexes were involved, and perhaps some papyri as well. Whether that was "large" or "small" obviously depends upon what one knows of other contemporary libraries. Cassiodorus is believed by recent scholarship to have had a more substantial collection than the next prominent figure in educational history, encyclopedist Isidor of Seville. But we do not know enough to be sure.

Can the *Institutes* be regarded as a catalog of the Vivarium library? In some respects, yes. Book I, "On Divine Letters," refers to nine codexes whose numbering corresponds almost exactly to chapter headings I through IX. That the term "codex" meant a physical unit is highly probable, because specific titles mentioned elsewhere are described as being multi-"book" or "-volume," in one or two "codexes." It seems reasonable to suppose, moreover, that Cassiodorus' allusions in Book I (XXXI. 2) to medical works "on the shelves of our library" was direct description, whether those shelves were inside an unmentioned *armarium* or somewhere else.

In other respects the *Institutes* is patently not a library catalog. The discussion of the literature of theology, agriculture, and medicine (Book I), and of the seven liberal arts (Book II), reads by and large like any guide. In line with customs already about 700 years old, or older still, it includes abstracts of some writing presumably not in the collection. Research has shown, moreover, that Cassiodorus normally used for "reading" verbs meaning "to read aloud," a practice believed to have been common throughout ancient and medieval times but hardly suited to the public premises of a library. If the scholars are correct in this interpretation, the guide aspect of the work was more significant than the catalog aspect.

That the *Institutes* was intended as a librarian's manual seems very doubtful. It includes a chapter about copying, expanded in the author's supplementary work on orthography, which he refers to. But apart from the few sample subject markings mentioned above, this treatise does not offer either location symbols or advice on the performance of any library function other than copying. The products of the scriptorium managed by Cassiodorus inspired admiration all over Europe, and imitation, especially by the Benedictines. The digest makers and encyclopedia makers were demonstrably aware of him; they and many others most likely profited from the bibliographical help in the *Institutes*. Instruction on the organization and operation of a library, however, awaited later efforts. For the time being, caring for books remained often the charge of one also responsible for sacred vessels or even food supplies.

Yet one cannot exclude the possibility of indirect influence represented by Cassiodorus' treatment of the traditional subjects often called jointly "philosophy," and the very arrangement of his *Institutes*. In Book II, "On Human Letters," he dealt with Theology as had his model Boëthius: together with Natural Science and Mathematics *(doctrinalis)* it was a branch of the Aristotelian "Theoretical" (III. 4 and 6). He defined this Theology only in a single-sentence allusion (III. 6) to God and "spiritual creatures," the latter expression long capable of hospitality to demons and magic. The other Theology, the Scriptural studies placed at the topmost level by Philo and Augustine, absorbed the bulk of Cassiodorus' Book I, "On Divine Letters." This order of precedence, emphasized most strongly by Augustine in his polemic against Varro (*City of God*, VI. 4), was to become characteristic of medieval library catalogs.

Early Christian Book Selection and Education

While Cassiodorus produced no full-scale catalog of his library, his writings provide us with a basis for inferences about Christian book selection which is perhaps more solid than the data in any surviving earlier source. It is thus appropriate to reflect on why the titles were at Vivarium which modern scholarship thinks were probably there.

Christian Criteria   The Christians' reliance on books lent an urgency to decisions about what to acquire and what to copy which quite likely had not confronted their pagan predecessors. Furthermore, the elaborate corporate structure of the church lodged authority and responsibility rather clearly. Officials had to concern themselves with the reading matter in church or monastery from the viewpoints of organizational and educational interests. Critical attention was therefore given to both writings purporting to be Christian and those manifestly pagan.

Determining the purity of doctrine was frequently complex and sometimes risky. When Jerome prepared a biobibliography, late in the fourth century, to defend the church against the pagan charge that its leaders were ignorant rustics, he repeated to a considerable extent what church historian Eusebius had long since established as authoritative. When it came to commenting on the writings of his contemporary, Bishop Ambrose of Milan, the scholar in semiretirement at Bethlehem balked: "I withhold my judgment of him, because he is still alive, fearing either to praise or blame lest in the one event I should be blamed for adulation and in the other from speaking the truth" (*Lives of Illustrious Men*, chap. 124). It took time to settle what would be admissible to the "canon" and approved supplementary reading, and what would not be. Cassiodorus frequently spoke of a cited theological work as "canonical."

Certain other book selection problems were solved more easily. Spurious and fictitious titles attributed to authoritative Fathers, and false martyrologies, were condemned and hunted down as defamatory misrepresentations of Christian principles. One of the earliest surviving lists of authors and titles (the *Pseudo-Gelasian Decretal*), compiled in Italy at the end of the fifth century or some time in the sixth—and still being reproduced bodily in a popular Parisian education manual of the twelfth century—includes a section of nearly sixty items explicitly repudiated by the Church, the authors and their followers "to be damned forever." Cassiodorus may possibly have had a few such writings in the private collection the *Institutes* refers to now and then; but it is hardly likely that he would have risked keeping any in the monks' library, and the evidence suggests nothing of that sort.

What it does indicate is that the Vivarium library was primarily theological. The collection embraced Christian writings in some other areas, and a few pagan works. Indeed, Cassiodorus may have had more like them in his personal library. Yet those of his cast of mind were perhaps already a minority among the literate of the West. The decline of the empire had taken its toll of schools and learning, although both were still available to the upper classes in much of Italy. By Cassiodorus' day, the relations between Christianity and several non-Christian bodies of thought had been hostile for well over a century. To appreciate what this meant to book selection, one must leave Cassiodorus and Vivarium briefly and consider some of the interrelations in the dying Roman Empire of Christianity, philosophy, literature, and education.

The Seven Liberal Arts The Greek curriculum for an "ordinary education," *enkyklios paideia,* was presented formally to the Romans at least by Varro's time, the first century B.C. In a lost work known to us through borrowings and citations by later writers, he reportedly described as the "nine disciplines" grammar, dialectic, rhetoric, arithmetic, geometry, music, astronomy, medicine, and architecture (in good part engineering). The last two represent in effect, if not consciously, an attempt to link the theoretical emphases of the Greeks and the Roman preference for practical applications. It failed, because "liberal education" was designed for those who would not be working with their hands. Medicine and architecture were exclusively earthly and material, said Apollo to Mercury in the early-fifth-century best seller, Martianus Capella's "Wedding of Mercury and Philology" (see below); they should accordingly be spurned. Although law had been discussed by Plato, Aristotle, and the Stoics, there seems to be nothing on the subject from Varro.

The seven liberal arts were the heart of Roman schooling. A great deal of general education was subsumed under the terms "grammar" and "rhetoric": hence the reasonableness of the first-century educator Quintilian's remark that a properly trained orator could speak on any subject.

Augustine It was precisely such training that initially shaped young Augustine, son of a Christian mother and pagan father. Indeed the future saint was for some years late in the fourth century a teacher of rhetoric, the most prestigious station for a general educator in that age. It is said to have been the eloquence of a preacher in Milan, the Ambrose who was also canonized, which first drew him to Christianity.

The Augustine thus challenged was well acquainted with Greek thought. He had been subscribing to the Platonic view that the only reality in a world of tension and change is the Idea, particularly the Idea of the Good. Platonism emphasized among other things justice and order. Augustine was repelled by contemporary injustice and disorder, and this distress was aggravated by a temperamental preference for precision. Finding the search for the Platonic Good inadequate, he undertook a church career. It was not long before Bishop Augustine was convinced that the highest Good was knowledge of God. Not unfriendly to his former masters, he nevertheless regarded any other knowledge as unimportant unless in the head of one whose heart was humble, a view quite different from Plato's.

In his text for studious and God-fearing young men. *On Christian Doctrine* (A.D. 426), he deprecated spending precious school time on rhetoric. He liked euphonious expression, he declared, and tried to achieve it in his own work. But it was not that valuable: finding graceful writing in the sacred authors "very rarely," he averred, pleased him "just as well" (IV. XX. 41). The rules were all right—"if any good man should happen to have the leisure for learning them" (IV. I. 2). Furthermore, he considered both rhetoric and grammar to be really elementary subjects, best learned not in classrooms but by imitating good examples. Even figures of speech, "said to be learned as a matter of a liberal education," could be heard in the "vulgar idiom" of persons never trained in grammar. One might teach rules to boys of quick mind; but they would not help the dull, and the mature should not need such assistance (IV. III. 4).

Latin "Grammar"   The subject knowledge represented by the seven liberal arts could not however be summarily abandoned. On the contrary, the trouble was that, as increasing participation of provincials in public service demanded greater attention to the teaching of Latin, the time given to "subjects" had been shrinking. Necessary now was a new approach sidestepping the traditional purpose of producing orators. New texts were written accordingly, intended simply for a general education as taught by "grammarians." While such texts may not have been adopted widely and promptly, they won their welcome when public political debate had largely disappeared and schooling was based on life in monastery and manor.

Capella's Encyclopedia   Augustine was keenly aware of this mode of meeting a clear social need. A Christendom profoundly influenced by him received enthusiastically for centuries the pagan Martianus Capella's "Wedding of Mercury and Philology," written almost literally within the sound of Augustine's voice. The work was cast in a form guaranteed to please. It opened with the allegory which furnished the title, a format apparently designed by the Stoics to make the popular Olympian gods respectable despite their unedifying personal behavior, and elaborated upon by later schools of thought. Mercury represented eloquence, Philology literary knowledge; "this delightful and fruitful copulation," to quote the mid-twelfth-century tribute of John of Salisbury's *Metalogicon* (book 1, chap. 1), was indispensable to civilized existence. Within the allegory envelope was a potpourri of the serious and the comic then well established as a form of entertainment. The rest was a version—his "geometry" was mainly geography—of the seven liberal arts. Later teachers and encyclopedists like Boëthius and Isidor of Seville utilized it in varying degrees. Thanks partly to the mnemonic advantages of its verse components, Capella's contribution helped the liberal arts to gather momentum.

Other Study Aids A major portion of the educational task was performed also by the anthologies, digests, and handbooks for students and other readers. That substantial literature has been classified as follow: (1) collections for school use of definitions of terms and glosses—explanations—on passages in earlier authors; (2) elementary manuals for various arts; (3) introductions to the ideas of a particular thinker, known after a famous explication of Aristotle as "isagoges"; (4) collections of opinion, especially on philosophical issues, called in Greek style "doxographies"; (5) reports of literary analysis and research in technical affairs, the "heuristic literature." From the fifth century on, moreover, enthusiasm mounted for (6) the general and miscellaneous anthologies known as *florilegia*. This "flower gathering," both the activity and the metaphor, was virtually routine during most of the Middle Ages, and the contents perhaps just as routinely included excerpts from pagan sources.

Catalog Entries Hardly any compiler's or editor's name is known to us today. But there is some reason to think that these derivative works were available in medieval libraries whether mentioned in surviving catalogs or not. In the first place, diverse titles often appeared together in a single codex and those occupying the second or later position in the contents list were seldom given independent entries. So we are told, with explicitness not common, in the French Benedictine abbey of St. Riquier's catalog of 831: the 256 listed were "of course" not a total picture of the library's holdings; recorded separately their number would exceed 500. (Presented in Edward Edwards' *Memoirs of Libraries,* London: Truebner, 1859, I:297–301; and in Gustavus Becker's *Catalogi Bibliothecarum Antiqui,* Bonn: Cohen, 1885, pp. 24–29.) Precisely what that means is not altogether clear. Many entries in the St. Riquier catalog refer to more than one title, the additions following like a string of beads or linked by "and." In fact, one of these multiple entries (no. 21 in the Becker edition) ends with the phrase, "all this in one volume." Evidently, then, just because an item is not a prime entry does not signify that it is not in the list. This procedure may account for the difference between the 256 and the 500-plus the catalog refers to. By actual count the 176 theological codexes in the cloister contained 195 "books"; but a "book" was not necessarily a separate title. Besides, were there in the indicated codexes any works not registered in the list?

Apart from recorded codexes, were others on hand but not recorded? Study aids perhaps, thought of differently, something like modern vertical file materials, and listed elsewhere or not at all?

Distortion and Survival Although the summarizers and popularizers in general subverted the reading of originals and conveyed an appalling amount of misrepresentation by way of careless or uninformed handling, they also contributed to the fame of particular ancient texts. Virgil, for instance, would probably have attained to preeminence in medieval book collections, poems and all, on his merits. It certainly helped that he was the favorite of the fourth-century Roman commentator-digester Macrobius, whose writings on dreams made his name a byword for centuries.

Pagan Works and Christendom   Given this framework of social change, literary and educational activity, and technical conditions, the acceptability of particular pagan classics was determined mainly by their respective literary characteristics. The Greek writings were not at first suspect because they were rich and varied, with much emphasis on abstraction; the salacious was a minor element. Brought up on these items, the early church Fathers were well acquainted with them. The Eastern Fathers, indeed, primarily Greek readers, continued friendly to the Greek classics; they were received in the East more or less hospitably all through the Middle Ages. Latin literature had a strikingly higher proportion of racy material. Many Western fathers thought it dangerous to unformed or half-formed Christian minds. The Latin classics never disappeared altogether; but on certain occasions in medieval times they came close to official proscription. Book selectors turning thumbs down could always refer to the denunciations by Pope Gregory or some of St. Augustine's statements. Defenders quoted other statements by Augustine, the Greek Fathers, or that outstanding lover of fine writing, St. Jerome.

Particular charm attaches to the tradition stemming from the widely influential Roman moralist of the first century, Seneca. Writing to a young friend whom he was trying to win from Epicureanism to Stoicism, he remarked joshingly that he himself had been reading Epicurus, because it was his habit "to cross over even into the enemy's camp—not as a deserter, but as a scout" (*Letters to Lucilius* II. 5-6). In later times, at least by the mid-twelfth century, an ecclesiastic asking for a copy of a pagan like Cicero was apt to use the Seneca formulation seriously, for protection.

Surviving in the West, by and large, were the pagan works associated with the tradition of the seven liberal arts, philosophy, or practical needs, and sufficiently intelligible to the ordinary student to survive the competition of the handbooks. The literary trivium was fairly well represented at Vivarium. When discussing rhetoric, Cassiodorus referred not merely to the polished gentleman Cicero but to Porphyry, third-century polemicist against Christianity, pupil and teacher of leading neoplatonists. Porphyry's critique of Aristotle's introduction to logic, the *Categories,* translated and edited by Boëthius, was probably in the Vivarium library; it certainly, as a matter of record, was in many collections all over later medieval Europe. Cassiodorus also alluded to Virgil, but his poetry was apparently not in that library. Nor did Cassiodorus speak of history or any historians outside the church fold except Josephus and Livy. The former had prepared late in the first century materials on Jewish history considered important enough to students of Christianity to be translated into Latin at Vivarium. Since Josephus seemed to Cassiodorus "almost a second Livy" (*Institutes,* I. XVII. 1), and no explanation was offered, the brethren were apparently presumed familiar with the latter, a leading light of the days of Emperor Augustus (27 B.C.–A.D. 14), famous for his Roman history then and since. Apart from its ecclesiastical branch, and the vital church administration tool, chronology, history had uncertain credentials as a subdivision of the liberal arts, theology or philosophy.

The mathematical quadrivium, more demanding than literary studies, did not do so well. Since the great Greek scholars of the third century the mathematical sciences had declined steadily; readers of Latin were even worse off. Although Cassiodorus' *Institutes* refers to such well-known pagans as the first-century text writer Nicomachus, the library probably owned practically nothing beyond Latin versions of Euclid's geometry and Ptolemy's geography, standard then and for centuries to come.

Isidor of Seville Fewer classics apparently were available to Bishop Isidor, educator of Seville in the generations just after Cassiodorus, patriotic Spaniard as well as loyal Catholic. The episcopal library remains famous for, among other things, Latin verses proclaiming the attractions of various writings, supposed to have been painted, in the traditional manner, on the walls near the *armaria*. They have been taken for a sort of catalog. Like inscriptions on modern library buildings, they are probably not a sure guide to the holdings. But their thrust should not be ignored: it pointed toward hospitality to all literature.

Isidor did not select the books—principally religious—for the library (or libraries) he used. Rough estimates of what had been chosen for them can nevertheless be made on the basis of his writing (analyzed masterfully in J. Fontaine's *Isidor de Séville . . .*, Paris: Études Augustiniennes, 1959). The bishop was called upon for guidance by the leadership of the Visigothic kingdom, recently consolidated after defeating the Byzantines and converted from Arianism to Roman Catholicism. This guidance he furnished in several works, most notably his encyclopedia, which dealt with the seven liberal arts, philosophy and religion, and several practical subjects like boundaries. The tone was not that familiar from the school tradition but what would be associated in modern terms with the invitation to (adult) learning. Owing to Isidor's documentation habits, sometimes naming a recognized authority but never the immediate secondary source he actually had in hand, scholarship has had to rely on comparing passages in his writing with those of earlier authors. It seems probable that his citing of renowned figures testifies far less to a rich library of original sources than to intelligent use of the unnamed derivative works quoting those sources.

The parlous state of knowledge in the early seventh century is reflected especially in the poverty of Isidor's treatment of the mathematical quadrivium. Minor points dealt with casually, as common property, in the works of Augustine, appear in Isidor as valuable nuggets requiring close study. The literary trivium fares little better. The presentation of dialectic is shabby; that of grammar by far outshines it, dominating indeed the whole encylopedia. Although Isidor was apparently the first encyclopedist to include jurisprudence (also medicine and chronology, but not architecture) as one of his ten subjects, his material was dated; he does not seem to have known of either Justinian's codification of Roman law (530s) or the contemporary collections of canon (church) law. The low level of audience understanding, it has been suggested, may have had more to do with the shallowness of his offering than his own limitations. Investigation of his ignorance of Greek, moreover, has produced the hypothesis that he could have learned it but deliberately neglected it on nonscholarly grounds: Greek was associated with the Arian opposition to Catholicism, and with the Byzantine military forces lately expelled by his sponsors.

If the impact of Isidor's encyclopedia upon subsequent culture and libraries was to be of little help in science or direct knowledge of Greek contributions, the work nevertheless had several positive effects. First, it was suffused with the holiness of writing, contrary to the early Greek tradition and the classical Roman view, but in harmony with Oriental paganism, neoplatonism, and the church Fathers.

Second, the bishop organized his material on each subject around the genesis of its principal words. Thus were projected the Platonic emphasis on ideas as the true reality and the corollary concern with words and letters as symbols, and also the theme common to many bodies of thought that the pinnacle of human achievement lay in the past, whether the pagan Golden Age or the Christian pre-Fall epoch or some other by-product of distress about the contemporary. It has been observed, in fact, that whereas the Greek *etymologia* focuses simply on the first meanings, the Latin *origines,* which Isidor is believed to have preferred as the title of his encyclopedia, denotes not just the "first" but the "best." This "etymological" method helped make possible a remarkably objective use of any source serving the immediate purpose, sacred or secular, Christian or pagan. In a number of instances Isidor even quoted Christian Fathers without mentioning either the source or the religious context. The neutrality of his tone has been compared to that of the modern encyclopedia. So broad gauge an enterprise evidently appealed strongly to Christian students and scholars for the next seven or eight centuries; it was undoubtedly responsible in part for the survival of secular and pagan writings in libraries.

Examining each subject from the viewpoint of the meaning of its principal vocabulary also produced an array of small-concept units easily recognizable as such and readily capable of rearrangement. Isidor himself, whether or not he had the talent to project a new structuring of knowledge, attempted none. But his encyclopedia was a powerful force clearing the ground for the many efforts in that direction to be made by later minds. His work was thus an important contributory factor in the development of the classification of knowledge, even though his own conformed to the familiar.

The hallmark of modern encyclopedia organization, alphabetical order, was not a feature of the "Origins." Except in Book X on words, statements about terms were grouped by their meanings; alphabetical order appeared only occasionally, as a subarrangement. Such combinations of the classified and the alphabetical were to become a feature of many systems of book classification, among them, nearly 1,300 years later, that of the Library of Congress.

Reading, the book, and the library were touched on. The Spanish educator penned rules for the local monks which included not only the usual requirements for reading but apparently exceptional specificity about the time for individual reading daily and the abbot's lecture each evening on difficult passages; yet there seems to have been nothing about copying. Of the library regulations very little appears. It was a festive occasion when the bishop inducted a new librarian with the words, "You are the keeper of the books and the supervisor of the scribes." There were amusing oft-cited mural verses about being quiet—not a new idea. The encyclopedia, however, differentiated between *codex, liber,* and *volumen,* something Cassiodorus had not undertaken; and the scribe and his tools were described, in a fashion which may go back to a lost work of Varro's.

The Oral and the Written   Most instructive is the bishop's treatment of the written as against the oral, in the perspective of 300 years. Donatus, fourth-century grammarian whose text was studied down to the nineteenth century, discussed sounds before the letters of the alphabet. Augustine, having denounced superstition and pagan symbolism, assured his students that letters and shorthand characters were respectable, provided their use was subordinated to divine purpose. (The point came up naturally, because the apparently magical was always suspect, and St. Pachomius—very likely others too—was reputed to have employed a sort of cipher in his official correspondence.) Cassiodorus, a century and a half after Augustine, still offered the traditional exercises in memory, diction, and voice. Isidor, about the year 625, eliminated those exercises from his presentation of rhetoric, although he himself was regarded by contemporaries as a good speaker. His discussion of the letters of the alphabet in his encyclopedia accompanied chapters on the alphabet as a whole, writing, and nonalphabetical signs, all of which preceded his consideration of the oral. Unlike Cassiodorus, moreover, he explicitly declared that too much lay at hand to be "learned by hearing and held in the memory" (*Origins,* I. 3. 2).

All this depended, mechanically, on copying. The name for it seems to have continued Roman Empire practice: the official court scribe was called *librarius* in the fourth-century Theodosian Code. Presumably, like most other items in law codes, that was not brand new but a recognition of the established and accepted. Likewise, at least at the beginning of the seventh century, he who transcribed books old and new, *librorum descriptor,* was known also as *librarius.* So we are told by Bishop Isidor; those who copied only the old manuscripts, said he, were *antiquarii.*

On the other hand, the social character of copying changed decidedly. In antiquity, it was primarily the labor of slaves or paid scribes, available on the whole simply to those with some money to spend. In much of medieval Christendom—and Islam—copying became a duty as well as an occupation, a function viewed as necessary socially and spiritually. Especially after the organization of monastic orders, it was the job of men unpaid individually but supported as a group by society. Yet copying, on a mass scale, for the sake of anything other than preserving what was copied, promised little for accuracy. Nor did occasional hurry calls for multiple copies for new monastery or church libraries necessarily produce response at high standards. The capacity of the supervisor of the scriptorium to maintain quality control doubtless varied with men and circumstances. That some did perceive a need for good copying and in the Cassiodorian tradition exerted themselves to obtain it, is one feature of the Carolingian Renaissance. Another is the assignment of some monks to teach writing to boys who were not preparing for the service of the church. By the late eighth or early ninth century the latter activity was well defined and was conducted separately in the *armarium,* while conventional copying and the book collection were located in the scriptorium.

The Carolingian Renaissance

In the latter part of the fifth century the wave of the future flowed from the far-off British Isles. As the Franks swept over Gaul, they threatened to isolate the Romans in Britain and Ireland. By 442 the legions and administrators had pulled out, leaving behind a few scattered seeds of Christian culture.

Irish Monks   For the next century and a half the religious and education story known to us was written mainly by Irish monasticism. St. Columba in 563 founded the meditation and copying center of Iona, whose influence was soon in astonishing contrast with the island's six square miles (off the midwestern coast of Scotland). Another evangelist, St. Columban, established a string of missionary posts complete with liturgical books along his way through France and Switzerland to Bobbio (30 miles northwest of Genoa). There, in 612 (or 614?), he initiated a monastery in the heart of the Lombard kingdom, Arian like most of the Germanic areas and therefore in orthodox eyes in need of reclaiming from heresy. Zeal to copy, and the cost of parchment, led the Bobbio monks of the seventh century to delete lines of earlier documents to make way for religious texts; theirs may be the first palimpsests. Of library and book life in England itself during those 150 years, or six generations, no data of consequence have survived.

Anglo-Saxon England   At the close of the sixth century, however, a step decisive in the culture of northwestern Europe was taken by Pope Gregory the Great. He dispatched the missionary Augustine to England, and a struggle ensued for the leadership of English church life between the Roman viewpoint and the Irish viewpoint. The victory of the "Romans," by the vote of a conference in 663, was of course significant for the future of Christianity in England. Very important also was the assembling in this connection of larger libraries than England had known before. Far less, thereafter, would Englishmen be moved to go to Ireland to find, as Bede put it a half-century later in his renowned *Ecclesiastical History of the English Nation* (book III, chap. 27), "books to read and free instruction."

The key man, wrote the same authority (*Lives of the Abbots,* 1), was Benedict Biscop. In 647 this "devout servant of Christ" built a monastery "by the mouth of the river Wear" (on the North Sea coast, near the border of Scotland), with the aid of a land grant from Northumbrian King Egfrid. The worthy abbot had already made a few trips abroad, even to Rome, and now made a few more. One purpose of his travels was to acquire books. To Bede, who used them in his long years at Wearmouth, they seemed (*Lives,* 4,

6) "a vast number" covering "all subjects of divine learning." It was his understanding that they had been bought by Biscop or "given him freely by his friends." Bede also mentioned other abbots who had performed like services.

The titles of the books thus provided are not recorded by Bede in his tributes to Benedict. But he does cite many in the *Ecclesiastical History.* Between that source and certain others, we know that there were several monastery and church libraries in seventh- and eighth-century England, possessing and probably loaning to each other as necessary not only approved religious materials but pagan works: the verse of Virgil, Horace, and Ovid; Roman law; and other items. It seems unlikely that the abbots transporting for long distrances the often bulky handwritten books called "codexes" added pagan writings to their orthodox burden. The Virgil and the others may have been in those libraries since earlier times, brought to England and copied there during the Roman period. Private collections doubtless played a part too, for classical culture was widely known in the better homes all over the Roman Empire. Thanks to the controversy over the correct date of Easter, moreover, English libraries were likely to have a body of calendar literature, one item of which was composed by Bede himself. (One of the "Roman" victories of 663 was the adoption of their reckoning of Easter in Northumbria.)

The "Roman"-Irish contest also dramatized the birth of a new epoch in education and publication, a new influence upon book selection. On the outer rim of the empire, those who were to learn Christian doctrine had first to grasp the elements of a foreign language, Latin. The Irish monks pioneered in developing the necessary pedagogy and texts. When they bowed to the "Romans" in the mid-seventh century they still had the advantage of greater numbers of personnel trained in this vital skill. To assure their own control of the education of Anglo-Saxon England, therefore, the victorious "Romans" were forced to undertake promptly their own approaches to the teaching of Latin. Turning to the classical grammars in their libraries proved unsatisfactory, because the old text writers, understandingly assuming that their students already possessed a knowledge of spoken Latin, had dealt little with ABC's. Bede and his fellow educators were obliged to write their own. That Bede's successful grammar was simple may account partly for the supposition, unproven and probably erroneous, that he taught children as well as youths and adults.

The maintaining and use of substantial libraries at such monasteries as Wearmouth and cathedrals like York was badly shaken up in the ninth century by successive waves of Danish invasion. Battles for the control of England were at a peak in the 860s and 870s. The church treasures and books, wrote King Alfred soon afterward, had been ravaged and burned; he knew of hardly anyone who could even translate a message from Latin to English. After defeating the Danes, he undertook titanic educational efforts. Among other things he translated and otherwise restored, in the words of the twelfth-century chronicler William of Malmesbury (*Deeds of the Kings of England,* II. 123), "the greater part of the Roman library." Thanks to the custom of using *bibliotheca* to mean St. Jerome's Latin Vulgate, the historian's tribute was long taken to refer only to the Bible. Later scholarship has demonstrated, however, that Alfred's enterprise gave his people a considerable sampling in their own tongue of the classic Latin authors.

Charlemagne Uninvited visitors from Scandinavia also punished repeatedly in that epoch other coastal areas of Western Europe, as far from home as Sicily. Yet they did not prevent Charlemagne and his immediate successors from establishing a stable government in France. The king recognized the need for administrators. To give candidates basic education, he lured from the English church and school center at York the veteran teacher Alcuin. The latter, accustomed to a cathedral library, was shocked by the feeble collections in the Irish-founded monasteries of France and the pitiful handful of competent scribes. Back to York went a call for the copying of many of the "flowers of Britain," that is, compilations of approved extracts, standard for study. England and secondarily Rome were to be the prime sources of book supply for the Carolingian world.

Judging from Alcuin's own writings, the main objective was to train priests to read Scripture, liturgy, and law books in Latin and to use Latin correctly. In limited areas of logic, mathematics, and astronomy, the pagan classics were given space on the shelves as repositories of subject knowledge. They also seem to have been utilized, sparingly, to show how the rules of rhetoric ought to be applied. But their quality as aesthetic models, vital to fourth-century Jerome and important to sixth-century Cassiodorus, was apparently a matter of indifference or even suspicion to the Master Teacher of the Carolingian Renaissance (eighth and ninth centuries)—without doubt a practical, able man.

The decline in the status and knowledge of Latin is documented with particular sharpness in approaches to the Bible itself. Jerome had lamented the neglect of Hebrew and Greek verse originals, comparing the Latin prose translations (in his preface to the *Chronicle* of Eusebius') to a "beautiful body concealed by a dirty gown." Even Isidor of Seville, early in the seventh century, cited biblical texts hardly at all in expounding rhetoric. But the good bishop flourished in Visigothic Spain, where Latin was well known to the upper classes. Circumstances were very different in the British Isles. Bede's teacher, Aldhelm, was able to regard the Bible as superior to all else not merely in moral authority but as a model for rhetoric; pagan authors were not to be read. Bede strained to find more of the necessary guidance in the Holy Scriptures.

That Alcuin drew upon pagan writings at all was a move toward relaxation, owing something perhaps to the stimulation of Charlemagne's court, where the influence of Spanish sophistication was felt, and solid scholars from Ireland were welcome. Certainly it was a larger area intellectually than York Cathedral. The resident learned did not hesitate to borrow books from other places like Fulda (founded in 744; 20 miles southwest of Frankfort-on-the-Main), to the recorded surprise of the loaning official, who had thought the imperial palace well stocked. Was it simply a matter of obtaining particular titles lacking in an otherwise adequate collection, or the absence of the expected catalog declaring what was on hand? However that may be, it was precisely from the Carolingian palace schools, rather than the monasteries, that the best examples have survived of the contemporary wave of new editions of the pagan Capella's noted encyclopedia.

Boniface   The unsteady flame of library life benefited not only from this stimulating work by Irish savants in the service of the Frankish king, and the pedagogical, text, and handwriting reforms of Alcuin, but from the far-flung efforts of another English expatriate. A generation or so before Alcuin, St. Boniface had left home as a Benedictine missionary. At many points in that major area of commerce and culture, the valley of the Rhine, he and his disciples reorganized existing religious foundations and established new ones both monastic and urban. By the time Alcuin was producing Latinists at the imperial court and books at the nearby abbey of St. Martin of Tours, much additional copying and library development was well under way at Fulda monastery, the archbishop's palace at Mainz (50 miles northwest of Frankfort), and several other locations soon to be famous.

Libraries in the Ninth to Eleventh Centuries

Records and Recorders   Thus were assembled in the future France, Switzerland, and Germany, some libraries apparently larger than what had been familiar, on the order of perhaps 500 or 600 codexes. (By 1100 Reichenau and St. Gallen—see below—boasted about 1,000 each.) That may have been the equivalent of upward of twice as many titles, for two reasons. First, as already noted (p. 44), a collection could have more titles than were considered in the codex count. Second, the annual review of "reading" was sometimes the only basis for compiling the abbreviated list of books borrowed and returned. A book not borrowed could apparently go unlisted indefinitely; for all we know, that may have been the fate of the most important item in the collection.

It is unlikely that enough documentation survives to yield the whole story. But we can do more with what we have. Consider for a moment three ninth-century catalogs of noted abbeys as treated in Becker (pp. 4–13, 24–28, 43–53). The 822 catalog of Reichenau (founded in 724, on an island in Lake Constance, where Switzerland, Bavaria, and Austria meet), lists holdings as numbered by Becker through 415. The above-mentioned 831 catalog of St. Riquier (f. mid-seventh century, some 50 miles south of Calais) reports items numbered through 243. In the 850 catalog of St. Gallen (then about 100 years old; in Switzerland's northeast corner), the last number is 428. From these data it is obvious that some libraries at least 100 years old held more than 400 codexes each. Closer examination reveals, besides, that these three have in common an internal arrangement based mainly on authors, a logical plan when a handful of well-known prolific writers like Augustine account for a large part of the collection. In fact, in two of the three, this arrangement is emphasized by the centering of the captions.

Highly probable, moreover, is the responsibility of the abbot rather than the librarian, at that stage, in reader guidance. A commentary of the mid-ninth century depicting the distribution of books at the beginning of

Lent is striking in these particulars: the librarian brings in the books to be assigned and reads the names of the brothers who are to return books; it is the abbot, however, who examines each brother on the book he is returning and discusses with him which book he will borrow next; even more, it is the abbot who judges whether the brother can understand the book he has asked for, and may well assign him another one instead. (Paraphrase courtesy of Sister M. Alfred Schroll, *Benedictine Monasticism as Reflected in the Warnefrid-Hildemar Commentaries on the Rule*, New York: Columbia University Press, 1967, pp. 120-121.)

Many other issues invite exploration. How often was the *armarius*, or registrar of the books, also the scheduler of routine reciting and chanting, the selector of personnel for such functions, the preparer of the weekly timetable? Was it general practice for him to add the names of the deceased to the martyrologies and calendars? How much of all this did he learn by serving first as *armarius junior*, i.e., as recorder of the list of books borrowed? In how many installations did both the junior and senior posts exist?

Latin Holdings   However they were staffed, the small libraries as well as the few large ones supported the teaching of enough Latin for the study of the Bible and the systematizing of patristic commentaries. At the same time, there were probably a few students here and there who kept alive the interest in classical and secular works nourished by a minority of scholars. Copying and library development correspondingly emphasized the religious sector without entirely neglecting the rest.

Systematizing the patristic literature revealed before long the numerous differences of opinion among the Fathers. Thanks to the Carolingian copying activity of the eighth and ninth centuries, not only text anthologies but nearly all the key original writings were furnished to even small monastery libraries. Despite the hazards of travel, moreover, there was beyond doubt considerable exchange of correspondence and transporting of books. Problems, debates, and fears arose. The necessity of self-protection then mothered a leading prelate's reinvention of the source citation. His advice was rarely followed: it was too revolutionary. Few writers of the preceding centuries had mentioned any of the writers they so often copied; those who did were normally careless with both copying and attributions, favoring, regardless of the facts, those whose names carried the greatest authority. To solve the problem required first the development of standards of textual criticism. Such canons were not yet available in the ninth century, and the first crude attempts were also the last for the time being. Furthermore, the powerful Cluniac reform movement of the tenth century stressed liturgy rather than study.

The pagan and secular classics, meanwhile, in the absence of a clear and felt need for them in libraries, might have suffered not merely neglect but eclipse. Their survival is accounted for partly by the marked increase in attention to "grammar" in the period roughly from 800 to 1100. Thus, the above-mentioned catalog of St. Riquier lists "Questions on the Seven Arts" among the seventy "books" devoted mainly to church council materials; but works by "grammarians" (writers versed in the liberal arts) appear separately, a group of twenty-six "books" including rhetoric and medicine, even "fables." Among the twenty-six was Priscian, whose grammar had been composed about the year 500 amid Byzantine influences and included many examples from pagan mythology; it was extremely popular.

Greek If knowledge of classical Latin had on the whole declined in the West, comprehension of Greek had almost disappeared. The Irish monks at Iona and elsewhere struggled with it on occasion; modern scholarship views their efforts as having been severely handicapped. Conspicuous for possessing significant command of Homer's tongue were a few savants like John Scotus Erigena. Even he, laboring at the mid-ninth-century French court of Charles the Bald, by invitation of that patron of learning, remarked that he had to quote Greek biblical passages by way of the Latin Vulgate translation; the celebrated Septuagint (Greek) was not at hand. Since Erigena was not only a confirmed Hellenist but a persistent researcher, this argues the rarity of Greek texts in Western libraries.

Italy, Latin, and Greek Circumstances assigned Italy a key role in preparing for the rebirth of classical knowledge. It did not rest on the size of Italian libraries. Bobbio's 666 codexes and considerably more titles in the tenth century (Becker, pp. 64–73) were comparable in numbers with the leading collections north of the Alps, at Fulda, Tours, and St. Gallen, although probably not with the reputedly much larger assemblages at Constantinople and Islamic Cairo. But Bobbio was not typical of Italy.

More important were the many small libraries in Italy's towns and villas, churches and monasteries, embodying the continuity of Roman traditions, pagan classics included. The bawdy verses of Catullus to be copied later by Renaissance humanists Petrarch and Salutati were in the Verona cathedral library. The spoken language was not very different from Latin, the book trade flourished, and there were scribes outside the ranks of the clergy. Lacking either the political or cultural motives generated further north, the Italian intellectuals did not turn their energies to educational reform.

In their company, however, were Irish monks like those who had founded Bobbio, men believed to have been more curious and imaginative than their continental brethren. Whether St. Columban's appreciation and knowledge of the old Latin literature—even poetry—lived on in them, is not certain. We know that, of the tenth-century Bobbio codexes just mentioned, about one-sixth contained works by pagan belletrists—not only Juvenal, Lucretius, Terence, and Virgil, but Ovid. We do not know how much they were read. As to Greek, members of the Bobbio community are thought likely to have been among those taking advantage of the opportunity for contact with readers of Greek increasingly drifting into north Italy from the east.

Influences from the East The life and culture of the Byzantine Empire, the Persian Empire, and the far-flung domains of Islam, during the epoch just discussed and the centuries immediately afterward, cannot be given their just due here. It is vital, however, that notice be taken of the principal points of contact, of influence upon Western library traditions.

Library services in the Byzantine Empire followed by and large familiar ways. At the capital, important collections were assembled, several times destroyed by fire, earthquake, or riot, and frequently reassembled or replaced. Lesser libraries were maintained just as they were in the West, in church schools in town, and in monasteries. This much is beyond doubt, thanks to the many passages in patristic correspondence and other writings advising the reader to go to a library. Nor is there any reason to think the larger of these institutions badly lacking in books of any particular type. As a matter of fact, when a century and a quarter of bitter politico-theological "iconoclastic" struggle ended, about the year 850, circumstances favored cautious scholarship and many chose to focus on philology. The fruits of these efforts, famous dictionaries and encyclopedias and anthologies, bear witness to the existence of substantial and varied book collections. Very little more is known, though, about either the library staffs or their work.

These libraries, presumed to have supported the reading of historically prominent figures like the Patriarch Photius, were to be found not only in Byzantine territory but in neighboring Persia and the wide-ranging caliphates of Islam. Some benefited from the militancy of orthodox Christianity in the fifth and sixth centuries. When vigorous efforts were made to establish religious uniformity in the Eastern Empire, considerable numbers of dissident Christians as well as Jews made their way to the friendlier Persian court and helped their hosts to absorb Greek philosophy and science. Then the Arabs swept over Persia in the seventh century and fell heir to those portions of Greek culture and to Persian literature. In the following 200 or 300 years the Arabic language and script carried from Persia and Arabia all over the Mediterranean littoral not only the Koran but the newly acquired non-Islamic learning. Notable indeed were the caliph-sponsored libraries of the ninth and tenth centuries in Baghdad, Spain's Cordova, Seville, and Toledo, and some centers in North Africa.

The process of conquest meanwhile spurred numerous Eastern monastic communities to depart northward and westward, from exposed areas to new quarters deemed safer. They often took with them their customary equipment and habits: manuscripts, copying materials, and copying routines. Thus, by the tenth and eleventh centuries, did many an important scriptorium develop in Byzantium and at isolated places in the Aegean islands and in the hills of Greece. Collections were further enhanced by gifts of the devout.

Greece itself, moreover, was subjected to pressures from the Persians, the Arabs, Slavic tribes, and political strife in Byzantium. Beginning probably in the seventh century, Greek refugees, including monastic groups, appeared in Sicily and southern Italy, easily accessible areas which had known Greek colonies in the days of Plato. Subsequent centuries found Greek abbeys further inland in Italy and further north, perhaps in part out of fear of the Mohammedan "Saracens" in control of Sicily in the ninth and tenth centuries, for the abbeys were regarded by Byzantium as official imperial outposts and were presumably fair game for Moslem or other hostile attack. Whether such abbeys functioned through the Sicilian occupation even before the Normans expelled the Saracens, or on the mainland alone, they seem to have had several libraries of consequence, from the eleventh century on, maintaining some of the traditions of Greek literature and the Greek language. Greek trickled into northern Italy at about the same time, thanks to commerce and other contacts between Constantinople and Venice and other towns. Then and there, perhaps, appeared for example the manuscript of Thucydides' *History of the Peloponnesian War* assigned by scholarship to the eleventh century, first noted in the collection of an Italian humanist early in the fifteenth.

Meanwhile, the scientific and other learned works available in Arabic were entering the Latin Christian world at several locations. A number of them were in the Norman kingdom of "The Two Sicilies" founded at Naples (1016–1189), under whose auspices arose the medical school at Salerno (30 miles south of Naples). A significant role was played in this episode by the combination of Benedictine traditions of nearby Monte Cassino, and the adventures which brought there in the eleventh century one Constantine of Africa. A man of wide travel and language gifts, he settled at the abbey as a monk and produced from the Arabic several Latin translations of Greco-Arabic medical thought. Another center developed meanwhile, under the Normans in Sicily itself. This exceptional intellectual entrepôt, bringing together the Byzantine Greek, the Islamic, the Jewish, and the Latin-Christian, is said to have been supported by libraries in each major town.

Furthermore, after Toledo (in almost the exact center of Spain) fell to the Christian forces in 1085, there emerged, thanks to wise leadership, energetic copying and translating of Arabic writings. Many of the Latin versions were the contributions of Italians like the celebrated Gerard of Cremona, and such Englishmen as Adelard of Bath, who carried back home numerous mathematical works.

Most fortunate was Western civilization in all this activity. Despite the loss of life and property, a precious fraction of Arabic-language scholarship was preserved, safe from the wholesale destruction of Arabic libraries and manuscripts wreaked by the Christians in Spain and North Africa in subsequent centuries. Probably more important, it yielded in the twelfth century that weighty portion of Aristotelian and certain other Greek literature which had not previously been known to the Latin world. The thinking embodied therein was to help generate Scholasticism, Humanism, and the many-faceted Renaissance, and the libraries which served them.

Pre-Scholastic Patterns of Life and Thought

Medicine and Law   The rise of the medical school at Salerno was one aspect of the rebirth of economic vigor in Italy. Commercial success aided by the Crusades contributed to the rise of bourgeois families to positions of power alongside the older aristocracy. Money was available for the physician's services as it had not been before; more was expected of him. The impetus thereby given to the advance of the medical sciences was profound, affecting in time the organization of study in many fields, interest in Greek writings on all subjects, the selection of books, bibliography, and classification of both nature and books.

Similarly, the transition in the chief mode of acquiring property from maneuvers on the battlefield to maneuvers in the law courts stimulated some fresh thinking. It was realized gradually that traditional rhetoric was not a satisfactory substitute for mastery of the law, and that new problems of property relations had to be solved by creative interpretation of existing law. Concepts, language, and modes of reasoning received close attention. The dynamic of change was soon felt in ecclesiastical law; beyond the law, in other subjects; and beyond the pioneer law school at Bologna, Italy, in other places.

Bibliographical Seeds   The eleventh- and twelfth-century expounders of law habitually introduced a text by giving the name of the author, the subject matter, its purpose, what "part of philosophy" it pertained to, and its "final cause." By "part of philosophy" was intended its classification in the Ethics-Logic-Physics scheme attributed to Plato. "Final cause" meant, in Aristotelian language, its role in the divine plan: its "true purpose," something a mere blindly fumbling human author could not hope to think of. The "canon" (church) law masters were notable for comparisons of texts; specification of time, place, and person; determination of the original cause of a statement; and other aspects of studying it in context.

These devices were a substantial equivalent to what would later be called respectively descriptive and analytical bibliography, and internal criticism. The bibliographical style was directly in line with the already mentioned practices of Servius and Boëthius, and was being recommended afresh at that very time, for teaching literature, by an influential Benedictine. How many others utilized it who never bothered to record the fact? Clearly, the broadened and perhaps refined application of a more or less standard bibliographical style, stimulated by new conditions, was strengthening the foundation for the bibliographical apparatus of the future. Not much longer would library catalogs suffice which listed only authors and titles, often rendered them incompletely, and not uncommonly included only those of the first item in each of the many codexes containing several. Indeed a new apparatus would soon be demanded by a world of more copies, more editions, more titles—then printed books with title pages—then more copies, editions, and titles.

New Meanings and Texts   Internal criticism, the study of context, by virtue of its advancing sophistication, contributed to the contemporary flux in the meanings of many subject terms. The span of variety was widening in what "rhetoric," "dialectic," and "logic" meant in different mouths, and how those subjects were thought to be related to one another. Theology and philosophy were separating as subjects; the juxtaposition of "faith" and "reason" was becoming familiar. The debate reached a climax in the second half of the twelfth century, when translation gave the Latin world for the first time the more complex portions of Aristotle's *Organon*. This "new logic" would probably have had a sharp impact in any case. Certainly the ground had been well prepared for it by dialectician Peter Abelard and his assembling (about 1100) of contradictory opinions of the Fathers under the title "Yes and No," without the customary exegesis designed to reconcile the contradictions. Provocative, and thereby offensive to many desirous of seeing the dust settle, Abelard helped create an audience eager for systematizers of source material whose tone was conciliatory. In the *Decretum* of 1140, the Bolognese monk Gratian thus treated canon law. His fellow countryman Peter Lombard, who arrived in Paris with a copy of Gratian and the sponsorship of the influential reformer-monk Bernard of Clairvaux, produced in his "Sentences" (1150) a kindred approach to theology, at once questioning and faithful, controlled and relaxed. These two texts became standard almost immediately. Gratian's is the first on the list of books inventoried after a fire, some time in the twelfth century, at the German Benedictine cloister of St. Peter in Wessobrunn; the others include several titles by Augustine, Ambrose, and Jerome, which usually precede anything nonpatristic. (The list is on view in *Serapeum*, 2:251-252, 1841.) Apparently even more popular, Lombard's work graced nearly every library for which records survive—often in multiple copies; the next century or two were soaked in commentaries on Lombard's effort and several "sentences" from other hands.

Wealth and Urbanization   If medicine, law, and theology in their respective ways generated special forces which affected civilization at large, those forces were entering an arena where a major act was already in progress. The monasteries had long followed predominantly the obedience-chastity-poverty formula of St. Benedict, but as organized economic units in a world of feudal manors they came in many instances to flourish as corporate bodies. The French abbey of St. Riquier, whose library catalog of 831 is referred to elsewhere, was not one of the larger establishments of the Carolingian Renaissance. Yet it was lord to 117 vassals, and from the 2,500 houses in the town which grew up around it the abbey was entitled to collect annually 10,000 chickens, 400 pounds of wax, other rent in kind, and money rent. Monks in Benedictine foundations seldom engaged any longer in physical labor; others were available for that.

Such circumstances subverted official poverty—sometimes moral fiber in general—and emphasis on material concerns mounted also as lay landowners interpenetrated with the upper church officialdom. Several efforts at reform were undertaken, the Cistercians, launched in 1098, being notable for establishing houses in remote, inauspicious localities where the achievement of creature comforts was almost sure to take a long time. Yet, within little more than a century, even those famous tamers of swamps had corporatively grown fat and somewhat soft. Monasticism now faced many enemies, and the acceleration of urbanism both reduced its serf-labor supply and increased its commercial competition from the bourgeoisie.

In the expanding towns were often cathedrals with various types of personnel performing a wide range of functions. They were quite likely to include a "chapter" of "canons" who might or might not live by a rule and who usually did not take a vow of poverty. To the schools they conducted came not only candidates for the priesthood but many with other objectives, who qualified technically by joining a "minor order." By the year 1000 the cathedral schools were more important in education than the monasteries: more and more isolated from the stream of life, the latter would henceforth decline and their codex collections suffer neglect and outright loss.

Two writers of the 1120s illustrate well the differences in environment and outlook. Bernard of Clairvaux, one of the last great figures in the tradition of monastic isolation and contemplation, denounced "curiosity" as the "beginning of all sin" (*The Steps of Humility*, 38); and insisted that the liberal arts were not required for salvation and therefore only an optional subject for the monks' study. He did concede that, so far as ordinary instruction was concerned, they held an honorable and useful place. Hugh of the famous Parisian abbey of St. Victor, was likewise an humble man of faith: he cautioned in the preface to his *Didascalicon* "lest mere study" interfere with "good works." Yet he was also an urban schoolmaster. He not only spoke of the liberal arts as the "foundation of all learning" (*Didascalicon*, book 3, chap. 4), but even cited enthusiastically the earnest struggles for knowledge of noted pagans of antiquity (book 3, chap. 14). Distinctions like this highlight the danger of bracketing the Bernards and the Hughs, without qualification, as "mystics"; indeed examination of the sources often undermines widely circulated generalizations.

Debate over Fit Reading   Both the enlargement of the scale of urban cathedral and abbey school instruction and publication and the last major bursts of scholarly activity in certain monasteries helped produce sophisticated analyses of the reading matter in the libraries. Now being examined on a large scale were the early attempts at reconciling the differences among the Western Fathers, the news from the broadening company of readers of Greek that even sharper differences awaited the investigator, the insights into Hebrew originals afforded by the Jewish scholars consulted by Abelard and many other Christians, the example of law scholarship moving toward order and reasoned thinking, the emergence via translation from the Arabic of mathematics—the very model of systematized abstraction—and the problems of the suitability for teaching of pagan works and contemporary vernacular reading matter.

Amid the welter of conflicting ideas of what was both reliable and pertinent, those concerned with education struggled for clarity and security. The idea of the "authorized" was not new: it had been known to Periclean Athens, the pupils of Aristotle, the Alexandrian scholars and dilettantes. The "canonical," moreover, ranging from simply "authentic" to "exclusively acceptable," had long been used to identify officially Christian writings of recognized authority. The concept now gave rise to the very name "canon law," by definition distinct from the Roman civil law of several well-known codes and the contemporary *Corpus Juris Civilis*. In the sphere of religious and secular literature, the idea of the "canonical" presumably further enhanced the standing of the "doctors" of the Church (Ambrose, Jerome, Augustine, and Pope Gregory) and the leading poets, Christian and pagan, such as Virgil. Certain works appear repeatedly in the library catalogs still extant, others appear seldom. Although not called a "canon," these lists of preferred books constituted in effect a standard catalog for book selection.

In terms of intellectual history, whether or not reflected in library holdings, there were really two such standard catalogs. One school of thought was even then marking off textbooks in the seven liberal arts or *artes*, under the traditionally very broad label "philosophy," as what really mattered beyond the sacred writings, while denoting as hardly more than excess baggage the poetic-literary balance. In the early twelfth century Hugh of St. Victor, expressing this very view, could also declare (*Didascalicon,* book 3, chap. 13) that "the wise student . . . gladly hears all, reads all, and looks down upon no writing, no person, no teaching," in order to meditate on his own ignorance. A century later such latitudinarianism would have receded as Scholasticism exerted a somewhat restrictive effect upon European library life in general. Significant also were such particular consequences as its combining with the national and class interests of the Norman conquerors of England: poetry in Anglo-Saxon, the language of the suppressed indigenous peasantry, was kept out of the libraries. On the other hand were equally articulate figures who thought the poets and prose writers of belles lettres still authoritative; they began by respecting the *artes* as well, but would shortly be forced to fight them and Scholastic "philosophy" in defense of Humanist ideas.

The new confrontation was nourished also by the circumstances in which literature was being produced, especially in France. Material comforts at courts provided subjects of interest to poets and their patrons. The frustrations of educated poor men of wit, who outnumbered the positions open to graduates of church schooling, sparked satire and other humor. For all this the Roman models were highly relevant, and employed. Pagan works, especially those amenable to allegorical interpretation, turn up in the library catalogs of the eleventh and twelfth centuries with markedly increased frequency. Although Ovid's *Art of Love* had long been rejected by most churchmen for its pagan sensuality, it was now widely read, even by nuns, as a series of allegorical religious lessons on familiar themes like the Church as Christ's Bride. As may be seen in the source materials assembled by Theodor Gottlieb (*Ueber mittelalterliche Bibliotheken,* Leipzig: Harrassowitz, 1890, Graz reprint, 1955, no. 183, p. 72), Ovid's is one of the few names on an Austrian abbey's loan list of the twelfth century, one of the oldest known. Also, the Roman poet held a place in the front rank in the anthologies. Extant copies of Capella's *De Nuptiis* ("Wedding of Mercury and Philology") prepared in the twelfth century and for some time afterward are usually incomplete, because readers sought only the allegorical Books I and II; the seven liberal arts balance was passé, except for Book VII on "astronomy" (heavily astrological), often issued as a separate item.

The twelfth century in particular saw also a striking wave of condensed versions of the writings of antiquity. This was in the first place a conscious tribute to brevity as a classical criterion of good style. It may also have been somewhat indebted to the burgeoning of a society in which time, like all else, can be measured in money.

Pre-Scholastic Library Patterns

The growth of a commodity economy, production primarily for exchange rather than for personal consumption, was in evidence in several phenomena of twelfth-century library life, and not all were entirely new even then.

The Book as Commodity   As early as 692 a church council had tried to illegalize cutting up, corrupting, or selling to book buyers or "those who are called perfumers"—presumably seeking parchment or vellum as raw materials—a portion of the Holy Scriptures or a patristic contribution ("Canon LXVII" of the Council in Trullo, *A Select Library of the Nicene and Post-Nicene Fathers of the Christian Church*, 2d ser., vol. XIV, p. 396). Disposing of these ideologically precious writings on the open market was declared permissible only if they had already been ruined by bookworms, water, or something else. How successful this effort proved does not appear in surviving records.

Library Support   Already on the scene also, here and there, was direct support to library services. A monastery might endow its library with a portion of the expected annual revenue or follow the example of the abbot of Fleury, who imposed (1146) a library tax upon the officers of his abbey and the dependent priories. (What each was to pay may be seen in Edwards' *Memoirs*, I:283-284.) A church might grant part of the tithes to its scriptorium. A center like the famous Abbey of St. Victor, founded in Paris in 1110, might develop an exceptional library with the aid of gifts from the royal family. Not yet, however, was cash the main basis of library operations. Monastery and church scriptoria were still very busy, especially in the areas which had been ravaged in the ninth and tenth centuries by Normans, Saracens, or Magyars, and needed replacements for their ruined book collections. Books were acquired by such means as the late-eleventh-century practice at the Abbey of Corvey: each novice about to graduate to the next stage in his career was expected to present the library with a codex. Standards of copying, having suffered noticeable depression since Carolingian days, were given new attention by men like Lanfranc, distinguished churchman and associate of William the Conqueror's.

Effects of the Growing Demand for Books   Although many religious houses attracted clusters of population around them, few villagers were literate or able to deposit the customary pledge to borrow a book. Loans to outsiders—laymen of standing or other libraries—were probably rather limited. In the large monastic houses, nevertheless, there arose by the twelfth century enough additional borrowing by the brothers themselves to encourage the formation of two separate collections, one of books loanable to the monks and to laymen, the other of books basic to the daily routine and often kept under lock and key. This precedent was probably beneficial to the latterly prominent cathedral libraries, still more to the newly important urban diocesan "chapter" and abbey libraries heavily patronized by students.

As students crowded into major towns, their wants stimulated the expansion of appropriate commercial enterprise. Manufacturing the books they needed, for cash sale, became in the twelfth century an industry supporting an unknown number of scribes and binders. New titles became available quickly in places distant from the scriptorium of original issue; in Paris, at least, books could be bought on the street. Students lacking the funds to buy the necessary texts either copied out what they needed or borrowed from their teachers. Indeed some copied for hire. By the end of the century there must have been great pressure on libraries in university towns to change their ways and loan books to impecunious students. For in 1212 a Paris council recommended cancellation of the curses traditionally laid upon persons removing books from a church or monastery library. A loan to the poor was a major act of mercy, it was pointed out, and should cover precisely this helping hand to the needy student. Indeed, refusing to loan books under these circumstances was to be forbidden.

The increase in the number and use of books obliged the newer libraries as well as those of the monasteries, in many instances, to divide the collection. It was not unusual in the twelfth century for a religious house to maintain one group of books for the adult residents, concentrated on theology and liturgy, and another for the lay students who came to school there, comprising largely texts in the liberal arts and supplementary classical writings. In some cloisters the area assigned to works of divinity was now a full scale "book room." Fairly familiar also was the division between heavily used items and the balance. The former had lately, precisely when is uncertain, been taken out of the locked chests or closets for easier access, and in the common interest chained to the desks they were laid upon. Functional convenience was likewise behind the separate location of two, sometimes three, self-contained portions of the collection. Books immediately related to the conduct of the services were often placed near the altar, a prototype for the standard subentry in modern catalogs, ". . . Liturgy and ritual." Books used in the singing were frequently stored "in the choir." The school, rather than the *bibliotheca,* was in many instances the repository of the grammar and other liberal arts holdings.

The type and number of divisions in any single establishment varied

Part of a single volume, showing the clasps, the ring for the chain, and the mode of attaching it: Hereford. (From John Clark, The Care of Books, *Cambridge University Press, 1901, p. 175)*

Piece of chain, showing the swivel: Hereford. (From John Clark, The Care of Books, *Cambridge University Press, 1901, p. 178)*

with circumstances. Very few instances have been verified, apparently, where there were more than three. Catalogs from those years listing theological and service items alone, or school items alone, are no proof that the other materials were not at hand.

Shelf Control Most of the handwritten bound volumes called "codexes" were, it seems, assigned fixed locations; an identifying Roman numeral was sometimes posted in the catalog next to the codex entry. Roman letters began to be called on, too, probably later. Actually, these developments cannot be dated closely: their emergence may have been as early as the eleventh century, and was almost surely no later than the twelfth. In a few striking cases like that of the Canterbury library cataloged in 1170, location symbols are known to have been marked in the books. More often, perhaps, codexes bore the device of the scriptorium of origin. But it remains largely undetermined whether "call numbers" appeared in the book as well as the catalog, whether they were on the outside or inside of the codex or both, whether they indicated an entire shelf or other group space or a particular space assigned to a particular work. The uncertainties are aggravated by varying use of the Latin terms for shelf, desk, location, etc.

Catalogs and Cataloging Furthermore, location symbols are not on view in a great many surviving catalogs of that age. Most of them were bare inventories, in many instances inscribed on blank pages of one of the books, mute testimony to service primarily to the protection of corporate property rather than the reader's convenience. Indeed *inventorium* was often the initial word in the title, and such documents frequently listed also other possessions like vestments and candlesticks. Even more expressive of property-consciousness, and perhaps responsive to the reawakening spirit of commerce, was the increasing utilization of "treasury" *(thesaurus)* instead of "inventory." At any rate, both these terms bespeak departure from the neutral flavor of *brevis,* or "short list," their predecessor of a few hundred years' standing but in the twelfth century seen much less often.

Codexes were still being listed as a rule in order of the official importance of the subjects and authors of the first works within them. It would be fascinating to learn what we probably never will learn, how often a given work known from some catalogs was actually in other collections too, but not so recorded because it was neither the first item in the codex containing it nor entered as a trailer after the first item. Why was it sometimes first, sometimes an after-item, sometimes perhaps not listed at all? Was there any work in the libraries of that age which was widely read although seldom registered in the catalogs?

Whatever the reader expected, whatever a teacher or someone else had told him, repeated handling of catalogs would in time accustom at least the more alert users of the library to the predominant patterns of arrangement. The Holy Scriptures, generally referred to as *bibliotheca,* usually enjoyed the place of honor. Church authorities customarily came next, first the Fathers, then the more recent figures. Augustine was evidently considered the most important, the leading "doctor" of the beatified four; his works were recorded before those of the others despite his being third chronologically and second alphabetically (after Ambrose). Secular writings were ordinarily listed after the sacred.

Certain types of material often appeared as a group entry. Continental library catalogs of the ninth to twelfth centuries speak of codexes in the "Scottish script," that is, the hand long used by Irish copyists which few Europeans if any could read. Some English catalogs of the twelfth century notice as such works in Anglo-Saxon. Almost any catalog was likely to refer to medical works as a group, and it was not unusual to list thus grammars or other "arts" titles; "books without titles" were sometimes entered simply that way, without any particulars. However the contents of the library might be grouped in these inventories, labeled divisions like those of the eleventh-century catalog of the French cathedral library of LePuy (No. 378 in Gottlieb, p. 137) were apparently still rare at the close of the twelfth.

The same applies to descriptive cataloging as thought of in later times. Normally, a twelfth-century entry provided a title; the author was given too, if known. The number of physical volumes was occasionally reported, but neither pagination nor date of "publication" had yet won that much attention. The scriptorium of origin might be indicated in the book's signature, but not in the catalog.

Operating Regulations Likewise not repeated in the catalog was the curse normally written at the end of a manuscript, until the thirteenth century at least and perhaps longer, to protect the book from overzealous borrowing or outright theft. Loan regulations often forbade a brother to read heavily used books anywhere but in the library area, and when a book could be carried off to his cell he usually signed for it with a pledge of some sort. The introduction of the carrel (*Karola, carola*—inspiration Charlemagne?), for those writing as well as reading, has been attributed to the lack of a scriptorium at certain houses. A borrower was limited as a rule to one or two codexes at a time. Important and expensive works could be loaned only by permission of the abbot. Physical care included prompt shelving in proper order and not too tightly; the closets now tended to have vertical partitions between shelves. At the Abbey of St. Victor in Paris, in what may represent many libraries' practice in that age, regulations stipulated that the book closets be protected from moisture with wooden linings and that the librarian inspect each book two or three times a year to repair damage done by moisture or vermin. The patching of damaged pages, however, was probably undertaken primarily in conjunction with the preparation of additional copies.

The Librarian The librarian, or caretaker of the books, was responsible to the abbot for all books. He controlled most of the use of the library, and told the scriptorium staff what to copy. His permission was required for erasures or changes. He was normally a monk or priest himself, and, at least in large urban establishments as well as at several famous monasteries, is likely to have been an educated man—William of Malmesbury, for example, monk-librarian-historian. Under some circumstances, monastic, usually, he was also the official in charge of the music books and the singing. Of at least one set of regulations, those of the recently organized Premonstratensians, it is said that the librarian's duties were spelled out with exceptional clarity and that his status was distinctively independent. That may account for their stipulating that the librarian handle the borrowing of books from outside sources, an assignment reportedly unique in the extant records, although the borrowing itself was well-established practice. Still, there is nothing to suggest that anyone was specifically guided and trained to be a librarian.

Hugh of St. Victor's Classification of Knowledge

Certain lineaments of the future, however, respecting both the practices and the training of librarians, were observable in a work produced for other purposes. The spectrum of educational effort in the twelfth century included many specialties like mathematics, law, poetry, and dialectics. It also harbored naturalistic rationalism, testifying among other things to the impact of revived commercial life. Both specialization and naturalistic rationalism distressed many minds of the time. One of them, educator Hugh of St. Victor, was also bothered by what seemed to him undisciplined dabbling and a sadly lacking sense of values.

He therefore undertook to prepare a corrective for the numerous students at the young but already celebrated Parisian Abbey of St. Victor. His text supported the Augustinian focus on balanced study, primarily of the seven liberal arts, in pursuit of the wisdom linking the student to God. This *Didascalicon* (late 1120s) was a success in at least two respects. It was often drawn upon and discussed by contemporaries and later writers. And the demand for it was sufficient to accord it wide distribution: some forty-five libraries all over Europe still possess copies dating from the days before printing.

Hugh's commitment to faith logically gave top status to Theology in the Philonic-Augustinian meaning of Biblical Revelation. In order of presentation he appears to run counter to Augustine's injunction and Cassiodorus' example, since this Theology follows (books 4 to 6) rather than precedes Philosophy (books 1 to 3). But he has simply chosen to build from the ground to the heights: the sacred writings alone are free from error, avows the noted Victorine (book 4, passim). He also explains (book 5, chap. 6) that "although it is clearly more important for us to be just than to be wise," he knows that "many" nevertheless seek in Scriptural studies "knowledge rather than virtue." Since he believes that "neither of these should be disapproved of, but that both are necessary and praiseworthy," he proposes to discuss both. Indeed, where Augustine had shrugged off good writing as unimportant in itself, Hugh urges readers of the Holy Scriptures (book 5, chap. 7) to be stirred "not only" by their literary appeal but by the beauty of their truth.

As for the mundane studies, said the author (book 2, chap. 29), he was offering only "the divisions and the names of things." This first half of his treatise was, in fact, a series of very brief introductions, none original. But the very focus on the organization of knowledge, and the systematic presentation, produced a more detailed but still coherent picture of the classification of knowledge than appears in any earlier surviving work.

In book 3, chapter 1, Hugh offered a retrospective synopsis of his scheme. In Appendix A he repeated that synopsis with brief explanations of his terms. Additional details on several topics can be found very easily in the discussion proper, which occupies most of book 2. Here is a composite rendering carried as far as Hugh carried it except where ellipsis is indicated:

Theoretical Arts
Theology (invisibles)
Natural science (invisible causes of visibles)
Mathematics (visible forms of visibles)
    Arithmetic (discrete quantities). . .
    Music (discrete quantities in relation to each other—proportion). . .
    Geometry (immobile continuous—space). . .
    Astronomy (mobile continuous—motion). . .

Practical
Solitary (personal ethics)
Private (family and household)
Public (political science)

Mechanical
Fabric making
Armament
    Construction. . .
    Crafts. . .

Commerce
Agriculture
  Arable
  Wooded and vine
  Pastoral
  Floral
Hunting
  Gaming
  Fowling
  Fishing
  Food preparation. . .
Medicine
  "Occasions" (health factors). . .
  "Operations" (medical practice). . .
Theatrics
  Theater: epics
  Porches: choral processions and dances
  Gymnasia: wrestling
  Amphitheatres: racing
  Arenas: boxing
  Banquets: songs and instruments; dice
  Temples: sacred singing
Logic
Grammar
Theory of argument
  Demonstrative
  Probable
    Dialectic
    Rhetoric
  Sophistic

This pattern of course owes a great deal to earlier thinkers, all the way back to the presocratic philosophers, although the formulations—and confusion—are largely derived from the earlier medieval intermediary writers like Martianus Capella and Isidor of Seville. Hugh's classification looks very much like Aristotle's as Hugh knew it mainly from the translations and commentaries of Boëthius. The kinship is rather close in the areas of the Practical and the Mechanical. Rhetoric, one subdivision of Aristotle's Practical (by way of Politics), appears in Hugh as a subdivision rather of Logic. Military Science, paired with Rhetoric as a division of Politics in Aristotle, does not seem to be treated in the *Didascalicon* at all.

The relationship is rather distant in the Theoretical division. Hugh could not have learned much natural science from his guides. In any case, Aristotle discussed at length, in several works, what are now called Physics and Astronomy, Zoology, Human Physiology and Psychology; the twelfth-century schoolmaster assigned these subjects largely, in a capsule statement (book 2, chap. 12), to two divisions of Music: "what belongs to the universe" and "what belongs to man." Between that and what he placed in certain subdivisions of the Mechanical, hardly anything was left for Natural Science (or Physics, as it was regularly called, down to the eighteenth century). Indeed, Hugh had little to say under that heading (book 2, chaps. 16 and 17).

Theology in what had long been its lesser sense Hugh presented briefly (book 2, chap. 2), first in the words of Boëthius about God and the soul, then in the language repeated by Isidor of Seville from Cassiodorus, on God and "spiritual creatures." Such discourse had, in the buffeting of centuries, departed some distance from its character in the writings of Aristotle.

Logic in Hugh's hands also displays a surface resemblance to the Aristotelian, but little more. Although the terms are all duly reported (book 2, chap. 30), the reader would certainly have acquired not even a glimmering of what had been meant by either "demonstration" (certainty, from axioms) or "dialectic" (reasoning about opinions). Furthermore, Hugh tailored Rhetoric to the Christian pattern of "what is suitable," where Aristotle had spoken only of persuasion as a process in itself, independent of morals, a division of Politics.

Hugh indicated that Grammar might cover portions of literature, as it had in the better days of schooling. He emphasized, however, that verse and fiction, ordinary history and fables, were only side issues, not really parts of the serious reading matter he called "Philosophy" (book 3, chap. 4). Yet, to understand the Bible allegorically, one surely needed "history"—which to him was a technique of reading as well as the reciting of "deeds" (book 6, chap. 3).

The fine arts and architecture do not appear as such in Hugh's classification. Construction, divided into Walls and a miscellany of other subdivisions, perhaps embraced important elements of both. Again, human behavior is touched on at various points, as in Book 3, Chapter 11, "Concerning Memory." But, in the manner familiar from the writings of Augustine and other church authorities, there is nothing so substantial and directly focused on psychology as Aristotle's On the Soul and Rhetoric.

Not mentioned in the body of the work, but dealt with in Appendix B, is Magic, eleven divisions of it—and all, he wrote, outside Philosophy.

Hugh did not refer to Law (apart from the Holy Scriptures), although he did write of the companion special fields of Medicine and Theology. This may derive in part from the fact that what he knew of Aristotle did not touch on matters legal.

Regardless of the differences between Aristotle and Hugh of St. Victor, the latter's pattern of classification acquired a significance of its own as his book was read and discussed. Not least of the reasons is the fact that his classification table was sufficiently detailed (more than preceding schemes) to pose the problem familiar to all students of the subject: what does one do with a subtopic which "belongs to" several different larger topics simultaneously? Hugh's reply (book 2, chap. 26) was as follows:

> Let no one be disturbed that among the means employed by medicine I count food and drink, which earlier I attributed to hunting. For these belong to both under different aspects. For instance, wine in the grape is the business of agriculture; in the barrel, of the cellarer; and in its consumption, of the doctor. Similarly, the preparing of food belongs to the

mill, the slaughterhouse, and the kitchen, but the strength given by its consumption, to medicine.

That the "different aspects" of subjects created problems for classifiers of books, that modes of announcing resources in various subjects would have to be devised to allow full representation in library catalogs for each "aspect," may or may not have been in Hugh's mind. As an educated man, he was probably aware of the fact that many codexes included more than one work and that the combination was not necessarily homogeneous subject-wise; whether or not he thought of such phenomena as a problem is so far unrevealed.

Obviously conscious of the interrelations among the myriad subdivisions of knowledge, Hugh chose to present the matter along Aristotelian lines. He could have chosen otherwise. The Physics-Ethics-Logic pattern associated with Plato had actually been adopted by most known writers on the subject for the 1,500 years in between. Why did Hugh reject the preference of the Stoics, Augustine, Cassiodorus, and Isidor and follow Boëthius?

There is no certain answer. The probability is, however, that he was acting consistently with his convictions about belles lettres and specialization. Both were prominent among the concerns of his contemporaries, especially at the great school of Chartres (about 40 miles west-southwest of Paris); and a powerful influence upon those thinkers was what they knew of Plato, mainly fragmentary or secondhand. Furthermore, many of the specialists were naturalistically or rationalistically inclined, and Hugh's allegiance was in the Augustinian camp of faith and humility. Did he choose "Aristotle's" classification rather than "Plato's" as a move against what he disapproved in philosophy and pedagogy? However that may be, the choice gave him coverage of the Mechanical, which he said he could not find in the Platonic scheme; and he bracketed the Mechanical with Ethics as important because of their respective "concern for works and morals" (book 2, chap. 16). Also, whereas the Platonic tradition gave Dialectic a tremendous, central role, and treated Rhetoric on the whole as less than fully respectable, an Aristotelian plan could be hospitable to both, modestly; the latter was by far the more appropriate to Hugh's objective and tactics.

When Hugh of St. Victor paired "works and morals" he was not offering an innovation in Christian ideology. Nor was Aristotle indigestible in a Christian diet, as Thomas Aquinas would soon demonstrate. But in the epoch about to open, the Late Middle Ages, great changes in the daily lives of thousands were to affect all three in varying ways, and these metamorphoses were to help modify religion, politics, education, and libraries.

Chapter Three

THE LATE MIDDLE AGES

On the eve of the Thirteenth century business and businessmen were important in north Italy and more than merely noticeable in the urban centers beyond the Alps. The subsequent conquest of the manor by the market steadily, if not often dramatically, pushed toward urbanism, nations, and bourgeois values. Many were the forces resisting such change, aiding it, or attempting as in the peasant revolts of the fourteenth century to go still further. Some aspects of the library life underwent major alteration; others were hardly touched.

Friars, Universities, and Books

The late twelfth and early thirteenth centuries saw great turbulence first in Italy, then in southern France. Rooted in sharp commercial competition, it was aggravated by political rivalries between emperors and popes, dukes and bishops, nobles and bourgeois, city and city; and by unrest in the Church over heresy, corruption, and revenue. Italy was ravaged by the wars of the Guelfs and Ghibellines, southern France shortly afterward by the "crusade" against the Albigensian "heretics"—and their challengingly prosperous economy. The reform impulse was manifest in the Fourth Lateran Council. Convened in 1215 by Pope Innocent III, its deliberations produced a substantial list of "canons" on non-Christians, heresy, misbehavior, and church administration. In particular did the Council decree that men should be appointed, in every diocese, to advance theology and instruct the people.

The Dominicans   Almost as though in response to the question "which men?" there emerged from the horrors in southern France a number of leaders with a plan. The clergy needed experts in doctrine, and the people needed sound daily guidance. Let the "Preaching Friars" be authorized, urged Dominic Guzman, to train men in theology and the languages spoken by the masses. The plan seemed good to the pope: by 1225 the Dominicans had well under way a system whereby each brother was supplied with basic textbooks, the warehousing and accounting being worked out thoroughly and recorded in great detail, tribute impressive if not necessarily conscious to the way of the bourgeois world. This property, however, was communal. Brothers were given money to pay scribes to copy the necessary texts. Those, and the others already on hand and loaned to the friar, often for life, reverted to the original convent when he died. Such policies, and gifts from outsiders, account largely for the libraries soon available to the Order of Preachers at their several houses. Brief rules for library management were composed in 1246, if not earlier, basically the same as those already familiar. So was the customary housing for books. Apparently still unusual, in the scheme of 1306 to 1308 for the Dominicans' new buildings at Toulouse, was the provision for one called *libraria*. From the same period, at Limoges in west central France, dates the earliest known reference to a building specifically constructed as a library.

It is perhaps worth noting that those same Dominicans were in 1231 entrusted with struggling against error also by other means, the Inquisition. Nor is it entirely coincidental that Toulouse, scene of the above-mentioned activity, was the heart of the territory where the Albigensians and other "heretics" had been fought.

The Franciscans   The sorrows of Italy meanwhile generated, among other things, the effort of Francis of Assisi to re-create the example of apostolic self-denial and service directly among the people. Reading did not play a central role at first. The focus was on walking in poverty and humility, and a breviary (book of public daily prayers) seemed enough to carry (a Bible would have been distressingly heavy anyway). But the Friars Minor (Franciscans) were soon involved in urban problems, and frequent debating of doctrine added other pressures for education. Not long after the passing of the founder in 1226, the order had many libraries, supplied and managed in very much the same fashion as those of the Dominicans. If St. Francis himself had not been keen on study, his outstanding successor, Bonaventure, assuredly was. Appointed professor at the University of Paris in 1253, elected General of the Order in 1257, the "Seraphic Doctor" promoted reading—of the secular too, the better to understand the Scriptures. So also had spoken Jerome, Cassiodorus, and Hugh of St. Victor. By 1336 Franciscan library management policies were stated in a decree by Pope Benedict XII (1334–1342), the "Benedictine Constitutions," whose first rule was that gifts should be distributed according to the donors' desires.

Scholarly Needs The emergence of the friars added noticeably to the demand for reading matter. The new-style preacher, equipped with core texts, might or might not require a library any more than the "master" who taught such arts as grammar. But others surely did. Thomas Aquinas, of the University of Paris "graduate school" of theology—almost unknown to contemporary undergraduates in the standard "arts" course, needed a good collection to fight the battle of orthodox doctrine against unsettling influences from Moslem, Jewish, and pagan sources, to buttress Christian revelation with impressive manipulation of the logic of Aristotle. His classic *Summa Theologica,* issued at mid-century, promptly became a key instrument in the intellectual and moral stock taking, analyzing, and systematizing characteristic of the age. What to read, what to have in a library, is not discussed in the *Summa:* the serious mind apparently wanted "everything." On the same basis one may suppose that books were likewise vital to the teachers of canon and civil law, sharpening church weapons of organization and control for the struggle with secular challengers; and to the professor of medicine, still denied human corpses to study; perhaps also to the monk like Matthew Paris who busied himself writing history.

Commercial Supply At Bologna, Italy, the combination of a long-established trade in books, and a law-focussed university consisting of strongly organized students determined to make their money and labor count quickly, produced the first regulations of the commercial supply machinery. Standards of accuracy and prices were issued in 1259. By 1289 the *stationarius* (publisher-dealer) could not sell authorized titles to any *studium* other than the Bologna law school, and quality control was being enforced by elected student inspectors. The teaching "masters" who constituted the University of Paris followed suit in 1275, with the difference that the inspectors were not students but *principales librarii* chosen from among the licensed *stationarii* and *librarii* (book-agents). Not even assiduous supervising, of course, could preclude all abuse or failure; the fourteenth century saw a good many more regulations designed to strengthen the university hand on the official book market. In like manner, under the law code developed from 1252 to 1285 by Alfonso X of Castile, licensing powers were conferred upon (or acknowledged in?), simultaneously, the several universities of Christian Spain.

The core of the system was the obligation of the "stationer" to produce a copy of a text pronounced satisfactory by the university, an obligation which soon included demonstrating that he was sufficiently learned to understand the importance as well as the market value of the books in his care. (The university also licensed illustrators, binders, paper makers, and parchment makers.) The number of titles involved might exceed 100, as it did at Bologna. The official copy—*exemplar*—was to be kept at the stationer's, accessible to copyists, unbound. The individual *pecia*—two sheets folded as four leaves (eight pages), something like the signature of later times—could be borrowed for a fee, and at the head of each *exemplar* was a record of the total number of *peciae* and the price for the opportunity to make a copy. The rules often stipulated the number of lines a *pecia* should have; insofar as they were enforced, the customer knew better what he was getting than the inquirer of later times who was furnished readily with the number of pages but rarely with the number of words.

Since a cash deposit was required as a pledge of accurate texts, and not all *peciae* were out earning fees all the time, entering the "stationer" business required a capital investment. Balancing this risk was the known advantage of being—as stationers were—"associates" *(propinqui)* of the university: they were exempt from royal and municipal taxes and night watch, and outside the jurisdiction of civil courts. Appealing also, perhaps, was the rather less predictable reward of a more or less assured market.

The pace of the scribes and illuminators employed to produce books at university centers like Paris was probably faster than that familiar in the scriptoria of the monasteries. Crowding more letters on a page was one means; the only other one, apparently, was speed-up, which presumably helped generate smaller letters and increased use of abbreviations. For the hours of daylight were not different, window design had not yet been altered conspicuously, and artificial light both adequate and safe was still by and large in the future; few but zealots did much writing or copying by candlelight. (Although spectacles were invented in the late thirteenth or early fourteenth century, they were not worn immediately by all who could have benefited from them. The oldest known pictorial evidence is the 1352 portrait of Cardinal Ugo di Probenza, in the chapter house of the North Italian church of San Nicolo di Treviso.) Perhaps these conditions in the commercial shops were reflected in new pressures in the abbeys. In 1279 the Carthusian monks, whose routine included much study and copying, were told by a statute of their order that failure to copy would bring down deprivation of wine. And when, more than a century later, the Paris Carthusians asked whether it was right to copy on holy days, Chancellor Gerson replied affirmatively, with a tract, "In Praise of Scribes." Quality may have suffered. Petrarch, apologizing for keeping a borrowed book more than four years, blamed the shortage of competent copyists.

Friar Domination If the flowering of the book trade around universities owed a good deal to the influx of students, one of the steadier sources of purchasing was precisely those whose mission was to strengthen the church against secular challenge by mastering theology and law, the Dominicans. The brother sent to the university had to have a few books, and money to buy more; that was the responsibility of the convent of origin. Complementarily, the *exemplares* approved by the University of Paris authorities—which in theology was likely to mean Dominicans—were the models for texts elsewhere. By these criteria did the Dominican field inspectors in each locality judge the reliability of the codexes in use. Psalters copied by nuns or other women were banned: how much for performance demonstrably inferior to the friars', how much for the inadequacy of the Latin instruction accessible to them, how much for prejudice?

Partly perhaps because of the 1292 decision that no friar could have a duplicate or any book he could not use, Franciscan students too were book buyers. In England, in the middle of the fourteenth century, an archbishop complained to the pope that all sorts of books were hard to obtain there because individual Franciscans were buying them so avidly; his point was that those friars should be satisfied with what their order furnished. The Friars Minor were in truth vulnerable. By papal pronouncements of 1255 and 1265 they enjoyed a privileged position even within the church: exemption from the papal tax (the "canonical portion") on the books and other gifts they received. Unlike the Dominicans, moreover, they were preoccupied with their "rule" of poverty, corporate as well as personal; conflict over its interpretation divided them for more than a century into strict and broad constructionist wings, even formal subdivisions of the Friars Minor. Yet all the orders of friars accumulated so much through the contributions of the faithful that they evoked as much critical comment by the fourteenth century as had the monks before them. "They have nothing but possess all," was the contemporary thrust.

The animus was probably nourished also by the seepage of commercialism into ecclesiastical precincts. The Dominicans emphasized from the outset study of and preaching from books copied by others. Some copying for cash occurred; a prior could sell duplicates if the convent members agreed, except for works on logic, natural philosophy, "questions," or sermons, which had to be assigned for use. But neither copying nor selling was ever, apparently, so widespread in Dominican circles as among the considerably more numerous and somewhat less tightly controlled Franciscans. The latter's Narbonne "Constitution" of 1260 tried to limit copying, and forbade a friar to write or have a book written for sale. Nearly a century afterward, besides repeating that injunction, presumably for good reasons, the "General Chapter"—that is, the convention—declared that no book should be sold at a price higher than its cost. Few, however, were the professional scribes among the friars. Their two original orders inclined to the hiring of laymen, insofar as they could not acquire enough books through gifts. The Austin Hermits, founded somewhat later, decided in 1290 that each convent should employ a lay scribe, and in the mid-fourteenth century that each master in theology in the house should be furnished a scribe (as well as a cook) paid by the convent.

English Exception   These phenomena were of earlier vintage in England. The reason was different: the Normans interested in reading found that the Danish raids preceding their own invasion had left an insufficiency of books and monks able to copy. The outside scribe thus became known to many English monastic houses long before the friars appeared on the scene. Indeed, the duties of the *armarius* (librarian) at such a monastery included not only furnishing the scribe with supplies but negotiating his wages. Book copying may have been the first industry conducted on the "putting-out" system, under which the workman takes the raw material home and returns to his employer with the finished product.

Book Economics and Library Ideology

The Victory of the Market   Evident, in perspective, is the advance of the new order, pushing aside the old. The monks, generally living in isolation, touched relatively little by the money economy, copied to serve God and keep busy. The friars served the church by studying and going among the restless masses to fight Mammon and heresy; they usually bought copyist labor on the market. The end of the Middle Ages added a combination of extremes. The Brothers of the Common Life, founded by the Dutch evangelist-educator, Gerard de Groot, in 1383, lived in their own establishments, praying and copying much like monks. But they also gave considerable effort, friarlike, to practical community service, especially in education. And this program rested financially upon the deliberate, well-organized manufacturing of didactic books for sale. Hardly different from the foreman of a commercial stationer's crew was he who in each house supervised the work and set the prices on the products, the *librarius*.

Trusteeship   The authorization of "moderate use" of worldly goods, the popes' thirteenth-century attempt (edicts over the years 1230 to 1288) to find middle ground between Franciscan factions and facilitate the labors of a Roger Bacon by letting him "own" pen and ink, marked a new phase in Christian ethics. Theoretically, the literal poverty associated with the apostles could be maintained in any world, even the new one proliferating with cash transactions, tax gatherers, bankers, and written titles to land. But the church would do so, in the thirteenth century, only at the cost of wholesale overturning of already existing relationships, not to speak of what was on the agenda with regard to the claims of secular powers. Pope Innocent IV did not outmaneuver Holy Roman Emperor Frederick II for the sake of the austerity program of St. Francis. On the contrary, he set the church on a definite course of aggrandizement, with steam up so high that change received serious consideration by the church decision makers only when the Reformation forced it upon them.

The ideological problem was solved, meanwhile, by reasoning that the church revenues, buildings, equipment, etc., represented legitimate "use" on behalf of the community of property "belonging" to all. This concept of trusteeship was to prove adaptable to the defense of wealth and minority power for centuries to come: first the church magnates, then the landed aristocracy, and eventually the tycoons of modern industry and property. Its later corollary, the board of trustees, would help preserve the atmosphere of minority control not only in privately owned museums and the like but even in the tax-supported public library.

The Cost of Hand-producing a Book   The medieval manuscript-book helped occasion these adjustments because it was more than likely to be "expensive." At what level? One of the fundamental items, the Breviary occupied 300-odd leaves, requiring at least thirty clean sheep hides. An experienced copyist could fill the two sides of each leaf in one hour. If he worked twelve hours a day, six days a week, he would turn out a Breviary in a little less than one month. To copy the whole Bible is believed to have required a minimum of 1,666 hours—more than five times the labor needed to do a Breviary. Peter Lombard's "Sentences" were about half the length of the Bible; Vincent of Beauvais' encyclopedia, in its 1244 version, three times the size of the Bible. It is hardly a surprise that extant catalogs list the "Sentences" much more often than the whole Bible—let alone Vincent's work.

Even the largest libraries of the early thirteenth century, at Durham Cathedral in England and Corbie monastery in France, each of which was one-fourth Biblical texts, reported having respectively two "complete" Bibles and none at all.

If money had to be spent not only on the hides and the writing materials and equipment, but on scribes, the buyer in fourteenth-century England had to reckon in his cost—on a big job—sixpence weekly wages beyond the scribe's room and board; on a small assignment the scribe earned two pence a day, the same as an agricultural laborer. If the bill for the "Sentences" was about five shillings in copyist wages for ten weeks, that item alone was only half a shilling less than the cost of a "quarter," or 480 pounds, of wheat. On that basis, a whole Bible cost about as much as a half ton of wheat. Is it strange that copies surviving from that era show little sign of wear? Or that the Breviary or New Testament in a friar's knapsack made him a walking treasure trove?

Besides, still more expensive manuscripts, usually illuminated, were manufactured for wealthy ecclesiastics and nobles as luxury items.

Paper Even the general run of books produced commercially were thus "expensive" because they consumed a great deal of skilled hand labor, and parchment was not cheap. Paper had been known in the Orient and to the Arabs and Jews long before a successful mill was opened at Fabriano, Italy, in 1276. The "new" material was clearly less substantial than parchment: officials mistrusted it. Nor were its Moslem and Jewish associations an asset. Its introduction was consciously hampered, moreover, legislatively and perhaps in other ways, by the parchment interests. But the acceptance of paper was aided by the technical advances in preparing pulp, and by the fourteenth-century swing to linen clothes, furnishing rags not only much better for paper than earlier materials had been but cheaper.

By 1348 the sponsors of the first paper mill in France were able to open for business with tax exemption. A century later bishops' and university representatives would still be struggling over the limited parchment supplies at the licensed dealers' shops and fairs, but the hours of parchment's supremacy were already numbered.

Beyond Church and Academe Favoring cheaper book production were not only paper technology, and the type of book demand discussed above, but the nonacademic and bourgeois markets. When the thirteenth century began, the noble household in many areas of Europe, and the bourgeois home in Northern Italy, were entertained often by oral readings of courtly romance, Arthurian legends, and the like. The next 200 years saw a pretty steady increase in the work of lay scribes and home book ownership; there was a lull from 1350 to 1360 thanks to the Black Death and the Hundred Years' War. Noteworthy was the composition in England in 1352 of a work on home remedies for sin, in Anglo-Norman, by a layman. At least one establishment is known to have existed by that time, devoted to making and selling books, in London, where the book trade was not under university control. There may have been others, wherever else a market of civil servants, merchants, and guildsmen lay at hand.

The merchants of Paris rose in revolt in 1357 under the leadership of Etienne Marcel, wealthy clothing merchant, prominent guildsman, member of the Estates-General, Provost of Paris, and nevertheless able to sympathize with desperate peasants—the Jacquerie. Who is to say that such men would not have been capable of interests in, even demands for, books? Perhaps some of them were among the thirty-seven purchasers of the French edition of the travels of "Sir John Mandeville." Considering extant copies alone, commercial enterprises were then well enough established and organized to issue in a short time not only a French edition but seventy-three copies in German or Dutch, fifty in Latin, and forty in English. Altogether, it seems quite comprehensible that, as the turn of the fifteenth century approached, there was already some production of books on a risk basis for a market at fairs and elsewhere (nonuniversity) rather than for known purchasers.

Indeed, the boundaries of the market would soon be still more capacious. Books were by now familiar objects not merely to those who read them in line of duty, or enjoyed the multifarious passages in contemporary literature comparing books or writing to the blood of martyrs, the human face, or the heart. The idea of the book was also projected in this metaphorical style in sermons: the preacher might even dramatize his spiritual point by explaining step by step how a book was made. Possibly relevant are the drawings of codexes which often appear in the margins of Gothic manuscripts (in the twelfth through fourteenth centuries) together with representations of clerics in ape or other animal form. What this mass education contributed to the awakening of interest in and demand for reading matter among largely illiterate peasants and ordinary townsmen is mainly in the realm of the unknown.

Gifts and Forfeits Libraries meeting known needs, in monasteries, cathedrals, and the convents of the friars, still dependent upon copying by residents or paid outsiders, relied increasingly upon gifts. That is plain from the large number of surviving catalogs of the later thirteenth and fourteenth centuries in which the first portion of the holdings is presented roughly by subject, but the balance—sometimes larger—is listed by donation, regardless of subject.

These donations were a constructive solution to a crisis. More and more students were enrolling at universities, attracted if not by hot debate and renowned lecturers then certainly by the economic and social advantages of bachelor's and master's degrees. Many of these students, perhaps most, were unable to buy books. The first few generations struggled through with the aid of church and abbey libraries; the Paris Council recommendation (1212) that books be loaned to poor students was apparently an early straw in the wind. Then the friars came, bringing books with them and cash for more; they soon had libraries "on campus." Next the monasteries sent some members to school too; with them, in several instances, arrived part of the home foundation's book collection, and they could draw upon the rest of it, at least in theory.

Those who were neither monks nor friars nor wealthy still needed help. The "seculars" at Merton College, Oxford (founded 1264) soon had books from donors: its catalog of 1360 reportedly includes no less than sixteen copies of Lombard's "Sentences," presumably from sixteen different contributors. Most of them were probably bequests, a prominent form of library gift in the thirteenth and fourteenth centuries. Conspicuous is a testament of 1297: the Chancellor of Notre Dame Cathedral was not to administer the legacy of books for the poor theology students in the customary fashion, as the property of the Cathedral Chapter; he was explicitly designated simply the custodian of books bequeathed directly to the students themselves, a concept of trusteeship destined to play a leading role in libraries, especially public libraries.

Also becoming a familiar part of the scene were libraries at individual faculties or student "nations," established often with gifts of cash or books or both. Outstanding was the Paris residence-with-library endowed about 1250 by the king's chaplain, Robert de Sorbon, for theology students of slim resources. Thanks to donations pouring in from all directions, more than 1,000 manuscripts could be listed in the Sorbonne catalog of 1290.

Necessary nevertheless were additional measures, old and new. The Sorbonne accepted certain books as satisfaction for debts; it was probably not unique. When Archbishop Kilwardby of Canterbury visited Merton in 1276, he decreed in the style routine to him as a Dominican that a fellow's books (like a friar's) would go to the college at his departure. The involuntary departure of the Jews from England in 1290 and from France in 1306 also enriched numerous libraries as their "nonmovable" property was confiscated. Yet the University of Paris in 1342 obliged the bookseller to loan copies to poor students for a nominal fee, set by the university.

Arrangement and Control of Library Books

Shelving and Chains   In the days when closets and chests sufficed for collections growing slowly if at all, books could be stored nearly anywhere. As the number of codexes for group use tended to increase more rapidly than before, logic produced an area coming to be called "the library" and the custom of chaining there the items in heavy demand. That meant few but service books like missals before the thirteenth century, but for perhaps the next 200 years the practice seems to have become common, on the one hand for any book in demand, on the other for those left over after the distribution to the students customary at least in English colleges of the fourteenth century. By 1360, at Merton College, Oxford, only the best copy of a title was chained, or a gift to be handled thus by the donor's stipulation; Merton may have been well ahead of its contemporaries.

These chained items were as a rule placed on inclined surfaces and anchored either directly to the desk or, as at the Sorbonne (1289 catalog), to the wall. As the inclined surface in turn became crowded the consequence was the development of furniture combining both that and horizontal shelves, foreshadowing after a fashion the reference-corner equipment of the mid-twentieth-century library. Unfortunately the chains did not always do what was expected. Many a catalog of this period denotes a codex as "chained"; but in the Sorbonne's 1338 list of the "Big library," the 330 items chained for the use of "all" (not just the theology teachers and students), certain entries of supposedly chained books include contrariwise a mournful "missing."

Subject Arrangement   Another consequence of growth of the collection was that the more-or-less subject arrangement in fixed locations, known since Carolingian days, was sometimes upset in a manner newly noticeable. When all codexes were shelved vertically, their order would depart from subject patterns here and there, because of a composite item with heterogeneous contents (a papal library of about 1400 reportedly held 4,000 titles in 1090 codexes). The same deviation would be produced occasionally, as in later times, by exceptional height. When a volume was placed flat on an inclined desk its height hardly mattered, and topical grouping was presumably a little easier. Then came additional titles claiming space on the same surfaces. A subject might occupy less than one, all of one, or more than one. Since the tenants already there were as a rule chained, the maneuvers necessary to anchor new ones may have produced departures from subject arrangement quite striking at times.

The surviving data suggest that an institution was unusual which planned its space utilization for expansion. Of course, those growing slowly did not necessarily face that problem: such, apparently, was the Benedictine cloister at Regensburg, Germany, which reportedly still lived happily at 1475 with the same thirty-two book desks it had had in 1347. Meanwhile, both space economy and ease of reading markings on a book's spine favored greater use of shelving on which the codexes were placed standing up.

Arrangement on the whole by subject was liable to deliberate exceptions as well as those deriving from the contents or size of the manuscript-book. At the convent of San Francisco at Assisi in 1340, at least one commentary was placed with each basic lecture item, while the other commentaries on the same questions were shelved elsewhere. This policy, tailored to study and therefore probably in use at other libraries too, seems to have been a prototype for the modern college reserve collection separate from the balance.

Markings   Whatever the arrangement, the growth of library collections meant more importance for markings, whether on the furniture alone, or also on books and in catalogs. The fixed positions on book closet shelves had been given symbols long before: letters, Roman numerals, or both. Desks were now equipped similarly. At the Sorbonne's "Big library" in 1330, for example, each of the twenty-eight desks to which reference works were chained was marked with both a single large letter and several small ones positioned to keep those codexes in order. Generally speaking, a particular closet or desk was likely to be designated by a large capital letter, a shelf or place on a desk by an additional smaller letter; a Roman numeral might be added for the individual codex. The first letter often stood for a subject as well as a location. The second probably did not, as a rule, because subject collections were not yet large enough to urge subdivision by topic rather than shelf. Likewise, the numeral for a particular work had no subject significance.

Recognition of broad subject groups was aided by the markings in some libraries, probably more often in combination with a fixed location symbol than independent of it. Richard de Fournival, theologian and poet of mid-thirteenth-century Paris and donor of 300 books to the Sorbonne library, not only urged using one desk for one subject, but recommended four different colors for the four Faculties of Theology, Law, Medicine, and Arts. He also advocated putting undersized books on top of one another to save space; this may explain the occasional occurrence in the old records of two books with identical call numbers.

The codex itself seems to have been marked with these symbols far less often than the furniture. At the Sorbonne, indeed, the classmark and individual book number were entered on the first page of each volume in the circulating collection ("Little library"), and the resulting call number was copied into the loan register when the work was borrowed. That, however, was reportedly unusual even for a large collection; in fact, quite a few eschewed markings on the outside of a book right into the nineteenth century. What was regarded as avoidable was evidently discouraged not only by the labor involved but by two sorts of confusion. One was the occasional effort to express subject as well as fixed location. The other was the frequent employment of cumbersome Roman numerals and the sporadic resort to Greek letters when Latin letters were found insufficient. Yet, if the men of the day were thereby inconvenienced, posterity gained, since the form of those handwritten letters and numerals helps experts determine where a given codex was originally held.

The last quarter of the fourteenth century saw a turn toward marking books outside, perhaps first at the papal library in 1375. The Dover Priory library in England was entering call numbers both outside and inside the codexes by 1389; others soon began to act likewise. By 1438 the Sorbonne system of marking inside only was recognized there as a major source of disorder.

Call Numbers in the Catalog New as a widespread phenomenon in the thirteenth century was the appearance of call numbers in the catalog. It is believed, in fact, that they were lacking in the period under consideration only where progress was impeded by severe isolation or some comparable obstacle. Fournival projected the call number on the later principle of subject, independent of location, but the Sorbonne's circulating library seems to have been the only one administered in that fashion. A "first" perhaps was the use of Arabic numerals in call numbers in the 1355 catalog of San Francisco convent, Pisa.

Catalog Arrangement Library catalogs continued by and large to follow the shelves. While the arrangement had a roughly subject profile there were several competing features. Familiar was the custom (requirement too?) of listing separately what had been donated, by donor; also books reposing in separate rooms. Further, like the traditional special reference to "Scottish script," catalogs were now likely to record books in Greek or Hebrew as simply a total number. Within subject groups of well-known titles by different authors, the arrangement was often author-chronological, an approach to subject materials still desired by readers in the twentieth century but rarely furnished by their libraries.

In 1338 the Sorbonne's reference library catalog listed the language subjects of the trivium first; then logic, physics, and morals; then the mathematical quadrivium. One wonders whether the recommendations of encyclopedist and court chaplain Vincent of Beauvais a century before had anything to do with it. More remarkable were the analytical entries under those subjects for the individual titles in the 330 codexes. The larger circulating collection, however, was presented traditionally, the Bible at the head, and without analytics.

The Classification of Knowledge   Nor were there any noteworthy advances in the late middle ages in the classification of knowledge. The earliest known Sorbonne catalog (1289?) expanded the quadrivium to include alchemy and medicine (shades of Varro, more than a millennium before!). And Robert Kilwardby, English Dominican, wrote about the same time a tract purporting to improve upon such earlier schemes as that of Hugh of St. Victor. He bracketed agriculture, dietetics, and medicine as a new "trivium" and treated as another "quadrivium" costuming, armor making, architecture, and commerce.

Description   Actually, for all the increase in demand for reading matter in libraries, subject analysis and control was rather incidental. The data at our disposal suggest that description and other property-serving practices were still attracting more attention. Among the few noteworthy instruments extant are those fashioned in 1389 on behalf of the Benedictine Priory at Dover, England (reported invaluably by C. R. Haines in *The Library,* 4th ser., 8:73-118, 1927-1928): a justly celebrated "register" of locations with unusual detail about each codex, a shelflist including all titles within all volumes, and an alphabetical list of all the works in the library. To list all the titles within a codex was not a novelty, but the record does not seem to show any earlier example of providing call numbers at the same time. On the other hand, it was fairly common by the end of the fourteenth century to use for the control medium the first few words on the second and the penultimate leaves of each codex rather than the first and last, because, as in many situations of later times, the first and last faced too much handling to be relied on.

Limited progress was made in descriptive cataloging despite the absence of a title page, the normal condition before the invention of printing. In the early thirteenth-century catalog of the abbey library at Savigny, in Normandy, many works customarily attributed to one of the Fathers were reportedly credited to their true, if less noted, authors; that was unusual; why it was done, whether the cataloger was right, and how he knew remain obscure. Although books did not yet include place, publisher, and date, they did sometimes bear a record of the scriptorium of origin; this, however, was not entered in the catalog. Nor, except in the Dover Priory catalog, so far as we know, was the total number of pages indicated. At that time it was habitual to assign sequence symbols—which might be letters—only to the gatherings, not individual pages; certainly moving ahead to the latter was not encouraged by the awkwardness of the Roman numeral system. Arabic numbers were available, but the newfangled notation overcame old attitudes generally only with the invention of printing.

Like arrangement on the shelves, the layout within the catalog underwent very little change. One reads only occasionally of a case in which lines were left blank for the insertion of added items. Conspicuous is the 1370 catalog of Admont, a Benedictine abbey in the mountains of southeastern Austria, in which each author has his individual page. In fact, the expansion of the collection put a strain on catalogs not always met. Quite likely more reliable than the catalogs with regard to what was actually available were the framed lists of items at a particular desk or shelf, attached to that desk or shelf in some libraries.

Union Lists   To seek elsewhere what one does not have on the premises is an old book-world habit. Since Carolingian days at least, short-title lists of holdings had been exchanged now and then. A monk of mid-eleventh-century Metz (northeastern France) presumably had seen something of that sort when he noted some books at a nearby monastery which his own did not possess (Gottlieb, no. 22, pp. 52-53); or was it hearsay? In 1253 the Dominican convention at Limoges (west central France) asked the priors at Toulouse and other large installations of the area to let the other convents know what books they had. That does not sound unique: in all probability the friars engaged in more movement of codexes than appears in surviving records.

Documents of varying degrees of union character date from the first half of the thirteenth century. The Savigny catalog of 1210 (or 1240?) listed the holdings not only of its own library but of other abbeys in the vicinity. The Sorbonne a few decades later developed a register of the holdings of the Parisian libraries open to theology students. In 1347 the Benedictines of St. Emmeram in Regensburg assembled the catalogs of several other libraries in that Upper Danube community, plus a few from other abbeys in the same region.

The Franciscans in England, meanwhile, were putting together an author-alphabetical book list with symbols to indicate which libraries among those in their seven "custodies" had a particular work, and a key to the symbols at the head of the list. This achievement is thought probably to have antedated 1251, because one of the named "custodies" (an administrative agency between the convents and the "province") no longer existed in that year; of course word of the change may have lagged behind the fact. The Friars Minor added about a half-century later a union catalog locating the works, chiefly biblical and controversial, of 94 authors not in Franciscan libraries in England but reportedly in one or another of 138 English and Scottish monasteries (i.e., non-Franciscan establishments), the renowned *Registrum librorum Angliae.*

Upon these efforts, and others from Jerome's biobibliography to Vincent of Beauvais' "Mirror of History," was built in the late fourteenth century the landmark *Catalogus* by Henry of Kirkestede, of Bury St. Edmunds (until lately attributed to John Boston of Bury). It dealt with 195 libraries, a few more than before, saying regrettably little about them; but the list of works had lengthened tenfold, and considerable biobibliographical information was furnished. Presumably this character was functional to the responsibilities of Kirkestede as librarian and master of novices: he regarded his labor as unfinished and urged others to carry it further.

Book Loans In the years from 1225 to 1400 books used by teachers and students tended to be divided as before, with some new shadings within the "circulating" category. At one extreme was the Dominican loan to a brother "for life." Then came the one-year type, common at Notre Dame and the Abbey of St. Victor in Paris from about 1270 on and in the English colleges soon afterward in the form of an annual redistribution of circulating copies, usually called the "election" because choice was often granted by seniority. Among the Dominicans at least there was also a very short-term loan arrangement, for a day or so, it seems—called *simpliciter.*

These books, to a considerable degree, could be and evidently were taken out of the building. Both Franciscan and Dominican convents were authorized to loan books to other convents; Franciscan priories recorded outside loans as early as 1233. This traffic was perhaps strictly local, inasmuch as the Franciscans did not permit it at the higher organizational level (covering a larger area) of the "custody," and the Dominicans were fewer and rather more scattered. In fact, under the "Constitutions" of reformer Pope Benedict XII, 1336, books were not to be moved about overreadily, certainly not if a convent were thereby deprived of any of its works on grammar, logic, philosophy, or theology; besides, no book was to be sold or exchanged except for a better copy. Meanwhile, from the papal library at Avignon, during the late thirteenth and early fourteenth centuries one of the largest in Europe, were loaned the numerous copies of popular works like Isidor of Seville's encyclopedic "Origins" (ca. 625) and Peter Comestor's more recent Bible-teaching aid, the "Scholastic History."

The early-thirteenth-century impetus toward book loans to students lacking funds, well developed in such libraries as that of Notre Dame in Paris, appears to have encountered obstacles here and there in the communities of the friars. A donor in Exeter, England, offered some books to the local Franciscans in 1266, but the gift was contingent upon the books' being available also to the town's Dominicans. In his eyes, evidently, the two original "mendicant" orders could stand some encouragement to cooperate. In 1328 indeed, perhaps because loans to non-Franciscan prelates and laymen were thought to be abused, the prior-general of the Friars Minor issued a letter discouraging loans outside the Franciscan ranks. Yet, in the English colleges, Franciscan books were at the end of that century available to non-friar students.

Book Security Security of the books loaned was as usual dependent on the good faith of the borrower, and his pledge. Taking a deposit of greater value for a loaned book was still general practice; the Franciscans reportedly required one only from "seculars" (clerics not in one of the several orders of the Church) borrowing a book for more than one month.

The additions to this arsenal of protection are known mainly in connection with those same Franciscans, who may well have maintained more library units than any other group. At the operational level, the Friars Minor charged the "custody" with supervising the record keeping of the convents in its jurisdiction. At the level of principle they produced a succession of legal documents insisting that the books be returned to the library. Notable in surviving records are the mid-fourteenth-century efforts to tighten control by the prior of the Tuscan Province: even books loaned "for life" were to be shown annually; until a bishop-elect returned his to the convent of origin he could not be consecrated; etc. (Modern scholarship doubts their enforcement.) One thinks of some twentieth-century institutions of higher learning which withhold a degree from a candidate delinquent as a borrower from the campus library.

Not really new, but probably applied with novel consistency, was the Dominican regulation that the name of the issuing convent or province be inscribed in each book issued.

Sorbonne data of 1338 indicate that allowing almost anyone associated with the university to borrow books from the circulating "Little library" for comparatively lengthy periods, leaving only his name, deposit, and a few facts about the book, was a clear handicap. Of the 1,722 titles nominally on hand, 500 could not be located.

Perhaps linked to security, perhaps not, is the apparently unusual rule adopted at Trinity Hall, Cambridge, in 1350. No book belonging to the college could be loaned unbound, for the purpose of copying. This was precisely the opposite of the obligation of the licensed book furnisher, the continental university "stationer." Whether or not copying was permitted from a bound book does not appear; perhaps the question did not arise.

The "Public"   In such records of operation as the celebrated 1381 catalog of the Franciscan convent library at Assisi, Italy, one of the largest of that epoch, one encounters the expression *bibliotheca publica*. At Assisi it distinguished the nontheological material from the theological. The latter was the "secret" library, reserved for resident scholars. The former was available to officials, visiting prelates, "and other clerics." Under these circumstances it is hard to tell whether *publica* defined the nature of the collection, or the (clerical) readers not admitted to the "secret" library, or both at once.

At the Sorbonne, in Paris, likewise one of the richest contemporary collections, admission to the chained-book room of a broader "public" seems virtually certain in the light of the regulations issued in 1321 for the use of that room. Attention is invited to rules 2 and 3 in particular, in the list offered herewith, freely rendered on the basis of the Latin original and French translation supplied by A. Franklin (*Les Anciennes Bibliothèques de Paris,* Paris, Impr. Imp., 1867–1870; Impr. Nat., 1873, I:239–240):

1   Robes and caps required.
2   No children or illiterates admitted.
3   Respectable learned men may enter if introduced by a member; their "valets" must remain outside.
4   Each member keeps his own key and loans it to no one.
5   Neither fire nor light permitted at any time.
6   No books issued without the permission of the Society.

7   A book should be laid upon a desk only after the dust has been removed.

8   No writing in or other abuse of a book.

9   Whether writing or reading, no bothering of others by talking or walking.

10   Maximum silence, as would be appropriate to premises "sacred and august."

11   Condemned books are available to professors of theology only—for use in line of duty only.

12   The professor is not to read such works for curiosity, lest he be poisoned.

13   Violators of that restraint are to be reprimanded.

Rule 2 would scarcely have been formulated if the admission policy had not been generous enough to raise such questions. Rule 3 nevertheless implies rather clearly that the nonmember to be received as a reader was very likely an individual customarily accompanied by a servant. Rule 10 claims the mantle of the classical library-in-temple tradition. (Concerning the "members" and the "Society," there were thirty-six bachelors or doctors constituting the "House and Society of Sorbonne," the poor *(socii bursales)* being paid maintenance allowances and the rich making up the difference; as *socii,* regardless of finances, age, or academic standing, all thirty-six were "equal.")

The Character of the Library Collections

Book selection and censorship in the thirteenth and fourteenth centuries differed only moderately from what was already established. The heritage of antiquity, savored anew in the twelfth, continued to find hospitality in numerous book assemblages, especially at the larger monasteries and cathedrals.

Greek Science   This tendency was aided by the transmission of Greek and Arab-Greek science, one principal stream flowing from Italian centers to Paris as Italian clerics went to the headquarters of theological education to teach. (Peter "the Lombard" and Thomas "of Aquino"—near Naples—were only two among many.) Although certain Aristotelian titles were forbidden to the undergraduates in the early thirteenth century, the limitation appears to have had little significance. Perhaps the materialist and other "more dangerous" ideas in the air made Aristotle seem tame, especially as Thomas Aquinas handled him. At any rate, quotations from The Philosopher's works on science became more varied and more accurate in Parisian writings during that century.

At the same time, Spanish centers like Toledo influenced English development with the aid of English students returned from Spain. Adelard of Bath's "Questions about Nature according to the Arabs" appears at least twice in the Benedictine library catalog (about 1300) of Christ Church, Canterbury (in codexes 96 and 368, among two different sets of items; as displayed in Edwards' *Memoirs,* I: 141 and 189). Yet quite a few scientific works were composed in that epoch which do not seem to have been recorded in library catalogs; perhaps they lay in the hands of individual scholars.

The Friars' Emphases   There were also contrary pressures. A great many university students sought training in theology and law, especially the latter, then the most promising career. The highly organized Dominicans supported this drive. Their libraries were strong in those two subjects and the literature of preaching; they usually held some Aristotle; but they were weak in other subjects. In fact, the Preaching Friars repeatedly banned the reading of books by pagans and works on philosophy, the liberal arts, and secular science. They also denounced alchemy and necromancy and told the younger men among them not to read Dante. As late as 1311 the Dominicans were rejecting codexes with Arabic numbers, still disconcerted, evidently, although those symbols had been introduced to the Latin world a century earlier.

The Franciscans were not quite so single-minded. Bonaventure endorsed reading some profane works; some Friars Minor appear to have done so principally in England, where indeed Franciscan libraries and scholarship were outstanding. But the prior-general, following Bernard of Clairvaux, also denounced "curiosity" in reading; and the convention decisions of 1260 (Narbonne) directed the Friars Minor not to buy *libri curiosi,* that is, physically sumptuous or secular-content books. Furthermore, their General Chapter of 1266 called for the burning of all biographies of St. Francis other than the new one by Bonaventure, which deliberately muted the mystic element in the founder, productive of heretical tendencies then and afterward. Franciscan collections included less of the Aristotle and Thomas favored by the Dominicans and more in the "mystical" tradition of Augustine and Bernard of Clairvaux, and such diverse critics of Thomist orthodoxy as Duns Scotus and Ockham.

Anticlassics Rumor   Also a factor discouraging to the pagan classics was the tale, apparently false but beyond conclusive evaluation, that Pope Gregory the Great (fl. 600) had destroyed the Palatine and Capitoline libraries in Rome. Of uncertain origin, it circulated very widely in the thirteenth century in an extemely popular work on the lives of the popes by a Dominican known as "Martin of Poland"; the alleged deed was hailed by many as a triumph for Christian virtue. Then questions began to arise, especially in the Italy of Dante and the early Humanists; by the early fifteenth century Gregory was being declared incapable of an act so narrow-minded, so inconsistent with his own known Roman civic pride.

Miscellaneous Restrictions   If the classical legacy was received now warmly now coolly, controversial items in theology were probably treated with less variation. Such works could be read at the Sorbonne, as indicated above, by masters only, for professional purposes only; and that custom is likely to have prevailed elsewhere too. Authority did its best, however, to keep entirely beyond the pale, as usual, tracts on alchemy, magic, and the occult. Books of this sort, some of which contributed to the mastering of nature, were occasionally attributed to individuals dead (like Aristotle) or controversial (like Roger Bacon); certain of these writings very likely did issue from the quills of the exploring minds of the age. Few appear in library catalogs. In fact the whole record is shrouded in thick mist. Early in the fourteenth century, for example, Pope John XXII promulgated a bull against books on magic; but one cannot be sure how much he was moved by custom or the urgings of associates, how much by a desire to protect his flock from the numerous swindlers advertising simple "solutions" to pressing problems.

Richard de Bury and his Philobiblon The broad view was upheld most interestingly in 1345 in *The Philobiblon,* or *Love of Books.* Although some scholars believe it to have been written mainly by Dominican Robert Holcot, it is associated historically with the patron of the circle Holcot belonged to, for a few years at least, Richard de Bury, Bishop of Durham (1287–1345). The author insists that every generation's knowledge is dependent upon the labors of those who went before; he praises the ancients for their lifelong devotion to study, quoting them frequently, sometimes inaccurately (Holcot has been shown careless), but usually pertinently. He excoriates the monks, the friars, and anyone else who favors wine, women, and song, "studies" in haste, and then expects appointment to a good job. He quotes ironically (?) the commentator who once said the brilliant ancients had left nothing for posterity to do but summarize their words. He pulverizes some critics of his commitment to books who "perchance would have praised . . . us, if we had spent our time in hunting, dice-playing, or courting the smiles of the ladies" (sec. 235).

De Bury was neither monk nor friar but a college man, a king's clerk, markedly successful in diplomacy and public administration, cherished by King Edward III and entrusted with positions of top importance. His career certainly brought him many gifts of books: by his own testimony he could be "reached" more easily that way than with a cash bribe. His mode of life probably helps explain his regret that poverty was driving potential churchmen away from study, back "to the mechanical arts solely" to make a living—a sort of "apostasy" (sec. 7). It may or may not bear on his impatience at the idea that anyone would haggle over the price of a book, or his remark that such prices are determined by "wisdom only" (sec. 39).

Observant, reflective, imaginative, he found a connection between the defeat of France in battle and the decline of philosophy at the University of Paris. This integrative approach helped shape his essay. God had "willed that books should be as it were an antidote to all evil" (sec. 190), and the Church desperately needed fresh forces properly educated. He proposed to assist by providing for student "support" (sec. 11), and leaving his books to one of the Halls at Oxford. (They never arrived there, so far as we know.)

Like many other striking figures he is intellectually the personification of some of the contradictions of his epoch. Determined upon the spiritual purpose of improving minds, he projects the book as the sovereign remedy, operating physically through the sensations. It not only impresses through the eye, but appeals "to the hearing when it is heard, and moreover in a manner to the touch" when it is "transcribed, bound, corrected, and preserved" (sec. 23). Ruining books by slovenly handling infuriates him.

Further, although accusations of "excess of curiosity, . . . exhibitions of vanity, . . . intemperance of delight in literature," bother him no more than "the barking of so many dogs" (sec. 230), he knows that passion for anything besides God and the Church is not altogether approved, and would avoid the "charge of excess." In familiar medieval style, therefore, he offers his heartfelt views as but a "slight matter," written correspondingly "in the lightest style of the moderns" (sec. 12). Support is sought from every possible quarter: first, Aristotle. Since "in moral science we do not insist upon demonstration"—that is, certainty—it is legitimate to base upon the value of books a "probable conclusion" (sec. 30).

He exhibits contradictory views not only about what people might say, but about the stars. Acknowledging the notable influence upon men's occupations of "the disposition of the heavenly bodies," he claims on behalf of his "blameless pleasure in books" the approval of Mercury—historically the symbol of change and commerce. In the very next breath he appeals to "the rule of right reason, over which no stars are dominant"; on that basis his commitment is linked to "the glory of the Supreme Being" (sec. 234). Precisely there is what matters: an act "otherwise . . . morally indifferent" is stamped with "moral rectitude . . . by the honesty of aim and purpose" (sec. 231).

Such expressions, like so many in the Christian tradition, owe a great deal to the pagan Stoics of antiquity. "Right reason" had been defined as a portion of the divine within a human, in the letters of the first-century Roman sage Seneca (*To Lucilius,* LXVI. 11-12); these letters were quoted in Vincent of Beauvais' encyclopedia and many other places, doubtless known to such men as those around De Bury. The stars had no direct part in that particular line of reasoning; but Nature was very prominent in Stoic thought, natural law virtually synonymous with right reason. Besides, the lore of the heavens and other unknown realms had long been very influential. Students of Augustine's *City of God* were familiar with the mysterious Hermes Trismegistus, and the more recent Albertus Magnus and Thomas Aquinas had displayed similar preoccupations—the former with Trismegistus and the rule of the stars, the latter with alchemy. More of the same appears in the *Philobiblon.* (Holcot was conscious of what was popular.)

The concept better known to later readers, that the end justifies the means, made it possible for De Bury to accord books extraordinary power to do well and wisely, with almost no reservation. He says nothing of condemned books and deprecates only "some treatises of small value" from which readers derive "strange heresies and apocryphal imbecilities." Even such works are not assailed for their authors' intent or error, but because the friars misuse them in their preaching (sec. 88).

Implementation of any idea depends upon action by persons able to make decisions. De Bury could declare that "man," undifferentiated, "is naturally fond of two things, namely, freedom from control and some pleasure in his activity" (sec. 179). But his targets here, those who "more than others . . . have need of wisdom" and therefore ought to cultivate books, are "the princes and prelates, judges and doctors. . . ." The "other leaders of the commonwealth" also mentioned (sec. 186) may in his thinking have included eminent merchants—but hardly the ordinary townsman, not to speak of peasants. A little more than one generation later, the "Wyclif" translation of the Bible into English would be accused of helping spark peasant revolt; one wonders whether De Bury would again have conceded only possible improper use.

Study Aids   Despite De Bury's dirge there was enough sober study in the late Middle Ages to evoke further development of several types of aid. The already venerable *florilegium* was by and large a collection of notes taken somewhat at random, not as a rule organized except perhaps by the sequence within the source used. On the scene since the eleventh century and conspicuous in the twelfth was an advance, the "book of sentences," which often rearranged the quoted or paraphrased passages around topics. The thirteenth century produced a still higher form, the *concordantia,* which pulled together under more specific heads the thought of a particular writer, usually, from either a single work or a whole group; the editor frequently added points of his own.

The concordance soon proved invaluable for accuracy in quoting. By 1315, Bible concordances were among the items required at any Dominican convent maintaining a *studium generale,* or school for "masters of theology."

Additional devices included a new version of the age-old abstract, the plainly titled *abbreviatio,* a recognized specialty of the Franciscans.

Encyclopedias   Both study aids and a principal medium of education were the new encyclopedias, imposing enough as a group to account significantly for the "systematizing" reputation of the thirteenth century. At a time when student numbers were pressing facilities and books were still beyond the means of most of them, a time also when the ordinary clergy were unlikely to negotiate the voluminous works of the Fathers, an audience was ready for an ordered arrangement of what "authority" had to say on every subject that might be coming up. The friars undertook the job, partly because their own ranks increased so fast that their corporate interests called for shortcuts to "education" as much as anyone else's.

In the years from 1225 to 1250 were turned out at least four such works of general scope and some consequence. Two, written by continental Dominicans mainly along traditional lines, are so clearly oriented toward the well-established, even the out-of-date, that they are thought to have been designed as weapons against the new and upsetting. A third was composed (in 1230?) by Bartholomew Glanville (?), an Oxford Franciscan who spent most of his career as a Bible teacher in Paris and elsewhere on the Continent and was usually referred to as *Anglicus,* "the Englishman."

His "On the Properties of Things" relied principally on Isidor's "Origins," the Bible, and Aristotle (as translated from the Arabic, not from the original Greek), and added such contemporary items as data on the Flemish wool trade. More unusual, he addressed the work to young scholars and general readers; he said they had trouble with allegorical renderings of the Scriptures, and while opening with theology he moved quickly to science, as a better basis for understanding Holy Writ (genuinely or only ostensibly?). His vocabulary was simple, his grammar unusually correct; he also cited his sources with care, a practice then extraordinary. At least by 1286 Bartholo-mew was among the works available to Paris students for rent at a fixed price in the book stores. The next century saw several translations.

The fourth of the Latin encyclopedias was the "Great Mirror" of Vin-cent of Beauvais, prepared in the early 1240s, apparently also in the Paris area. Quoting some 450 authors from Aristotle to Virgil, with the help of known *florilegia* rather than the large library he would otherwise have needed, he explained his effort on the ground that it was high time to counteract the injustice of leaving sources unidentified. Actually, Bartholo-mew had already named his in many instances; Vincent may not have known his work, or perhaps, as a Dominican, he was consciously trying to outdo a Franciscan. His mammoth product had no peer for five centuries. But it was three times the size of the Bible, a tremendous chore to copy; also it was classified in arrangement but apparently not indexed. It remained more admired than used.

Besides these Latin instruments written by clerics for students and found in many libraries, at least four semipopular works of the same range of content, in French, came in the middle third of the thirteenth century from the hands of laymen. All were issued in several editions and transla-tions. But they do not turn up so often as the scholarly type in extant library catalogs, and their use, not to speak of their "influence," is known hardly at all.

Even a vernacular encyclopedia did not in the early fourteenth century include biographies. Worth mentioning accordingly is the biographical dic-tionary of "philosophers" by Walter of Burley (1275–1337), who taught phi-losophy at universities in England and France. Initially in Latin, it was soon translated, testimony to its secular and individualist thrusts.

Language Dictionaries and Alphabetical Access   Those same thrusts lent new strength to the alphabetical. Bilingual dictionaries of Latin go back at least to tenth-century England, remote from Rome and early in need of bridges between Latin and the local vernaculars. When some educator com-posed that Latin–Anglo-Saxon dictionary, believed to be the oldest extant, he was taking an important step beyond the long-familiar writing of ver-nacular equivalents on the margins and between the lines of Latin manu-scripts. The language of the church tended soon afterward to become more widely known. But the Dominicans thought the peoples' tongues significant enough to stress their use in preaching: it is hard to avoid the hypothesis that libraries and individuals in the late Middle Ages possessed more such aids, giving variously Celtic, Romance, or Teutonic meanings for Latin words, than surviving codexes account for. Nor is there much doubt that the dictionaries of Arabic, Greek, and Hebrew long since penned in Byzantium, Persia, and Spain, contributed to the resources of Christian centers of learn-ing from the twelfth century on.

The alphabetical order often utilized in such efforts was also applied here and there in encyclopedias and other educational instruments, princi-pally in the explanatory word lists they commonly included. Some 3,200 terms are thus treated in the school-subjects section *(Doctrinale)* of Vincent's encyclopedia. Another such contribution occupies most of John Balbi's *Catholicon* of 1286, a treatise on the Latin language, said to have been chained in many a French and English church and one of the first books printed.

Further, whether the idea came from the advantages of the language dictionaries or the disadvantages of the classified arrangement of many concordances (keyed to individual words), educational and scholarly materials began in the late thirteenth century to be equipped with either alphabetical arrangement or an alphabetical index. Of the former one may cite an edition of a pagan favorite, the proverbs of the Roman Stoic Seneca, reported about 1300 to be in the library of Christ Church, Canterbury, one of twenty items in codex 62 (set forth in Edwards' *Memoirs,* I:135). The latter may be represented by the late thirteenth-century index to the principal canon law texts known as *Margarita decreti* (literally, "little pearl of the decree").

Alphabetical arrangement of titles in catalogs, however, was apparently unknown before the twelfth century, and long remained rare.

Alphabetizing beyond the first letter was unusual before the ninth century. By the tenth a number of compilers were carrying it to the second letter. Full alphabetizing was probably not considered until about 1240, when Robert Grosseteste, scholarly Bishop of Lincoln and founder of Oxford University, prepared his influential Bible concordance. Nor did it necessarily carry over in translations: Bartholomew Anglicus' Latin encyclopedia presented the names of places and natural phenomena in alphabetical order; but John of Trevisa's Middle English version of the 1390s left the sequence unchanged, and the result was no longer alphabetical.

Reference Resources and Scholars' Habits In these varied ways were the reference resources in libraries enriched during the thirteenth century. Even a minor figure, Simon of Hinton, studying science and technology in the Dominican convent at Oxford, must have been surrounded, concludes modern authority, by encyclopedias and dictionaries. At the same time, repetition and duplication abounded, as in the evolution of the gloss. Some advanced students were not satisfied with translation alone, others unable to comprehend particular texts. The familiar gloss, occasional marginal or interlinear comment, was now outdone. Interpretations written literally between the lines absorbed the energies of scores of experts and would-be experts. The desks and book closets of numerous libraries soon groaned with codexes in which nearly every word was followed by explication: a whole new genre was created in the later thirteenth century, known correspondingly as "postills" *(post illa verba).*

A great part of this labor unwittingly retraversed ground gone over by earlier generations. Why? Didn't the scholars know that? The paucity of bibliographies and union catalogs is certainly one reason; another, the time required to seek and obtain books and information about books. Perhaps also the friars' and monks' interest in their work picked up such momentum that it would not have been slowed appreciably even by better communication and bibliographies. In any case, this was by no means the last appearance of the phenomenon.

National Differentiation and Libraries

The bearing of exceptional distance from Rome upon knowledge of Latin in England, noted above, is but one facet of that most complicated phenomenon, the development of a nation.

The International   Still vigorous to all appearances were Europe-wide patterns well rooted in the old: the church and the clergy, Latin and Christian education, the depressed status of the peasantry, women, and Jews. Much of the new was also international: the Crusades, commodity society, the stable gold florin of 1252, the ambitions of guildsmen and burghers, the Black Death (1348–1349 and twice again in the 1360s), the unrest of both peasants and bourgeois, the friars, and the Inquisition.

The book itself, indubitably international, was both old and new, the latter as a symbol. By the second half of the fourteenth century its image was an element in university seals, representing either the Bible or a text in the hands of sometimes a teacher, sometimes a female figure symbolizing wisdom. (The book would likewise be incorporated in the coats of arms adopted by universities in the fifteenth and sixteenth centuries as one means of defending their privileges from church or state challenge.) At the same time, nonetheless, significant differences were emerging in different European environments, some already "national," others only laying foundations for what would mature as national later on.

Latin, Vernaculars, and Libraries   Antedating even the impact of the Romans were many bodies of law usually called "Germanic," featuring secular concepts rooted in tribal property relations. The coloring of that material by Roman ideas of contract and individual rights, partially conflicting Christian notions—especially about marriage and the family, and the use of Latin, blurred many distinctions. Yet differences survived, thanks in some measure to variation in economic and political conditions from area to area. Seeds of national tradition were also evident within the culture of the church itself. The chronicles penned since the eighth-century days of the Venerable Bede, in Latin, ecclesiastical in authorship and general purpose, were nonetheless harbingers of the future in their occasional focus on events and personalities of a particular locality, often the one in which the chronicler lived and worked. These contributions were now to be joined on library shelves by companions in the vernacular and of more clearly national bent.

The rise to significance of vernacular writings in the later Middle Ages, together with the limited education of women, affected arrangements at some libraries. Certain monasteries and abbeys had an "interior" library of Latin books for the permanent inhabitants and an "exterior" collection in the vernacular for visitors and perhaps local loan. In a number of convents for women, on the contrary, their reading matter, vernacular of necessity, was the "interior" library; the Latin titles for the few priests in attendance were in the *bibliotheca exterior*. The extent to which books in local languages fed national feeling in the surrounding area is a question not easily answered.

France and French   By the late thirteenth century Paris had become the first city of Europe, numbering working people, guildsmen, merchants, students, teachers, prelates, and courtiers somewhere between 125,000 and 175,000, more than twice the population of any other center. They and their (Old) French, the *langue d'oeil,* dominated the northern half, more or less, of what came to be called France. Notable among the reasons for this turn of events were the city's location astride major road and river routes, and the smart military, economic, and administrative moves of the principal French kings of the era. Furthermore, their language had been in literary use since the tenth century, the celebrated national-sentiment-building *Song of Roland* marked the twelfth, and the idea of narrative history involving Frenchmen was embedded in two notable thirteenth-century efforts: Villehardouin's chronicle (about 1210) of the Fourth Crusade (to Constantinople), and Joinville's life of Saint Louis. One aspect of the Albigensian "Crusade" at home, moreover, was the enlargement southward of the dominance of the *langue d'oeil,* reducing the territory of the doomed southern cousin, the *langue d'oc.* Chronicles of France initiated in Latin in the late thirteenth century were continued in the fourteenth in French. The thirteenth century also saw, initially in French, a treatise on husbandry, a popular bestiary-geography, and encyclopedic miscellanies. In addition to these works mainly in the aristocratic tradition the urban bourgeois element in French life of that century was reflected in the distinctively satiric *Reynard the Fox* and *fabliaux,* as well as the not-so-distinctive love verses of the first portion of the *Romance of the Rose.*

Of all the contributors to what George Sarton called "science" (virtually everything but literature and the fine arts; *Introduction to the History of Science;* Baltimore: Williams & Wilkins for The Carnegie Institution of Washington, 1927–1948), authors using Latin still dominated the fourteenth century. But the number of those expressing themselves in vernaculars increased 50 percent from the first half of the century to the second (XIV-1 to XIV-2, Sarton-style), partly at the expense of Latin. And French led the advance (among European tongues), from 22, one-fourth of the 82 vernacular authors in XIV-1 to 51, well over one-third of the 137 in XIV-2.

Translations from Latin into French likewise multiplied, beginning with the "Mirror of the World" wanted by a French duke in 1245, and portions of Aristotle's "Meteorology" (about 1250). During the fourteenth century there were two translations of the best-selling compilation of the lives of the saints and miracles known as the "Golden Legend," drawn upon by preachers everywhere for examples edifying and entertaining; also French, Dutch, and English versions of the Bible.

French Libraries   Vernacular works, familiar in castle, court, and tavern, seem to have been accepted in the largest libraries, the Sorbonne and the papal collections at Avignon. But they were a tiny handful so far as extant catalogs tell the story. Did such works also penetrate into ordinary cathedral and abbey libraries? Finding out may depend upon close search of records little studied to date, especially the Franciscans'. And so much in libraries was destroyed by neglect and individual catastrophes, not to speak of the

Hundred Years' War (1337–1453) and the others that followed, that the full picture may never be known.

That library life in general was changing little is suggested by the outstanding fruit of recent scholarly investigation. When Archbishop Eudes of Rouen (northwest France) made his rounds in the third quarter of the thirteenth century, he repeatedly directed the local abbot or prior to mend books and the roof, prepare some sort of book inventory, and be less liberal about book loans. Nothing in his travel *Register* (New York: Columbia University Press, 1964) points to the presence in those libraries of works different from the traditional religious items, "liberal arts," classical metaphysics and ethics, and Ovid; the material was largely in the form of extracts, *florilegia,* and books of "sentences." Many collections covered much less, hardly more than church service books, to judge from extant inventories. Even the library of King ("Saint") Louis IX was not spectacular in holdings, if the sparse clearly verified evidence is representative. At the University of Paris, however, the prominence of theology and law were doubtless reflected in the book collections. More important, the Sorbonne portion of the university was a leading college in the largest and probably most advanced city in Christendom. The powers and obligations of the library directors, the *librarii* elected annually by the members of the college, may therefore be taken as the forward limit of a long-settled body of practices. The Sorbonne regulations of 1321 (on view in Franklin, I: 237–238) assigned to them the evaluation of the considerable stock of unbound and ephemeral items, largely student notes and old sermons. Such materials might be retained, or disposed of through sale, exchange, or gift. The men deemed competent to perform these tasks were also thought capable of substituting inferior copies for the library's good ones and selling the latter.

Accordingly, there was a special register of the books in the care of each successive *librarius;* each had his own page, and the requirement was emphatic that the customary entry for a book was not enough: the work must be clearly identified by recording also the first few words of the second leaf. Indeed, whoever was taking his turn as librarian was on notice to loan his key to no one, and that he would be held fully accountable for the collection; "otherwise," said the regulation, "calling them custodians is pointless." Despite these recognitions of professional judgment, the documents say nothing of special training beyond what any Sorbonnist would have acquired anyway.

England and Its Languages The unique position in France of Paris and its institutions had no counterpart in England. Since the Norman Conquest of 1066 that area had seen far less fighting than had France. A land of country houses developed, together with important cathedral towns and a commercial-political capital, London, of population about one-third that of Paris. Unlike Paris, London was neither the ecclesiastical capital nor a university community; but it was the largest urban center in England. That its dialect, the "Midland," should triumph over other dialects is not surprising; the process may have been facilitated by a book trade not controlled by a university and beginning to cater to a commercial market. Yet two other tongues had to be conquered as well, Latin and Anglo-Norman (a variant of Norman French).

Latin was the lesser problem, having been from the outset a foreign language in England, less widely used outside church environs, probably, than in western and southern Europe. On the other hand, Norman rule meant the development of an unusually sharp division between ruling class culture and popular culture, thanks to the official and literary use of Anglo-Norman while the underlying peasantry and villagers continued largely in their own ways. Anglo-Saxon and other pre-Norman vernaculars had been employed since perhaps the seventh century not just for daily speech but for royal ordinances, chronicles, Bible glosses, and cognate Latin-vernacular word lists; "Beowulf" was composed probably around 750, and codexes bearing that and other Anglo-Saxon poems survive from the later tenth century. By the reign of Edward I in the late thirteenth century, class and cultural relations had been reshaped to the point where the significant literary challenger to Latin was no longer Anglo-Norman but the newly emerging (Middle) English, whose victory was sealed a mere century later by Chaucer's "Canterbury Tales."

English Libraries   The library profile accordingly differed somewhat from that of France. Norman nobles and squires raising families in the countryside were often served by a chaplain and were likely to own some books. When the books went out of fashion, they found their way, in many instances, to the shelves of the monastery the chaplain came from, or perhaps simply the nearest one. Many romances and epics in (Old) French arrived thus in English abbeys in the thirteenth century, although they seldom appear in the catalogs known today. The donors may have thought them "dated," or out of keeping with the serious tone urged by the Fourth Lateran Council, or too reminiscent of the French domains the English king had lately lost (1204). Accordingly, the "public library" collection would seem to have taken on a more varied appearance not in response to demand but precisely because the newly added titles furnishing the variety were no longer in demand. Monastery libraries were also dumping grounds for texts addressed to the laity once their owners had had enough of them. In general, however, the libraries of abbeys and cathedrals were apparently much like those of France.

The English and French university records differ in some important respects. The two-headed leadership of Oxford and Cambridge is in obvious contrast with the status of the University of Paris; likewise their location a day's journey, more or less, in different directions from London, the capital. Furthermore, thanks in part to the scholarly connections between England and Christian Spain, the Franciscans at Oxford rapidly moved into a noteworthy pursuit of science. Theology at the English schools did not enjoy its standing at Paris. The law so vital at the latter center came to be taught in England not at the universities but at the "Inns of the Court" in London.

Whatever this implied for book collections, difference was not striking in library administration. Oxford, although aided in its rise by two "migrations" of dissatisfied teachers and students from Paris, developed a clearly non-Parisian general university library before any particular unit's library gained renown. At Cambridge, on the contrary, as at Paris, the first libraries were individual college collections, led by that of Peterhouse, launched in 1284.

When Bishop Thomas Cobham left his books for a library at Oxford, a statute was passed in 1367 appointing a full-time chaplain to say prayers for his soul and take care of the putative library. (Litigation delayed its materializing until 1410.) For these services he was to be paid out of the yield on an investment, and the money for the latter was to be obtained by selling some of the more valuable books. This may have been a step "forward," although stipends for library service were already customary in English cathedrals; they do not seem to have been the practice in English monasteries, or in France.

The Low Countries Across the Channel from England and north of France, the towns later called Dutch and Belgian had been important and increasingly privileged for a century, thanks to trade, textile making, and favorable political conditions. The leading encyclopedias were translated into Flemish in the second half of the thirteenth century. Not yet, however, was there any notable interest in books and libraries beyond what was well established in the religious institutions; in fact the wave of enthusiasm for study and books in the later fourteenth century was intimately associated with monastic reform. Still less was secular library development to be expected at that stage in the emerging municipalities of the Rhine, of the North and Baltic Sea coasts, following somewhat the same course as that of the Low Countries but less advanced upon it.

Central Europe Yet central Europe, long seeded by commerce, missionaries, and religious foundations, was not altogether lacking in book activity. University instruction revolved around the writing down of the lecture; this *pronuntatio* was soon the focus of a body of regulations, the first at Prague in 1367. Book collections also began to develop in individual colleges and faculties somewhat after the Paris fashion. Conspicuous in the record is Heidelberg, similar to Paris in its control of the *stationarii,* but dissimilar in that all books were from the outset the property of the university as a whole. It may be that stationers are not mentioned in most other German university records because the few students with money to patronize them went elsewhere, perhaps for prestige, especially to Paris and Bologna. Worthy of remark too is the dissemination of vernacular reading matter in the convents of the Dominicans' "Teutonia" Province in the fourteenth century: thanks apparently to the traditionally second-class citizenship of women, the nuns could not read Latin.

Striking indeed was the widespread crystallization in speech and literature of a congeries of Germanic tongues, and an unknown number of dictionaries bridging them to Latin. Although the early secular—often pagan—verse was apparently unable to survive church disapproval, religious poetry and prose enjoyed the active support of church teachers and missionaries. Latin and the dialects of the central and upper Rhine Valley, represented literarily by Old High German, were linked perhaps in the eighth century in a version of Isidor of Seville's essay on faith, surely in the labors about the year 1000 of the St. Gallen monk Notker; and in dictionaries as well. The late twelfth and early thirteenth centuries saw the flowering of Middle High German: the religious and German-patriotic verse of Walter von der Vogelweide, the *Nibelungenlied* and other folk epics, and important lyric poetry. All this was more or less in the chivalric tradition, and much of it composed by clerics. By the late thirteenth century peasants and townsmen were finding written expression, but not thus far in any work noteworthy as literature. Nor, despite their long use in speech, was anything of lasting consequence produced further north and northwest, in the Low German media—Saxon, Dutch, Flemish, and so on.

How this uneven development in literary productivity and progress toward the national is to be explained is a most complicated question. One notes that Thomas of Cantimpré's Latin encyclopedia of the early thirteenth century was rendered within one generation into Flemish, and by the mid-fourteenth century into the Bavarian-Austrian dialect spoken around Regensburg (65 miles northeast of Munich). The latter choice is significant, because it judges the literary language, Middle High German, to be less likely to reach the intended audience—townspeople and women. Between that choice, indeed, and larding the translation with good stories and moralizing, the translator (Conrad of Megensburg, ca. 1309–1374) was very successful. Yet he was far less so with the leading semipopular work on astronomy by "Sacrobosco" (John of Holywood), apparently because astronomy readers preferred the Latin and those without Latin ignored astronomy.

Diversity had survived the rather brief period of strong Holy Roman Empire leadership, particularly among the common people. One can hardly doubt that it was favored by the virtual collapse of the Empire in the thirteenth century and the control of Europe between the Alps and the northern coasts by church and lay princes, who traditionally elected the "emperor," and in a few instances town fathers.

Perimeters North and East Least of all could one hope to find circumstances friendly to nonreligious library life in the lands of the Scandinavians, Balts, Slavs, and Hungarians. While they were equipped with some churches and church libraries, their trade and towns were on the whole barely above the rudimentary level, and traditions of learning, planted by missionaries, monasteries, and students returning from Paris, were in their infancy. Nor were they encouraged by the ravages of the Teutonic knights in the Baltic littoral, or the Tatars and Mongols in eastern and southeastern Europe. Distinctive, again, were the several vernaculars. Those of Scandinavia (including Iceland) had been since the ninth century the vehicles of poetry later famous, and prose was now appearing too. In the Slav lands, quite different thanks to such factors as the Byzantine state-supported Greek Church rather than Roman Church inspiration, they carried not only folk literature and prayer books but selections from the literature of theology.

Iberia There was no lack of either towns or traditions of learning in the Iberian peninsula. Yet the defeat of the Moors by militant Christianity had not been an experience like that in Eastern Europe, overcoming lower cultures as local pagan tribes were conquered or Oriental pagan invaders repulsed. The shapers of Spain and Portugal-to-be had on the contrary been driving out the Moorish (and Jewish) creators of a civilization in many respects higher than their own. When Alfonso the Learned, king of Castile and Leon (1252–1284), sponsored new astronomical tables of importance, he continued rather than initiated; for such purposes, indeed, he, unlike his successors, maintained the rights of the Jews. In the process of Christian reconquest largely completed by his predecessors, however, the Spanish nobles had become more powerful than before: when Alfonso tried to weld their particularisms into unity on the basis of absolute monarchy, they resisted rather successfully. Contributing perhaps was the vigor of several different tongues, some boasting a ballad literature already a few hundred years old, especially the Catalan of the northeast and the Galician of the northwest; Castilian, geographically between them, had only recently become prominent, thanks heavily to the celebrated epic "The Cid" and the "General Chronicle" prepared at Alfonso's direction.

Yet the libraries of the vanquished Arabs were now no more, not to speak of those of the Visigoths before them. When universities were founded (or refounded) in the thirteenth century, they did not emulate Paris or Oxford in assembling either particular unit or general university libraries but left the provision of reading matter to the commercial stationers, by legal monopoly, as at Italy's Bologna.

Italy   Italy may be regarded as the most contradictory of all. The lower half of the peninsula, and Sicily, were largely settled in agricultural routines destined to change little for centuries, and sufficiently adjusted to the Saracen presence to virtually ignore the calls to crusade. Most of the catalytic industrial and business activity, including a conspicuously cash-oriented approach to the Crusades, was located between Rome and the Alps. Politics and culture were shaped substantially by a dizzying kaleidoscope of conflict: popes, Holy Roman emperors, kings of various countries, Italian nobles and powerful merchant families, career soldiers and city managers, ideologists, and often the ordinary populace—all were engaged for several hundred years, on and off, in combinations of shifting configuration. The popes' vision was much grander than the merely national, most of the kings on the scene were foreigners with their own home concerns, and many towns were shaking off baronial control without the help from kings so noticeable in France and England. Although the Norman-German emperor, Frederick II, was Italian-born, his efforts at civilization building, like the university he founded at Naples in 1224, were favored by circumstances only in the south, and survived his death in 1250 only in part.

Education, in the heartland of the Roman Catholic Church, was by no means a clerical monopoly. Santa Maria Novella, a Dominican convent in Florence, was but one of many clerical establishments allowing laymen access to its books. Indeed higher schooling as well as publication was frequently a commercial enterprise. Even in the mid-eleventh century, we are told, records were being kept in Milan which made possible the statement that the city then boasted 200 jurists, 200 physicians, 80 schoolmasters, and 50 "writers of books." Whether that phrase means professional copyists, a vital group in the law- and account-conscious towns of northern Italy, or authors, or some of each, their inclusion in reports of the era is striking.

Although Latin was still the language of learning and diplomacy as well as church ritual, several closely related vernaculars were spoken and written. Yet the diffusion of Latin and learning among laymen as well as churchmen and the pervasive traditions of Rome, among other factors, appear to have retarded the emergence of national cultural phenomena like those in evidence in other countries. Much of the recorded early vernacular verse of Italy was composed in the language of the socially approved southern French model, Provençal; and the noted thirteenth-century popular "encyclopedia," Brunetto Latini's "Little Treasure," was but one of many items offered initially in (Old) French. Only at the dawn of the fourteenth century was a work created which exerted the impact necessary to launch one of the Italian vernaculars as the literary standard. The "Divine Comedy" was written in the language of Florence and its region, Tuscany, by a friend and pupil of Latini's, well grounded in Latin and French and the Provençal tradition. It reflected no political or military triumph: the poet, Dante Alighieri, was already out of favor and died in exile from Tuscany. But when it was added about 1400 to the library at Avignon by the "anti-pope" Benedict XIII, it was the first "in the Italian vernacular."

Church literature and the Greek and Roman classics were familiar in cathedral and cloister libraries. Nor was there any striking change in the university pattern. Except perhaps at Naples in the days of Frederick II's patronage, there were no university libraries: reading matter was on the contrary the preserve of the booksellers, the *stationarii*. Even when new impulses shot through the world of Latin as translations from the Greek and Arabic emerged from Naples, Salerno, and other centers of scientific labor, and the receiving agency was a university, little or nothing is said of a university library.

Yet, for all the apparent stagnation, one of the most fascinating paradoxes in human history was about to unfold. Princes fashioning new states out of collapsing feudalism would sponsor worship of classical antiquity. Monuments of secular learning would be drawn into the glare of publicity from old monastic *armaria*. Greek and classical Latin texts would absorb enormous energy from men more likely day by day to speak and write the national language. And the library would be thrust into public consciousness by the establishment of magnificent collections owned privately.

Chapter Four

THE RENAISSANCE AND REFORMATION

None of the phenomena covered by the chapter title fit neatly the two-hundred-year period from 1400 to 1600. Humanism and the other waves customarily associated with the Renaissance, beginning before 1400, reached successive crests in different countries at different times for different reasons, with different characteristics. Likewise the Reformation: if it required the invention of printing from movable type to go into high gear, the phase most immediately influential for England's North American colonies ran well into the seventeenth century. The chronological limits of 1400 to 1600 are nevertheless a convenient framework in which to consider how the supersession of medieval civilization by capitalism and national states, in large portions of Europe, affected book making and distribution, book selection, and some major phenomena of library life.

Renaissance Humanism

Italian Roots Italy of the fourteenth and fifteenth centuries was still marked by sociopolitical turmoil in the leading cities, and an absence of Italian national or imperial power. That absence was now conspicuous, however, owing to the repeated appearance in Italy of forces and influences originating in the former provinces of Rome such as French and Provençal poetry, philosophical tracts by Englishmen, and troops under the orders of a German Holy Roman Emperor or French or Spanish king. Numerous sensitive minds turned for solace and inspiration to Italy's own past, the apogee of republican culture or the glories of the empire: Cicero and his classical Latin, the historians and the poets. A search began for works heard of but not yet seen; as more items were found, allusions within them brought up still others: a passionate hunt developed for titles rare, often gone or even imaginary.

French Nourishment The first phase of this vigorous effort, sometimes merely antiquarian but frequently scholarly, took shape in France. It was thence, notably to the towns not far from Italy, that hundreds of Italians fled from sharp turns of political fortune at home. Among these refugees were the fathers of Petrarch and Boccaccio. Young Petrarch (1304–1370), most of whose first thirty-five years were spent in France, almost surely acquired his basic knowledge of classical literature from books and readers at the Avignon court of the exiled popes and the Sorbonne library in Paris. He may have been equipped for classical studies within the framework of his distasteful law course at Montpellier (50 miles southwest of Avignon): the training of jurists and notaries had for perhaps two centuries been leaning heavily, to a degree not yet fully clear, upon materials in classical Latin, apparently because the early medieval breed succeeding it had been found wanting when it came to precision and sophistication.

Although these experiences indebted Italians like Petrarch and the Italian Renaissance to some four centuries of copying in the Carolingian tradition in the Frankish territories, the debtors' response was not unqualified appreciation. Petrarch among others criticized the French for their acceptance of extracts and stressed full original sources. That preference was obviously harmonious with the Italian rejection as insignificant of all events between the fall of Rome and their own rise to prominence; the French on the contrary stood by their achievements from Charlemagne on.

The Age of Discovery of Manuscripts The second phase of the search for the classic past was the ransacking of every ancient cloister the emissaries of the collectors could reach. Sometimes the sponsor was a duke or merchant prince, sometimes a pope. The worship of Roman antiquity thus brought to Italy what could be cajoled or extorted (with the pope's warrant) from priors and abbots all over present-day Switzerland and the Rhine valley and beyond. The materials, thought men like Poggio Braccolini, an outstanding early fifteenth-century hunter, were being "saved" from "barbarians." Neither in Bohemia's Prague, which occasioned his remark, nor in many other such localities, was there yet enough national sentiment or political power to allow much resistance; that all the dogged, often frenzied activity yielded few manuscripts of real consequence may have played a part too.

The very fact that manuscripts of the Latin classics were found in French and German ecclesiastical libraries on a scale not matched in Italy itself underscores an important contrast. France was the center of European culture from Charlemagne, late in the eighth century, to about the middle of the fourteenth. Not just the principal libraries but a good many smaller ones were passably stocked in Latin literature. Carolingian impulses were likewise felt and encouraged at many points in the Germanic-language areas as well. This was far less true of Italy. Carolingian civilization did not cross the Alps so easily as the Rhine, partly for physical reasons, perhaps more because Italian conditions did not so readily nourish it.

Meanwhile, a fair number of aristocrats in central and southern Germany and the Danube valley now caught the fever and assembled respectable codex collections. The impulse owed something to Italians like Niccolò Niccoli (1363-1437), one of the many scholars around Cosimo de' Medici, who in his seventies traveled all over Germany and wrote about what he found and what he did not find. The gathering of desired titles, moreover, depended in many instances upon certain Italian bookdealers, especially another celebrated Florentine, Vespasiano da Bisticchi (1421-1498), whose customers were an international who's who including Englishmen.

Hungary; The Corviniana Nowhere was this transmission of Humanism more conspicuous than in Hungary. Early fifteenth-century King Sigismund happened also to be the Holy Roman Emperor, and the royal family's relatives included the Naples branch of the Angevin (French) dynasts. Poggio and others appeared as envoys; educator P. P. Vergerio stayed for twenty-five years; young Hungarians coming back from school in Italy were often kindred spirits. The Bishop of Pécs (100-odd miles southwest of Budapest) soon had the first Hungarian collection with Greek as well as Latin codexes. In the latter half of the century King Matthias Corvinus (1458-1490) sponsored what was by 1490 the leading library north of the Alps: from 2,000 to 2,500 volumes mainly codexes, including probably from 4,000 to 5,000 titles; the Greek holdings were second only to those of the Vatican; the glories of Corvinian illumination and bindings became a specialty among art historians. This treasure survived the king's death in 1490, but not the neglect by his successors, aggravated by the Turkish War of 1526-1529. The sultan failed to conquer, but he did carry off to Constantinople a major portion of the Bibliotheca Corviniana.

Italian Humanism Flowers If politico-economic strife was plentiful everywhere, it was long engaged in north of the Alps by peoples and potentates who shared common focal points in a common religion, the pope, and the Holy Roman emperor, and whose educated elements were mainly clerics, schooled in Carolingian traditions. In Italy these foci were rivaled and given a somewhat different character by Greek and Byzantine influences, the immediacy of papal politics, and the long tradition of educated laymen. Grammar and rhetoric, secular eloquence, were the specialty of those who served as teachers, secretaries to nobles and merchants, speech makers or speech writers for, or advisers to, political chieftains. These men were a peculiarly Italian type called *dictatores* in the twelfth century and by the fourteenth *dettatori;* the designation thus changed from the Latin to the Italian form, and a good deal more was changing with it.

Neither the earlier *dictatores* nor their clients, apparently, were very much concerned with the poetry, history, or ethics included in the grammar and rhetoric of classical times molded by a Quintilian. But it is probable that interest in those subjects was stimulated by what Petrarch and others found in French literary circles and libraries. As war, pestilence, politics and the other developments noted by Richard de Bury took cultural leadership away from France in the late fourteenth century, a deep-running enthusiasm for all Latin writings of yore arose in Italy, an enthusiasm Italian-nationalistic in part but also philological, revolving around original classical sources, the hallmark of the Humanist. He might be a man of wealth who paid for Latin works on literature, history, and ethics, perhaps enough of them to be considered by history a library; or a secretary to such a man, who might perform many library functions; or a teacher of those subjects in secondary school or university (called in Italian universities *umanista*, as the canon law professor, for example, was long since known as a *canonista*). He might write some "philosophy"—really just ethics, on the whole; far more often did he compose orations, letters, poems, and historical works that were accepted by contemporaries with much greater interest than the neglect by later scholars suggests. Likewise, he might copy Latin writings. Many were of course known to the Middle Ages, but others were not; and the great increase in the number of copies in circulation was in any case a new situation, both preparing a market for the printed book and helping determine which particular books were to be printed first.

Furthermore, as events ecclesiastical and military brought many learned Greeks to Italy after the middle of the fourteenth century, Humanism expanded its working concerns to embrace the Greek heritage in translation, and a modest handful of Humanists actually learned Greek to read the originals. (We are told that Boccaccio demanded in 1360 that the University of Florence offer Greek, that a chair was actually established, but that Boccaccio himself was apparently the sole student.) If Marsilio Ficino (1433-1499) and other *quattrocento* Florentine intellectuals were not the first in a turbulent world to study eagerly Plato's presentation of the Idea and Justice—and mysticism, if the study circles they called "academies" were inspired by the Greek model, their scholarly attention to original sources was on the whole a novelty. It was made possible by the Greek visitors and refugees.

Two collections of Greek manuscripts became available at about the same time, the early 1460s, the Platonic materials and the *Corpus Hermeticum,* writings attributed to a philosopher-king-magician of Egypt, contemporary with Moses and therefore the "source" for such later figures as Plato. This extraordinary personage, known as Hermes Trismegistus ("Thrice-Great"), had been respected by Christian Fathers Lactantius and Augustine and almost everyone after them. Cosimo de' Medici directed Ficino to translate Hermes first (our authority is Ficino himself); he did so, in a few months. Then, for most of the years from 1464 to 1483, he rendered from Greek into Latin the whole of Plato and others in his tradition, utilizing materials previously in the hands only of Greek readers in the Byzantine East. Launching the *Republic,* as well as other items, into the Western world apparently for the first time, was shortly to set in motion shock waves permeating an entire culture. The Plato of the semiscientific *Timaeus* left the center of the stage to the Plato of an ideal "republic" ruled by philosopher-kings and supported by slaves.

Nor need that have been a surprising turn of events. The Renaissance Humanists enriched contemporary and later literary and educational life by accenting the Latin classic style in oratory, poetry, history, and ethics. But they were neither scientifically inclined nor serious students of philosophy as antiquity and the Middle Ages had known it. Petrarch at the Sorbonne Library in Paris copied Plato's *Phaedo,* a dialogue on the importance of pure reason and acceptance thereby of immortality of the soul; he did not copy the *Timaeus,* which was until Ficino's labors the best known in the Latin (and Arabic and Hebrew) world of Plato's works. Many called "Renaissance men" did probe nature and seek to advance man's control of it. But by that very token they were not Humanists (as understood here), neither the professors in the medical schools nor he who discovered perspective (F. Brunelleschi, 1377-1446) nor he who discovered America nor Leonardo da Vinci and the other luminaries of the sixteenth century.

Nature attracted attention, on the other hand, among the very Schoolmen the Humanists often spurned. In the fourteenth century, contemporary with Petrarch, they examined questions of matter, motion, force, and time, especially at the numerous points where those issues impinged upon theological commitments to the authority of the Bible and the powers of God. These efforts and others induced close analysis of accepted texts: Church scholars in France and England had indeed been demanding and getting patristic literature *in originalium* (at full length) before Petrarch was born; his charge that "the French" were satisfied with extracts was an exaggeration spawned by ignorance.

The Aristotelian writing and method central to much of that discussion continued in vogue during the Renaissance in the university classes in theology and law, Italy not excepted. In fact, at the celebrated medical school of the University of Padua (a few miles southwest of Venice), a succession of sharp Greek readers applied themselves to Aristotle's logic and psychology and laid foundations for "Galileo's" scientific method. Furthermore, the mainly Aristotelian classification modified to embrace everyday concerns like cooking, familiar thanks to Hugh of St. Victor and Brunetto Latini among others, was offered anew by Florentine scholar-poet Angelo Poliziano in 1491 and German popular encyclopedist Gregor Reisch in 1503.

Interest in Plato rose considerably, nevertheless, when the learned of the Greek and Roman churches argued Plato and Aristotle as they pondered ecumenical action in the 1430s and 1440s, the young manhood of Ficino. Plato's ethical and social views were further promoted when bibliophile and former librarian Parentucelli, as Pope Nicholas V (1447-1455), sponsored translations from the Greek calculated to favor Roman doctrinal positions, incidentally enriching library collections. Then Ficino's Plato project was aided by an original polemic from the pen of Humanistically inclined scholar Bessarion, a Greek in Rome for church negotiations who remained to join the Catholics and become a cardinal. In 1465 he published a defense of his preference (Plato) without maligning the other side (Aristotle), something then extraordinary. If consequent publicity attracted welcome support to Ficino's translation of Plato, it did not help him to reconcile Plato and Aristotle, a futile enterprise seldom attempted by serious philosophy students.

Although the Humanists of the Italian Renaissance were not philosophers, the educators among them developed a most influential philosophy and style of education. Details varied from P. P. Vergerio's landmark treatise published in 1404 in Padua, to the younger and better known Vittorino da Feltre, and others. But classic Latinity was to them the stuff of which instructional materials were made, and Greek occasionally added where feasible. Lecturing and recitation thereon began to replace the texts paraphrasing and extracting the Scriptures and Church Fathers. The seven liberal arts were still subjects to be taught, but history, literature, and ethics were deemed more important. Aristotle the logician deferred to the Aristotle who said a properly educated man was not only well schooled but active in civic affairs. The focus was not on the acquisition of knowledge but on the development of the habits and image of hard work, modesty, and brevity. In an Italy of seething city-states that could hardly have seemed more natural, at any rate for the sons—and some daughters—of merchants and nobles who were doubtless the majority of the pupils.

Humanism and Libraries

Humanism and Book Selection For all their stress on reading good books, the new type educators did not, apparently, direct attention to libraries as such. And libraries of the familiar more or less public sort did not suddenly discard the patristic literature for the histories and poems of the Greeks and Romans. Suggestive of the climate among leading citizens is the *Canone bibliografico,* or book selection guide, drawn up about 1440 by library consultant Tommaso Parentucelli (later Pope Nicholas V) for Cosimo de' Medici, and according to bookseller Bisticchi the basis of many princes' collections. As can be seen in Parentucelli's text, reproduced as Appendix A to Giovanni Sforza's biography of the Pope (pp. 359–381 in *Atti delle R. Acc. Lucchesa di Scienze, Lettere ed Arti,* t. XXIII, 1884), the stamp of the epoch was mainly negative. The compiler recommended the customary staples: the Bible, the Fathers, the principal pagan philosophers like Aristotle and Averroës (vastly influential scientist-philosopher of twelfth-century Moslem Spain), Virgil, elementary texts for grammar, and so forth. Striking is the absence of the retinue of commentary, postill, etc., usual in medieval libraries.

On the positive side for Humanism one can cite little more than a bit of history, Plutarch's "Lives of Eminent Greeks and Romans."

The Private Collection and Insecurity Humanism was of course much better reflected in collections entirely or mainly private. For book gathering in the Renaissance differed from what had preceded it not just in the Humanistic preoccupation with classical pagan titles in literature, history, and ethics, but in its social character. The acquisitions were flowing not so much to group-serving abbey, cathedral, or university libraries as to private collections usually lacking any relationship to a group tradition. The merchant-prince or nobleman, the courtier or poet he patronized, might adore classical Latin poetry; he might warm to the historian of Rome's glories. In the home library of the Medici there were now enough such works to assign binding colors accordingly, violet for poetry and red for history as well as white for long-established philosophy. But these attitudes and interests did not always suffice to assure the collection's preservation after the collector's death. Books had long been among the spoils of war, and in a society dominated by cash and the instability of fortune building they were also likely to be seized by creditors. Privately owned libraries were somewhat more vulnerable than those belonging to corporate bodies.

If the Corvinian library was scattered after the Hungarian king's death, leaving a few tracks followed wistfully by modern scholarship, if the treasures of book hunter Poggio and collector Petrarch were dispersed without even that much trace, there was at any rate an effort to forestall the tragedy, something of a useful precedent. Petrarch journeyed widely (not always voluntarily), and by age forty had assembled a considerable number of books. The uncertainties of income of a man who was not a peasant or craftsman and had no landed or commercial property most of his life, the reality moreover of daggers under cloaks, threw doubt on the future of his books after his passing. And after many years of energetic participation in politics he was at fifty-eight becoming tired.

Having sounded out his friend the chancellor of the Venetian Republic, he offered a bargain: a restful home in exchange for his library. The petition has not survived, but the Major Council minutes of September 4, 1362, summarize them. The government was to keep his collection "'in perpetuity in some appointed place,'" safe from burning and moisture; while he lived the books and he were to occupy a house "'not large, but respectable.'" He thought it likely that other private persons might be moved to offer like donations, that additional materials might be obtained "'at the public expense,'" that "'a great and famous library, equal to those of the ancients'" would arise, that "'the scholars and gentlemen of the said city'" might benefit thereby, and that "'this State'" would thus acquire glory "'understood by learned and ignorant alike.'" (From James Harvey Robinson's translation in his *Petrarch,* New York: Putnam, 1914, pp. 29–30. The Latin may be seen in Ernest H. Wilkins' *Petrarch's Later Years,* Cambridge: Medieval Academy of America, 1959, p. 37; "Major Council" was still in use although constitutional change had ended the earlier famous one in 1297.)

The formula was not really new in any component: Petrarch himself had earlier contemplated giving his books to an ecclesiastical library, and wondered why anything as obvious as his "public library" gambit had not been tried before. Still, to acquire books "at public expense," even if only for "scholars and gentlemen," was a notion with the ring of novelty since it had apparently not been voiced since the days of Rome. Evidence is lacking as to a follow-up of the Major Council's vote to accept his proposal; the poet-politician's 1370 testament says nothing about his books, and it was stated a few years later at the funeral of Niccolò Niccoli that Petrarch's collection had gone no man knew where after his death. One may suppose, however, that Cosimo, the Medici magnate who paid Niccoli's debts, was not just performing honorably his duty as an executor but was sympathetic to the dead man's philosophy of access to books for all, stipulated in his will, when he deposited Niccoli's books in the San Marco convent in Florence and placed a Niccoli relative in charge of them.

The Library's Purpose Thus did princes of the blood, the church, and the countinghouse, and their intellectual servitors, think of libraries not only to display their sensitivity to classical Latin (and Greek now and then) but as a means of protection for their books, or even a social instrument. Probably most of them, like the Florentine civic official Coluccio Salutati (1331-1406), saw a library as a working tool for scholars. Fewer, it seems, shared the broader view implied (rather uncertainly) by the "all" of Niccolò Niccoli, and the "for the use of the community of man" of Cardinal Bessarion's great book legacy to the Marciana Library in Venice. The difference of focus was destined to continue important in library thinking for several hundred years—as late as the 1850s in the United States.

Individualism, Irony, Ambiguity The genius of Renaissance Humanism, moreover, like so much else of that age, was predominantly individualistic. This newly enlarged model of the rhetorician, so to speak, was on occasion a priest or a monk: Ficino the former rather seriously from middle age on, Erasmus of Rotterdam (1466-1536) the latter only technically. But the traditional group discipline was not for their minds. Especially in promoting the use of classical sources did they encounter opposition and debate, although the company a Humanist kept might divide one way on, say, the immortality of the soul, and another way on some other issue. As promoters of the "new" they tended to be more concerned than their antagonists with the right and ability of the individual human mind to deal with ideas independently of and if necessary in opposition to those approved by institutional thinking. But when such efforts, together with other conditions, produced conflicts like peasant revolts, involving large numbers of people and threatening their individualism with new institutionalization, Humanists often stepped aside. Erasmus, a notable example, wrote bitterly of the church and scholastic thinking, but declined association with Luther's rebellion. He spent most of his life in the world of study and publication, contributing vitally to the scholar's shelves of editions and translations from Greek and Latin Testaments and commentaries. But his comments on books and scholarship, in *The Praise of Folly* (1512) and the *Colloquies* (1529) (Bantam Matrix ed., pp. 89-91, 109, 130, 403), are ambiguous or ironic, book display being mentioned only in connection with book shops, and libraries apparently not at all.

Irony and ambiguity about the world of writing and ideas were not new with Erasmus. War on received opinion, in diverse forms, was many centuries old. Some argumentation had been scholarly, some quite unscholarly. Noteworthy in the fifteenth and sixteenth centuries was the spectacle of dissenting scholars fighting the dominant schools partly by appearing to mock scholarship itself. In the case of Nicholas of Cusa (1401-1464), brilliant mathematician and philosopher of religion who was born in Germany and flourished in Italy, the irony was not intentional. But in attempting to reduce the ambiguity about the relationship between the individual and the cosmos, he found it appropriate to entitle his thoughts, "Of Learned Ignorance" (1440).

Where Cusa addressed his peers in Latin, another German, half a century later, aimed vernacular rhymed verses at his fellow townsmen and other ordinary citizens. Sebastian Brant (1458–1521), sometime teacher of canon law at the University of Basel, Switzerland, wrote in 1494 his "Ship of Fools." Following a tried and tested Humanist pattern, the South German moralist called on biblical and classical writers to witness human vices. Quoted substantially more often than anything else are, first, the Book of Proverbs, and second, the satires of Rome's pagan Juvenal. Moses and David, Plato and Alexander, are referred to about a dozen times each; Cicero and Boëthius, standbys of the Middle Ages, only twice and thrice, respectively. On the other hand, Brant wrote in the local Swabian dialect; woodcuts executed under his direction, characteristic of the age, both supported the satire of the text and supplemented it with a bit of humor.

The very first verse is entitled, "Of Useless Books." I sit in the front row of the fools, says the poet, because I am surrounded by books and understand virtually nothing of what is in them. With this observation goes a picture of a "scholar" amid his tomes, attired in jester's cape, tassels and all, and obviously fake spectacles. If the drawing is Holbein-like, the spirit is more nearly that of a Hieronymous Bosch caricature.

The impact must have been considerable, for there were soon translations or adaptations in Latin and the principal vernaculars; seventeen German editions within the century. Bibliographer Johann Tritheim, ecclesiastic, Humanist, and opponent of the abuse of peasants and Jews, hailed the "divine satire." Plausible indeed seems the view that Brant was known in many a modest corner never reached by such as Erasmus.

Why should an educated man apparently decry books and reading? Actually, just what he is up to is not altogether clear. The satirist does not condemn either the books or the reading directly and unequivocally, but blames himself for failure to understand the contents. Left ambiguous are the answers to several questions: how he felt about books, what he thought the burghers' attitudes were, why he considered it politic to play the fool, etc. Yet, where Cusa deals in abstractions, never mentioning books or reading, Brant begins by lampooning the model student. Although neither his verse nor his illustrations argue that books are not worthwhile, depicting their contribution as beyond even a scholar cannot have aroused much desire to read them. Was his target bibliomania—passion for books regardless of content, much satirized at that time? Whatever specifically local explanation there may be, it is evident that scholar Brant, unlike earlier scholar Cusa, felt a need for the sympathy and support of the nonscholar, and thought self-demeaning humor a good tactic by which to obtain them.

Nor, as already suggested, did the idea of reading benefit from Erasmus' attack on stupidity in thinking and behavior. Where Brant deliberately turned to the populace in dialect, Erasmus, like Cusa, wrote in the tongue only the educated could read. His Latin message of 1512, punning on his friend Thomas More's name, *Encomium Moriae* ("The Praise of Folly"), described as higher folly the inner spiritual life, a subject familiar to those capable of following Cusa. But it also deals with the lower folly of ordinary existence, and may thereby have carried to the educated the sort of theme the large masses of uneducated had lately heard about from Brant.

More's *Utopia* was issued (1516) a few years after Erasmus' contribution, in the same language, perhaps with the same audience in mind. It reacted to misery and folly in a fashion entirely different from Brant's and Erasmus' irony and ambiguity. Inspired in part by Plato's *Republic,* it counterposes to a description of grim reality an ideal society. There is much lament in the first part; innocent joy in the second. More was not a savage wit. His "reporter," seaman Ralph Hythloday, says he found a few classics in the hands of the Utopians and gave them a few more he happened to have with him. He names these titles (*Famous Utopias,* ed. Andrews, p. 196). But that is all.

Still slimmer is the thread linking Humanism to books and libraries in the celebrated satiric *Letters of Obscure Men . . .* (1515–1517) associated primarily with reformer Ulrich von Hütten (1488–1523). Among the second group (1517) of supposed letter writers helping expose, again in Latin, stuffy behavior and thinking is "Demetrius Phalerius" (ed. F. G. Stokes, London: Chatto & Windus, 1925, letter 38, p. 213), a name borrowed from the roster of the founding librarians at the great institution of ancient Alexandria.

In 1532–1534 appeared the first two books of the prime French contribution to this literature, Rabelais' *Gargantua and Pantagruel.* Father Gargantua enjoyed a medieval education, reading mainly identifiable items, over preposterous lengths of time (LeClercq trans., book I, chaps. 14 and 23). "(Printing had not yet been invented, and the young student had to write out his own texts)" (chap. 14). Son Pantagruel had the advantages of the library of the Abbey of St. Victor (real enough); "some of" its holdings "were already printed." As for the "admirable books" he found there, the titles were distorted almost beyond recognition (book II, chap. 7). Rabelais was apparently venting his spleen, like some other contemporary Humanists, over the fact that the St. Victor library, perhaps the best in France, had shown some potential for a Humanist orientation but failed to develop it. Humanism had lost a battle to the conservatives of the Sorbonne.

What he would have preferred at that stage is suggested in the celebrated letter "from Utopia," from father to son (chap. 8). The message praises classical reading but does not mention history or poetry; it urges acquiring "a knowledge of nature" but does not speak of studying nature directly. Perhaps more important is the brief tribute to progress, which presumably exerted some influence regardless of how much the physician-humorist really meant it:

> Today the world is full of learned men, brilliant teachers and vast libraries: I do not believe that the ages of Plato, Cicero or Papinian [second-century expert on Roman law] afforded such facilities for culture. From now on it is unthinkable to come before the public or move in polite circles without having worshipped at Minerva's shrine. Why, the robbers, hangmen, adventurers and jockeys of today are infinitely better educated than the doctors and preachers of my time. More, even women and girls aspire to the glory, the heavenly manna of learning.

At Rabelais' own Utopia, the abbey of Thélème, contrary to the triple vows of monasticism, each was to marry if he or she chose, enjoy wealth, and live in "perfect freedom"; no clock or dial of any sort was tolerated (book I, chap. 52). The main gate welcomed in thirteen stanzas "gallants and noble gentlemen, . . . loyal scholars who expound novel interpretations of the Holy Writ. . . . ladies fair of eminent degree, . . ." Not wanted were "legal knaves! . . . loan shark[s], . . . badgers bred in schools of hate; . . ." (chap. 54). Thanks presumably to the servants mentioned in one fleeting phrase (chap. 55), life was a dream combination of knightly-courtly ease and Humanist tastes (chap. 55–56) much like that cherished at the new palace of King Francis I. Indeed, each member of the community was able among other things to "speak five or six languages and readily compose verse and prose in any of them" (chap. 57). Serving that purpose, perhaps, were the "rich libraries of Greek, Latin, Hebrew, French, Italian, and Spanish volumes, grouped in their respective sections"; no human resource is mentioned (chap. 53).

A decade or so after producing the first two portions of his tale, Rabelais issued Books III and IV (V was posthumous). The great Humanist scholars were now departed, and new intellectual currents were washing France. The edge of the doctor's satire turned away from Scholasticism to the very antiquity he had been adoring; the work of scientists important to him (for example, Vesalius, "On the Makeup of the Human Body," 1543) moved some of his thinking from books to experience; and with that shift apparently developed a closer sympathy with the bourgeois audience. The deprecatory attitude toward women in the world of property and contract was reflected in his debates with contemporary feminists, and the admiring portrayal of gentlewomen at Thélème gave way to crudities about domestic relations such as those in Book III (chaps. 32–35). Thélème itself he now described less flatteringly: a mysterious painting of a rape could be seen there (book IV, chap. 2), and fanciful devices for avoiding cannon balls were reported to be "a common pastime and harmless sport among the Thélèmites" (chap. 62).

Rabelais, writing in French, evidently sought like Brant a broader audience than Latin readers. Almost as evidently, his ambiguity and irony worked against the sort of attention library advance required. Contrariwise, Juan Luis Vives, the well-known Spanish Humanist, speaks explicitly and positively of the library in a short dialogue of 1539, on the Latin language, dedicated to the eleven-year-old Prince Philip. Yet, offered in Latin, its audience was presumably not very large. And Vives' comments on library decoration and the measures needed to deal with moths and wood borers are clearly subordinate to his promoting of the best writers of the past.

By the time Michel de Montaigne penned his long influential *Essays* in the 1570s, the old and the new were plainly in conflict. The country gentleman is never without books, he says; he is sorry for anyone not thus equipped. His massive ruminations are in fact filled with allusions to and quotations from the writers of the past. Yet he frequently shrugs off their significance. Despite Cicero's conviction—as Montaigne puts it—that nothing is so "sweet as involvement with letters," the Humanist critic thinks of "a thousand silly women in country towns" who have lived satisfactory lives "sweeter and steadier than" Cicero's (*Essais*, II: XII). He is sure that books hard to understand are not widely read, and declares that he himself prefers the light and easy. His only reference to libraries is an opinion that, as encouragement to sedentary behavior, they account for the weakening of military capability.

He is strong for reason, moderation, and intellectual humility; he opposes compulsion in child rearing and in book censorship. He is also shrewd enough to observe that books tend to become "that much more saleable and public as they are suppressed" (III:V). His annoyance with honorifics cluttering title pages seems very democratic, but he discusses with uncomprehending indifference the new cosmology of Copernicus, and sneers at the "new experience" (II: XII) in medicine of Paracelsus, who for all his occultism and other confusion had drawn men's attention to the relationship between chemistry and health, out of clinical experience with sick miners.

Altogether, the late Humanist Montaigne illustrates with exceptional clarity the contradictions of his age. Intensely individual, he is also literally isolated. He searches the past fretfully but finds little promise in the present and has no confidence in the future. The new profit-focused order offers him no compensation for the loss of the old virtues like honor. His faith in free reason would be an asset to libraries, but the social underpinning they needed would have to be sought elsewhere. (Quotations from *Oeuvres complètes,* ed. Thibaudet et Rat, Editions Gallimard, 1962, pp. 468, 763, 554.)

Humanism did indeed expand reading horizons. But the figures here discussed were mainly not organization men but prophets. Such minds tended to use libraries as they needed them. Their concern with thinking and morals, however, rarely if ever focused on the problems of library service. The required additional pressure was generated in some quarters, especially in Italy, by the concern of collectors for what would become of their collections. The problem was solved otherwise in large areas north of the Alps.

Print, Conflict, and Criteria of Acceptability

Despite the obstacles referred to, Humanism exerted a profound influence upon library collections and the entire life of the mind because it was shaped in the epoch of printing and the Reformation.

Northern Humanism Humanism traveled from Italy to Switzerland and Germany in the fifteenth century primarily under the leadership of Germanic-speaking scholars who visited Italy to study and returned home. Scholarship could be continued there thanks to the patronage of the imperial court at Vienna, lesser courts elsewhere, and the numerous strong cities. These conditions were not then paralleled in war-torn France and England, the former lacking support for scholars and the latter absorbing them in public affairs. Whereas France had no cadre of scholars before about 1550, and England's famous Humanists of Thomas More's generation (died 1535) were not matched during the rest of the sixteenth century, Erasmus and his contemporaries of Germany and the Low Countries were already the third generation in those parts who were versed in classical studies. Their predecessors had prepared (1465–1475) the first printed editions of most of the Latin classics, and their own day was that of the *editio princeps* for most of the Greek (1493–1518), Erasmus himself being very prominent in such efforts.

The flood of printed matter seemed to the great Dutch Humanist, and perhaps some others, composed largely of mud. Whereas his widely appreciated anthology of ancient life and thought in proverbs, the *Adages,* included no editorial criticism in its original form in 1508, comment was added in later editions: in the 1533 version he revealed his mounting distress at the printing of what he considered trash and seditious materials. Nor, like such later humanists as Thomas Jefferson, did he take kindly to the spirit of capitalism.

On the other hand, nonetheless, these advances rendered possible a new solution to an old educational problem. The classical heritage had been drawn upon throughout the Middle Ages, in varying degrees—that is, what was known of it, and at hand. Now, thanks to Humanism and printing, virtually all of it was available—even if Erasmus thought it necessary in 1507 to go to Italy for Greek source materials not at his disposal in Paris, London, Oxford, or Louvain. (Aldus Manutius is said to have chosen Venice for his printing enterprise because he would thus have close at hand the great Greek manuscript collections presented by Cardinal Bessarion to the Marciana Library.) More important, the desired classics were appearing in versions more reliable than their predecessors because of Humanist scholarship, and far more stable once in print than anything the manuscript age could have produced. The educator had sought before Latin readings which would convey the sort of knowledge a Christian youngster should have, in good clear style and with a minimum of material generating unwanted thoughts and images. No longer, however, need he overemphasize style to underemphasize dubious content; no longer need he camouflage much of the pagan by calling it allegory. Indeed the resources obtainable were considerably more than his pupils could possibly use. He was therefore able to choose works or parts of works from antiquity which exemplified good prose and the near-Christian Stoic morality.

This approach, initiated in the essays of Erasmus, was carried into the schoolroom by Luther's educational coadjutor Philip Melanchthon, and further refined and systematized by other Protestant schoolmasters, with the Catholic reformers quickly following suit. The new education was most welcome where religious revivalism demanded clarity; business, brevity and accuracy; and nationalism, tight organization of indoctrination. One consequence later minds found distressing was the practically motivated concentration on the rules of Latin which tended to elbow aside concern with the ideas in the texts analyzed. Another was the strengthening of the censorship of reading matter; not new, but consciously developed on behalf of powers secular and religious.

Luther   Such is the context of the library-related ideas of Martin Luther. In his celebrated letter of 1524, *To the Councilmen of All Cities in Germany* (*Works,* American ed., vol. 45, ed. W. I. Brandt, Muhlenberg Press, 1962), the great reformer argued at length for public schools with libraries. He began by reviewing the weakness of the universities and the deterioration of the monasteries. He then observed that the right sort of teachers were available for a new instructional enterprise. Finally, he declared that it was God's command to educate the young: it was bad enough to "despoil virgins or wives (. . . bodily and recognized sin, may be atoned for)," but despoiling a soul was far worse—there could be no atonement (p. 354). "By the grace of God," he added (p. 369), "it is now possible for children to study with pleasure and in play languages, or other arts, or history"; he recommended also "singing and music together with the whole of mathematics."

The challenge was presented to the upper-middle-class councillors because too many parents lacked the talent or resources to raise their children properly, and the princes and lords were too busy "in cellar, kitchen, and bedroom." It was up to the civic leaders to sustain the production of "men able to rule well over land and people, women able to manage the household and train children and servants aright" (p. 368). They could find the cash: plenty was being spent annually on "guns, roads, bridges, and dams" and there was no reason why they could not apply to schools at least the funds no longer wasted on "indulgences, masses, . . . mendicant friars, . . . pilgrimages, and similar nonsense" (pp. 350–351).

The proposed course of study laid great emphasis on Latin, Greek, and Hebrew. Like Jerome, Augustine, and the humanism-absorbing contemporary Schoolmen of Germany, Luther directed attention to the sources as the only sure way of getting the scriptural message correctly. He defended this program, moreover, on the ground that Germans were too provincial; he promoted the German language, but simultaneously pronounced "fools and beasts" (p. 358) those supposing that their native tongue was enough. The "doing and saying of the entire world" must be grasped (p. 368).

To support this saving of souls, "no effort or expense should be spared to provide good libraries or book repositories, especially in the larger cities which can well afford them" (p. 373). The commentaries, sermons, etc., should in general be ignored; one should seek "the right sort . . . consulting with scholars." The Holy Scriptures should be on hand in Latin, Greek, Hebrew, and German, with the best commentaries, especially ancient ones. Language teaching should be serviced with the poets and orators, pagan and Christian, Latin and Greek. The liberal arts should be there, and "all the other arts"; law and medicine too. "Among the foremost" in the collection should stand chronicles and history, so that Germans might see the hand of God in events and cease being boors (p. 376).

Thus reasoned Luther about "judicious selection" of types of books, so much more important than mere numbers (p. 375). He had already, four years earlier, made plain his view of freedom of thought, publication, and reading. On June 15, 1520, he had been excommunicated. On December 6, after his own works had been burned by emissaries of the pope, he in turn burned several church-approved items. Why he did so was explained in a tract composed December 10 and published about a fortnight later: "Firstly, it is an ancient custom to burn poisonous and evil books"; St. Paul's own teaching had led to some such activity. Second, it was his sworn duty "to destroy false, seductive, and unchristian doctrines, or at least to rebut them." Third, the opposition had burned his. Fourth, the pope was probably not directly involved, but whether or not the pope liked the books burned "was not an issue with me"; also, the destruction of his books in the name of the emperor was fakery (he knew bribes had been passed to certain officials). Fifth, "I burned the books of my enemies because it was hopeless to teach them any better." And a parting shot: "Samson. Judges 15: as they have done to me, so I have done to them" (*Reformation Writings*, trans. from the Weimar ed. by B. L. Woolf, Philosophical Library, 1956, II:76–77).

Luther's attitude toward printed books was further elaborated a few months afterward, when he offered advice to his followers who might run into trouble with their confessors over possession of his writings. While his own books were open, under his own name, he noted in "A Word to Penitents," it was "unfortunately true that there are many scandalous books in circulation without name or title. It would be reasonable to forbid them, and they should in fact be forbidden; for they are not only contrary to Christian love but also against natural ethics" (*Reformation Writings*, II:97).

Calvin Nothing equally explicit about libraries or categories of reading matter appears in the *Institutes of the Christian Religion* first released by John Calvin in 1536. But in view of his firm support (ed. John T. McNeill, trans., F. L. Battles, Philadelphia: Westminster Press, 1960, book IV, chap. XX) of civil government, magistrates, and kings—even bad ones, and his injunction (IV:XX:29) to leave the correction of evil to God, there is no reason to doubt a readiness to censor publication and reading very much like Luther's.

Censorship

These views were of course in no way exceptional. In the manuscript age, when the bulk of the production of books was in ecclesiastical hands, censorship had been managed rather easily most of the time, and the principal violators of the rules had themselves been clerics on the whole, dissident or heretical. The age of printing by movable type was quite different: large numbers of publications were prepared on all sorts of subjects by all sorts of writers, and printing facilities tended to become available somehow for nearly any of them, initially in the Rhine Valley, then especially in the towns of what became the Netherlands.

Adult Censorship Lists, 1520–1546 The church reacted soon after Gutenberg's achievements with type and ink. Rome pressed (1479, 1501) the leading archbishops of Germany to exert more influence in their jurisdictions. In 1515 the Lateran Council decreed that nothing should be printed until after examination by appropriate ecclesiastical authority and threatened resisters with excommunication, their books with confiscation and destruction. This meant little to the Lutherans for the moment. But in June 1520, after much high-level debate at the Vatican, Pope Leo X issued the bull *Exsurge Domine,* condemning Luther's "errors," demanding recantation within a stated period on pain of excommunication, and meanwhile commanding that the rebel's books be burned. (One of the two official announcers was Leo's librarian, Italian humanist Aleander, distinguished as a teacher and diplomat.) However calmly the Lutherans might have absorbed that expected blow, the new Holy Roman emperor, Charles V, shortly altered the situation. Unlike his predecessors he saw advantages in an alliance with the pope; its consequences expressed at the Diet of Worms (1521) included a ban on Luther's translation of the Bible and on all new doctrines in general.

Within one year, the church had at its disposal a catalog of "heretical" writings compiled by no less than the inquisitor for the Archdioceses of Cologne, Mainz, and Trier, Dominican Bernard of Luxemburg (d. 1535). The next seventeen years saw six successive ever larger editions. In 1548 and 1549 appeared the logical complement, Johannes Cochläus' "brief" guide to refutations of heresy. It was a fitting product for a Catholic humanist most prolific in anti-Lutheran polemics (1479–1522). No corresponding Protestant work was produced until much later.

Meanwhile, numerous warnings were being directed to the general public. By 1523, according to surviving evidence which may be a small portion of the original, placards were posted in the name of the emperor against two Lutheran religious tracts, in Flemish, presumably in Flemish-speaking areas. Two years afterward were issued enlarged announcements explicitly condemning de boucken and other writings of Martin Luther, his principal—named—associates, and his other adherenten, whether in Dutch, Flemish, or "Walsche" (Walloon French). Any such items found were to be burned in a public place, and anyone connected with their publication to be banished for life from the county of Flanders. (On view, pp. 23–24, Heinrich Reusch's collection, Die Indices Librorum Prohibitorum des Sechzehnten Jahrhunderts, Niewkoop, de Graaf, 1866; 1961 reprint.)

This message was restated more elaborately in French in 1529 and 1531 (Reusch, pp. 24–25), adding the names of developers of Protestantism Wyclif of England, Hus of Bohemia, and Zwingli of Switzerland; also Italian reformer-of-church-government Marsilius of Padua, and three printers held responsible for condemned editions of the New Testament. In the document too were warnings against making offensive illustrations or images of God, the Virgin Mary, or the saints, or maltreating those then approved.

Another proclamation issued in Flemish in 1540, and directed against the same authors, listed particular books, apparently for the first time in this series. There was no visible order, the first word being from the title in nearly every instance. The works thus named seem to have been theological or mystical; nothing clearly classical or political.

The repetition of these injunctions suggests that they were not altogether successful. Across the Channel in England, moreover, cries could be heard against dangerous imports. Whether or not the first known English list of prohibited books (1526) contained items brought over from the Low Countries is not evident from the document itself (Reusch, p. 5). Listed are eight works in English and ten in Latin: Luther appears in both groups, also a few tracts with politicoeconomic overtones; Hus and Zwingli appear among the Latin only, whereas the English portion is notable for the "New Testament of Tindall." But Lutheran books importati are explicitly proscribed in a City of London blacklist given a probable date of 1529; fifty-odd items appear, all in Latin, entered mainly by title in no apparent order (Reusch, pp. 6–10). Most of the titles so far noticed, plus many more like them, were denounced in several lists of the 1530s, sometimes in English, sometimes in Latin (Reusch, pp. 10-15).

The "injunctions" of 1539 (Reusch, pp. 15-19), naming several English writers and translators, indicate that while some English prohibited books may have found printers only in the Low Countries, there were plenty of Englishmen to write them. In 1535, four years after Henry VIII broke with Rome and the very year of the execution of Sir Thomas More, works favorable to the Catholic Church were labeled seditious. But that turn of events did not promptly relieve the previously banned Protestants. Tyndale, "Calvyn," Luther, and the rest were still off limits in 1542, 1546, and 1555; indeed the 1546 list denounced the new Protestant Bible of Miles Coverdale. The proclamation of 1555, issued during the temporary Catholic restoration under Queen Mary, demanded that no one "from henceforth presume to bring or convey, or cause to be brought or conveyed into this realm" any work "in the Latin tongue, Dutch tongue, English tongue, Italian tongue, or French tongue" against the Catholic Church or the "church of England" (Reusch, pp. 21-22).

Meanwhile, continental Catholic authorities continued to move against heresy in various ways. Whereas in 1513 Louis XII had encouraged printing by relieving the printer-booksellers of taxes, 1533 saw the doctors of the Sorbonne demanding that Francis I protect the Catholic faith by forbidding any printing whatever (most North European printers were Reformers). Cooler heads at first stemmed this tide, but the insistence of some Reform elements upon decorating Paris walls (October 1534) with nasty attacks on the mass and the Roman clergy led promptly to severe persecution, including public burnings. By January 1535 the king had been induced to prohibit any printing in France and order all bookshops closed. This too proved unacceptably extreme: resistance materialized in the Paris Parlement and within one month Francis decreed instead that the Parlement should nominate twenty-four suitable persons from whom he would choose twelve who alone would be authorized to print in Paris what was needed and approved. Two years later emerged the renowned "first" provision for legal deposit (see below).

The Church itself took an unequivocal policy step, in the 1536 edition of the bull issued annually (1364-1869) on Lord's Supper day and titled accordingly In Coena Domini. A new sin was added to those which could be absolved from sentence of excommunication (except on the deathbed) by the pope alone: keeping or reading heretical books. That offense thus joined a long list including piracy on the papal seas and appeals from ecclesiastical to secular courts. Soon afterward (1540-1550) the inquisitor-general at Toulouse, in the old Albigensian heresy country of southern France, issued a document denouncing ninety-two numbered items, Latin and French, headed by the works of John Wyclif, and including Rabelais and several songs scandaleuses et contenantes erreurs contre Dieu et l'église. Striking was the demand that any book dealer or other person of any estat et condition be reported who handled, bought, sold, printed or had printed, bound or had bound, works on the list (Reusch, pp. 130-135).

The theologians at the Sorbonne in Paris likewise made their concern known, in a series of edicts beginning in 1542. Four, from 1544 to 1556, were markedly longer than the initial list, and an attempt was made at alphabetical arrangement by surname, announced each time at the end of the preface. Considering the novelty of the practice the announcement was well-advised, particularly since the results were shaky: Arsatus Schopfer, for example, appeared under both A and S (Reusch, pp. 95, 109). Possibly significant also, the first three of the four lists concluded with the statement in Latin that the faculty had examined and censured the named books, whereas the fourth (1556) submitted that testimony in French (Reusch, pp. 128-129).

School Concerns Too, 1546-1559 The lists so far considered were directed, to judge from their contents, at Protestant editions and translations of and commentaries on the Holy Scriptures and the Fathers, polemics by well-known Reformers, and miscellaneous tracts deemed dangerous to church or state or both, often issued without any author's or printer's name and sometimes expressing a left-wing viewpoint.

Classics from antiquity, the common interest of Humanists on both sides of the contemporary religious fence, were referred to probably for the first time in the 1546 Brussels announcement about books, made in the name of the emperor. Opening with the same general warning already noticed in the Toulouse French Index of 1540, here however in Flemish, it designated the Theological Faculty at the University of Louvain as the judges of what should or should not be printed and read. Next, it specified what should be read: for children the religious staples like the Paternoster, and in the *particulier scholen* where the seven liberal arts, ethics, and history were studied, numerous pertinent textbooks and Latin and Greek classics. Included were not only old safe standbys like Cicero and Virgil and bland Humanist additions like Plutarch, but even the long controversial Ovid and the newly available, similarly controversial drama of Aristophanes and Menander (Reusch, pp. 27–28). Were these latter in editions cleaned up for school use?

To these recommendations was joined the *Cathalogum* of prohibited books of the Louvain theologians. Its first few pages (Reusch, pp. 28–32) were devoted to the rationale and recent history of the struggle against heresy and related ills. Jurisdiction was claimed explicitly over "all libraries, bookshops, and books" (Reusch, p. 29). Among the dangers signalled were books in the local vernaculars, near-heretical works, titles better not read than read, Bible translations and interpretations. The next portion of the document is a list (Reusch, pp. 33–36) of proscribed Bibles, grouped by language, for which are provided the place of publication, printer's name, and date of publication. This practice, not yet customary with books in general, will be seen to have been adopted promptly in many localities, in part no doubt because there was no author and control of the work's circulation seemed vital. After the Bibles comes a list of banned items in Latin, largely but not entirely theological in nature; noteworthy (Reusch, p. 38) are three textbooks by Johannes Sturm, Lutheran pedagogue par excellence. The arrangement, like that of the Sorbonne, is alphabetical usually by the author's surname (whether the first word in the entry or not) or, in the absence of an author, the first word of the title. These items are followed by Dutch, High Dutch, and Walloon-French lists, again mainly religious, in no apparent order. The concluding paragraphs repeat the general ban on Luther, Wyclif, etc., and the warnings of the Theological Faculty and His Imperial Majesty (Reusch, pp. 36–43).

Neither threats nor book selection positive and negative brought results satisfactory to the authorities. A new communication was offered to the Christian reader in 1550 by the rector of Louvain University on behalf of the emperor. His majesty, he said, had asked him to try again to save ordinary citizens from the troubles certainly in store if they read or kept proscribed books. Of concern also were children in school: the emperor wanted a list of books for school use which would be most appropriate and agreeable without restricting too narrowly youthful study and understanding, even where there was no question of endangering religion or morals.

Much thought had been given to available reading matter openly heretical or otherwise, continued the rector. It was realized among other things that evil could be conveyed by way of grammar and other textbooks; also through little Latin books ostensibly devoted to teaching good style such as *colloques familiers* (a swing at Erasmus' *Familiar Colloquies,* a primarily didactic and partially satiric work then known to two generations of Latin students). Keeping such *pernicieux livres* out of popular hands was not a new idea. If it seemed drastic to deprive youth of books condemned or purged of error, for heresy or association with heretics or dubious passages, it should be understood that his majesty allowed their use on a showing that he who wished to utilize such books had solid scholarly reasons. Incidentally, readers were not to undertake any corrections of authors' mistakes on their own account (Reusch, pp. 45–49).

The list of prohibited books (Reusch, pp. 52–70) is very much the same as that of 1546 but somewhat enriched and more closely organized. Not only are both Bibles and other works listed by language groups; anonymous titles are now separated, language by language, from the books with named authors (Reusch, pp. 63–70). Noteworthy in the main alphabet, characteristically under C (Reusch, p. 54), is Conrad Gesner's *Bibliotheca Universalis* ("Universal Bibliography"), only a few years in print. An attempt by a humanist of reformer Zwingli's Zürich to make known to scholars the basic data about every Greek, Hebrew, and Latin volume in existence, and to do so explicitly without reference to an author's vocation, religion, or viewpoint, it was evidently in conflict with the concepts of reading guidance then dominant at Catholic Louvain, very likely elsewhere too. On the positive side, the 1550 catalog recommends a few more books for children in school, in six groups: Latin, Greek, and Hebrew grammars, rhetoric-oratory, poets, and dialecticians.

By 1558, eight years after the promulgation of the above, the rector of the university again addressed the devout reader, this time with a "salute." Despite the dedicated efforts led by the emperor, the Catholic faith continued to be assailed by "damnable opinions," in subversive prefaces, arguments, marginal annotation, summaries, and text editing. His majesty was still trying to protect the common people from these bad books; his sanctions were thoroughly grounded in the best traditions of burning the offensive. But what use were laws "often published and never observed"? When prohibited items were "surreptitiously introduced"? Nonetheless, another effort had to be made to fend off "the tumults of this unhappy century." The faculty had therefore assembled with "great effort" a blacklist of books in various languages, some with authors, some without names of authors or printers. Readers would please cooperate, and read with wisdom and discretion the books coming into their hands (Reusch, pp. 49–52).

The sweep of prohibition in 1558 was about twice as great as in 1550, although apparently not different in character. Conspicuous additions are the German and French books listed separately according to the presence or absence of author's names (Reusch, pp. 67–70). The arrangement is the same as that of 1550, new titles having been brigaded into lists of the earlier document; although the main section is ordered alphabetically, the pattern elsewhere is alphabetical at most only remotely.

These endeavors evidently met a need. In 1549 and 1550 Cologne church officials issued a reading guide (Reusch, pp. 78–81) very similar to the Louvain document of 1546. The Louvain product of 1550 was copied bodily a year later by the Spanish inquisitor-general, who added thereto a long list of works condemned by the Inquisition; many items thus enjoyed the distinction of being mentioned twice. Also proscribed were the Koran and other titles in Arabic with Moslem "errors" (Reusch, pp. 73–77), testimony to the persistence of ideas in print two generations after the expulsion of the Moors and Jews from Spain. The same authority turned out in 1559 a considerably more elaborate *Cathalogus.* It bars among other works all vernacular Bibles, various "Books of Hours" judged infected with *curiosa et superstitiosa,* and numerous titles in Dutch (taken from the Louvain 1546 list), German, French, and "Romance" (Spanish). Excluded from respectability also are several *comedias,* and the *Novelas* of Boccaccio, who seems to be named here for the first time. Whatever impact these edicts had, the next hundred years of Spanish literature were to be the greatest, the "Golden Century."

The Italians too were ready to offer advice on reading, if only because Lutheran and other heterodox items circulated persistently. Banned wholesale in successive announcements (Reusch, pp. 136–142) by the Holy Office at Lucca, 1545, and papal representatives at Venice, 1549, were all the works of the continental Reformers, although England's Wyclif appears to have been overlooked. On the other hand a considerable number of Italians are named who drew little if any notice elsewhere. The "Catalog of Heretics" issued at Milan in 1554 was prefaced with a long orientation essay in Italian, which in the manner observed in earlier instances placed (Reusch, pp. 144–145) unmistakable responsibility upon the bookdealer, the bookbinder, and anyone distributing or selling books, whether at the shop or in "his own home." The list, perhaps the first entitled *Index Librorum . . .* (by then a common title for any book list), includes besides the stock content such other items as Dante's "On Monarchy" and the corpus of Jewish rabbinical learning known as the Talmud. The Venetians released a virtually identical document at the same time. One of its differences was a section following the main list, also alphabetically arranged, devoted principally to entries like "The Book called Treasure" (Reusch, pp. 148–175).

The "Indexes of Prohibited Books" of 1559 and 1564   The decree of January 1559 usually cited as the first "official" Index of Prohibited Books was promulgated at Rome, in the name of the Roman "and universal" Inquisition on behalf of the "universal Christian Republic" and sponsored by Pope Paul IV. It begins by referring to authoritative precedent, the above-mentioned bull on the sinfulness of contact with forbidden books, *In Coena Domini*. But the Latin introduction is otherwise very brief; no detailed rationale; hardly more than a plain explanation of the organization of the list (Reusch, pp. 176–178). Entries are grouped alphabetically, being subgrouped within each letter as follows: (1) writers proscribed entirely, (2) particular titles by known authors, and (3) anonymous works. Most of the persons designated appear under their first names, in Latin, which can mean a transfer from "William" (Tyndale) to "Gulielmus." Desiderius Erasmus can be found under both D and E, Martin Luther under both M and L (Reusch, pp. 183–203); the duplication looks deliberate.

Pope Paul's Index of January 1559 may have provoked no debate among Catholics in Italy or Spain, where Reform carried little weight, or in France, where the balance of power was most delicate. But the situation in southern Germany was quite different. "'People in all appearance excellent Catholics are not afraid to reject and condemn its severity!'" wrote Peter Canisius, Jesuit educator for southern Germany, Bohemia, and Poland, to his superior in Rome (quoted, p. 464 of James Brodrick's *Saint Peter Canisius;* Chicago: Loyola University Press, 1962). That was a virtually immediate response, early in March; other protests soon followed it, for Canisius and the other Jesuits struggling to improve schooling and repulse powerful Lutheranism were torn between duty and the practical necessities of the classroom. The inquisitor-general offered a concession: the German Jesuits might expurgate the bad books and then use them; they might allow a three-month period of grace for parishioners still using banned items to clear their records.

To Canisius, however, that was not good enough. In May he remarked, "'I hear that the legislation cannot be maintained even among yourselves, either in Venice or Milan, in spite of the efforts of the inquisitors. Much less chance is there of its having any force in Germany.'" (Quoted in Brodrick, p. 465.) And shortly afterward he declared that the "'great lack of books on the humanities and other classical arts'" was tragic; Erasmus' collections of such readings were not permitted by the standards of the Index, and no adequate substitute was available. Should the three-month dispensation not be considerably extended, "'I am afraid that we may have to close our schools'" (quoted in Brodrick, p. 466).

In brief, the contemporary scholarly editions of the pagan classics, which were not themselves on the Index, were not within the reach of the classrooms in Canisius' jurisdiction. But the Humanist, often Protestant, texts based on them were officially proscribed. The Jesuits' resistance to the Dominican-administered rules bore some fruit, with the aid of other events and influences. Pope Paul IV died in August, to be replaced by Pius IV. And the new (third) series of meetings of the Catholic Council of Trent opening in January 1562 (the earlier ones convened 1545–1548, 1551–1552) was under great political pressure to go easy on leading Protestant documents like the Augustinian Confession of Faith of 1530. Although Canisius was not directly involved in the deliberations of the Council's special commission to prepare a new Index, his views were taken into account and in 1562 he said that what was going on pleased him. Incidentally, he furnished the Council with the latest news and books from the Frankfort fairs, including every new Protestant work he thought important; he is said to have packed them personally.

The so-called Tridentine Index of March 4, 1564, differed from its predecessors in giving half the lengthy Latin preface to ten regulations, an aide to enforcement presumably inspired by discussion and debate. Rule I declares that books condemned by pontifical or council decisions before 1515 remain so, even if not on the present list. Rule II is a blanket prohibition of certain authors like Luther, with permission to utilize writings by other heretics on nonreligious subjects which have been passed by appropriate bishops and inquisitors. Rule III is an injunction to be most careful about editions and versions of the Latin Bible; Rule IV, the same about vernacular Bibles. Rule V allows controlled use of reference tools and other scholarship contributed by heretics. Rule VI bans vernacular polemics; Rule VII the obscene; Rule VIII, works on divination or superstitions; Rule IX, those on witchcraft, the occult, and the magical. Rule X details the procedures under which the bishops may expurgate items only partially offensive and then authorize their use. (Reusch, pp. 247–251.)

Comparison of the 1559 and 1564 Indexes reveals a number of significant modifications that look deliberate. In 1559 Erasmus is in class 1, banned outright. In 1564 he rates class 2, treated selectively: a few items are still proscribed, certain others are spoken of as unacceptable "as long as they have not been expurgated" by the Paris or Louvain authorities—as though such action were being anticipated, and an appropriately expurgated edition of the *Adages* is "permitted" (Reusch, pp. 183, 259). Furthermore, an edition of selected letters of Erasmus' is on the earlier list but not on the later one (Reusch, pp. 178, 259).

Similarly, Boccaccio's bawdy tales appear in both documents in class 2, but in 1564 there is a hint of hope: the work is condemned "until expurgated" (Reusch, pp. 180, 255). The Talmud and all related glosses, annotations, interpretations and expositions are rejected without qualification in Paul IV's Index. The Tridentine list states that "without the name Talmud and without the injuries to and calumnies about the Christian religion, they will be tolerated" (Reusch, pp. 203, 289). Such an edition was actually published in Basel, Switzerland, in 1580, thanks to the demand from Italian Jews who had seen numerous earlier editions burned, acceptance of the censorship by those underwriting the expense and a rabbi whose approval was needed, and publisher Ambrosius Froben's desire to take advantage of circumstances.

Evidences of growing bibliographical sophistication also mark the later of these two Indexes. Although as usual most authors are entered once, under their first names, and a few twice, the 1564 product adds what is perhaps the first see reference: *"Erasmus Roterodamus, vide supra in littera 'D,'"* where the works follow the man's name (in the customary genitive case), "Desiderii Erasmi Roterodami" (Reusch, pp. 260, 259). Another device, likewise used possibly for the first time, indicates that a work held anonymous in 1559 may no longer have to be so treated: the entry of 1564 adds, "the author is believed to be Calvin" (Reusch, pp. 186, 263).

One wonders also at certain features which did not change. Why did both Indexes name dialectician Peter Abelard but not the more or less materialist, equally controversial Spanish Moslem master Averroës? Why should early Humanist teacher Vergerio have fallen under the ban but not Catullus, the risqué Roman poet whom the Renaissance Humanists "discovered"? (Reusch, pp. 200, 275.)

The pre-1515 proscriptions mentioned may have a bearing. Another factor was ignorance. In 1572 the Jesuit provincial—i.e., supervisor—at Naples wrote to Canisius that news was a long time traveling between southern Italy and France and Germany, and added this enlightening comment:

> As for the principal heresies that are abroad, the prevalent views of the sectaries, and the books circulated to seduce the people, nobody knows anything about them. You cannot be unaware of the strict laws under which we have lived during the past few years; of the obstacles put in the way of heretics who desire to visit Italy; of the ban on the importation of new books; and of the great difficulty experienced by those seeking permission to read heretical books, even when they might do so to the glory of Christ. . . .These are the reasons why Italy has produced few champions against heresy. . . .You in Germany are on the battlefield (Quoted in Brodrick, pp. 720–721).

"Indexes" and Library Acquisitions, 1560–1582 How men of Canisius' bent and temper carried the banner of the Roman Church into the schools and colleges of southern Germany may be judged in part from the surviving testimony of book selection. Undoubtedly intended to harmonize with the Index as modified at Trent was the book-order list (Brodrick, pp. 519–521) prepared by Canisius in July 1562 for the new College of Innsbruck, Austria. The largest group, eighteen Greek and Roman classic writers, includes an edition of Virgil's poetry by teacher Peter Ramus of France, who had become a Protestant the year before (Canisius of course may not have known it) and would die ten years later in the St. Bartholomew's Eve massacre. Among the fourteen rhetoric-grammar titles one finds another Ramus offering, Aristotle on rhetoric. The Humanist strain is especially evident in the presence of nine works on history and archaeology, the last being the landmark biobibliography of ecclesiastical writers (1494) by Johann Tritheim, respected abbot of Sponheim, a Bavarian monastery, and in 1500 notable also for the first modern treatise on cryptography. The nine authors recommended for mathematics and physics include geniuses of antiquity Archimedes and Ptolemy, tribute perhaps to the positive side of Humanist scholarship; the negative side is witnessed by the absence of near-contemporary Copernicus, whose epoch-making study had been published twenty years before.

Broader guidance was provided in a complex series of documents issued by the Munich ecclesiastical authorities: I (1566), a substantial general statement in German about forbidden books, without a list; II (1569), a reprint of the Tridentine Index plus a list of books recommended for use in Bavarian monasteries, all in Latin; III (1569), an ordinance for the schools of Upper and Lower Bavaria, in German, discussing book needs, dangers, and recommendations; IV (1582), a new Index, in Latin, expanded beyond the Council of Trent's product by the addition of varying numbers of items to each group of authors totally proscribed (but not to selective class 2 or anonymous class 3).

In the first document (Reusch, pp. 324–348), every book handler is warned not to bring in, display, or sell, any book of theology, prayer, or song in Latin or "Teutsch," unless originating in an approved place of publication. A long list is furnished, all being individual cities except "Hispania." Tradesmen dealing in German works are advised to be especially careful about their merchandise. Several church titles such as old translations of the Bible are mentioned as quite acceptable but not being printed currently for lack of demand. Certain groups of books are recommended explicitly: Bibles, catechisms, prayerbooks, tracts, and polemics. They are said to be obtainable locally, at Dillingen and Ingolstadt. (At about that time Canisius reported to Rome that the burdens of publishing officially approved material had driven the Dillingen man out of business; he urged a church subsidy for such enterprises. He also observed that the official monopoly on church publications held by an Italian printer had raised prices to the point where some German Catholics were buying reprints from Protestants; he thought such reprinting ought to be allowed to Catholic printers.)

The classics readers and the others need differentiated attention, the 1566 essay continues. Those versed in Latin and Greek have much at their disposal if they have the purchase price; some is good and some is bad, and they should be judicious in their selection. Strong recommendation goes to the evangels and materials on saints and martyrs. Quite satisfactory also are the books in any language on history and the secular arts, issued by Catholic printers, who ought to be patronized. But certain writers are banned, whether in German or in Latin, owing to their incorrect or evil materialistic, political, or historical concepts. Among those thus proscribed is John Foxe of England, noted for his Protestant martyrology (*Acts and Monuments,* 1554 first Latin edition, 1563 complete English edition), gruesome and very popular. The statement concludes with a denunciation of tracts attributed to fanciful authors named " . . . -Devil."

The second brochure, for the Bavarian monasteries, after reprinting the Tridentine Index, goes on to provide specific guidance positive and negative (Reusch, pp. 330–337). A paragraph is given to acceptable legal and medical literature; all is classical or medieval, neither Vesalius ("On the Makeup of the Human Body," 1543) nor any other contemporary being mentioned. Another warns against Calvinist editions from France, advises that anything from Spain, Italy, or Belgium will be safely Catholic, and names the proper procurement sources in France and Germany. The balance is a select list of recommended authors in Catholic editions, embracing a wide range of works from Aristotle and Herodotus through the Fathers and Cassiodorus, on to the medieval authorities, and down to Thomas More (dead only some thirty years). One of the very few titles mentioned after an author's name is Ptolemy's *Geographia.* Humanism is reflected in the inclusion of history and ethics, of Petrarch and Juan Luis Vives, the Spanish-born educational philosopher. But belles lettres are conspicuous by their absence: neither poets nor dramatists nor fabulists like "Aesop." Bibliographer Tritheim is endorsed, but not the more comprehensive, evidently too comprehensive, Gesner (see below).

The *Ordnung* for the Bavarian schools devotes section 6 to reading and books (Reusch, pp. 337–341). To be acceptable, printed matter must have been issued under Catholic auspices. Melanchthon's and other hostile writers' works are forbidden; but it is urged that specified inoffensive school materials be used, such as the grammatical texts by Erasmus. Joined oddly in support of the study of dialectic, rhetoric, and nature are Aristotle, Cicero, and several lesser lights. Models of letter writing and oratory may be admired in any edition from a Catholic printer and unmarred by annotations from heretical hands. The Greek and Latin historians are mentioned with enthusiasm; especially good for the souls of the boys is the spiritually oriented sort, like Eusebius and Josephus. Besides, more Catholic-sponsored history is being produced all the time. It would be grand to have expurgated editions of the classic poets, like the version of Martial published in the Netherlands; but until they are available, Ovid's *Metamorphoses* and *Amatoria* and similar items must be rejected. Meanwhile, most of Virgil, Horace, Seneca, and some others, is safe. Latin may be studied to advantage through heathen poets, but the schoolmasters are not to venture beyond approved media. Specified Catholic editions of pagan poets are named; likewise approved versions of letters and fables.

Finally, the enriched Index of 1582 (Reusch, pp. 341–350) was issued, according to the Latin *Mandatum* preceding the list, to combat ignorance, carelessness, and malice. Every item added to the Tridentine original is apparently an author's name; nearly all are obscure by twentieth-century standards.

New Purposes and Techniques in Bibliography

The publications just described were generated by the desires of major religious and political forces to control the reading, thinking, and behavior of the tens of thousands newly involved in public life by printing. This objective occasioned some attempts at careful bibliography, but was often blocked by the dissident author's or printer's interest in remaining off the record; besides, a tradition of meticulous book description did not yet exist.

Opposing pressure arose from another aspect of economic and social transformation. Perhaps as revolutionary as the Reformation was the shift from book production mainly ecclesiastical-corporate and nonprofit to book production by individual lay enterprisers devoted of necessity, if not by conviction, to profitable operation. Where a codex's origins had sometimes been a matter of importance from the standpoint of reliability or aesthetic value, a book producer's investment in quarters, equipment, and materials demanded that he sell his wares and become known for them. Within twenty years after the first printed books appeared, printer-publishers were advertising in leaflets and handbills the splendors of their own offerings and the shortcomings of those of their rivals.

Further motivation to be precise bibliographically derived from considerations of national and local prestige, Humanist scholarship, and individualism.

Particularistic Bibliography Probably the earliest list of books printed was the 1470 announcement of their own wares by Sweynheym and Pannartz, the German printers only seven years in business in Italy. Initially serving the Benedictines at Subiaco Abbey, near Rome, they apparently moved into the Eternal City about the time they published their catalog; Spanish Cardinal Torquemada of Inquisition fame, supervisor of the abbey, seems to have had a role in their moving.

Impelled by the national sentiment which soon became more sharply defined in the Protestant camps, Catholic abbot of Sponheim Johann Tritheim, Humanist collector of Greek manuscripts, assembled in Latin not only a practically oriented bibliography of ecclesiastical authors (1494) but a similar list of writings by eminent Germans (1495). Each bibliography bore the medieval stamp of chronological order and Christian names, but the alphabetical index to those names was rather a novelty. More in harmony with the medieval features than with the national focus of his second product was his conviction that parchment manuscripts would far outlast printed books: he even urged scribes to copy by hand the unreliable experiments. (Some Scotch Franciscans reportedly paid the neighboring Benedictines to do precisely that in 1501 and 1502 with whole sets of books.)

Half a century afterward, presumably untroubled by printing, Bishop John Bale issued another biobibliography chronologically arranged and indexed by forenames. The 1548 "Summary . . . " listed the "illustrious" British authors, furnishing for each in Latin a brief biography and the opening words of the title of each of his works. Bale explicitly based his effort on the labors of John Leland (more below), and like him indicated in this first edition no knowledge of the late-fourteenth-century record composed by Henry of Kirkestede. To judge from the enlarged second edition, issued from 1557 to 1559 in a Basel friendly to an outspoken Reformer, Bale improved upon his exile from the England of Catholic Queen Mary: he credits directly in his title a long line of earlier bibliographer-biographers, including Kirkestede (as "Boston of Bury"), Tritheim, and Gesner (see below).

The first bibliography of a particular vernacular was perhaps the effort of Florentine priest-dilettante Antonio Francesco Doni to list all books in Italian. It was striking also for the inclusion in the first edition (1550) of printed music, and in the second (1551) of a descriptive list of Italian academies.

The full-scale Renaissance phenomenon, the individual advertising himself, appears in the bibliographies of Erasmus' writings, the first (1519) by a printer, then three more (1523, 1524, 1540) by the author himself; he ultimately added a classification as a foundation for their arrangement in his "Collected Works." Personal bibliographies emanated also from two poets, one English (Skelton, 1523), the other French (Gascoigne, 1573).

By that time, biobibliography could be found in locality-centered context. Possibly the earliest Latin work of that genre was a book about Padua published in 1558 (in Basel!) by Bernardino Scardeoni (1478-1574), who seems to have written nothing else of consequence. Priest-historian Michele Poccianti's Latin bibliography (1589) of Florentine authors was both alphabetical and classified.

"Universal" Bibliography; Gesner Perhaps representative of many others not so well known was the alphabetical dictionary of proper names in poetry put together by Herman van Baeck ("Torrentinus, " 1450-1520), a Dutch Brother of the Common Life and teacher of grammar and rhetoric. First issued in Strasbourg in 1505, expanding through several successive editions, it served as the nucleus of a true dictionary of universal biography, the "Historical Dictionary" assembled in 1553 by Charles Estienne (1504-1564), of a famous French publishing family.

More legitimately considered bibliography was the fabulous effort to cover "everything" made by Conrad Gesner (1516-1565). His *Bibliotheca Universalis* has been described most usefully by Zürich librarian Hermann Escher in the 1934 *Vierteljahrschrift der Naturf. Gesellschaft in Zürich*, 79:174-194. Like Catholic Tritheim at the end of the fifteenth century, Zwinglian Protestant Gesner two generations later included profane as well as Christian authors of the Christian Era, and offered remarks on their lives and works. He ignored vernacular publications, considering them of no consequence to learning.

There the resemblance ends. Starting from the data on about 1,000 personages (perhaps 7,000 titles) in Tritheim and those for some 280 in the works of the ninth-century Byzantine litterateur-diplomat Photius, Gesner energetically moved on. Traveling, corresponding, and taking notes at a rate evidently extraordinary, he utilized the catalogs of great libraries such as the Vatican, publishers' trade catalogs (he was the only bibliographer of his epoch to speak of them), tips from all over Europe, and as much library visiting and reading as he could cram into his days and nights. For example, sometime early in the 1540s he met at the Leipzig Fair a librarian from Venice, the man in charge of the noted collection of Hurtado de Mendoza, Spanish ambassador to Venice; a few years later we find Gesner using those resources in Venice at the diplomat's invitation; a causal connection seems likely. In three years of extraordinary labor he produced an annotated biobibliography of 3,000 writers (10,000 to 12,000 titles), all he could find in Greek, Hebrew, and Latin, "important" or "unimportant." Of the forty-five works of that sort printed between 1494 and 1598, Gesner's *Bibliotheca Universalis* was the first general European bibliography.

Why the "unimportant"? He had begun with only the better items in mind, but soon concluded that reporting "all" would be less work. He took comfort in this reflection: printing provided so much to examine which was not worth the trouble that he was serving readers by giving solid and perceptive descriptions. Insofar as the controversial was concerned, he would leave the decisions to the kings and princes. (The church responded, as noted earlier, by putting him on the Index of Prohibited Books.)

Actually, Gesner's main point was to save civilization from the consequences of losses like those of the Alexandrian and Corvinian libraries. He did not think printing solved the entire problem with its multiple copies at lower unit costs, because printed works often remained available only in their homelands and disappeared easily, and some books were plentiful in one place but rare in others. Besides, tastes and conceptions of importance changed: many items once much read were now forgotten. He hoped his contribution would be recognized as a guide to the materials covered and as a model catalog by which to develop libraries public and private. It immediately was, by the banker-bibliophile Fugger family, who invited him to their headquarters; but Protestant Gesner was uneasy about Catholic Augsburg and went to Heidelberg instead.

The coverage of the *Bibliotheca Universalis* was thoughtfully designed. Vernacular publications were excluded and anonymous works, those *bêtes noires* of both bibliographers and authorities, put off until a later volume. On the other hand, thanks no doubt to the modesty and appreciation of cooperation for which Gesner was famous, he was able to list even works projected but not yet written. Longer or shorter treatment was determined, apparently, not so much by a writer's rating as a scholar—ignored by the compiler—as by his position in the alphabet. While he began his toil presenting authors generously, taking full advantage of his omnivorous reading and evaluating, that could not go on: L to Z received one-third the space given A to K. Gesner apologized, citing printer pressure, fatigue, and tedium. Apart from that, he tended to scant the medieval writings, perhaps because he was a non-French Humanist.

Although, like his predecessors and most of his contemporaries, Gesner entered authors under their Christian names, he differed in adding their birth and death dates. The data were gathered largely from his huge correspondence, so carefully that his work remains creditable as a biographical dictionary, even though he failed to update some of what he copied (with acknowledgment) from Tritheim about "the living."

Clearly a step ahead was the "index" at the end of the *Bibliotheca Universalis,* where authors' names were listed "inverted," thus alphabetically by (Latin) surname; because, acknowledged the headnote, many were thought to know the surnames but not the forenames.

Gesner's titles, moreover, were established so meticulously that they were more reliable than those in any other source antedating him. When he was able, he added the publication year, the place of publication, and the printer's name. Of course, for reasons already indicated, that was not always possible; his results are not altogether consistent. He made the effort because he appreciated the difference in quality among various printers, the advances in their art which made dates important, and the usefulness of place of publication data to a prospective buyer, who might expect to obtain the item if not from the printer himself at least in the nearest library. Yet he did not transcribe the title page, imprint included, with the deliberation displayed first in the Frankfort Fair catalogs.

Gesner did report when he could the number of sheets, a step short of pages. Contents were indicated variously: abstracts of short items, chapter headings from long ones, and individual part titles along with collected works.

Subject Access; Gesner's "Pandects" Furnishing thus the descriptive data traditionally entered in library catalogs ever since, albeit with some important changes, was not enough for the Zürich natural scientist, physician, and classical linguist. He was a Humanist in the age when Humanism's particular energies and skills were no longer needed by such distinctive groups as physicians and lawyers; the Humanists were already moving steadily into isolated and low-appeal specialization. Among the earlier known subject-bibliographical attempts were one in law in 1522 by an Italian in Latin, and an elaborately classified *Catalogus* of works on rural life appended to a 1577 Latin treatise on that subject by a German; the 1559 "Summary" of the books published by Aldus Manutius for the Academy of Venice was subject-arranged. A good many more were soon to come. How well these items were used remains unclear. Perhaps more successful was the device of incorporating catchword, sometimes even subject heading, guidance in a scholarly edition of a classic writer, as Erasmus did for Augustine.

Whatever Gesner may have known of such developments or thought about them, however devoted he himself was—manifestly—to the bibliography of particular branches of natural science, he also maintained possibly the broadest view of his generation. He was eager to make the essential substance of all branches of knowledge easily available. Many familiar models were in view, encyclopedias, books of source readings organized by topic, and schemes of classification. His professor of Hebrew, Conrad Pellican (1478–1556), had crystallized some of these influences in a four-part catalog plan unveiled in 1532:

1   Authors, alphabetized by first letter precisely but thereafter "freely"
2   A location list-inventory utilizing for location the ordinary succession of simple numbers, together with the authors' names and brief titles but no publication dates
3   Subjects arrayed systematically under twenty-one main heads
4   Alphabetical arrangement of titles by *Schlagwort* (that is, more or less, the most striking term in the title)

Gesner's *Bibliotheca Universalis* surpassed Pellican's part 1, not just in coverage but in furnishing guidance. His execution of part 3, in a mere three years, was likewise an event.

With the 1548 *Pandects* ("all embracing"—748 folio pages), Gesner undertook to organize by subject the information in the writings listed in the *Bibliotheca Universalis.* The contents of the new volume were arranged in nineteen classes, each divided into *tituli,* subdivided into *partes,* and finally broken into *segmenta.* Ordered thus were approximately 30,000 topic entries averaging 120 per *titulus.* The authors drawn on are usually named, but not particular works; for titles one must consult the earlier volume.

Most of the classes were traditional: the seven liberal arts, established university faculty areas such as Jurisprudence, and other subjects venerable (like Mechanical Arts) but not necessarily respectable (like Magic). Late medieval church-versus-state literature and Renaissance political science were recognized in the State and Politics category; humanism, in the Poetry and

History classes separate from Grammar and Rhetoric. That he did not treat Philology likewise, independent of Grammar, evoked sharp criticism; since the two were by no means so distinct then as they became a century or so afterwards, the objections may have been parochial. The complete scheme of twenty-one classes of course included Medicine and Theology. Physician Gesner was perhaps never satisfied with his drafts of the former or amenable to letting someone else do it for him; it never appeared. Theology, by far the largest part of his guide project, was issued later.

On the plus side for bibliography and libraries, in addition to the classification, are two groups of the data presented in the *Pandects*. Book I, Grammar, in *Titulus* XIII, part VII, entitled "On Libraries" lists libraries old and new and treats of author bibliography. Far more important, each class in the work is introduced with a dedication to a Swiss, German, French, or Italian printer, with either a summary of his leading publication or a list of his wares. Advertised thus at the head of the volume, Class I, is Gesner's own publisher, Froschauer: only his output then in stock, to be sure, since the entire list would have been too long. In a word, this was a trade bibliography, most welcome to enterprisers headquartered at the Frankfort Fair but not yet equipped with a means of disseminating news of the latest books. Georg Willer's fair catalogs were then fifteen years off (1564).

On the minus side is Gesner's rather crude venture into shelf arrangement and catalog construction, laid out in Book I, in Titulus XIII, part II, "On Access to Books." Whatever it may owe to part 2 of Pellican's plan, it was no better. The more books to be accommodated in his fixed-location system, the more complex became the web of expedients to control them: none was an advance beyond the techniques of the Middle Ages. Gesner troubled to explain step by step how to make book indexes, but his fascination with the contents of a book collection does not seem to have been matched by any notable talent for shelf classification.

His achievement in bibliographical access may be marked both plus and minus. The *Pandects* rarely mentioned a specific title, and one had to repair to the *Bibliotheca Universalis* to identify a desired work; besides, its arrangement was classified, like the medieval encyclopedias and concordances. Gesner had originally intended, apparently, to alleviate the latter burden with a volume rearranging the *Pandects* topical entries alphabetically. That would have been a significant broadening of the established dictionary tradition. But he never found time for it.

Instead, when the *Pandects* was printed, the preface among other things rationalized the change of plan with the comment that anyone who wanted material on subject X would surely know how to find it in the systematic arrangement. That notion was to be acted on often in the centuries to come, in Europe's scholarly libraries, and occasionally in those of the United States. The comeback in the later nineteenth century of the alphabetical subject approach was to seem to many one of the peculiar products of those unsophisticated Americans. In point of fact, the classified arrangement without an alphabetical key did not find ready acceptance even in Gesner's day. Part 4 of Pellican's scheme provided an array of titles alphabetized by key word and reportedly included other key words not actually in titles in the collection but expected to turn up, in effect, advance subject headings.

Nor could Gesner, busy as he was, altogether sidestep the responsibility of providing better access to the *Pandects.* A year after issuing the nineteen-class compendium without the projected medical and theological sections, he produced the latter as a separate 340-page folio volume. Appended to it was an alphabetical list of about 4,000 key words supported by references to numbered pages and columns not just in Theology but throughout the preceding offering, the *Pandects.* This was not, indeed, his whole classified encyclopedia reordered alphabetically, but it may have helped.

Rivalry from Brevity The awkwardness of using Gesner's ponderous tomes, and perhaps the price, soon stimulated the preparation of abridgments. Gesner himself was already absorbed in his zoology book, and very shortly would be engaged on bibliographies in botany and medicine. Partly for that reason the first short version of his universal bibliography was produced (1551), without his knowledge, by his mentor Pellican's nephew, philologist Conrad Wolffhart ("Lycosthenes," 1518–1561). The new tool abbreviated the biographies, and omitted places and dates of publication and the evaluative annotations; it also had quite a few errors. But the compiler claimed to have added many new names, his 1,100 pages in small quarto were more easily handled than Gesner's folios, and the price was considerably lower than that of the *Bibliotheca Universalis.*

Gesner's own publisher, Froschauer, promptly pressed him for counteraction. By 1555 an *Appendix Bibliothecae* of 210 folio pages was ready, updating the original, for the first and last time, with 2,000 additional names old and new. The work apparently enjoyed substantial assistance from Gesner's young associate Josias Simler (1530–1576), who in the same year turned out the desired shortcut, an *Epitome* of 184 four-column double pages (368 physical pages) of reduction in the Wolffhart editorial style. Medieval scholar Albertus Magnus received one column instead of the three pages in the *Bibliotheca Universalis;* Aristotle, two and a half columns instead of thirty-seven pages. A statement on the title page says that the publication will not be "necessary" for public and private libraries but that it will be "most helpful" to those engaged in independent study. Both the *Appendix* and the *Epitome* were outfitted, like the *Bibliotheca Universalis,* with alphabetical indexes of the listed authors' surnames (1966 reprints by Zeller of Osnabrück).

Thanks largely to data from the fair catalogs, the 1574 edition of the *Epitome* was larger; and the 1583 version by J. J. Fries (1547–1611), presenting 9,000 names in 834 pages, was three times the size of Gesner's main volume and almost twice as large as that and the 1555 *Appendix* together. The added matter included both new vernacular titles, listed in Latin translation (!) and certain old titles missed by Gesner but since found available. Authors' names continued to be Latinized, viz., Meistersinger Hans "Sachsius."

Simler stated in the foreword to the 1574 *Epitome* that the fair catalogs were soon—at the latest, next year—to be equipped with a Fries-designed subject grouping of authors, akin to that of Gesner's *Pandects.* The same forecast reappeared (by accident?) in the 1583 edition handled by Fries himself. But no such subject guide to books in print materialized, perhaps because Froschauer's successor Christoffel did not think it would pay. Meanwhile, the Willer fair catalogs issued each fall and spring (1568–1618), organized first by language, were already listing Latin and German publications in university faculty-related subject groups, although the considerably fewer items in the Romance tongues were presented jointly, without distinction by either language or subject.

Innovation: Trefler, Fries, and Spach   The flood of printed matter was rendering impractical the familiar rough instruments of subject approach. Where subject lists had been detailed primarily in classifications of knowledge, rather than in book arrangement schemes, the relationship between subjects and physical books began to enter expressed thinking in the later sixteenth century. If bibliographer Gesner moved halfheartedly, not developing any intimate connection between his vast author-title guide and his encyclopedia of subject information, two men directly concerned with libraries essayed specific steps in that direction.

His predecessor Pellican, as mentioned before, provided subject groupings in a systematic catalog, and an independent alphabetical approach via key words in titles. Florian Trefler, a contemporary German Benedictine, published in 1560 a treatise on library management urging among other things that every library have a classified subject index to the contents of all its books and an alphabetical index thereto. That was in principle no advance beyond Gesner. But Trefler, decidedly ahead of Gesner on this point, recommended that a broad subject (letter) symbol be one of the three assigned to each book for shelf control. The other two letters were to record respectively the size and color of the volume. Trefler, it seems, had thus broken away from fixed-location shelving to flexible shelving, and since only three sizes and three colors were mentioned in his remarks, as against seventeen subjects, it was flexible shelving primarily by subject. Fries likewise combined subject classification and relative location, in a Zürich church library in 1587.

Closer to the general level of late-sixteenth-century practice was the contribution of Israel Spach, a Strasbourg physician and professor. In each of two specialized bibliographies, published in the 1590s, entries were arranged under a large number of subject headings and subdivisions—a refined subject classification. This apparatus was not, like Gesner's in the *Pandects,* for information, but specific titles. And it was reportedly a considerably closer classification than Trefler's sixteen categories for books or Gesner's twenty-one or Fries' twenty-three. Equally important, Spach's product had in each instance two alphabetical indexes, one for the subject headings and the other for the listed authors' Christian names.

It is interesting to note on the other hand that neither Trefler nor Spach, for all their zeal, made any claim to have covered everything that might, objectively considered, be relevant. Trefler urged that the (five) catalogs exclude any work superseded by a better more recent one, and (says scholarship) would probably have barred any item antagonistic to the theories or other interests of the Roman Catholic Church. Spach announces flatly in his later (1598) publication that he has certainly not included "'frivolous works

. . . without the names of authors or publishers'" or the "'almost infinite number of writings for the vulgar'" or the "'notorious booklets that fly about by night and avoid the light of day'" (quoted p. 65 of Archer Taylor's *Subject Indexes since 1548,* University of Pennsylvania Press, 1966). It is possible that a large portion of the indicated material was ignored by Gesner too, because it was in a vernacular; but surely not all of it. In any case, to a twentieth-century ear, the Gesner accents sound much more attractive than Spach's.

Library Responses to Social Change

The massive forces thus affecting book selection and bibliography also bore upon library life in general.

Spain To begin with the extreme of Catholic stability, fifteenth-century Spain saw the unification (1479) of Aragon and Castile, the organization of substantial dominions in America, the expulsion of the Jews (1492) and Moors (1502) who declined to become Christians, and much destruction of books. Not long after Ferdinand and Isabella were succeeded (1516) by Charles I (Emperor Charles V), Humanist impulses became manifest. Just a year later Cardinal Ximenes invited Erasmus to Spain (he declined), but Erasmian influences were prominent enough to worry the conservatives. They appear to have won the support they needed in a society top heavy with nonproductive nobles, knights, hidalgos, and ecclesiastics; a society in which royal power was suffocating both the merchants and local government. The magnificent art and literature of the "Golden Century" concealed widespread decay.

So far as Christian Spain is concerned, library history may be said to begin with the addition in 1480 of the University of Valladolid Library to ancient Salamanca's. During the sixteenth century progress consisted of the establishment of three more university libraries, and (about 1575, under Philip II) the royal collection in the new group of buildings called the Escorial. The latter may represent acceptance of one of the suggestions from Humanist scholar and official chronicler Juan Paez de Castro (1514?–1570), who had earlier but vainly urged Charles I to found a royal library. Another good idea from the same source, to locate said library at the true intellectual center, the University of Valladolid, was evidently rejected.

Possibly typical of dominant thinking and behavior was Juan Bautista Cardona, bibliographer and antiquarian, inquisitor and bishop. A zealot at expurgation from books of the names of "heretics," he wrote in Rome (1576) in his sixties a Latin treatise on the subject. (It will be recalled that contemporary Catholic educators doing battle in southern Germany were confident that books published in Spain were acceptable.) During that sojourn at the capital of Catholicism, devoted largely to scholarly editorial services to the pope, Cardona's mind was apparently drawn also to library questions. For upon returning he soon (1586) dedicated to the king a memoir on "the right way to establish the Escorial library" which may have owed to two Italians (see below) some inspiration, even style, but certainly not practical guidance.

Prepared in both Spanish and Latin, it may have had some influence at the library in question; in any case it presumably helped preserve the Italians' memory until the German scholar Mader in the mid-seventeenth century edited the whole corpus as one volume.

Spanish America   Spanish America was meanwhile yielding silver and other treasure and absorbing the energies of numerous Spaniards. The earliest "library" seems to have been established by Augustinians in Mexico, in 1537, for their own purposes. A more important one arose in Lima, Peru, at the University of San Marcos, organized in the 1550s by the Dominicans. The major influence in both cases was Spain's Salamanca, and the prime responsibility missionary labor. When the Jesuits arrived, first in Mexico in 1572, their options were limited: they concentrated on schools for young Spaniards of both the first and second ("Creole") generations. Although the Society's "Constitutions" were by then well developed and the half-clerical half-janitorial "librarian" characteristic of the epoch was alluded to, the soon numerous *colegios* in New Spain apparently furnished book service mainly without any such staff.

Italy   The Renaissance was in Italy a period of great politico-military turmoil, especially in the cities of the center and north, despite which many private libraries of distinction were founded and maintained. Furthermore, action was required to reinvigorate the Vatican Library, languishing ever since the popes had been exiled to Avignon and assembled a fine library there. The "Roman" pontiff returned to Rome in 1376; but none of the books of the Avignonese establishment came back with him, partly because for another forty years—the "Great Schism"—there continued to be a pope at Avignon, a rival, elected by the French cardinals. In some respects therefore the interested popes at the Vatican were starting afresh.

   Nicholas V (1447–1455), versed in library matters, laid sound foundations which survived the indifference of would-be crusader Calixtus III (1455–1458). Under Sixtus IV (1471–1484) the collections became world-famous, triple their size under Nicholas V; the staff, including a bookbinder and specialists in Greek, Latin, and Hebrew manuscripts, earned a high reputation for service; and by a bull of June 14, 1475, the library was authorized an annual allocation of funds. Invading imperial troops damaged it in 1527, but within a few years the popes took restorative action. (Raphael's 1517–1518 portrait of the art patron Medici, Pope Leo X and Cardinal Julio, depicts the pope's hand on an open book, evidently an illuminated manuscript; in plain sight also is a reading-glass.)

   The intellectual struggles accompanying the sixteenth-century wars of religion induced the Roman church leadership to adopt a strong policy of support to scholarship, as well as an Inquisition and an Index of Prohibited Books. The printed book, condemned by fifteenth-century Florentine bookseller Bisticchi and some equally famous book collectors, was soon welcomed nonetheless in the Vatican Library. The demand curve for shelf space turned up faster. Under Pope Gregory XIII (1572–1585) the holdings were made more accessible: Montaigne reported that in 1580 and 1581 the library was open almost daily. By the years 1585 to 1590, the papacy of Sixtus V, the pressure had reached the point where a new building (1588) was considered the solution. Some of the materials for it were obtained by despoiling an ancient Roman edifice, to the expressed but ineffectual dismay of certain contemporaries. On the other hand, Sixtus set up along with the new library quarters a printing office whose purpose was to expedite the printing of the Vulgate Bible and several other items of significance.

As already indicated, moreover, at least two tracts on libraries were penned in Latin by Italian clerical scholars at some time prior to the departure from Rome of Spanish Bishop Cardona. One, by antiquarian and librarian Fulvio Orsini, apparently impressed many later writers by quoting classic tributes to famous libraries. The other, by Panvinio, an epigrapher who served a short time on the Vatican Library staff, was a brief history of its collections and leadership. Both documents look back, Orsini's in the Humanist spirit, Panvinio's on behalf of the church. Neither appears to offer any data on planning or operating a library (printed versions are in J. J. Mader's *De Bibliothecis . . .,* Helmstadt, Müller, 1666). No more than Spain, it seems, was Italy then capable of producing anything directly practical even as limited as what Trefler contributed in Germany and Pellican in Switzerland.

The Libraries of Germanica before Luther   Indeed, the fortunes of libraries north of the Pyrenees and the Alps were affected by a greater diversity of forces than those operative in Spain and Italy. The oldest existing libraries, at monastic foundations, were given another—short—lease on life by the conjunction of Humanism and church reform discussions. Not surprisingly, this occurred primarily in the Swiss-South German region around Constance and Basel, the seats of the stock-taking church councils of 1414 to 1418 and 1431. Tegernsee Abbey, outstanding in this regard, reported a book collection increase from 1,100 in 1484 to more than 1,800 in 1524—in a class, for the moment, with the Vatican Library. The future, however, lay with other forms of library service.

The latter part of the fourteenth century had already seen the rise of universities with libraries at or near power centers all the way from southwest Germany's Heidelberg (1356) to Bohemia's Prague (1361) and the Cracow (1364) of Poland's King Casimir the Great. Humanism brought many more to Switzerland and southern Germany in the late fifteenth and sixteenth centuries; those further east and north were fewer and more scattered. More than one absorbed by bequest the books initially in the castle library of a Humanistic prince of church or state. Humanist Conrad Celtes, lately expelled from Leipzig University, was appointed (about 1500) by Holy Roman Emperor Maximilian librarian of the University of Vienna and professor of poetry.

Meanwhile, many trading or ecclesiastical centers in South Germany— Nürnberg, reportedly, as early as 1370—developed in the fifteenth century a "council" library for the ready reference of the city fathers, built around books owned originally by churches and Latin-schools. Gradually such books were utilized by broader circles, professional men especially; some evolved into a "city library." In evidence also is the phenomenon already noticed in Italy: the presentation, in Germany by a burgher, of books to a church or city council with the stipulation "for the common use." Roughly in parallel was the appearance in several coastal and Hanse towns of North Germany of church or school libraries serving presumably the merchant element.

Interacting Social and Cultural Conflicts in Germanica   Yet, even before the Lutheran reform was officially initiated in 1517, both Humanism and practical bourgeois education presented problems as well as advantages. In the towns of the Rhine Valley and the coasts the commercially oriented "arithmetic" schools already rivalled the "Latin" lower schools of the church. As the attacks on Scholasticism by the Humanists and the early Reformers mounted in the late fifteenth century, as trade and manufactures rapidly broadened, the new style training promised more market appeal than the old. The established university faculties were divided into factions holding diverse views about Scholasticism and Humanist critiques. And Catholic instruction at every level was affected adversely by the change of attitude toward gifts and bequests, a symptom of basic social change. Reform attacked reliance, for mediation with God, upon a huge corporation requiring taxes and contributions of all sorts, a chartered monopoly whose unique commodity was the salvation of souls. It accented instead individual responsibility, and those most eager for religious reform were often determined individualists in acquiring wealth as well as in communing with their Maker; such persons no longer gave generously to the church.

When these forces broke their bonds in open revolt, the very substantial educational apparatus of northwest Germany and the Low Countries was weakened rapidly. Catholic premises were often harassed, teaching staffs driven off; voluntary exodus contributed; all this well before the Reformers had personnel or plans ready to replace what was rejected. The Humanists did not fill the breach because they shared with the Lutherans only opposition to university Scholasticism: they mocked Scholasticism for studying the wrong materials in the wrong ways, but feared that popular preaching and the antilearning moods stirred up by Luther's polemics would wreck culture itself. For his part, Luther saw the universities as the heavy artillery of the Roman church, and the Humanists as too friendly to them. University enrollment declined sharply even at his own Wittenberg in the period roughly from 1515 to 1530.

Aggravating the distress was the confluence in the early sixteenth century of two other powerful streams more influential in Germany than elsewhere at that time. Mysticism, often including the idea of direct communion with God—bypassing the church, had long played an important role among European Christians and Jews. On the Christian side it drew sustenance from some of the writings of St. Augustine, then from Bernard of Clairvaux in the twelfth century, and Francis of Assisi at the turn of the thirteenth, latterly from Germany's own Meister Johannes Eckhart (1260?–1327) and Henry Suso (1300–1366). Certain mystic notions fitted well into the framework of church orthodoxy; but others did not. Repeatedly, antisacramental or antipapal or even antichurch sects appeared, and heresy spread, frequently embracing demands for social or political change. The result was usually brutal suppression.

Exceptional militancy emerged once more, especially among the town lower orders and unlettered peasants, in the 1520s: the Anabaptist revolt. The mystical and social extremism of the left wing of Protestantism coincided in action with a phase of the peasant wars then rocking portions of Germany. Whatever else was in the minds of the Anabaptists, or rebellious peasants and petty nobles, they generally identified existing monastery and church libraries with their ecclesiastical and secular oppressors. Nor were they calmed by Luther's injunction to obey their princes. Many were mystics who respected little but the Bible as reading matter. Many others could not read. Abbey libraries suffered badly.

Similar losses ensued for many generations thereafter, all over Europe, the combination of factors usually including class and religious conflict and frequently national liberation as well. The subject is greatly in need of systematic study.

German Struggles over Books and Libraries Under these turbulent circumstances, in which the Catholic-Lutheran conflict was central, Catholic book collections in monasteries, churches, and schools were widely damaged, even ruined. By the mid-1520s the consequences moved Luther and his associates to take constructive steps. Thus was fashioned the above-mentioned appeal to the city councillors. Where a guide like fine organizer Johann Bugenhagen was in charge, as in Hamburg, Lübeck, and Pomerania, the enabling ordinances (1529, 1531, 1535) and subsequent action focused on improving what the Catholics had developed. Some Catholic holdings helped form Lutheran university libraries. Probably more of them enriched the city libraries; many localities in central and northern Germany were thereby equipped in the sixteenth century as the southern cities had been in the fifteenth.

The Catholic forces were not idle. They had been trying to defend the faith as they understood it for centuries. Both argument and burning had been applied to dissenters and heretics and their writings. The Jews too were harassed on and off: Catholic Hebraist Johannes Reuchlin (1455-1522) gave much energy to sabotaging the imperial edict of 1509 which condemned Hebrew writings and was widely carried out. As the Reformation gathered strength, the archbishops in the heart of printing country tried to establish control of the book trade. The Cologne *Hochschule* had been an official censor since the mid-fourteenth century. Even more powerful potentially, as archchancellor of the empire, was the Archbishop of Mainz. In 1486 he attempted to halt the flow of vernacular translations of the Bible, and a papal bull of 1496 declared that no book should be printed without his approval, on pain of excommunication. The next half-century was marked by constant struggle between the church and imperial censors on the one hand; and on the other, the bookdealers of Cologne, the participants in the Frankfort Fairs, and the Frankfort (on-the-Main) Town Council.

The center of the book trade was Frankfort, which until the Reformation was allowed to do its own censoring, although literary property in the other free cities of the empire fell under imperial authority. By 1530 the wide circulation of polemics led the Imperial Diet to issue new control decrees: the imperial supervisor of literature and superintendent of printing, at

Strasbourg since the first appointment in 1455, became a commission. The Society of Jesus, established in 1534, soon made its influence felt in these very quarters, and by 1555 the Frankfort Protestants were explicitly opposing the Jesuit pressure. When Georg Willer began in 1564 to issue his landmark series of fair catalogs of books actually in stock, place of publication and name of publisher were very often lacking: such was the impact of censorship on the one hand and competition on the other.

The struggle reached a peak in 1567: the town lagged in suppressing certain allegedly libelous brochures, and when pressed by the Imperial Book Commission asked for its help. The emperor sent a court clerk to organize a local censorship body, soon independent of the town council. The latter meanwhile dragged its feet about inspecting dealers' stocks at the fair and collecting the *Pflichtexemplare,* the copies supposed to be deposited when permission was sought to publish. That was not just a censorship device but also furnished some protection against pirating of literary property. In 1579 the Imperial Book Commission itself moved into Frankfort and promptly strengthened both the censoring and the deposit and antipiracy machinery. Finding the latter advantage insufficient to outweigh the censorship and costs, many publishers moved north to the more moderately controlled (since 1553) Leipzig Fair in Lutheran Saxony. Thus began a rivalry of nearly a century and a half.

France France reached the level of enacting legal deposit several years earlier than the Holy Roman Empire, partly because it was far ahead of Germany in national development. The wars and bargains of the fifteenth century gradually filled out what became known as France. One by-product was the seizure of the books of the kings of Aragon by the troops of Charles VIII, at Naples in 1495. More important was the direct exposure to the Italian Renaissance, which in the sixteenth century paid back some of its debt to France. Louis XII (1498–1515) set precedent by treating the Royal Library as an institution of permanence, legitimately accessible to scholars rather than just the royal household. Francis I (1515-1547), frequently absorbed in fighting and politicking abroad, remembered to keep his Venetian ambassador buying manuscripts.

Francis also set another precedent by establishing legal deposit, on December 28, 1537. That is, the royal "library guardian" was supposed to receive, before it was placed on sale, a copy of every title to be released in France. The first reason given was to make sure that everything "worth being seen," past and future, original or modified, remained available even if it was forgotten. In the case of a book imported from abroad the copy was to be submitted to the Royal Council and judges, to see whether it was "tolerable," for one had to guard against foreign "wicked works and errors" (meaning Protestant writings). (The documents are quoted in *Bulletin des Bibliothèques de France,* 5:283-284; 1960.) The receiver of these deposit copies was at the palace at Blois, about 100 miles south of Paris, until in 1544 that collection was united with the royal library at Fontainebleau, less than 30 miles from the capital. He was never well posted on current publications, and legal deposit in France remained for a long time poorly enforced. Of course what did arrive built up the royal collections, although at the king's death in 1547 the approximately 3,000 volumes were mainly manuscripts, only 200 being printed books.

In 1530, moreover, Francis was persuaded by his venerable librarian, the great Humanist scholar Budé (1468-1540), to establish Royal Readerships in Greek and Latin, minus ecclesiastical strings; but university life did not change notably. The brand new Collège de France could not counteract quickly the dead weight of established institutions, and within a generation the torch of progress was already off the campus altogether, in the hands of the new literary-artistic academies and the pioneer scholars in a few abbeys. Nor is it likely that many church libraries differed substantially from the collection in Troyes Cathedral, which in 1500 comprised about 400 volumes, half liturgical and another fourth theological.

The Renaissance tone of the new academies seeped into society and letters at court by way of the numerous Italians flocking to Fontainebleau in the train of Catherine de' Medici, who left Florence in 1530 to marry Francis' son. Humanism found successively warmer receptions in the generations of social critics Rabelais (1494-1553) and Montaigne (1533-1592). Yet political-religious armed conflict obstructed a great deal, library advance apparently included. Besides, in sharp contrast with Germany and what was about to become The Netherlands, bourgeois development was not vigorous enough to produce municipal libraries of consequence. Only one such institution appeared, about 1530, founded under the patronage of the king at Lyons, active in textiles, prime publishing center north of the Alps, the intellectual capital of France, and at that juncture about to become the home base of satirical doctor François Rabelais.

English Life and Libraries in the Fifteenth Century Bourgeois development and her semidetached location contributed substantially to the shaping in this epoch of England's book and library life. The fifteenth century was marked by intermittent conflict with France and then the Wars of the Roses (1455-1485). At the turn of the century England was ruled by the new Tudors, the old aristocracy had virtually been wiped out, another one was developing, and the "liveried companies" of London, with the exclusive right to buy and sell commodities in that "corporation's" jurisdiction, were enjoying increasing influence. The next fifty years or so witnessed the growth of the partnership between the king and the leading merchants, a wave of chartered monopolies, and the domestication of the church under Henry VIII. By the last quarter of the sixteenth century, both commerce and culture had risen to the point where monopolies were being challenged with some success.

Literacy became more widespread. In 1400 schooling was well established at churches and under the roofs of the London merchant and craft guilds. Most books were in abbeys or churches or the church-influenced colleges. The early fifteenth century saw the flow of bequests away from the monasteries toward "chantry foundations," private posts whose incumbents said prayers for the family but usually had no parish duties and gave much time to elementary instruction in the neighborhood. The disappearance of serfdom and incorporation of municipalities tended to encourage that activity; late in the fifteenth and more in the sixteenth century it was supplemented by the rise of "Latin grammar" (secondary) schools sponsored by the country squires and better-off town craftsmen. These institutions were on the whole undisturbed or even enriched by the confiscations and conversions of the 1530s.

Taking these advances economic and educational into account, it is not surprising that a publisher was ready to try the English market fifteen years after Gutenberg opened the new era. William Caxton was a member of the Mercers Company and by that token may have dealt in such luxuries as manuscripts. Observing the course of trade from the strategic position of consul to the British trader "nation" at Bruges, Belgium, favored by the aristocratic friends he cultivated shrewdly both there and in England, Caxton found the 1470s ripe. He went to Cologne to learn printing, then (1476) to England to begin publishing. Making each move with a keen eye for political change, he served with his choice of books now the aristocrats, now the merchants; averse to large commitments he never published a Bible.

That the middle-class buyer tended to favor devotional and how-to-do-it books, the aristocrats "history" and light literature, is but one indication of the very uneven impact of Humanism upon England. Interest in ancient languages, in history and poetry, in personal expression, took root in greatly varying degrees. What arrived as an import and on the whole kept its character through domestication on the Continent, found less receptive soil in England and tended to rely heavily on foreign nourishment. Collector Poggio tried to find valuable classical manuscripts in Albion's abbeys in 1418, but failed. Several Englishmen of the next generation or two imbibed some Humanist spirit in Italy, to which they repaired for education because war denied them access to Paris. And when the return of the pope to Rome shifted the papal staff coloration from French to Italian, Vatican legations abroad often became centers generating new interest in polished Latin. But the university Latin tradition apparently gave English graduates the impression that Humanism was not really new; unlike Italy, no chairs were endowed for Humanists, and relevant manuscript collections were skimpy.

This was the atmosphere in which Humphrey, Duke of Gloucester, developed his book collection, largely traditional, but more varied than any English contemporary's, and favored with expert advice and procurement aid from Italian Humanists. Had the noble bibliophile been ready to pay such agents for searching service as well as for books delivered, it is reported, he might have assembled an even more distinguished library and staff. Although the bulk of it, bequeathed to Oxford, disappeared, at least two batches of manuscripts were actually deposited there during his lifetime (1439, 1444). Only the donor could take an item out of the library; but it may be supposed that some who taught or studied at the university were privileged to read on the premises books from "Duke Humphrey's Library."

Books and Libraries under the Tudors After the Wars of the Roses (1455–1485) a bourgeois tone became manifest in the concern for sound administration and trained cadres in public service, and national patriotism. The central establishment was equipped with personnel shaped in the new law schools, the "Inns of the Court," whose three library starts (1497, 1540, 1555) apparently outnumber those of any other sort during that period. The

English headquarters also boasted, like the French and imperial (Vienna) courts, Latin secretaries and a royal librarian. This was not fullblown Humanism. Efforts thus directed were made at new (1516-1517) Corpus Christi College at Oxford, outfitted with a library including classics ordered from renowned printer Aldus Manutius in Venice. And both Erasmus and Thomas More tried to promote Greek as a vital means of tracing the roots of Christianity for the common man. But the contemporary university student was increasingly of the lower gentry and middle strata and had no such interest. Nor was there then any mass conflict to challenge him like the contemporary continental struggles of Lutherans and Catholics. Career interests thus encouraged the maintenance of a Latin but not a Humanist curriculum: Corpus Christi College remained for many years unusual.

When Henry VIII moved in the latter 1530s to eliminate the authority and influence of the pope, more than 800 monastic houses were dissolved, and something like 6,000 books dispersed without control. As contemporary John Bale observed, there were despoilers who bought monasteries partly for their books, "'some to serve theyr jakes [toilets], some to scoure theyr candlestyckes, and some to rubbe their boots'" (quoted by William Roberts, *The Earlier History of English Bookselling,* London: Low et al., 1889; Gale reprint, 1967, p. 16). Libraries in undisturbed surroundings like churches also changed in certain respects, Catholic tomes exiting and newly approved Protestant titles entering. More purging was visited upon libraries under Edward VI and Mary, this time at Oxford and Cambridge. If the experience was bad for the college libraries, endowed, it was markedly worse for the university libraries, vulnerable for lack of endowment.

The tragedy of the "Great Dispersal" did not unfold without notice. Young John Leland had started school at St. Paul's, founded by celebrated Humanistic educator John Colet, and after finding Oxford too old-fashioned, had moved on to Paris to sit at the feet of leading classical scholar Budé. By about 1530 Leland had some connection with the English royal palace libraries, and may have handled for Henry VIII the books being taken from some monastic houses even before the official Acts of Suppression. Soon afterward he traveled all over England, from 1535 to 1543, making notes topographical and bibliographical. He acquired little of consequence for the king's book collections, but his ideas throw light on contemporary attitudes.

Leland was passionately nationalistic: his mission as he defined it was to salvage from the old repositories what he could find of English historical and biographical importance. He delighted to serve a house which had named its first son Arthur, Duke of Cornwall (1488-1502). One of his arguments for attention was that "Germans" (at least some were apparently Swiss) were at that very moment sending "scholars" to look for those same treasures, who "cutteth them out of libraries" (Leland's *Itinerary* . . ., ed. L. T. Smith, Carbondale: Southern Illinois University Press, 1965, I:xi). He was a Protestant of a practical turn of mind. Although the abuse of benefices (pastorates with real income but duties often nominal) was one of the sore points producing the Reformation, Leland accepted no less than four of them as support for his efforts in the last year (1533) the pope's authority was recognized in England. After finishing his travels, moreover, he was able to write to the king in 1546 that his objectives had been to advance the "publique

wealthe," publicize the king's generosity and his "most magnificent libraries," and fight popery; and at the same time state that he was modeling his
biographical dictionary after Jerome, Gennadius, Cassiodorus, and Tritheim—all faithful Catholics (Leland, pp. xxxviii-xxxix).

However familiar Leland's adaptability may have been, there were but a
few besides him who labored to save England's ancient manuscripts and
monuments. Conspicuous was John Dee, widely respected mathematician-
astronomer who provided calculations for the abortive calendar reform of
1584. (England did not change until 1752.) In January 1555 and 1556 he
petitioned Queen Mary on behalf of the treasures in dispersal, spoke of the
opportunity to form a fine library at small cost, and as a veteran traveler (he
signed Conrad Gesner's "Book of Friends" in Zürich in 1563) offered to
procure for it copies of famous documents at the Vatican and other celebrated repositories. By 1568 Elizabeth's Privy Council expressed a like concern; and 1586 saw the chartering of the Society of Antiquaries. Meanwhile,
explorer Sir Humphrey Gilbert dreamed (about 1572?) of a "'Queen Elizabeth's Academy'" whose "'Keeper of the Liberarie'" was to look after the
binding, arrangement, and safety of the books, and choose additional titles
from those to be submitted by the book-importers; he was to have £40 a
year for those commitments and £26 salary, quite respectable. (The phrases
from Gilbert's papers are in W. Prideaux, "Library Economy in the Sixteenth
Century," *Library Association Record,* 11:161, 1909.) Contemporaneously,
moreover, there was a rebirth of vigor in university life, owing in part to the
rise of Puritanism.

Until that point, however, educated men as a whole, absorbed in state
affairs, apparently found no reason to encourage antiquarianism or libraries
of a public character. A gap opened between cultural pursuits and practical
schooling. Perhaps on this account among others, sixteenth-century England
produced no cumulating tradition of scholarly depth in Humanistic studies.
When Elizabeth's day brought a local Renaissance it was based on classical
literature in English, and most of the materials came by way of Italian and
French intermediaries. If Shakespeare had little Latin and less Greek it was
because neither he nor his generation needed any more to tap the classical
tradition.

As observed above, library advance required more than Humanism;
involvement was necessary in conflict of one sort or another. A struggle was
in fact germinating in the book trade, the stakes both thought control and
profits. Attempts to suppress dissident writings were of course no novelty. In
1410 Parliament had banned Wyclifite and other heretical materials; English
translations of the Bible were among the proscribed. Such precedents were
ready to hand when the English bishops began in 1521 to cooperate in the
papal and imperial onslaught against Lutheran works. It was a halfhearted
beginning, because the London merchants were at that moment needed by
the throne for loans. By 1524, however, the demand for cooperation was
more vigorous, partly because the bookdealers were known to have sympathy for the continental Reform and partly because statutes of 1523 had just
favored local business by pushing out the formerly welcome foreign printers. Yet the flow of disapproved books went on.

Meanwhile, the business-political side of the question had been underlined in a grant of monopoly privilege in publishing in 1517. Chartered monopolies, indeed, uniting the more powerful merchants and the king, were to become very familiar in Tudor and Stuart England. For the next twenty years, the ambiguous implication hung over the situation that royal privilege meant an acceptable book. But in 1538 a specific case was decided by Henry VIII in such a fashion as to end the uncertainty: the privilege was exclusively a printer's property right over the text produced; acceptability of the contents had to be determined separately before the work could be licensed to appear, normally by church officials. When the century-and-a-half-old, powerful printers' and booksellers' guild was chartered in 1557, by Queen Mary, as the Stationers' Company, it was authorized not merely to monopolize publishing but to seek out and apprehend for punishment those who engaged in pirating or other challenges. Twenty years later Elizabeth I was granting monopolies to others for special types of books like Bibles; the Company leaders complained, to no avail. On their second try they won some concessions; but non-Company operators continued in business, and renascent Cambridge (1581) and Oxford (1585) successfully fought the Stationers' Company for autonomy in these matters. In 1585 Elizabeth's Court of Star Chamber was empowered to police the restrictions on printers and presses in both the university towns and London. By 1600 the Company "monopoly" had been greatly reduced.

New Roles for Books and Libraries   Thus, in a period of somewhat less than two centuries of Western life, the reproduction and distribution of recorded thought had been detached completely from composition. In England, corporate secular organization had become decisive in publishing while corporate ecclesiastical organization was giving way to the secular in publishing and the individual in writing. The medieval guild, a form modified out of Roman predecessors, had gradually become modified further into the chartered monopoly which merged the interests of powerful merchants and ambitious kings. This private organization performed the public functions of censoring writing and policing printer and bookdealer behavior. In "the Germanies" there was no comparably dominant axis; those duties were carried out directly by church or civic officials, not the guildsmen. The book remained an instrument of Scholastic or Humanist, Catholic or Protestant, sovereign or rebel; but it had become just as much in some localities and even more in others, a commodity, a source of profit.

In such an atmosphere, shaped by fortune building and thought control, registration copies of books were not as a rule given to a library. The known exceptions emphasize the point. Legal deposit in France brought a copy of each book to the Royal Library, bearing witness to the relative weakness of the merchant class, the power of the king, and the appeal of the Renaissance literary and social impulses sweeping in from Italy, late waves of a phenomenon past peak. Similarly, although the celebrated ducal Library of Burgundy, in Antwerp, was granted in 1594 the right to legal deposit copies of all books published in the Spanish Netherlands (present Belgium), one by-product of the Dutch wars of liberation was the closing of the mouth of the Scheldt, finishing Antwerp as a seaport: by the mid-seventeenth century the

Library of Burgundy, despite its apparent advantage, would be going downhill for good.

The library was not an institution by nature profitable. Like other kindred enterprises its character and role in society had to be rethought in several respects before it could be fitted properly into the emerging epoch of capitalism. The Reformation and Counter-Reformation indicated how important it would be in mass education. The founding of four leading libraries under public auspices, during the struggle for the independence of the Seven United Provinces ("Holland") in the last quarter of the sixteenth century, testifies to the possibilities of nationalism as a favorable factor. Above all would the bourgeois, especially Protestant bourgeois, concerned with usefulness and productivity, on the one hand lead the scientists and many philosophers to bypass libraries, and on the other urge upon the libraries a better handling of the rising tide of printed matter and potential readers.

Chapter Five

THE SEVENTEENTH CENTURY

As the sixteenth century came to a close, different patterns were in evidence in European life. Some would have changed a good deal by 1700, others very little even beyond that point. In most of Europe life was punctuated by wars, several of which were much larger scale than earlier conflicts: mercenaries played an increasingly prominent part, and their employers had to find more money to pay the mounting bills. Conspicuous accordingly was on the one hand the transformation of public finance from individual bankers' loans into a state operation complete with tax-"farmers" and a mushrooming bureaucracy. Thus crystallized new social types, bourgeois and would-be aristocrats, bound more or less to the throne and its inevitable pressure toward centralization. On the other hand, the desperate urge to stretch ducats, livres, florins, etc., put on the spot of royal notice those elements of society, mainly the landowning nobility, which in most of Europe were so far tax-exempt and as a rule preferred to remain so.

With the financial exposé went frequently a moral drive for less luxury, more austerity. In England the puritans were often Puritans, in the Netherlands Reformers; but in France they were more likely Catholic and in Spain exclusively so. The issue was not at bottom religious but political: which class would hold enough state power to make and enforce tax decisions? At the end of the century the great landlords were for the moment secure, with more serfs than ever, in all Europe except the northwest sector, England and the Netherlands. The mid-century revolts produced considerable change in England and finished what had begun earlier in the Netherlands by way of independence from Spain, but disturbed little elsewhere: royal absolutism predominated. Libraries not ruined by hostilities were primarily display items, largely ignored by the craftsmen and scientists shaping challenges that would sooner or later alter almost everything.

The outset of the century was marked by the rebirth of the noted "library" tradition at Oxford University associated with Duke Humphrey. That event and others following it reveal both the impact of contemporary conflicts and the continued momentum of certain library practices and thinking rooted in earlier circumstances.

Bodley and the Bodleian

Bodley and His Purposes The founder, Thomas Bodley, was born in 1545, the son of a Protestant active enough to be exiled during the reign of fervent Catholic Queen Mary. Thomas' early adolescence was spent among the large English congregations in southern Germany and (about 1557) Geneva, Switzerland. When Mary's death allowed the family's safe repatriation, Thomas was well grounded in Greek and Hebrew—as well as Latin—and became associated with Merton College, Oxford. In 1565 he lectured on Greek and in 1569 on "natural philosophy," that is, physical science, for which Merton was conspicuous. Seeking additional equipment, he then undertook continental travel, the first requisite being to obtain (1576)—through his college—from the Crown the required license; apparently a two-year passport, it was renewed in 1578. Bodley acquired Italian, French, and Spanish. He returned in 1580 and thanks to his connections became an official at Elizabeth's court. Running for Parliament in 1584, he was defeated for one seat but shortly found himself "representing" another electorate; in 1586 he "represented" a third locality. Meanwhile he married the rich widow of a Bristol merchant. In the 1590s he performed many important diplomatic missions abroad. Reappearing at court in 1597, he discovered himself on the wrong side of current factionalism, and withdrew, declining flattering new foreign service assignments.

Of the four prerequisites he laid down retrospectively (1609) for founding a library, Bodley now had not only (1) knowledge of ancient and modern languages and "sundry other sorts of scholastical literature" (*Life,* ed. Dana and Kent, 1906, p. 58), (2) "purse-ability," and (3) "Honourable Friends," but (4) time. As he explained in 1609, he had "resolved . . . to possess my soul in peace, all the Residue of my Days" (*Life,* p. 52). The best way, he thought, to do his "Duty towards God," to satisfy "the Expectation of the World," his own inclinations, and "very Morality," was to "set up my Staff at the Library-Door in Oxon" (Oxford). He was sure he could not "busy" himself to better purpose, than by "reducing that Place (. . . ruined and wast) to the publick use of Students" (*Life,* pp. 56–57).

On February 23, "1597/8" (Catholic Europe had reformed the calendar but England had not), Bodley offered to fit up the old quarters with shelves and seats, procure benefactions of books, and endow the library with an annual income. These proposals were promptly accepted by the university, and the restoration and expansion of "Duke Humphrey's Library" was initiated at once by varied means. Bodley's confidence in Thomas James, whom he had mentally marked as librarian some time before the post existed, may have been strengthened when in 1601 James gave the Bodleian a mass of manuscripts he had been permitted to remove from several college libraries at Oxford.

Beginning the Bodleian Collections   As for more systematic and respectable steps, Bodley, the erstwhile traveling scholar, engaged London bookseller John Bill (or Bille) to buy books on the Continent. "You need make no doubt," he assured librarian James on June 23, 1603, that Bill had been trying to do an effective job, "for his commission was large, his leisure very good, and his paiment sure at home" (*Letters . . . to Thomas James,* ed. G. W. Wheeler, Oxford: Clarendon Press, 1926—hereafter LBJ—p. 90). The only untoward note was sounded late in 1604—a time of chilly relations with France—when Bill is reported "utterly discouraged" by his reception at a French town because "usage towards all of our nation is so cruel and malicious" (Bodley to James, November 14, 1604, LBJ, p. 118). In addition, Bodley furnished James in 1602 with the sales catalogs from the Frankfort (on the Main) book fairs. He did not think the Oxford booksellers a promising source. In general, he emphasized to James in 1607, no book would be "lost" for want of buying—from Bodley's private pocket if necessary; if James did not tell him what the library needed, it would be his own fault.

Meanwhile the word went out for donations. On March 6, 1598, Sir Dudley Carleton, future diplomat, wrote from his country seat in Devonshire that Bodley's offer to the university had made a fine impression; that the former ambassador was "'daily expected at Oxford to make good his word,'" and that "'every man bethinks himself how by some good book or other he may be written down in the scroll of benefactors.'" Carleton added that his cousin wanted to be among the first, but was dissuaded by his wife on the ground that so strange an act "'would be ascribed to some planet which possessed all men with a sudden humour'"; yet, having heard that the previous contents of the library had been burned she wished the new collection "'longer endurance.'" (Quoted p. 16 of W. D. Macray's *Annals of the Bodleian Library . . .,* 2d ed., Oxford, 1890.)

The indicated skepticism is supported by the judgment—published in 1621—of the more celebrated contemporary, Robert Burton. Having discoursed richly on the contribution of study to "Exercise Rectified of . . . Mind," he noted "how barbarously and basely for the most part our ruder Gentry esteem of Libraries and Books . . . through error, ignorance, and want of education." He thought a solicitor for financial support to "College, Lecture, Library, or whatsoever else may tend to the Advancement of Learning" would surely be rebuffed by any of these hound-loving gourmandizers; for they were so irritated by such institutions that they wanted even the existing ones to be "utterly ruined, demolished, or otherwise employed." (*The Anatomy of Melancholy,* ed. Shilleto, London: Bell, 1903, II:100–106 passim, especially pp. 105–106.)

While realist Bodley cautioned that more talk was to be expected than action, he also acknowledged handsomely what did arrive. (In fact, setting up the register of gifts was one of the three evidences of progress he mentioned to the vice-chancellor in June 1600.) Among the more interesting donations were £50 from Sir Walter Raleigh in 1603, on the eve of that remarkable man's second jailing in the Tower of London, and in 1605 a copy of Francis Bacon's new *Advancement of Learning,* presented by the author with a salute to the "'ark'" Bodley had built to "'save learning from the deluge'" (quoted in Macray, *Annals,* p. 35). There was some hope of a gift of books from King James' library, but it never materialized.

Most striking of all, perhaps, were the volumes contributed by individuals on record as Roman Catholics and in some instances publicly known as such, despite the disadvantages then attaching to that commitment in England. If one considers in conjunction therewith the high probability that the Bodleian Library was established in part as a weapon in the struggle against Catholicism, it is evident that both the donors and the beneficiary were able to separate religious differences from their common interest in the library. Indeed, when Bodley undertook to chain many books (see below), he borrowed the necessary craftsman from the staff of a friend unequivocally Catholic, Ralph Sheldon.

Bodley's Humanism, the Renaissance, and the Bodleian   Bodley did not welcome every possible acquisition. His humanist tastes were refined and his convictions strong. Like Conrad Gesner and many others he plainly preferred materials in the classical tongues. The poor coverage of vernacular works other than German in the Frankfort Fair catalogs does not seem to have bothered him, any more than the decided discrimination against Catholic titles in that commercial product of a Protestant business center. The "Arts" or general (mainly undergraduate) section of the Bodleian 1605 catalog displays only thirty-six books in English, one the 1561 *Works* of Chaucer.

Although translations into English were an important feature of the English Renaissance, some scholars and aristocrats apparently thought that step appropriate only for the Bible and patristic writings, not for anything less weighty. In 1570 the distinguished Dr. Thomas Dee had introduced the first English version of Euclid's *Geometry* with the dry observation that the faculty and students at the renowned University of Padua somehow survived the translation of the classics into Italian. In 1603 John Florio prefaced his soon famous translation of the essays of Montaigne with a vigorous attack on resisters, ridiculing the thought that "conversion" (i.e., translation) of books should amount to "subversion" of the universities, that the "turning" (again, translating) of books should be the "overturning of Libraries." In the spirit of Montaigne himself he linked translation boldly with assault on class privilege: "Learning cannot be too common, and the commoner the better" (Modern Library ed., pp. xx-xxi).

That the founder had some acquaintance with Florio's effort is evident from his notes in the 1602 manuscript catalog of the library. But it is most unlikely that Bodley paid any attention to such arguments. He was personally a paladin of the read-it-in-the-original school. And contemporary translation was moving away from the classics toward light materials offensive to the previously friendly conservative Protestant humanists as a whole. Not one translation of even a Latin or Greek work appears in the 1620 catalog, although the 1610 English version of William Camden's *Britannia* surpassed the Latin original of 1607 in its important county maps, and Tacitus had been rendered into the home tongue by distinguished backer of the library Sir Henry Saville. There seems to have been just one lonely translation from French or Italian, and it was *not* Florio's Montaigne!

In general, the belletristic side of the Renaissance was little respected at the Bodleian. Lack of demand from university readers may have been a reason, and seems at the least to have been an excuse.

Theology was prime (half the collection in 1605 and 1612) and Protestant coloration dominant. Yet the Renaissance was visible in decoration, Bodley's individualism, and moderate attention to science. In the upper gallery was a frieze: after the neoclassical fashion lately set by the Escorial in Spain and to become familiar in libraries of the next century and a half, it memorialized 200 writers of many persuasions from classical antiquity right up to Bodley's own day. Among them were such pre-Reformation dissidents as Wyclif, Hus, and Savonarola; also such revolutionaries of science as astronomer Copernicus, physician Paracelsus, and cartographer Mercator.

The individualism emerged vigorously when librarian James hesitated to list two titles by the celebrated Scotch controversialist George Buchanan (died 1582), because they had been proscribed in Scotland by King James and were now (1603) banned in England at his accession to the English throne. Bodley balked. He would rather plead ignorance of the law and would if necessary argue that they had been bought legally, under Elizabeth. (One work promoted popular sovereignty against royal absolutism; the other was an anti-English-"lies" history of Scotland.)

The science holdings did not of course compare with the riches in theology. And the customary titles from arithmetic to astronomy and optics in the arts section betokened traditionalism. The images in the gallery, however, reflected the admiration of numerous Englishmen for the pathfinders of science and silently rebuked those largely excluding them from the laggard English universities. In 1603 Bodley asked James to be sure to obtain the last book by cosmographer Tycho Brahe. Brahe's data were shortly to facilitate Kepler's decisive blow for heliocentrism: Bodley may or may not have anticipated that, but he probably knew that a great many contemporaries, including George Buchanan, rejected Copernicus and stood by the geocentrism of Ptolemy. Besides, Brahe himself offered a short-lived compromise theory. At any rate, Bodley's request does at least argue the alertness of the erstwhile Merton science lecturer to scholarship produced abroad.

Possibly relevant here also is the fact that Bodley advised James to dedicate the 1605 catalog not to the king, who was thus acknowledged so often that he might not respond, but to Henry, Prince of Wales. That young man, friend of Puritanism and science, maintained a court rivaling his father's, frequented by live-wire scholars and scientists operating apart from the universities. Whether, like the university expert on ancient Greek mathematics, Sir Henry Savile, they displayed any interest in Bodley's library, is so far undetermined. The single pertinent fact, apparently, is the use of the Bodleian between November 1602 and November 1603 by Thomas Lyddiat (or Lydiat), a thirty-year-old cleric who left the faculty in

1603 to write—on his partrimony—and later became chronographer and cosmographer to the prince. Of course we shall never know what might have transpired had not the latter died in his early twenties in 1612, the year before the Reaper took Bodley at sixty-eight.

Image Problems; the Stationers Company Agreement The holdings assembled at the new library were in 1602 by no means "all of any worth"; Bodley reproached James for incautious remarks to library users implying the contrary (March 17, 1602, LBJ, p. 32). Indeed, he delayed opening the library until November 8 of that year because the number of books on hand before that date (almost as many more were in his house in London) was not in his eyes impressive enough. In 1604, although the collection had almost doubled, he complained of "the general conceat abroad and at home" that "nothing" was lacking in the Bodleian: expectations generated thereby were bound to leave some inquirers "greatly frustrat" (January 26, 1604, LBJ, p. 114). Repeatedly he called James' attention to the presence of titles not listed in the latter's catalogs. Reminding him of what could be overlooked, because several items were often bound together in medieval style and a catalog entry might be accorded only the first of them, he exhorted James in preparing the catalogs to work with the book in hand, not just the lists affixed to the ends of the respective bookcases. In 1607 he was still nervous about users becoming frustrated.

High-quality service was to be assured when plainly called for: in 1606, the scholars working on the King James version of the Bible being expected, Bodley warned librarian James to have ready for them a listing of the materials likely to be pertinent to their labors. Yet the law books were to be arranged for the library's advantage rather than the readers': "we are not to provide for every little inconvenience" (May 8, 1605, LBJ, p. 138). And when tales arrived about defects in the catalogs and the books, a stiff-necked Bodley rejected them, blaming those who "knewe so muche" but had heretofore been silent (to James, April 3, 1607, LBJ, pp. 165–166).

The grubby side of good service, familiar to all librarians before and since, was treated by the well-traveled knight in this wise. "The inconveniences of spitting," he responded to James early in 1603, could be "remedied" only by the "increase of his diligence, that is to cleanse the Librarie" (February 18, 1603, LBJ, p. 76). A few weeks later, Bodley declared that alertness on the part of the same functionary could prevent the development of mold in the books; but "the breeding of worms in your deskes we cannot prevent" (April 13, 1603, LBJ, p. 84).

No stranger to diplomatic maneuver, Bodley was meanwhile knighted by King James, in April 1604, and the library shortly afterward granted "letters patent" in his name. (That is, an open rather than sealed communication implementing one of the sovereign's powers; in this instance apparently a gesture of recognition.) The next year the king paid one of several visits to Oxford. Bodley tipped off his librarian in advance, but vetoed placing the sovereign's writings in an expensive binding; rather, he counseled, hide them or say they are at London being bound.

Well developed also were the gentleman scholar's sense of timing and capacity for restraint. At the outset he instructed James not to offer advice to inspecting university delegates unless asked; he would comment on their proceedings "in time convenient, and when neede is" (November 3, 1602, LBJ, pp. 59-60). A few years later, when librarian James published one of his numerous controversial religious works, Bodley read him a mild lecture: "For whatsoever is printed under your name, in regard to the office and place that you hold, will be thought to be the act of the whole Universitie" (December 31, 1607, LBJ, p. 173). Advising foreman James that there had been no need to pay for transporting sand, because the university had bought it and would doubtless have covered the delivery too, employer Bodley noted that he was not really obliged to respond to the billing but would do so this time.

By 1610 the library's image had survived Bodley's worries, and his own talents and connections had proven equally durable. Acting on a suggestion of James', he negotiated an agreement with the authorized publishers' guild, the Stationers Company. Signed on December 12, it brought to the Bodleian one perfect copy of every book printed by a member of the Company, and granted in return certain borrowing privileges from the library.

That the agreement carried prestige is beyond doubt. The books presented to the library did not, however, strike Bodley as altogether satisfactory. "Some" English books were among the many titles listed by James in January 1611 which were not worthwhile (Bodley to James, January 30, 1611, LBJ, p. 203). A year later he was declaring that James should not have cataloged "our London Bookes" without checking with him: "There are many idle bookes, & riffe raffes among them, which shall never come into the Librarie, & I feare me that little, which you have done alreadie, will raise a scandal upon it, when it shall be given out by suche as would disgrace it, that I have made up a number, with Almanackes, plaies, & proclamacions: of which I will have none, but suche as are singular" (January 1, 1612, LBJ, p. 219). In particular, "some plaies may be worthy the keeping; but hardly one in fortie"; English plays were inferior to foreign drama, because the latter were written by men of "wisdom and learning, which is seldome or never seen among us." He feared ill repute from talk that "we stuffe" the library with "baggage bookes" (January 15, 1612, LBJ, p. 222).

Bodley's attitude toward the stage—legally printed works, not to speak of the illegal—was matched by those of the playwrights toward libraries. Shakespeare, for example, referred to libraries in only two plays, one before the founding of the Bodleian (*Titus Andronicus*, IV:1:34, 1593-1594) and one after that event (*The Tempest*, I:2:109, 167, 1611); and the passages in question clearly allude in like language to private collections. The Bard apparently never mentioned the Bodleian, although numerous other contemporary phenomena, especially those well known to the public, find recognition in his works.

For all his objections, Bodley did agree that the Stationers Company contribution was "a gifte of great moment" (February 26, 1611, LBJ, p. 206). According to the 1620 catalog, issued seven years after Bodley's death, the number of volumes had by that year reached 16,000. Some of them may have been among those initially accepted and bound by James without entering them in the earlier catalogs, because Bodley disapproved of them.

Even now there were listed but two contemporary English plays; Shakespeare waited until the First Folio edition arrived from the Stationers Company in 1623. James was thus stretching the terms he used in the title of the 1620 catalog, which had not been in the 1605 document, *universalis* and *omnium* ("all"). Would Bodley have authorized that if he had still been on the scene?

Bodley's "Publick" The Bodleian Library was accessible to a very limited clientele. The sponsor's philosophy is plainly set forth in the "first draught" of the *Statutes* he worked up, from a list of topics in 1602, to the document officially adopted with amendments, from 1610 to 1613. (First printed in 1703, readily available in a 1906 reprint, part of *Literature of Libraries in the Seventeenth and Eighteenth Centuries*, edited by American librarians John Cotton Dana and Henry W. Kent, Chicago: McClurg; in turn reprinted by Scarecrow, 1967):

> Now because it is apparent, that Nothing makes more for the Ease of the Keeper, the Quietness of the Students, the Security of the books, and the Honour and Dignity of the University, than that we should proceed with some choice Limitation, in the Admission of such Persons, as are to study in the Library; we do utterly reject the Opinion of those, that would have no Exception to no Man's Access . . . (p. 93).

Certainly the serious are not to be inconvenienced by "gazing . . . babling, and trampling up and down." Admissible are "only Doctors and Licentiates" of the three graduate faculties (Theology, Law, and Medicine) and certain closely defined groups of bachelors (*Statutes*, p. 94), as long as they behave. The same applies to the sons of members of the House of Lords, "(for of the Lords themselves there may be no question)." Also eligible as a matter of gratitude are book donors "of all Degrees," but they too must for safety's sake swear "Fidelity to . . . the Publick Library of this University" (*Statutes*, pp. 95–96).

"Publick" thus meant essentially no more than that the Latin- or Greek-reading bachelors and doctors of a particular college, ordinarily allowed to use only that college's library, could draw upon the Bodleian, a service to the university as a whole. Undergraduates were still barred, during the very period when the educational emphasis at Oxford and Cambridge was shifting from the graduate students to them. In what almost seems a mid-twentieth-century manner, James proposed in 1609 that a special section of the library and a special selection of its books be organized for the benefit of the undergraduates of the Faculty of Arts, but Bodley flatly refused. (It was for them that James designed the subject catalog to the "Arts" he worked on after his resignation in 1620.) These young men—no longer the boys of the medieval college—were of course mainly from the families of gentlemen; neither farm nor urban working youth, nor young women of any sort, were yet in the picture. How clearly all that was understood afterward, by Gabriel Naudé and others who lauded the Bodleian's example, is not presently known and may never be.

Book Shelving and Access The collection was first housed in the refurbished "Duke Humphrey" quarters pursuant to Bodley's original proposals. Emulating the then quite up-to-date style at Hereford Cathedral, each bookcase consisted of three shelves of which the lowest was at the height of a seated reader's eye and hand, with a slightly sloping desk between reader and books. All those on the upper two shelves were chained to horizontal

Hasps opened to remove chain from rod: Hereford. (From B. H. Streeter, The Chained Library, *Macmillan, London, 1931, p. 59)*

rods along the fore edges of the shelves, the lowest group to a similar rod just below the shelf. The rods were maneuverable when the controlling hasps were unlocked. The bookcases in question ("presses") were fixed at right angles to the walls between the windows, and back to back benches for readers between each pair of presses took full advantage of window light. Whether it was deliberate or not in the original construction, the benches and reading surfaces thus ran north-south, normally an advantage. One end of each bookcase being against the wall, the other was free, on the center aisle, and a list of the books therein was affixed to it in a wooden frame. Thus, as one walked down the aisle between two lines of presses, one walked also between two parallel sets of shelf lists. (The twentieth-century stacks have posted of course only the terminal call numbers of a range, since locations are rarely fixed and the catalog is the prime guide.) This version of

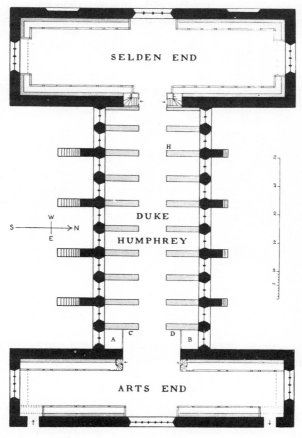

THE BODLEIAN

Plan of the Bodleian Library. (From B. H. Streeter, The Chained Library, *Macmillan, London, 1931, p. 201)*

the "stall system" may well have benefited from Bodley's connections and style, for the Oxford vice-chancellor in 1599 was a man closely associated with Hereford Cathedral and more than likely called on by Bodley much as later librarians would employ consultants.

The unchained books were shelved in locked cabinets at one end of the library.

These arrangements sufficed for about one decade. By 1609, as the collection grew steadily, Bodley not only endowed the library, but further displayed his confidence and resources by building (1610–1612) the first of two new sections, the "Arts End." Breaking with the stall system, he followed the new wall system. Shelving was parallel to and flush against the wall. Only the lower shelves bore chained books; those beyond reach were approached by means of a gallery, and gallery access depended upon an enclosed stairway to which the librarian had the key. Although the wall system and its spacious uncommitted central area were already (1584) featured in the library of the Spanish Renaissance Escorial and were soon to become familiar in Baroque Europe, the Bodleian eminence induced many libraries, especially in England, to adopt for the time being the stall system.

Admission to the treasures thus presented did not imply unhampered use of every book. James states in the preface to the 1620 catalog that heretical and schismatic works are available only by permission of the vice-chancellor and the Regius Professor of Divinity. How long that had been the custom at the Bodleian is not indicated; but the idea was certainly no novelty, as the practices touched on earlier in this work attest.

Such exceptions apart, readers could go directly to any chained volume, the folios and larger quartos; they were to be left as they had been found, their clasps properly fastened and their chains "untangled" (Statutes, p. 81). This ease of control probably accounts in good part for Bodley's known preference for the large-format volumes, about three-fifths of the collection in 1605 and still over half in 1652; when James in 1602 indicated some nervousness about running out of chains before finishing the Hebrew books, Bodley noted that "fear of embezzling will be smalle" and advised calm (LBJ, p. 24). The smaller quartos and the octavos, locked up, had to be obtained from the keeper, read "in Sight," and returned on pain of payment of double the book's value, or, if the misdeed was deliberate, "perpetual Expulsion" (Statutes, pp. 81–82). In general, readers were bound by their oaths before the vice-chancellor, in the presence of the keeper, that they would "Study with Modesty and Silence," handle books protectively, and report within three days any wrongful act witnessed on the part of another. Anyone charged with and convicted of such behavior would be "excluded out of Hand" from not only the library but the university. (Statutes, pp. 96–101 passim.) Taking inventory, however, seems not to have been mentioned until the Visitors' first meeting after Bodley's death.

The basic policy barred circulation off the premises. From the outset Bodley called James sharply to account when deviations came to his notice, adding on one such occasion (1605) that neither the university nor the vice-chancellor was to meddle in this matter. He himself is known to have made an exception now and then. The only one, it seems, which he acknowledged, involved Sir Henry Savile (1549–1622), Greek and mathematics savant, a power at Oxford and Eton, and to Bodley a firm friend and principal donor. Bodley was most defensive about it, noting that the statutes barring his act were not yet "confirmed" (a technicality of uncertain pertinence, since they had been passed and were then being amended); he insisted that James tell no one but the underkeeper.

In support of the emphasis on use on the premises only, Bodley reproved James when complaints (he gave examples) indicated that the building was "oftener shutte than it should be" (August 8, 1606, LBJ, p. 162). The stated schedule was six hours daily, except Sundays and festival days (more generous than most, for another 250 years). No one could enter "by Night, with a Torch, Link, Lamp, Candle, or other kind of Fire-Light," on pain of dismissal—if the 1610 *Statutes* (p. 80) were enforced. All these restrictions were justified therein as the lessons of sad experience in earlier libraries.

The First Year's Recorded Use Actual patronage of a library was seldom recorded in those days before charging-out on a mass scale. It is posterity's rare good fortune that data survive concerning the Bodleian for the period from November 8, 1602, to November 7, 1603; that is, the year between inspections (see below), or as later times would put it, the fiscal year. According to the close reporting of Bodleian scholar G. W. Wheeler (*Bodleian Quarterly Record,* III:214–217, 1922), the library was open that year 239 mornings and 185 afternoons. Its "rather less than 3,000" volumes were used by 248 readers on 3,510 occasions, traffic being slightly heavier mornings than afternoons. Callers averaged seventeen a day; the peak was thirty-five, on July 6 and August 8, 1603. Only the masters of arts and bachelors and doctors of the three graduate faculties who were resident enjoyed ready access. Qualified bachelors of arts and outsiders had to apply for special permission. Only one bachelor of arts did, but the *Extranei* were as a group the most regular readers, among them many from abroad who came to Oxford precisely for that purpose. Their average use was 47 occasions each; the top graduate student's record was 142, and the most frequent patron overall came 151 times. How the collection was utilized is unknown, but it is presumed that attention focussed primarily on the rich holdings in theology by Protestant authors.

Bodleian Finance Like many library leaders since, Bodley was faced from the start with expenses greater than anticipated. Examination of the old library quarters in 1599 disclosed a considerably larger number of rotten timbers than had been estimated. Next James pressed for a salary boost soon after reporting for work. Then came the matter of helpers: pay for the two "Underlinges" is first mentioned in June 1606 (LBJ, p. 158). According to the *Statutes* adopted in 1610 the eight annual inspectors were to have a pair of gloves each (to handle books?), at prices meticulously differentiated according to the social standing of the wearer, and a 40-shilling allowance for dinner (5 shillings was then the weekly pay of many a skilled craftsman). Other obligations mentioned included tips and book repair.

Until perhaps 1609 the bills were apparently paid from Bodley's pocket. On May 31 of that year he endowed the library with the rent from a manor and some houses in London. The *Statutes* speak in addition of an annual stipend granted the keeper originally by direction of King Henry IV (1399–1413) and evidently still in force. They also stipulate that the state of the library's funds be reviewed within fifteen days after the inspection, by the vice-chancellor, the Visitors, and the keeper: anything questionable will be dealt with appropriately, to protect "a Treasure to Students of incomparable worth" (*Statutes,* p. 116). Bodley's death in 1613 revealed no large untouched treasure. His principal beneficiary was the university. Much laudatory verse was evoked: Robert Burton, for one, apostrophized the learned and the libraries of antiquity. Some relatives and friends complained of token bequests.

However that may be, Bodley's cash and other contributions seem to have worked reasonably well in his relations with the university authorities. He was also human enough to confess (to James, LBJ, p. 34) as early as March 27, 1602, "I am so weery of writing to Mr Vicech [ancellor]."

Additional revenues, probably modest, were collected under the *Statutes* of 1610 to 1613 and associated rules, if not earlier. That the traditional deposit exacted in advance from borrowers generally gave way to the penalty mentioned (double the price, for not returning a book as directed) was perhaps an improvement if not necessarily a novelty. One supposes that it enhanced public relations; did it net more money than forfeited deposits would have? Perfectly clear, on the other hand, are the two fees collected from 1610 on, from every individual admitted to the library; 8 pence to the keeper and 4 to the underkeeper. Ten years later, the library user was also obliged to buy the new catalog: 2s. 8d. for nonstaff persons and 2s. 6d. for booksellers, amounts exceeding slightly what the underkeeper was paid for one week's work.

Bodley and James Bodley's prime test as a manager was of course his relationship with Thomas James. That both men were sons of Marian exiles, that James was a passionate Protestant who had to earn a living, Bodley a firm but not passionate Protestant who had already made his fortune, was not extraordinary. From a class point of view it had been familiar since the Italian Renaissance: the religious facet was secondary. What may have been unusual, and certainly remains interesting, is the picture (derived of necessity entirely from Bodley's side) of a determined but flexible master, trying to utilize and also keep happy a talented servant who often strained against the leading strings.

When Bodley moved toward founding his library, James, already a fledgling scholar at age twenty-two, dedicated his new edition (1599) of De Bury's *Philobiblon* to Bodley, then fifty-four. Whether or not that step was as calculated as it may seem, James turned up in 1601 as Bodley's librarian, at an annual salary of close to £23. (That came to about 8 and ⅔ shillings per week, when top carpenter pay during the years from 1583 to 1642 averaged a trifle over 7 shillings a week. The comparison may be pursued in James E. T. Rogers' invaluable *History of Agriculture and Prices in England . . .*, Oxford: Clarendon Press, 1866–1902, V:792 and passim.) Within a few months James asked for more, and permission to marry, something Bodley opposed as too great a distraction, together with outside jobs.

On the pay question Bodley responded (September 11, 1601, LBJ, p. 18) that he had promised "in time" an increase to £40 or £50; the following year he did grant James a £4 raise. Meanwhile the latter sought curateships, partly for greater income and partly because he apparently wanted to leave the library job (harder than he had anticipated) as soon as he could line up enough church posts of the sort that would support him without taking much time. His heart lay, not in the library, but in exposing alleged mishandling or worse of patristic manuscripts by Roman Catholic editors. Employer Bodley was convinced that the library duties would take all the energy the librarian could muster and therefore opposed moonlighting. (So also thought Hugo Blotius, librarian at the emperor's court in Vienna, 1575–1608.) Yet he seems to have meant what he said about his affection for James. When the latter tried to add more church livings to the curateship he held in Oxford (since 1602), Bodley supported him on several occasions (if his own letters can be trusted: LBJ, pp. 162, 165, 184–85). James did obtain a second such position in 1609, but no more.

This indifferent success is explainable partly because some supposed sinecures were not so regarded by those controlling the appointment and were therefore withheld from James. There may have been other reasons: the inquiries he made about them—Bodley denounced "such motions at random" (December 12, 1606, LBJ, p. 165); James' alleged (by Bodley, September 11, 1601, LBJ, p. 20) reputation for starting more than he finished; bad luck perhaps. What does seem probable is that he remained as librarian until 1620 only because he had to.

Early in 1608 James wrote what Bodley interpreted as a hint at resigning. Bodley demanded straight talk, for the sake of the library whose leadership he must replace; he also told James he would find no one more favorably inclined to himself than Bodley.

Accordingly understandable is the sequence of events beginning with the completion late in 1604 of the manuscript of the first printed catalog. James asked for a deputy; on October 10, 1604, Bodley declined, on the ground that no one suitable would work under James and that after all the latter's labors he would hardly accept a new man as his equal. Just after this exchange, apparently, Bodley heard that James might work on the King James translation of the Bible: if he had not asked for the assignment, wrote Bodley on October 31, 1604, he could easily withdraw, citing the demands of the library. A week later the sponsor exploded: so James *had* asked; it was astonishing in view of his complaints about the work load at the library; his statements "did not hang together" (November 7, 1604, LBJ, p. 116). Nonetheless, early in 1606, Bodley was ready to pay an underkeeper a salary somewhat less than one-third of James' initial compensation, or a weekly rate near the bottom of the scale for that time, only slightly higher than the pay for women's labor (Rogers, V:792). James was authorized to make the appointment if he had "found a fitte scholler" to his "fantasie" (February 25, 1606, LBJ, p. 157). The underkeeper was not, however, to be a true deputy (in the judgment of expert Wheeler): should the keeper have to be away, he must be spelled by a graduate appointed deputy for that occasion.

Meanwhile, the Bible project proceeded. Unlike his learned friend Sir Henry Savile, neither Bodley nor the zealous James is among the forty-seven official translators listed in 1604 (as presented, p. 208, Charles C. Butterworth's *The Literary Lineage of the King James Bible, 1340–1611*, Philadelphia:, University of Pennsylvania Press, 1941). James does seem to have become involved, with rather grudging permission from Bodley. By 1608, his share was supposedly handed over to a committee (of the forty-seven?), but there were more recriminations in 1610. In March of that year Bodley brought James to London on library business; James apparently said nothing about his intention regarding the scholarly undertaking; a few days later Bodley reproached him for that silence and urged him to plan better.

The marriage question was settled more easily. The stipulation against it may have derived in part from Bodley's own apparent need for a wife—he was past forty when married—mainly as a source of wealth. (A man of his time, he opined to James on May 1, 1605, LBJ, p. 136, "But wordes are women, and deedes are men.") James on the other hand was very eager to wed, and seems to have pushed the matter very soon after his appointment, with references to what he called assurances of accommodation. On September 11, 1601, Bodley wrote that he could not recall any promise of a waiver—he had merely remarked that he would bear with James above all others; James had conceded that he should not be an exception to the rules, and if he was not serious about his commitments he should not have taken the job. Yet, within a year, Bodley gave in. He may have thought replacing James too high a price to pay for the maintenance of his rule that the keeper be married, as it were, only to the library. But the surrender note to James speaks only of the "love" he bears him, and declares that the sponsor would rather suffer public accusation of "defective proceeding" than inconvenience his protégé by "stifnesse" (August 11, 1602, LBJ, p. 52).

In the area then the heart of James' duties as a professional, catalog preparation, Bodley was more demanding. As recorded above, he repeatedly called James' attention to titles the catalog overlooked. Furthermore, in at least two missives of August 1604, he noted errors in the transcription of Hebrew, the confusion of ו (V) and ז (Z), ו (V) and ר (R), and כ (KH) and ב (B). A few months later, when a gentleman likewise versed in Hebrew and also competent in "Chaldee," Greek, and Syriac called on him before going to Oxford, Bodley gave him a letter of introduction to James and told James he was coming (LBJ, pp. 102, 107, 141). There were other differences too, to be discussed shortly. But Bodley remained conscious always of the human element: more than one lecture to James on cataloging "mistakes" was softened with the suggestion that James check the matter with his "learned friends."

Bodley's Job Descriptions In parallel with Bodley's relationship to James and his thoughts thereon, perhaps also influenced by that experience, there emerged in the founder's *Statutes* a job description for the librarian and supplementary points about his helpers. He who may be given "Custody" of the library is to be "noted and known for a diligent Student . . . Trusty, Active, and Discreet; a Graduat also, and a linguist," with no private distractions whatever (Dana and Kent ed., p. 66). His post is secure except for detection of "some heinous Offence, or apparent insufficiency." He is responsible "first" for recording donations of books or money in "the great Register Book." "An other chief Point" is to arrange the holdings according to faculties, preparing corresponding catalogs including full imprint, and to see that "the Books and Things" are in proper physical condition. (*Statutes,* pp. 70–74.)

As for public service, hours are to be posted and the "Keeper himself in person" is to be on hand, except for seven days off every quarter, when "some learned, able Graduate" substitutes for him. For the customary daily necessities he is to have "a slender Allowance" in that he may briefly be relieved by his assistant, a person capable of finding and issuing requested books (*Statutes,* pp. 78–87 passim).

The keeper is expected at all times to "carry himself uprightly and content every Student with due respect to his Degree" (*Statutes,* p. 84).

He receives money and accounts therefor to the university vice-chancellor. If a gift appears as "Ready Money" for purchase "at his Discretion and Election," he buys as promptly as possible, otherwise placing the funds with the vice-chancellor as a library reserve. Books thus bought are to be inscribed with the price, while the list of benefactions includes titles only. (*Statutes,* pp. 75–76.)

Salaries are stated for the keeper and his two aides. One is "some honest poor scholar, or Servant of the Keeper," paid four pounds a year for cleaning the books and the library (*Statutes,* p. 90). The other is his £10 assistant.

The foregoing notwithstanding, the experience of "other like Foundations" teaches the importance of the outside check. Annually, on November 8, the library is to be inspected by "eight principal Graduats who have been appointed perpetual Overseers and Visitors"—a concept and formula destined to become familiar on campuses in the American colonies. (*Statutes,* pp. 101–102.) They are to examine the keeper thoroughly on the performance of his duties, paying due heed to the grave dangers of "a small Toleration of abuses at first." It is for them to decide whether certain books should be "Exchanged for better editions" and which ones should be discarded as worthless or "superfluous." (*Statutes,* pp. 106–108.)

From these data it is evident that the librarian was regarded by Bodley (and how many others?) somewhat as the book selector but more as the registrar of donations, arranger and cataloger; not as the mentor of patrons but as their servant skilled in classical languages and in finding what they wanted; as defender of the holdings and furnishings against losses to man or lower forms of life, but not a maker of decisions about building the collection or premises. By and large, Bodley's librarian, suitably altered in religious commitment, would have been at home in at least some of the later medieval libraries, and a number of his functions were well established much earlier. Obtaining the binding of printed books donated and not yet bound (though supposed to be) may have been a new responsibility, as technical conditions changed and the rate of book arrival rose; but Bodley kept that in his own hands, presumably because he was by choice the solicitor of gifts and was paying the unavoidable binding bills.

Above all, Bodley sets forth neither concern nor plan for training either the keeper or his subordinates. Western medieval libraries had no library science texts either, so far as we know, but provision seems to have been made in that religious corporate framework for juniors to learn the trade from seniors. In this vital respect English Renaissance scholar Bodley, in tune with his increasingly bourgeois individualist times, is a step backward.

James' 1605 Catalog Whatever improvement training might have afforded, James did produce two printed catalogs and a number of manuscripts of related character. The Bodleian catalog of 1605 is often called the first printed general catalog of a public library. In 1575 the city of Augsburg had sponsored what was reputedly the first separately produced printed catalog of an institutional library; a record of the municipality's notable Greek manuscripts, it was presumably "public" but patently not "general." The Leyden "Academia" (University? founded in 1575, its library in 1587) is credited with a printed catalog in 1595, how "public" or "general" being undeterminable in the absence of readily available description. Meanwhile, there is no doubt that the Bodleian item circulated rather widely and presumably exerted influence.

James had assembled a manuscript catalog in 1601. Printing was contemplated perhaps early in 1603, but plague during the summer in both London and Oxford brought activity to a standstill until mid-1604. James then finished the basic document, but Bodley insisted on incorporating an appendix listing more than 2,000 recent acquisitions. Owing to the student demand for service, Bodley brought James to London, putting him up in his own home, to catalog the many books still there. When James returned to Oxford he tried to add call numbers to his lists, without the books. But, not knowing just how the cataloged items had been bound, he soon gave up his effort as hopeless; the numbers were added later when the books were delivered. The catalog appeared in the summer of 1605, the appendix occupying about one-third of it, with a diversity of type faces testifying to numerous shortages in the font used at first.

The catalog listed the 5,611 main entries, printed and manuscript together, plus analytical entries for a considerable additional number of items which were parts of other works or bound with them. It did not include certain folios in the archives. Fundamentally a shelf list, the main part consisted of 324 pages, one for each shelf housing the chained folios and large quartos. These shelf positions were determined first by the presumed pertinence of the work to one of the four faculties—Theology, Medicine, Jurisprudence, or Arts (undergraduate), each of which was served by several bookcases. Each page had a corresponding heading, like the *Libri Artium* on page 300 (viewable at the back of G. W. Wheeler, *The Earliest Catalogues of the Bodleian Library,* Oxford: University Press, 1928). Within a given faculty group, these chained works were arranged by letters and numbers; the letter referred not to the bookcase but to the initial letter of the respective authors' surnames, and the numbers kept the volumes of that subgroup in a rough alphabetical order. The call number, or "press mark," comprised an author letter, a shelf number, a position-on-the-shelf number, and an abbreviation for the faculty, like "Th." To this extent, a given group of pages in the catalog replaced one of the wood-framed lists which in then customary fashion had been affixed to the individual bookcases.

The page thus begun tended to have some space unoccupied. It was therefore advantageous to add on a particular page entries referring to material of the same faculty and author letter but shelved elsewhere. Entries beginning with the paragraph (or "section") symbol were analyticals, designating items bound with something else, and the call number was included in the reference. Asterisks denoted the smaller quartos and the octavos kept in locked cases and available only through the librarian. These works were shelved by (1) faculty, (2) author, and (3) more or less chance sequence; their call numbers included a 4° or 8° for quarto or octavo, respectively, an author letter, and an integral number (that is, one providing a bare record of relative location but not per se a particular physical location).

The practical advantage of this feature is evident from a comparison of the 1605 catalog and its manuscript predecessors. Whereas the call numbers for the folios had been altered several times as new books were shelved among them, the call numbers for the smaller books had remained unchanged despite additions to their company.

Assignment of integral numbers to books grouped by format or faculty or both, ignoring a particular shelf or even a particular bookcase, had been tried as early as 1407 at Avignon and at various other places afterward. By 1590 the Ducal Library at Munich and Imperial Library at Vienna had arrived at a stage of arrangement first by format, then by subject, and finally by integral number. None were truly relative-locational, because certain bookcases were understood, whether by reason of vertical dimensions of the shelving or simply by usage, especially where chains were involved. An important step beyond may have been taken at Zürich in 1587 when Johann Jacob Fries disposed the books of the Grossmünster (a church) by subject, unchained and without regard to format. Whatever the experience of these practices may have taught, whether any word of them reached Bodley, who had seen and heard of so much, does not seem to have been recorded.

In general, within any of Bodley's lists, alphabeting was prominent for the first letter but less evident thereafter.

Although arrangement followed surnames, like the new (1595) Maunsell book trade catalog, the first names continued to be recorded first. And the emphasis on surnames, italicized, carried over, inappropriately, to authors known by forename: they were here filed on the contrary by sobriquets like *Anglicus*. Known pseudonyms usually appeared as a cross-reference to the real name; sometimes the work was entered under both names. If a title page furnished initials only, the work was treated as anonymous. (The *Anonymi* were numerous enough to make section A of the Theology folios, together with the Bible-holding section B, a leading subdivision.) If authorship was stated but questioned, the name was followed by a cautionary "apparently."

Some works entered under title, for lack of author, yielded a bit of subject guidance. If a place was mentioned, it was employed twice, first as the entry term and again in the title. Furthermore, whenever the same word was the first significant term in several successive entries by title, it was not repeated, the balance of each title being listed in turn as though under a subject heading. This practice seems to have harmonized with the custom of abbreviating the fairly numerous longer titles.

As for the rest, description normally included place and date of publication but not edition data. Size was left to the call number, absence of a symbol meaning a folio. There were no added entries for editors.

If the shelving and the 1605 catalog were both classified first by the four faculties, i.e., broadly by subject, a unified alphabetical approach was provided in the catalog's index. Listed therein were the authors and titles, both the latter and the pseudonymous works being filed by first word or catchword. James also incorporated in it a forty-six-column list of commentaries on the Bible and its parts, and another pertaining to Aristotle. All these items were followed by page references. Call numbers were given instead for certain books listed in the index because they had been accidentally overlooked in the catalog proper.

The appendix to the 1605 catalog was by origin an assemblage, on the same plan, of entries for the lately added books Bodley wanted in the volume. Thanks to printing delays it also embraced (about half the total) analytics to large sets, a concession by Bodley to James after some exchange of opposing opinions. Besides, James accommodated Bodley by inserting lists of references to Law and Medicine, much briefer however than what had been prepared with enthusiasm for the Bible. Finally, to bring together references to authors appearing in both catalog and appendix, the latter was equipped with an index of its own.

James' Descriptive Cataloging in 1620   James made only two noteworthy changes in descriptive cataloging in the 1620 catalog. Works by more than one author were entered under each, and works in English were signalled by boldface type.

James' Subject Cataloging   If description had here made no net advance beyond earlier practice, and does not seem to have concerned James as much as his employer, subject cataloging was very much on the keeper's mind. In 1599, very much like some kindred earlier (1577) spirits at Strasbourg who issued a union list of Greek manuscripts in nine libraries in Constantinople, he prepared a comparable register of manuscripts at the several Oxford libraries, as an appendix to his edition of *Philobiblon*. And the next year he added not only the Cambridge holdings but a subject index (the *Eclogae . . .*). The 1605 Bodleian catalog included certain subject guidance: lists of commentators on the Bible and its parts, like Maunsell's subsections within "Divinitie" (see below), and on Aristotle, law and medicine; also occasional entry under place. Yet the numerous works of critical commentary, entered under their authors, were not entered also under the writings they dealt with. Nor were biographies entered under the biographee, just the biographer.

James was clearly dissatisfied with that apparatus, at least in the area of Theology. Whether or not the effort was related to the contemporary Bible-revision project or his own scholarly editing of some Church Fathers, he set about developing a subject guide to the Theology materials in the Bodleian. Within a year or two (no work acquired later than 1607 is listed) he had a 784-page folio manuscript catalog, with some 10,000 references to both books and parts of books, giving call number and quite often page numbers. *Christus* and its ninety-two subdivisions tap the contents of about 400 works. *Fides* ("Faith") has fifty-seven subdivisions (notes Wheeler, *Earliest Catalogues*, pp. 98–99). The chief headings sometimes have numbered subdivisions; all are in (Latin) alphabetical order.

Deliberately excluded is the list of references to Bible commentaries already printed in the 1605 catalog. A serious deficiency is the close dependence of subject heading formulation upon title terms. The materials on Holy Communion, for example, are to be found not only under that rubric but also, thanks to varying titles, under *Coena Domini, Eucharista,* and *Missa.* (Wheeler, p. 99.)

James next rendered similar service to readers attracted to the Bodleian's resources in Medicine, Law, and the Arts. The subject guide to Medicine seems to be lost. The Law guide, prepared apparently in the years 1612 to 1614, varies slightly from the style of the Theology catalog. On the one hand it updates the list of commentaries published in the 1605 catalog. On the other, it contains no reference to either English law or books in English.

The Arts guide was a distinctive venture, oriented by definition to the undergraduates, whose satisfactions meant little to Bodley but a good deal to James. He began it after failing to persuade his master to organize an undergraduate library and brought the guide to completion after several years in retirement (1624 or 1625). The main headings are Grammar (including Philology), Geometry, Astronomy, Architecture, Arithmetic, Optics, Cosmography, Geography, Chronology (one of the two sections being the chroniclers), Music, Logic, Commentaries on Aristotle, Metaphysics, Military Arts, Politics (poaching on Law Faculty territory), Natural Philosophy, Rhetoric, and History (including Biography). The debt to the past speaks for itself. History-Biography consumes 117 of the 258 pages. Eighteen sections on matters like historical method come first, then names of persons and places, alphabetically; altogether, there are more than seventy subdivisions. Grammar is developed somewhat similarly, the subdivisions for particular languages being brought together in the alphabetical sequence by the common beginning, *De lingua* . . . (Wheeler, pp. 109–110). At the head is an alphabetical index composed mainly of subject subdivisions.

James did not aim at total coverage, but utilized only the 5,000 or 6,000 works which seemed to him best for the undergraduate in terms of the library's anti-Catholic purpose, content, and accessibility. English history appears little; literature not at all. The scope is still considerable, however, and under most headings there are accordingly few entries. Geometry has twenty-nine subdivisions leading to 123 books; in at least one instance there is but one book under the heading, and that heading simply duplicates the title. A subclass so specific that the heading is the same as the solitary title entered beneath it is dubious. Its recurrence would in the course of time inspire the rule for "dictionary" card catalog entries that a title identical with a subject heading is normally not provided.

How this performance compares with the specificity and standardization achieved in Conrad Gesner's contributions is a matter for research apparently not yet on record. A few tentative conclusions may be offered. Where Gesner's *Pandects* linked subjects only with authors and one had to consult the main catalog for more information, James takes the reader directly to specific works and even pages. Gesner drew upon everything he could find in Greek, Hebrew, and Latin; James confines himself to a single library, obviously restrictive but permitting him easily to add the convenience of a call number. How subject heading specificity differs in Gesner and James is largely unexamined. Not very much in Theology, apparently: each utilizes some subdivisions not employed by the other. As for the rest, one must at the moment be content with an hypothesis. Gesner worked from the classification of knowledge, a good framework for subject headings of a standardized character; James, probably aware of the advantage, nevertheless found himself succumbing to the powerful undertow of specific titles in his own library, and may have produced subject guidance considerably less stable and reliable as a whole than Gesner's.

To match this subject guidance with subject arrangement on the shelves had quickly been recognized by James among others as impracticable—impracticable, that is, given books of varied content, volumes containing more than one bibliographical unit, and a small choice of subject classification schemes (either the various long-accepted classifications of knowledge or the more recent four-faculties patterns). James' solution, to leave subject control to catalogs and shelve the materials in the simplest manner possible, more or less alphabetically, was explicitly recommended in the preface to the 1620 catalog. This was of course not entirely new, but the emphasis probably influenced some librarians. It was long to remain a respected policy wherever library collections were in stacks closed to the public, especially if they included works with more than one principal subject or more than one defensible main entry. Not all concerned with the problem were satisfied, however, and an additional approach was soon to emerge.

In these respects, the age of printing was little different from the age of the codex. Two metamorphoses were in the making: the rising number of printed works in libraries, and later the rising number of persons desiring to find information or other satisfactions in them, would create a situation qualitatively new, which was not to yield easily even in the age of the computer. But James dealt with a small clientele and in 1620 with a mere 16,000 volumes.

Libraries and Librarianship

Paradox in "Public" Service   If a new English university "public" library, under Protestant-humanist, strictly scholarly auspices, faced firmly backward in most respects, the surprise should not be total. Although there had long been "libraries" (rarely librarians) at parish churches or rectories or schools, their heavily theological character and clerical patronage were hardly "public." The debates between the Established Church and its challengers in Elizabethan and early Stuart England brought many scholars and gentlemen to such book collections, indeed a skilled craftsman or small merchant now and then; and the same need called forth "libraries" under municipal auspices as well, first in the late sixteenth century in vigorously Presbyterian Scotland. The accepted "public" was thus expanding in the heat of church and state controversy, particularly in the more substantial towns capable of supporting a dissenting as well as an orthodox minister.

But gifts to nonuniversity libraries were a drop in the English philanthropic bucket (see the data on pp. 369 and 373 of W. K. Jordan's *Philanthropy in England, 1480-1660* . . ., New York: Russell Sage Foundation, 1959). There was no stable revenue for the purchase of books. And however nominal may have been the "librarian" listings in dozens of Rhine Valley cities and towns, the English nonacademic scene had very little of even that. The first known instance, decidedly lonely for many years, was the library at Manchester, whose regular funds for a librarian (1656) and book purchase (1661) were provided by the 1653 bequest of successful textile merchant Humphrey Chetham.

Protestantism had not made that kind of progress in France. The clergy of the famous Atlantic port, La Rochelle, organized a library in 1604 which they opened to the public, but within a single generation it became a casualty of Cardinal-Prime Minister Richelieu's pressure against the Huguenots. Numerous other French towns were notable for ecclesiastical libraries with a liberal orientation toward service, thanks to donations by bibliophiles who required that their gifts be available to teachers and students. Toulouse, a leading southern community, possessed four such institutions. Yet the model was basically medieval.

Paradoxically, the combination of welcome to a nonacademic public, and stability of staff and operations, was for good reasons more readily associated with an environment superficially just as traditional. In 1608 (or 1609) in Milan, Italy, a brand new library was founded by Cardinal Federigo Borromeo (1564-1631) and serviced by friars. If the Bodleian was a Reformation instrument and James a conscious cutting edge, the Ambrosiana, named for the Father whose preaching had once converted to Christianity a pagan Augustine, expressed one aspect of the Counter-Reformation. It was open to anyone capable of using its 12,000 books and 9,000 manuscripts (and who presumably had occasionally some daylight hours free from other commitments). That the institution provided readers with paper, pens, and inkstands could be regarded as a piece of ostentation—aristocratic largesse; at any rate the service was surely an appreciated convenience, and may have been essential to some who studied there with heads full but pockets empty. On the other hand, no catalog was then available; perhaps that handicap was minimized by shelving all the books in plain sight, reportedly a practice contrary to the custom of most Italian libraries.

In the spirit of Petrarch and many subsequent figures, the model was the Library of Alexandria: the Ambrosiana too was the seat of a body of scholars governed by a committee of leading *dottori* from the archbishopric of Milan, one of whom was designated librarian, a post of honor. The administrative and technical staff, the *conservatori,* were supposed to serve but not interfere with the scholars. The facilities included a printshop for Oriental materials. In 1618 a gallery for paintings was added, and in 1621 an art school.

A few years later (1620), the Angelica Library, established in Rome also under ecclesiastical rather than university or noble or municipal auspices, followed suit in that "laymen" were welcome twice daily except Thursdays. That term's meaning should probably be taken as limited by social and educational circumstances, just as at the Ambrosiana at Milan. One does not easily picture ordinary working people, or peasants from the nearby villages, or their wives or daughters, utilizing such an institution. (The 1676 rules of the Sorbonne differ conspicuously from those of 1321 in referring to the possible, "bound to be rare," arrival of a female researcher; the prescribed treatment is insultingly restrictive. See pp. 178-182, Alfred Franklin's *La Sorbonne,* Paris 1875, reprinted 1968 by Van Heusden, Amsterdam.) Yet the cited practices appear to have been an advance upon those at the Bodleian, even though England was then moving ahead in general much faster than Italy.

Possibly the most remarkable of all, as an indication of things to come, were the new public libraries of northern Switzerland. No wealthy aristocrat or merchant prince stepped forward with an endowment. The pace was set by four successful businessmen, who were stimulated by what they had seen on their travels to organize (1629) in Zürich a Library Society which apparently held title to the books in corporate style. Operation was to be in the hands of two permanent librarians and two temporary unpaid associates, Society members taking turns at two-year stints. By 1631 the Society had obtained quarters for the library in the "Water-Church" (on the left bank of the Limnat near its junction with Lake Zürich), and three years later the institution was open to the public. Gifts came from all directions; they were no doubt encouraged by their announcement, from 1645 on, in the columns of a "New Year's Sheet" issued annually by the Society, soon imitated in several other cantons. Subject and author catalogs were begun in 1656.

Naudé　The open door as he understood it, at the Bodleian and the two Italian libraries mentioned, impressed energetic Parisian Gabriel Naudé. Born of modest forbears in a period of fierce religious and political strife, he reached age eighteen the year (1618) the tight censorship of publication was formalized, and age twenty-four just as Cardinal Richelieu emerged the key man in France. By this time Naudé had already issued (1620) a polemic against libels and (1623) an attack on the Rosicrucians: he considered imposture their particular brand of mysticism, transmutation of gross metals and human qualities into higher forms of both. Like most of his keen contemporaries, however, he had favorite brands of his own. In 1625 he defended great men from what he called false accusations of belief in magic; he meant that they were innocent of indulgence in "evil" magic, mainly witchcraft, the several other categories being entirely or partially "good."

The first of these products presumably helped bring Naudé to the attention of Henri de Mesmes, president of the Paris *Parlement,* that primarily judicial institution which had lately exercised much political influence. Appointed in 1620 librarian of the "Memmiana," Naudé served briefly but decided to drop the job and pursue his medical studies at Padua. Soon afterward he returned to Paris to finish his degree, delivering by election of the faculty a paean to its antiquity and dignity, in Latin. A humanist commitment of the Bodley stamp was however by no means implied thereby. Like Montaigne, one of his models, Naudé had already (1627) set forth in his celebrated *Advice on Establishing a Library* (ed. A. Taylor, Berkeley: University of California Press, 1950), dedicated to De Mesmes, the view that books should be selected for their internal value rather than their rarity or cost, and from the writers of all ages, viewpoints, and—by implication—languages.

Naudé's achievements now came to the ears of the papal nuncio, Guido di Bagni. In 1623, Bagni had been thought sufficiently interested in libraries for Greek expert Leone Allacio, later Vatican librarian, to describe to him from Heidelberg some of the problems of moving the Palatine Library from that location to Rome. Bagni was elected a cardinal in 1629; when he left Paris for Rome in 1631, he took Naudé with him.

For the next ten years Naudé busied himself in the vicinities of the two towns to which, successively, his master was assigned as bishop, from 1631 to 1635 near Ravenna (thus also near Padua and Venice) and from 1635 to 1642 near Rome. Partly on account of his duties as the cardinal's librarian, he maintained an active correspondence. One partner had admired him since his graduation address and had met him as he traveled from Paris to Italy: Nicolas-Charles Peiresc, aristocrat and wealthy lawyer, well known in his own day as a broad-gauge patron of science and letters—also faithful to the culture of his native Provence. Naudé spent many an hour searching Italian bookshops, libraries, and catalogs for items of interest to his influential friend. The young man's letters to him (*Bulletin du Bibliophile*, Paris, 1886) reveal among other things that shipping a library catalog was not a rarity but not a practice without restrictions, either; that in 1633 Naudé prepared a tract on censorship but did not publish it; that in 1634 he intrigued in vain for an Italian university teaching post.

Peiresc and many other acquaintances of Naudé's shared a strong interest in science; a few, like Peiresc himself, had been members of the renowned Accademia dei Lincei (1603–1630), in which Galileo participated. Indeed, Naudé's role as a science information center in Rome might be compared with that of his close friend in Paris, the celebrated monk Marin Mersenne. Possibly typical of their contribution was the publicizing of Descartes' *Discours sur la Méthode*, issued in 1637 in Amsterdam, thanks to French censorship. Mersenne wrote about it to Naudé, and the latter began spreading the news by telling a leading Roman patron of literature and the arts, wealthy archaeologist Cassiano dal Pozzo. Naudé's sympathy for offbeat thinker Tommaso Campanella generated sabotage of some of his own publishing efforts; but the shabbiness of Campanella's data on a contemporary eclipse led him to remark that *"ces Messieurs les Italiens"* (*Bulletin du Bibliophile*, 1886, p. 151) were not to be compared in such matters with scientists like Peiresc himself and abbé Pierre Gassendi. (In his utopian *City of the Sun*, the main basis of his continued repute, Campanella alludes only fleetingly and fancifully to a library, revealing not a trace of what might have been learned from Naudé.)

The rising star was meanwhile appreciated at home as well. He was in touch constantly with Gassendi, noted reviver of Greek atom theory who tried stripping it of its materialist character but could not do so altogether, and the other *libertins*. In 1633 he was appointed to the nominal post of physician to Louis XIII. When Cardinal Richelieu sent his librarian to Italy to buy book rarities, Naudé helped him with both that task and personal problems. In 1638, influenced perhaps by the maneuvers he had witnessed in Italy as well as France, Naudé wrote a pamphlet on *coups d'état* which found justification for the 1572 Massacre of St. Bartholomew's Eve. This contribution, one of several on various subjects, may have made him no less attractive to Richelieu. When debate arose in 1641 over the authorship of *The Imitation of Christ,* an extraordinarily popular religious guide ever since its appearance in 1418 (first printed edition Augsburg 1471/1472), Naudé was asked by Richelieu to examine the four key manuscripts in Rome. He did so, reaching conclusions offensive to the Benedictines; criticism became nasty, Naudé responded in kind, and litigation ensued which was not resolved until 1652.

The incident actually worked out well for Naudé. When Cardinal Bagni died in 1641 he became librarian for another cardinal in Rome, but seems to have had no hesitation accepting a similar call from Richelieu early in 1642. The latter himself died a few months later and Naudé joined the staff of his successor, Cardinal Mazarin. Still another death made available the 6,000 volumes of an ecclesiastic named Descordes; Naudé cataloged them, and his new employer on his recommendation bought them in 1643.

Naudé was already truly eminent in the circles of the learned: Mersenne dedicated the enlarged and revised version (1639) of his earlier (1623) essay on magnetism, "to that most erudite man." And when Jesuit Athanasius Kircher, restless prober of many fields of science and "scier.ce," issued in 1641 his work on magnetic declination, he spoke of Naudé as one "most erudite and most zealous for the common good." It is not surprising that Mersenne's friend and biographer should state of Naudé that, thanks to his knowledge of science and books, one could "without exaggeration" pronounce him "a walking library." (From the sources assembled in Mersenne's *Correspondence,* ed. De Waard, Paris: Presses Universitaires, 1933–1965, VIII:754–75, IX:454, I:xli.)

It was very likely thus that Naudé's brochure on establishing a library was translated in English in 1661. John Evelyn, aristocrat and royalist, made a hit with a book on gardening in that year and decided to improve upon his success quickly by translating in his popular style works on "the most polite and useful arts" (*Diary,* ed. De Beer, Oxford: Clarendon Press, 1955, I:42). Among other items, he rendered Naudé as *Instructions concerning Erecting of a Library.* Evelyn's comments on the many libraries he visited are uniformly superficial. He knew nothing whatever of the problems or the efforts made to solve them. Was this piece of good fortune for the fame of the already deceased (1653) Naudé really important to the advance of the "polite and useful arts"?

In two major respects long since recognized, it clearly was. First, suffering for himself and his "curious" fellows, those searching for new standards in a world upset by severe political and intellectual conflict but unable to afford books individually, twenty-seven-year-old Naudé offered his distinguished employer *Advice on Establishing a Library,* for "public use" (p. 16). He had at that moment some notoriety as a pamphleteer but no comparable reputation as a librarian; Monsieur le Président de Mesmes indeed was accustomed to buying books without consulting him. Contrary to what might have been expected, moreover, a document in Latin like all the others on the subject for another half-century yet, Naudé made his *démarche* in French, in public. It seems very likely that he wanted De Mesmes to enrich his collection, to assemble in fact a model, encyclopedic library which he would then throw open to the "curious"; Naudé was apparently appealing at least to those "curious" to stir up support. The projected joy was not to be savored, however, for another seventeen years, and at another library.

Second, library development benefitted also from his strong personal feeling that all schools of thought should be kept at arm's length. Although he had more respect for ancient academicians than for the moderns, he readily urged collecting "all the principal authors" and all works of good quality without worrying about points of view or standing. He is here similar to objective bibliographer Gesner so far as ideological criteria are concerned, but moves beyond him (thanks to French tradition?) in recommending inclusion of modern authors emphatically and vernacular works by implication. Yet he too observes limits. As the great critic (and librarian) Sainte-Beuve pointed out 200 years later, when romances had become accepted as a major category, Naudé regarded novels as "purely frivolous, as though Rabelais and Cervantes had never existed," and "paid no attention" to those in vernaculars (C.-A. Sainte-Beuve, "Gabriel Naudé," *Oeuvres*, ed. Leroy, Paris: Gallimard, 1960, II:483, 488,).

Was this not related to his ignoring of women in his work as well as personally?

To assemble and organize for the use of the men sorely needing it a grand, encyclopedic library was, Sainte-Beuve assures us (*Oeuvres*, II:482), what Naudé meant by *dresser* in his original title, *Avis pour Dresser une Bibliothèque*. Taken more narrowly, it invites attention to his rather backward notions of shelf control and cataloging access. Favoring "natural magic" and "natural memory," in line with the conservative view of the appropriate, he rejects mnemonic devices because they would "spoil and pervert it" (*Advice*, p. 64). He thus strikes a blow against the radical practitioners of magic, whose elaborate use of codes, symbols, and star lore favored fluidity in thinking on many fronts and was considered a threat by his church associates. Partly for this reason, which obviously had no immediate bearing on library management, he opposes shelf arrangement whose use depends on devices aiding the memory. He argues vigorously for what is "easiest, least intricate, most natural, most used" (*Advice*, p. 65): by this he means the grouping of books by subject and exact classification, and the provision of both a systematic subject and alphabetical author catalog. The two-catalogs idea is less sophisticated than various earlier ones like Pellican's plan of 1532, but for lack of implementation of those models Naudé's still sounds novel in 1627. His main "subjects" are a version of the familiar four faculties, Philosophy being expanded into History-Philosophy-Mathematics-Belles lettres. The shelving scheme(s) disapproved are not identified in his pamphlet. Nothing is said there about either the Bodleian practices he would presumably have endorsed or the critique of those practices by Thomas James.

That he considers a minor problem the allegedly "very few books . . . not reducible to some order," and would "at worst" (*Advice*, p. 67) put them all in a location of their own, suggests ignorance of pertinent recent experience and discussion, and perhaps underestimation of the rate at which libraries would soon grow. Both the library of Jacques de Thou, probably the outstanding collection in the Paris of Naudé's young manhood, and the comparably significant holdings of Descordes which Naudé cataloged in 1643, assembled over many years, numbered less than 10,000 volumes. Naudé himself did much buying for his own library and on a larger scale for Cardinal Mazarin; in fact he acquired thereby not only books but a rather unsavory reputation for subordinating ethics to determination. He seems to have had less concern for organizing the material acquired, and, at least in 1627, to have thought little about the library-technical implications of the expansion just over the horizon.

Buying abroad and opening the collection to "*hommes de lettres et d'érudition*" were well-established traditions, acceptable to the author of the quoted phrase, Cardinal Richelieu, who sent representatives traveling to acquire books and left a sketch for public service in his private papers (quoted from the imperial archives by Franklin, *Anciennes Bibliothéques de Paris*, III:45). Whether inspired thereby, or simply taking advantage of a powerful helping hand from the grave, Naudé pursued both courses on behalf of Richelieu's successor, Cardinal Mazarin. The library Naudé organized, called the Mazarine, was in January 1644 thrown open to the "public" on Thursdays. The *Gazette de France* of January 30 reported an impressive response from "'the learned and the curious, who go there in droves'" (quoted by Franklin, III:43). Five years later Naudé said the library had attracted 80 to 100 persons on those Thursdays: theologians, magistrates, scholars, and dilettantes. No complaint has been found that such a public was narrower than what he had had in mind.

There seems to be no reason to expect broader vision. Naudé was neither an ecclesiastic nor a member of one of those comfortable families which by custom purchased government positions like the royal librarianship. His experience, except for school, was confined to the domestic establishments and private collections of the French judicial dignitaries who sponsored him at first and eminent Catholic churchmen in Italy and France, men of generous bent in matters of reading. In 1627 he had projected a major library in Paris in terms of the realities as he knew them: housed in a palatial private home where income was ample, and open to men like himself, a few steps down the economic and social ladder. In 1644 he was able to realize that dream. Very practically too: aware of the touchiness (Sainte-Beuve says "savagery"; *Oeuvres*, II:483) of proud, impecunious, and hitherto frustrated scholars and dilettantes, he furnished them a private side door to avoid incidents with the cardinal's front-door staff, the *grands laquais* who seemed likely to disdain the visitors. Doubtless nourishing the latter's self-esteem was the inscription over the private entrance in Latin. The ordinary run of Paris humanity did not of course figure at all.

The masses did figure, nevertheless, in the disturbances over taxes, civil oppression, and high politics, which mounted through the 1640s. One phase, the aristocratic "Fronde" revolt of 1644, temporarily unseated Mazarin and crushed Naudé by demanding the surrender of that very library, "the most beautiful, the best and the largest library which had ever been brought together in the world, containing," he declared, more than 40,000 volumes; it was a ghastly deprivation of "the public" (*Surrender of the Library of Cardinal Mazarin*, in *The Literature of Libraries*, eds. Dana and Kent, pp. 52–53).

Responding like many others in similar circumstances, Naudé accepted an invitation to join the savants around Queen Christina of Sweden. It was a two-month trip, overland—not too uncomfortable, he wrote Gassendi. The sovereign impressed him enormously, partly because her new *Bibliotequaire de la Reyne,* as he signed his letter, was given "absolute charge" of the library. He also noted apparently with forebodings that Stockholm was much colder than the France he had lately left (Gassendi's *Epistolae,* Lugduni: Anisson, 1667, 6:336–337). It is unlikely that he knew how unimportant his presence would be, at a court then seething with struggle over political power. Perhaps it did not matter, since acquisitions-specialist Naudé had shown his indifference to public service at the Mazarine by frequently paying a substitute to work at the desk. At any rate, just before Christina outsmarted all her opponents, Mazarin regained power in Paris; Naudé set off for home but died of illness on the way (July 1653) at fifty-three.

He left neither a new library tradition nor—like those he admired—a single syllable about the training of librarians. But Louis Jacob, initiator of current national bibliography in France, was not the only individual who considered Naudé his friend and inspirer. Naudé was destined to be cited often for his *Advice,* with all its library ideas good and bad. It is one of history's ironies that the ignorant amateur Evelyn should have played a considerable part in the process—and another that Naudé's career in science information should have been recorded long ago by students of the history of science but left almost unmentioned by library historians.

Libraries and Nonlibrarians' Views of "Usefulness" If little that was new appeared in the writings of library people like Bodley, James, and Naudé, the first half of the seventeenth century did bring to the library world some striking contributions from nonlibrarians. Contemporary with Bodley was Justus Lipsius (1547–1604), a Belgian Latinist well known in his later years as a teacher. Continuing the library history tradition begun feebly by a few servants of the Catholic Church during his middle years, he published in 1595 a much more impressive little treatise on the same subject, *De Bibliothecis Syntagma* (Antwerp; again in 1602, 1620, and 1629; reprint in *Literature of Libraries,* eds. Dana and Kent).

He begins by defining *bibliotheca* (building, bookcase, book collection) and *libraria* (bookshop); whether he was original or not, his formulations have been accepted ever since insofar as the Latin and Romance terms are concerned. He then writes of the libraries of antiquity, drawing heavily upon classical sources. Only once does he give an exact page reference (to Pliny; see Dana and Kent version, p. 97). And he is not critical, accepting for instance the hoary myth that Caesar deliberately burned the Alexandrian Library. Besides, perhaps because he was a non-French humanist, he deals only with classical times, going no further than Emperor Diocletian (284–305). But his quoting, direct and indirect, is lavish, and many successors seem to have mined his work without acknowledgment.

So far, he differs from earlier laborers in the history vineyard only in more thorough scholarship. But he was a flexible man, a north European who more than once changed his religious affiliation with his employer. Was this in part a product of life where bourgeois values were contending with earlier commitments? Consider these remarks, apparently most unusual for a scholar of his day, with which Lipsius opens his last chapter:

> I have nothing further that seems worth saying on this subject of libraries, except a few words about their use. If they stand empty, or with only an occasional visitor; if students do not frequent them and make use of their books, why were they ever established, and what are they save that 'idle luxury in the garb of scholarship' to which Seneca alludes. (*Syntagma*, p. 111.)

The idea of usefulness was assuredly not new, but its prominence was bound to benefit where productivity was honored economically and ethically.

Usefulness was of course a main thread in the writings of Francis Bacon. While much of Book II of the *Advancement of Learning* (1605) is devoted to his influential classification of knowledge, a scheme differing fundamentally from the medieval pattern and its "faculty" offshoot (see below), the discussion opens with a review of the "defects" in the state of learning. Progress hinges on money, sound direction, and collective effort to overcome "the frailty of man." Direction is really the most important, and the trouble is that activity so far tends "rather to augment the mass of learning in the multitude of learned men than to rectify or raise the sciences themselves"; libraries "are as the shrines where all the relics of the ancient saints . . . are preserved." Just as the secretaries and spies "of princes and states" are paid for information, "so you must allow the spials and intelligencers of nature to bring in their bills. . . ." Yet he also declares that the crisis "is not to be remedied by making no more books, but by making more good books, which, as the serpent of Moses, might devour the serpents of the enchanters." (Modern Library ed., pp. 222–223, 228.) In a frame of mind to be useful, no doubt, he presented a copy of this very work to the Bodleian Library.

To collect "books, instruments and patterns of every kind" was among the proposals he circulated even earlier, at Elizabeth's court, but it became generally known only in 1624 *(New Atlantis)* in the plans of his philosopher-kings. A voyage to that purpose is dispatched every twelve years, he reports: responsible for the collecting are the professionals, "three of the Fellows or Brethren of Salomon's House," that "Order or Society . . . dedicated to the study of the Works and Creatures of God . . . sometimes called . . . the College of the Six Days Works" (Modern Library ed., p. 582–583). Thus ingeniously does Bacon weave together the traditions of the church, the Renaissance academy and the English college. Forty years later, the members of the various preliminary scientific groupings on the scene for many decades finally attended the birth of the Royal Society: "Salomon's House" was on many a lip. No more than the prophet's own remarks, however, do the celebrated *Philosophical Transactions* yield any reference (in the indexes of the first century) to a particular library or libraries generally, or to Sir Thomas Bodley. The *Correspondence* of Henry Oldenburg (eds. Hall and Hall, University of Wisconsin Press, 1865-   ), the Society's first secretary, discloses interest in books occasionally but in libraries hardly at all. Bringing science and libraries together had to wait on circumstances not yet ripe.

Yet they plainly were receptive to Bacon's related contentions: that the struggle to master nature must be conducted by teamwork rather than in isolation, cumulatively rather than hit and miss; that reporting and discussion should be honest and straightforward, not encumbered by the verbal and symbolic camouflage of the magicians; and that the purpose ought to be the service of mankind, not the enhancement of the power and prestige of an elite, however lofty or even blessed the hoarder of secrets fancied his objective to be.

The target was neither imaginary nor unimportant. Side by side with the humanist tradition of mastery of the best recorded thinking had run the Hermetic tradition of mastery of nature and life via magical symbolism and practice. For the Humanists, despite their many virtues, sought ethical and literary guidance on the printed page and mainly in the past, whereas life demanded also direct attention to nature and the present. That the state of science and technology limited what could be done soundly was not exceptional; nor was there any novelty in the notion that the ignorance gap could be bridged by ritual and formula along with experiment. But in the very year of Gutenberg's invention were translated from the Greek a body of documents associated with the supposed philosopher-king and master magician of ancient Egypt, Hermes Trismegistus. He had been taken as historical for centuries, and continued to evoke great respect, even though the Humanists tended to believe that the printed book had brought knowledge so much closer that magic was no longer needed. In 1614, however, Greek expert Isaac Casaubon proved by analyzing the texts that they originated not in Moses' day or even earlier but much later—perhaps the third century. That was a mortal blow, because it meant that Hermetism could not have been the "real" source of Greek, Jewish, and Christian wisdom. Numerous contemporaries of Bacon and Naudé, like the Rosicrucians and Jesuit Kircher, stood by the Hermetic tradition, blandly ignoring the annoyance. But the influence of Hermetism in its many variations, for centuries vast, was now inevitably to shrink rather steadily in educated circles.

On the negative side it had nourished self-seeking individualism, secrecy, and obscurantism and furnished a nominal target for persecutors whose definitions of the "black arts" often stretched readily to hinder true scientific experiment. On the positive side, its animistic universe operated by magic, especially "reading" astral patterns and influences with the aid of numbers, geometric figures, etc., well organized in appearance, had helped prepare the seventeenth-century mind for a mechanical universe operated by mathematics. Bacon opposed the magicians in the name of straight thinking and expression; on the other hand his cool view of the writings of the past was partially a rejection of the Humanist emphasis.

Very little is known so far about the representation of magic in libraries of the epoch under review. In 1587 the Rhine Province of the Society of Jesus asked the General (their chief executive) whether such works should be kept with the books by heretics. His response was that heretical writings were of some advantage as a target for refutation, but that those on magic, containing nothing refutable by arguments or reason, served no valid purpose and should be burned. How many titles thus proscribed were actually on hand in any library? How many, once identified, were indeed destroyed?

If Bacon was concerned with clarity, integrity, and substance, with scientific effort organized socially for society's benefit; if the Jesuits subordinated science and social benefit to the promotion of the Roman Catholic faith, René Descartes examined the process of reasoning. Where the magicians utilized numbers in a variety of ways usually permeated with mysticism, where Bacon dealt with them not at all, the fount of Cartesianism placed mathematics at the center, as the model of precision, the very heart of abstract thinking, like Plato long before. His logical base is directly related, the Aristotelian distinction between the probable and the certain: living in the precalculus age, he still associates the scientific with the traditional "certain." So far as "the sciences found in books" are concerned, at least those "whose reasonings are only probable," truth is more readily apprehended by "the simple reasoning which a man of common sense" can apply to "the things which come immediately before him." (*Discourse on the Method of Guiding Reason Properly and Seeking Truth in the Science,* 1637; in *Philosophical Works* eds. Haldane and Ross, Cambridge University Press, 1931, I:88.) Thus also had Montaigne spoken explicitly on occasion and Bacon by constant implication. A "man of common sense" was evidently the antithesis of the man schooled traditionally, but not a sharply defined image. These thinkers could see that the old order was cracking; the difference between men of bourgeois property and the propertyless seems however to have been no clearer to them than to Richard DeBury, 200 years earlier.

Descartes' psychology is also somewhat discouraging to immersion in books. Thanks to the impressions registered on a child's mind by his physical environment, decisively important at that stage, thanks further to the tenacity of memory and the preservation of false notions as well as sound ones, and finally to the fatigue of thinking abstractly, "most men . . . perceive nothing but in a confused way." This condition is aggravated by habituation to words rather than things. (*Principles of Philosophy,* 1644; in *Philosophical Works,* eds. Haldane and Ross, I:251-252.) Neither Montaigne, who quoted past writers voluminously, nor Bacon, who referred to them a good deal less often, seems to have given any sustained thought to libraries. Hardly a surprise is it, therefore, that Descartes, whose deference to the past was hardly more than perfunctory, apparently said nothing on the subject.

How much nonphilosopher John Durie's attention to the matter was the hand of fate, or, as he would doubtless have put it, God, will never be known. For a man engaged in library work for a mere four years of his eighty-four (1596-1680), he managed to sound a number of helpful notes, on both usefulness and other themes. Durie (or Dury) was the son and grandson of determined Scotch Presbyterians and was himself an equally determined seeker after peace among men of all convictions. Educated at several institutions in Europe, he was attracted early to ecumenical effort and gave it his young manhood. Arriving in England in 1640/1641, aged forty-four, he chose inopportunely to join the royalists, who were just about to suffer severe setbacks. For the moment he was fortunate, obtaining some foreign assignments; but they did not suit him and he was again in London in 1645, in time to help write the celebrated Westminster Confession—one of the stiffer of the various Calvinistic credos—and new catechisms, the "long" for ministers and the "short" for children. He held some curateships but was apparently happy to assume the actual operating of the "King's Library" in 1649, the librarian not wanting to be bothered. Parliamentary party zealots who knew his background harassed him, and he left England again in 1654; meanwhile his daughter married German-born Henry Oldenburg, soon to become the first secretary of the Royal Society. When the Restoration brought back a king for the "King's Library" in 1660, Durie tried to reestablish himself at home. The new masters, however, were no more charitable about his service under the Cromwellian Protectorate than their predecessors had been about his royalism, and he spent the rest of his life unhappily in Germany.

Durie's ideas for library development and management were expressed briefly, as he undertook his "drudgery" in 1649, in two letters addressed to Samuel Hartlib, the well-known friend of education and agriculture, who published them together with several other items in 1650. His peroration, at the end of the second letter, is a splendid illustration of the interweaving in England of the pressures of capitalist accumulation of wealth, nation building, learning, and religion: "It is the Glorie and Riches of Nations and of great Cities, to make themselves the Center of Trade," and if they can manage it, to oblige their neighbors to buy from them. Thus is it also in learning. Blessed in such activity, "from whence much Glorie to God in the Gospel, and honor will redound to the Nation." The goal indeed must be "the advancement of the Kingdom" of God "over the Souls of men." Otherwise, "the increas of knowledge will increas nothing but strife, pride, and confusion." (Durie, *The Reformed Librarie-Keeper,* in *The Literature of Libraries,* eds. Dana and Kent, pp. 66–67, 70.)

How does this apply to libraries? Nearly everywhere, declares this observer of many places and institutions in northern Europe, the post of librarian is approached for "profit and gain," not "in regard of the service" to be rendered. Even at famous Oxford, he has been told, the librarian is paid no more than £50 or £60 a year and ekes out his income in ways "I have not been curious to search after." The incumbents protect their jobs and the books, "and this is all." (Durie, pp. 39–41.)

Concern for one's "profit and gain" was on the one hand entirely consistent with the blooming bourgeois order; Durie probably understood that very well. On the other hand, himself the embodiment of dedication to the human spirit, he wrestles with the contradiction between that dedication, more congenial to an order passing away, and the pressures inherent in the new one. He urges, almost desperately, that librarians should have £50, that they should be not "Mercenarie, but rather Honoraries." Thus recognized, he implies, they can more readily understand "the nature of their work . . . their places in a publick waie." Their "proper emploiments" are to become "Agents for the advancement of universal Learning." They should have "more than a bare keeping of the Books" to think about: thus would "a dead Bodie" perhaps be "animated with a publick Spirit." Only those should be eligible who had demonstrated zeal "in some publick waies of Learning"; their tasks should be listed and described. (Durie, pp. 41–44.)

The librarian's responsibilities are to build collections, care for them, and as "dispenser to applie them to use, or to see them well used, or at least not abused" (Durie p. 45). Collection building is to proceed with heavy emphasis on exchanges. Durie's own language is plainly borrowed from contemporary political economy: "for the increas of the stock" the librarian should correspond with those "eminent in every Science, to Trade with them" for mutual satisfaction. Domestic contacts should even be given notice of what has arrived from abroad but is not yet known to the public, in exchange for gifts such persons are peculiarly able to make. Thus does the librarian "multiplie the publick stock, whereof hee is a Treasurer and Factor," producing "an useful commoditie." (Durie, pp. 46–48, 43.) And for the expense of these "correspondencies and transcriptions" he should have "some Revenues" (Durie, p. 52).

Furthermore, Durie envisages this activity more broadly than merely collection building. He would thereby put Englishmen of various "faculties" in correspondence "with men of their own strain" at home and abroad, "for the beating out of matters not yet elaborated in Sciences." The scholars thus become the "Assistants and subordinate Factors" in the librarian's "Trade" and their own (Durie, p. 49). This "trade" seems to approach the international communication of knowledge. Gabriel Naudé had been plying it for some twenty-five years, but Durie, for all his associations (including Descartes) seems not to have heard of the Frenchman, nor the latter of him.

Book selection Durie places in the hands of the university "doctors." The librarian is to furnish them once a year a list of "the particulars . . . gained from abroad" so that they may decide what is "fit to be added to the publick stock" (Durie, p. 51); and also a list of the deposit copies received from the Stationers Company, which are to undergo the same critical review. For, says he: "I do not think that all Books and Treati[s]es which in this age are Printed in all kindes, should bee inserted into the Catalogue, and added to the stock of the Librarie" (Durie, p. 54).

What survives the weeding is to be listed in the "Catalogue of Additionals" to be issued "in writing" (Durie, p. 51) annually within the library; and whenever an appropriate number of titles accumulates (triennially, more or less, he thinks), to be published for circulation outside. Since, moreover, "there is seldom anie Book wherein there is not something useful, and Books freely given are not to be cast away," Durie urges placing all rejected volumes in their own "peculiar place." An alphabetical author register of such works is to be made, each with a "note of distinction" as to its subject (Durie, p. 55). His view of book values brings to mind the very recent (1644) *Areopagitica* by John Milton; one wonders how he viewed the "popery and open superstition" or "impious or evil absolutely either against faith or manners" which Milton excluded from his otherwise broad spectrum of the defensible (ed., Gollancz, Boston: Beacon, 1951, p. 64). Durie's reluctance to surrender the "freely given" is understandable enough but unusual in its candor. The special storing of disapproved books had a precedent in the Dominican-controlled assemblage in Rome of books prohibited by the Index, but he may not have known about it, and the idea was in any case uncommon.

In connection with the advancement of learning, noted Durie, a great stir had been created by the "Palatine" Library at Heidelberg. (Since 1356, each successive Count Palatine had been one of the seven Electors of the Holy Roman Empire.) At the opening of the century it was reportedly larger than the Vatican collection. "But," queried Durie, "what use was made of it?" Its capture in 1622 by Catholic forces, and its shipment to Rome on a train of 100 mules, the "gift" of victorious Duke Maximilian of Bavaria to Pope Gregory XV, seemed to Durie a consequence of error not far short of sin. Since the library had been made "an Idol to be respected and worshipped for a raritie . . . without anie benefit to those who" admired it from afar, deserved was its fate of falling into the hands of "those that in all things follow an Idolatrous waie . . ." (Durie, pp. 60–63). For a militant Protestant to condemn Catholic use of images was virtually routine. That a fervent Calvinist should have been distressed by nonuse of a product of human effort or expense is no surprise, either. Fascinatingly unusual, however, is the focusing of these shafts upon precisely a library—and by an outsider, at that.

There was little likelihood of similar neglect in the Calvinist portion of the New World. Defense of orthodoxy in Massachusetts was the purpose of the Puritan preacher training school founded in 1636 at Cambridge. Book gifts are known to have arrived within two years. And in 1642 the " 'Hon[ore]d Magistrates & Rev[eren]d Elders' " of the legislature ("General Court") cooperated with more, for " 'A Library that might be of publick use to the Students therein' " (quoted from the sources by Louis Shores, *Origins of the American College Library, 1638-1800*, Nashville: George Peabody College for Teachers, 1934, p. 12). The "court" recorder could almost have been quoting Bodley. In the same year, moreover, Harvard was also provided by the legislature with a corporate charter and, like Oxford, a Board of Overseers. Continuing an even older tradition, the newly chartered corporation adopted in 1643 its well-known seal, three open books with clasps, the lowest face down, *veritas* ("truth") inscribed on them, one syllable on each. The Harvard College Library reached about 2,000 volumes by 1680, but its glory was so far solitary in the Protestant New World.

At that point Catholic culture had been flourishing in Lima, Peru, vice-regal headquarters, for a century. The Jesuits' San Bartolomé, in Bogotá (capital-to-be of Colombia), founded in 1604, had since 1628 been granting university degrees as a *colegio máximo*. The use of the associated libraries, however, was certainly no more "publick" than Harvard's: by and large the benefits accrued to students only through the minds of the faculties.

The Bibliophilic Commitment The idea of usefulness had not, however, eliminated either the bibliophilic impulse or appreciation of its history. In 1639 Carmelite Louis Jacob (1608–1670), one of Naudé's admirers, was induced by the latter to set aside his proposed retrospective biobibliography of French writers for some other tasks which seemed to Naudé more pressing. The first was to prepare a new edition of the master's *Advice,* at Naudé's plea that he himself was too busy developing the library of Cardinal Mazarin. Young Jacob began with the idea of enriching the original with five or six pages' worth of additional data. But the friends whom he apparently queried (the first library questionnaire?), and his own researches, despite being limited to collections of at least 3,000 volumes strong in one or more recognized major categories, yielded material so substantial that he published in 1644 a "Treatise on the Most Attractive Libraries Public and Private" (*Traicté des Plus Belles Bibliothèques. . .;* Paris: Chez Rolet le Duc). (So Jacob tells us in his prefatory address to the reader.)

He salutes a score of predecessors, noting, accurately, that their works were brief and concerned more with antiquity than with modern times. His own does seem to be the largest to date, not because any one library is reported in depth but simply because he mentions so many. He draws on an impressive array of resources, library catalogs included, but he is no more critical than earlier writers, crediting the mythical Hermes Trismegistus, for instance, with a library of 6,525 volumes, and submitting without comment the figure of 55,722 volumes for the collection of the twelfth-century ruler of much of Spain and the nearby areas of Africa, known as Jacob Almanzor (*Traicté*, pp. 48, 51). He speaks now and then of a particular work like Sebastian Münster's well-known encyclopedic "cosmography" of the 1540s (*Traicté*, p. 236), but on the whole devotes his story to sponsors, owners, and the transfers of collections.

With the end of the warfare in Germany came more of the same. Lipsius' history was reissued in 1666 in a volume containing also several more or less similar tracts, most of them of still earlier vintage. The assemblage begins with the two-page "chapter" on libraries from Isidor of Seville's seventh-century encyclopedia and ends with a group of items on the Vatican Library, one of which treats briefly of twenty-one successive Vatican librarians. Emphasized are antiquity in general, Rome in particular, and the leading Renaissance libraries of Italy, France, and Spain. Several contributors refer to philosopher-physician Galen; a few offer documentation. The assembler, Joachim J. Mader, historian-antiquarian, was evidently thinking in individualistic humanist fashion, for his title is "On the Libraries and Archives of the Most Enlightened Men," disregarding the corporate auspices element.

Narrow though it may have been, there was a market for such wares. Mader's compilation was lavishly praised only two years later in a "dissertation" on "illustrious libraries" by another nonlibrarian, Gottlieb Spitzel, enough of a neoclassicist to affect the Greek style for his published name ("Theophilus") but not enough of a student of bibliography to mention Gesner. In 1703 Spitzel's essay appeared again, as the third component in Johann A. Schmid's "supplement" to Mader. The first was Cardinal Bessarion's letter to the Venetian authorities presenting his great collection of Greek manuscripts; the second, a Latin translation of Naudé's *Avis*.

Two Practical Observers: Hottinger and Lomeier   Meanwhile, stimulated apparently by renewed use of libraries, and perhaps also by the curious (not yet investigated?) failure of librarians to speak up, other nonlibrarians in the Germanic area were writing in a contemporary vein about library service, classification, or both. J. H. Hottinger, brilliant Oriental philologist, died (1667) at forty-seven when a summer storm caught him and his family out on the lake near his beloved native Zürich. Before that tragedy deprived the leading University of Leyden of the services he had been preparing to render, he had published in 1664 a substantial tome with the unusual title, *Bibliothecarius Quadripartitus,* or "The Librarian/Bibliographer in Four Parts." Hottinger took note of the use of *bibliotheca* to mean a building or a collection of books and declared that he was adding a third application: a well-chosen collection of books organized by means of catalogs. He was here—and elsewhere—walking in the steps of Naudé, as he himself acknowledged; but Hottinger's distinctive way of formulating the idea was clearly a contribution, accepted as common currency in library discussion long after the coiner was forgotten.

He was not a librarian, although he reportedly had some influence upon and may have had an official connection with the City Library in Zürich. Of the four parts of his book, moreover, three are guides to the literature of theology. Nevertheless, Part I, entitled after the style of a widely known essay by Cicero, "On the Duties of the Librarian," considers in seven chapters that subject and the functions of libraries. (Again we are indebted to the labors of Hermann Escher, "Der Bibliothecarius Quadripartitus des J. H. Hottinger," in *Zentralblatt für Bibliothekswesen,* 51:505–522, 1934.) The first reviews the librarian from Greek times to the Vatican, noting that he was often an archivist too and is now also "at least" the city chronicler. A person of energy, dedication, and intelligence is needed, with good health and a good memory; one who can pick the right book as readily as a pharmacist finds the right drug; one who will not be likely to falter for lack of knowledge of various alphabets. That sounds as though Hottinger's study wall bore a portrait of Conrad Gesner; it certainly owes little to the James shaped by Bodley. The additional remarks, about catalogs, we put aside for the moment.

His second chapter is devoted first to annotated bibliography, classified by traditional broad subjects and by language. He bemoans the failure to continue what Gesner began, appreciates Georg Draud (see below) and some others, and displays an impressive familiarity with both general and special bibliographies. Next comes a list of fifty-odd celebrated libraries, in alphabetical order, with notes on their character and holdings and a sample catalog. Noteworthy is the neglect of the medieval abbey libraries, mainly ignored by Humanism and the Renaissance and quite likely unknown to Hottinger. English writers on theology, and the matters dealt with in that literature (no less than 400 names are mentioned), occupy the third chapter.

Book selection and procurement are the subjects of the fourth chapter. Again in the Naudéan manner he first stresses usefulness and having the principal works on each subject. Going further, he observes that a large library should also satisfy curiosity and honor the appeal of the attractive book. In good humanist fashion he argues for originals, but agrees that translations are needed too. His particular accent on Hebrew Bibles is a direct reflection of contemporary polemics over variant texts, a tradition going back at least to Jerome in the late fourth century and deeply rooted in Northern Humanism. On the question of acquiring books, he illuminates his times with the contention that the task will be easier if one starts by buying an existing library. That does not seem to have occurred very often. But it is certainly a fact that many a library had within living memory been greatly strengthened or weakened, or moved bodily by the fortunes of war;

more pertinently, peaceful transfer by sale was already familiar to book men and was shortly going to be conspicuous.

The fifth chapter is given to subject classification, with particular attention to theology and philology (in its classic broad meaning). Hottinger here contributes nothing noteworthy. No more significant to the main stream is his sixth chapter, responding to some questions of a friend about private library management.

A number of other matters related primarily to cataloging are dealt with partly in the first chapter and more extensively in the seventh. In the first chapter, like a good many catalogers of later times, Orientalist Hottinger calls for subject entries " 'neither too elaborate nor too meager' " (quoted by Escher, p. 515); homely examples are offered. It should be remembered, he urges, that a single page can be more enlightening than an entire volume. He is confident that subject access (by the staff) means more to good service than (author) alphabetical catalogs. The latter, if secondary, should nevertheless give not only the author's name but edition and other descriptive data. (This *catalogus nominalis* is literally a name catalog and does not include anonyma.)

Chapter 7 opens with the reflection that comprehensive library catalogs are hard to produce and rarely found. The problem is the labor of analyzing the contents of several thousand books. Such work really requires scholars, but is usually thought unworthy of their time, child's play; besides, few sponsors are willing to pay for a proper cataloging performance. Despite this lugubrious confession Hottinger doggedly proposes an apparatus of unusual complexity, going even beyond Pellican's plan of 1532.

Most important is the *catalogus logicus,* or systematic catalog arranging material under subjects. The pattern is conventional, Theology-Philology-Jurisprudence-Medicine-Philosophy. Yet he includes not only books but academic theses and the addresses read at German school ceremonies, and speaks of serving anyone uncertain in his search, whether educated or uneducated; perhaps this reflects the known increase in demands on library service in the German cities of his day. The author himself, however, has not always found what he wanted, readily, in this instrument, the classified catalog. He therefore prescribes another of the sort already familiar, in which entries are arranged alphabetically according to the key word in the title. This *catalogus realis* can be limited to book titles or carried out precisely enough to include analytical entries for parts of books. He is aware nonetheless of the unreliability of titles for subject guidance.

The balance of the suggested apparatus is subject-oriented only in part or not at all. The *catalogus theologicus* would protect the unwary against a religious point of view not plainly stated, by listing authors by faith. How many libraries acquired such works? The *catalogus chronologicus* arranges entries by authors' lives, a device employed in limited fashion in many medieval catalogs, breaking up the long list into three parts, ancient, medieval, and modern. The *catalogus topographicus* distributes authors by their homelands, obviously a national-bibliography feature. There is also a possible *catalogus personalis,* an author-alphabetical catalog.

Hottinger said little about shelving, perhaps because he was not a librarian. Separating the tall books from the short appealed to him aesthetically, and he favored keeping books of like content together. But he was shrewd enough to know that classification is highly subjective, and to recognize that when shelves are closed to the public it does not matter very much what the scheme is. How many hours have been wasted by librarians who did not reason thus?

Johannes Lomeier, a Dutch pastor (1636–1699), likewise perceived that arranging books is bound to be in large measure arbitrary. He did indicate a preference for a seven-part pattern in which "philosophy" was associated with the mechanical arts dependent on it, chemistry linked with medicine, and provision made (part seven) for encyclopedias, dictionaries, collections, and bibliographical/library tools. Most of his substantial work (*De Bibliothecis*, 1669; enlarged ed., 1680) was, however, given to a survey of the libraries of Europe, including considerable history and citing authorities in the spirit of the recently developed sober historiography. He apparently checked little or nothing by visiting libraries himself; he was occasionally wrong in details and overlooked some important libraries altogether. But his data were more numerous and more reliable than any predecessor's, according to John W. Montgomery, who translated and annotated the lengthy Chapter X (Berkeley: University of California Press, 1962); and for a generation or two Lomeier was respected enough to be plagiarized, errors and all.

The Librarian's Uncertain Standing   There was now enough consciousness of libraries to evoke in classification schemes provision for bibliographical literature, and some library literature may have been included. The cautionary "may" is required by the dual meaning of *bibliotheca* and the impossibility of inspecting all the books under that title. So far as the evidence in Julius Petzholdt's great collection tells the story (*Bibliotheca Bibliographica*, Leipzig: Englemann, 1866, pp. 25ff.), Naudé was the first: the third category of writers listed in his Cordesiana catalog (1643) is *Bibliothecarii*, which usually means "librarians." In 1649 one Alexandre Fichet published in Lyons a bibliographical guide in which Section IX, the last, was devoted to *Curiosa Bibliotheca*; there, the key word probably means "bibliography." Hottinger's ruminations of 1664 included a rather elaborate classification sketch: in the science branch *(Physicos)* appears a division for *Scholasticos*, which may embrace library catalogs, unless the subdivision *de Indicibus Bibliothecis* means not that but either indexes to bibliographies or subject indexes. Lomeier's allowance for library/bibliographical tools in 1669 was noted a moment ago. Also clearer than many is the last heading in Ismael Bouillaud's famous Thuana catalog (1679), *Academiae, Bibliothecae, Catalogi Librorum et Scriptorum.* The second term may mean bibliographies or sets of books; the last phrase is bookseller language for bibliographies.

Recognition of bibliography was a logical consequence of the proliferation of bibliographies, for the trade and national types (to be discussed shortly) dominated the early portion of the seventeenth century; and subject lists, together with printed library and sales catalogs, its closing quarter. Librarianship, however, was germinating more slowly. The grammar schools of England, for example, continuing the medieval chantry tradition of instruction in Latin, were by the 1620s furnishing classical education to boys (not girls, as a rule) of nearly all social strata, backed up often by a "library" of dictionaries and anthologies of classical writers produced by the Humanists. The trend was encouraged by pedagogue Charles Hoole's *A New Discovery of the Old Art of Teaching School* . . . (London: Crook, 1659-1660), in which precisely such a "Schoole Library" is urged frequently, especially in connection with the schemes for the upper grades (Scholar press facsimile reprint, 1969, pp. 144, 155, 171, 179, 200, 205, for instance). The grammar schools continued to multiply for about another generation, and at least one, the Westminister School, actually built a library between 1655 and 1660. In none of this evidence, however, is a librarian so much as mentioned.

There were librarians in the universities. Yet, in the century ending in 1680, whether the incumbents were would-be scholars or ministers tarrying in the library briefly (as so often on English campuses), or amenable sons of wealth or connection in posts all over Europe filled by family purchase, or professors who developed scholarly collections of classics, Orientalia, theology, law or medicine, often on the basis of gifts from private collectors (fairly common in Germanica and some other places), "librarianship" seems often to have differed little from "minding the store." How much more was needed when in 1590 the Jesuit field inspector for Germany, asked whether the library really must be swept twice a week, replied that once in two weeks would suffice because the library was entered rarely? Or at an institution like North Germany's University of Rostock, whose forty professors are recorded as having borrowed in the forty years from 1650 to 1690 a grand total of 300 books? Thomas James was officially "Bodley's Librarian," but his attempt via his "Arts catalog" to exercise professional judgment in selecting books for undergraduates was strictly unofficial, the fruit of labor on his own time, and never printed.

The marginal character of librarianship by comparison with the scholarly or literary life is plain enough in Naudé's reputation. The separation was downright stark at an outstanding institution in Naudé's Paris, representing on the one hand long established ecclesiastical tradition and on the other the new scholarship kindled by Humanism, the Renaissance academy tradition, religious competition, and nationalism. At the Paris Abbey of St. Germain-des-Prés about 1645, the Benedictines of the reform "Congregation of St. Maur" (founded in 1621) were operating a historical research center based on remarkable book and manuscript collections and a corresponding scholarly staff assembled from various cloisters. At least by 1681, the year of publication of Jean Mabillon's landmark paleography manual, *De Re Diplomatica*, they were the recognized leaders in the scientific treatment of documents, inspiring much rival emulation on the part of the Jesuits and others.

But the modified Benedictine rules governing the Maurists at St. Germain-des-Prés, apparently formulated early in the seventeenth century, charge the librarian with no striking responsibilities and grant him no authority worth mentioning. He records acquisitions, "distributes" the books in classes, and watches over circulation. Whoever laid out those classes, the convent superior must always be asked about anything beyond narrow routine, obviously a practice unchanged over some three centuries if not longer. The only novelty (?) is the three-paragraph section in the reformed rule devoted to the "Prefect of the Library," the first portion of which states that the librarian ought to be a brother versed in the sciences *"'et bibliographi-*

ca.'" What the last term meant to those then using it is uncertain: perhaps book matters generally, inasmuch as the most numerous group of published book lists, the trade product, were most often called *catalogi*. In any case, by whatever means the brother was to become thus *"'versatus,'"* training is not mentioned. (Quoted in Franklin, *Anciennes Bibliothèques*, I:110.)

That the librarian element in the scholar-in-library equation was nevertheless pushing forward may be seen in the contrasting case of Peter Lambeck (1628–1680), originally of Hamburg and later of Vienna. The City Library of Hamburg was not only part of the tradition of municipal institutions known in the Germanic area for well over a century, but fortunate enough to be rooted in German's leading port and trade center and to emerge from the Thirty Years' War hardly touched. It was further favored in the 1640s by substantial bequests and the timely return from travels of native son Peter Lambeck, a promising and well-connected young history student. His organizing of the newly expanded library in 1648 seems to have helped sustain the local momentum, for in 1650 the library was authorized a (permanent?) librarian, and stated hours of public service a year later. Lambeck himself went off to Vienna in 1663, to direct the library of Emperor Leopold I. His arrangement of the 80,000-plus Palatina volumes by subject, without regard to format, drew much attention; and his fame was secured by the printing, from 1665 to 1679, of the first eight volumes of his projected twenty-five-volume catalog based thereon.

There were of course other scholars serving as librarians, but they were not always appreciated as librarians quite the way they were as scholars. These were but tender shoots of recognition, nourished by perceptions of a body of technique and policy going somehow beyond the confines of any given familiar specialty but not yet clearly defined and not yet illuminated by any systematic theoretical literature or formal instruction.

Acquisitions policy was indeed debated, at some of the colleges in England before the Revolution, during the Protectorate, and under the Restoration; also in the Paris salons throughout the century, especially with reference to the increasingly prominent private libraries; also in Germany after 1648. The number of books available for purchase was mounting rapidly enough to encourage the proliferation of bibliographies of all kinds; if the subject variety often focused on the past, the national and regional varieties were more catholic, and the trade bibliographies conspicuously oriented on the present. Did one build with the traditionalists around the old masters? Or with the modernists around recent and contemporary writing? The public attention granted the issue was at times quite heated. Yet the issue was far less a question of library philosophy than of rival positions in philosophy and science, literature and literary criticism. Naudé's conviction that both old and new were appropriate remained unusual; more than two generations later, Leibniz' similar emphasis on the inherent importance of a work was still worthy of remark.

On that question and several others, full understanding of the role and status of librarians awaits study of important contemporary evidence, especially the pertinent encyclopedia materials from Alsted (1620) to Ephraim Chambers (1728), and the book-related sections of works like Daniel Morhof's *Polyhistor* (1688).

Meanwhile, an assessment is within reach which is unlikely to be amended by closer acquaintance with contemporary writings. Full authority and responsibility depend in the last analysis on a stable income, controlled by the librarian. That was coming very slowly, as might be anticipated. In 1578, Hieronymous Wolf, Swabian classics scholar and director and librarian (1557–1580) of the Augsburg Gymnasium, had written that a library must have a firm annual appropriation for acquisitions; his proposal was clearly premature. The Great Elector, Frederick William of Brandenburg-Prussia, applied his familiar firm grip in 1659 to the Royal Library in Berlin. Advantageous was the furnishing, then unusual, of an annual appropriation, from 1664 to 1692, dependent upon the collection of penalty fees from nobles delinquent on certain feudal obligations. The sum available to the librarian varied, it was never enough to support a regular budget or planning, and he could buy nothing without the Elector's signature. But it was regular and fairly stable: a step forward.

Organizing Information

Whether those caring for libraries were really scholars or merely dilettantes, whether their own hearts were in their library duties or not, whatever funds they had at their disposal, they were obliged to give increasing attention to building and organizing the collections they managed.

The Booksellers and the Scientists Enlarge Book Information Current trade bibliography had been initiated in 1564, on an international scale, by Georg Willer, in connection with the Frankfort Fairs. The book trade as a distinctive enterprise had come of age, albeit little is known of booksellers who were not also printers. National bibliography appeared a generation later (1595), developing in fits and starts under various circumstances until it was temporarily sidetracked early in the eighteenth century by selective critical bibliography.

Libraries were affected in two major activities. Collection building was made easier, obviously, insofar as it became possible to learn about new publications promptly if not always accurately. The Frankfort Fair catalogs, and some others entering the arena soon afterward, announced Latin and German imprints acceptable in a Protestant market and neither of purely local interest nor otherwise "minor" in Willer's judgment. (The authorities at Mainz meanwhile countered with lists of works by Catholics, but only intermittently from 1606 to 1625.) Certain titles in French, Italian, and Spanish were included from the outset. The first Dutch items appeared in these listings in 1600; English publications (none however *in* English!) were advertised much earlier (1578), but presumably because they were not on hand in the shops were not listed until 1608. When the Frankfort Fair catalog cumulations of 1602, 1611, and 1625 were produced, quite a few more were advertised: significant pre-1564 works and especially contemporary French writings. Actually (see below), these added categories were not always included in the fair catalogs supporting the cumulations, and not all are known to have been on hand in the bookshops.

In England, on the contrary, the predominant practice was to register books regardless of their availability in the shops. This characteristic in due course appeared elsewhere too, helping to differentiate "national" bibliography from "trade" bibliography, wherein availability for purchase (or being "in print") is a prime consideration. The English national bibliographies are also distinguished by their very attention to English publications. Andrew Maunsell may even have been moved to assemble his 1595 *Catalogue of English Printed Bookes* (see also 1965 London reprint by Gregg Press) partly because the 1592 cumulation of Frankfort Fair catalogs listed nothing of English origin. Certainly he reproaches those who "soare so hie[gh], that they looke not so low, as on their own countrie writers." And he contends, in his prefatory salute to the book trade, that he is informing the learned of many titles "they would not thinke were in our owne tongue." In his how-to-use-this-book section he explains that translators' names are italicized like authors' if made known in the book.

He is a businessman. He sounds like Gesner in his regret at "seeing . . . mainly singular books . . . after the first impression [i.e., printing], so spent and gone, that they lie even as it were buried in some few studies." His concern, however, is not the survival of civilization but the interests of his fellow booksellers, for whom the catalog is just as "necessarie" as a dictionary to a schoolmaster. He does not mention the catalogs from the Frankfort Fairs.

Clearly individualistic is his stress on study at home, where a man need only open the Maunsell product to discover "what Books are written, and how many translated." Understandably, he says nothing of libraries, although many of his potential customers must have held library privileges. Overtones of bourgeois egalitarianism as well as English nationalism can be heard in his remark that he did not bother to look up foreign authors' pedigrees or academic titles.

A most practical patriot, Maunsell emphasizes in the "Epistle Dedicatory" to Queen Elizabeth, in *The First Part of the Catalogue . . . Divinitie,* that "these divine books" have "mightily increased" during her reign; also, that "your MA[jesty's] loving subjects may freely use all those good bookes within this Catalogue specifyed, and many more, only by your Majesties most godly & Soveraigne Authoritie. . . ." In the same spirit, his address to the clergy and other readers of "Divinitie" closes with the statement that his list includes "the ancient Popish Bookes" printed in England; but "the Bookes written by fugitive Papistes, as also those that are written against the present government, I doe not thinke meete for me to meddle withall."

He says nothing, as the Frankfort dealers would, of all books being on hand; but does declare that he has "seene" every work listed, and calls attention to the space provided for the addition of books overlooked or brand new. That had been known in the Middle Ages. But Maunsell represents the future rather than the past in listing printed books only, without manuscripts, explaining to the reader how to use the book, and adopting some advanced styles in cataloging (as will be seen below).

Neither Maunsell nor anyone else in England produced a current bibliography until 1618, when John Bill, who had served Bodley and visited the Frankfort Fair regularly from 1605 to 1622, undertook a London edition of the fair catalogs. He ignored the German section but reproduced the Latin lists; and in his second issue, Fall 1618, appended thirteen English titles, barely 10 percent of the works of that sort published within the six-month report period. A competitive effort was made simultaneously by printer William Jaggard, but his catalog purportedly of current English books included fewer of those than of pre-1618 imprints and did not list all of 1618. Since no sequel appeared, Bill in 1622 turned out another fair-related list of English books, longer than Jaggard's. A few more similar stabs were made, but the heavy hand of Church of England censorship under Charles I injured the book trade much more severely than the Thirty Years' War's impact on continental activities. A catalog of Latin and English books printed in England between 1626 and 1631 was offered in 1631, anonymously. No more appeared until nearly the end of the Cromwell Protectorate.

William London's trade bibliography of 1658 listed more than 3,000 of "the most vendible books in England," mainly recent works he thought important, mainly in English, and all allegedly in his stock, a feature then more German than English. Included as well was a 1657–1658 supplement with about 100 titles, the first of its kind in England. Dealer London spoke of expanding his product to become an annual guide to all new books. But he operated at Newcastle-on-Tyne, near Scotland and quite a journey from the London center. (Since the 1585 order of the Star Chamber, books could be printed legally only in London, Oxford, and Cambridge.) He did manage to turn out another two-year supplement in 1660 covering about 400 titles, but that was the end.

Meanwhile, despite the (final) war with Spain, an Amsterdam printer, Broer Jansz (or Jansson), issued between 1640 and 1652 the first current national bibliography released periodically. Sometimes annual and sometimes semiannual, it listed Netherlands publications, first by language, the largest group being Latin. Not all High Dutch and Low Dutch items were reported, but Jansz announced far more Dutch books than the contemporary international bibliography based on the Frankfort Fair. A kindred Belgian enterprise lasted only three years, from 1641 to 1644, partly because the compiler was not a printer and, unlike the earlier Frankfort Fair catalog cumulators, was not sought out by the book trade but himself tried to take the initiative. He was apparently the first current-bibliographer to suffer from such grave handicaps. In his three years' activity, nevertheless, he managed to record more than 300 products of Belgian presses.

The failure of the Frankfort Fair catalogs to post readers properly on the rapidly expanding output of French scholars was on Gabriel Naudé's mind when Louis Jacob called on him in Rome in 1639. Besides urging him (as noted above, p. 177) to work on a new edition of the celebrated *Advice,* Naudé contended that France needed not a retrospective but a current national bibliography. Jacob's first issue (1645) listed 845 Paris imprints of 1643 and 1644. By 1654, when political turmoil in France and other factors blocked continuation of his *Bibliotheca Parisina* and *Bibliotheca Gallica,* the patriot-priest had registered over 3,500 works, of which 2,351 were in French and 3,100 published in Paris.

None of the current national bibliographies launched on the continent during the Thirty Years' War lasted long. National sentiment of the Naudé-

Jacob sort was evidently a weaker magnet than the broadest coverage obtainable, and national bibliographies were accepted only while war interfered with the distribution of international listings. Perhaps the matrix of the well-established semiannual fair (the book trade accounted for about one-twelfth of its revenue) buttressed by certain legal privileges, was also indispensable for stability. The Frankfort and Leipzig fairs not only continued throughout the war but became more lively after it. Yet the emergence of large-scale publishing houses was going soon to reduce the importance of a fair; meanwhile, Frankfort steadily lost ground to Leipzig as Latin and the older type of scholarship took second place in published output behind the vernaculars, science, and belles lettres.

The vernaculars and science, and the divergence of interest in science from interest in belles lettres and philosophy, now exerted a decisive influence in altering the book-reporting scene. For approximately forty years the handful of publicly known academies deriving from Italian Renaissance models had been supplemented by discussion groups in private homes in France and England, labeled variously—the *"Cabinet,"* for example, of Naudé's friends, the brothers Dupuy. Devoted predominantly to literary and philosophical discussion, they eventually moved their science-oriented members to form groups of their own, sometimes with provision for experimentation. Beholden to this tradition, and others, were the Royal Society (1662) and the Académie des Sciences (1666). Contact among the groups was maintained primarily by correspondence; a prime purpose was to learn about new books and brochures, especially those on scientific questions. If this curiosity leaned somewhat on a host's private library and had no recorded bearing upon collections open to the public, it did emphasize speed of reportage and in France exposed the fact that few read English.

In response to these needs appeared, in January 1665, the *Journal des Sçavans*. Like the "newsbooks" already on the scene since about 1620, it was a weekly, decidedly a novelty in the book world. That high frequency had been chosen deliberately, in preference to monthly intervals, said editor Denis de Sallo, lawyer and amateur historian, lest the desired audience think the contents badly out of date. One wonders whether the postal service or the subscribers' time and energies really matched that effort. In any case, certain other characteristics seem to have been most welcome. The language was French rather than Latin, and very soon the columns passed along from the *Philosophical Transactions* of the Royal Society materials of interest to the non-English-readers. Besides, the coverage was both selective rather than "complete," and broad enough to appeal, reportedly, to many beyond the "Learned" of the journal's title.

Probably more important, the *Journal,* beginning its bibliographical service eleven years after Louis Jacob's last contribution, explicitly rejected the mere listing of titles as insufficient for the serious mind. The foreword in the first number (January 5, 1665) declared that to make known what was new in *"La République des lettres"* required not only mentioning the principal new books but indicating what they dealt with and "in what way they can be useful." Thus joined the philosophical accents of Montaigne and Bacon, the university teacher plea of a Lipsius, and the concerns of the scientists still relying much more on pamphlets and correspondence than on books and libraries. Present also, in all likelihood, were the interests of the bookdealers, especially those who in the half-century then beginning, whether outright owners of the journals or otherwise, would shape journal policies, choosing editors and speaking authoritatively as to which books would be reviewed and which reviews printed.

Editor de Sallo's emphases and tone promptly displeased the royal and Jesuit keepers of orthodoxy, and he was removed after three months. Thanks partly to the launching meanwhile of the *Philosophical Transactions*, which utilized quite a few items from the *Journal*, French national pride evidently played some part in its almost immediate resumption under new and more respectable management; the price, understandably, was a decline in references to it in contemporary correspondence.

On the record, nonetheless, book reviews were a principal contribution of both this journal and the later (1682–   ) Leipzig *Acta Eruditorum* ("Works of the Learned"). The former carried 1,234 reviews in the years from 1680 to 1689, the latter 1,332 in the period from 1682 to 1689. On the other hand, the *Philosophical Transactions* of the Royal Society of London was from the start (1665) a repository primarily of scientific, and pseudoscientific, papers rather than book notices. Each of these types found imitators among the numerous periodicals established afterward, and in-between brands emerged as well.

Whatever the paucity of book information in the Royal Society *Transactions* had to do with it, whether or not the Restoration of Charles II stimulated the local book trade, England was now to produce the first current national bibliography of notable longevity. An obscure attempt was made in 1664, covering works published between Christmas 1662 and Christmas 1663; continuation was apparently intended but failed to materialize. More important, the plague of 1665 and the great fire of 1666 badly damaged the book trade as well as London life in general.

Two years later, recovery could be measured by the lists of 50 to 100 newly released books distributed by John Starkey at the end of each term of the law courts (November, February, May, and June). Most of the titles were in English; some, a distinct group, were reprints; prices were stated, an unusual step. Immediate success seems to have led Starkey to require a fee from the publishers whose works were to be listed. That was not a new practice: the prominent pioneer newspaper, *A Perfect Diurnal*, had been running book advertising frequently since May 13, 1650. But the publishers reacted by organizing their own catalog, denouncing not only Starkey's fees but omissions from his *Mercurius Librarius*, and indeed presenting eighty-six titles where he mentioned forty-one. Starkey's associate Robert Clavell then defected to the other side. The original series ended with the eighth issue in June 1670, and the traders' *A Catalogue . . .* pursued the established pattern under Clavell until his death in 1711, the aggregate being known to history as the "Term Catalogues."

Like Bassé at Frankfort almost a century before him (see below), Clavell initiated a series of cumulations. In the first, 1673, the book buyer could find a great many of the works published in England between the fire of 1666 and November 1672. A supplement dealt with the next two years. By 1675 the second edition, including all the foregoing, down to November 1674, registered 2500 titles on 119 pages. To furnish also select data about Latin imports (published between 1670 and 1680) was too difficult at that point, but they occupied half of the 191-page third edition of 1681, listing altogether 3,500 works. The next cumulation was available in 1696, a 126-page record of English publication from 1666 to 1695; although it included only select Catholic items and no "minor" writings, the number thus announced was some 8,500. Clavell was in 1698 and 1699 Master of the Company of Stationers.

To what extent did those involved with library acquisitions anywhere use the contemporary lists of new publications? Bodley and James regularly consulted fair and other sales catalogs. Naudé, developing the Mazarine Library, was still in 1647 the energetic traveler, thumbing foreign bookdealer catalogs as well as the domestic output, and going to the leading London shop in person. In 1658 the Jesuit authorities in Germany, soon to dominate Catholic education in that area, directed their university and school officials to utilize those same means of keeping their libraries up to date. And the countermoves by the Evangelical pastorate were similar. The city libraries, moreover, were under burgher pressure after the war ended to modernize their holdings and service; they probably turned to the catalogs of the book trade. How representative these activities were will not be established until a mass of individual-library data is examined carefully and summarized.

Book Trade Advances in Bibliographic Control   Although little seems to be known about library utilization of current bibliography for acquisitions, hindsight wisdom tells us that library practice helped shape but probably was more to be shaped by, if tardily, trade bibliographic style. Use of the author's surname as the main entry first became prominent in 1595, in the pioneer national bibliography, Andrew Maunsell's never-finished listing of England's book output. Full and faithful transcription of the title page had already been adopted in the Frankfort Fair catalogs; place, publisher, date, and format (such as "quarto") likewise, but not the number of pages. Prices were seldom mentioned; but they were then seldom fixed, either. This level of development presumably corresponded closely to the needs of the book trade as its members saw them, for bookdealers' catalogs soon emulated Willer in following title pages in their listings. In one way or another this ever-increasing assemblage of data was affecting library thinking and behavior, even if the libraries, not directly a part of the world of business and bourgeois values, did not feel the same need to be meticulous.

Additional advances imitated sooner or later by the libraries may be observed in both Maunsell and the cumulations of the Frankfort Fair catalogs published between 1592 and 1625. (Thanks to the invaluable close reporting of Rudolf Blum, *Vor- und Frühgeschichte der nationalen Allgemeinbibliographie*, Frankfurt-a.M.: Büchhandler-Vereinigung, 1959? pp. 16ff.; also in *Archiv für Geschichte des Buchwesens*, II:233–303, 1960.) The first was produced in 1592 by Nicolaus Bassé, a French-born printer and bookdealer of Frankfort. Cumulating fifty-seven of Willer's semiannual lists of the years from 1564 to 1592, each arranged first by language, then broad subject, then author, he introduced subject entries for places and events notable in historical literature in the form of alphabetically located see-references to the appropriate books. Any given broad subject group, like medicine, might thus comprise (mainly) author entries, title entries (where no author was recorded), and subject entries for events and historically related places: all in a single alphabet, a dictionary catalog of sorts. This device was also employed by Latin teacher Johannes Cless in a Frankfort cumulation of 1602 issued by Bassé's son-in-law Peter Kopf, drawing upon seventy-one fair catalogs and including some pre-1564 titles.

England's Maunsell meanwhile was disingenuous in implying that his choice of subject arrangement, rather than the author alphabets of "*Gesner, Simler,* and our countriman *John Bale,*" was a bold departure. He may not have known about Gesner's *Pandects* scheme of twenty-one classes with lavish subdivision; partly because they led only to topics, not titles, they had drawn little attention. He may not have known either that J. J. Fries in Zürich had lately (1587) improved upon his mentor Gesner by adding to the latter's twenty-one classes two more for general works, and building class numbers upon subjects, independent of particular shelf locations. But it is probable that he was cognizant of the four to seven divisions called the "faculty" classification, and of the fact that its use was then spreading steadily. Besides, his contemporary Bassé utilized thirty subject groups for the small company of Romance language entries in his fair catalog cumulation. (With the much larger assemblage of Latin and German titles, Bassé, like many a later librarian, shuddered and settled for the easier seven conventional groups.) Maunsell does not allude to Fries or Bassé.

The London bookdealer's work is on the surface rather ordinary. *The First Part* deals with theology, *The Second Part* (also 1595) with mathematics, medicine, and other applied sciences. And in his bow to the book trade in the latter item, Maunsell voices his hope to produce soon a complementary guide to "Humanity," or "Gramer, Logick, Rhetoricke, Lawe, Historie, Poetrie, Policie, &c." But it is harder "to get sight of" such books and to settle on a pattern of listing; anyway, they are less "necessary." He died that very year, 1595, and the putative third part was never done.

Closer examination reveals, however, certain features deserving particular notice. In the spirit of the elaborate breakdown urged by Gesner but generally neglected, Maunsell furnishes his exclusively English-language listings under "Divinitie" with ninety centered subdivisions, from "Ag[ainst] *Adultery and Fornication*" to "Of Good *Workes.*" "Bible" is conspicuous among them for further refinement, by parts of the Bible, subject subdivisions, and special subdivisions like *"Concordances"* (Did Thomas James see it before finishing his own larger model?). *The Second Part* arrays scientific and technical books likewise, in thirty-three sections from "Of Anathomie" to "Of the Art of *Warre.*"

Although these headings look very much like the usual phrases plucked from book titles, they are in several instances derived on the contrary from ideas. Under "Of *Oathes*" (p. 76) is listed a single see-reference to an authorless title, in which the word "oaths" does not appear. Similarly, under *"Recantations"* (p. 91) are posted one see-reference and two full entries, none of which employs the term "recantations." More examples could be cited. In short, Maunsell is using what later times would call subject headings. And quite consciously too. Speaking, in his preface to the book trade, of anonyma, he notes that he has used either (the customary) entry under title or entry under "the matter they entreate of" or "both, for the easier finding of them." These subject headings, moreover, are in alphabetical sequence with authors and titles without authors, each of his two *Parts* being thus a dictionary catalog in a fuller sense than the first two cumulations of the Frankfort Fair catalogs.

The third of those German offerings deviated from local precedent by substantial use of sources beyond the fair catalogs, placing one foot somewhat belligerently in the camp of scholarly bibliography with the explicit contention that the importance of a work justified listing it even if it was not "in print." In like manner preacher Georg Draud titled this multipart product with the *Bibliotheca* of the learned rather than the *Catalogus* of the bookdealers. Probably more significant were the innovations in the apparatus of subject access. They were not unveiled in his first contribution, the *Biblioteca Exotica* of 1610. Devoted to works in languages other than Latin and German, it arranged the 168 pages (of a total of 219) of French listings not by the customary six or seven subject groups but by nineteen; at least two rubrics, "Satire" and "Erotica and Gynecology," were unusual, but the others were familiar and did not include either polygraphy or bibliography.

Draud was dissatisfied with these means of subject access. He considered organizing the more substantial Latin and German lists more elaborately, twenty or thirty groups rather than six or seven, but apparently did not. To apply to all nonfiction the see-references used for historical places and events would have been too laborious. And he did not like (for reasons not entirely clear) the subject indexes sometimes appended to learned bibliographies. His second and third products were accordingly designed on the contrasting *Schlagwort* or catchword plan. He took Cless' materials, added more, and arranged them to begin with under the conventional seven broad headings. But within each such group books were entered no longer in an author alphabet but by title, in alphabetical order by catchwords. Since these catchwords had subject significance, and were repeated in several titles, subgroups were produced. These he called "classes" and his two catalogs ". . . .classica," one devoted to Latin works and the other to the German, both being issued in 1611. Only within one of the usually small subgroups were the entries arranged by author surname.

It is noteworthy, moreover, that government decrees were treated exceptionally, entered not under an "author" but by the *Land* ("county") which promulgated them, a striking prototype of the corporate entry so prominent in later times.

Achieved thus was greater sophistication in subject access. The see-reference, signaled by an asterisk, was now utilized to refer the user from old-fashioned terms to new ones. And titles not providing any catchword were followed by references to a subject expression, plus, usually, an author's name. Other problems proved less easily solved. One was the degree of directness and specificity desired, still a poser in the mid-twentieth century. If one catchword yielded by the titles under theology was "marriage," a sacrament, and another was "sacraments," the user was confronted with a list of subject entries on the same level which were not equal in substantive scope. To many minds, apparently a majority then, this violation of the hierarchical nature of knowledge was unacceptable; Draud found few disciples. Full scale application of his atomistic approach awaited the age of documentation and such devices as "uniterms."

Furthermore the *Schlagwort* system—until in the late nineteenth (?) century it came to mean also "subject headings"—has certain inherent defects. (They may explain why, though in use since the fourteenth century, in some but certainly not all libraries, it was apparently subordinate always to other controls.) First, its success hinges on the recurrence in every relevant title of one particular word, the one used as the catchword. Works of similar content but not using that term in the title can easily be overlooked in preparing the catalog, and are lost to readers not familiar with them beforehand. Draud recognized the need for compensating instruments: he ended numerous "classes" with *Vide etiam* in the Latin catalog and *Such auch* in the German, that is, a "see also" followed by pertinent terms or titles.

In the second place, a catchword might well express a topic truly without telling the whole truth by labeling a point of view. Nor indeed would that facet always be thought the business of the later subject cataloger, since it sometimes required a judgment rather than mere reporting of a book's contents. Draud, in contrast with Gesner before him and strict constructionists after him, considered it necessary and proper to announce points of view, at least in the theology section of his 1625 (second) edition. There, every *Schlagwort* "class" presented Lutheran works first, then Calvinist titles signaled by single asterisks, and finally Catholic contributions, each with a double asterisk. This very instance would turn up again in the exceptional Library of Congress subject subdivision, "—CATHOLIC [etc.] AUTHORS."

Third, as already noted, not every title yields a catchword. Librarians of later days would solve the problem of personal papers with such entries as "AUTHORS, FRENCH—CORRESPONDENCE, REMINISCENCES, ETC."; the conference documents problem, with headings like "CHURCH AND STATE—CONGRESSES." But bibliographical ingenuity had not gone that far in the early seventeenth century. Even Draud's stop-gap see-references, apparently too time-consuming, did not reappear in the second editions (1625) of his catalogs.

Finally, to search seven subject group author-alphabets for a particular author is nuisance enough; to check the scores of author-alphabets generated by the "class" pattern, out of the question. This obstacle Draud surmounted by providing both his Latin and his German catalogs with author indexes.

The unusually detailed subject headings utilized by Maunsell in his 1595 English catalog may have come to Draud's attention. Those of James in his catalogs of the Bodleian collections, unpublished, could have played no role before Draud worked on his second editions (1625). But he was already familiar with the subject-heading tradition, Gesner perhaps included, and it therefore seems unlikely that Maunsell's and James' method would have appealed to him in any case.

Draud's own efforts were apparently little known, partly no doubt because of the turmoil of the Thirty Years' War (1618–1648). History identifies only one conscious imitator, Martin Lipenius. This theologian-bibliographer produced between 1679 and 1685 a catalog relying on a base of carefully alphabetized catchwords; but he had no division by language and thus only four main alphabets, by faculty, where Draud confronted the user with twenty-two. And when that approach, bringing out subject resources by capitalizing or italicizing a key word in each responsive title, enjoyed a renaissance in the nineteenth century, it was one more case of starting from scratch unnecessarily, thanks to ignorance of earlier work. The main stream of German bibliography was to develop with the catchword section playing second fiddle to the Gesner-type list: an author-alphabet with a subject index, often called the *Stichwort* system. (The use of the two in tandem would be labeled *Stich- und Schlagwort.*)

While Draud tried catchwords, most others preferred to elaborate upon the familiar subject patterns. Thus Englishman Jaggard in 1618, perhaps knowing of Maunsell's and James' labors, arranged his list of books under 204 subjects, with subdivision by publisher. Louis Jacob was satisfied with thirty, of which twelve concerned theology; the *Bibliotheca* section provided for library catalogs and works related to the book trade, in the fashion newly (?) set by Naudé's "Cordesiana" catalog (1643). Actually, bibliography of current publication seemed to require little detail in subject arrangement. The "Term Catalogues," the last significant seventeenth-century achievement in the area, returned to just a few large groups.

Worth notice, meanwhile, are, first, the fact that format was given little attention in the continental bibliographies, but remained important enough to be the primary basis of arrangement within the "Term Catalogue" subject groups, as it had been in the Bodleian catalog of 1605. Since, generally speaking, booksellers aim to dispose of their books and libraries to keep theirs, format, a factor bearing upon shelving and layout, could be expected to interest dealers little and librarians considerably.

Further, the question of the language of a work was declining in importance. The Bodleian catalog of 1620 put the few English entries in bold face. William London in 1657 contrariwise printed the scattering of Latin items in italics, but language did not affect the order of entry in his broad-subject lists. It was the basis only of the brief final list, of "Hebrew, Greek, and Latin Bookes, such as falls not directly under the Heads of Divinity, Physick, or Law etc. but are properly usefull for Schooles and Scholars," Greek characters being used only for the main portion of the title and Hebrew books apparently being represented only by English equivalents of their titles.

Nor, by and large, did language of publication affect library book arrangement, inasmuch as their holdings were so largely in Latin.

The Frankfort Fair catalogs and their cumulations followed precisely the opposite policy of organizing by language first. The pioneer Dutch and Belgian current bibliographies and the 1681 cumulation of the "Term Catalogues" (the only one including non-English works) were structured similarly. Naudé's "Cordesiana" catalog of 1643 held to the library catalog tradition, making no language distinctions of that kind, and Jacob's current bibliographies followed suit. Differing thus from the Frankfort Fair catalogs before him and the "Term Catalogue" cumulation of 1681 after him, Jacob may have given more weight to Naudé's view than to the attitudes of the bookdealers.

A column-long, numbered contents note appears in Maunsell, preceding imprint and format data, for the works of Thomas Becon, a very popular propagandist of Puritan-leaning theology who in Mary's day served time in exile and in the Tower. Similar attention is given to the sermons of a few other Protestant luminaries. But in this practice, so familiar to later libraries, the pioneering Maunsell seems to have been well ahead of his times: imitation was rare.

Subject Classification In seventeenth-century libraries, so far as we know, books were arranged by and large as they had been before. Subject content, format, and author's names played varying roles in determining placement and marking. Although certain libraries were increasing their holdings conspicuously, Jacob could in 1644 regard as "truly royal" (*Traicté*, p. 51) a twelfth-century collection of 55,722 volumes. Even in 1700 very few exceeded 50,000, mainly private: ease of access for the casual reader was not a pressing question in practice. The challenge of finding shelf space at the "right place" for the new acquisitions, arriving in some libraries at a more rapid rate than before, engaged Naudé's and other minds. Naudé recommended leaving one end of each shelf vacant when the shelving began. Johannes Rhodius, the Danish librarian at the University of Padua, urged in 1631 that for each group of books some location numbers be left unassigned initially, a feature to be seen often in later times in such places as the Library of Congress classification. But thinking of that stripe was not yet central.

Most catalogs of book collections were organized similarly, by broad subject, whether of private libraries, dealers' stocks, or institutional libraries. A few are known to have been organized contrariwise, by author, alphabetically, notably the Bodleian catalogs of 1620 and 1674. Indeed the latter became famous (copies were sent to other leading libraries) for presenting in its preface rules of entry: every item was to be listed by author, that is, an individual person; unless neither name nor initials nor pseudonym was identifiable, in which case title would do. This approach was to be preserved in the German tradition when in the mid-nineteenth century Panizzi, Jewett, and Cutter abandoned it for the "corporate entry" and the "anonymous classic."

From the evidence available, mainly university library "catalogs" of the sort familiar since the Middle Ages, arranged in shelf order, the expected seems obvious. The medieval curriculum pattern was being modified, mainly in the elaboration of philosophy, thanks largely to the increase in the number and distribution of titles following the invention of printing. More specific categories such as mathematics were provided, and Renaissance Humanist emphases helped generate more or less new ones like history and ethics. As the number of published bibliographies mounted in the course of the century, an entirely new category was born, the problem of relating it to the others being solved variously by different catalog composers. Furthermore, this classification activity threw a sharper light on two old problems, the bibliography in the form of the catalog of another library, and volumes so general or miscellaneous that they did not fit easily into any of the usual groups. Here and there attention was given also to another new species, the brochure on library matters.

Certain other categories, plays and romances, were at least in late-seventeenth-century England popular enough for publishers to risk their own money, whereas for research and new editions of classics they took subscriptions. Yet drama and fiction do not appear in classification schemes directly. In some they emerge under other rubrics: Jesuit Father Garnier's 1678 catalog of his college library in Paris, for instance, includes prose fiction and similar poetry in *Historia fabulosa*. Or the shelving might not be distinctive: when the Académie Royale des Sciences began to function in Paris in 1666, according to Diderot nearly a century afterward, the physicists and mathematicians held their section meetings in the physics and mathematics room of the Bibliothèque Royale, the historians theirs in the history room; those "uniquely occupied with what is called distinctively Belles-Lettres; that is, Grammar, Eloquence, and Poetry" met too, but no corresponding room in the library is mentioned (*Encyclopédie,* nouv. éd., Génève: Pellet, 1777, 1:230-231). In a good many other situations, however, such reading matter was not yet regarded as library material. Still less was it then thought necessary to assign library classification to certain nonbook items which were recognized as major categories by the government licensers, at least in England until the lapse of the statute in 1694: heraldry, portraits, pictures, and the like.

In addition to its vital role in increasing the number and variety of titles issued, the invention of printing had by this time affected the classification of knowledge directly, thanks to the pedagogical advantages of the diagram. To conceive of nearly any entity as divisible into parts was an old behavior pattern. One of the most popular devices for expressing it was "Porphyry's Tree," named for the third-century Neoplatonist considered its creator, wherein any given branch could be divided into two subbranches. Diagrams of the parts of knowledge, and often of other bodies of material, became fairly common soon after the advent of printing and the associated advances in the engraving of line drawings. A mere century beyond Gutenberg appeared Peter Ramus (d. 1572), extraordinarily influential as a teacher partly because he simplified and systematized instruction in "logic," possibly even more because he illustrated his points with diagrams. By no means all writers on the classification of knowledge used diagrams, but their spreading familiarity doubtless encouraged more construction of classification schemes.

The period under review was accordingly characterized by the crystallization of two classification traditions and the birth of a third, and by a divergence in the manner of application to book shelving. The oldest scheme was philosophical, the several arrangements of "subjects" derived from classical antiquity: the "Aristotelian" Theoretical-Practical-Mechanical, the "Platonic-Stoic" Logic-Ethics-Physics, and so on. For example, Protestant educator J. H. Alsted's briefly popular (1620, 1630) encyclopedia apportions its seven volumes in a manner appropriate to an eclectic outlook inspired by the author's passion for harmony. Like his associates of the Herborn School, he is a Neoplatonist who regards all ideas as originally "forms" in the Divine Mind, a powerful argument for unity. The realization of those ideas among men is the job of educators, and here he draws on both Aristotelian precision and the psychology of the Humanist and Reformation pedagogues. Thus his first part begins with remarks *(praecognita)* on overall unity and system. It then defines the several branches of knowledge and sketches their organization *(archelogia);* outlines the psychology of cognition and action *(hexilogia);* introduces the particular arts and science *(technologia);* and concludes with a treatment of how to teach *(canonics).* Having laid these foundations, Alsted apportions the six remaining parts of his encyclopedia traditionally: Philology (the old trivium plus word study and poetry); Theoretical Philosophy (like Aristotle's embracing ethics, economics, politics, and education); the three usual Graduate Faculties; Mechanics (like Aristotle's applied arts); and Miscellaneous. This last was decidedly a mixed bag, from alchemy to polygraphy, and including biography.

Nearly as venerable were the curriculum-related patterns the philosophical schemes helped father, which by the end of the Middle Ages were very powerful indeed. This "faculty" classification, Theology-Medicine-Law-Philosophy (Arts), was developed by Conrad Gesner into a quite elaborate array of subject subdivisions. The idea appealed to a few librarians here and there, especially in small libraries, where change was less risky than in large ones. A rather precise breakdown of subject shelving was installed at the Duke's library in Königsberg (eastern Prussia) apparently within a few years after the release of Gesner's *Pandects.* Interest spread. At the University of Strasbourg in 1613 it was even contended that thorough systematic subject arrangement could render the catalog unnecessary. And when

Artist's sketch of the subject catalogs at Leyden University Library, early seventeenth century. (Courtesy of The Bettmann Archive, Inc.)

Naudé enlarged the collections at the Mazarine in the 1640s the acquisitions so far outran the cataloging that access actually did depend—though not by plan!—upon a systematic arrangement much more sophisticated than the thirteen main groups and a few subdivisions (History had the most, twelve) of his 1643 "Cordesiana" catalog.

The second half of the seventeenth century found the "systematic" shelf arrangement invading the larger library. Complex subject subdivision featured the Lambeck style at Vienna in 1662, the Garnier college pattern (Paris) of 1678, and Bouillaud's sale catalog design (also Paris) of 1679. Bibliographically, Garnier's 481 subdivisions were probably the extreme of the epoch. From the shelving point of view the extreme was Lambeck's, wherein the many small subject subdivisions were unified irrespective of differences of format.

On the whole, however, the larger seventeenth-century libraries, and some small ones, were content with more modest advance. Provision for library-bibliographical items or polygraphy might be added to a major division by faculties, a step toward the so-called library-practical classification. Thus French Jesuit Claude Clémens (or Clément), teacher of Latin and Greek at the Imperial College in Madrid, concluded (1635) from his observations at the Escorial library that twelve classes were desirable. Classes I, II, and VI covered the three "graduate faculties"; all the others but one, like Naudé's, divided among them the parts of philosophy. Unique was class IX, given to polygraphy, a category obviously based on book-binding practices rather than subject content alone; this may have been a first.

But the faculty groups, four to seven, as a rule, were seldom subdivided more than once. Very often, moreover, they were broken up not by subject but, as in the case of the Bodleian, by format. The Ambrosiana as a matter of fact arranged books (1608) entirely by format and likeness of binding. And in Berlin in 1659 the Elector allowed sets to be distributed by subject only if the individual parts belonged to different faculties. (Compare Class AC of the Library of Congress scheme, which keeps certain distributable sets together without exception.) Most librarians, or their employers, apparently agreed with James of the Bodleian 1620 catalog and LeTonnelier of St. Victor in Paris, who in 1677 declared that the great variety of content as well as format made exact subject control via shelving impracticable and that the catalog was the only answer.

The Bourgeois Revolution Brings Man-Centered Classification

For the moment, the most striking bid for change originated far from the library. Of the essence of Renaissance Humanism was a renewed attention to individual capacities. Psychological insights discussed intermittently at least since Aristotle were now regarded by some thinkers as a better framework for classification than such objective abstractions as Logic, The Practical, and Physics. The long-dominant categories were challenged by Memory, Imagination, and Reason.

The first modern protagonist of this approach, apparently, was Juan Huarte, a Spanish physician who wrote in his forties (1575) a book on what would later be called differential psychology. It was very popular and frequently translated, seventy versions before 1700. One reason, perhaps, is the emphasis on individual differences: the contention that a person might well study "all the daies of his life" in vain a subject not suited to him, whereas, properly advised about his "naturall abilitie," he could master his subject or skill "in two daies" (*The Examination of Men's Wits;* English version by R. Carew, 1594; Gainesville, Fla.: Scholars' Facsimiles & Reprints, 1959, p. 102). A declared disciple of Aristotle and the great second-century physician-philosopher Galen, Huarte relies heavily upon the ancient four humors, linking memory with a moist brain and understanding with a dry brain. Much of his disquisition is an effort to unravel that contradiction and account for imagination, which Galen had not altogether explained and was still rather a mystery.

Each of the three is in his view an integral part of activity of the (Aristotelian) "rational soul." It is therefore logical to group subjects according to the "soul" faculty with which they are most intimately associated. To Memory are assigned the grammar of any language, the theory of law, "Divinitie positive" (what is "verified" only), the heavens, and arithmetic. Reason is thought the best means of learning "School divinitie" (whatever is taught), medical theory, logic, natural and moral philosophy, and law practice. From "a good imagination spring all the Arts and Sciences, which consist in figure, correspondence, harmonie, and proportion" (Huarte, p. 103). The roster includes all the fine and creative arts, embracing not only poetry but pulpit and other eloquence and medical practice (bedside eloquence?); mathematics, astrology, and invention; and perhaps less expectedly government and warfare.

The old categories tended to approach objectively a reality independent of the observer. Huarte, a Renaissance man, moves to the observer himself, a subjective outlook and by that criterion less scientific. Partly on that account he separates theory from practice, another liability. At the same time, the best assurance of individual flowering is collective guidance: "Well ordered commonwealths ought to have men of great wisdom and knowledge, who might in their tender age discover each one's wit and natural sharpnesse, to the end they might be set to learne that art which was agreeable, and not leave it to their own election" (Huarte, p. 23).

This interpenetration of opposites, or dialectical unity, is even more marked in the thought of Francis Bacon. Reflecting the contradictions of life in his age, he accents human control of nature and considers the larger part of knowledge to be that acquired through the physical senses; yet, like his less revolutionary contemporaries, he also leaves part of knowledge to revelation. Further, eager to reject much of the old way of thinking and acting, he abandons the broad curriculum-related subject patterns established for centuries. Instead, in the manner of Huarte, whose work was probably familiar to him, he strives to tie all sense-perceived data to the human capacities of memory, imagination, and reason.

Of course his circumstances are quite different. He is not a physician; not indeed even interested, so far as we know, in the contemporary epochal advance in physiology of William Harvey or the navigation craftsmanship of William Norman or the reasoning on magnetism of Humphrey Gilbert. But he lives in the atmosphere they help shape, also the England of joint stock companies and a belligerent Parliament. All this is a far cry from a Spain of outward sparkle and inner decay. Huarte urges joint guidance counseling. Bacon becomes a prime promoter of joint investigation and discussion of everything, because knowledge, like wealth, is pursued better that way than in isolation.

His classification of knowledge is a major weapon in a fight on two fronts. On the one hand, he tries to break away from Scholastic and Humanist dependence upon the past, and does so much more pointedly and economically than Montaigne a generation earlier. On the other hand, he apparently aims to take the play away from the Hermetic magicians. (His polemic may have seemed perfectly clear to his contemporaries, but one cannot be sure some 300 years later.) A Galileo in astronomy and mechanics or a Harvey in the circulation of the blood could undercut magic by demonstrating what systematic experiment and verification were capable of; charlatanry could be exposed. Likewise a Casaubon or a Valla could deal severe blows to Hermetic or papal-superiority legend by irrefutable document analysis. Bacon is neither a natural nor a social scientist in those senses. Although he takes the same path as Huarte, he does not rest his case on the physiological psychology of Aristotle and Galen. His contribution is unique: to acknowledge the mass concern with memory as the key to learning, and by giving it top billing in his classification to mount a challenge able to draw minds from the magicians' tent to that of the scientists.

Perhaps for those very reasons he feels free to attack under Memory (in the Natural History section), "books of fabulous experiments and secrets, and frivolous impostures for pleasure and strangeness," and to decry the lack of "due rejection of fables and popular errors" (Bacon, *Advancement of Learning,* Modern Library ed., p. 231). Similarly, under Reason (in the Nature section), he condemns "this degenerate Natural Magic, Alchemy, Astrology, and the like," in whose "propositions the description of the means is ever more monstrous than the pretence or end" (Bacon, p. 263). Yet, just as Naudé would defend "good magic" twenty years later, an area of caution remains in Bacon: he is not ready to condemn "superstitious narrations of sorceries, witchcrafts, dreams, divinations" because not enough is known about the "natural causes" which might account for them (Bacon, p. 232).

Memorizing had always leaned heavily on imagery and association. (One venerable technique was to picture a building with standard internal arrangement and relate a sequence of data to the sequence of rooms.) Bacon pays his respects promptly. The three kinds of Civil History (another part of Memory) are "not unfitly to be compared with the three kinds of pictures or images," of which "some are unfinished, some are perfect, and some are defaced" (Bacon, p. 234). To these he parallels the three kinds of history, unfinished Memorials, Perfect Histories, and the scattered remnants called Antiquities.

Pursuing the development of his pattern logically, Bacon crosses from Memory to Imagination. The role of the latter is obvious at the level of words: he assigns it and other "arts of speech" (Bacon, p. 244) to Reason, discussed later. Here he is concerned with the level of "matter." The "Poesy" dealt with by the Imagination is "nothing else but Feigned History." Its "use" is "to give some shadow of satisfaction to the mind of man in those points wherein the nature of things doth deny it": opportunity for the spirit to enjoy "a more ample greatness, a more exact goodness, and a more absolute variation" than are afforded by known objective reality. True history is often disappointing and dull; poesy provides relief and hope, whence "it was ever thought to have some participation of divineness" (Bacon, p. 244). For the understanding of Man, moreover, the poets have contributed more than the philosophers. Thus does Bacon appeal to the many who despaired of authority and drew solace and inspiration from the magicians. Dreaming, daring, and enjoying are a respectable adjunct to sober study.

Again, leaving Poesy, or "the Theatre," for "the judicial place or palace of the mind" (Bacon, p. 247), Bacon's first remarks on Philosophy, the domain of Reason, are very critical. Not enough questions are answered, says he, with examples which may have been more enlightening in the early seventeenth century than they seem in the mid-twentieth. And the tone of what follows implies quite often that any sensible person could raise such questions himself. Predictably, moreover, among his comments introducing "Natural Philosophy," he asks leave to "revive and reintegrate the misapplied and abused name of Natural Magic." It is "in the true sense. . . . Natural Wisdom," long familiar, of course "purged from vanity and superstition" (Bacon, p. 252).

The total classification scheme is tightly structured in terms of Bacon's goals and psychological presuppositions. As a pattern for arranging containers of knowledge, books, it is marred by defects recognized by many observers from the outset. Its application would set in immediate sequence materials on the "histories" of Nature, Mechanical Invention, the Churches, Man in general, and Literature, and miscellaneous supplements to History such as government reports. The "sciences" of Nature appear later (after Poetry); political science very much later. The separation of related resources on Nature and Government seems rather obvious; more instances could probably be found. Bibliography is not mentioned. And a classification of knowledge owes no recognition to such problems of format as polygraphic volumes. It is not surprising that of the numerous classifications circulated in the seventeenth century, only one, apparently issued by theology professor and librarian Jean Garnier for his Parisian Jesuit College library in 1678, betrays any Baconian markings of consequence.

Yet Bacon's ideas were by no means without impact. What probably gave them momentum despite their impracticality for the shelves was the tight inner logic, an element not common in prior schemes. That human activity served God's purposes had long been taken for granted, but the assumption had no striking effect on classification systems. Bacon was challenging dominant views enough to pick his way with care. His outlook too was teleological, but the purpose was the service of humanity. Thus he protests repeatedly his respectability as a Believer, and spins a closeknit classification, in which each category is dependent upon what precedes it and leads to what follows. Man receives (most of) his data through the senses, then processes this store with the aid of mental images and imagination, and finally applies the resources thus acquired to problem solving. That is why Bacon begins with Memory-dependent "History" and concludes with

Reason-dependent "Philosophy." In the successive patterned worlds of the students of Descartes and Newton; of the eighteenth-century encyclopedists, Comteians, Hegelians and Darwinians, this was frequently to be admired aesthetically as well as otherwise. In due time it would help support a tradition, exemplified in the sequences and modulations of the Dewey Decimal Classification.

Among the next generation of Englishmen none was to be more influential in the thirteen North American colonies than Thomas Hobbes, several of whose ideas and phrases eventually found their way into the Declaration of Independence and the Constitution of the United States of America. If his views of natural equality and popular sovereignty, and his support of absolute monarchy, were in some respects contradictory, no less so were his absorption with the materialism of Galileo, Mersenne, and Gassendi on the one hand, and on the other his indifference to experimentation and his bitter exchanges with the founders of the Royal Society. For all his conventional aspersions upon Aristotle and others of the past, his own syllogistic logic is heavily Aristotelian and his classification of knowledge grounded on the objective world, rather than the capacities of the human observer from which Bacon started. Bacon for example makes Imagination a major division and approaches "Poesy" as a category of psychological need. Hobbes treats Imagination as an aspect of Memory, among the Facts acquired by the senses: "absolutes." Poetry he places at the end of one of his "Science" chains of "names appertaining to the subject in hand," all "conditionalls": Bodies Permanent-Terrestrial-Organic-Man-Speech-Poetry (Leviathan, ed. W. E. Pogson Smith, Oxford: Clarendon Press, 1909, pp. 36, 64–65). His scheme concludes with a list of subjects very much like those of yore. Its impact would strengthen in the English colonies the classical tradition going back to Varro. Its omission of prose literature may be natural in a man devoted to political science and theological polemics. Medicine is a conspicuous lack, so far as labels are concerned. The absence of bibliography testifies to Hobbes' impatience with the past ("Read thy self," Leviathan, p. 9) as well as to his remoteness from the scholarship of libraries.

The problems of political organization in an era of fundamental social change were however producing a mounting literature, and the industrial revolution was soon going to add more. To put across new ideas would require a great deal of grappling with old ones. The role of reading matter was expanding, even if Hobbes thought the invention of printing, by comparison with the invention of "letters," "ingenious" but "no great matter" (Leviathan, p. 23). For little more than another two generations would it be possible to satisfy the needs of thinking persons without libraries of a public character.

Chapter Six

THE EIGHTEENTH CENTURY

In the years between 1680 and the French Revolution, differentiation in the conditions of life became much more striking than before to tens of thousands of people. There were perhaps 125 million human beings in Europe in 1700 and close to 190 million in 1800. Most of them were peasants, whose reading if any was probably confined to coins at markets and fairs, public announcements posted on walls, and portions of the Bible; notably literate were those who worked the land in the British North American colonies, sufficiently exceptional from the outset to be called "farmers" rather than "peasants." Cities accounted for a small percentage overall, but their role was enlarging with capitalism. By the later eighteenth century England's population, pushed in part from countryside to factory villages, was half urban; those of France, Prussia (northeastern Germany), and Württemberg (southern Germany), one-quarter urban. (Borrowed largely from Josef Kulischer, *Allgemeine Wirtschaftsgeschichte . . . Bd. II: Die Neuzeit,* München: Oldenbourg, 1965, pp. 7–8; and from Marcel R. Reinhard, *Histoire de la Population Mondiale de 1700 à 1948,* Paris: Domat-Montchrestien, 1949, p. 44.)

The largest single agglomeration of people under a single sovereign was France, where the population mounted, broadly speaking, from 18 millon to 26 million during the eighteenth century. England and Spain were meanwhile doubling to 9 million and 10 million, respectively. Multiplying from about 1 million to more than 5 million was Prussia, while the British colonists in North America reached 5 millions in 1800 from a 1713 level of

250,000. Significant urban concentration was primarily a tale of France and England, though not just of two cities. In 1700 London (674,000) had already passed Paris (600,000); eighteenth-century England became the most urbanized area in Europe. Yet, until the industrial revolution's full bloom, festering new factory towns and deserted nonfactory villages, no English communities besides London matched the second-rank cities of France; Lyons reported more than 100,000 in 1700 and five other centers more than 50,000 each. Amsterdam, Vienna, and Rome boasted populations of 150,000 to 200,000 in the eighteenth century. Berlin had only 100,000 in 1750, but that was tenfold expansion since 1650. (Kulischer, pp. 7–8; Reinhard, pp. 62, 73, 103, 107, 115–116, 148, 154.)

Mortality rates and life expectancy may not have changed in fact; but the statistics called into being by the needs of tax collection and the insurance business—"political arithmetic," as founder Sir William Petty called it (1690)—drew more attention to these and other measurable phenomena than they had attracted before. At midcentury, about one fourth of Europeans born alive died before age three, another fourth before age twenty-five, and a third quarter before age fifty. (Kulischer, p. 10.)

How many surviving infancy could read? A rough estimate is possible on the basis of class composition and the degree of urbanization. England may be taken as a benchmark, since it was in 1700 becoming the most urbanized community and would soon afterward be the most industrialized, which is to say, the community most in need of mass literacy. At the bottom of its social structure in 1700 were three large groups numbering more than 4.5 million (of a total of 5 million) which probably included very few able to read beyond the rudimentary: the families of the rural poor and relief clients, laborers and servants, and small farmers. Of the other 550,000, the most literate were presumably the 35,000 professional men, the 10,000 large merchants, and the 10,000 government employees. The women of the middle and upper classes, urban and rural, were increasingly becoming readers, but the opportunities for children were considerably narrower. Thus the number able to read magazines and books undoubtedly fell far short of the estimated 330,000 in the families of the 55,000 men referred to (Reinhard, p. 105). One may surmise that, of England's 5 million in 1700, perhaps as many as a quarter million, or 1 in 20, were literate enough to be of interest to booksellers and library sponsors. That the ratio was higher elsewhere is of course possible, but unlikely so far as Europe is concerned.

The epoch was dominated politically by the rivalries of the sovereigns, businessmen, and landowners of England and France; others played roles of varying significance. That French Bourbon power was rotting at the roots owed something not only to archaic land tenure, taxation, and privilege, but to the life of the mind: this was the age of Montesquieu and Voltaire, Rousseau and the Encyclopédistes. If their political and cultural challenge invigorated all Western life, it was not exhaustive. The classical political science and political economy were being established primarily by English heads with bourgeois perceptions: John Locke, law-commentator William Blackstone, Adam Smith, and so on. Notable for advance in serious philosophy were the politically backward Germans, whose Leibniz and Kant registered seminal achievements. Science was conspicuously international. Leibniz and Newton invented the calculus independently; advances in electricity and magnetism were greatly facilitated by the terminology of British colonial Benjamin Franklin (the Royal Society awarded him the Copley Medal in 1753, long before he made his marks in diplomacy or gadgetry); and contributions from many quarters aided the emergence of scientific biology and botany, chemistry, geology, anthropology, and psychology.

Through it all, controversy swirled around conceptions of God and man, truth and error, and innumerable lesser points of theology and social policy. Many certainly rejected Alexander Pope's sanctimonious "Whatever is, is right." But few, it seems, would have disagreed with the slogan on which Johann Sebastian Bach composed in 1735 his Cantata no. 100, "What God does is well done."

Library life benefited from the crackle of debate and the spread of literacy, but rather little. Theological polemics were added to many academic library collections; but libraries were slow to receive contemporary science or politics, and the flowering periodical press scarcely touched them, except for serial publication of an explicitly learned character. The new wave of encyclopedias and self-educator works were almost by definition an alternative to library use. And the rising national libraries, if associated occasionally with the idea of service to a public, were basically expressions rather of antiquarian- and display-partriotism. Harbingers of the future included on the one hand the small-town book collections generated by the struggles of the religious dissenters and on the other the fiction and popular reading "libraries" sponsored for profit by imaginative book dealers; both were phenomena then most familiar in Britain and British North America. The shape of things to come was also suggested by the lonely adventure of the University of Göttingen, admitting undergraduates to library privileges.

Except in such isolated instances, indeed, the class composition of library users—aristocrats, professionals, and their staffs—did not change markedly. But the years under review were the seed time for great metamorphoses later. Aristocratic and bourgeois women acquired much more opportunity than before to read, material to read, and reason to read. Their children began to be seen more clearly and even heard, at least by the theorists of education and writers of children's books. Furthermore, great need was being created for an industrial labor supply which would require carrying literacy to the lower depths of society on a large scale, both for the sake of efficient production and to provide access to their minds for those desiring to guide them in channels politically safe.

These undercurrents were to be felt among library staffs too. It was the day of the rise of the legal and medical professions, the birth of civil and mechanical engineering out of what had been called very imprecisely "architecture" as well as metal crafts and mathematics; but it was a rare person who made a living writing, and librarians still tended to be primarily something else, albeit scholarly. If the techniques of acquisitions and cataloging and building management were fairly well developed, the service aspect of librarianship still awaited the emergence of the masses of the people as a library factor. The literature of librarianship was correspondingly oriented to the scholarly library, and until the nonscholarly library rounded out the scene, there would be no defining of professional librarianship or education designed to produce it.

Reading, Education, and Libraries in Britain

Reading in Britain As befitted a nation long embroiled in religious and church-state controversy, and on the brink of assuming industrial leadership, England at the opening of the eighteenth century was notable for the number of persons who read not only the Bible and theological writings but classics, belles lettres, and popular science, not only books and pamphlets but newspapers and magazines. Belles lettres seeking alternatives to the grip of the monopolist publishers and the 1709 Copyright Act encouraged those magazines. By 1740 the firm of Dyche and Pardon could formalize the recent developments in the book trade by adopting the distinctive label "Publisher." Forty years later, the book market was large enough for a writer to make a living writing.

As so often before, there were sharp disagreements between old and new: a notable defense of traditional reading was Jonathan Swift's polemic, characteristically satiric, "The Battle of the Books" (1710). In *A Tale of a Tub* (1704) the explosive Swift scores those who "have discovered a shorter, and more prudent method, to become scholars and wits, without the fatigue of reading or thinking." They memorize titles, or acquire "a thorough insight into the index," just as "physicians discover the state of the whole body, by consulting only what comes from behind." In the sciences, much can be absorbed quickly, thanks to "systems and abstracts"; the "labour" of their composers, he adds, "is the seed of idleness" on the part of the beneficiaries. "Large indexes and little compendiums—booked in alphabet" allow "any writers" to handle any subject; works produced thus "make a very comely figure on a bookseller's shelf . . . never to be thumbed or greased by students, nor bound to everlasting chains of darkness in a library. . . ." (Swift's *Prose Works,* London: Bell, 1897, I:103–105.)

By midcentury there was also a debate over what was proper English. Benjamin Martin's good reform dictionary appeared in 1749, and Dr. Johnson's better one six years later.

Collecting books for show was now a pastime of numerous merchants and gentlemen. In the libraries of town houses and country seats, ornate bindings precious in value and *précieux* in tone were conspicuous examples of the rule of rococo, as well as of the advances in leather and other craftsmanship. One of the delights in *The Spectator,* issued from March 1711 to December 1712 by the celebrated essayists Joseph Addison and Richard Steele, was the facetious extreme of a set of striking "spines" without any books behind them. Little could have been more harmonious with the emptiness of contemporary speculative "Bubbles" (the "South Sea" scheme collapsed in 1720) and political corruption.

Of course, it was by no means all false-back. By the late seventeenth century, at least in England, some publishers had come to furnish a book bound. Probably for that reason one finds in the "Term Catalogues" a feature not encountered in the other comparable bibliographies of the era, description of the binding as a normal element in the entry. Yet, selling books unbound was to remain the general practice until the day of buckram bindings, about 1830.

The consequences for libraries were neither very powerful nor altogether favorable. Thinking of reference resources as within arm's reach was presumably encouraged by such publications as John Harris' *Lexicon Technicum* of 1704. In contrast with the encyclopedias already on hand, devoted to old "liberal arts," and religious and humanistic matters, this new model by a fellow of the Royal Society stressed practical and scientific subjects, in English. There were several reprints and expansions. And they probably helped broaden the compass of what was covered in the "general reader"–oriented successive *Cyclopaedia's* by Ephraim Chambers (first edition, 1728); and, thanks to "a Society of Gentlemen in Scotland," by *Encyclopaedia Britannica,* the first two of whose hundred "parts" were released in December 1768 at six or eight pence each depending upon the quality of the paper. Within three years the entire work was available in three bound volumes; a second edition was issued between 1777 and 1784, and a third between 1788 and 1797.

Academic and Religious Patterns and Libraries; Bray, Kirkwood British higher education had long differed from the continental pattern insofar as the product was not the scholar-preacher, jurist, or physician, but the scholar-and-gentleman. Upon this had been grafted at several institutions, especially in Scotland, the hard-nosed humanistic Latinism of the Reformation educators, although the Puritan Commonwealth was no more successful than the Church of England authorities in enforcing daily use of the language of Cicero. The steady decline in tone and spirit at tradition-bound Oxford and Cambridge, evidenced in their failure to produce a leading figure, probably contributed to the popularity of foreign travel (by students who could afford it) as an alternative to university education. Yet there were at least two countercurrents. The study of mathematics and experimental science took a turn for the better in the 1640s at a few university centers: one consequence was the foundation of the Royal Society (chartered in 1662; library apparently in 1667); another, the flourishing of mathematics at a Cambridge enjoying the twenty-first to fifty-first years (1663–1693) of Isaac Newton. Besides, the "equal and opposite reaction," so to speak, of the philosophical idealist movement called "Cambridge Platonism" was also stimulating to scholarship.

In 1683 Elias Ashmole (1617–1692), a lawyer of craftsman origins who married wealth, gave Oxford a museum largely devoted to scientific specimens and equipment. The incidental expenses were such that the university budget had to ignore the Bodleian Library for a few years. But the museum became the meeting place of a chemistry colloquium led by the first Ashmolean Professor of that subject, and a "library" was organized to support the deliberations. Seventeen of the twenty-three donated books were in Latin. Were Robert Boyle's *Skeptical Chymist* (1680) and *New Experiments* (1681/ 1682) and the other two English titles the only ones respected? The only ones known? The only ones actually available? As might be expected under the circumstances, no librarian is mentioned. And the larger literature which might have justified seeking one was meanwhile being discouraged by the popularity of such summary-outlines as Charles Morton's *Compendium Physicae* (about 1680). A declared foe of the large volume as an evil, he did not receive the hoped-for presidency of Harvard, but his book was adopted as the Harvard science text in 1687 and enjoyed that standing for nearly forty years.

Like the dissenters who had established Harvard half a century earlier, those who stayed home were active in education, contributing a fresh element which overlapped the new attention to science. Soon after they felt the lash of enforcement of the Act of Uniformity, their first (1670) "academy" (a term originally applied to universities established without the sanction of the pope) appeared. In the years 1680 to 1780 some thirty-five academies furnished a solid and balanced education to young men who did not want to take the loyalty oaths required at Cambridge and Oxford, and others as well. Information about their book resources does not appear in the readily accessible descriptions. It is safe to assume that they were not in a class with the Bodleian, inasmuch as nothing in England then was, not even at Cambridge. But it is appropriate to wonder whether curriculum support may not have occasioned the presence of a respectable number of works in science, vocational subjects, and modern languages. If so, the dissenting academies had the first modern campus book collections. Betraying almost surely the influence of university training is the little we know of life in the long-established cathedral chapter libraries, collections meant primarily for the men assigned to a particular cathedral. They were noteworthy in the eighteenth century for the apparent devotion of their borrowers to Greek and Latin rather than English literature, by then a somewhat unusual preference.

Book collections accessible not only to the clergy but to their parishioners were also familiar. The years under review witnessed however some changes deserving notice. Of the approximately 160 "endowed"—subsidized in some fashion—parish collections in the small towns and villages of England, one third were organized in the years from 1680 to 1720. The reactions of the pious to the easy styles of the Restoration doubtless played an important part. In particular, some of the orthodox were disturbed by the novel availability in the 1680s of truly varied reading matter, disseminated in the country districts by way of both fairs and a great wave of auctions.

Still more important, in all likelihood, was political persecution. Under the Corporation Act of 1661, anyone not sharing the Church of England's ritual of the Lord's Supper was excluded from civil, military, and municipal office; and the First Conventical Act of 1664 illegalized any meeting of more than five persons additional to the family in the house. The following year the Five-Mile Act declared that anyone detected violating the above-mentioned strictures was not to be found, except when traveling, within five miles of any municipality sending a representative to Parliament. Dozens of dissenting ministers who stuck to their convictions were thus isolated from their parishioners, and sought both a new living and new followers by moving to the smaller towns and villages. The "libraries" which began to appear after 1680 in those communities were so often the product of effort by dissenting clergymen that the sequence of events cannot be dismissed as entirely coincidental.

One obvious exception was the celebrated Church of England divine, Dr. Thomas Bray. Entering the ministry in 1678, he held several pastorates and soon became sensitive to the problems of putting reading within the reach of impecunious clerics. Once when a colleague died, he checked the books, and found them very few; the deceased had drawn on two "'very Considerable Libraries in his Parish,'" noted Bray. (The source quotations come from B. C. Steiner, "Rev. Thomas Bray and his American Libraries,"

American Historical Review, II:59–75; 1896–1897.) But that was not possible for all the thousands of vicars and curates too poor to buy books themselves. Thus was born the idea, printed and circulated, of *"'Parochial* and *Lending Libraries.'"* Response was not immediate; it awaited another death, that of a minister who left his many books to the town for the use of clergymen of the vicinity. Then it became *"'usual for some of us to Ride even Ten miles to Borrow out of it the Book we had Occasion for.'"*

The proposals Bray first submitted had focused on the colonies, urging the distribution of books strictly for the parson's use *"'as unalienable* as any other Rights and Dues of the Church.'"* Donations were to be sought and the ministers held accountable, much as the fourteenth-century friars had operated. The church approved the plan. More formally, in a published *Essay* of 1697, the library promoter expanded his vista, with much greater emphasis on *"'lending libraries in all the Deanaries of England.'"* (The deanary, supervising several parishes, is an administrative device between parish and diocese.) Suggested titles filled six pages, heavily theological but representative of other branches too. The books were intended not only for the clergy but also for the gentry, and both groups were called upon to finance the project, the collections to be worth about £30 each.

He hoped in particular that the books could be loaned off the premises: *"'Standing libraries will signifie little in the Country, where Persons must ride some miles to look into a Book; such Journeys being too expensive of Time and Money: But Lending Libraries,* which come home to 'em without Charge, may tolerable well supply the Vacancies in their own Studies, till such time as these *Lending* may be improv'd into *Parochial Libraries.'"* If the English parochial library was to be mainly "standing" the deanary library or the library in the colonies was "lending," a substitute for and supplement to the former. That is, the central collection at the deanary would provide a sort of extension service pending the establishment of local libraries at the parishes. *"'And, whereas it may be objected, that the Books will be so often Borrow'd, that it will be hard for anyone to have the book he wants, I am so far from being much concern'd to answer it, that I heartily wish the great Use and frequent Borrowing of Books out of these Libraries, may make it a real Objection.'"*

Bray based his campaign explicitly on the idea of the aristocracy of the intellect, appealing to *"'Gentlemen, Physicians, and Lawyers.'"* Nor did he overlook the concern of *"'Persons of Quality,'"* who found their eldest sons deprived by country life of books suitable to develop their talents and too often drawn into filling up their *"'Discourse'"* with *"'the Porterly Language of Swearing and Obscenity.' "* Yet his basic target remained the clergy. They are *"'the Persons whose Chief Business it is to be men of Knowledge . . . because they are to instruct others.'"* They must know what they teach, knowledge is in books, and the purpose of libraries is *"'to give Requisite Helps to Considerable Attainments in All the Parts of necessary and Usefull Knowledge.'"*

These views were not altogether new, but the lending feature was unusual, and Bray's persistent campaigning made a difference. The Society for Promoting Christian Knowledge (S.P.C.K.), founded in 1699, was by 1705 ready to sponsor such lending libraries. Some of its leaders chose that same year to devote themselves to the labor more intensively, as a separate group, establishing more than sixty like collections in England and Wales. And in 1723 arose the Associates of Dr. Bray, who performed similar services for many years beyond the inspirer's death in 1730. Most of those in Wales were reportedly libraries for the clergy.

The older endowed libraries were thereby influenced in the same direction. The drift toward lending books was aided, moreover, by the gradual abandonment of chaining and, by midcentury, the utilization of the folio format only for reference volumes. Still fairly common, however, was the requirement of a deposit against the book borrowed, usually 125 percent of its value.

For the more advanced notion of supporting libraries by means of a property tax we are apparently indebted to another determined promoter, James Kirkwood of Scotland, who despite repeated loss of jobs for refusal to take various loyalty oaths, managed to stir up organizational activity by both the General Assembly of the Scotch Presbyterians and the Society for Promoting Christian Knowledge. Forced out of a rural Scottish post in 1681 he moved with several kindred spirits to England, where after a while he obtained a small rectory. In 1690 he began corresponding with Robert Boyle, who was like Isaac Newton not only a key thinker in the transition to modern science but deeply preoccupied with problems theological. Boyle's particular interest in Bible translation merged with Kirkwood's direct observation of ignorance in Scottish Highlands: the upshot was that, with Boyle's massive aid, and despite English objections to keeping Gaelic alive, more than 3,000 Gaelic Bibles were distributed to northern Scotland.

In 1699 Kirkwood published anonymously in Edinburgh *An Overture for Establishing Bibliothecks in Every Paroch throughout This Kingdom,* a proposition clearly reminiscent of Luther's move nearly two centuries earlier. Familar enough was the idea that the minister's own books were to be the nucleus. Less familiar were the recommendations that the schoolmaster should act as librarian, that cataloging should be uniform, and that the whole should be financed by a tax on the landlords of the respective parishes. Kirkwood is said to have established also in the same year a library in the Highlands for the clergy; but the broad plan dependent for execution upon the church General Assembly was merely approved without implementation.

In 1702 he lost his English pulpit over another loyalty oath. But the following year the S.P.C.K. saluted him with a Corresponding membership, and perhaps some shrewd advice. At any rate, he shortly produced a more modest library plan, for the Highlands alone. The Scotland given its tone by Calvinist John Knox was by no means devoid of books and libraries, and the peasantry of the Lowlands were then better educated than any other in Europe. Now that Kirkwood had revised his plans to eliminate what seemed superfluous, and perhaps encouraged by S.P.C.K. help in gathering books and money, the Assembly between 1704 and 1708 distributed seventy-seven "libraries" among the presbyteries and parishes of the Highlands and the islands. If Kirkwood's rules were followed, the books were carefully kept in dry places under lock and key and loaned only two at a time to approved ministers, schoolmasters, and students, against a deposit 125 percent of the value recorded in the catalog. In 1709, apparently soon after Kirkwood's death, the church assembly called on the presbyteries lacking libraries to raise money and obtain them; but no official aid was given, and the entire movement declined. It had nonetheless set an example, in contrast with the predominant practice in England, of trying to reach beyond the clergy and the men of standing, not to speak of the principle of tax support. The full story has yet to be told.

Secular and Commercial Libraries Whatever the memory of those events may have had to do with it, the first of three known miners' reading societies was launched at Leadhills, Scotland, in the 1730s. As one part of the program of reform-minded manager James Stirling (1692–1770), who raised wages, shortened the workweek, and furnished a battery of social aids, it anticipated the better known activities of Robert Owen and the Utopian Socialists half a century later. Tax support was not involved. Dependent initially on individual founders' gifts, this collection and its followers (1758, 1792) at other miners' centers looked back to medieval tradition and forward to Carnegie. Insofar as the miners themselves controlled the operation of the library—possibly the reason why Stirling himself, for example, was never a member—a new model was set forth which was to inspire the flattery of imitation rather seldom. Did the initiating sponsor think of the books as something of a toy, and the miners as children?

At about the same moment that the Leadhills venture was being launched, the scene was entered also by the "school library" of Shrewsbury (30 miles northwest of Birmingham). The borrowers recorded between 1737 and 1821 numbered 137, of whom 17 were schoolmasters and 120 citizens of various stations; 10 were women. To all appearances a school library regarded also as a community agency, this institution reminds us that the story of an entire type of library service is so far virtually unknown.

Perhaps more nearly "public" in spirit than most of the foregoing, although plainly not in tax support, were two other forms of group attention to books, the book club and the circulating or rental "library." The origin of the book club is apparently connected with the coffeehouses of the Restoration: the earliest one reported as the scene of a book club is dated 1668. There were soon many more. In 1700 London had some 2,000, many of which were also in part periodical reading rooms, and apparently contributed thereby to the formation of the custom of offering such facilities separately from libraries, a custom strong enough to survive for nearly a century after the creation of institutions providing both at once. The larger coffeehouses may have maintained book collections too. They are known to have been the site of book auctions in the late seventeenth and early eighteenth centuries, and occasionally of a bookdealers' meeting. By 1742 the habit of buying one copy of a book for the use of the coffeehouse clientele evoked a bitter protest from the booksellers. (Were they indifferent or disorganized before that?)

Just when the book club independent of the coffeehouses began to function is not clear. The celebrated nonconformist minister Philip Doddridge, for example, wrote in 1725 of having membership for a nominal annual fee in a society, far from London, which developed a common stock of books he thought entertaining and useful. Benjamin Franklin, then in London and aware of the capital's clubs and bookstores, may have heard of such ventures. There seem to have been two types. One brought together middle-class folk, all over eighteenth-century England—and by midcentury in Wales—meeting as a rule monthly, choosing whom to admit or reject, and constituting a channel for the sale of many books. Quite a few accepted women members, and a few were composed of women only. The focus was current issues; the books and pamphlets chosen by a majority vote were concentrated accordingly, and religion was represented weakly.

A second type of book club moved gradually toward what became a proprietary library, based on shares, often possessing permanent quarters, with business conducted at an annual meeting. Throughout the century, the term "book Club" was used flexibly, being at times a synonym for a literary society which never bought a book, whereas some "literary societies" were in effect book clubs.

If the emphasis in the book club was on current serious issues, it was partly because the circulating or rental "libraries" gave prominence to fiction. Those agencies evidently grew out of the bookseller device of renting out some of the copies of books that were slow to sell; not surprisingly they appeared first in Edinburgh and London. Benjamin Franklin, writing in 1771 in London, of his earlier days there (December 1724 to July 1726), remarked that circulating libraries did not exist then but that a bookseller next door to his first lodgings, "on certain reasonable Terms which I have now forgotten," allowed him to borrow anything in his stock—all second-hand books, according to Franklin (*Autobiography*, ed. Labaree et al., New Haven: Yale University Press, 1964, p. 197).

Before long bookstore proprietors were advertising rentable wares in printed catalogs. Novels soon proved to be a favorite of the customers, who included working people. Rental outlets were widespread in the provinces long before the publication of Samuel Richardson's *Pamela* (1740) heralded the modern novel. A circulating library advertisement has been found in a newspaper of 1718; perhaps it was not the first (mentioned, p. 192, in Paul Kaufman's indispensable *Libraries and Their Users*, London: The Library Association, 1969). Colonizing in Ireland then brought similar agencies to Dublin, and Anglicizing, to many a locality in Wales. These developments were undoubtedly an important reason for the success of the novel.

By 1742, a commercial proprietor could announce a "public circulating library" of several thousand volumes. In 1754, if not sooner, a list of books for a "Polite Circulating Library" was being offered satirically in *The Connoisseur*. Not long afterward, the moralists were sufficiently upset to launch a broad campaign against the "immoral," a drama to be replayed repeatedly in both Great Britain and the United States. Richard Brinsley Sheridan's success, *The Rivals* (1775), gave posterity this picture (Act I, Scene 2):

> *Sir Anthony Absolute.* In my way hither, Mrs. Malaprop, I observed your niece's maid coming forth from a circulating library!—She had a book in each hand—they were half-bound volumes, with marble covers!—From that moment I guessed how full of duty I should see her mistress!

Mrs. Malaprop. Those are vile places, indeed!
Sir. A. A. Madam, a circulating library in a town is an evergreen tree of diabolical knowledge! . . .
Mrs. M. . . . I don't think so much learning becomes a young woman. . . .Above all, Sir Anthony, she should be mistress of orthodoxy, that she might not mis-spell. . . .

Since the circulating library reached the servant and other lower ranks, whoever could muster a few pennies a week to rent a book, the institution was potentially a threat to certain aspects of the status quo. Thus, in all likelihood, arose disquiet manifested partly in the resistance to the education of women, both satiric and cold sober, the custom of associating the popularity of cheap romances with women readers, and disparaging both the books and the ladies. That the sparse records extant point on the contrary to a majority of male subscribers seems to support the Kaufman view (*Libraries and Their Users,* chap. XVII) of the common hypothesis as sheer assumption, an example of male-supremacist thinking.

A decade or so after Bray had passed on, and the circulating library had made its mark, the center of gravity was leaving the old parish and "town" libraries (usually parochial rather than municipal, although the distinction may have been important only in law). Thanks to better living for the middle classes, the popularization of both science and belles lettres through lectures and the new magazines, and the stimulus of the "dissenting academies," variety was in demand on a scale the traditional libraries could not satisfy. Yet books were not cheap; nor was it easy even with the required cash in hand to obtain whatever work one might desire outside London. Thus, at the very time the industrial revolution was hitting full stride, about 1740, emerged the subscription library.

Precedent was ample: the ventures undertaken in Liverpool in 1758 and in many other locations soon afterward differed from the parochial libraries in being strictly secular, in emphasizing popular history, biography, and travel. In the small communities, the provincial gentlemen and scholars and their ladies, far from the big-city bookstores, apparently sought their own means of access to this variety, by procedures perhaps little-recorded because long familiar, especially among dissenters accustomed to close and discreet cooperation to survive persecution. Those sufficiently determined about reading organized jointly a book fund; annual fees were fairly common too. They may have had more books than a book club, and less availability; not all is clear.

In the larger centers, these sharing operations occasionally became more tightly organized as proprietary libraries, and the proprietors usually acquired a building. They were also likely to employ a "librarian" who kept an eye on the books, maintained a catalog, and saw to the fire in the grate. At the Bristol Library Society in 1772 this functionary was on duty two mornings and three evenings weekly; his annual compensation was 10 guineas or £10½, which means that he earned on his half-time job 25 percent more than a (full time?) deputy sheriff and clearly more than what a "man-servant" was offered (from £5 10s. to £8) for one year (Rogers' *History,* VII:515). The evidence does not suggest that the "librarian" of this "social library" had any particular training or that the matter was discussed. The subscribers or proprietors themselves evidently made such decisions as those excluding controversial materials, like polemics in the Unitarian-Trinitarian debates, and the ephemeral romances they said they despised.

The British Museum　At the beginning of the events just sketched, certain observers were troubled by the fact that in London, of all places, the home of the bookseller and coffeehouse, there was but one library considered "public," a modest and rather obscure charitable affair founded in 1684 by Archbishop Tenison. Diarist John Evelyn wrote about it in 1689 to diarist Samuel Pepys, but more than that was needed to initiate the necessary action. Some was provided two days before Christmas, 1693, when Richard Bentley, classics expert and literary critic, assumed responsibility for directing the Royal Library.

His first major step was to demand of the Stationers' Company the deposit copies of books printed in England required under the Licensing Act of 1662. Since the stipulation had lain dormant most of the intervening years, the awakening was rude: the publishers took heavy advantage of a key defect in the statute, delivering about one thousand volumes unbound. Furthermore, the renewable two-year life of the statute was at that very time expiring, and in contrast with the practice on most similar occasions since 1662, it was now allowed to lapse. Thanks to the struggle in Parliament against the monopolist inner circle in the Stationers' Company, there were no more registrations or deposit copies until the passage of the Copyright Act effective in 1710.

Bentley had meanwhile accumulated considerable knowledge of the library in his care and partly by reason of antiquarian Humphrey Wanley's labors had further developed the collection. Either from Bentley's own hand or with his blessing there appeared, some time before 1710 (say the scholars), an anonymous printed *Proposal for building a Royal Library, and establishing it by Act of Parliament.* It deplored the state of the manuscripts and of the books bound and unbound, the failure to provide money for binding, and the absence of any titles from abroad issued during the past sixty years. It spoke of the "public" for which the library had supposedly (no proof is known) been founded and called for remedial action. Urged first were a new building and a residence for the keeper, the preferred location being praised for its elevations and "dry sandy ground" and fire-protective distance from the nearest structure.

Furthermore, like Leibniz a few years earlier (see below), the writer was concerned with "'a perpetual yearly revenue for the purchase of books,'" which he thought Parliament ought to provide by statute; the funds would be "'under the direction and disposal of the curators'" who would report to the king "'from time to time.'" It was up to Parliament to find the money, but he did suggest renewing the paper tax about to expire, the renewal to fall only upon the imported product, an obvious advantage to local manufacturers. As for the stationers, who might have doubts about a narrow paper supply, the revenue was to be used to buy books, by implication mainly from them. Altogether, the substantial increase anticipated in the use of the library, especially by students from abroad, would bring not only prestige to king and Parliament but enough daily spending to pay for "'the whole charge and revenue of this library.'" (Reproduced in Edwards, *Memoirs,* I: 423–426.)

Particular note should be taken of Bentley's argument that a stable annual income would permit the curators to borrow sums two or three times that size. His point was that many large book collections were being thrown on the market; he who had plenty of cash in hand could obtain remarkable bargains; the curators should be so equipped. Bentley knew what he was talking about. For one thing, enlarging an existing library or establishing a new one by purchasing book collections wholesale, private libraries or bookdealers' stocks, was already a well-rooted custom. Cardinal Borromeo, for example, had thus launched the Ambrosiana. By 1664 these tactics were being urged as better than piecemeal buying from retail catalogs, by J. H. Hottinger, the Zürich Orientalist whose writings on libraries and librarianship noted above were probably the most significant since Bodley's "Statutes." One feature of the next seventy-five years, more or less, was the bloc sale of great private collections, often because the heirs of a deceased aristocratic assembler either needed or at any rate preferred hard cash to books. Quite a few such libraries, of both printed matter and manuscripts, moved through several stages of private ownership to an old university or a new university or national library.

Besides this general trend, the Cromwell period had seen much travel abroad by Englishmen unhappy at home, and the Restoration found many booksellers importing foreign works in greater numbers than domestic demand required. An earlier Dutch solution, the auction, was first imitated in 1676, and repeated with enough success to spread to the provinces. More than 100 auctions of private book collections were conducted by 1700, disposing of 350,000 books; the largest was the three-part sale between 1686 and 1688 of the holdings of Richard Davis, nationally known Oxford bookseller. To reason as Bentley did was perhaps as sound as anything in the later annals of library acquisitions. It seems overwhelmingly "natural" in the England which had just established its central bank and a national debt.

Harmonious therewith was national sentiment. It was known to some that the French Royal Library was already open to readers, albeit not officially until 1753. The gentlemen scientists of the Royal Society of London, who occasionally used its library and admired its exhibits, included a number of friends of the national library idea. And certain active political figures were ready to struggle for it, notably Arthur Onslow, a trustee of the Cottonian collection deeply affected by the fire of 1731 which nearly ruined that seventeenth-century antiquarian treasure. Onslow was in 1753 Speaker of the House, instrumental in accepting the Sloane plan, and destined to serve as trustee of the British Museum.

The Sloane plan emanated from Sir Hans Sloane, distinguished physician, and successively secretary and president of the Royal Society. As early as 1707 he expressed an interest in uniting with its resources the valuable materials of the Royal Library and the Cottonian collection, in order to have "'a Public Library in London'" (quoted in Edwards, *Memoirs,* I:432). More such thinking may have been induced by the numerous catalogs of manuscript collections published during that epoch (from the Cottonian catalog of

1697 on). However that may be, at Sloane's death in 1753 his own library was offered first to the king, and declined on grounds of lacking the £20,000 asked. The trustees then reshaped the proposal for purchase by the state. Some contemporaries disparaged scientist Sloane as a "toyman"; some who liked the idea feared their ridicule; others balked at the lottery required to raise the money, lotteries being then under a cloud. Thanks to Onslow's efforts among other factors, Parliament nevertheless chose to approve the idea, in 1753. Speaker Onslow was soon to become ex officio one of the three trustees who nominated candidates for Crown appointment as the principal librarian, the other two being the Archbishop of Canterbury and the Lord Chancellor.

The lottery was authorized. Prizes absorbed £200,000 and the net proceeds for the library amounted to £95,000. Despite the scandals—one agent is said to have pocketed £40,000 by selling some lottery tickets at unofficial premium prices—the enterprises moved ahead. The Sloane purchase took £20,000, a bargain price; £10,000 more went for the acquisition of the Harleian collection, rare manuscripts assembled early in the eighteenth century mainly by palaeographer Humphrey Wanley, its librarian for many years. About half the balance, £36,000, was needed for the transfer of the collections to Montagu House, and the remaining £29,000 invested in government securities as an endowment against maintenance expenses. For the Cottonian particularly these steps brought a welcome end to an odyssey full of moves, neglect, and even the above-mentioned fire. In 1757, half a century after the original notion was expressed, the Royal Library joined the group by grace of King George II.

The purpose of the new institution, as formulated in Sloane's will, was to further "'the glory of God, the confutation of atheism and its consequences, the use and improvement of arts and sciences, and benefit of mankind.'" That is mainly traditional. Striking for novelty is the allusion to "atheism." It could hardly refer to the genuine article, barely visible then. Very likely it embraced both the hot and cold critics of the Church of England, i.e., the Dissenters, and those who rejected both them and the church, the men of "reason" and "natural religion" rather than ritual and revelation. Perhaps more significant is the immediately following explicit focus on "'the city of London, where . . . the great confluence of people'" would assure the projected library of the "'most use'" (quoted in Edwards, *Memoirs*, I:441–442).

In pursuit of these goals as they understood them, the twenty-odd ex-officio trustees, the most prestigious office holders in governmental, learned society, and church life, elected in 1753 fifteen operating trustees, mainly statesmen of literary sympathies. Four years later emerged their first *Statutes and Rules*. Its preamble declared that, while the institution was

> ". . . chiefly designed for the use of learned and studious men, both natives and foreigners, in their researches into the several parts of knowledge; yet being founded at the expence of the public, it may be judged reasonable, that the advantages accruing from it should be rendered as general as may be consistent with the several considerations above mentioned." (Quoted in A. Esdaile, *The British Museum Library*, London: Allen & Unwin, 1948, p. 37.)

Days and hours of opening were set forth, the ticket of admission established (which had to be asked for the previous day), admission fees prohibited, rules of admission for study laid down, provision made for catalogs and labeling, and lending banned except under extraordinary circumstances. (The full text may be seen in Esdaile, pp. 329–331.)

When the museum officially opened in 1759 service was offered Monday through Friday from 9 A.M. to 3 P.M., September to April; and from May through August, Monday and Friday from 4 P.M. to 8 P.M. and Tuesday through Thursday from 9 A.M. to 3 P.M. No artificial light could be brought in. Catalogs of the Harleian collection were on sale, but the reader had no comprehensive index to consult until an alphabetical author catalog was printed in 1787. The holdings were arranged as the shelf space in the several rooms seemed to recommend; not until 1790 was a shelflist produced.

The staff initially consisted of a principal librarian paid £160 annually, and five part-time associates, clergymen and physicians assigned free lodgings right there at Montagu House. Each of the first three principal librarians (1756–1798) carried an M.D. after his name. The second had upon appointment in 1772 already served since 1756 as keeper of the printed books; the third, promoted in 1776, had been for twenty years keeper of the manuscripts. "Reverends" seem to have been prominent among the early assistant keepers. Not included in this august company was the personage doubtless best known to the library's users, the keeper of the reading room. The first incumbent, paid £100 and quarters, departed after two years, dissatisfied with the quarters and perhaps not missed by his superiors, who reportedly found him too flexible in dealing with reader requests.

The nature of the clientele attracted in those early years, and able to respond to the attraction, is indicated in a contemporary diarist's entry of July 23, 1759. In the reading room was this

". . . good company . . . a man that writes for Lord Royston; a man that writes for Dr. Burton of York; a third that writes for the Emperor of Germany, or Dr. Pocock, for he speaks the worst English I ever heard; Dr. Stukeley, who writes for himself, the very worst person he could write for; and I, who only read to know if there were anything worth writing, and that not without some difficulty." (Quoted in G. F. Barwick, *The Reading Room of the British Museum*, London: Benn, 1929, p. 26.)

By 1774 the traffic apparently justified providing a new reading room with 120 seats, free of the darkness and dampness which had led users of the original one to complain.

Whatever this indicates with reference to the library's public, there was still no parliamentary financial support. Derived entirely from gifts and income from investments, the library's income was initially less than £1,000 annually and did not reach £3,000 until the next century. If the famed Dr. Johnson's view was representative, it was right for any "public library" to depend upon a succession of donations of various authors' works and materials related thereto, each developed by an individual collector with means and taste.

Life and Libraries in the New World

Colonial Variations on English Themes: College Libraries Although the British Museum could not then count on regular funds for book purchase, the Harvard College Library was favored with a £500 endowment for that purpose in 1775, by the will of Thomas Hollis, great-nephew of the earlier benefactor (1659–1731) of the same name. From 1775 to 1844, the younger Hollis' legacy furnished half the library's income. (He was similarly generous to libraries in Berne and Zürich, Switzerland, but the colonials do not seem to have noticed their cousins.)

Up to that point (1775), and at other institutions well beyond it, the colonial college library pattern was very much like that of England. In the first place there were more books on "divinity" than on any other subject. Still, the domination became gradually less marked, thanks to the emergence of law as an alternative career, and rising interest in fine literature and the latest in political science and natural science. Whereas John Harvard's 1638 book gift had been 75 percent theology, the College of William and Mary opened in 1695 with a library only 42 percent of that character, the lowest of any colonial college. Yale literally began in 1701 with book donations as the basis for a college: "Divinity" accounted for 46 percent of the collection, which until 1718 moved several times, with losses along the way. Elihu Yale's gift of 1718, providing a set location, included books more than half on religious subjects. But the outstanding donation of the colonial era, the thousand volumes presented to Yale in 1733 by philosopher-bishop George Berkeley, were only 25 percent "theology" and 28 percent "literature." Judged by their respective catalogs, Yale had in 1743 a smaller percentage of books on "divinity" than Harvard in 1735.

That is most interesting, inasmuch as Yale had been organized in good part to counteract the alleged backsliding at Harvard from puritan Calvinism. Actually the Yale book collections were reportedly never so limited as the theology officially professed. Among the best known graduates of the early days were Samuel Johnson, afterwards president of King's College (later Columbia), and several others who declared, to the consternation of many local divines, their preference for the Church of England, or what would soon be called Episcopalianism. By 1760, when the four-year-old College of New Jersey (later Princeton) library was catalogued, the older puritan writings were noticeably less in evidence than they had been at Harvard and Yale.

In point of fact, none of the colonial colleges were narrowly exclusive in their book selection in that area. Whatever the expressed views, they seem in practice to have absorbed the advice of the elder Thomas Hollis to the Harvard Corporation in 1724, offered in connection with some gifts:

> "If there happen to be some books not quite orthodox, in search after truth with an honest design, don't be afraid of them. A public library ought to be furnished, if it can, with *con* as well as *pro*, that students may read, try, judge; see for themselves, and believe upon argument and just reasonings of the Scriptures. 'Thus saith Aristotle,' 'Thus said Calvin,' will not now pass for proof in our London disputations."

Latin and Greek classic writers were fairly well represented, often in translation. Modern literature began rather weakly at Harvard, whose 1723 catalog reveals little beyond Chaucer, Shakespeare, and Milton. Yale quickly set a stronger example in this respect, acquiring an impressive range of contemporary English writing. Largely responsible were the 517 volumes obtained in 1714 as gifts from Englishmen, authors included, by Jeremiah Dummer, for many years the agent in England of the colony of Connecticut and other clients.Very little French writing seems to have reached colonial college library shelves. Only a few items were widely held: the two celebrated seventeenth-century "dictionaries" by Catholic Louis Moréri and rationalistic critic (of Moréri) Pierre Bayle, a long since forgotten general guide to behavior called "The French Academy," and the ethics and educational thoughts of Bishop Fénélon. Descartes was at hand, but not for literary appeal. Neither the great French plays nor any classic German, Spanish, or Italian literature, apparently, was in those library collections. There were a few works in some libraries in those tongues, but far more consistent was the provision of a wide-ranging collection of foreign-language dictionaries. Instruction in the classical languages was an undergraduate affair, if not secondary school; and it was late in the eighteenth century before a teacher of French was recognized at any colonial college with full faculty status.

If the campus libraries were uneven in their acquisition of English literature and rather feeble in recognition of continental belles lettres, they were rather prompt in obtaining the new English general periodicals like *The Spectator* and *The Tatler*. These resources contributed significantly to the formation of not only literary taste but political attitudes, transmitting among other things the celebrated *Cato's Letters* (1720–1721), whence the fathers of the Founding Fathers learned much of their political science.

That ground was of course well seeded by several works still thought important: the sixteenth-century Frenchman Jean Bodin's, those of the celebrated seventeenth-century English trio—James Harrington, Thomas Hobbes, and John Locke—and Dutchman Hugo Grotius; likewise from the eighteenth century those of Montesquieu and Voltaire. There were others of significance, now forgotten.

Speaking to scientific and technical interests from some colonial college libraries were the *Transactions* of the Royal Society of London, and the two leading learned journals published in Germany (both in Latin). Harvard bought the latter pair at the end of the seventeenth-century with the proceeds of the sale of 100 duplicate books; Yale's set of the *Acta Eruditorum* was among the works received from Bishop Berkeley in 1733. Curiously enough, there seems to be no evidence of attention to the French *Journal des Sçavans*.

Reading the news of scholarship and science in English and Latin were several colonials, some of whom appeared in the pages of the Royal Society's *Transactions*. From 1711 on, the faculty of William and Mary College included a professor of mathematics. By 1723, thanks to a Hollis gift, Harvard had a professorship of "natural philosophy" (physics and astronomy) and mathematics; it was occupied from 1738 to 1779 by Professor John Winthrop, who cultivated a still broader potential library demand by giving popular lectures on astronomy. Yet the landmark works from Copernicus through Newton's *Mathematical Principles of Natural Philosophy* (1687) began to arrive on the library shelves to join prescience and magic (Hermes Trismegistus at Harvard, for instance) only in the second quarter of the eighteenth century; Newton's *Optics* (1704), on hand earlier, was a rare exception. A reverse lag, another product of colonial circumstances, saw "natural history" (botany, mineralogy, and zoology) first taught more than half a century after campus libraries acquired the botanical classics of Nehemiah Grew (1682) and John Ray (1682). Chemistry was heralded by a few books like Boerhaave's (1732) several decades before the organization of medical schools in the 1760s urged its recognition as a college course. The so-called Georgian or neoclassical style in architecture may have been nurtured in part by library books. Several campus collections had one of Inigo Jones' English editions (1715, etc.) of the renowned sixteenth-century treatise by Italian Andrea Palladio.

The sciences were also promoted by the display of astronomical and physical apparatus, in several instances, in the college library. Franklin had a hand in a number of these acquisitions, normally gifts. The custom was probably patterned after the examples then familiar to many European intellectuals and their North American correspondents and visitors.

The history holdings were for some time more weighty at the ecclesiastical than at the secular end. Noteworthy is the *History of the Council of Trent* by the Italian friar Paolo Sarpi, first issued anonymously in England in 1618. Charging the Church of Rome with inability to reform, it went through twenty-four editions in Protestant countries by 1700, and five in Catholic lands. Milton's laudatory allusion to it in *Areopagitica* was doubtless understood much better in the early colonial colleges than subsequently. How many of Sarpi's admirers sympathized with his inclination to attribute a bit more influence to circumstances than to leaders? In addition to this and cognate works, a college library was likely to have a few titles in English history, and the pioneer attempts to chronicle life in the colonies.

Texts in the basic seven arts, and moral philosophy, were of course on hand everywhere. Standard items also were foreign-language grammars as well as dictionaries.

No less traditional initially were the encyclopedias. Harvard early acquired the medieval standby attributed to Bartholomew Anglicus, and the related seventeenth-century compendia, also in Latin, by German Protestant educators Johann Alsted and Bartholomew Keckermann (1573–1609). The latter two were of the Reformed group, who in the early seventeenth century enthusiastically promoted reliance on reason and experience as well as revelation. Their philosophical eclecticism, optimism about universal harmony, and carefully organized pedagogical style brought them great popularity, unfortunately upset by the disharmonies of the Thirty Years' War. The college libraries also picked up soon after publication John Harris' English-language and practically oriented *Lexicon Technicum* (1704) and Ephraim Chambers' 1728 general encyclopedia. They were apparently not equipped with the comparable works in other languages.

The Harvard Library owned the 1605 Bodleian catalog, Georg Draud's 1611 classified bibliography of Latin and German publications, John Bale's sixteenth-century English national bibliography, an edition of the *Index Ex-*

purgatorius—or books cleaned up enough for approval by the Catholic Church—and a few other resources of like nature. If the famed Cotton Mather consulted these works as a senior (1678) or later as an alumnus and fellow, it would help account for his recognition about 1700 that the Harvard collection was "at this day, far from a *Vatican,* or a *Bodleian* Dimension" (*Magnalia Christi Americana,* London: Parkhurst, 1702; book IV, sec. 3, p. 127). Whether the other colleges possessed such tools or not, they are known to have engaged occasionally in interlibrary lending.

Collection building, as already indicated, was almost entirely a question of gifts. Probably the most famous individual contributions were those of John Harvard to Harvard in 1638, Elihu Yale to Yale in 1718, and George Berkeley to Yale in 1733. In importance they were certainly matched by the composite donation assembled by Jeremiah Dummer for Yale in 1714 and by the replacement and expansion items which flowed to Harvard from all directions soon after the 1764 fire destroyed something like 500 volumes. Owing to that catastrophe, Yale's 4,000 books were in 1766 the largest college library collection in the colonies. But Harvard soon regained the lead: its 1790 catalog listed 12,000 to 13,000 volumes. Most other campus libraries were considerably smaller.

Fire was indeed the principal enemy of those libraries, doing far more damage than the marauding soldiery during the Revolution. As a rule, the only items escaping such destruction were those in circulation, which were unfortunately a very small portion of any particular collection.

Academic library service was still quite exclusive. The virtually universal practice until well into the eighteenth century was to allow the use of library books only to the faculty and officers, resident graduates, local dignitaries, and seniors. Harvard gave borrowing privileges to the seniors in 1667; juniors waited until 1767. That is fairly representative, and for the most part lower classmen entered the charmed circle only after several decades more had elapsed. Furthermore, the usual custom with respect to students was to charge and discharge books at the door; they were not admitted to the Harvard "library room" until the mid-eighteenth century. President Clap of Yale was in 1743 probably the first to prepare reading guidance for students of all classes.

Borrowers were limited to a very few books at a time, often just one, and penalties were carefully detailed in college rules for mistreatment of books or tardiness in returning them. At William and Mary from a date not yet known, and at several other colleges in the later eighteenth century, the students paid either a flat library fee or fees scaled according to the format of the book borrowed. Issuing a book, registering all the particulars about borrower, book, and term of the loan, and accepting its return, was the business transacted by the librarian for a few hours once or twice a week. Reading on the premises was for many years a privilege accorded to hardly anyone but a visiting minister or gentleman. In 1755 President Clap recommended 32 titles to Yale freshmen and sophomores; to upper classmen, about 400, of which 170 were "divinity" and 80 "science." But physical separation of books for undergraduates seems to have occurred first twenty years later, at the largest library, Harvard's. As recorded in a *Catalogus. . . Selectus,* theology led with 30 percent rather evenly divided between Anglican and Puritan works, but with only one known Catholic.

The great 1764 fire at Harvard spared what was in circulation, 260 titles in 404 volumes, a little less than one-tenth of the collection. Borrowers had off the premises (not all are identifiable) 146 folios, 36 quartos, and 212 smaller books. Most of them had been borrowed within the preceding year, but as many as 100 had been in the hands of this or that trustee ("Overseer") for anywhere from one to fourteen years! All but two of the forty-six men receiving bachelor's degrees in 1764 were among those charged with books; also charged were three master's candidates and some faculty members. Half of the 120 works in use by students were theological; the most frequently registered, with seven entries, was John Leland's *View of the Principal Deistical Writers,* a recent (1754) English historical-critical analysis of high repute, helping to fix in the public mind the association of deism with moderate rationalism in thought and opposition to formal church organization. Science titles numbered 23. (For the vital details, from a Harvard manuscript probably of 1764, we are obliged to Joe Walker Kraus, *Book Collections of Five Colonial College Libraries . . .,* Ann Arbor, Mich.: University Microfilms, 1964, pp. 255–259.)

It was presumed that students owned at least some of the books they ought to read. Whatever the foundation for that view may have been at first, it was evidently too narrow for satisfaction by the later eighteenth century. Just before the Revolution, the Linoneans at Yale and a few others of the new literary societies were already assembling books in their meeting rooms or some other easily accessible place. This rivulet was soon to become a substantial stream.

Students did not then enjoy the benefits of public library service. Yet the idea was advanced on at least one occasion. In connection with the search for a permanent site for the College of Rhode Island (later Brown) in the late 1760s, Newport and Providence supported their bids with warm praise of their respective "public" libraries. Newport indicated that use of the Redwood Library collections might be "'allowed the pupils, under the discreet care of the president and tutors'" (quoted in Shores, p. 42). Providence won the competition, and at least some members of the college community reportedly profited from the resources of the Providence Library Company (afterwards the Athenaeum).

In harmony with established English tradition the college library was first usually "kept" by a recent graduate or junior faculty member (tutor) who awaited a call to a pulpit. If one adds to that the Reformation emphasis on books, and the small number of both students and teachers at any colonial institution, it is not surprising that the post was frequently held by someone later distinguished in public or intellectual life. Thus the Harvard librarian for most of the year 1674 was twenty-two-year-old Samuel Sewall (Harvard, 1671) who became a politician and merchant and the only Salem witchcraft trial judge to admit his error publicly, wrote one of the earliest North American antislavery tracts, and gave posterity a diary of high value. As the colleges expanded, the library might be operated by a tutor, or a professor, or even the president, but he was controlled narrowly by regulations composed by the trustees.

The college president was very likely to play a key role. Just as he generally taught "moral philosophy" to the seniors, developing the library was his concern both educationally and financially. To take the most famous instance, President Clap of Yale himself directed the production of the Yale catalog of 1743 as a guide to reading. For Samuel Davis of Princeton to have served two years as both president and college librarian was only a little unusual; one outcome was the 1760 catalog.

The library-keeper function brought £5 annually to tutors at Harvard in 1693, £8 in 1698. A senior tutor at Yale drew £5 for that task in the 1720s when the college was very young. In 1763 King's College paid a professor of mathematics £10 for library service. Comparisons are very hard to make, because many an instructor was paid according to the number of students in his care, there were at times competing currencies, the value of money changed from time to time, and the college histories say almost nothing about compensation of the staff in those days. It is established that John Rogers was voted £100 salary and £50 for expenses to preside over Harvard in 1682; that a brass kettle cost a little more than £5 at about the same time that President Clap of Yale in 1722 valued his official home at £115.

Plainly, while the library was regarded as vital by these Protestant higher educators, "library-keeping" rated a few notches below teaching. Since book selection and procurement were in practice faculty, presidential, or trustee activities, the "librarian's" job was primarily to keep records, and frequently to keep the premises clean too. For such duties one does not anticipate finding discussion of training. (In 1674 the Harvard library was presumably prepared thus for a solemn flogging, preceded and followed by presidential prayers. Later days continued to see nonlibrary rituals in college libraries, but as a rule they were agreeable to all participants.)

The only work expected of a librarian at a colonial college which might be considered "professional" was the preparation of a catalog. Actually, the primary reason for that unique semiskilled labor until about midcentury was the solicitation of gifts, and the president often assumed the burden personally. Not very surprising, accordingly, is the Harvard 1765 rule number 1 that donations worth £50 or more are to be shelved in particular alcoves, with the donor's name in plain sight. Rule number 3 goes on: "'A written Catalogue of all the Books in each Alcove shall be hung up therein; and an alphabetic Catalogue of the whole Library, divided into Chapters, according to the Diversity of Subjects, shall be printed and a copy chain'd in each window of the Library'" (quoted in Shores, p. 186).

The extant catalogs are a valuable record of educational and cultural growth in the British North American colonies; but as samples of the bibliographical art they are in no way significant. Mainly no doubt because the collections were so small, there was no urgency to adopt even the few refinements displayed in the Leyden catalog of 1595 and the Bodleian guides of 1605 and 1674, despite their availability at Harvard at least until the great fire of 1764. Yale, for instance, decided in 1740 that if library revenues yielded any surplus, it could be applied in part to the assembling of subject catalogs. But modern scholarship has not yet reported any awareness of the contemporary advances (see below) by Leibniz and J. M. Francke at court libraries in Germany and the guiding spirits at the University of Göttingen. Sophistication in library matters awaited the expansion of campus book holdings and the surge of quasi-public urban library development in the years ahead.

More Variations: The Noncampus Library Matrix The colleges and college libraries in the colonies were more or less English, modified within ready recognition. Other libraries also followed several home precedents, as will appear shortly, but the difference in fundamental conditions was much more evident in their development than on the campus.

The population of the colonies originated in several different places. Those arriving involuntarily from Africa were not to influence libraries, except perhaps as building craftsmen, for many years to come. Of the largely voluntary migration from Europe, at least 60 percent were English, by far the predominant element; and most of them were Protestant. Not every settler was a booklover, but such persons were to be found in every colony, and their numbers in New England were striking. A bookbinder opened for business in Boston in 1637, just one year after Harvard; at least one merchant ten years later was advertising books imported for sale. By 1690 twenty bookdealers had been operating in that town for twenty years. Not for a century did the "Athens of America" face any serious competition as the prime book trade center, serving far beyond the corporation limits.

Why was Boston the key location? Why not Williamsburg, Virginia, where able men from the plantations made laws, or Charleston, South Carolina, seat of a well-supported culture; or Philadelphia or New York? The last two, despite their steady rise to population leadership in 1790, with about 22,000 persons each, are not candidates partly for special reasons. Quaker tradition emphasized meditation rather than reading, and the admixture of other traditions during the eighteenth century did not promptly delete what was there already. In New York City, although the Dutch Reformed Church and the later Anglicans sponsored schooling, culture found no devotion comparable to that accorded commerce.

Considering just the South and New England, as early as 1700 the population of the latter already exceeded the total in Virginia and Maryland, by roughly 113,000 to 93,000; New England had about 4,500 Negroes, nearly all slaves; the two Southern colonies had 10,000. The reading and book preferences of educated whites were much the same in both areas, but life was shaped very differently by conditions of production. Tobacco was the South's big cash crop; tobacco cultivation favored dispersion, and land tenure laws did not obstruct it. Population density was low in Virginia, there being only two counties with more than 30 persons per square mile at the end of the colonial period. The density in Maryland was somewhat higher. Slaves were by then (1790) one-third of the Southern population.

In "old," or southern, New England, diversified agriculture and the town system of land tenure produced an individual ownership average for the eighteenth century of about 100 acres. That was actually larger than the average holding of the small-farmer majority of Virginia; but where Virginia also knew plantations of over 1,000 acres, the New England maximum was 200 acres. Further, several New England ports flourished on the basis first of fisheries, then commerce and shipbuilding, and finally the sugar-into-rum part of the slave trade, the greatest money-maker of all. The colonial period ended with population densities as follows: Massachusetts (not counting Maine, soon to be independent) 35 persons per square mile, Connecticut 39, Rhode Island 45. Such averages are obviously higher than those of the

South. But, like any average, they do not report the contrast in full: the New England densities were produced partly by populations in excess of 7,500 (in the 1770s) in Boston and Brockton, Massachusetts; New Haven and Norwich, Connecticut; and Newport City, Rhode Island. Besides, there were nine additional Connecticut towns, half a dozen in extreme eastern Massachusetts, and coastal Portsmouth, New Hampshire, boasting at least 4,000 inhabitants. (The source data are assembled in Evarts B. Greene and Virginia D. Harrington, *American Population before the Federal Census of 1790,* New York: Columbia University Press, 1932.)

These differentiating facts of life overbore the common cultural heritage. Church of England educational traditions survived but did not flourish in the South. The more intense Calvinist concern with Scripture lessons made only modest contributions in cosmopolitan New Netherlands; the British takeover in the 1670s does not seem to have strengthened them notably. New England was far more homogeneous, and led by numerous determined "Puritans," largely from the more settled eastern end. Such persons may well have regarded their above-average population density as a challenge politically as well as a threat to public health and safety. It was certainly the justification in their thinking for some of their pastoral and political behavior. Perhaps these phenomena are the main reasons why New England advanced more rapidly than the South in the provision of the rudiments of education to the children of the struggling mass as well as those few enjoying wealth. Massachusetts had the extra advantage initially of the highest percentage of (English) college graduates in the colonies.

If the diffusion of culture was shaped considerably by differences in population density, slavery was surely not without influence. In 1755 South Kingstown, Rhode Island, in the south-central swamp area, was apparently about one-fourth Black, and Newport something less than one-fifth; but the ratio of Negroes to the total was lower elsewhere in that colony, and very much lower in Connecticut and Massachusetts. To most New Englanders Negroes were known, if at all, as objects of trade: commodities. They seem accordingly to have played little or no part in the thinking in those communities about schools and libraries.

Remote abstractions to most New England townspeople, the Blacks were a daily visible fact of life to substantial numbers of Southerners. The slaves sometimes moved a master or mistress to behave understandingly or generously. But their primary character as an indispensable work force was bound to determine most of their treatment. Potentially sharers as well as builders of a civilization, they were largely deprived of education out of fear that such improvements would unsettle them and endanger white supremacy. The home and furnishings of William Byrd of Westover, Virginia, and the headquarters of the Charleston (South Carolina) Library Society, might stand partly to the credit of slave craftsmen. But neither of these outstanding mid-eighteenth-century book collections, one private the other semipublic, was in any way accessible to nearby Blacks, or, for that matter, to poor whites.

The cultural condition of women is difficult to define. Most of them in New England were literate; how they became so is not clear, except for families known to have employed tutors and scattered evidence about "boarding schools" in Boston and certain "dame" schools. That the ladies of the Southern aristocrats frequently could read seems evident: William Byrd of Westover reported a quarrel with his wife "because I was not willing to let her have a book out of the library" (*The Secret Diary . . . 1709-1712*, eds. Wright and Tinling, Richmond, Va.: Dietz, 1941, p. 461), but expressed no surprise at her request. It is not likely that literacy was widespread among the female portion of either the slave or white small-farmer population.

Public Ownership, 1656-1730   The campus libraries tended to follow English tradition with considerable challenge to the discouragements of the immediate environment; being small and poor, they vigorously solicited support in England as well as locally. The noncampus library was by no means uninfluenced by English models, but local circumstances made for noticeable difference. The first venture was not altogether typical of what followed. In 1656, Captain Robert Keayne, a successful merchant of less than sterling reputation, left the town of Boston £300 for a public market well protected from fire and dampness, together with quarters for courts of justice, conference and social rooms, and "'a Library & a gallery'" (quoted in Jesse H. Shera, *Foundations of the Public Library*, Chicago: University of Chicago Press, 1949, p. 17). He also bequeathed to his fellow citizens his unfinished Bible commentaries, and authorized his executors to set aside for said library any of his books "'as they shall thinke profitable & usefull for such a Library (not simply for show but properly for use) they being all English none Lattine or Greeke. . . . [He hoped that] after this beginning the Lord may stirr up some others that will add more to them & helpe to carry the worke on by bookes of more valew, antiquity, use and esteeme.'" (Quoted in Shera, p. 20.) Keayne tried to leave no loose ends. If the town failed to build the market, the money was to be transferred to Harvard, already a going concern. And if there were no library room within three years after his death, his books' destination likewise would be Harvard.

   The building duly arose, and its existence sounded promising to some ears: a donation of 1674 brought several religious titles, Euclid's geometry, and two bibliographical pillars, Tritheim's late fifteenth-century ecclesiastical biobibliography and "'the Catalogue of Oxford Library'" (see Shera, p. 21). This last may have been the third Bodleian catalog, just issued (1674), or one of the earlier guides by Thomas James. The Town House was damaged by fire in 1711, but the books survived, and either their usefulness or some other factor produced enough contributions for restoration. By 1747, when a worse blaze utterly leveled the institution, Bostonians interested in books did not choose to support a replacement. Part of the explanation is that the Harvard graduates among them could use the Harvard Library. One wonders how green were the memories of the Town House disaster when the college library was burned in 1764; certainly a torrent of donations for a new Harvard Library blotted out the ashes in record time. In any case, strength in one library limb depriving another of nourishment was to become painfully familiar on the United States scene.

   Public ownership of "useful" books seemed fitting to rugged individualistic Robert Keayne, whether or not he was consciously echoing Francis Bacon and John Durie. Like views may be found also in a small New England town. By 1672, if not earlier there or elsewhere, the selectmen (city council) of Concord, Massachusetts, were alluding to "'the bookes of marters & other bookes that belong to the Towne'" (quoted in Shera, p. 25). The phrase occurs in a document requiring careful handling of books loaned and a limit of one month in loans; the authorities were apparently referring in particular to Foxe's "Book of Martyrs," a century-old best seller. Thus was set down a precedent for public ownership of books in a small community (population 1,564 in 1765). A few more Massachusetts villages used public authority to acquire—sometimes even buy—books, in those days before Benjamin Franklin offered a different model. That similar practices were then a part of behavior in the middle colonies seems very doubtful; scholarship has apparently brought none to light so far.

The "useful" in 1656 was substantially divinity and little or no belles lettres. It is hardly accidental that the only work indicated specifically by the Concord fathers in 1672 was the English classic of Protestant struggle. Yet the jealous God of Calvinist predestination would soon have to fight leisured culture, rationalism and optimism, ideas of the self-sufficiency of nature and the intellect. Successive reading patterns were to reduce the role of self-flagellation texts and increase those of gentle improvement of the mind, science, and plain fun.

By the same token, the range of books appropriate to the home needed no special guidance merely because it was in a public place. In fact, it is unlikely that any but the Boston, large town, specimen, is properly described as a library in the sense that it had distinctive quarters. The campus library, vital to the faculty and advanced students, required a guard-recorder-janitor and therefore employed a "library-keeper." The noncampus library had apparently no such steady use and no such need for protection, and as a rule no "librarian" in the pre-Franklin age. Its usefulness being a function of independent continuing education rather than professional study with regular obligations, there was no regular budget, either.

The Bray Chapter   At the turn of the century, before any further progress was made along public authority lines, so far as we know, there was an interlude of book provision of an older sort. Together with his labors for small-town libraries at home, Dr. Thomas Bray gave much thought and energy to the book needs of the Church of England ministers in the North American colonies. Some time prior to his visit, he sketched plans for a deanary library to serve five parishes, and a classification scheme to go with it. These collections for the clergy were to comprise the Holy Scriptures, some outstanding commentaries on them, and some leading treatises on particular points of theology. Nonreligious works like law, mathematics, natural history, and medicine, could be furnished only at the province level; but they were to serve any interested reader. Actually, as many as twenty libraries seem to have been shipped directly to the parishes with the backing of the Bishop of London, before the organizer examined the scene in person.

Word of Bray's plans and hopes reached sympathetic colonial officials rather soon. In 1697 Governor Francis Nicholson asked the Maryland Legislature for an appropriation to add to the books donated to Annapolis by the king, place the collection under the care of the province commisary, and open it to "'all persons'" wishing to consult it, "'under proper restrictions'" (quoted by Steiner, p. 67). The Assembly thanked Bray for his efforts but declined to vote any money. Like appreciation was formally expressed in November 1698 by the South Carolina Legislature.

By the following year, when promoter Bray departed for Maryland, the foundations had been laid for the Society for Promoting Christian knowledge, a vital aid in financing his enterprises, and he reported that the four years' labor just ended had produced nearly £2,500 worth of books for the colonies. His accounts reveal that one-third of that amount had been invested in Maryland, another £300 in Carolina, and £69 in New York. Smaller collections had been sent to the other continental and West Indian colonies, and a few to other parts of the world. The money had been donated mainly by numerous upper- and middle-class Englishmen and women, the largest sum being the more than £600 turned in through the S.P.C.K. Certain "'Societies and Companies'" contributed corporatively, led by "'The Colony of Carolina at present and in promise . . . £225/0/0'" (quoted from the original records by Edgar L. Pennington, "The Beginnings of the Library in Charles Town, South Carolina," American Antiquarian Society *Proceedings*, new ser., 44; p. 160, April 18, 1934).

Bray regarded thirty of the libraries as "'advanc'd . . . some of them to a considerable Perfection'" (quoted by Steiner, p. 67), and seventy more as having been started. He spoke of sixteen in Maryland and one each in Boston; New York City; East Jersey, Pennsylvania; and Charleston, South Carolina. Although his official inspection trip led him to conclude that he could do more for the Established Church in Maryland from England than on the ground, the library venture proceeded famously. Beginning in 1700, "laymen's libraries" (exclusively theological) were sent out, for distribution at the discretion of the minister. Some items were provided in 100 copies, many no doubt to serve propaganda purposes. Including titles directed at dissenters, Quakers, and Roman Catholics, such libraries were intended for many centers outside Maryland. They were to be in the hands of key governors and magistrates, and in some instances they were to be placed where they were accessible to the public.

Although the church in Maryland did not benefit particularly from Bray's contributions as quickly as he had hoped, the province was conspicuous for its thirty "Bray Libraries." Nearly every one of the thirty parishes received one in the years beginning in 1698. The largest was the provincial library at Annapolis, 1,095 books kept in the state house until the fire of 1704 and then transferred to King William School, the library's home for about eighty years. It was probably the first library in North America both circulating and free. Five other collections held at least 100 books; most were smaller, nine small parishes being allotted "libraries" of 10 books each. The collections were predominantly religious but frequently had a handful of secular works too.

Books from the same source were dispatched on a smaller scale to other colonies. The Anglican King's Chapel in Boston received in 1698 some 200 volumes, and others were added later; all remained in the rector's study until the Revolution, after which the survivors were moved a number of times, ultimately to the Boston Athenaeum. Collections also arrived, from Bray sources, in Rhode Island; Albany; New York City; Perth Amboy, New Jersey; Philadelphia; several parishes in Virginia (not generally, thanks to resistance from a key official); and South Carolina.

The South Carolina Assembly had in 1698 appropriated £70 for books for a public library. That same body accepted the Bray contribution, and placed it by statute (1700) in the custody of a Charleston minister; the churchwardens were to take charge if he resigned or died. The General Assembly was to appoint nine commissioners responsible for judging the books and examining them annually on November 5. The arrangement reminds one of the Visitors at the Bodleian, but there was a notable difference. These books were to circulate, and it was necessary to stipulate that they all be on the shelves each October 26. Fulfilling that requirement was most difficult, because any book could be borrowed by "'any Inhabitant'" (quoted by Steiner, p. 71) without a fee, and the loan was controlled only by the borrower's signature on a receipt and his knowledge that failure to return the book on time and in good condition would bring down upon him a bill for three times the value of the book. Much delinquency apparently did occur: a law of 1712 authorized the keeper of the library to deny books to applicants when he thought such action appropriate.

The vital records were the catalog and the registration-and-loan book maintained on the premises. Six other copies of the catalog were furnished to various parties including Dr. Bray and the commissioners.

The latter were charged not only with the duties mentioned but with supervision of the parochial libraries, designation of persons to catalog their collections, and appointment of trustees to govern them. In other words, the South Carolina Commissioners were a noteworthy prototype of the later state library commission, and an unusually powerful one at that. Not quite a commission were the library visitors directed by an act of 1704 to inspect the parish libraries of Maryland and report to the governor and council. The governor appointed the visitors; the libraries they checked were in the care of the parish ministers. The North Carolina Act of 1715 directed the principal officers of the province and an additional ten named citizens to serve as a board of commissioners for a free circulating library in St. Thomas' Parish. The statute is striking because it designated a librarian, selected primarily for that position; suspended for the time being was the custom of regarding that responsibility as the incidental task of a nearby college president or other clergyman.

Thus accumulated useful precedents in state responsibility for the management and supervision of local libraries. They were not accompanied, however, by any provision for adding to the 34,000 books provided by the Bray mechanism, or assuring stable budgetary support, or improving the library skills of the person in charge. The impulse generated by Bray, in fact, did not long survive him. Legislative bodies were not yet ready to pay for libraries, and the torch had to be picked up by men whose background and purpose differed considerably from those of both the Puritan and the Anglican library advocates.

The Subscription Library, Franklin Style The very forces eroding those traditions now produced a new type of library. Journeyman printer Benjamin

Franklin, deist and student of all manner of new ideas, was like most educated colonials aware of the clubs of England. Not long after returning from his eighteen months there he gathered several kindred spirits into a junto. Launched in 1727, the new discussion group soon became in its founder's judgment "the best School of Philosophy, Morals and Politics that then existed in the Province" of Pennsylvania. Certainly the members' use of books increased. For one thing, each member was expected to produce and read once every three months an original paper on a topic of his own choice. Perhaps more important, questions were announced each week for examination at the next meeting, which "put us on Reading with Attention" (*Autobiography,* ed. Labaree, p. 118); and "our Books were often referr'd to in our Disquisitions upon the Queries" and would be more convenient if at hand. Since the club had just left a tavern to meet in private quarters it was possible to assemble books safely. Franklin proposed just that, successfully, and "clubbing our books to a common Library"was engaged in for about one year. The collection of such Books as each "could best spare . . . fill'd one end of the room"and was of "great Use"; but fewer books were there than "were expected" (*Autobiography,* p. 130). In any case, abuses spoiled the experiment and each member took his books back.

Such was Franklin's testimony in the portion of his memoirs apparently penned mainly in England in 1771. Thirteen years afterward, in France, he turned to the same subject, to be sure of recording the origins of the "Philadelphia Publick Library." Writing without access to his earlier account, he recollected that for lack of "a good Bookseller's Shop in any of the Colonies to the Southward of Boston," in 1730, "those who lov'd reading were oblig'd" to send for books to England. The members of the junto had "each a few" (*Autobiography,* pp. 141–142).

Partial failure of the junto's experiment promptly moved the imaginative printer to organize what he called in 1771 "my first Project of a public Nature, that for a Subscription Library." With the help of his junto associates he found in 1731 fifty persons who put down 40 shillings each and pledged 10 more annually for fifty years to come, "the Term our Company was to continue." Then they obtained a charter for "the Mother of all the N American Subscription Libraries" (*Autobiography,* p. 130). To these data Franklin added in 1784 the following: "each subscriber engag'd to pay a certain Sum down for the first purchase of Books and an annual Contribution for encreasing them. So few were the Readers at that time in Philadelphia, and the Majority of us so poor, that I was not able with great Industry to find more than Fifty Persons, mostly young Tradesmen, willing. . . . On this little Fund we began." (*Autobiography,*p. 142.)

The first step was to obtain James Logan's advice on book purchase, since that statesman and scholar—then Pennsylvania's chief justice—was by common consent the best read person available. On March 31, 1732, a list of books recommended by Logan was sent to Peter Collinson of London, Quaker textile merchant, antiquary, and leading clearinghouse on matters scientific for Anglo-America. The titles desired were heavily scientific and practical, with some political science and belles lettres, one spy tale, and no theology; the last item was "Catalogues," evidently an open-end request for the bookdealer variety. (The details are on pp. 9–10 of Austin K. Gray,

Benjamin Franklin's Library; New York: Macmillan, 1937.) Nearly half the company's funds, £45, were committed in this manner, with misgivings about pirates and other menaces. But all went well, the books arriving in October. They were arranged first by size. Franklin soon afterward indicated that he would present each subscriber with a printed catalog; he did so in 1733.

Franklin himself, according to his recollections in 1789, had "in the scheme of the library . . . provided only for English books" (*The Writings of Benjamin Franklin,* ed. Smyth, New York: Macmillan, 1907, X:9). Whether Logan, guide and donor, or the others who contributed books afterward, knew that or simply thought like Franklin, the collection does seem to have developed in that manner.

Meanwhile, in November 1732, the associates deemed it desirable to employ a librarian. They selected Louis Timothée, originally a refugee from France after the revocation of the Edict of Nantes, by way of Holland, latterly Franklin's protégé, and soon to become an enterprising printer in South Carolina. For the next three months, ran the contract, he was to give "due Attendance" on Wednesdays from 2 P.M. to 3 P.M. and on Saturdays from 10 A.M. to 4 P.M. permitting "any civil Gentlemen" to use the library books on the premises. He might loan available books to the Library Company of Philadelphia subscribers but not to any others save only book selection consultant James Logan; borrowers must sign a promissory note against failure to return books as agreed. The authorized duration of the loan and the size of the pledge were specified for each title in the "Catalogue," and no one might borrow more than one unless it was mentioned in that catalog that they could be "lent together." The librarian was not to act on any promissory note in default without approval from a majority of the directors' committee. He was to attend their meetings when asked to. For these services he was to receive at the end of the three months "Three Pounds lawful Money certain" plus such bonus as was thought deserved. (*The Papers of Benjamin Franklin,* ed. Labaree, New Haven: Yale University Press, 1959, I:250-252.)

For all his promoting and organizing, and even though he served as librarian for a few months after Timothée resigned in 1733, the future diplomat held both reading and libraries at arm's length. During the very period in which the junto moved out of the alehouse to its own room, Franklin was opening a stationery shop. To protect his "Credit and Character as a Tradesman" he was not only industrious and frugal in fact but deliberate in avoiding "all Appearances" to the contrary: no fancy clothes, no idle diversions. "A Book, indeed, sometimes debauch'd me from my Work; but that was seldom, snug, and gave no Scandal" (*Autobiography,* pp. 125-126). He was glad to discover the woman he married of much the same disposition. Among her services in the shop were"folding and stitching Pamphlets" (*Autobiography,* p. 145).

The problems of launching the first subscription library, moreover, remained prominent in his memory. In 1771 he made a note to himself to write about them. In 1784 he unburdened himself thus:

The Objections, and Reluctances I met with in Soliciting the subscriptions, made me soon feel the Impropriety of presenting one's self as the Proposer of any useful Project that might be suppos'd to raise one's Reputation in the smallest degree above that of one's Neighbours, when one has need of their Assistance to accomplish that Project. I therefore put myself as much as I could out of sight, and stated it as a Scheme of a *Number of Friends,* who had requested me to go about and propose it to such as they thought Lovers of Reading. In this way my Affair went on more smoothly, and I ever after practis'd it on such Occasions. . . . If it remains a while uncertain to whom the Merit belongs, some one more vain than yourself will be encourag'd to claim it, and even then Envy will be dispos'd to do you Justice, by plucking those assum'd Feathers, and restoring them to their rightful Owner. (*Autobiography,* p. 143.)

If the Library Company of Philadelphia was established despite difficulties, some credit is due the political wisdom of its leadership. When the new proprietor of the Province of Pennsylvania, Thomas Penn, arrived from England in 1733, the directors greeted him on May 16 in the name of "Among the Rest, the Subscribers to the Library." Climate, constitution, and native genius were all favorable, they noted, "but when colonies are in their infancy, the Refinements of Life, it seems, cannot be much attended to." It was the task of the "first Founders" to provide for agriculture, commerce, and "good Laws." The "other Arts and Sciences" were "less immediately necessary"; neither in Pennsylvania nor in the neighboring provinces was there yet "any Provision for a publick generous Education." The deficiency would they thought be remedied in part by a "Common Library." Surely a son of "the great and good, and ever memorable William Penn would smile on efforts to advance knowledge by rendering "useful Science more cheap and easy of access." Penn's reply warmly approved anything "so useful to the

Painter C. E. Mills' conception of Benjamin Franklin welcoming the first patrons to the Library Company of Philadelphia in 1731. (Courtesy of The Bettmann Archive, Inc.)

Country, as that of erecting a *common Library* in this City" (Franklin, *Papers,* 1:320–321). The exchange of compliments was repeated after the arrival a year or so later of John Penn. This time the tribute was to "so good and necessary an Undertaking, as the erecting a Publick Library" (*Papers,* 2:35).

How rapidly the institution became truly "common" is not readily ascertainable from the record. We do know that while Franklin served as librarian, from December 1733 to March 1734, the library was opened to nonsubscribers prepared to leave a deposit equal to the value of the book plus a rental fee. On the other hand, a number of other subscription libraries were organized before long (1746, 1757), in Philadelphia, apparently because the Library Company's subscription fee was too high for some persons interested. The Reverend Jacob Duché (1738–1798) reportedly learned from the librarian at the Library Company in 1772 that, for every gentleman using the collections there were twenty "'tradesmen.'" (Another observer declared that "'obscure mechanicks'" with a bent for mathematics were the regulars at the rather similar Loganian Library, also in Philadelphia. Both items are quoted in Carl Bridenbaugh, *Cities in Revolt,* New York: Knopf, 1955, p. 383.) Duché was the son of a colonel and a member of the first (1757) graduating class of the College of Philadelphia (later the University of Pennsylvania). In the 1760s he helped select books for its library. When the city was occupied during the Revolution, he turned Loyalist after a brief spell in General Howe's jail. One wonders whether the remark about skilled workers at the Library Company seemed to him particularly welcome or unwelcome and was accordingly exaggerated in his comment.

In any case, Franklin's institution grew steadily in holdings and reputation. Gifts began to arrive: usually books, sometimes money, and on several occasions scientific instruments and botanical and zoological samples. Visitors favorably impressed ranged from evangelist George Whitefield and reformer John Wesley to botanist John Bartram, who became an honorary director. By 1739 the institution owned enough property to bring up the question of incorporation. Much debate ensued, but the idea was finally accepted, and the document incorporating the company in perpetuity was approved in March 1742. A few months later a formal thank-you letter was dispatched to the "true and absolute Proprietaries" of the province. They responded with complimentary allusions to "an undertaking calculated to form [the inhabitants'] Minds and influence them to good and Virtuous Actions" (Franklin, *Papers,* 1:347–349). The note of thanks does not mention explicitly the proprietors' gift of a tract of land for a library building. The directors evidently calculated that their undertaking would be better off by renting it, but collecting the rent proved troublesome. Meanwhile, the library vacated its private quarters and from 1739 to 1772 occupied part of the state house (subsequently Independence Hall).

Other troubles emanated from the shortage of certain virtuous actions among the directors and subscribers. The second long-term librarian, serving from 1746 to 1763, ran afoul of directorial rank pulling. Book losses were under the by-laws deductible from the librarian's salary. Enforcement was demanded, and the librarian's protest that the directors and subscribers were themselves the delinquents did not suffice to protect him. He boycotted their meetings. They in turn persisted in seeking the money, first from him and then from his widow and estate; but they failed, and the by-law became a dead letter.

The directors, incidentally, missed meetings often enough to annoy the librarian and founder Franklin. The latter urged a fine for nonattendance, and they submitted. But a mere shilling penalty proved no control. Then their well-informed leader suggested that proxies would do: two good bottles of wine. The proxies probably livened up the proceedings, at various restaurants, with perhaps some debt to the presiding "Widows" (some real and some by courtesy). This noble experiment also, in due time, went the way of all flesh.

That the Library Company should have accepted poetry in 1757, Pope's *Essay on Man*, certain very respectable novels like Dr. Johnson's *Rasselas* but not those of the daring Messrs. Fielding, Richardson, and Defoe, and a few plays is not particularly remarkable. Such works were on the campus too. When the Revolution interrupted commerce with the British Isles from 1774 to the peace of 1783, no fiction was bought; but in September of the latter year the directors promptly ordered 200 books from London. They were mainly from the variety already established, history and biography, poetry, chemistry, and electricity.

While gifts remained welcome, book purchase was at least from 1745 on (perhaps earlier?) based on a regular subscription income, an advantage not yet known at Harvard or the British Museum (Franklin suggested precisely that, for Harvard, in 1755, but no action is on record). The Company, wrote Franklin to commercial correspondent William Strahan in London on December 11, 1745, was then spending on books annually about twenty pounds sterling. James Logan, asking in March 1747 for a list of additions to the collection, was embarrassed to learn that they were "so considerable since the year 1742 as to require the Press," that is, a twenty-eight-page catalog, issued in 1746 as a supplement to the library *Charter* (Franklin, *Papers,* 3:113). By 1752 the scale of outlay had enlarged to an annual rate of £50. In June, Franklin advised Strahan, then beginning his tenure as London book buyer for the Library Company, to reduce the want list as necessary, to hold the total cost to that figure. The directors' "Money comes in but once a Year," he pointed out, "and they do not chuse to lie so long in Debt" (*Papers,* 4:323).

The prices on Strahan's invoice of August 26 (*Papers,* 4:351–353) vary from 1s. 6d., for an explanation of the Julian and Gregorian calendars (the Protestant world was just changing from the former to the latter), to 11s. 6d. for Montesquieu's *Spirit of the Laws* in two volumes. The Company also paid 17s. for six volumes of the *Rambler* magazine, and £17 16s. for a twelve-volume set of tracts. The bill, including insurance for the voyage, came to £48 9s., nearly the stipulated maximum. If it exceeded what was in the till, explained Franklin to another correspondent in 1758, the difference would normally be made up by collecting "one or two Years Payment of their Subscriptions" in advance from a few subscribers (*Papers,* 8:85). Was any other library anywhere that well off? Germany's University of Göttingen library (1737), the semipublic Royal Library of France under A. J. Bignon (1743–1772), and the older and still private library of the Italian Dukes of

Este, in Modena, may have been. Comparison of the four operations, involving among other things different currencies, does not seem to have been undertaken to date.

The limitations on what could be bought were brought home sharply in 1769. Franklin suggested that the Royal Society *Transactions* ought to be joined on the company's shelves by those of other European learned societies, and the directors asked him to investigate the cost. His findings put an end to the discussion for the time being.

Like most library operators since, the Philadelphians checked what was received against their purchase orders, and occasionally found discrepancies. Illustrative is this description, submitted by Franklin to Strahan on December 11, 1752; after acknowledging that most of the merchandise was in good order—

> . . . not D'Argens Philosophy of Common Sense . . . but another thing of his instead of it. The Life of Boerhave sent is an old and small Book; what was intended was a new Life lately published in (I think) 4 Vols. 8ᵛᵒ . . . And instead of Chaucers' whole Works, in his old original English; only the Canterbury tale's moderniz'd, are come. These two, we had before, or we should keep them; tho' I think they are imperfect Books, and two of the Volumes intermix'd with each other in the Binding . . . (*Papers,* 4:379).

The same missive assured Strahan that he was right to suppose that the Company did not want to buy a "dictionary of trade" lately translated from the French and being published in parts (like so many books in those days); the company did indeed "chuse rather to have" the work "entire, than in Numbers" (*Papers,* 4:379). Involved here was the annoyance of binding. A few years after the remark about the trade dictionary, Franklin mailed Peter Collinson a list of missing numbers of magazines: "We are about to bind them up, and should have our Sets compleat" (*Papers,* 6:171). A year and a half later, on January 31, 1757, Franklin tried again, informing Collinson that the items desired were "still wanting" (*Papers,* 7:114). Such letters were soon to become routine in the correspondence of libraries.

So also were those indicating a change of agent because his prices were too high.

However such problems may have struck Franklin, he had no hesitation in crediting Collinson with key contributions of time, books, and money to the rise of the Library Company of Philadelphia. Worth noting in particular is the remark in his condolence message (of 1768 or 1769) to his friend's son, that the late Peter Collinson had assisted in "the Choice of the Books" (*Writings,* V:185–186).

By the close of the year 1763, better known for the transfer of Canada by treaty from French to British rule, and the Proclamation Line supposed to hold the American settlers east of the Alleghenies, the Library Company of Philadelphia found it desirable to promulgate a set of rules for the use of the collection, some of them old, some new. The librarian was to be on hand from 5 P.M. to 8 P.M. each Saturday, to loan and receive books, and to keep a full record of loans, borrowers, and penalties. A borrower was to deposit a promissory note in the amount at which the book was priced in the catalog.

Nonmembers loaned books also paid a weekly rental fee for the privilege, 8d. for folios, 6d. for quartos, and 4d. for smaller works, "to be applyed towards the repairing of Bindings, encreases of the Books &c." The librarian was to inspect a returned book for damage. Anyone in default on either that ground or tardiness could borrow no more until he paid his bill. No borrower could lend a book to anyone else "out of his House." Each Saturday at closing time the librarian was to check his record of forfeitures and list them in a separate book; on the second Monday of each month he would lay the blacklist for the preceding month before the directors.

None of the foregoing was strikingly new. What may have been novel, however, were the rules about reserves and new books. Rule 9 provides that should a member desire a book out on loan and ask that it be held for him upon return, a reserve memorandum is to be filed and the borrower reading it cannot renew his loan. According to rule 10, one person may borrow at one time two octavo volumes, three duodecimos, or four pamphlets, "provided they have been in the Library at least Twelve Months" (*Papers*, 10:-387–388). The shape of the twentieth-century library was beginning to emerge.

It was perhaps in those years also that attention began to turn increasingly toward the matter of more spacious quarters. The Library Company made an attempt at obtaining legislative support but had to settle in 1773 for a suite in Carpenters Hall. The First Continental Congress met in their club room; it may have been familiar to the eleven delegates who held memberships in the Company. There the institution remained through the war, partly for lack of a quorum to authorize moving out of occupied Philadelphia (some British officers used it). By 1789, when the landlord raised the rent, other circumstances had altered too, and the company finally won its own building.

Twenty years earlier, when Franklin sent his regrets to Peter Collinson's son, he observed that the organization Collinson had so favored had been a model increasingly emulated:

> It is supposed there are now upwards of 30 subsisting in the several Colonies . . . [devoted to diffusing] Useful Knowledge . . . The Books [Collinson] recommended being all of that kind, and the Catalogue of this first Library being much respected and followed by those of Libraries that succeeded [i.e., came after it] (*Writings*, V:186).

At approximately the time that the lack of "publick generous Education" was being regretted in Philadelphia, prominent citizens were getting together for that purpose in several Connecticut towns. Durham was the first so far as we know. Of the eight founders who invested 20 shillings each and wrote detailed rules of operation, all were white males. Five had military titles; two were members of the legislature and served as officers in the hostilities against French Canada in the later 1740s. It is supposed by the probers of the old records that many more groups than the few which have left traces assembled funds by joint subscription for buying books, adopted regulations, and sometimes even employed a "library keeper." At least in the case of Durham (founded in 1733), the collection was of sufficiently high calibre for books to have been made available, despite a company rule to the contrary, to President Clap of Yale and some of his students.

There is no proof that the Connecticut ventures, sometimes called "social libraries," owed anything to the example of the Library Company of Philadelphia, although Franklin had many contacts and advertised his activities widely through the *Pennsylvania Gazette,* correspondence, and conversation. A closer link seems indicated in the subscription libraries organized a little later, in the 1740s and 1750s, in a number of towns in southeastern Pennsylvania and southwestern New Jersey, near Philadelphia. Associates of either Franklin's or James Logan's were often leaders in those enterprises. Some small-town libraries managed to operate on the basis of 20-shilling subscriptions and 5 shilling-a-year fees, perhaps because they had low-rent or no-rent quarters. However that may be, such financing was apparently inadequate in Philadelphia, because two such libraries founded (1747, 1757) at lower rates than that of the Library Company gave up in 1769, to be absorbed by the latter.

Likewise, the larger-town enterprise was the more likely to acquire property and incorporate. (The labels "social," "subscription," and "proprietary" were used too variously to be a reliable basis for generalizations.) This has been noted in the remarks of the Library Company of Philadelphia; it was also a feature of another big-town institution probably the first of its kind in the colonies, the Redwood Library of Newport, Rhode Island.

Older Seeds in the New Soil Newport was in the eighteenth century, before the Revolution disrupted its foreign trade patterns, a leading town enjoying the fruits of the triangle trade (slaves-sugar-rum) of mournful memory. Merchant princes were numerous and the arts patronized. Good relations with England were important commercially and the Anglican congregation was the largest in New England. When the celebrated idealist philosopher, Bishop George Berkeley, arrived in 1729, he was received with enough interest to keep him there for about two years.

One apparent byproduct of this toning up was the foundation in 1730 of the Literary and Philosophical Society. And one may suppose that the society's activities stimulated among others the twenty-year-old Maecenas born in Antigua, West Indies, Abraham Redwood (1709-1788). Redwood had been raised in Philadelphia. In 1724, at age fifteen, he fell heir to plantations in Antigua. Three years later he married, adopted his wife's Quaker faith, and settled in Newport. Before long he had become a shipping magnate as well as a successful absentee owner of slave labor. At some point in the mid-1740s, a fellow merchant of Newport gave a tract of land for a library and Redwood was moved to pledge 500 pounds sterling for books. The building was financed by donations from various others. The library, duly incorporated, opened in 1747.

Some years afterward the Quaker founder was registering distress at what he considered the infiltration of the library's board of directors by the Anglicans and their voting as a unit to block a greater variation of the membership. Operations were still supposed to be nonpartisan, he protested to Ezra Stiles, Redwood librarian from 1756 to 1775 and later president of Yale. No one seemed to notice; Redwood finally withdrew from the board's deliberations.Whether or not his charges were valid appears to be unsettled. How many library board rooms have been the scene of private conflict affecting the public weal?

In 1749, a young Swedish science student, Peter Kalm, heard in Philadelphia that "a rich gentleman from Rhode Island" had been at the Library Company and left for home with plans to emulate it. As Kalm understood the episode, the visitor had in fact "persuaded some gentlemen . . . to build a house for a library to which he made" the gift just mentioned. Kalm's diary does not reveal precisely when Redwood was at the Library Company. (*Travels in North America,* ed. Adolph B. Benson; New York: Wilson-Erickson, 1937, p. 638.) Evidently, whatever contributed to the library event in Newport, only Redwood's role was common talk at the Library Company in Philadelphia. This incomplete appreciation may well have been repeated with regard to many other libraries of the epoch, and would help account for Franklin's somewhat exaggerated view of the influence of the Library Company.

That model remained unusual insofar as it began without any books on divinity and apparently gave very little attention to the matter afterward. The Redwood Library, though launched sixteen years later, in a large town, was more traditional. According to the first catalog, dated 1764, books on science accounted for 19 percent of the 700 titles; those on theology and philosophy, 13 percent. The leading category, with one-third, was belles lettres and the arts. History was second (16 percent). Yet theology and philosophy were better represented than biography (4 percent), travel (3 percent) or technical books. Manifestly, a large-town library was not necessarily very much different from a small-town library in its book selection just because the community was large. The intellectual interests of the leaders counted heavily, and the Philadelphia library promoters followed a course shaped partly by a craftsman outlook not detectible in the style at Newport.

What noncampus users preferred is suggested by the registry book of the Library Company of Providence, Rhode Island. A fire on Christmas Eve, 1758, ruined what was on hand, but titles in circulation were on the surviving record (furnished by Shera, pp. 117–118). Among the books owned by the library the largest group were the 136 labeled scientific-medical-reference. The history and biography collection was roughly half that size, literature about the same, theology a little smaller (51), and geography and travel petty (17). The loan data are rather different, starting with history and biography at 21 and ending with divinity books at 4.

Although conventional libraries are not known to have kept such titles, Ovid's *Art of Love* and Richardson's *Pamela* did very well at a Boston auction of 1744. Works of that sort were also staples at the circulating libraries operated for profit at least by 1762. Some rented books for fees scaled according to the size of the item rented, on the order of 25 cents down to 5 cents for a pamphlet or magazine. Others sold annual memberships for 7 dollars; the "member" could then borrow a stated number of books. An enterprise of this character was not greatly different from certain subscription libraries, but the latter did not purvey other commodities whereas the circulating library proprietors frequently did.

Nor, of course, did the commercial "library" employ a librarian. A functionary so designated was by the later eighteenth century a fairly familiar personage in the voluntary libraries. From the records of the above-mentioned Providence institution we have a statement of his duties (quoted by Shera, p. 108). He was to "'see that'" the books and premises were kept clean and orderly and that the registry book was maintained according to the rules. This may mean that he was supervising one or more subordinates. He was also to "'deliver out books and replace them'" on the single afternoon each week when the library was open, keep records up to date and go after delinquent borrowers, and "'show the Library to all Strangers who are Gentlemen and who desire to visit it.'" These latter duties are plainly his personal tasks. The pattern seems to follow, more or less, the practices at campus libraries. Considering the numerous college graduates in towns with libraries, ministers particularly, some direct influence may reasonably be presumed; but proof is apparently lacking. In at least one instance on record, an interested Englishman accompanied a gift of books to a Connecticut town library with a list of recommended rules for its management; the outcome is unknown. By that time, however, 1739, such guidance was probably not needed.

All the institutions mentioned so far were in a sense special libraries. The campus libraries were designed specifically for the faculty and advanced students, Bray's collections for ministers and their most God-fearing parishioners, and the voluntary secular breed for off-campus devotees of serious study. Hardly any offered light reading: that was left almost entirely to the bookstores and the college literary societies of the latter part of the century—not to mention private collections.

Special "libraries" in the twentieth-century meaning of the phrase began to appear in the 1760s. Whatever they may have done before that time, the colonial "associates" of Dr. Bray were by 1760 under the chairmanship of Benjamin Franklin, and spending some money on "'Books for Negroe Schools,'" a little more than £7 in the fiscal year March 1761-March 1762. (Quoted on p. 70 of Margaret B. Korty's massive report, *Benjamin Franklin and Eighteenth-Century American Libraries,* American Philosophical Society *Transactions,* Philadelphia, 1965, new ser. vol. 55, part 9.) Closed by the Revolution, these schools—in New York City; Newport, Rhode Island; Philadelphia; and Williamsburg, Virginia—were reopened soon afterward.

Perhaps more explicitly oriented to religious education was the Philadelphia Lutheran School, whose library was first advertised by a printed catalog of 1763. The collection of German books was outstanding in the colonies. (Franklin had long since regretted his earlier churlish outburst against the German settlers' preference for their own tongue.)

At the other extreme was the medical collection launched in 1762 by a gift from a British physician to the Pennsylvania Hospital. Its catalog of 1790 listed 528 volumes.

Leaning toward science but not confined to it was the first of many learned groups, the American Philosophical Society. Formally organized in 1743, it moved rather hesitantly for a quarter-century, stirred to notable activity in 1768 partly by the emergence of a rival group. Political axes were being ground on behalf of both the proprietors of the province and their principal opposition. Franklin's influence was exerted against this sort of obstacle, and the two groups merged in 1769. Not much attention had so far been given to books. As Franklin had noted in his 1743 circular, Philadelphia was the logical place for the Society partly because it already had "a good growing library" (Franklin, *Papers*, 2:381), and a large number of members were also subscribers to the Library Company. By 1774, however, books had been assembled, and were kept mainly in the home of the librarian, astronomer David Rittenhouse. They found normal quarters when the Society's building was erected between 1785 and 1789.

Publishing one's own proceedings, and exchanging them for those of other similar bodies, was then a principal means of developing a learned library. According to the manuscript minutes of the American Philosophical Society for February 1, 1771, a copy of the first volume of its transactions was to be presented by the Society's secretaries "to the Proprietaries [of Pennsylvania], the Governor, to each member of Assembly, the Assemblies Library, the Library of Philadelphia [i.e., the Library Company], to the Library of every College, in America, to the Royal Society in London, each of the foreign Philosophical Societies and to the Pennsylvania Hospital . . ." (*Early Proceedings . .. from 1744 to 1838,* Philadelphia: McCalla & Stavely, 1884, p. 62). The hazards of transoceanic mail sometimes interrupted such activities. An entry in the minutes of August 15, 1788, notes that materials sent from Milan were somehow more than two years on their way; the secretaries were directed to dispatch thanks promptly, with an explanation for the delay; a copy of the recently (1786) published second volume of the *Transactions* was to be sent to Milan.

Among those who wrote thank-you notes for the first volume was Princess Ekaterina Dashkova (1744–1810), an important link between the Russia of Catherine the Great and the French *philosophes.* Founder (1783) and the first president of the "Russian Academy," devoted to Russian language and literature and absorbed in 1841 by the Imperial Academy, she led French-style efforts to improve the Russian language. She was also prominent in the Academy of Sciences, sharing the production of an atlas; that may have played a part in her election to membership in the United States group in 1789.

The idea of a legislative reference library was perhaps in the air when the New York Corporation "Library" was established in 1730 at city hall, and when the Library Company deposited a good part of its collections, in 1739, on the premises of the Pennsylvania General Assembly. Neither, it seems, really was that sort of library. The New York collection, although it had a "keeper" from 1734 to 1742, was absorbed in 1754 by the just-organized New York Society Library. The Pennsylvania legislature did buy some books of its own in 1753 and appointed a librarian a year or so later, but the Library Company holdings must have remained dominant in the Penns' province for many years. While Franklin was abroad, he often sent books to the Continental Congress. He knew it had no library of its own, and may have thought it should not to have to go on relying on the hospitality of the learned societies in the towns where it convened. Such hospitality was certainly preferred. When the Continental Congress opened at Philadelphia, September 6, 1774, an extract was read from the Library Company's minutes, directing that books be furnished the Congressmen, "'during their

Sitting, taking a Receipt for them'" (Quoted in W. D. Johnston, *History of the Library of Congress, 1800–1864;* Washington: Government Printing Office, 1904, 1:17). Likewise, the First Congress, convening in the New York city hall, in March 1789, was invited to use the New York Society Library, which happened to be shelved at that time in the very same building. And when Philadelphia became the seat of the national government the following year, the Library Company tendered the President and congressmen all the book privileges of members. Some congressmen had already inquired into the feasibility of a library of Congress' own, but the necessary funds were not then forthcoming.

Spanish and French America   In neighboring French Canada, and the Spanish dominions of Central and South America, life was more closely controlled than in the British North American colonies. The wealth produced by the Indians at the Spanish-owned estates and mines was channeled largely home to Spain, but enough remained to fuel a long-useful flame of clergy-operated education and a book trade patronized by the urban upper classes. At the close of the colonial period there were in New Spain more than a score of institutions furnishing collegiate instruction, ten of which could reasonably be called "universities" and were as large as the largest of New England's colleges. Their purposes were primarily ecclesiastical but, in contrast with custom in white Protestant English America, they admitted Indians to train them as Christians. Until 1784, indeed, the natives were taught their own language too. Negroes and mixed-bloods were also accepted at first; their entry into the field of law in the mid-eighteenth century, however, aroused opposition which soon expanded into widespread exclusion from the universities. Of the 150,000 students who were granted degrees from Spanish-American universities during the colonial epoch, some were Indians and a few Negroes or mixed-bloods.

This measure of success was regarded by some contemporary New England church leaders as a mortal challenge. As the celebrated Cotton Mather put it in the fourth book of *Magnalia* (1702), they founded Harvard to produce something "more significant than the seminaries of *Canada* and *Mexico*" (p. "126"). In the later eighteenth century, nevertheless, these "seminaries" began to disintegrate, to the great loss of the nonwhites in particular, thanks to economic troubles and the culmination of long-festering rivalries in the expulsion of the Jesuits in 1767. Imperial policy sent the books of the Company of Jesus to bishops and archbishops for episcopal libraries unless an approved university was at hand; many of these books ultimately found their way to the national libraries established in later years.

The stakes are illuminated by the events in Guatemala, which boasted the approved University of San Carlos, named after sixteenth-century reformer cardinal Carlo Borromeo (canonized in 1610). What the Dominicans had begun in the late sixteenth century was aided substantially about 1650 by funds from a comfortably retired Inquisition officer; when the Jesuits characteristically opened their own college, San Francisco de Borja, in 1667, the battle was joined for a century. The expulsion found the San Carlos faculty eager to enrich their library collections with spoils from San Francisco de Borja. Such action was authorized by the king, and a librarian appointed in 1779. Unfortunately, the faculty soon learned that the new acquisitions were no more up to date than the San Carlos holdings, and the students were on the whole able to buy the few books they needed. The library was neglected, the librarian resigned within two years, and his replacement was directed among other things to weed the "extras"; those were sold between 1781 and 1784 and brought in some 125 pesos, at a time when the ordinary professor's annual salary was 200. The operation continued downhill.

The episode reveals pretty plainly that competition among the religious orders was not the only factor in keeping university libraries at a rather low level of esteem. It is known that the book trade was vigorous in the major cities, and that as early as 1683 a Mexico City bookseller reported to the Holy Office a list of recent imports which included the latest titles from Spain and several from other countries; the putative purchasers were probably better off than their contemporaries in Spain or even Boston. In fact, by the 1780s, the Inquisition was campaigning against subversive works like those of Macchiavelli, Montesquieu, and the Encyclopedists, and the viceroy in Lima assigned a commission the task of removing them from the "public" libraries. Whatever the upper-class book owners may have felt about libraries other than their own, the large money gifts needed were rarely forthcoming.

The royal government itself seems to have maintained some important collections about which too little is yet known. One has been identified at the Royal Botanical Station at Mariquita, a provincial capital in what is now west-central Colombia. Whether men like the San Carlos teachers knew about it or not, they apparently had no access to its scientific resources, possibly the best of their sort in the hemisphere. Intimacy between government scientific installations and higher education was still a century in the future.

Development was far slower in New France. Neither its agriculture nor its fur trade yielded much wealth, and the culture of Quebec and Montreal depended heavily on church and state functionaries supported by the mother country. By the late seventeenth century there were numerous private book collections in the hands of administrators, jurists, lawyers, and doctors, and a few at ecclesiastical institutions; of the approximately fifty on record, the largest held perhaps 20,000 volumes. The institutional collections were predominantly theological. Hardly any works were in English: the 1782 catalog of the Séminaire de Québec, a foreign mission agency, listed them with medieval brevity simply as "'ouvrages anglais'" (quoted, p. 55 of A. Drolet, *Les Bibliothèques Canadiennes, 1604–1960,* Ottawa: Le Cercle du Livre de France, 1965). The earliest indication of an interest in broadening book use was the 1760 legacy of Msgr. Pontbriand, the last bishop under the French regime. His books were left to his successor, to organize "'une bibliothèque publique ou épiscopale'" (quoted by Drolet, p. 63); if he bracketed "public" with "episcopal," traditionally, even that was unique for its time and place.

Although it is known that there was no bookdealer in 1759, a circulating library seems to have existed in Quebec City in 1764. By this time, English books had come to challenge French. Canada became an English possession in 1760, and the Navigation Acts made it very difficult to obtain French books. Some did arrive by way of American traders and immigrants, but the new settlers also brought disquieting works like those of Voltaire. Nor, apparently, did the Loyalists who fled to Canada during the American Revolution represent more acceptable reading preferences.

The first library comparable with English and American social libraries was launched by Sir Frederick Haldimand, British Governor General from 1778 to 1784. A Swiss Protestant by origin, he worked tactfully with the French Catholic clergy, seeing to it among other things that the library had French books. The Anglo-French wars interrupted book imports, and national feeling obstructed these efforts, French participation in the library's directorate soon dropping to one or none. In 1785 the library possessed some 1500 volumes, half in each language, the lion's share divided between the category of history and travel books and literature. Soon afterward it was reported housed in a room in the bishop's palace, its circulation mainly of romances, to Quebec women.

Secondary school libraries were a part of the facilities under clerical auspices, first in Quebec, and after 1773 in Montreal. Secular "higher" education seems to have begun under the British rule imposed upon Nova Scotia in 1755. The Acadians were expelled, New Englanders immigrated, and in 1788 King's College boasted a library.

Library Development on the Continent

In the years between 1680 and 1789, as the English and French and their colonist cousins pushed out the boundaries of empire, the Anglo-Americans also brought book collections to the middle class and craftsmen in many a small town or village which had not known such advantages before. In old England this seldom meant inclusion of farmers working their land; in Scotland and New England it often did. Such advances were aspects basically of the rise of the upper bourgeoisie, the struggle for control of state power, and religious conflict. They owe something also to the increasing involvement in public life of the lower middle class and skilled workers.

Communication played an important role, inasmuch as the English politico-religious world was at least partly conscious of events colonial, when not utterly absorbed in matters closer to home, and a large number of colonial preachers, lawyers, and merchants followed European developments as well as the press, correspondence, and travel permitted. Yet, if the colonials were sensitive to most of Europe politically and militarily, if their leading minds knew the social science emerging from England, France, and Holland, very little seems to have reached them concerning the institutional and cultural life of the Continent. They could read about great cities, palaces, cathedrals, and libraries in contemporary encyclopedias, sometimes in the newspapers and magazines too. But very few were acquainted with German or life in the Germanic area. The English Channel was no obstacle to cross-fertilization between English and continental art, architecture, music, and librarianship. The Atlantic Ocean did tend for some time to isolate the North American colonies. Until the latter part of the eighteenth century brought Franklin, John Adams, and others abroad, the flavors of France and Holland were remote. And the tone of Germanica remained so until after independence was established, when the first of the new nation's college graduates went to Germany to study further.

Rulers, Educators, and Libraries, 1680–1740 The first third, by and large, of the period under consideration was featured most obviously by a wave of national libraries and regulations for legal deposit of new books. Noteworthy also are the flourishing of scholarship in the ecclesiastical libraries of the Paris area particularly, and in the French Royal Library; the emergence of secondary schools with libraries; the changes in certain universities of Protestant North Germany; the splendor of the libraries of numerous German aristocrats; and the contributions to library management by Leibniz and others. (The apogee of "title-bibliography" and Daniel Morhof's challenge to it will be examined later.)

Neither the "national" library nor legal deposit was new. The latter institution had been unveiled in 1537 in France, and in the early seventeenth century manipulated to control the book trade in certain areas by way of the local universities: Giessen-Marburg (1614), for example, was held responsible in the Duchy of Hesse-Darmstadt. Granting the right to receive deposit copies of all books published in Sweden had rendered the Swedish Royal Library in 1661 virtually a national library; in 1692 another deposit copy was required for the University of Uppsala. Similar action strengthened the Elector's Library in Berlin in 1699, at least potentially—enforcement proved difficult—and in 1716 the Spanish "national" library, which until 1712 had been the king's own collection. The imperial library at Vienna had been "national" in a sense for perhaps two centuries; a new building provided by Emperor Charles VI in 1726 helped give its character formal recognition. Besides, the already noted English copyright act of 1709 named as depositories, in addition to those in England and Ireland, three Scotch university libraries and the renowned Advocates' Library in Edinburgh, destined to become some time later the National Library of Scotland.

Records of deposit copies were often maintained in the official archives of various jurisdictions, but their printing for public use does not seem to have been considered at that time.

Learned labors with manuscripts were by this time one of the glories of France, especially in the four ecclesiastical collections long since accessible to the scholar-public. A vistior of 1728 observed that one of them, the library St. Germain-des-Prés, possessed 50,000 books and was open four hours daily. In 1732, the unique expansion of the Royal Library despite hard times, thanks to royal grants and miscellaneous gifts, was memorialized on a medal sponsored by the Académie des Inscriptions. Unfortunately, no medal was yet appropriate for service to the public. When Voltaire, that very year, wanted "a few English books" allegedly not available to him otherwise, he wrote a most humble petition to librarian Bignon, promising to return the books within one month, and declaring that he made bold to apply because Bignon had so fine a reputation for understanding. The records show that several loans were made to Voltaire. (*Correspondence*, ed. T. Besterman, Paris: Gallimard, 1963, I:321, 1362.) But Voltaire was a special case, obviously. It was another three years (1735) before the nearly fifteen-year-old behind-the-scenes debate was resolved in favor of opening the great collections to the general public, twice a week from 9 A.M. to 2 P.M.; scholars were admitted nearly any time. In 1739 was begun a printed catalog which ultimately occupied six folio volumes. The capital relied far less on academic facilities, the Sorbonne College Library being one of the few then in respectable condition. A project of 1725–1726 for a University of Paris library remained on paper. Altogether, French library life had no influence in those quarters comparable to that of French literary and social life on the French language.

Ecclesiastical libraries were vital to scholars also in Germanica and Italy. Milan's Ambrosiana under L. A. Muratori (1695–1700) contributed substantially to scientific methodology in historical work. Similar efforts were made by clerics in the German Catholic cloisters and cathedrals, punctuated by such interruptions as their occupation by French troops in 1689; fortunately, the damage was not so serious as it had been in the Thirty Years' War. Both war and peaceful purchase occasioned more transfer of valuable materials than is witnessed in surviving records. We know only of results: the abbot of St. Florian's (a few miles south of Linz, Austria), for example, in these years, sent agents as far as Rome and the Hague and reportedly built a collection with more contemporary scholarly resources than the average university library offered.

Of consequence too were the "colleges," boarding schools at the secondary education level, maintained by the Jesuits (until their dissolution) by the hundreds in France, Germany, and the Low Countries; and in France by the municipalities. The latter included book collections more advanced than those of the Jesuits: little of classic writers, most French writers since 1500, and ample general history, natural history, science, and magic.

The Protestant portion of Germany was meanwhile the scene of other developments important for library service. Evangelical authorities had established *Hochschulen* comparing very favorably with the universities already in existence. Owing partly to their challenge, perhaps more to the impulse to experiment with both philosophy and pedagogy, several older universities were reorganized and a few new ones were founded. Particularly interesting, if not necessarily representative of the whole picture, is Halle, transformed in 1694 from an upper-class boys' academy into a university. The leaders were minds sufficiently active to have run into trouble elsewhere: among other things they separated philosophy from theology and lectured in German rather than Latin. There were conflicts with both royal authorities and the conservative theologians of the Pietist school. Whether despite those struggles or because of them, Halle's enrolment in the first half of the eighteenth century was exceeded only by that of Jena.

Yet the only university book collections at Halle, apart from those in professors' sanctums, were housed in three rooms at the City Wagon-Weighing House; indeed the university then had no buildings of its own of any sort. Theology and philosophy students, moreover, were better served by the rich materials assembled at the new orphanage in a working-class suburb of Halle. At first thought, a more unlikely combination is hard to imagine. Not really, however: August Herman Francke (1663–1727) had begun with a solid classical education and become strong enough in Greek and Oriental tongues to teach them at Halle University. His psychology was Pietist, or good will- and behavior-centered; as an educator he was anxious to shape all young minds from the beginning, the poor as well as the comfortable. He settled among the poor deliberately. A whole series of schools arose in the 1690s in the Halle suburb, from elementary to teacher-training, and including for a few years (1698–1705) a *Gynacaeum* for girls; several were soon emulated elsewhere. Probably none of these institutions needed Francke's scholarly book collection—but there it was, and his university students used it.

Other evidences of progress may be seen in the university area. At Duisburg, for example, library reform in the years beginning with 1714 crystallized such budgetary practices as allocating fixed portions of the funds to particular subjects on a steady basis, and the purchase, transportation, and binding cost of general items like the *Acta Eruditorum* equally to each faculty.

As much significant activity, indeed very likely more, was occurring at the private establishments of princes, dukes, and the like. No less than 180 of their libraries are said to have been important in Germany of the years 1700 to 1738. The Elector's Library in Berlin was by 1687 open afternoons to readers and even provided with a room heated in winter, with eight work places. In 1695 it could be used from 9 A.M. to noon and 3 P.M. to 7 P.M. in summer, 10 A.M. to noon and 2 P.M. to 4 P.M. in winter. Taking books off the premises was allowed in 1710 to privy councillors, and in 1711 to members of the Academy of Sciences; others needed special permission. An independent building was projected, but various delays prevented its completion until after the Wolfenbüttel Library had won the accolade as the first structure so designed in modern times.

That institution was not a rarity in making books available to the "public" daily since 1666; or in being thought of by its owners as a display piece, together with art objects and scientific instruments, a principal part of the baroque style. Nor does interest attach to it as the property of a ducal family based at nearby Hanover (80 miles south of Hamburg), which maintained a library at its home too. What commends this particular venture to our attention is the fact that the librarian, from 1690 through most of the planning of the new building opened in 1723, was the great philosopher–mathematician–political advisor Gottfried Wilhelm Leibniz (1646–1716). At age twenty-two he was already well known in mathematics and political science, and offered a professorship immediately after the conferring (1666) of his doctorate. Among other things, he petitioned Emperor Leopold I to sponsor the publication of abstracts with best-books guidance, and a new encyclopedia, to counter the increasing flood of printed matter. His pen was frequently in demand by potentates, but his concern with science remained vigorous enough for him to win election as a fellow of the Royal Society in 1673, shortly after demonstrating a calculating machine at a society meeting. In that same year began his long service with the Dukes of Brunswick-Lüneberg; in 1676 at their request he took residence in Hanover. He was soon submitting memoranda on the selection of useful books; on keeping abreast of new publications by means of bookseller and fair catalogs, correspondence, the *Journal des Sçavans,* and the Royal Society *Transactions;* on developing wisdom in retrospective bibliography with the aid of auction and bookseller catalogs of collections about to be sold.

The death in 1679 of the duke most responsive to him, John Frederick, meant for several years thereafter less ear for his thoughts. He was considered for the temporarily vacant post of librarian at the imperial court in Vienna, but the incumbent had to be a Roman Catholic, and Leibniz was not. At this point his patrons directed him to write the story of the House of Brunswick, in addition to caring for the library, and he traveled (1687–1690) for materials in Germany, Austria, and Italy. His nine months in Vienna surely gave him much data; librarian Daniel von Nessel may have given him some stimulation in librarianship. At any rate his mind returned to "best books" bibliography. During his 1689 stay in Italy he composed a list of some 2,500 titles, arranged first by subject and then roughly by date; based on both classics and recent science, it was designed only as a guide, and closed many a section with a general allusion to the existence of other worthy materials. He returned from these travels knowing bibliophile Magliabecchi of Florence and scholar-librarian Muratori of Milan. Furthermore, he had then been offered and turned down library positions at the Vatican and the French Royal Library which would have obliged him to become a Roman Catholic.

In 1690 Leibniz was invited to preside over the Augustan Library at Wolfenbüttel (40 miles southwest of Hanover), the prized possession of another branch of the family he served. The beginnings were inauspicious: he had to remain in Hanover until his family history writing was finished, "operating" the Wolfenbüttel institution mainly by correspondence; and in 1692 his patrons' political ambitions were satisfied by their advance to Elector status, after which Leibniz' value as political secretary and ghost-writer seems to have dropped considerably. In 1700 he was in Berlin, helping launch the learned academy he had sketched by invitation and serving as its first president; it was to lead not only by research in the various branches of learning but by serving as censor and as inspector of manufacturing, to unite theory and practice. He also submitted plans, by request of Peter the Great, for a similar institution in Petrograd (it materialized in 1724), and dreamed of still others. This activity seemed to him very important for the protection of scientific progress. In an age of powerful monarchs, achievement could be destroyed overnight by a whim, and with the scientists themselves disagreeing sharply over their methods, positive organized counteraction was called for: hence, the academy. (Diderot would soon be offering related arguments.) Almost as though to document this reasoning emerged the historic unpleasant debate over Leibniz' and Newton's contributions to the invention of the calculus. In his last years (1712–1714), the great German was in Vienna, a privy councillor.

Although his attention to the Wolfenbüttel Library was intermittent and hampered by his location elsewhere, he managed to reinforce most of the advanced ideas of the time about library operation. In 1695 he complained that the supposed annual allocation was not arriving regularly. Whatever effect that move may have had, he returned to the struggle in 1702, with a dossier which may have been a first and certainly remains impressive. Emphasized therein were the increasing rate of book production, the rising costs of books and binding, the state of the library's holdings, and comparable data from other collections. There was also some deprecatory comment on the provision of state funds to transitory attractions like comedies and music. For revenue Leibniz recommended not only the currently fashionable stamp tax on documents and the advertising of duplicates for sale or exchange, but also investing in mulberry plants and silkworm breeding, an enterprise not so fashionable but much discussed, especially at the French court. Duke Rudolph Augustus is not known to have responded.

The man who succeeded Rudolph Augustus at his death a few years later (1704), Duke Anton Ulrich, was much more interested in the library. The pace of acquisitions was stepped up sharply, and books soon had to be placed in temporary quarters. Leibniz' suggestion for a new building physically detached was accepted. It was erected between 1706 and 1710, four rectangular stories topped by an oval dome. The twenty-four arched windows in the dome provided considerable overhead light for the inner room on the ground floor; that lighting was not obstructed because the three upper stories were only galleries. The dome was supported by an oval ring of twelve columns. Shelving was installed directly on those columns and along the walls forming the ground floor oval and also in the five-sided rooms in the four corners of the ground floor; this use of space was widely admired. There was in addition some passing fame for an independent library building. Unfortunately, the whole structure was wood, and Leibniz' testimony about the experience of other libraries did not persuade the duke to allow artificial heat in it. Despite the librarian's devotion to service to "all," a traveler of 1731—eight years after the books had been placed there—found just a few scholars using the collection, the staff absorbed in niceties of cataloging.

That the Wolfenbüttel Library was used little did not apparently make it conspicuous. A professor visiting the Elector's library in Dresden in 1727 found it covered with dust and cobwebs, appreciated more by rats and mice than by humans; the whole scene in the capital of Saxony seemed to him playacting, the "librarian's" behavior included. Even where the situation was not so repulsive, where books and manuscripts were being added, provision of appropriate space seldom kept up with the acquisitions. The Imperial Library in Vienna was acknowledged as the leader of Europe in manuscript holdings, but that achievement was matched negatively by appalling neglect of the physical conditions.

Evidently, these circumstances did not bother many contemporaries. One of the young men of the turn of the century who followed his university studies with travel, and wrote about it, was Zacharias Conrad von Uffenbach (1683–1735) of Frankfort. After stopping at more than 100 libraries (nearly half of them private) in Germany, the Low Countries, and England between 1709 and 1711, he was struck by the crowding and disorganization. He also expressed strong preference for vernaculars over Latin, and for the alphabetical over the systematic catalog. That sounds forward-looking; yet he wrote that the virtual absence of belles lettres from "public" libraries was appropriate because such works did not comport with the dignity supposed to attach to a library. Thus spoke not merely the aristocratic bibliophile.

Even the good bourgeois who patronized the city libraries of Germany and Switzerland, while apparently indifferent to theology and the classics, and Latin, were asking not for contemporary literature but for practical, self-help reading. Their needs were met partly by precisely such books and partly by the new home encyclopedia, all as a rule in the vernacular.

The cataloging and classification of the period, and the character and status of the men directing the libraries, will be discussed separately, below.

1740-1770: New Service to the Campus and the Provinces The next phase, roughly 1740 to 1770, is known for a new model of a familiar machine, the University of Göttingen, and for several at least partly new library developments in Germany and France both like and unlike those already touched in connection with Anglo-America. How promptly they responded to the new needs society generated is not altogether clear. Political economy and political science were introduced at the universities of Sweden in the 1740s, at Glasgow soon thereafter in the lectures of Professor of Moral Philosophy Adam Smith, and in the 1760s at Göttingen; but the impact on university and research library acquisitions has apparently not been illuminated. It is known nevertheless that all the library mutations under review owed something to the Age of Reason; all involved both aristocrats and bourgeois of several levels; all were hostile to a share for women.

Noteworthy in the second quarter of the eighteenth century was increasing dissatisfaction in Protestant Germany with the Pietists who dominated Halle University and much else in education. Recognizing that instruction in the Greek and Latin classics had become depressingly grammar-centered and otherwise narrow, the New Humanists attempted rather to encourage the use of the ancient writers on behalf of better thought and expression, in the contemporary vein. They were given a magnificent opportunity at Göttingen.

That celebrated institution was created by men who aimed at giving Hanover a university even more respected than those of arch-rival Prussia (Leipzig University) and Saxony (Halle University). They enjoyed certain advantages: Hanover's new importance since one of the ruling family had (1714) become king of England, the challenge of rationalism to Pietism as well as Catholicism, and the related weariness of many minds with polemics and other sharp differences of opinion. The new university explicitly sought out keen young scholars who agreed to pursue learning in a nonpartisan fashion, eschewing name calling; top status was given not only to theology but to statecraft and law. The faculty were not an independent corporation but an arm of the state, financed by its revenues and swearing loyalty to it. In return they were theoretically uninhibited in their research and writing— and incidental teaching—and enjoyed numerous fringe benefits like tax privileges. The institution was administered by rectors; between them and the state operated a group of curators. One such functionary was Baron G. A. von Münchhausen (1688-1770), whose achievements were quite the opposite of those of his legendary namesake: the library benefited greatly, budgetarily and otherwise.

The Göttingen University library was logically and avowedly designed neither as a warehouse nor for courtly show nor for the amusement of dilettantes, but for the working scholars assembled at the university. It was placed in the care of two New Humanist professors of classical philology, first (1736-1761) J. M. Gesner, then (1763-1812) C. G. Heyne. Gesner began with some 12,000 volumes, of which perhaps 9,000 were a legacy to the Hanoverian government from Baron J. H. von Bülow (d. 1724), the balance from the local *Gymnasium;* unlike virtually all other university librarians of that epoch, Gesner obtained a steadily increasing budget. Procurement was based on systematic use of auction and antiquarian catalogs, as well as the right to deposit copies of all books printed in England (ruled now by the Hanoverians). A unique advantage was added when an academy of science was started in 1751 (in emulation of the several already functioning) and undertook almost immediately to issue a regular periodical with book reviews and information. The library staff kept in touch. By 1765 there were some 60,000 volumes and 100,000 pamphlets. The author catalog and shelf-list were reportedly kept up to date, but the systematic catalog steadily fell behind, presenting by 1790 a crisis calling for heroic measures. Not clear is the degree to which this situation was affected by faculty participation in collection development.

Offering service daily except Sundays, ten hours weekly, was not then extraordinary. But Göttingen made unusual efforts to serve the faculty and local dignitaries; even undergraduates could borrow four to six books—more, with the endorsing signature of a professor. Of still greater importance was the spirit of "friendliness and thorough-going service" (as Gesner wrote in 1748) which should be maintained despite the bad manners and ingratitude too familiar among "so-called scholars." Gesner is said to have practiced this preaching. (For details and the Göttingen rules of 1761, we are indebted to Georg Leyh's report in *Zentralblatt für Bibliothekswesen,* 37:- 1-30, 1920.) If Gesner and his associates succeeded in making the library the center of the campus, they may well have owed some thanks to the accident that Göttingen had unusually few manuscripts by comparison with its holdings of printed books.

While campus library service was thus being extended to the undergraduates, the general public off the campus was benefiting by other contemporary developments. Even in the 1690s the University of Basel Library, "public," had been supported by gifts from professional people and other interested parties. German university libraries occasionally gained richly by grace of a professor or other scholar, many of whom possessed specialized collections superior to those of nearly any other library in Germanica. (Bibliographer J. A. Fabricius, 1668-1736, had 20,000 volumes.) After midcentury, moreover, personal records of the sort once deposited as a rule in a monastery were now turned over to city libraries. In certain towns like Zürich and Berne that was fine, because the Swiss burghers there already had a strong tradition of public libraries committed to serving the public; the former issued a printed catalog in 1744, the latter between 1760 and 1769. But city libraries generally were much less active at this time than the university libraries: their hours of service were frequently nominal, and the legacies used hardly at all.

The trend to the secular in donations was meanwhile somewhat more lively in France. As early as 1731, for example, a jurist friend of the renowned Montesquieu bequeathed his Bordeaux home and library, and an endowment, to the local academy on condition that they be open to all. After 1750 this pattern became notable.

Striking too was the proliferation of the provincial academies which often, like that in Bordeaux, maintained libraries. There were twenty in France in 1748 and nearly forty in 1770. One reason was the retirement home from the Versailles court of nobles impoverished financially but still seeking social recognition or cultural opportunity. Another was the desire of numerous local business and professional men to show their mettle in a world dominated by king, aristocracy, and Paris. Montesquieu was associated with the academy of Bordeaux (southwest coast), Rousseau with that of Dijon (eastern France), and Robespierre with the Arras academy (northwestern France). Group effort itself was not new: salon, club, and café were familiar. Yet the academies certainly differed in excluding women, and may have differed in their acceptance of petit-bourgeois associate and corresponding members. While a few functioned as branches of the Académie Française and the Académie des Sciences, the majority guarded their autonomy jealously. These organizations sponsored not only libraries but lectures, exhibitions, and contests with prizes; one of the elements preparing the atmosphere for the revolution was the steady rise 1710–1789 in the number of public disputations at the academies.

The contemporary (1751) first volume of the *Encyclopédie* adds dimensions to the foregoing, first, in the *"Discours Préliminaire"* (p. lii). Jean-Jacques Rousseau is noticed for his attack on the arts and sciences as subversive of the morality given us by unspoiled Nature. D'Alembert rejects this thesis; he remarks in a footnote that it was unveiled in a lecture before the Académie de Dijon, very well received, and soon thereafter printed. (He does not mention that the occasion was an annual oratorical contest, in which, medieval-style, the topic for disputation was chosen by the sponsors; probably his readers knew that without being told. Also not mentioned, possibly for other reasons, are the facts that Rousseau visited the young radical in jail at Vincennes, in the summer of 1749, and that the publication referred to was handled by precisely Diderot, after his release!)

Under *"Académie,"* Diderot pursues the subject. He not only declares that the number of academies is growing day by day, and lists a dozen or more towns in which they have been established, he also observes that a good many other communities lacking academies do have literary societies which engage in "about the same activity." This is promising, as a solution to a gigantic problem. The age is known as the century of *"la philosophie"* but he prefers to call it "the century of half-knowledge": the journals and dictionaries account for some of the worst. The public nevertheless takes the scholars seriously. The latter must rise to the challenge, publishing transactions and monographs which respect just two rules, truth and decency. Let them repress, even "crush, if necessary" (*"écraser"*—the word Voltaire made famous), the opposition of incapacity, insolence, and depravity. That is bound to be "advantageous to all the rest of humanity." (Nouv. éd.; Génève: Pellet, 1777; 1: 232, 252, 254.)

Apparently rather similar if not identical reading rooms and reading circles meanwhile appeared in Germany too, particularly in the smaller communities without universities, but also in large and university towns. Their collections, cataloged, were catholic except for books of entertainment (no belles lettres); journals and works of reference were normally in the place of honor. Bookdealers displayed there the latest titles. The quarters were usually heated and lighted, in contrast with the cold which the Dresden court librarian complained of in March 1763 as preventing him from doing his work. Also, smoking and refreshment rooms were provided, and patrons could hold meetings on the premises and take books out. All told, they were decidedly more appealing than the public libraries. The organizers, bookdealers, bibliophiles, writers, and some professors, generally barred women.

The rising secular, the broadening connection between scholarship and the "public," and the spread of the idea of collective study and discussion, appeared also in another new institution in Germany in the 1760s. Stimulated additionally, perhaps, by pride in a regional sovereignty which had ceased to exist in England and France, was that unique product of the German Enlightenment, the *Landesbibliothek,* or public research library at the province or state level. Among the best known were those of Württemburg (in Stüttgart), Bavaria (in Munich), and Saxony (in Dresden). Common to these three, and very likely to others as well, was the sympathy or even the leadership of the decision maker, in Munich and Dresden the elector, and in Stüttgart, the duke. Also, history was very prominent in those collections, and one principal purpose in organizing the new libraries was to open them to at least the learned public.

Details vary. The Stüttgart story seems to be the earliest, beginning in 1750 with the duke's combining of his librarian's collection with those of the local ecclesiastical and secular ruling bodies. At Dresden the start was quite different: The elector possessed some 70,000 books of his own in 1768, and bought (1764, 1768) the also substantial private libraries of Counts Bünau (42,000) and Brühl (62,000). Learned academies played an important role in several instances. The duke of Württemburg for example, launched an Académie des Arts in 1761 and proposed an Akademie der Wissenschaften the following year, but the "supporting" library, functioning since 1750 despite difficulties, developed much more readily than the desired society itself. At Munich, on the other hand, an academy was organized first, in 1759, the library soon afterward.

Again, we defer consideration of the development of cataloging and librarianship.

From the Anti-Jesuit Moves to 1789 It would be very difficult to identify any events with greater significance for libraries in Catholic Europe, in the generation before the French Revolution, than the actions taken against the Jesuit order. The Society of Jesus had long been regarded with jealousy and other negative feelings by numerous rival Catholic organizations, not to mention Protestant and secular forces. War and social unrest were giving chancelleries everywhere much to think about, and the Jesuits' involvement in some contemporary financial adventurism provided the necessary excuse to start what became a chain reaction. Known misdeeds were widely referred to, and additional ones invented. In the period 1759–1768 the members of the order were deported from Latin America; in 1767 from

Spain,more than 5,000 of them. France in 1764 pronounced the Society of Jesus illegal but did not exile the 3,500-odd individual priests. In 1773 the order as a whole was officially dissolved by Pope Clement XIV.

The impact was particularly noticeable in the Habsburg dominions, which confiscated Jesuit property worth 400 million florins and annual revenues of 4 million. Cloister and collegiate book and manuscript collections all over present-day Austria, Hungary, Czechoslovakia, northern Italy, and northern Yugoslavia, were removed from Jesuit hands and applied to the advantage of non-Jesuit institutions. In 1777, for example, approximately fifty Austrian Jesuit cloister libraries were thus "lawfully" expropriated on behalf of the new University of Vienna; Graz and Innsbruck benefited similarly soon afterward. Altogether, under the direction of Maria Theresa's son Joseph, coregent from 1765 to 1780 and emperor from 1780 to 1790, some 1,300 cloisters were dissolved outright and the collections at the other 700 sharply reduced.

These rather messy affairs were one aspect of the secularizing and vernacularizing of education, for which history awards Joseph II some credit. In Bohemia-Moravia, Latin was supposed to be replaced by German rather than Czech. In the villages, however, less ready to be Germanized than the larger towns, both Czech and the priests teaching it held on. What this meant for library collections and service does not seem to be reported in any readily accessible record. It is known, however, that in Slovakia, controlled by the Hungarian nobles most of the time from the eleventh century to the Hungarian Revolution in 1849, the erstwhile Jesuit treasures were not applied to the benefit of the local population. About one-third of the library holdings of Slovakia, they were instead carried off to Budapest: one more element was added to the accumulating forces distinguishing Slovak national development from that in Bohemia-Moravia.

The Hungarians were cast in a similar role in Croatia, their southern neighbor, when in 1779 the Austro-Hungarian emperor placed that area under their jurisdiction. An immediate consequence was the collapse of a promising three-year-old library development effort at the Academy in Zagreb, owing partly to the rising importance of the University Library in Pest (united with Buda formally in 1872). The Croatian cloisters had not taken the best of care of their holdings, works published primarily in Germany, Austria, and northern Italy; fire and vermin did much damage, and the Turks' raids inflicted more. When the sequestration decrees of 1782 were enforced, the surviving books were placed first at the disposal of the Pest University Library, which absorbed a great many historical and literary titles, mainly in Latin. Numerous others, lacking interest, were sold for paper, most of the Croatian books apparently among them. The record reportedly includes a decree of 1788 designed to save for posterity one copy each of the titles destined for the mill, but the move seems to have failed for lack of trained personnel and bibliographic aids. Insofar as any of these acts were debated, the issue was the cost of transportation, the distance to Budapest from the Augustinians' cloister in Rijeka, for example, being 250 miles by the flight of a crow crossing many mountains.

Slovenia, further west, remained under Austrian administration to some advantage. The dispossessed Jesuits had in many instances enlarged their collections by absorbing the abbey libraries of earlier religious orders, and the absence of either a prince's court or a university meant that hardly any nontheological ("profane")books were on hand. There was no local printing. The vernacular works joining the Latin titles from the later sixteenth century on were in German at first, then in French or Italian, but not, it seems, in Slovenian. Hardly surprising is the fact that the sporadically rebellious peasants were no more respectful of books than the Turkish invaders of 1630. One advantage did accrue to Slovenia from the 1782 assault on the Company of Jesus; although the best books went to the court library in Vienna and some others to the university library at Graz, a number also moved to the Slovene capital, Laibach (today's Ljubljana). Surviving French and Austrian occupations and other trials, they were to become part of the library of the University of Ljubljana after World War I.

Secularization was accompanied by additional grants of the right to receive deposit copies of new books. In 1782 the cited privilege was conferred upon at least two important libraries under Austrian (Imperial) jurisdiction. The Biblioteca di Brera in Milan, then six years old as a "public" library, was assigned deposit copies of the imprints of Lombardy. The Public-and-University Library of Prague was to be the corresponding repository for books issued in Prague—and soon afterward for books issued anywhere in Bohemia.

Likewise worthy of note is a strikingly modern institution established at that time in Denmark. What would later be called special libraries had begun to appear, at least since the 1735 foundation by Hamburg merchants of their Commerzbibliothek, intended as both an aid to business and a means of enlightenment (printed catalog, 1750); other business, and medical and historical libraries seem likely to have been launched too, more than are mentioned in the standard reference works. Evidently distinctive was the library established in 1783 by the Danes to support the instruction in a school of veterinary medicine and agricultural economics.

The Epoch as a Whole: The Library Rather Neglected The use of continental libraries during the years from 1680 to 1789 is not known well, for lack of statistics. Maintaining such records was seldom thought of, and little pressure for them was generated in an age keyed more to ideas than to books, and on the whole more to books than to libraries. (Lending libraries conducted at booksellers' stores became numerous: Paris is said to have had 123 dealers in 1721, of whom several probably rented books; by 1783, if not sooner, they were the object of satire.) The leading German thinkers were frequently educators and occasionally librarians. Some English luminaries like David Hume and Adam Smith served as librarians, to earn a living, without leaving any remarkable traces in the area. Italy also offered a few scholars employed as librarians; but librarianship gained little as such from them, and nothing so far discovered from the truly creative thinker Giambattista Vico.

Least encouraging of all, in this respect, is the story of the French Enlightenment. Voltaire wrote to a friend in July 1733 that a couple of conversations with him were worth the whole Sainte-Geneviève library. Montesquieu's extensive travel notes refer to libraries now and then, but far more in the art critic vein than with respect to their holdings or service. The *Encyclopédie* (first volume,1751) was intended to counteract the flood of shortcut "dictionaries," "libraries," and handbooks; it would furnish the ordinary literate citizen with enough information, in the vernacular, to comprehend whatever he looked up, but no more. The editors acknowledge the courtesies received, especially at the Bibliothèque Royale, but their product is projected in familiar style as an alternative to a library: if the ancient Alexandrians had turned out a grand encyclopedia which alone escaped the fate of the rest of the celebrated library's collection, that surviving item, "we dare say, would have been able to console us for the loss of the others" (1:1x). Besides, there seemed to be too many books in the sciences, too many bad ones in the arts, and not nearly enough in the mechanic arts; the editors had gone for information to the craftsmen in their shops.

Prominent in the earlier portion of the period were the Protestant universities of northern Germanica, which tended to emphasize limited student borrowing of books for use off the premises; perhaps this was encouraged by the general fact that the leading professors so often had the principal books in their own libraries, and the special additional fact that pioneering Halle had no premises. Yet there was no tidal wave of liberal circulation policies before the days of Göttingen. Some of the very same Protestant professors also took the position that library use should be restricted lest it interfere with attention to their lectures.

In the southern portion of the area, especially in the later years of the century, the scene was featured more sharply by the revived old Benedictine foundations and several new universities, especially in Austria, seat of the Holy Roman Empire. Less ready to loan books for home use, they furnished many more hours of service in the library, reportedly averaging twenty weekly. The hospitality of the Strahov monastery in Prague was legendary. In neither north nor south, however, was access easy to anatomy books.

The years under review also witnessed what was perhaps the first effort to approach the use of book resources as a part of the total educational process. Confronted with a steady increase in available titles, thanks in part to the rival publishing activities of opposing schools of theology, philosophy, and so forth, the student could obtain some guidance from his professors; but, in the judgment of certain contemporaries, not enough. Library use was both explained and encouraged in orientation lectures at a few North German Protestant universities late in the seventeenth century, owing in some degree to the Pietist educational movement already mentioned. Outstanding in this labor was Daniel Georg Morhof (1639–1691), who taught at Kiel University, poetry and eloquence first, history later; in the 1680s he directed the library. His library talks began in 1672, and the first portion, on books and scholarship, was published in 1688 as *Polyhistor . . . literarius*. In this work he discussed scholarly institutions and associations and aids to learning, including libraries, bibliographies, and biography (Book 1); how to study (Books 2 and 3); and the particular branches of knowledge, their origin and history and above all their literature. For knowledge of *notitia bibliothecarius* in both meanings, "bibliographical manuals" and "library guides," seemed to him the sole road to full grasp of any field. Morhof not only tried to acquaint students with all published bibliographical literature but urged princes to subsidize the cooperative preparation of the numerous manuals still lacking.

The assumption that "everything known" was written down seemed natural. Nor was there any novelty in the idea that one needed help to find one's way in the literature; but the tangible implications had not been thought through by many. Morhof's pioneering drew enthusiastic praise from some contemporaries. His book was finished by coadjutors in 1708, and by 1747 had reached a fourth edition: hardly a best seller, but not neglected either. It was still current as supplementary reading in 1765, reminisced Goethe in his sixties (*Dichtung und Wahrheit*, 1811–1814); he had "skimmed through" *Polyhistor* as part of his "encyclopedism" phase as a sixteen-year-old student fresh at Leipzig (*Dichtung und Wahrheit*, 6. Buch; ed. Meyer, Stuttgart: Cotta, 1902–1907, II:29; Jubiläums-Ausgabe, 23. Bd.). None other just like it has come to notice. Meanwhile, one finds strewn through eighteenth-century records references to other orientation efforts at universities: the weekly sessions at which the Duisburg librarian examined with students the latest learned journals, the weekly two-hour tours initiated at Greifswald in 1775 to acquaint students with the key works in each area, etc.

For a librarian to learn what was being published was in these years more difficult than it had been in the preceding century. The Frankfort Fair catalogs ceased in 1749; not only was the Leipzig Fair continuing to purvey more modern types of writing, under far less censorship, but after 1710 Latin publications were increasingly outnumbered by German works. The Leipzig Fair catalogs were apparently the only current bibliographies issued throughout the period, the English "Term Catalogues" having ended with the number for Easter Term, 1711. Besides, the Fair catalogs avoided price information, and the "Term Catalogues" had provided it less and less after 1680. Theoretically, these sources could have been supplemented or even surpassed in quality by official lists of works accepted through legal deposit. After all, that device was being adopted by one jurisdiction after another. The fact remains, however, that the years 1680 to 1789 saw no such publication.

Greater dependence was evidently placed on bibliographies largely if not entirely retrospective. There were catalogs of famous "public" libraries, those announcing the glories of private collections (about 100 in Germany alone between 1700 and 1750), and a substantial number of sales and auction catalogs printed mainly by booksellers. What these circumstances meant to the casual book buyer may be indicated by Montesquieu's note to himself, at Venice in 1728, that Vico's "New Science" was to be obtained in Naples. (*Scienza nuova* was first published there in 1725.)

The latter part of the century was marked partly by a new wave of subject bibliographies, no longer blocked by the popularity of the informational encyclopedia, and by some rene··ed attention also to national bibliography. Both types were retrospective. Neither could have meant very much in buying current publications. Did the scholars and the dealers want them? Are they simply evidences of the determination of a compiler answering a personal compulsion?

Better data would not necessarily have helped very much at least in the nonprivate area, because so few such libraries had a regular income for collection building. Through most of the eighteenth century the "public libraries" were mainly in poor shape financially, even though their holdings benefited in the later years as private collections were transferred to them. More important, to ignore the private sector, were the libraries of the German-speaking areas. Excluding state-supported Göttingen, long a rare bird, one finds a pattern of expedients, straw clutching, and net uncertainty. Library expenses were met in part from student fees of various sorts, even from marriage licenses. The faculty were in command, and doubtless kept in mind the fact that professors often owned the books they needed: their agent, the rector, allocated funds to the library when he thought he could. Tübingen's library, for example, was supposed to receive thus 50 florins each semester; but the annual average actually provided in the years before 1750 never exceeded 13 florins. The income of the university library at Greifswald varied during the years from 1747 to 1756, between 88 and 286 Taler. In addition to student fee sources and copies of professors' new books, Jena supposedly received a regular allowance from the Weimar court, and deposit copies of the books printed in Jena (in the first third of the eighteenth century, second in that activity only to Leipzig). Actually, the court subvention was often little more than half of the "due" sum, and the Jena printers frequently dodged their obligations just like printers elsewhere. Now and then the problem was solved by auctioning off duplicate books. For a major special purchase, of course, it was frequently possible to find an underwriter; but that did not pay operating expenses. Indeed a university librarian was known, at Innsbruck for instance (1760–1779), to pay the staff helpers out of his own pocket. There were even occasions when obligations had to be met in kind rather than cash.

The style of handling money varied considerably. While Duisburg University was notable for its budget reforms of the 1710s—fixed percentages for each faculty, etc., several practices taken for granted in later times, such as distinguishing between staff pay and other classes of expenditure, were not then widely familiar. Besides, university-library record keeping was often primitive, either because book purchasing was handled through the deans of the respective faculties without regard to the library's plans or desires, or because of the latter's own shortcomings. In any case, the results probably did little to persuade the financial authorities that more funds should be placed at the library's disposal.

Nor, it seems, did librarians have much to do with designing their libraries. As holdings increased, more room had to be found. In many a library the result was the distressing state of affairs already mentioned. At some others, especially those enjoying aristocratic financial and moral support, the noblemen and their architects debated the issues. Was a room in the palace still appropriate, or was an independent building better? Should there be one large rectangular room or a central room with several smaller satellites? Should the area enclosed by the walls be reserved in good part for display or surrendered to book shelves? A Leibniz might participate in the discussion, but the librarian share generally, such as it was, has been given little attention.

From the library at Wolfenbüttel on, there were independent library buildings. The evidence does not suggest, however, that physical distinctiveness thus carried to the ultimate degree was generally desired and paid for. Neither the interests of display nor those of privately patronized scholarship, still less those of use by a broader public, were so far strong enough.

Predominant was the style called by many "Italian," the characteristics of which had emerged notably in the seventeenth-century Italy and were being adopted elsewhere: a long room in a multipurpose building, with books shelved along the walls, high enough to invite the addition of galleries. Challenging it were two contrary tendencies, the oval style at Wolfenbüttel, and the "magazine" device, an outgrowth of the earlier occasional placement of book stacks at right angles to the wall rather than against it, but no longer necessarily in contact with the wall. The oval plan somewhat, and the "magazine" decidedly, favored filling library space with books more densely than before. Depending on circumstances, this threatened either the reader or displays or both.

The Baroque Age, however, and succeeding Rococo, cherished "cabinets" and collections, from gems to models of the universe, and lavish decoration. In fact, a Jesuit father had been making a notable impression on library owners, along these lines, ever since he published in 1635 his *Musaei sive Bibliothecae,* or "Museums and Libraries." The library, Claude Clémens (1594–1642) had argued, was the latter-day temple of the muses; it should sit atop high ground; it should memorialize good men with statues; it should hold up bad ones like the horrid Dr. Rabelais to permanent obloquy by treating them the way the ancient Greeks had treated prisoners of war, by carving their visages at the head of the columns. Clémens' thoughts circulated widely and in one respect or another influenced many libraries in the late seventeenth and early eighteenth centuries.

In all likelihood all this worked against the grossly utilitarian covering of floor and wall by structures bearing only books. The library of the printed book was destined to use its space mainly for those books and their readers, like the library of the medieval codex, but it would take a little more time for the artistic and public relations features to be scaled down by the new society in the making.

The utilitarian tide was probably supported by the gradual introduction of heat in libraries north of the Alps. Several potentates sponsoring scholarship began to offer heated areas for readers late in the seventeenth century. The unmistakably bourgeois "Waterchurch" Library in Zürich may have been the first to heat the staff workroom, an undertaking far from common in 1718. If word reached continental libraries fifty years later, of Benjamin Franklin's stove, or his long-handled plucker to take small things off high shelves, the historians do not seem to have mentioned either device.

Access to Library Materials and Information

Shelving, Catalogs, and Control Numbers How the books were to be arranged was not yet an urgent question to library users, it seems, because fetching and shelving the items desired continued to be primarily a staff function. Nor have we any evidence that the matter absorbed large numbers of librarians during the years under review: in 1789 libraries with more than 50,000 volumes were still unusual, and those with more than 100,000 really conspicuous.

It is nevertheless plain that the growth of collections, campus and other scholarly library service, and interest in the classification of all sorts of things, as well as personal proclivities here and there, drew considerable attention to the organization of library materials for use. Three basic problems were attacked: How to shelve books in a fashion conducive to finding them despite the lag in space, and protect them from heat, fire, damp, and vermin; how to provide access to the information in them, by subject; and how to maintain both bibliographical and inventory control by means of marking and registering which could involve books or shelves or particular catalogs or indexes or a combination thereof.

Shelving as a rule followed seventeenth-century precedent: broad "faculty" groups, with generous accommodation of variations in format. Some broke the faculty groups into subject divisions. The so-called Lambeck (Vienna) style, a strictly subject arrangement ignoring format, provoked observation and comment, but no widespread emulation so far traced.

As long as collections remained modest, inventory control was accomplished in familiar fashion. The shelf record that monastic times had called the catalog now became distinctively a shelflist composed of four (or a few more) registers of books according to faculties. Its character is plain from the German expression which became common in the eighteenth century, *Standortskatalog,* meaning "location catalog." If a large library (say, more than 50,000 volumes) continued, like Göttingen, to separate the list only by faculties, control was still achievable. But when, as frequently happened, the faculty groups and their records were either subdivided by format or subdivisions of format divisions, and one had twelve or sixteen series of call numbers to check, control was no longer satisfactory. Many libraries accordingly returned to the original inventory idea: in addition to the shelf record they kept an accession book or journal, registering—at least theoretically— every item in the collection in a single master list. In eighteenth-century Germany that device was known as the *Accessionskatalog;* it was sometimes the only complete record of a library's holdings, and often the key to other devices for bibliographic access.

Of the instruments well established in 1680, printed catalogs of a library or a bookseller's stock, complete or partial, alphabetical or classified, main lists or indexes—all were known for both their good points and their defects. Was there a clear preference in practice? The preceding period had made alphabetically arranged subject guides familiar. Morhof in 1685 thought strange the 1674 Bodleian catalog, which Thomas Hyde organized by authors; and it is said that many complaints were heard, accusing Hyde of defaulting on an alleged promise to produce a subject index to it. Then, with the new century, came a swing to general encyclopedias for the bourgeois and intellectuals on the one hand, and specialized bibliography for scholars and collectors on the other. Related to the latter, it would seem, was the success of Paris bookdealer Gabriel Martin, who turned out more than 100 subject-organized catalogs during the years from 1705 to 1761, of which at least 22 are reported to have had author indexes. Meanwhile, comprehensive subject bibliography suffered neglect: a plan of 1700 to create a classified guide to the most helpful books, based on outstanding library catalogs, was never implemented. Whatever librarians may have thought of these developments, they were obliged to grapple with the challenge of the increase in book stocks. The larger a collection, the more important became the machinery of access to the information in it. The questions arose: must the catalog scatter cognate materials by format simply because it is mechanically advantageous to shelve them that way? Could not a single subject be approached through a single page or sequence of pages in the catalog?

By way of response there appeared, perhaps more often than before, subject catalogs of two principal kinds. The systematic catalog began with the books, in the spirit of Francis Bacon's recommendations, sorting them by faculties and the subdivisions thereof. The outcome was a set of lists under subjects, each author-alphabetical within, the whole usually arranged in classified order. Later, transformed into catalog cards, this apparatus was to remain a principal tool in the scholarly libraries of Europe.

Devised on the basis of reverse logic was another variety of catalog, which began with a classification of knowledge and then tried to fit it to the books in a given library. Of those who either adapted an existing classification to this purpose or shaped one of his own, an outstanding representative was Johann Michael Francke (1717–1775). His famous 1750 *Realkatalog* of the Bünau library was prepared under circumstances then fairly common: Count Bünau was ready to sell his great collection, the Saxon elector's court was hesitating over the expenditure because of other involvements—not least the three "Silesian" wars (1740–1742, 1744–1745, 1756–1763), and Francke anticipated that his master would resort to sale by auction. (The labor was enormous, and he evaded pressure to prepare also a *Nominal,* or author, catalog.) The Saxon court did finally buy the books, Francke became the elector's librarian at Dresden, and between 1769 and 1771 he reorganized the newly enlarged collections there. He was so confident about his classified shelf arrangement, built around places and sovereignties, that a catalog of the substantially new library was allowed to wait twenty years.

How much difference was there between the systematic and the *Realkatalog* (or, with annotations added, *catalogue raisonné*)? They were bound to overlap somewhat, because when sorting books one can exclude ideas of classification only with difficulty; and when creating classification schemes, in a library environment, for libraries, actual books are likely to intrude on one's theorizing. Which method was better for any particular library at that time must remain an intriguing speculation. Later times were to accord standardized schemes high respect, particularly in the United States, but European practice was to remain substantially faithful to patterns built on the books originally at hand.

Paradoxically, *Realkatalog* also came to be used widely to mean, not a particular sort of logical or classified arrangement, but the altogether different alphabetical arrangement. That practice had of course a number of precedents, in the first place the nearly always alphabetical catchword-entry pattern, in which position in the list was determined not by the author's name but by the key word in the title, whether a place name or some other name or a topic. Closely related was the alphabetical catchword index to a catalog organized by subject groups. Paris librarian Adrien Baillet assembled in 1680 to 1682 an index of that type to his gigantic manuscript catalog of a private library; although remaining unpublished, its repute seems to have reached quite a few eighteenth-century students of the subject. Besides, there were some listings utilizing true subject headings rather than catch-words from titles, broadening what pioneers like bookdealer Maunsell had done (1595) just at particular points where a satisfactory catchword was not available.

Probably the most influential example, though not the first, of the alphabetical subject *Realkatalog* was produced in 1776 at the University of Greifswald (100 miles due north of Berlin, close to the Baltic shore). Librarian J. C. Daehnert was working with a two-volume author catalog listing some 52,000 titles; he chose to add a third volume, *Repertorium reale*, in which the same materials were alphabetized by place and personal names and *Schlagwörter* from titles. The high standing of his work among librarians of his own day and some time afterward patently owes nothing to subject headings, since he used none; but it may rest in part on the fact that one-third of his entries were dissertations, monographs, and journal articles.

These materials were fairly new in libraries, in large measure a product of the Age of Reason and the learned societies. Hardly surprising is it that France, birthplace of Cartesianism, had started using *raisonné* as a synonym for "logical" late in the seventeenth century and that the term came in the eighteenth to be applied to subject catalogs organized logically rather than alphabetically, especially those annotated. Even more intimately related to the transformation of the social scene was the application of *real* to alphabetizing in early eighteenth-century Germany. Akin to the vocationally oriented *Realschule* then challenging classical secondary education, it owed much directly to the bourgeois spirit of practicality.

If shelf records controlled books physically, and subject catalogs of one sort or another offered guidance to informational resources, a number of problems still remained. Defense against the attacks of heat, fire, damp, and vermin was still inadequate. Physical control was also upset when books could reach a reader's hands before being entered in any of the library's major records. Precisely that was the case in a great many eighteenth-century libraries. Cataloging was very often an extra, paid for as such and even regarded as the cataloger's private property (when Reuss left Tübingen for Göttingen in 1782 he took the Tübingen catalog he had prepared with him); it was quite likely to be incomplete and was seldom up to date. The leading professor on the other hand was accustomed to handling books freely, if only because he had in many instances as good or better a collection at home. When the great library at Dresden decided in 1790 that henceforth no book would be loanable unless it was entered in the catalog, a new era was signalled.

Insofar as books were processed sufficiently to be assigned a place on the shelves, the librarian was confronted by a dilemma already noted in the seventeenth century but during the eighteenth becoming a nightmare. One could maintain a particular subject arrangement, or shelve books in permanent locations, but one could not do both, consistently, unless one ceased to add books to the collection. Naudé had advised leaving the end of a shelf vacant when one began, and the Padua librarian had suggested skipping some numbers in each group of numbers. When those expansion outlets were gone, moreover, a certain amount of squeezing in was feasible for a while. But it became necessary sooner or later to shelve new volumes by placing them in front of or on top of those already there. The limits of tolerance were narrowing. The increase in holdings was creating a qualitatively new situation; a better plan for shelving books was becoming in many localities an urgent necessity.

The wisdom of hindsight notes two possible escape routes. If the bulk of the collection remained in closed stacks, books need not be classified by subject contents: any control system would do provided the staff understood it and could find desired books. That does not seem to have been perceived in the eighteenth century, partly because interest in classification (of data and things of all sorts) was at a higher level than ever, and partly because so many libraries were furnishing substantial reading-room collections necessarily arranged by subject for direct reader access. On the other hand, one could base the call number on the book rather than a fixed shelf location. This "relative location" plan had been proposed and apparently used in Zürich in 1587 (and elsewhere?), but it found no more acceptance than fixed location free of subject classification functions.

It appears that most libraries were content to muddle through with makeshifts of arbitrary decisions. Thus Francke, at Bünau and Dresden, held rigidly to his fixed shelving and minute classifying; supplements to items on hand were treated not as supplements but as new items, shelved somewhere else. Daehnert at Greifswald put in his catalogs only the accession number, the location symbols being entered only in the accession book. At Göttingen, Gesner was so proud of his classifying that he banned book numbers as superfluous; it was left to his successors to record full call numbers in the accession catalog. Such practices were doubtless encouraged by the occasional necessity to alter shelving and the location symbols governed by it, and the conviction of a librarian here and there that he could certainly improve upon what had gone before. Anticipation of change led many of those charged with doing the work to avoid commitments, and to write down "permanently" as little as possible.

Whether call numbers were registered in the accession record only, or in one or more catalogs, markings on books were far from standardized. The major elements were the symbols permanently assigned to particular sections of shelving and individual shelves, those associated with either a traditional faculty or the more recent narrower subject grouping called in Germany a *Fach* (literally, "occupation"), and format indicators. How often the respective letters or Roman or Arabic numerals were marked on bookcases or shelves, how often outside or inside the book or both, is a matter beyond certain knowledge.

We do know that descriptive cataloging continued basically its established patterns, place and year of publication being handled inconsistently, and titles not originally in Latin often being Latinized for the catalog record. Yet entry upon the library scene of learned society transactions, academic dissertations, and learned journals confronted the cataloger with numerous volumes of multiple authorship. Some rose to the challenge. Baillet, and very likely some other librarians, prepared entries not only for whole books but for parts of composite works and for pamphlets. Such entries were among the improvements proposed in 1697, at the Bodleian curators' invitation to their staff, by twenty-five-year-old assistant Humfrey Wanley. Daehnert's attention to individual journal articles was probably not unique either. Such analytics were to become familiar and valued in many libraries, especially those in the scholarly tradition.

The old custom of simplifying descriptive cataloging with abbreviations had occasionally suffered some pressure from protagonists of bibliography as a fine art. An opposite drive now emerged, on economic grounds, from the increasing frequency with which libraries printed their catalogs. Among the institutions so equipped in the eighteenth century were Uppsala in 1706, Moscow and Harvard in 1723, and Alcobaça, Portugal, in 1775. By the end of the period here considered, scholars generally expected to find a printed catalog in a library, especially at a major university. Oddly enough, the British Museum first had one only in 1787.

Library catalogs in the vernacular were beginning to become noticeable during this period—about a century after the book trade had given the vernacular prominence in published bibliography. It is very doubtful that vernacular catalogs became as numerous as those in Latin in the libraries of the eighteenth century. But the problems created by differing forms of names may have contributed to the intensification, as early as 1700, of the discussion of anonymous works and pseudonyms.

A catalog with only one entry on each (midget) page was reportedly in use in 1757 at the Cistercian Abbey of Hohenfurt, Bohemia. It was to remain rare, if not unique, for a century and more.

Bibliography and Classification At the higher level of bibliographical control was the progress of union catalogs and bibliographies. Of the former, the early-eighteenth-century effort of Abbé Montfaucon (1655–1741) to assemble data on Western manuscripts promptly became legendary. A few German librarians reportedly tried to enrich their own institutions' catalogs with union features, but the results are not clear.

Bibliography, understood as lists of books which were not library or dealers' catalogs, fared unevenly in the years under review. Although impressive work had been done by the end of the seventeenth century, only some of it reached printed form. The next hundred years saw, in the realm of current national and trade bibliography, a number of English efforts under the auspices of periodicals. The most impressive contributions were the lists in the *Gentleman's Magazine,* from 1731 to 1751 and *The London Magazine,* from 1732 to 1766 (available in Gregg reprints of 1966).Their common feature was price. *The London Magazine,* apparently from the second number on (May 1732), arranged both the lists and the annual indexes in subject groups; its rival followed suit with the lists in 1735, but not with its indexes, not even the twenty-year index issued in 1751. Both journals registered titles in divinity, entertainment, history, poetry, and prose; only *The London Magazine* seems to have attended to the listing of "Law, Parliamentary Affairs, and Trade," "Arts and Sciences" (including architecture and horticulture, for example), and the"Physical," or medicine.

France was meanwhile served by a succession of registers published by booksellers beginning in 1759, covering French, German, English, Dutch, and Italian publications. The range of reportage was early narrowed somewhat by a proprietary challenge from the well-established *Journal des Sçavans*.

A number of retrospective compilations appeared, such as the Maurists' *Histoire Littéraire de la France* (12 vols., 1733–1763); they are primarily specialists' aids today. On the other hand, scholarly biobibliography was enriched by two works long of rather broad utility. J. P. Niceron (1685-1738) produced celebrated *Mémoires,* a forty-three-volume assemblage (1727-1743) of data on writers and writings since the Renaissance. Equally serviceable then and afterwards was the *Allgemeines Gelehrten Lexikon* ("General Dictionary of Scholars") compiled in 1750 and 1751 by C. G. Jöcher (1694-1758) and resumed later by others.

Subject bibliography was heavily colored by attention to the pagan and Christian heritage at one extreme, and medicine and natural history at the other. Such products, however, frequently massive, were too expensive to find wide use quickly; besides, for all their scholarship, they were spattered with some of the sarcasm directed by conservatives against the popularization of knowledge by subject indexes and other means. When Alexander Pope exclaimed in 1728 (*The Dunciad,* I:279-280)

> How Index-learning turns no student pale,
> Yet holds the eel of science by the tail

he was beating a horse, as it were, far from dead, but already well flayed.

Actually, much of the contemporary mind, popular or scholarly, was focused less on the past than on the present and future: the *Encyclopédie* of 1751 was of the essence in that respect. Two enormous rival German undertakings (Zedler's, 1732-1754, and Krüntz's, 1773-1855) did sow seeds of consequence by incorporating in their offerings select bibliographical references. It is worth noticing, moreover, that the convenience of the alphabetical arrangement in these tools by no means smothered interest in the classified. When the contents of the *Encyclopédie* were reorganized as a series of subject handbooks, Pancoucke's *Encyclopédie Méthodique* (1782-1832), many readers responded with enthusiasm, among them Thomas Jefferson, then in Paris, who promoted the new work among his acquaintances back home.

How best to classify information continued to be a matter of importance to librarians, bookdealers, and others. Of the numerous patterns devised between 1680 and 1789, none seems to have diverged substantially from those already familiar. Now and then emerged terminology of distinctly contemporary flavor, like "Artificial and Technical Knowledge" in Chambers' 1728 encyclopedia. There also appeared such deviations as Johann Michael Denis' contribution of 1774, derived according to its author from the seven pillars of wisdom of Solomon's Temple: to the standbys of the "French System" (theology, law, philosophy, medicine, history) he added mathematics and philology. Conceivably he was reacting to notable published achievements in his time, for example D'Alembert's eight-volume *Opuscules Mathématiques* (Paris, 1761-1768) and the Latin and Russian works by mathematician Leonard Euler (various places, 1748–   ). In any case he was a self-styled disciple of D'Alembert's, wanting his classification scheme to show relationships among subjects; thus was a Baconian tradition carried on.

Precious few of these schemes, however, provided visible homes for the categories of recent vintage. Fiction *(romans)* was apparently recognized in the scheme of the learned Samuel Formey of Berlin, issued in 1746 and several times again until 1775. It was one of the twelve major classes in his "advice" on choosing books for a library. Another class was assigned to *journaux*, perhaps reflecting his intimate association with the local Academy of Science, whose secretary he became in 1748. As late as 1774, however, in the above-mentioned Denis plan, fiction appeared conventionally as a subdivision of history. Francke's select catalog of Dresden books, issued between 1773 and 1777, gave one of sixty-six classes to *Fabulae Romanenses &c*, but that sounds classical rather than contemporary.

Provision was made more often, it seems, for polygraphy. Prosper Marchand of Paris, producing in 1709 a sale catalog for a private library, placed in an appendix composite works (including dictionaries), miscellaneous, and writings which did not fit into any of the preceding classes. A German scholar offered in 1747 a scheme including slots for bibliographers and encyclopedists. In Francke's great Bünau catalog of 1748, Volume I, Part I, Book 5 was reserved for works pertinent to various departments of learning simultaneously. His later select catalog of the Dresden collections assigned Class XXIX (of the sixty-six) to encyclopedias and miscellaneous works.

What is not clear from the data readily available is the difference, if any, between medieval composite volumes and what the seventeenth and eighteenth centuries called polygraphy. Although the years from 1680 to 1789 witnessed the organization of many learned societies and the publication of numerous scholarly journals and monographic proceedings and other collections, acquired certainly in several libraries, the classification schemes rarely refer to those materials as such. Were they assigned arbitrarily to a particular subject area, or grouped as polygraphy or collections? Were the librarians and readers satisfied by the sort of analytical entries furnished by Daehnert at Greifswald? Was that a fairly common practice?

A classification position for library matters turned up now and then. In Morhof's *Polyhistor* (1688) it led the procession. Marchand (1709) placed bibliography and book trade affairs in his "introduction," while polygraphical reference works were listed in the appendix. Leibniz, in thoughts dated 1718, paired literary history and "that which concerns the librarian," *"Generalia & Miscellanea"* being next and last. Yet a great many classification plans of those years (as displayed in Petzholdt, *Bibliotheca Bibliographica*, pp. 29–35) do not mention explicitly either libraries or bibliography. Presumably, such works were frequently treated as a portion of something else.

A great deal of the labor just sketched was intended to be comprehensive. Selectivity was nevertheless attracting more attention. It was not a new notion, obviously. Long on the scene were discrimination on political or religious grounds, the favoring of rare or beautiful books, strong convictions as to the importance brought simply by publication in an ancient tongue rather than a contemporary vernacular. Yet discussion was now enriched, thanks to the mounting numbers of books and university students and the great wave of popularization of knowledge associated mainly with the advance of the middle class. The Morhof approach was to emphasize bibliographical guides to all known reading resources, an approach destined to live long and well. But many contemporary observers, some pedagogues some not, thought selection a more desirable route: Morhof found himself satirized. Still others, on the contrary, especially conservative essayists, poked fun at the notion that knowledge could be acquired by way of abbreviated or simplified versions; they were not usually aiming at guides to reading, but their shafts may have had a dampening effect. Decidedly unfavorable to either the comprehensive view or selection based only on quality was the contemporary drive to focus on "nature" rather than books, paradoxically derived largely from Bacon just as much as certain notions of classification.

The Library Staff, the Library in the Encyclopedias, and the Promise of New Patronage

Librarians and Librarianship   Whether putative employers counted on them to select rather than merely acquire, whatever subject areas or skill in description might be involved, academic and court librarians and some others were being pictured more and more as persons of specific educational attainments. When young Wanley, for example, submitted his above-mentioned thoughts at the Bodleian in 1697, he envisaged a long agenda of library policy questions being pondered "'so many times a week, for a month or two,'" by "'a dozen or more Learned men, who are likewise supposed to *know books* better than others.'" He expected them to guide wisely not only on classification and arrangement and numerous points of description but "'whether books with gilt backs should stand with their backs out or not'" (quoted by D. M. Norris, *A History of Cataloguing. . .;* London: Grafton, 1939, p. 152). Although Wanley himself was already known as a manuscript cataloger and enjoyed the esteem of his superior, Thomas Hyde, much as Bodley had appreciated James, his application (1699) for the post of deputy to Richard Bentley at the king's library was ruled inadmissible because he lacked a university degree.

Additional significant details may be found in the process by which the staff of Emperor Leopold I chose a successor to imperial librarian Daniel Nessel, who died in March 1700. Within six months after Nessel's passing, the court's chief administrator (*Obersthofmeister*) reported to the emperor on his impressions, or in effect the initial screening of candidates. Abbot Paolo Franceschini submitted that the emperor had promised to take care of him. Wolff Weckhardt von Rain cited the services of his forefathers as officials, etc., and his own devotion to books since childhood. F. A. Harmanseg asserted that he had completed studies in philosophy and jurisprudence, had traveled, and knew somewhat "the vernaculars." E. F. Schollberg had taught the history of public law at the Agrarian Academy of Lower Austria. F. Wirtz identified himself as tutor to several sons of courtiers and alleged that the emperor liked his Latin style. J. H. de Sapogne of Luxembourg had served in the University of Vienna Company during the siege (of 1683, by the Turks) and with the cavalry, and now appeared to seek quiet. J. B. Comazzi wanted income beyond his job as imperial historian, to make up for a series of losses. Interpreter J. B. Podesta approached the position as a means of getting printed his Turkish "Calapini" (that is, dictionary). The same objective moved Benedictine Thomas Maphäus (Maffei) from Naples, professor of theology, philosophy, and mathematics, who had writtten on philosophy.

The right man, it seemed, was Spanish priest Nicolaus Garzia de Londono, minister of the king, general historian, Cavalier of St. George, aide to the Duke of Parma. He wanted to come to Vienna, and claimed wide acquaintance with books, Oriental languages, and Latin and Greek as well as Spanish and French. Language knowledge was also prominent in the claims of J. J. Haakius, exiled from his northern home by the French war; he was living by writing verse and would be glad to oblige the emperor with Latin poetry. One candidate, J. Berger, described himself as a librarian and "Dr. Phil.," but he proved to be only a subordinate.

The *Obersthofmeister* was particularly concerned about the backlog of unprocessed materials from the Corvinian Library (Budapest acknowledged the Austrian king since 1683); knowledge of Greek was very important, of Hebrew nearly as much so; he wanted the manuscript translated into German. He was afraid that a man able to handle such traffic would not come for what was offered, 900 gulden a year without quarters at court; lodgings in Vienna would involve a tax of 150 gulden (besides rent?). The appointee would have also 1,000 gulden for such library expenses as binding, import duties on books, and a secretary. So many books still unbound had turned up after Nessel's death, however, that the allowance just mentioned had not stretched far enough. In fact, it had been required to keep the assistant, whose memory of the books and their locations was indispensable in the continued absence of a catalog.

The emperor concluded that the candidates with apparently the best language equipment, Londono and Haakius, were the men to examine. Also invited was one Alberti, who had tutored the son of the Austrian envoy to Constantinople, and was taken as knowing the Oriental tongues.

There were at first no examiners. The Jesuits, asked for help in the emergency, produced some "old-character"-Latin, Greek prose, Greek poetry, and Hebrew. For the last-mentioned they provided a translation on a separate sheet so that the examiner need not know Hebrew himself. Nevertheless, they also sent a fully qualified examiner, a Rome-trained canon with a library certificate. The proceedings were conducted at the Jesuits' Library, the committee consisting of the librarian thereof, the above-mentioned canon, and the court administrator's secretary.

Londono could not handle the old Latin or the Hebrew without guides to the letters, but was satisfactory on Greek. Asked to translate into German, he stated that he had not been told to expect a test of that kind and that he would need dictionaries. Haakius stumbled with Latin and Chaldean, but performed well with Greek and Hebrew. He had the necessary preparation but was a Protestant; he said he would accept Catholicism—only, noted the *Obersthofmeister,* for the sake of the job. Haakius was told he was in the running and was asked for a transcript of his studies. Alberti appeared, but after observing what was transpiring excused himself. He explained afterward that he had learned his Greek and Hebrew ten years earlier and lost much of them since. The upshot of the session was that no one was judged satisfactory and the post remained vacant for the next five years, until Emperor Leopold I died in 1705. (Assembled from the imperial archives by F. Hadamowsky, in *Biblos,* 2:11–14, 1953.)

A generation later (1728), Montesquieu remarked on the satisfying service at the Ambrosiana Library in Milan, especially the catalog notes which enabled the user to judge promptly the age of a manuscript, and praised those responsible, *"bibliothécaires savants"* (*Oeuvres Complets,* ed. Caillois; Paris: Gallimard, 1949, I:594).

The wisdom required of the librarian at the Weimar court is indicated by the examination of 1743. Much emphasis was given to private and public law, history, mathematics, geography, languages, and literature. The written tests also covered tax and other land problems rural and urban, and the "Duties and Characteristics of a librarian and the direction of a library." A report on the performance of an unsuccessful candidate, issued in 1747, noted that he was weak on the history of literature, pretty good on public law, and foggy on theology (he didn't know what a polyglot Bible was). He was also regarded as ignorant of political history, fair on German historiography and on some rare books though not on others. He seemed unfamiliar with many names in scholarship and the learned journals in foreign languages. His geography had ended with his schooling. He was thought to have no clear objective in life. (Presented by Werner Deetjen in *Zentralblatt für Bibliothekswesen,* 45:303–305, 1928.)

J. M. Gesner of Göttingen had in 1748 no comment on personal philosophy, but contributed a sophisticated view of a librarian's education. A man equipped only with the history of scholarship (a Morhof favorite) and not himself a scholar would probably find his knowledge sterile, but he had better know at least that much; in fact the library staff regularly provided the university with three lectures on the subject. Furthermore, Gesner had learned the library trade at the ducal library at Weimar, and at Göttingen found high-powered professors less helpful than those worthies imagined they were: he told Baron Münchhausen he would much rather have two or three beginners, who would do what they were told. The personality side of the matter was developed still more keenly by Francke at Dresden about 1768. His distinguished colleague Crusius, thought Francke, was certainly a learned man, but his attitude toward people was a grave liability. To protect and improve the collections was indeed a necessity, but the librarian "'must not be a dragon in the library'" (quoted by Hans Henning from Francke's papers, in *Zentralblatt,* 72:294, 1958).

Diderot meanwhile (1751) explained the role of the librarian thus: the person charged with "protecting, maintaining, properly arranging, and adding to the books in a library." Few *"fonctions littéraires"* demanded that much talent. Indeed, the librarian of a major collection like the Royal Library had to know ancient and modern languages and everything pertaining to books, the history of letters, the book trade, and typography. ("BIBLIOTHÉCAIRE," *Encyclopédie,* V:17.) Whatever he may have thought about the librarian's ability to work with others and serve readers, his definition does not touch those subjects.

If much was defined, standards were hardly more than implied. It is not known whether any two employers interpreted in the same way such expressions as "knowledge of Greek"; nor was there any set of criteria manifestly applied in more than one library. Nonetheless, those making decisions about candidates for library leadership posts, or like Diderot affecting the decisions, were frequently influential in various other ways. Their views may have meant little in ordinary libraries, but insofar as they became known, the stimulus may have been as beneficial as what some later standards (often unenforceable) were to provide.

A considerable number of the men—and all were men—serving as librarians had been educated comparatively well, and several were like Leibniz acknowledged scholars. Personal careers naturally varied. Armand-Jérôme Bignon, French royal librarian from 1764 to 1771 by grace of family connections, was also a member of several learned societies, *Conseiller d'État,* and *Prévôt des Marchands.* (This last personage supervised, at least officially, trash collectors, bridge tenders, and other municipal "officers"; since numerous associates worked with him, his obligations were probably no more burdensome than the pastoral duties of the hundreds of church scholars and staff men assigned livings at one time or another.) J. Oriot des Auberts, graduate of a Jesuit secondary school, began as librarian at a *Ritterakademie* in Poland, turned to the stage in 1741, and settled at the Bayreuth court (east central Germany, near the Czech border) in 1744, becoming tutor to the local princess. From 1759 on he held several posts successively at the Stüttgart court, among them the librarianship; piquant is the fact that in 1763 his books became part of the duke's collection. The remarkable professional life of J. D. Reuss opened at Tübingen University in 1774; in 1782, while he was traveling to improve his knowledge of library operation, at his own expense, he was recruited by C. G. Heyne to reorganize the cataloging at Göttingen.

Heyne (1729–1812), indeed, set a noteworthy example for the library administrator. He learned his trade at Count Brühl's library, one of those merged into the Saxon elector's assemblage at Dresden. A trained philologist, he also knew how to organize, lead, and inspire loyalty in his staff. His stated conception of first things first was to give prescribed duties top priority; family obligations came next, then the expectations of the learned world, and last, his personal desires. A sound executive, he required semiannual reports from his principal subordinates, but left to them the details of their performance. It is a measure of how far librarianship still had to go, however, that Baron Münchhausen, devoted and serious backer of the Göttingen University library, kept financial decisions in his own hands. Only after his death in 1770 was Heyne able to buy books entirely on his own authority.

This state of affairs probably owed something not only to the uneven development of the art but to social circumstances. The librarian usually came from some stratum of the middle class, occasionally from the lesser aristocracy. He might be an employee of standing and repute, especially if he were a scholar; but he was still an employee, and his employer was seldom accountable to anyone but himself. User comment, probably received now and then, could rise no higher than its source. Although Göttingen carried further than ever before the idea of making a library useful, the users were at most the German academic community. Neither in that world nor in the off-campus academies and reading-circle libraries was the potential clientele yet thought to include everyone who could read and wanted a library book.

Insofar as library literature reflected either the accepted or the desired, contemporary writings deserve more analysis than they have received in the English-speaking world. The period opened with the enlarged edition of Johannes Lomeier's meaty Latin survey of libraries; it is recorded as having 414 pages of rather small format, 16.5 centimeters. Like the travelers of the next generation or two, he dealt with library holdings and decoration rather than service. A few years later (1685–1686) librarian Adrien Baillet released an extensive work on literary criticism, *Jugemens des Sçavans*, which included some discussion of the rules he had formulated and applied in cataloging his master's collection. Perhaps it contributed to the thinking of Frederik Rostgaard, a young Dane then a student in Paris, who published in 1697 a plan for systematic catalog, to counteract shelf separation by format, and eventually became a distinguished librarian in his home country.

An annotated guide to earlier writings, occasionally critical, was contributed in 1688 by D. G. Morhof, in the form of several chapters (mostly seven-page) in his Latin *Polyhistor Literarius*, Book I. Chapter III on libraries generally and Chapter IV on origins and decoration are not strikingly novel, but Morhof emphasizes the three stages of purpose: "public custody," then "love of study," and finally "usefulness to the public" (pp. 21 and 26 in the Lübeck 1747 edition). Chapter V unites brief remarks on organization, alluding to Naudé among others, and reflections on disorganization through human failings and bad luck. Chapter VI pays tribute to numerous librarians, Chapter VII to manuscript caretakers. Chapter XVI offers observations on many writers significant in the history of "letters" (not just "literature") as well as libraries; noteworthy are the inclusion of and accurate statements about the Royal Society *Transactions*, the *Journal des Sçavans*, and the *Acta Eruditorum*. The next chapter concentrates on "librarian-writers," treating a second time several individuals like Naudé, already noticed for nonlibrary writings. Longest of the group is Chapter XVIII (pp. 196–214), on the literature of cataloging. It begins with Philip Labbé's history of bibliographical effort, noting both the first (1664) and the second (1682) editions. Morhof then moves successively to universal-scope writers like Gesner, national bibliographers by country, subject bibliographers, the catalogs of "public" libraries, and the catalogs of private libraries—these last including the book collections at the famous printing establishments.

Morhof covered a great deal of ground, with the bibliographical care characteristic of his epoch; but he was neither deeply perceptive nor given to interpretation on the grand scale. Although he was concerned with ideas, his recital tends to give more prominence to the names of writers and their writings. It helps explain why some contemporaries rejected title bibliography.

Of the many subsequent writings one might consider, the first was a collection of reprints. Mader's 1666 assemblage of library tracts reappeared from 1702 to 1705 in a much enlarged edition, three volumes in quarto, the third occupied mainly by Lomeier's survey. Neither basic policy nor the techniques of library operation were examined in these narratives; their appreciation turned far more on holdings, decoration of the premises, and scholar-librarians; just what a Baroque audience was likely to want. Quite different was "The Library Newly Revealed," addressing to "school youth and other curious amateurs" instruction on organizing and operating libraries "usefully."*(Die Neu eröffnete Bibliothek . . . studirenden Jugend und andern courieusen Liebhabern . . . nützlich zu gebrauchen.)* It was issued in 1711 in Hamburg, leading port long hospitable to the library idea; no author was named. In the handy (pocket?) size of duodecimo, its 298 pages dealt in seven "books" with (1) establishing a library, (2) what a librarian should know, (3) manuscripts, (4) books on libraries, (5) library operation, particularly bibliographic control, and an introduction to the literature of those subjects, (6) decoration and (7) useful types and styles thereof. The final "book" added data on the leading libraries of Europe and writings about them. (As reported by J. Petzholdt in his *Neue Anzeiger,* 25:2–3, 1864.)

Several other works with "library" in the title were offered during these years, but none seemed truly important to expert Petzholdt, who examined most of them, if not all. The day of the fundamental treatise on library science was yet to dawn.

The Library in the Encyclopedias   If in that sense library science had not yet been born, the bourgeoisification of life was creating new potential library users. One means was the gradual emergence of articles on libraries in general encyclopedias. Thanks to predecessors like Lipsius and Lomeier, the compilers had both data and patterns of discussion at their disposal.

The French Royal Library bulks large in the French tradition. Louis Moréri's *Grand Dictionnaire Historique* includes only a routine two columns on pages 454 and 455 of Volume 2 under *"Bibliothèque"* in the 1759 *"nouvelle édition"* (actually the twentieth) in ten folio volumes (Paris: Libraires Associés); Lomeier is the first source cited at the end. Immediately afterward, however, Moréri provides a longer article (pp. 455–460) on the Royal Library. (Since each successive edition is known to have been enriched, it is not possible to report here how much of that contribution graced the first edition in 1674.) Pierre Bayle's encyclopedia critique of Moréri and others (1697) is silent on libraries. But the *Encyclopédie* of the *philosophes* is lavish: pages 17 to 38 in Volume 5 of the forty-five volumes composing the "Geneva edition" (Geneva: Pellet, 1777–1779). While early-eighteenth-century events are treated, the article as a whole has probably changed a good deal less since the first printing, twenty years earlier, than in the case of Moréri. The coverage is broad gauge, including medieval libraries; the last six pages are devoted to the Royal Library. Within the text are numerous references to older authorities, and a few cross-references to other articles like *"LIVRE"* ("Book").

The English tradition developed differently. John Harris' *Lexicon Technicum* (1725 edition) does not offer an entry for "Library." The article so titled in Ephraim Chambers' 1728 Cyclopaedia (London; 2:973) does: about 500 words, conventional coverage owing a good deal to earlier accounts like that of Lipsius. Chambers relies heavily upon classical writers, cites Lambeck for data on the Imperial Library in Vienna, and stresses gently the glories of the Bodleian.

The Chambers article was copied in turn by *Encyclopaedia Britannica* and Abraham Rees. In the first two editions (1768, 1776–1784), the former somewhat abridges Chambers and adds an original statement about the University Library and the Advocates' Library (later the Scottish National Library) in Edinburgh. The University Library is praised for the protection given the collection by "wire doors that none but the Keeper can open," and for the deposit required against the loan of a book, preferred to "the multitude of chains used in other libraries." (Actually, chains were well on their way out; was the charge based on hearsay?) The Advocates' Library is simply mentioned, with a see-reference to the article "Advocate." (1st ed., 1768, 5:795–796, photocopies and other data courtesy of Encyclopedia Britannica, Chicago.)

In the third edition (1797) through the sixth (1820–1823)—to go beyond chapter boundaries for a moment—the *Britannica* article is doubled in length, primarily by restoring material earlier deleted from Chambers. Besides, a substantial new paragraph identifies briefly numerous English college, medical, law, ecclesiastical, and family libraries, principally in London. The statement on Edinburgh remarks that the University Library is "deficient in a catalogue," and goes on with an appreciation of the library of "the society of writers to the signet" (law specialists responsible for preparing many government documents). The Advocates' Library is treated as before. (3d ed., 1797, 5:795–796.) A separate article is furnished on catalogs.

Meanwhile, however, there was apparently no such material in the distinguished yearbook of current events, *The Annual Register,* from its beginning in 1758 through 1789.

Altogether, the reader of the principal encyclopedia articles on libraries would have gained during this period only a basic acquaintance with institutional history, some stray facts about famous collections, and a bit of bibliographical guidance. Few traces can be seen of the new bourgeois commitment or the emergence of new facets in library life. In Moréri the French reader would have had a very similar experience, except for the extensive essay on the Royal Library and its librarians. Only in the *Encyclopédie* of Diderot would he have found a really deep treatment, including philosophical considerations. As for readers of German, the outstanding sixty-four-volume compilation initiated by bookdealer J. H. Zedler, issued between 1731 and 1750, offered several articles on book questions but none on libraries.

Inasmuch as cataloging is an intellectual rather than a recreational topic, it is hardly surprising that the first entrant in the genre here discussed appeared in the *Encyclopédie*. The catalog, declares the essayist (1777 ed., 6:510), is like a library, each being a bibliographic system for arranging books in classes and subclasses, "to find easily the books wanted." It is noted that "learned bibliographers and skillful bookdealers" have fashioned different systems; it will suffice to submit that of Gabriel Martin (which occupies nearly all of the eleven-page entry). One may incline toward that exceptionally popular plan or toward one of the many others available (names are mentioned). In any case, the diversity "seems to prove that it's all rather arbitrary" (p. 520).

Women and Children   Whatever recreational or intellectual interest the encyclopedia articles on libraries and cataloging may have served or aroused, producing goods to sell was the way of the world, printed matter primarily a commodity, and the emergence of a new market welcome. In England, the leader in technological progress, economic and political change developed among the town middle class and the country squires' families a female audience to which writers and printers consciously addressed products new or partly new. These women responded, servant girls sometimes included, but they were for the time being obliged either to buy books or to patronize commercial lending libraries. In France the challenges at home and abroad were partly responsible for Louis XIV's absolutism, the continuance of Paris as the main center of European culture, the salons and influence of upper-classwomen, and increasing attention to the education of such women. If admittance to the Sorbonne library was permitted, there seems to be no evidence to suggest widespread hospitality to women in French libraries. Germany, lacking a national center, had no comparable assemblage of salons, and its outstandingly numerous universities did not accept female students any more than those elsewhere. The many women with secondary-school education, in France and Germany, were no more welcome at the provincial academies, although some doubtless had access to a private library. As for opportunity in Vienna and points south, Mozart's librettist Da Ponte gives his impression in *Don Giovanni* (1787). After aristocrat Elvira denounces the Don, his servant Leporello is heard to mutter, "Just like a printed book!" (*"Pare un libro stampato!"*—Act I, Scene 2.)

In New England and parts of the Middle Colonies of British North America, organized schooling for women was less developed; but the Calvinist preoccupation with Bible literacy, and the enormous importance of the woman to the life of the characteristically small farm were preparing a vast potential readership which became obvious after the Revolution. In this new society where one spoke of "farmers" rather than "peasants," the idea of the library's possible audience thus took a great leap forward.

Reading matter for children had been available for centuries, whether moralistic or imaginative or simply instructional; church-sponsored items had probably dominated. But the rise of the printed pamphlet in the seventeenth century included the emergence of the chapbook, with contents secular and often offensive to church-minded pedagogues. Besides, many ecclesiastics were working toward inviting rather than forcing as a teaching method: in 1693 John Locke crystallized these trends in *Some Thoughts Concerning Education*. Two generations later an enterprising English publisher reckoned that the time was ripe to offer children's books as a distinctive product. Thus appeared in 1744 *A Little Pretty Pocket Book,* issued by John Newbery, who had risen from country near-rags to near-riches through the newspaper business. The step succeeded, partly because Newbery was a businessman and partly because a new wave of didactic items spread over the bookmarts after the publication of Rousseau's *Émile* (1764). Of course, not all such wares were as acceptable as the Newbery line. A German schoolmaster who regularly went to the Leipzig book fairs wrote in 1787 that the books and periodicals for children displayed there were countless but often worthless; he protested the ethic of moneymaking.

These contradictory forces, reader desire versus moral "needs,"and book quality versus book salability, were before long to concern also the operators of library service to children. Admitting minors to libraries, however, required new circumstances, notably the development of a struggle over the minds of those newly able to vote, white males without property.

Chapter Seven

THE BEGINNINGS OF GREAT CHANGE

The years between the French Revolution and the first number (January 15, 1840) of the library periodical called *Serapeum* were characterized primarily by struggles producing recognition of the white male rank and file. Prominent also were contests between the landed and industrial-and-urban interests, between defenders of classical education and promoters of the new professions. National differences became ever sharper not only in economic progress and political patterns but in numerous aspects of culture: new ideas about nature and man, ultimately international, took root variously according to circumstances. Several bases for a vast broadening of library services were laid in the young and highly self-conscious United States of America, but the advance of the science and art of librarianship remained on the whole a German achievement.

The French Revolution and Its Consequences for Libraries

In France In 1789 the truth could no longer be concealed. France wanted big changes, and they were effected with resounding éclat, although not to universal applause. On July 14 the hated symbol, the Bastille, was destroyed, and nobles began emigrating. In November the Constituent Assembly issued a basic decree confiscating ecclesiastical property, and others later confiscated the property of émigrés. Altogether, by the time of the Directory (late 1795), decrees bearing on libraries numbered twenty. Most of these documents were produced by committees of the National Convention (September 1792 to October 1795), especially that on public instruction.

The confiscated books and manuscripts were brought to the *dépôts littéraires* established at several locations in Paris and numerous points elsewhere, throughout the eighty-three departments into which the former provinces had been reorganized under the Constitution of 1790. Precise plans for library service were developed, to strengthen both the famous "public" libraries in Paris and the significant collections in many other principal towns, and to assemble a union catalog *(Bibliographie générale)*. Supporting these schemes were elaborate directions distributed to the provincial centers on preparing entry cards for the books to be transported to Paris, on moving and storing books, and on the measures necessary to protect them from damp, vermin, etc. Obviously, the men of the committees represented not only love of books but considerable experience handling them.

The plan for the *Bibliographie générale* was appealingly simple. The staff at each *dépôt* was to record on cards the basic particulars about each item held. These cards were then to be bound up in bundles and sent to the Paris Bureau de Bibliographie. The Bureau would develop a union catalog and allocate books among the existing libraries and those supposed to be created; the allocation procedure included a distinction between "good books" and others. Actually, the bureau did materialize, with an executive, eight bibliographers, and three catalogers for anonymous works; and by April 1794 about 1.4 million cards had reached them from the departments. But the scope of the task was evidently underestimated: if key figure Abbé Henri Gregoire was correct, the provincial *dépôts* had some 12 million volumes when the project began, and to keep up with even the limited shipments soon proved impossible. The *Bibliographie générale* rapidly withered and died.

The shipments were limited mainly on two accounts. Although provincial society had flourished, especially in the numerous academies, the revolutionary situation found few persons on hand ready, willing, and able to follow Paris cataloging instructions: many a card duly submitted was unusable. Furthermore, local pride and bourgeois sentiments about property nourished behavior much like that of the peasants who concealed what they could from the tax agents: many a book and manuscript was not reported for fear it would be demanded by Paris and never returned. The central authorities, for their part, desperately dispatched more detailed guidance on cataloging and proclaimed the theses of national public ownership. The libraries of Strasbourg, Lille, and Perpignan, for example, they insisted, "'don't belong to those communities any more than their fortifications' "; the citizens of Brest, Dunkirk, and Besançon, and so on " 'have just as much right to them' "(quoted in Milkau, III-I:711). By comparison with the public ownership of books in the towns of New England nearly a century earlier, this was an advance in thinking, but clearly premature.

The partly developed, partly contradictory plans for book selection and book disposal, deprived of the *Bibliographie générale,* staggered forward. The sequestered collections of nobles and bourgeois included books attractive for their content, and a vain attempt was made to establish a commission of three scholars to choose the best for addition to the Bibliothèque

Nationale. On the other hand, there was an immense number of works on theology and law, and others representing *ancien régime* thinking, necessarily absorbing a great deal of energy. Of interest mainly as a possible source of revenue, they stimulated varied ideas. One school urged selling the "detestable" writings to the enemies of the Revolution, retaining just a copy or two of each as a record of Unreason. Another recommended selling abroad anything but rarities, on the theory that revolutionary ideas would be exported thus to the advantage of men's souls as well as of the pocket of revolutionary France. Both of these philosophies were friendly to the notion of preparing an "Index de la raison," a riposte to the Catholic Church's *Index librorum prohibitorum,* but the Index of Reason never appeared.

In practice, books were soon being sold at the *dépôts* in defiance of the rules, and the Convention (1794-1795) felt obliged to halt such acts. A National Institute was organized to work out guidelines, the provincial *dépôts* were told to cease sales until further notice, and the Paris *dépôts* authorized to dispose only of such titles in theology and law as were not claimed by the major libraries of the capital. Enough disposition ensued to saturate the market and ruin many bookdealers. Meanwhile, the ban on provincial *dépôt* sales was undercut by the Council of 500 (legislative body created in 1795), which allowed numerous exceptions supposedly under careful controls: the whole arrangement broke down within a few years. The moves toward moderation following the Reign of Terror included restoration—on paper—of some collections to those formerly condemned (who had survived), but the *dépôts* had few books left and few old ecclesiastical libraries gained much by the change of policy. One of the fortunate ones was the Archbishop of Paris, who recovered 15,000 volumes in 1802.

The events of the revolutionary epoch produced also not only rhetoric favorable to book and library appreciation but tangible benefits. In Paris, despite extremist demands to get rid of every trace of aristocratic heraldry on book covers, repulsed by determined defenders of the book arts, substantial advantage was reaped by libraries old and new. In 1793 the Bibliothèque Nationale was granted the privilege of removing manuscripts from the *dépôts* and thus acquired much of what had been in the confiscated collections. In 1795 this authorization was expanded to cover books. Soon afterward the library was given the power to engage in purchase and exchange with *dépôts* anywhere in France, and eventually no book, theoretically, could leave a *dépôt* without permission of the Bibliothèque Nationale. These circumstances rapidly doubled the latter's holdings, the inadequacy of time and space being regarded by Joseph Van Praet (1754-1837), chief for printed books, as problems to be dealt with later. More arrived as Napoleon's troops moved through several countries at the turn of the century and shipped booty home; some of these items were returned to their owners in 1814 and 1815. During Napoleon's rule as First Consul (1799-1804) grandiose plans were made for a move to the Louvre but never materialized, nor did the funds appear which he reportedly promised for the "rounding out" of the collections.

Acquisition by sharp bargaining and maneuvering did take place. In the years 1801-1806, sponsored by a national commission, former Benedictine Jean-Baptiste Maugérard (1740-1814) directed agents in scouring areas not normally French. This involved primarily the left bank of the Rhine (Mainz for example), first the scene of political competition between émigrés and government representatives and then a battleground, ending with its award to France by the Peace of Basel in 1795. The yield included 4,000 manuscripts and 15,000 books, mainly incunabula; it may be supposed that Maugérard's talents as a palaeographer and knowledge of literature played a part. (Had he laid some groundwork while in his temporary exile of 1791 in Erfurt, virtually the geographic center of Germany?) Other talents played parts too. In 1809, for example, the treasures of the imperial library in Vienna were raided with an efficiency testifying to the French officials' familiarity with the monumental catalog (1665–1679) of Peter Lambeck. The bibliographic control of the Bibliothèque Nationale's massive collections remained to bedevil the future.

The extreme left phase of the Revolution heard the cry that having a single director for the library was inconsistent with revolutionary principles, and for a few years the great institution was operated by an eight-man collective, each taking his turn for one year as chairman. In 1800 Lucien Bonaparte began a reversal, and additional steps during the next fifty years gradually reestablished authority and responsibility together in a single pair of hands.

Privileged access to *dépôt* holdings was early extended to the other major Paris libraries, all "public" in the sense that almost any male was welcome to use them. The Bibliothèque de l'Arsenal, named for the artillery headquarters in which it was originally lodged by its private owner in 1765, gained 50,000 volumes. The Mazarine, renamed Bibliothèque des Quatre-Nations after its street-address, received 50,000; 20,000 went to the Bibliothèque du Panthéon, known in earlier days as Sainte-Geneviève. Furthermore, the reduction of stocks at the Paris *dépôts* led to consolidation; only one remained in 1801, and what was still on its shelves in 1811 was turned over to the Arsenal. The Royal Library suffered great losses but did survive.

The *dépôt* treasures also permitted the establishment of new libraries associated with government agencies like the Chamber of Deputies, museums like the Louvre, and schools like the Saint-Cyr military academy.

Characteristically for France, conditions in the provinces were rather different from those in Paris. When the Revolution broke out, most cities of consequence had "public" libraries as well as church and abbey book collections. Whether they were used appreciatively or simply ignored is not easily determinable, but it was clearly an advantage for them that they were not mentioned in the celebrated *cahiers* of complaint. Their role at first was negligible. The process of confiscation and assembling of books at the provincial *dépôts* varied a great deal according to the capacities and attitudes of the personnel involved; vandalism was the subject of three reports by Abbé Gregoire. By 1795, nevertheless, some 8 million volumes were on hand, and the Paris leaders were trying hard to counteract abuse and inefficiency.

Although the city libraries had been recognized in January 1794, the *dépôts* were instructed on October 25, 1795 to assign appropriate books to the new central secondary schools, one in each major city (ninety-seven in the first two years under the "Law of Daunou"). The libraries therein were to be open to the public, and each was to be administered by a librarian designated as such and named a member of the school's faculty. Often, however, the selection process proved to be too much for the persons available; perhaps one-third of the *dépôt* holdings were really examined. Whatever the respective effects of modernizing the curriculum, the antireligious tone, the weaknesses of administration under the Directory, and private-school competition, the episode came to an end after six years. By a decree of January 28, 1803, the central schools supported by department (public) funds were abolished and the books finally allotted to the " 'bibliothèques municipales' " and " 'bibliothèques de la ville' " (quoted in Milkau, III-I:744). The 7 million volumes thus transferred remained legally the property of the national government and became the basis of state supervision of the libraries possessing them.

The collections of the learned were on the whole among those confiscated. The original Sorbonne library disappeared in that fashion; the assemblages which were to assume its name long afterward (1860) were established in 1794 when the library of the Jesuit college of Louis-Le-Grand was renamed *Bibliothèque du Collège Égalité*. As in Paris, provincial academy and university libraries went to the *dépòts*. There were exceptions. If the Académie Française was undisturbed at the capital, the *mission littéraire* under Napoleon's Consulate, bringing numerous books and manuscripts from the provinces to Paris, spared the Medical School of the University of Montpellier (southeast France) because a high mission official happened to be a professor on its faculty who saw to it that his institution benefited. Many of the books of the old provincial scholarly institutions came ultimately to the stocks of the city libraries. Beginning about 1820, new academies were organized, and tended to found new libraries. The universities and their libraries, however, remained largely in the doldrums until much later.

All told, the fact that France, after twenty-five years of "vicissitudes," boasted nearly 150 "public libraries" distributed among the principal cities of the realm, with more than 3 million volumes "available to the public" daily, seemed astonishing to the librarian of the Mazarine, L.-C.-F. Petit-Radel. He thought it timely to investigate and explain how France had accumulated so large a number of "these permanent resources for general instruction" *(Recherches sur les Bibliothèques Anciennes et Modernes . . .*, Paris: Rey et Gravier, 1819, pp. 1–2). Noting the meager numbers of manuscripts held by even famous libraries, in comparison with the quantities of works produced since the invention of printing, and the coincidence with that event of the Turkish conquest of Constantinople, he had been fascinated by the transmission of the classical tradition in France; since surviving catalogs were few, he had hunted "first" citations of Latin and Greek authors wherever they could be found. His book-selection–oriented results he carefully distinguished from those of Louis Jacob's *Traicté des Plus Belles Bibliothèques* (1644) "and others of the same sort" (p. iv), focused on collectors, notable acquisitions, and library décor. If his mainly careful documentation followed precedent, his emphasis was apparently new, an attractive expression of both French nationalism and contemporary neoclassicism.

In Germany   The French Revolution also exerted a substantial influence on library life in Germany. The invasion by French armies and numerous important battles, and the transfer of books by conquest and purchase just mentioned, were only the direct consequences. The award of the left bank of the Rhine to France in 1795 generated pressures for compensation from the ousted German rulers; those pressures, and various other considerations, led to complex negotiations settled largely in 1803, with modifications after the defeat of Prussia in 1806 and 1807. Numerous small jurisdictions, including the erstwhile imperial cities, now became part of larger states. Many a fine collection of manuscripts, incunabula, and so on, became the property of a larger library, either a *Landesbibliothek* or a court or university library. Interweaving with these developments and frequently dominant was the belated secularization of certain church properties—accomplished a generation earlier in the Habsburg Empire territories (as noted above, pp. 251–253).

Among the numerous institutions suddenly enjoying greater repute than before was the Bavarian court library at Munich, enriched under Christoph von Aretin's leadership (1806–1807) mainly by significant transfers from about 150 cloister collections—more than 2,000 manuscripts from Tegernsee Abbey alone. In Protestant North Germany there was less to sequester.

Secularization also produced, particularly in both Bavaria and Prussia, regional book depots and so-called area *(Kreis)* Libraries. As in France the impact was minor, many of these collections ultimately being added to either a university or a city library.

The university libraries were affected variously. Some were divided among other collections: little Herborn University (45 miles north of Frankfort on the Main) broke up in 1812, for example; in 1817, while the Theological Faculty remained to become a seminary, most of the books arrived in 1817 in the Royal library in Berlin. Certain others moved bodily: thus in 1810 the university library of Frankfort on the Oder (50 miles east of Berlin) migrated about 125 miles southeast to Breslau, and was merged the next year with confiscated elements from various abbeys in a new "Royal and University Library." Still others, like the Mainz University library, remained where they were but became city institutions.

On the whole, these libraries remained weak. Except at Göttingen, there was still no government support, and most research depended on the professors' own collections. Space was often short for both collections and staff. Marburg for instance was in 1804 shelving books three deep and depending upon staff memory to find them; the book–cubic-foot ratio was evidently no better than it had been in many German libraries a century earlier. As late as 1812, Göttingen, the exemplar of loan service to students as well as professors, controlled the issue of books from a desk in the history lecture and exhibit hall, and had not yet even considered designating particular rooms for either reading or circulation transactions. In fact, the catalogers had had a workroom only since 1787. And that was the state of affairs at the institution which Napoleon treated far better than the others in his path—because, American student (1815) George Ticknor was told, he had thought of it as belonging " 'neither to Hanover nor to Germany but to Europe and the world' "(quoted in Ticknor's *Life and Letters,* 6th ed., Boston: Osgood, 1817, I:75).

Noteworthy on the other hand is the resumption of a practice once known in medieval libraries, limited though it was, of allowing an outsider to use the collection. Perhaps the earliest, acting thus in 1819, was Bonn University. More old wine in new bottles may be detected in the 1820 regulations governing the exchange of university publications among Prussia's universities.

Goethe's view was rather detached and skeptical, like Erasmus' before him and Emerson's after him. In 1796, when certain romances written by others were being credited to him, he wrote to Schiller that it was too bad they didn't live in the Dark Ages; in that case, posterity would have had to name a beautiful library after him. In 1801 he mused, in a strikingly bourgeois fashion, that at a library one seemed to be in the presence of "a great principal, the interest on which is being dispensed silently and beyond reckoning." But he was also concerned by the inability of libraries to keep control of the flood of printed matter received; and as late as 1821 he said sardonically that the librarian with no mysteries, no locked rooms, "is no true librarian"(ed. Richard Dobel, *Lexikon der Goethe-Zitate,* Zürich: Artemis, 1968, cols. 72–73).

If the great writer-scientist focused on the human condition at large, his day was nevertheless colored considerably by the rise of German nationalism. It had emerged in the mid-eighteenth century with heightening bourgeois consciousness and the German Enlightenment. Despite the basically localized and backward character of economic life—more than 300 sovereignties and a thick web of customs barriers—a new spirit was stirring. Compulsory school legislation had been developed in Prussia in 1716, 1763, and 1787, then codified in 1794. The bourgeois impulse in political economy and the practical arts was evident in the secondary-level *Realschulen;* and in such phenomena as the Physical-Economic Society established near Heidelberg in 1789, an academy with a library, its name suggesting affinity with the reform-minded Physiocrats of France. The elector soon afterward established a higher school for such studies which absorbed both the library and the funds of the society and in 1784 added the books to the Heidelberg University collection. While these steps were organization-oriented and exclusively male, there was taking shape also a broad market of both sexes, aristocratic and bourgeois, eager for a ready-reference home encyclopedia. Toward such readers were directed the efforts begun in 1796 by the Leipzig scholar R. G. Löbel, which emerged complete *(Conversations-Lexikon)* in 1809 under the management of the celebrated F. A. Brockhaus (1772–1823).

The French Revolution and the battlefield defeats by Napoleon meanwhile evoked many responses among the Germans, one of them a determination to reorganize German life. Deeply affected by the French Revolution were such men as Heinrich Stephani (1761–1850), a progressive teacher of reading and leader of the forces seeking to broaden state-backed education to cover all Germans, and Julius von Massow (1750–1816), Prussian Minister of State and Justice, who favored more and better practical instruction for the middle classes but argued against sharing such wealth with the manual laborers. Popular libraries alone, contended Stephani, would fulfill the promise of the invention of printing; some municipalities were already sponsoring them, but the state ought to pitch in, to absolve itself from sin and to counteract confusion. The last, indeed, Stephani called a "political necessity" (*Grundriss der Staatserziehungs-Wissenschaft,* Leipzig: Severin, 1797, pp. 24–25 of selective reproduction in Karl-Wolfgang Mirbt's invaluable *Pioniere des öffentlichen Bibliothekswesens*, Wiesbaden: Harrassowitz, 1969).

Massow responded encouragingly on several counts. The books needed for adult education but not yet written he would have stimulated by offering premiums and then recommending them officially. A few copies could be presented to the poorer libraries; in fact, said he, Prussia and some other states were already doing that and even supplying them with copies of articles on statecraft and public finance from a leading encyclopedia. He thought reading circles ought to be welcomed at "collegiate centers, schools, and the headquarters of merchant and craft groups." The book collections ought to serve youth as well as adults. But he meant primarily the youth of "the classes who have to be able to read," and he could not see providing such opportunities for laborers—actually better off, he was sure, if in the mean real world they could not read. Besides, there were not enough persons available with the skill to indoctrinate all the youth. (Massow seems here to document the problem attacked in 1810 by introducing teacher certification.)

On the other hand, an Enlightenment note is clear in Massow's concern lest the libraries' challenge to the contemporary successes of "low quality" fiction and other publications seem to infringe on the citizen's natural right to choose his own reading. He hoped to avoid such unpleasantness with sound book selection and reader guidance. But he did not rely for that upon "whoever happens to preside over" a reading circle or library; university faculties and other official educators were apparently to have the determining roles. (From Massow's monograph on improving public education, in the *Annalen des preussischen Schul- und Kirchwesens*, 1800, 1:76–143, 181–260, 361–395, as extracted, pp. 27–34 of Mirbt.)

Stephani returned to the fray in 1805 with a 415-page *System der öffentlichen Erziehung* (Berlin: Froelich), or "System of Public Education," from which emerge Prussian patterns of belief and commitment significantly different from those of the French. On behalf of the rural masses spurned by business-oriented Massow, Stephani argued their potential as the "producing class"; that was good Physiocratic doctrine, but few French Physiocrats would also have agreed with his basic belief in the church as the integrating element in society. Furthermore, whereas the French were more occupied with moving books around from one library to another than planning a national network, Stephani set forth a detailed outline for an entire hierarchy: national, provincial, city, and village; even some observations about special units for governmental and other technical needs. (A politico-historical library had been established in the Berlin Foreign Office in 1798.) Also in contrast with the French, he submitted that city and village library service needed attention much more than the national center. (Extracts in Mirbt, pp. 36–43.) A second edition of his *System* appeared in Erlangen in 1813.

The national library did nevertheless engage important energies. In 1780 it had been furnished with a new building by Frederick the Great, but Minister Massow in 1798 placed it under the Academy of Sciences in harmony with his utilitarian view of serving technical advance, and before long it was neglecting other concerns and trying to meet reader needs without any catalogs. At that very time celebrated philologist Wilhelm von Humboldt (1767-1835) was ending twelve years of foreign travel, during which he visited nearly every European library of consequence. Instrumental in the planning of the new University of Berlin, favored with the close friendship of a high official in the Ministry of Education and the backing of King Frederick William III, he was able to lay the groundwork of change for the benefit of the coming university even while serving from 1801 to 1808 as envoy in Rome. In 1809 the Royal Frederick William University was opened; and the Royal Library was transferred from the Academy to the direct oversight of the Ministry, beginning a new career of high distinction.

Complementarily, while several romantic popular writers appealed to the mass audience to take heart, philosopher Johann Gottlieb Fichte, in fourteen lectures to Berlin intellectuals (1807-1808), called for recognizing a German national genius independent of "Roman" elements and cultivating it by means of schooling open to all, regardless of customary class limitations. Thanks to this conjunction of bourgeois enlightenment and nationalism, enough sympathy was awakened in the Prussian bureaucracy to permit some reform. The famous Baron Karl vom Stein, a noble with experience in both mining and local government, was able to obtain (1807-1811) some alleviation of the feudal burdens upon the peasantry and greater self-government for the municipalities, advances which probably facilitated the creation of troops capable of repulsing and then defeating Napoleon. Although the Junker landowners of East Prussia obtained partial reversal of the reforms in 1816, serfdom was ended in one German state after another.

The momentum worked to the advantage of several German libraries. The restitutions of 1815 by the French were enlarged and improved partly because men like Josef Görres of the *Rheinische Merkur* thundered in their columns to drum up public pressure. Nor was France the only target. The negotiations of 1815-1816 which moved Europe into the conservatism-dominated age of Metternich included the return to Heidelberg, 200 years after its abduction to the Vatican, of a large portion of the Palatine Library.

How deep the new impulses were felt is not altogether clear. The reforms of Stein and his associates left important marks on centralization and standardization in German education, reported at length not long afterward by such influential foreign observers as the Frenchman Victor Cousin and the Americans Horace Mann and Henry Barnard. That the book collections in the *Gymnasia* and other secondary schools were affected seems likely, but the cited evaluators hardly mention them. Whether school libraries in early nineteenth-century Germany—and France—were indeed inconsequential, or have been undeservedly neglected by historians, is one more matter for research.

Elsewhere in Europe and in Latin America The events in France affected library life in other places, too, in varying degrees. Evidently a direct product was the founding of the university library in Naples in 1812, under the rule of Napoleon's brother-in-law Murat. Direct at one remove, so to speak, was the emergence of cantonal libraries in Switzerland; the French-managed "Helvetian Republic" of 1798 projected a centralized plan, and part of the rebellion ending French rule in 1803 was a decentralizing emphasis on the several cantons. Somewhat similar were the events of 1793 and 1794 in Poland. Citing Jacobinism as an excuse (that is, the French revolutionary virus), the Prussians joined the invasion of Poland in 1793, which led to the Second Partition. The next year saw the noble but hopeless revolt led by Kosciuszko and the removal to St. Petersburg of the library of Count Zaluski, regarded as the unofficial national Polish collection. (It was returned to the Poles after the Bolshevik Revolution.) The final partition (1795) placed Polish Galicia under the Austrians, who allowed cultural autonomy; taking advantage of that and the eleven-year-old university library at Lemberg (present Lvov), the Poles by 1817 managed to organize an institute to perpetuate their traditions and attract to it many documents and books.

The stolen Zaluski collection meanwhile occasioned the erection of a new building in St. Petersburg; opened to the public in 1814 was the Imperial Public Library (renamed in 1932 for satirist Saltykov-Shchedrin) with 300,000 volumes and the right to legally deposit copies of new books. The Russians also established a university with a library in Warsaw in 1817; it likewise enjoyed legal deposit rights, but only to Russian publications, Polish imprints being ignored.

More attractive to posterity is the rise of significant private collections in Russia's leading cities, spurred initially in the eighteenth century by the French enlightenment and after 1812 often manifesting nationalist coloration. Notable was the subsidizing of document publication and history writing by N. P. Rumiantsev (1754–1826), diplomat, promoter of commerce (as a minister, 1801–11), and bibliophile; his own remarkable book "museum," founded in St. Petersburg posthumously (1831) and transferred to Moscow in 1861, became eventually the heart of the Lenin Library. Favoring the prominence of the private collections was the otherwise distressing fact that state and religious holidays kept the state libraries closed no less than 100 days each year. Yet the Rumiantsevs and appreciative readers were a handful, whereas true popularity attached only to newspapers and light novels. Academy of Science publications were often unsalable and distributed to members at cost; indeed their disposition for 4.5 rubles per pound, in St. Petersburg in 1808, was not a unique event. Healthy library life would require expanded business, industry, and literacy.

More remotely affected, but still owing something to the bourgeois-national impulse of the French Revolution, were the new national or royal libraries in Lisbon (1796), The Hague (1798), Budapest (1802), Oslo (then Christiania, 1811), and Reykjavik (1818).

In South America, Napoleon's invasion of Spain and Portugal produced contradictory effects. The exiled "legitimate" ruler of Spain was supported by the upper classes of Argentina and opposed by those of Chile; the expanded activity of the town councils in Buenos Aires and Santiago de Chile included founding national libraries in 1810 and 1813, respectively. Rio de Janeiro's leading citizens welcomed the exiled sovereign of Portugal and among other things founded a similar library in 1810.

Little Touched by the French Revolution: Anglo-American Library Life

Owing very little to the great changes in Western Europe were the libraries of Great Britain and the United States of America. In both countries there was bitter partisanship in the 1790s, colored distinctly by the French Revolution, expressed in part by assaults on certain political and religious publications. Since the circulating libaries in both countries and some English book clubs possessed a few of these items, they were fair game for such organs of strident respectability as the *Anti-Jacobin*. One consequence in England was the success of those who advertised moderation in their wares, like the celebrated bookdealer James Lackington. The nationalism evoked or strengthened on the Continent and in South America by way of reaction against Napoleon meant little in England or the United States. But the war-induced inflation sent up the price of library subscriptions in England, and the perspective for libraries and everything clse in the United States was altered profoundly by Thomas Jefferson's decision to buy from Napoleon the great central third of a continent then called "Louisiana."

Nationalism may have played some part in Parliament's passing a new copyright act in 1814, which extended the author's rights to twenty-eight years, required that all published works be registered, and obliged the publisher to deliver one copy immediately to the British Museum and ten others on demand to the other libraries with depository privileges. The British Museum responded with alacrity, assigning an agent to Stationers' Hall, where 500 works were collected in 1814 and 1,000 in 1815. The other copyright depository institutions also rose to the opportunity, sparking resentment which later led to a deflation of the depository system. In the newly independent and very self-conscious United States, meanwhile, local copyright acts of the 1780s were capped by a federal act of 1790 protecting authors and their heirs, and a supplement of 1802 extending copyright privilege to the creators of prints; but copyright deposit was not yet involved.

Britain When the Bastille fell, the libraries of Great Britain continued mainly their familiar ways, but variation did occur. Perhaps most traditional were the university and college libraries, broad in holdings but quite restrictive in use permitted. Ecclesiastical collectiors, especially in the parishes, were managed more liberally, but their offerings were usually very narrow. This proved to be true of rebels as well as orthodox. When the Wesleyans organized in 1792 the New Circulating Library in Manchester, and when a breakaway group established Zion's Temple there in 1804, drama and light literature were excluded, although a great deal of sensational reading matter was on hand in the shape of criminal trials and the sufferings of missionaries and travelers. Besides, the moral suasion element long sustained by the S. P. C. K. gained new strength when the Religious Tract Society undertook in 1799 an evangelical publication program to contest "weakness" in or indifference to Christian views and soon rivalled the S. P. C. K. in stocking libraries.

So far as essentially secular types are concerned, changing times exerted influence differentially. As the industrial revolution flowered, the immediate negative effect was the migration of unlettered working people from the countryside of Ireland and west England to the factory towns of Yorkshire and Lancashire. One consequence was the educational crisis resolved for the moment by means of the Sunday School movement and the monitorial system of instruction. On the positive side was the rapid rise in industrial productivity, more well-being for the upper strata, and the increasing interest in libraries on the part of the upper middle class, notably in the industrial centers. Some of these professional men, business and manufacturing officials, gentry and clergy, were members of the recently organized Literary and Philosophical Societies, normally outfitted with libraries, serving individuals of scientific bent and at least modest means who were as a rule not of the university world. Quite a few others enjoyed neither academic nor learned society opportunities, and were not satisfied with either church collections or the lighter fare in the book clubs or subscription libraries, let alone the circulating libraries, outstanding for plays and fiction and particularly on the latter count less than fully respectable.

Thus did a new wave of book clubs appear in the 1790s, quite similar to the first, a century earlier. In 1821 there were reportedly more than 500. The stronger among them were soon adding annually 300 titles or even more, thanks in part to the increasing number of learned society publications issued and the sets of historical records distributed by the government. They therefore had to consider a permanent home for their resources. Unlike many an earlier model, they had no endowment or substantial bequest, and if any corporate auspices were to be furnished they had to organize it themselves. Accordingly emerged the latest of a series of joint-stock type of ventures, often, but not always, called a "proprietary" library. The members met once a year to determine policy; the librarian was not a colleague but an employee who enforced rather strict regulations and collected rather stiff fines for infractions thereof. The group at industrial center Leeds erected a building in 1807, and paid off in 1852 the last installment of debt on 100 loans (with interest) of £50 each; this was apparently not uncommon.

Although the libraries of cultural and educational institutions—including novel science-serving collections (medical, 1773 and 1800; Linnaean Society, 1788)—outnumbered the church and middle-class subscription libraries, they did not on the whole reach the working class. Furthermore, if the subscription libraries appeared early in the nineteenth century not only in metropolitan centers but in market towns, their fees were too high for the mass of country readers and their buildings often beyond easy reach of those readers' homes. The latter were served, here and there, as before, by parish collections of vicar-encouraged "libraries" of secular stripe; financing varied.

Conspicuous in the post-Napoleonic unrest was the "itinerating" library plan launched by small-town merchant Samuel Brown in 1817, in the Scottish county of East Lothian. Some fifty volumes, more than half religious, would be deposited for two years in every village and hamlet where a "librarian" could be found to care for them; the idea was to have no resident more than a mile and a half from a "library"; at the end of the two years, each collection would move to another location. By 1830 there were perhaps fifty such installations, underwritten by Brown and his friends; that was the peak. If the sponsors were not (?) consciously counteracting challenge ultimately political, some later emulators of their technique explicitly were, as in Glamorgan County, Wales, in 1831.

None of these types, apparently, satisfied all needs for pamphlets and periodical material. At any rate, in parallel with the book club, the early nineteenth century witnessed pamphlet clubs and magazine- and newspaper-reading societies. The magazine groups were more numerous than the book groups, and the newspaper societies by far the most numerous, until the newspaper tax was reduced in 1836 and individual purchase rapidly broadened. To this extent was continued the predominant separation: books in libraries and nonscholarly periodicals elsewhere.

Finally, it must be noted that the commercial circulating library enjoyed strikingly enhanced success, along with the novel and play so important to its stock. William Lane of the Minerva Press pioneered in promoting such enterprise in the provincial towns, announcing in the local press in the late 1780s his

> "GENERAL CATALOGUE . . ., containing several Thousand Volumes on every Subject . . . the Result of Twenty Years Care and Attention. . . . In order that an *immediate* Supply may be received, a large Collection is kept ready bound, and a *Library* from *Twenty* to *Five Hundred Pounds,* properly arranged and classed with a Printed *Catalogue* may be ready at a Week's Notice. . . ." (*Leeds Intelligencer,* May 1, 1787, as quoted by Dorothy Blakey in *The Minerva Press, 1790-1820,* London: Printed for the Bibliographical Society at Oxford, 1939, pp. 120–121.)

Thousands were more than ready to rent a novel, although few would have been able to buy one. Lane was a solid success. New York City bookstore owner H. Caritat became an agent of his for a few years starting in 1802; Lane's "Minerva" merchandise was also known as far as the haunts of the British in India. In 1826 a popular annual declared that " 'almost every small town in the kingdom' " had one (quoted in Kaufman, p. 193). Thanks to these enterprises, fiction was to flourish on a rental basis side by side with what was thought appropriate for "libraries," until years later fiction too was partly absorbed by those libraries.

Canada   Rather similarly, the publisher of the *Quebec Mercury* opened in 1797, in the capital of the new (1791) British province of Lower Canada (Quebec), a library and periodical reading room. He even announced that he would buy for it such French books as their possessors would sell him. The Lower Canada Assembly had its own book collection, which by 1817 reportedly held 1,000 volumes. Loyalists departing the new United States tended to go to English-speaking provinces. In 1800 they founded a "public" library at Niagara in Upper Canada (Ontario); the income from subscriptions and annual fees produced by 1818 £500, of which one-fourth was paid to the librarian. In 1820 the latter assumed full control and converted the enterprise into a rental library. A like outlet is said to have been established meanwhile by other Loyalists in eastern Quebec.

U.S. Public Libraries   In the new United States of America, even more than in Great Britain, the French Revolution and Napoleon were rather remote apart from their impact on shipping near European ports. As in Poland, Jacobinism was allegedly detected, in the views of the Jeffersonians of the 1790s. General unhappiness over the Reign of Terror helped fuel a new

wave of pulpit denunciation of backsliders: among those pilloried were athe-
ists, drunkards, and consumers of cheap fiction.

On the other hand, with the war of independence over, and the federal
Constitution well on its way to ratification, life was kinder to substantial
portions of the white population. Among the classic observations of Henry
Adams upon conditions in 1800 was the judgment that "all the public libraries in the United States—collegiate, scientific, or popular, endowed or unen-
dowed—could hardly show fifty thousand volumes, including duplicates. . . ." Adams further mentioned particularly the "numerous small
subscription libraries" thought to be modeled after Franklin's Library Company, "containing fifty or a hundred volumes . . . scattered in country
towns." (*History of the United States of America,* New York: Scribner, 1889,
1:61.)

Although such writing was a useful precedent for American historiography, it must be noted that Adams made no use of available corrective data.
He was apparently not aware of the rapid increase at the end of the century
of social libraries in New England and commercial circulating libraries in the
large towns everywhere. At least 50 social libraries had been founded in
New England through the 1780s; the next decade brought nearly 60 more;
the years 1790 to 1815 added more than 500. Hard times induced partly by
the Embargo Act of December 1807 and the struggles with Britain ending in
1814 then interrupted library advance harshly in the northeast, and in the
ensuing years the social library center of gravity shifted to the west.

The victory over the Indians at Fallen Timbers in 1794 and the treaty
the next year with the Spanish which opened New Orleans to United States
merchants encouraged heavy migration across the Alleghenies, mainly under New England leadership. A few who settled near Marietta, Ohio, established in 1796 the strikingly (and perhaps uniquely) named Belpré Farmers
Library, which lasted about twenty years. The same year witnessed the more
conventionally titled Lexington, Kentucky, Library Society. Although it began with a mere 400 volumes, its future was brighter than that of the Belpré
venture because, until the rise of Cincinnati in the 1830s, Lexington was to
remain second only to New Orleans in commercial and cultural significance.
Noteworthy in Lexington's annals are the two legislatively authorized lotteries by which the library raised money before 1818, and the absorption of the
four (?)-year-old Lexington Junvenile Library said to have been organized by
a group of boys, some of their "directors" being invited to sit with the
Lexington Library board. Altogether, neither the books carried with emi-
grants nor those sold in the bookshops of towns like Cincinnati were
enough to satisfy the settlers' desires: in 1840 Ohio alone boasted 160 social
or more nearly public libraries.

The basic pattern of these institutions continued to be the voluntary
association of subscribers, most of whom were persons of modest means:
professionals, businessmen, and some farmers and craftsmen. Toward the
end of the eighteenth century, the larger associations, if not already chartered as corporations, found that device advantageous to the enforcement of
their regulations and generally businesslike conduct of their affairs.
("Larger" meant, up to 1800, the six holding 10,000 or more volumes, and
perhaps also the twenty-five with collections of less than 10,000, but at least

3,000.) Their internal procedures were democratic. A few, founded in the leading cities by groups of prominent persons frequently called "proprietors," preferred the closer control of the partnership, allowing the use of their books by outsiders for fees. The first law conferring corporate character upon a library was the detailed guide enacted in New York in 1796. But libraries did not touch any private competitive interest beyond a bit of real estate, and such concern was hardly worth the trouble. Whether the legislators elsewhere reasoned thus or not, the subsequent statutes for library incorporation tended to be briefer and more general.

Tribute to the impact of contemporary events is the conspicuous provision, in several charters of the years toward 1820, forbidding the incorporators of the library from engaging in banking. Since the shortage of hard currency was particularly felt in the West, and bank ingenuity was considerable, it is not surprising that four such charters were issued in 1819 and 1820 by the state of Kentucky alone.

No more than private book collections were these libraries now dominated by theology. North as well as South, histories and biographies were prominent, and in some social libraries more numerous than religious works. Literature was close behind, and fiction was rising fast. Science was still weak: the famous real estate agent and diarist Manasseh Cutler (1742–1823) noted in 1799 "few" books in the public libraries on "natural history . . . and those mostly ancient authors who wrote before the Linnaean system was formed"; he also thought "our booksellers" were importing nothing in that line (*Life, Journals and Correspondence,* eds. W. P. Cutler and J. P. Cutler, Cincinnati: Clark, 1888, II:298). Thaddeus Harris, a Harvard librarian, offered in 1793 a book selection guide for social libraries. Concerned for morality and relying on respectable English reviews, even he included eleven novels among the 276 titles recommended. His suggested eighteen in applied science were certainly not common in the social library holdings on record, and it is very probable that they did have more fiction than he advised. Whether or not anyone used his pamphlet is not known. But he is credited with having advised the "Coonskin Library" (Ohio) representative who was applying (1803–1804) to fifty-one books his $70 from the sale of furs.

While romances were as much as one-fifth of the titles in social libraries, they composed 20 to perhaps 50 percent of the stock of the commercial circulating libraries. During the years under review those outlets multiplied not only in major centers like Boston and New York but in many smaller communities. Disapproving observers were not lacking; some attacked the fiction purveyors publicly. It seems, however, that the circulating library proprietors were hampered less by ideological opposition than by business problems. Dealing in books alone was possible for some enterprisers in the large towns, but even there and certainly in the smaller communities books were handled together with various other commodities. This custom was to remain familiar.

U. S. Campus Libraries, Old and New   Fiction and light reading were also responsible, together with liberal loan policies, for the rise at this time of the college literary society libraries. The restrictions upon lower classmen at the college libraries had evoked the new instrument as early as 1769 at Yale, whose Linonia Society collection reached 475 volumes by 1800 and was housed in the college library building. Perhaps the largest of these undertakings was the combination of two at Dartmouth. The aggregate collection numbered 2,000 in 1799, and upon parting company at the end of that year, each of the two erstwhile partners soon reached that size individually. Many decades were to elapse before this service was rendered unnecessary by the character of the official libraries of the colleges.

The resources of the college libraries were still very modest, not just across the Alleghenies at Transylvania University in Kentucky, but in the numerous institutions in the long-settled areas. British traveler Isaac Weld wrote of Princeton in June 1795, "The library, which we were shewn, is most wretched; consisting, for the most part, of old theological books, not even arranged with any regularity" (*Travels through the States of North America,* 1807; Johnson Reprint, 1968, 1:259). When George Ticknor read in 1814 the recent work on Germany by Madame de Staël, he looked in vain for a German book in the shops of Boston and Cambridge and the Harvard College library; he could not even find a good teacher of the language. As Henry Adams wrote many years afterward, Goethe and Schiller were in 1800 known in translation if at all, and "as for deeper studies, search in America would be useless for what was rare in England or France . . . the Western nations knew no more of German thought than of Egyptian hieroglyphics" (*History,* I:123).

Harvard's own president, John T. Kirkland, declared in 1818 that "however respectable" the colleges might be, in relation to undergraduates or "the mass of readers," they were "as general repositories of knowledge, of course, inconsiderable" (*North American Review,* 8:193, December 1818). He went on to point out that Harvard itself, with some 28,000 volumes, second only to the Library Company of Philadelphia (30,000), was far from holding more than a paltry selection of what was then at the disposal of readers in the Western world. He rapidly sized up the situation in one category after another. Among the numerous items lacking even at Harvard were "several periodical works of deserved reputation, and the transactions of different learned societies," the latest in belles lettres "republished in this country" (he could have said "pirated" but did not), and "the American authors, not contained in the University library, which ought to be collected and preserved there" (*North American Review,* 8:196–197).

Such was the state of affairs at a Harvard which lately had established chairs in science and the literatures of France, Spain and Germany. True, thanks to several gifts, it had been possible to register certain advances. George Ticknor, then studying at Göttingen, had in January 1817 accepted appointment as professor of French and Spanish on condition that his salary start with the date of the offer, July 1816, and that it be applied to the purchase of books in those fields. At that, he long afterward told the compiler of his memoirs, the Harvard library suddenly seemed to him, upon his return from Göttingen, no more than " 'a closetful of books' " (Ticknor, *Life, Letters, and Journals,* footnote, I:72). Librarian Andrews Norton was meanwhile appealing to editors and publishers to contribute to Harvard periodicals, newspapers, pamphlets, "&c," promising that they would be bound; he added that "in consequence of a request lately made" several were already sending in "different publications" (*North American Review*, 5:431-432, September 1817).

Sharp struggles then characterized affairs in both the Harvard Corporation—as for example it broadened the Board of Overseers beyond the principal elected state officials and Congregational ministers—and the legislature. Harvard had lately lost some ancient privileges such as the tolls from the ferry over the Charles River, the compensatory annuity being regarded as substantially less promising. President Kirkland found it necessary to challenge an articulate opposition which applauded efforts to achieve national glory but doubted the need for "a great library . . . and whether we have not now more books than we can read.—It is said, that a selection is better than a whole Göttingen library. We may ask, Better for whom, for what? The notion is not that each student or each professor is to read the whole, but what his purpose requires." (*North American Review*, 8:197-198.)

One could of course buy thousands of volumes not worth "half the expense of their freight." What mattered was "the literary selection, that is, what author,—the bibliographical, what edition. . . ." Further, "Regard should be had to what the library already has, what other collections within· reach have, to what is first wanted as being of common use and essential service, and to what is wanted in particular departments." (*North American Review,* 8:198.) The proper way to proceed was to send abroad, not a professor who would inevitably acquire at auctions what he knew best and probably serve badly the other interests of the library, but a "faithful agent" armed with the desires of all the various departments.

After all, did we not want "something written, that will give a tone to the nation, that will promote general taste in the people, that will furnish our children something to boast of?" (*North American Review,* 8:199.) Such a work could not be guaranteed even with a great library but was inconceivable without it.

During the next two decades more white youth went to college, and advocates of "modern" studies challenged (vainly, for the moment) the classical curriculum. But the institutions were still quite small and usually poor, the style was austerely practical, and neither the faculty nor the students were concerned much with library books. Most of the latter were gifts (sometimes cast-offs), and a librarian fit to stimulate change was a rarity. Perhaps the best feature of this generally depressing scene was the frequent presence in the collection of transactions of learned societies.

Urban Sophistication and Libraries in the United States   If the educated were not ready for innovation on the campus, there were signs of it in town. As the nineteenth century opened with independence still new and not entirely free of challenge, to demonstrate that the new nation's writers could match England's literary achievements became a prime objective with a group of Bostonians. They respected the scientific color of the enlightenment, were determined to link high-quality writing and morals, and were conscious of the female and youthful portions of the white population. They began in 1803 by putting up their own money on behalf of a journal of "polite literature," *The Monthly Anthology and Boston Review.* (Did that event hasten the appearance in January 1804 of the first *Catalogue of All the Books Printed in the United States, with the Prices, and Places Where Published . . . Published by the Booksellers in Boston . . . that the public may see the rapid progress of book printing in a country, where, twenty years since, scarcely a book was published?)* By October 1805 they chose to become a society and within three weeks voted to form a library of periodicals for their own use, in the fashion of the magazine societies and certain new libraries in contemporary England. The associates began by contributing some of their own possessions to the common store. In May 1806 they agreed upon an "Anthology Reading-Room" and advertised for subscriptions: it was to be a " *'Public Reading-room, ' "* affording the subscribers " 'not only . . . an agreeable place of resort, but opportunities of literary intercourse, and the pleasure of perusing the principal European and American periodical publications, at an expense not exceeding that of a single *daily* paper.' "

To this end were proposed quarters " 'easy of access, in a central part of the town,' " open from 9 A.M. to 9 P.M., furnished with paper, pens, and ink. The stock would include newspapers from Boston and other towns in the United States and from Paris and London; " 'magazines, reviews, and scientific journals' "; Parlimentary debates and Army and Navy lists; " 'the most interesting literary and political pamphlets in Europe and America' "; bibliographies, the catalogs of London and Paris bookdealers, and " 'works of useful reference' "; and maps and charts. The magazines and newspapers would be bound in semiannaul volumes. (The quoted "Proposal" is reproduced on pp. 6-7 of Josiah Quincy's *History of the Boston Athenaeum,* Cambridge: Metcalf, 1851.)

A subscription cost 10 dollars a year. More than 100 were bought promptly, bringing in the very tidy sum of $1,600.

In October 1806 the sponsors obtained a charter which contemplated eventually converting the entire enterprise into a " 'Public Library, one of those institutions, of which every scholar in most parts of our country feels the want.' " Since government " 'from its nature' " was not to be counted on, the " 'industry and munificence of individuals' " had to meet the need. The appropriate channel, they suggested, was an increase in the receipts of their journal, *The Monthly Anthology,* the profits of which would be so applied. (Quoted by Quincy, pp. 8-9, from the Editors' Address in vol. 7.) By November 1807 they were congratulating all concerned on the progress made. Wealth was increasing, and one would best " 'guard against the pernicious effects of luxury' " by stimulating " 'a taste for intellectual enjoyment.' " Law should be maintained "'by manners, manners by opinion, and opinion by works in which genius and taste unite to embellish the truth.'" A letter was printed from one of the group who was visiting England and waxed eloquent over the books and journals "'always accessible to every man of letters, who wishes to consult them,'" in the Liverpool Athenaeum; he pleaded for comparable achievement in "'our dearly cherished Athenaeum'" (in Boston). (Quincy, pp. 9-10.)

The Boston Athenaeum was formally projected on January 1, 1807, in a document signed by eleven gentlemen, two of whom were "Hon." and three of whom were "Rev." Among them was twenty-four-year-old Obadiah

Rich, son of a successful fish merchant, already a member of the Massachusetts Historical Society, and later to win fame in the book trade. They noted that the "'Anthology Reading-Room and Library'" had to date more than 1,000 volumes, mainly donations, and that they the trustees intended to found an institution similar to the

> "Athenaeum and Lyceum of Liverpool; combining the advantages of a public library, containing the great works of learning and science in all languages, particularly such rare and expensive publications as are not generally to be obtained in this country; with a reading or news room, furnished with all the celebrated political, literary, and commercial journals of the day, foreign and domestic. And no book, pamphlet, or newspaper is ever to be permitted to be taken from the rooms by subscribers; so that the patrons of the institution may be certain at all times of finding any publications, which they may have occasion to read or refer to." (Quoted in Quincy, p. 12.)

The already mentioned policies for book and journal selection were stated again, in point 2 of the appended rules. Point 5 invited subscribers to recommend for acquisition "'any book'" thought proper for the library, and "'any'" newspaper or journal for the reading room. Number 6 provided for placing new books and magazine issues "'on the tables of the library reading-room'" long enough for their "'perusal.'" (Quoted in Quincy, p. 14.)

The library was open (point 8) to Bostonians who were subscribers, and each was entitled to bring in one guest "'not residing within five miles of the library.'" Tickets of admission were to be issued when individuals from some distance visited Boston who had given the library a "'valuable present'" (point 10). Honorary memberships were authorized (point 11) for the supreme, circuit, and district court judges, the Harvard faculty, and the presidents of the nearby learned societies. (Quoted in Quincy, pp. 14-15.)

Following this guidance was a list of the periodicals already ordered. It included more than a score of English titles, and fifteen in French. None named was in German, Spanish, Italian, or Russian. "'All the American publications,'" it was emphasized, were received in exchange for the *Anthology* and cost the subscribers to the library nothing. (Quoted in Quincy, p. 17.)

The catalogs of "'public libraries, . . . museums and botanical institutions, literary projects, &c. &c.'" were solicited. "'Booksellers and printers in any part of the United States'" were urged to send promptly any books or pamphlets newly issued. Efforts were being made to obtain material likewise from Europe; that would take longer, and loans of French and English periodicals would be appreciated meanwhile. A catalog of the library was to be published as soon as possible, including the names of the subscribers and donors. (Quoted in Quincy, pp. 17-18.)

These tactics relative to periodicals were doubtless well advised. The history of serials acquisitions is well larded with entries like this minute of the American Philosophical Society, dated October 17, 1800: "Mr. Vaughan [the librarian] handed [in] the 2d & 3d numbers of the Recreations in Agriculture &c which had lain in the Custom house many months for want of a letter of advice" (*Early Proceedings*, p. 304).

The Proprietors of the Boston Athenaeum were incorporated by the Commonwealth of Massachusetts on February 13, 1807. Duly noted in the legislative charter was the national advantage of providing books and other items, such as "'models of new and useful machines, and . . . paintings . . . more especially of our native artists . . . not usually to be met with in our country, but which are deemed indispensable to those who would perfect themselves in the sciences. . . .'" There was also local advantage to "'this Commonwealth,'" which lacked what "'have long since partially existed in many of our sister States.'" To the customary corporate privileges were added provision (section 5) for free access "'for the time being'" by the legislators and chief executives, and (section 6) the right of the Legislature to check the conduct of the corporation's affairs. (Quoted in Quincy, pp. 18–21.)

In May 1807 the Proprietors submitted a "'memoir'" to the "'friends of improvement,'" repeating most of the foregoing and adding the following appeals, first to "'parents, who consider the temptations surrounding young men, and the connection between employment and innocence.'" Those of "'proper age and deportment'" might have access to the Athenaeum like an adult. Rather than spending their time wastefully, foolishly, or dangerously, they would employ it usefully, sharpening their curiosity and improving their taste. (Quoted in Quincy, pp. 25, 34.)

What the institution might do for the "'character of men,'" moreover, was of clear albeit indirect benefit to the women. The Athenaeum would go further. Lectures would be offered to which the ladies would be invited, and they would enjoy also "'the use of the circulating books of the library.'" (Quoted in Quincy, p. 34.)

The usefulness of lectures on chemistry, natural philosophy, astronomy, "'and other related subjects, calculated to interest the young of both sexes'" and diffuse knowledge of nature, could be taken for granted. (Quoted in Quincy, p. 35.)

Altogether, the institution represented "'additional security to public and private morals.'" It would offset "'show and equipage, convivial entertainments, festive assemblies, and theatrical exhibitions.'" In a society where "'the love of pleasure and the means of it are continually augmenting . . . the wise and patriotic'" might confidently be expected to bless the Athenaeum. Let it be noted that the library was so planned as "'not to interfere with the interest of any other in operation,'" and that the other departments of the institution were unique. Boston ought to have what Charleston, Baltimore, Philadelphia, and New York already had. In days when "'we are not called upon for large contributions to national purposes'" a better local investment than the Athenaeum was hard to imagine. (Quoted in Quincy, pp. 36–40, passim.)

Only a few weeks later, on June 22, 1807, the British frigate *Leopard* fired on the American frigate *Chesapeake,* and burdens on the pocket were plainly in prospect. By August the proprietors decided to drop the scheduled campaign for a new building. If they regarded this disappointment as further vindication of upper-class Boston's opposition to the embargo, of Federalist resistance to the policies of Mr. Jefferson, it would not be surprising.

That the Athenaeum Proprietors were offering books and periodicals on the same premises was in harmony with the latest practice in similar libraries elsewhere, not only abroad but in the Philadelphia library of the sixty-year-old American Philosophical Society. The Athenaeum rule that all materials remain in the library was also quite familiar, but differed from the Philosophical Society's just-adopted (1803) policy of allowing members to take "from the hall . . . any volume" other than "the latest and the loose numbers" of the journals received. (*Early Proceedings*, p. 342). How to meet the convenience of the individual reader of the moment and also protect the rights of all readers was indeed a poser. Conditions in the United States of America were going to nourish the first horn of the dilemma more than ever before.

In two other respects, the older organization seems to have advanced beyond the newer one. On October 19, 1804, the officers of the Philosophical Society suggested that a "lion's mouth" be provided for the deposit of the members' proposals for book purchase; the device was reported ready for use two months later, but the precedent does not appear in Quincy's narrative of the Athenaeum Library. In 1809 the American Philosophical Society officers recommended that some money be appropriated for translating portions of "eminent German Books" likely to be "beneficial to this country" and not already available in French or English. No action was taken by the Philadelphia group; the Boston gentlemen are not reported as even discussing the matter.

Sketch of the 1804 innovation at the American Philosophical Society Library in Philadelphia. (Courtesy of The Bettmann Archive, Inc.)

On the other hand, the Athenaeum Proprietors were perhaps pioneers in their consideration for the ladies and the youth. White male youth were shortly to be favored with several instruments of library service oriented specifically toward those with some ambition and skills. The Boston manifestation was not thus specific; indeed it seems to have been generated rather by talk of restlessness among the youth of the comfortable element. White female youth, mentioned fleetingly, were perhaps thought of similarly. Adult white women were offered a bit of library service cautiously and apologetically, a remarkable fact when one observes that women writing under their own names (several others preferred to use male or neuter pseudonyms) were prominent among the leading contemporary producers of didactic novels and other guides to behavior widely represented on social and circulating library shelves. Extant evidence reveals almost nothing of the part such women may have played at such libraries. Why were the Boston gentlemen the first, apparently, to take their notable step? Was it the influence of the women they knew? Or something else? Scholarship has not yet accounted for the lag in the other libraries. As for the Negroes, the Athenaeum advances did not cover even the handful who were free.

Whatever may have been known in the West about Boston's Athenaeum, it was that term rather than "library" which the sponsors on at least one occasion applied to an institution whose resources included periodicals and newspapers. Such was the character of the Lexington, Kentucky, Athenaeum, launched in 1818 with the aid of a lottery. Perhaps search of local data will reveal others.

Meanwhile, other men of the proprietors' stripe were eager to outdo their peers of New York and Philadelphia, who had some time since led the way with the Library Company, the American Philosophical Society, and the New York Society Library. The Bostonians organized the American Academy of Arts and Sciences in 1780, which soon boasted a significant collection of books in physical science, listed in a printed catalog in 1802. By 1800, of the twenty-odd additional libraries of that gentlemen-scholarly sort in the United States, one-third were in Massachusetts. The Massachusetts Historical Society was founded in Boston in 1791 and incorporated three years afterward, its library quickly renowned and emulated in other states. Altogether, the more or less public collections of Boston and Cambridge were in 1817 believed to hold perhaps 60,000 volumes, including considerable duplications; that was probably more than New York City but less than Philadelphia. Boston was active in less public fashion too. In 1804 was begun the collection incorporated in 1814 and later known as the Social Law Library; in 1808 the Boston Female Asylum was equipped with some books; in 1815 the reading resources of the Handel and Haydn Society were organized as the first music library in the United States.

The State and Libraries in the United States Of tremendous importance were the vote of the Massachusetts Legislature in 1811 to exchange its official papers with the other states, and the agreement of Congress on December 27, 1813, to furnish to each state's executive department one copy each of its journals and documents. State libraries were not then a novelty, at least in principle (the facts of their realization are somewhat in doubt), but their prospects had thus been strikingly enhanced. South Carolina boasted one in 1814, and twenty-three more states and territories had acquired similar assets by 1840, mainly law-centered and dependent in part on exchanges.

Furthermore, the 1813 federal statute prescribed furnishing the congressional journals and documents to each college, university, and historical society in the United States. Subsequent actions added more, such as the 1817 provision for distributing sets of state papers. Besides, in 1814, the American Antiquarian Society Library at Worcester, Massachusetts, was placed on the distribution list, one reason it became an invaluable repository of Americana.

Early tariff rates were also designed in part to assist cultural enrichment. Although the comprehensive act of July 4, 1789, imposed a 5 percent duty on imported books and maps, as well as on nearly all other imported articles, the law of August 10, 1790, exempted books owned by persons coming to reside in the United States, and scientific instruments imported for the use of institutions of learning. These protected categories were in April 1816 broadened to include works of art; and the purpose could be not just the benefit of colleges but nearly anything literary. In May 1824 sophisticated distinctions were introduced, levying different charges according to date of publication, language of publication, and whether or not the book was bound. Local industry was protected by widely applicable rates of 26 cents per pound on books in sheets or boards and 30 cents per pound on bound books. Books printed in Latin or Greek paid half those rates. For those in other foreign languages, or printed before 1775, the charge was 4 cents a volume.

United States "Public" Libraries Evaluated The precise impact of these measures on United States libraries does not seem to have been studied. But there evidently was a basis for the mainly harsh English judgment published in *Blackwood's Edinburgh Magazine* in 1819, and answered the same year in the *North American Review* by Sidney Willard (1780-1856), librarian at Harvard in his early twenties, and thereafter professor of Hebrew and Oriental languages. The public libraries of the United States, wrote the critics, were "'for the most part pitiful,'" despite the progress at Harvard. Most of the college libraries were "'inconsiderable'"; none of those of the literary and scientific societies were "'important enough to be mentioned particularly.'" Hardly worth counting were "'the social libraries, as they are called, being small collections of books, made up in the country towns by subscription, which are about equal in value and number to those nicely matched octodecimos, that are put into a gift and lacquered box for children, and distinguished by the name of a juvenile library.'" If there were some 500,000 printed individual titles "'in the world,'" the United States was furnishing about "'one-seventeenth of the means necessary for extending learning to the utmost'" and about one-thirteenth of what was available in Paris alone. (Quoted by Willard in *North American Review*, 9:246-247.)

There was no reason to question the figures, responded Willard, but it should be realized that the public libraries had been assembled under difficulties, that Harvard had had to start anew after the fire of 1764, and that the other colleges were "either situated in parts of the country where there is not much wealth, or in small states, where there is little public munificence";

or they were too young to have obtained much money for books so far. "We are very far from being reconciled to our poverty" in books, he concluded, "but we wish it to appear no greater than it is." Of the future there should be no doubt. (*North American Review,* 9:248.)

The Library of Congress, 1800–1840 Despite the sweep of the remarks by the English observers and the contributors to the *North American Review,* no reference seems to have been made to the Library of Congress, possibly because they were discussing resources open to readers generally and it did not fit that definition of a "public" library. Its birth and early character, indeed, were different also from those of the numerous royal and/or national libraries of Europe.

The lawmakers at first used what was right at hand, thanks to the hospitality of the leading libraries of Philadelphia and New York. Moving the capital to Washington, D. C., threw another light on the matter: the act of April 24, 1800, included a section appropriating $5,000 to buy books and house them for the use of the members of Congress. By January 26, 1802, Congress voted to pay a "librarian" $2 for each day that he was needed; it stipulated the bond he must deposit but said nothing of qualifications (political acceptability being understood). The functions of this office were part of the responsibilities of the Clerk of the House, but the governing rules were up to the President of the Senate and the Speaker of the House.

The selection of books was at first narrowly practical: parliamentary procedure, the law of nature and nations, encyclopedias, and foreign language dictionaries. In February 1804 they numbered about 1,500. But the elaboration of congressional business generated pressure for broader resources, and by 1812 the collection had reached 3,000, with numerous scientific and technical works, surveys, travel reports, and even some fiction. Furthermore, under a law of January 2, 1805, the library was directed to store 300 copies of each law and the journals of the two houses; in 1809 the responsibility was extended to the printed reports and public documents laid before Congress at each session. By that time the regulations for use of the library were detailed, the most striking one perhaps being the provision of service during sessions of Congress daily except Sunday from 9 A.M. to 3 P.M. and 5 P.M. to 7 P.M..

On Monday night, July 22, 1814, British troops attacked Washington and set the Capitol afire, thus destroying the library. (The officer in charge testified afterward that he had not known books were there and that there would have been no such action if he had known.) A fresh start was necessary, and the key step was Thomas Jefferson's offer in October to sell his personal library (destined in his view to some public purpose sooner or later) to Congress, on its own terms. After much pulling and hauling, with division usually along political lines, it was decided on January 30, 1815, by a vote of 81 to 71, to pay $23,950 for the former president's 6,000-odd volumes. Jefferson himself superintended the packing, and the books arrived at Washington from Monticello late in April.

Meanwhile, on March 21, Congress separated the librarian post from the office of the Clerk of the House. The first incumbent, George Watterston, an acquaintance of Jefferson's and one of his supporters, was chosen primarily for his reputation about town as something of a poet and novelist. He began with vigor, notifying President Madison that the library was supposed to have space suitable for its use, a theme to be heard often thereafter. Such progress as he could make was virtually cancelled by the fire of 1825, and his successors' efforts were to be crippled similarly in 1851: not until that point was fireproof construction taken seriously. Before the catastrophe of 1825, however, Watterston managed to organize the collections in harmony with their treatment by the previous owner. The forty-four main classes and numerous subclasses of the Baconian scheme of Jefferson's were the framework in the 1815 catalog and were to dominate the library until the end of the century.

The absence of a national library evoked now and then proposals that the Library of Congress assume that character. Cited were both prestige and the distance from Washington of the largest (in 1840 less than 50,000 volumes) libraries in the nation, located in Philadephia and Cambridge. Congress was not then ready for such thinking. It did, however, authorize in 1832 expansion of the law section, for the Justices of the Supreme Court; and in 1839 and 1840 the improvement of the documents service and the exchange of public papers with other countries.

Library Service Expands

Collars Blue and White The aristocrats and the business and professional classes were served well in the large towns of the Western world and not always badly in the small ones. University College opened in London in 1828, financed by a joint-stock company for the London middle class, beholden to no church, nonresidential, and emphasizing lectures rather than the tutorial intimacy long common in England. As reported in Henry Barnard's *American Journal of Education* for September-October 1829 (4:464-471 passim), a library of "more than eight thousand volumes" supporting their studies, "daily increasing," was open "every day" from 10 A.M. to 4 P.M. to "all students of the University." Separate libraries were available evenings to law and medical students. Among the offerings were lectures on the Italian language by "Professor Panizzi," soon to be far better known for his achievements at the British Museum library.

The manual working population of Great Britain, however, was not contemplated in that effort, useful as it was. That the majority rural portion should have continued to be more or less dependent upon books in the care of the village curate and the current wares of the peddler is understandable: for another century, until the internal combustion engine and other forces brought the bookmobile, it would be virtually impossible to overcome the obstacles of low density of population and financial resources. The condition of man in the burgeoning towns of Europe and the Atlantic coast of the United States was on the contrary productive of recognition of better things in this world and pressure to obtain them.

Notable in the early drive for access to books were some lettered and ambitious Presbyterian craftsmen of Scotland. They were paid well enough to support lectures and related book collections in Glasgow in 1760; the efforts of Dr. George Birkbeck (1776–1841) generated another wave of such activity in 1799. There were others like those in the English industrial center of Birmingham, who in 1795 organized a subscription Artisans Library, with a rate of a penny a week. Meanwhile, the Sunday School activists and the Wesleyan Methodists were carrying to workmen and shopkeepers the idea of advance through study, and trying to counteract the vast semiunderground literature of radical reform.

With the defeat of Napoleon, controls relaxed; the hitherto severely harassed demand for political and social reform, more nearly legal, came out into the open widely. But the agitation, the riots against machinery, and other factors led shortly to new repressive legislation in 1819. For several years debate filled cheap pamphlets and newspapers. The Mechanics' Institutes in the major cities, whether under partial worker control at first (London) or under businessman's control from the outset (industrial Manchester, Birmingham, and Leeds) became rapidly less attractive to the workers. In 1823 there was a dramatic secession from the original institution, the Andersonian in Glasgow; 374 members soon joined the new Glasgow Mechanics' Institution. In the same year the opening of the Liverpool Mechanics' and Apprentices' Library was enlivened by the unfurling of a silk banner dispatched for the occasion by "The Apprentices of New York."

As these centers and the coffeehouses provided forums for working-class thinking which was beginning to turn sharply away from middle-class liberalism, liberal reformer Henry Brougham (1778–1868) counterattacked in 1825 with his *Practical Observations upon the Education of the People*, dedicated to Birkbeck, and the following year saw the birth of the similarly oriented Society for the Diffusion of Useful Knowledge. The proof of the pudding, the Reform Bill of 1832, made unacceptable eating to many working-class elements; they did not get the right to vote they had been demanding. They promptly derided the *Penny Magazine* and other products of the S. D. U. K. on the one hand and on the other exhorted their followers to strengthen their unions and their cooperatives and develop a wide array of activities, including reading circles. One such leader, William Lovett, opened his own "Coffee and Conversation Rooms" in London in 1834, with several hundred books and twenty-eight journals freely at the disposal of patrons. By 1838 these elements and others merged for the time being into the Chartist movement.

Meanwhile, the clientele of the older institutes became primarily middle class and expanded downward to include children. That could have done no harm, for in 1838, nearly half of those registering their marriages in England signed with an X.

The S. D. U. K. had by no means given up, however. In 1835, impressed by the London Mechanics' Institute and some others, it sent them a questionnaire about their practices. The responses disclosed among other things that the institutes varied markedly but that the one common feature was to ignore women. Partly with the help of the other data thus gathered, the society published four years later *A Manual for Mechanics' Institutes*. The cards were plainly on the table: the defects of the institutes and their middle-class character were frankly conceded. Offered nonetheless were a model layout for an institute in which the lion's share went to the library, stress on careful arrangement and cataloging to help the reader, model regulations (rather generous as to borrowing but with stiff fines for overdues), a confession that fiction could not be barred, and a model book selection list.

Perhaps for the first time in Anglo-America, although not in Europe (see below), the *Manual* also called attention to the other book resources a mechanics' institute might draw upon, at a good many county seats: the library of the cathedral dean and chapter, municipal archives, book clubs, circulating libraries, and the collections of religious sects. Notable is the section speculating on the advantage of merging all those materials in one repository open to all and suggesting that a government grant would be a proper foundation for it. That suggestion was to return to mind occasionally, during the subsequent struggles over the device adopted instead, the property tax.

Merging is not the same as cooperation. During the very year of the *Manual's* release, S. D. U. K. secretary Thomas Coates visited numerous institutes to check the frame of mind: very little interest was detected even in the exchange of books.

Revealing noticeably less community interest in library service for the working people was the vigorous but rather isolated and largely ineffective propagandizing, in newly industrialized Saxony of the 1830s, by Karl Benjamin Preusker (1786–1871). The son of a weaver, he spent his twenties working in the book business, then a few years as a regimental supply officer in the Saxon army, taking the opportunity to visit libraries in South Germany and France and even reportedly leading a reading circle in Lille in 1816. In 1824 he settled down as an internal revenue agent in Grossenhain, a town of some 6,000, not far from Dresden, the Saxon capital, and gave countless leisure hours thereafter to the promotion of publicly encouraged self-education revolving around libraries and reading circles. He served as librarian of a reading circle in 1826, and helped found a school library in 1828 and a Sunday School for young workers' continuing education in 1829. The city library opened in 1833 owed a great deal to his efforts, and a year later he organized a reading circle for those with miscellaneous book interests. Although Saxony awarded him a medal in 1833 and Prussia another one in 1841, the Grossenhain city library received no regular budgetary support from the municipality until long afterward (1869); actually, Preusker had not made a point of it, apparently satisfied with the traditional path of soliciting gifts.

Considerably more elaborate and advanced were his published argumentation and proposals (accessible very conveniently in Mirbt, pp. 53–125). He was moved in general by J. G. von Herder's (1744–1803) philosophy of feeling and language; in particular, by zeal to defend the individual worker and his tools from the menace of mass production. He labored hard for education and for libraries as the heart of popular education: not just the familiar scholarly type but village and parish libraries, traveling libraries, and libraries for schools, hospitals, military installations, and prisons; not just good moral reading but vocational self-help reading. Owing to both direct observation and wide-ranging correspondence with librarians and other men of letters, he could speak with assurance on catalogs. One proposal was to print systematic indexes to the various classes of books as a means of public enlightenment, a step akin to Poole's "finding lists" some forty years later in Chicago. His business background is plain in his prescriptions for library cash records.

Preusker was especially preoccupied with the needs of those who could at best reach a village library and might be dependent upon a traveling collection. Although he is not known to have read Stephani's writings, he clearly did respond to Henry Brougham's *Practical Observations* (in German translation, 1827), particularly the allusions therein to Samuel Brown's "itinerating" libraries in Scotland. He contributed a number of terms to the library vocabulary, *Kinderbibliothek* ("children's library") among them. Except for the masterworks of German literature and outstanding poetry, romances and drama seemed to him unsuited to general popular (as distinct from scholarly) libraries. Of a piece with this, and his mentor Herder's Lutheranism, was the matter-of-fact fashion in which he looked to the clergy as well as the schoolmasters for leadership and control in the smaller libraries.

At least one of Preusker's German contemporaries was anxious for evening hours at libraries for working people. A squib in the literary journal *Europa,* in 1838 (3:181–183), noted that the French Minister of Public Instruction had lately ordered the Paris municipal libraries to render that service and that the major provincial cities were following suit. Libraries were available in Germany, the writer ("H——k") contended, only in capital cities, university towns, and other famous places; if Germans could associate for the improvement of wine and for temperance, why not for people's libraries *(Volksbibliotheken)*? The actual nature of those French library operations would be worth some research time.

The patterns in the United States were at once similar and dissimilar. Furnishing practical books and light reading as well as the traditional range was largely the same. Well established were awareness of the need for a literate work force, desire to spread knowledge of sciences and other current ideas as good in itself, and confidence that education was the door to opportunity and a potent damper on radicalism. Likewise familiar was the opposition of conservatives who feared enhancing the capabilities of their employees any further than was essential. Such resistance did not suffice to halt the movement, which was in full swing in the 1820s and 1830s, first in Eastern towns (Bristol, Connecticut, 1818) and then west of the Allegheny (Cincinnati, 1829). It was aimed at the young white men. The young women were mainly ignored in this connection, just as in Europe, although a voice like Jesse Torrey's (see below) could be heard on their behalf now and then.

There were also important differences. If workers themselves had taken the initiative here and there in late eighteenth-century Scotland to form reading groups of some sort, that was certainly not common in England or on the Continent. Yet, soon after the mechanics' institute and apprentices' libraries of the United States, there arose in the 1820s and 1830s mercantile library associations, distinctive for being often organized and led by the young beneficiaries themselves, the most truly Franklinesque of all contemporary types. Surely this experience strengthened the belief of the young men in their chance to make good in a fluid society with plenty of "free" land, a prospect seldom taken seriously in a restrictive England where opportunity was recognized by the rank and file as something that had to be fought for politically. No glorious vista gladdened the eye of the slave, however; and the record seems to disclose nothing by way of consideration at these libraries for the handful of Blacks who were freedmen.

The contrast in sponsorship possessed another dimension as well. Promotion of mass education and library service in Prussia and Saxony was in the hands of men thoroughly committed to Lutheran church-and-state thinking. In Great Britain the clergyman, whether established church or dissenting, played an important part in the small towns and the countryside but seems to have had no role in the mechanics' institutes or other urban installations. The record of the young mechanics' and clerks' libraries in the United States displays nothing of that sort; the spirit of secularism was dominant.

In two respects these libraries were noteworthy whether or not they were actually different from their parallels in the Old World. They were in at least some cases open strikingly long hours: perhaps extreme was the Ohio Mechanics Institute in Cincinnati, which was reported in 1850 to be serving its public "six days in the week from sunrise till 10 o'clock P.M.; Sundays, from sunrise to sunset." How long that had been going on is not mentioned by Charles C. Jewett in his classic *Appendix* to the *Fourth Annual Report of the Smithsonian Institution* (Washington, 1850). But he does allude to the founding date, 1829, and the first printed catalog, 1841; and states that the library has "for the last ten years" been acquiring about 200 volumes annually at a cost of about $100, the annual revenue being $3 "use" fees from "members" and 50 cents each from "ladies and minors" (Jewett, p. 170).

Besides long hours, especially Sunday and evening hours, these libraries deserve some attention for their share in cataloging achievements. At the peak was the series of printed catalogs produced by the Mercantile Library Association of New York: first, four which were alphabetical lists, then a systematic arrangement in 1834, and finally another of that type both brought up to date and enriched with bibliographical notes and annotations, printed in 1837 by Harper and Brothers.

The United States "School District" Library The broad representation of nonfiction plainly implied by "systematic" catalogs was accompanied as a rule by some fiction and other light fare, whether it was regarded as a necessary evil or welcomed as legitimate. The question hardly arose among the elders striving to organize good reading for children. That such nourishment should serve character formation was never in doubt: the issues were simply what kind of book and under which roof?

Since about the middle of the eighteenth century, Calvinist ideas about religion and children had been faced with challenge. The promise of the New World to white men seemed to contradict the pessimistic theology of Original Sin and predestination, and the spectrum of commitment gradually changed. The kindly God of the Quakers, Unitarians, and Universalists became more popular, just as Rousseau's view of the child as a fundamentally good product of unspoiled Nature reached a widening audience. The consequences did not so far include hospitality to children's reading for recreation as it would be thought of in later times. (Fairy stories were then accepted in Western Europe but not yet in the United States.) They did come to focus in two major conflicting traditions. To some minds, in a society about to become industrial and rapidly granting—state by state—the vote to white men of whatever economic standing, education seemed important enough to subordinate denominational concerns over the proper translation of and approach to scriptural and catechitical literature, to regard the elementary school as a "common" state enterprise barred to any sort of particularistic church influence. Others on the contrary regarded the "correct" reading matter as far more significant than any benefit obtainable from a lowest-common-denominator strategy.

The common school forces were first in the field, with their "school district libraries," an expression meaning different things under different circumstances. The first stage was the organization of "common" elementary schools in Massachusetts. The legislature authorized local school committees in 1826. An amendment of 1827 stipulated that such a committee "'shall never direct any school books to be purchased or used, in any of the schools under their superintendence, which are calculated to favor any particular religious sect or tenet.'" (*Laws of Mass.,* chap. 143, sec. 7; quoted by Raymond B. Culver, *Horace Mann and Religion in the Massachusetts Public Schools,* New Haven: Yale University Press, 1929, p. 22.) As revealed several years later, the legislators' conscious purpose was to protect the common school from the kind of book selection which might occur when zealots controlled a school committee.

The contest acknowledged by the statute rose to a new peak after the creation in 1834 of a school fund and in 1837 of a state board of education. The very first report of its distinguished secretary, Horace Mann, on January 1, 1838, noted that of all the works expounding revealed religion, none had so far been approved by a committee. "'The beautiful and sublime truths of ethics and natural religion,'" he was distressed to observe, were the message of only three of the books used in the schools, and those three were to be found in only six of the 2,918 schools from which returns to his inquiries had been received. He thought it extremely important that a book be available, explaining the proper subordination of passions to principles "'with a simplicity adapted to the simplicity of childhood . . . not a book written for the copy right's sake'" but from comprehension of the pressing need. (Quotations from Mann in Culver, p. 42.)

Although the legislature had on April 12, 1837, authorized the districts to raise by taxation, for school libraries, $30 the first year and $10 each subsequent year, little action if any had transpired when Mann's report and the board's were distributed. Mann therefore proposed at the board's annual meeting on January 31, 1838, that machinery be devised for the selection of books which the board could recommend to the district committees. By April plans had been made for two series of "Libraries," to be produced under contract with a commercial publisher. The leading conservative board member objected that unless each book was examined personally by each of his associates, he could not cooperate any further; soon thereafter he resigned. That body, still including several orthodox members, rejoined with a reaffirmation of the policy of the 1827 statute and emphasized that offering guidance was the best way to preclude any sales to individual districts, by "'individual enterprise . . . that would be objectionable'" (quoted by Culver, p. 47). A "library" to the board's taste was published by Capen & Lyon of Boston, in September 1839. The board was careful to insist that purchase was optional with the local committees, even as it promoted the books in articles in the *Common School Journal.*

At the same time, the American Sunday School Union's editor of publications, Frederick A. Packard (1794-1867), made several vigorous efforts to place in school "libraries" the evangelical Calvinist works whose promotion was one of its reasons for existence. (The Union screening committee comprised two Baptists, two Episcopalians, two Methodists, and two Presbyterians.) Mann's opinion was solicited concerning an approved book, and he obliged by denouncing its sectarian character. Although the opposition carried the battle to convention, press, and legislature, Mann triumphed. His own liberal views (he later became a Unitarian) were only partly responsible. The explanation lay rather in the fact that the public of Massachusetts and much of the rest of the Northeast, regardless of denomination, was quite prepared to support education without religious sectarianism. Of course this was within the framework of Protestantism; problems of a different sort would soon appear with the rise of Irish immigration and Catholicism.

The schools of New York State, shortly to be the scene of classic struggles on that issue, were in the years here discussed drawn into "school district library" activity mainly on bases far less religion-connected than was the case in Massachusetts. The idea of the free school and good reading matter, for character formation, had been broached at least since the governor's message to the legislature in 1812; patriotic purpose was added in the 1825 recommendations of Governor DeWitt Clinton, sponsor of the Erie Canal and many other progressive undertakings. Meanwhile, steady agitation emanated from the celebrated Jesse Torrey of the upstate town of Ballston Spa, who was concerned specifically not just with children "'over ten or twelve years of age'" but with the girls neglected by the very mercantile and mechanics' libraries he had encouraged, and with "'Free Circulating Libraries'" in even the smallest communities, open to "'all classes'" (quoted by Sidney Ditzion in "The District-School Library, 1835-1855," *Library Quarterly,* 10:546, 1940). He was thinking not only of the practical advantages of education to make a good living but of democratic opportunity. Government aid to universities was known in Europe, legislative aid in the United States; Torrey wanted knowledge diffused among all the people. Not surprisingly for a reformer of his day, he urged that free libraries and schools be financed by a tax on liquor.

However the foregoing may have contributed to public sentiment, the law enacted in New York was directly the product of a conventional lobbying by James Wadsworth of Geneseo, whose farm produce benefited greatly by the opening of the Erie Canal. Campaigning hard after 1827 he buttonholed legislators in 1833 and 1834 and was most instrumental in obtaining the law of 1835. The authorization to local committees to tax themselves for books was very much like the earlier legislation in Massachusetts. It did not, however, allude to sectarian materials, and it did speak of a "librarian," although such a person was plainly regarded not in any professional but simply in a custodial sense. Permission to tax did not at first induce local committees to act, despite much publicity to that end, and an act of 1838 shifted the base to the matching principle. A district taxing itself would receive the same amount in addition from the state's share of the money President Andrew Jackson had just withdrawn from the United States Bank; the state's own appropriation for the school account was $55,000. District libraries had first call on the funds for three years; after that they were to be available for either library purposes or teachers' wages. But the act was amended in 1838 to extend the three years to five, and in 1843 to establish the library advantage indefinitely.

Neither in their major aim of serving the children nor in their supplemental aim of offering continuing education to adults lacking easy access to another library were these institutions notably successful. The population were neither avid readers nor enthusiastic taxpayers and a district was seldom wealthy. Perhaps reflecting early realization thereof was the 1839 statute permitting establishment of "union" library districts which crossed the usual lines. Resistance was probably aggravated by the New York state education authorities' readiness, greater than that of their Massachusetts contemporaries, to issue guide lines and offer advice to local citizens supposedly running things themselves. Whether the officials' choices would have been any different from those of the townsmen is doubtful, but the book selection policy was on the one hand catholic and practical and on the other hand opposed to religious or sectarian partisanship, statutory proscription of the Massachusetts sort proving to be unnecessary. Recommended were the books published by the American Society for the Diffusion of Useful Knowledge. A commercial bid was received on behalf of Harpers' School District Library, but sidelined for some time because the state officials were not informed about the books.

Similar events were occurring in Connecticut and Rhode Island under the leadership of Henry Barnard, and in Ohio, Michigan, and the Iowa Territory. Involved was elementary school book service. State aid for secondary school book service was as old as the Literary Fund established in New York in 1813, intended to support the classical-curriculum academies. In 1827 and 1828 forty-five of them were reported to have received $10,000 thus, presumably benefiting some 3,000 tuition-paying students, although the precise amount allotted to books is not indicated. (*American Journal of Education*, 3:357, June 1828). Like undertakings of varying degrees of health marked the operations of several other states, but the day of the tax-supported free high school was still in the future.

All told, the school district library, taken in its meaning of a book collection in a school paid for by public funds and intended primarily for the pupils in that school, helped establish the principle of tax support for the provision of books. It continued the established requirement of quality in the collection as defined by educated elders. It also continued the assumption that books for children were properly handled by parents, ministers, and teachers; professional librarianship was not discussed.

Other Book Service to Children   Nor did that element enter the campaigning of the American Sunday School Union. Launched in 1824 on an interde-

nominational basis, a "home mission" enterprise supported by church revenues, it responded to the advances of common school education by
organizing in 1830 a major publication program. Collections numbered as a
rule between 200 and 300 books, occasionally as large as 1,200. They were
normally lodged in a church and accessible only on Sunday; the person in
charge, often the janitor, issued to children the items they selected from a
printed list. Thus might a child borrow what the Union regarded as (1)
unquestionably moral and religious, (2) graded, (3) presentable as literature,
and (4) unmistakably American. For all the limitations thus evident, the
Union is to be credited with a pioneering policy on books for children.
Besides, at the end of the very first year it claimed to have furnished with
such materials every Sunday School in the United States. Whether that is
precisely accurate or not, the Union's "libraries" were for the next thirty or
forty years the most readily borrowable books for children in large portions
of the United States.

Partly in these traditions, though not primarily for children, was the
Peterborough, New Hampshire, Library. It is worth a moment here for its
illumination of the variety of forces bearing on libraries, political, religious,
educational, and individual-inspirational. The legislature had tried to alter
the charter of Dartmouth College and in a celebrated decision of 1819 had
been rebuffed by the Supreme Court of the United States. A tax was then
levied on the capital stock of banks doing business in New Hampshire, to
finance a rival state university; but it produced only money, not a university.
Thus in 1828 was the modest "Literary Fund" apportioned among the
"towns" (i.e., townships), destined for the "'support and maintenance of
common free schools, or to other purposes of education'" (quoted in Shera,
pp. 162–163). While most New Hampshire towns did apply the revenue to
such schools, Peterborough earned fame in library annals by spending its
share on a town library, the responsibility being laid upon a committee
composed of one representative from each school district (in the township).
On April 8, 1834, the library was reported open.

Pictured here in microcosm are many of the forces then operative in the
northeastern United States. Noted already is the connection between politi-
cal-constitutional struggle, and benefit to culture somewhat by accident.
Evident also is the standard school district structure on the one hand, and on
the other, local initiative to utilize both that structure and the statutory
phrase in a deviant manner. To this must be added what the records of the
1834 triumph reveal: that substantial portions of the collection came respectively from a "Juvenile Library" organized in 1828 and from a Bible Society
grant for moral and religious books which was twice the size of the town's
own original grant; and that a key role throughout was played by the Reverend Abiel Abbott, vigorous in his sixties, a theological liberal and promoter
of several different libraries as well as other public service ventures.

Professional Views of Library Tasks

If book collections for children were on the order of a few hundred volumes,
and no academic or research library in the United States held more than

about 40,000, it is evident that the organization and operation of large book collections remained a European challenge. During the half-century under discussion, indeed, nearly all contributions, from the multiplication of acquisitions source tools to the proposal of organized training for librarians, were European, forming a literature which, like so many other bodies of material, reached American eyes piecemeal and after some lag in transit.

Book Sources, Records, and Space The outstanding current bibliography already on the scene, although declining, was the continuing catalog of the Leipzig book fairs. To it were added during the period under review several other information media, notably the semiannual register of new books in German launched in 1797 by the Hinrichs firm, which afterward sponsored also like media of greater frequency; and in 1834 the first weekly *Börsenblatt* issued by the Union of Book Dealers at Leipzig. The leading product in France was what became known as the *Bibliographie de la France,* a weekly launched in 1811 shortly after Napoleon first confiscated all periodicals and then relented moderately. England was furnished sporadically with new versions of the *London Catalogue* first published in 1773, but in 1837 favored with the first weekly number of the *Publisher's Circular,* later cumulated into the annual *English Catalogue of Books.* The Netherlands was similarly equipped in 1833, Belgium in 1838. The nearest approach to such service in the United States, apart from the Boston booksellers' catalog of 1804, was the succession of notices of new books in leading magazines like the *North American Review* (1815–   ). Instruments of this type normally included not only the basic library information about the items announced but their prices.

In retrospective national bibliography, the Germans pretty well had the field to themselves. Setting a remarkable pace were the work begun in 1812 by W. Heinsius, devoted to German-language output from 1700 to 1797, and the subsequent achievement by C. G. Kayser, initiated in 1834, covering the literature issued from 1750 to 1832.

The librarian wishing to keep up with specialized publishing was in increasingly good shape from 1822 on. From Tübingen University emanated the first of the countless annual summaries later so familiar, the *Jahresberichte* for progress in the physical sciences. For the next thirty years all such products were German, save only the botany (1825–   ) and zoology (1826–   ) series contributed from Stockholm. The same pattern also characterized retrospective specialized bibliography. Hain's great register of incunabula, *Repertorium bibliographicum,* was issued in Stuttgart beginning in 1825, to be followed by several other German landmarks. The year 1837 saw the emergence on this scene of a French work, on entomology, and in 1839 arrived the *Rara Mathematica* by England's J. O. Halliwell.

Coverage not limited to either an individual nation or language or to a particular subject became available in a number of works more or less distinctively reflecting the times. In 1790 two Frenchmen compiled a guide to the sort of book made conspicuous by the French Revolution—. . . *rare, précieux, singuliers, curieux* . . .—and sought after, with their best judgment of prices on the basis of public auction records. From this developed twenty years later Jacques-Charles Brunet's renowned *Manuel du libraire et de l'amateur des livres,* or "Manual for book-dealers and book-lovers." Focused not on rare, precious, or sought-after works, but general British (most of the items listed) and foreign writings, was the *Bibliotheca Britannica* by Robert Watt, published posthumously in 1824. Unlike Brunet, Watt included analytical entries to hundreds of monographs in learned society transactions, and magazine articles, such as this:

> "Adamson, W. esq.—a Short Account of Horizontal Water Wheels. Phil. Mag. 1. 256. 1817" (vol. I, position 7A)

Watt's preface makes no reference to predecessors in that type of service. Nevertheless, an *Allgemeines Sachregister,* or "Comprehensive Subject Index" to the most important German periodicals had appeared in 1790. And J. D. Reuss of Göttingen soon afterward began issuing his sixteen volume classified guide to the publications of learned organizations in all fields, down to 1800, the celebrated *Repertorium . . .* (1801–1821).

That academy publication should have reached such dimensions will occasion no surprise. It may not be appreciated, however, that the 14 known periodicals of 1640, the 68 of 1690, had become in 1761, according to Voltaire, 173 "which appear monthly in Europe" (*Oeuvres Complètes,* nouv. éd, Paris: Garnier, 1877, t. 44, p. 414). Advance soon afterward became explosive, 910 being recorded in 1800 and 3,179 in 1826 (M. B. Iwinski, "La statistique internationale des imprimés; . . . ," *Bulletin de l'Institut International de Bibliographie,* 16. année, 1911, pp. 1–139, especially p. 58).

To acquire books or journals required several methods, some old, some new. Gifts were as old as libraries. Nearly as old, perhaps, were exchanges. How to date the money gifts called endowments depends on definitions legal and fiduciary: since the later Middle Ages, probably. Legal deposit was now nearly two centuries old, but by its nature could not directly benefit more than a few libraries in any one jurisdiction. Book purchase funds from subscription fees were available here and there before the eighteenth century but became prominent only during that epoch. The German Enlightenment, and the French Revolutionary spur to nationalism, then produced a vital advance in exchange technique. In 1816 a professor of medicine at Marburg induced the University Senate to sponsor a plan for exchanging with other similar institutions dissertations, programs, and occasional papers. The following year saw invitations extended to twenty-two German universities, Prague and Vienna included. Surviving the blows of academic politics, the arrangement was officially recognized by the Prussian Ministry of Instruction in 1820, and had become three years later a network of eighteen German and eight foreign universities; one of the many learned units joining it in the next half-century was the Smithsonian Institution. Besides, numerous bilateral links were established: that of the Royal Library of Berlin with the Imperial University of Vilna in 1828 was Berlin's first with an Eastern European institution. The event documents the growth of the latter from an originally Jesuit college (1570) to a university with a 60,000-volume library in 1832, thanks in part to the influence of Göttingen's Heyne upon his pupil, the Lithuanian scholar G. E. Grodeckas (1762–1825).

In the early 1830s, certain leading institutions were spending these sums (expressed in thousands of francs by pioneer library statistician Adrien Balbi, as translated in the *North American Review,* 43:121, July 1837):

Bodleian	75
Imperial Library, Vienna	47.5
Royal Library, Berlin	29.68
Advocates Library, Edinburgh	25
Göttingen University Library	20

The Royal Library of France in Paris yielded at that time no overall figure, but for the Prints Department alone was reported 15,000 francs.

The same authority had examined the history of claims with sufficient care and sophistication to warn that "with the exception of a few . . . the exact number of volumes is unknown"; extracts appeared in translation in the U.S. Bureau of Education's *Public Libraries in the United States . . .* (especially p. 746). In 1835 he arrived at the following estimates of the holdings of the largest libraries (*North American Review,* 45:126–127):

	Thousands of Bound Volumes	Manuscripts
Royal Library, Paris	626	80
Royal Library, Munich	540	16
Imperial Library, St. Petersburg	432	15(?)
Royal Library, Copenhagen	410	16(?)

Balbi was confident also that neither the Bodleian nor Göttingen actually held more than 200,000.

The accommodation of increasing numbers of volumes stimulated some bold proposals for architectural emphasis on practical management of space, at the expense of the ornate and monumental. Outstanding was Leopoldo della Santa's plan, published in Florence in 1816 and publicized by the writings of Danish Royal Librarian Christian Molbech (1783–1857) in the late 1820s on library science, in turn translated into German in 1833 (*Über Bibliothekswissenschaft,* Leipzig: Hinrichs). The key proposal was to shelve the books apart from the reading area, in forty-eight small rooms which were in the aggregate virtually stacks; they were later to become so in fact, under the label *magasin,* with the removal of most of the internal walls. Molbech's only cavil was that della Santa naturally was unconcerned with artificial heat, something one could not overlook in Northern Europe.

Molbech may have been the first to give his whole twenty-page initial chapter to the library building, which he describes as "the first condition for outward useful existence" (p. 19); the librarian must think about it even though it is more the business of the builder than his own. His remarks on roominess and convenience, and protection from dampness, are as old as Naudé, as he knew; but in certain respects Molbech is unusual. He urges that no library be more than two stories high. He hopes that recent discoveries with steam heat will "make all use of fire-places in the library superfluous" (p. 23), thus facilitating security against fire. And he stresses weighing not just what is on hand but the future, the likelihood of need for more space for books and readers, and the urgency of providing for it. This is a dynamic view, harmonious with the contemporary dialectic of Hegel, whose work was known to Molbech.

Meanwhile, Bavarian monk and librarian Martin Schrettinger (1772–1851) devoted part of the work which first used the term "library science" *(Bibliothekswissenschaft)* to these very questions of money and space, in 1808 in the first *Heft* of his book, and again in 1829 in his supplementary comments (*Versuch eines vollständigen Lehrbuchs der Bibliothek-Wissenschaft,* Munich: Lindau; or "Attempt at a Comprehensive Textbook on Library Science"). A library intended for public use required appropriate premises and "adequate endowment" (1829, II:174). Without sufficient space "the poor books must be packed together like Negroes on a slaveship" (II:175). One should avoid excess in length and height, and corners and nooks. The objectives are adequate light, adequate and safe heat, and clear "communication in all directions" (II:178). Having many small rooms leads to difficulty in orienting visitors. He submits numerous practical suggestions. Library finance lessons have been learned the hard way, in connection with the recent transfers of ownership: "Libraries turned over to municipalities or corporate agencies by gift or bequest, without the funds needed for their administration and growth, are only library-cadavers" (II:187). A smart librarian, he says, can pick up some more revenue by running on the side an institute for journal reading whose patrons pay fees.

Internal Bibliographic Control   These new currents of thought did not overcome established preferences rapidly, and librarians of large libraries perforce continued to give much thought to the problems of shelving books and providing access by way of catalogs and markings. The half-century under review was featured by sharp debate between advocates of the logically arranged systematic catalog and those who regarded as far better the contemporary *Realkatalog,* in which the subject groups followed the alphabetical order of the subjects. Usually involved also were observations on the author catalog, the shelflist, or both.

The opening gun was a 1790 brochure on library cataloging and shelf control, perhaps the first addressed to the "public," composed by Albrecht Christoph Kayser (1756–1811). Trained at Leipzig University, he was long a counselor to the Princes of Thurn and Taxis and seems to have had practical experience at the Regensburg (Bavaria) City Library.

He is convinced that manipulating a catalog can be made understandable to all, whence the beginning of his title, *Über die Manipulation bey der Einrichtung einer Bibliothek und der Verfertigung der Bücherverzeichnisse . . .* (Bayreuth, 1790). But one must first dispose of the half-baked meddlers who think that if they put German historians under "German history" they have mastered cataloging. Another handicap is the influence of the systematic catalog. It does not serve its purposes: neither the quick overview nor the expeditious location of the book on the shelves. A very good one might, but the Göttingen and Weimar systematic catalogs are actually available only in manuscript; would it not be appropriate to organize an academy which would publish them? Really though, the alphabetical approach is so much better.

Having ended his preface thus, he opens his text proper with the explanation that he is writing it because such a work is lacking. An inserted reference calls attention to an encyclopedia article just published, read by him after his own work was finished; he invites comparison. What he has to say may not be so good for someone else's library as for his own, but let argument throw light. The trouble to date has been the inclination of librarians to behave as though they were immortal, writing down almost nothing and wasting much of their successors' time. They need not attempt to tie posterity's hands, but some guidance as to what they have done would help.

Kayser's basic plea for the alphabetical catalog is of course no novelty in principle. But in laying out the reasoning and the details of procedure he enriches the record. He is confident that library users know the author and title of the work desired often enough to justify concentrating on the alphabetical catalog and effective links with the shelflist. Emphasis on accurate transcription of the title page is demanded first by current bad habits like skipping an author's given names; there are enough common surnames to cause trouble, not to mention false names or names masked in Latin form. True names are often found in dedications, prefaces, a statement of privilege to publish, or the censor's permission. If two forms of a name appear, both should be entered in the catalog, cross-referenced. How to handle pseudonyma and anonyma has been well presented in a manual which he recommends.

Utilizing the title for subject guidance is evidently taken for granted, for Kayser bemoans the lack of standard procedure in general, and the brevity and obscurity of titles in particular. The tendency in titling dissertations seems to approach a frightening ultimate in both respects. The cataloger cannot of course provide what is not there, but at least he can transcribe the whole title. Whatever contribution might be made by subject headings, Kayser does not suggest any relationship.

Curious in the light of his drive for precision is the author's silence on the lack of it in the narrative guides to the more important books in various fields which eighteenth-century Germany called *Historia litteraria*. Archer Taylor notes (*General Subject-Indexes since 1548*, p. 211) that they scanted conventional bibliographical details and sometimes omitted titles altogether; and that this was accepted practice. Perhaps the otherwise voluble Kayser did not feel called upon to complain about a qualitative guide which was not the catalog of a particular library.

But his concern on the latter count is evident again as he urges more care than is customary in recording the format. He contends that with small numbers, omission or error is easy.

Kayser's comments on other items of description throw further light on several contemporary conceptions and practices. He refers to incunabula as "so-called" (p. 19) and defines them as works published up to 1530, a later date by thirty years than that more often accepted in Western bibliographical practice. Further, a proper catalog ought to record publisher or printer or both even though, he says, the bookdealers normally leave out such data. Kayser would also like to incorporate in this connection (?) literary anecdotes about the publication cataloged. Is that an echo of discussions at a local salon? He exhorts writers to reduce current confusion about parts of books by avoiding *Band* ("volume") where some other term will do; leave it, he advises, to the binders, who can use it uniquely for what is between two covers. Librarians, he concludes, ought to put down faithfully information on copperplate illustrations and maps, above all because the value of the book is affected. Does he exaggerate?

The next stage in the discussion is the technique of assigning each book an integral number for permanent inventory, and permanent location symbols. Five pages (23-28) are devoted to this task.

The rest of his text, some forty pages, sets forth the steps by which individual slips, each with the entry for a single work, can be utilized first to prepare an alphabetical catalog and then as the basis for a subject catalog, either systematic or alphabetical. His introductory point is the reminder that all writings are either by a stated author or anonymous. Suggestions follow as to multiple entry of the latter by various words in a title, cross-referencing, and the use of underlining or a different script for emphasis. Arrangement of the entries is no less complex. Kayser regards it as necessary to defend faithful alphabetizing "even" when it means placing a son before his father. He also warns that he is ignoring differences of format here in the catalog, although he respects it in shelving. Step-by-step alphabetizing absorbs pages 38 to 45: the characteristics of German usage necessitate reliance on the nominative case as an anchor (regardless of how a name or key word actually appears on the title page), and a separation between U and V; he confesses that ü (or ue) has not been solved yet. (Librarians many generations later would still be nodding in sympathy.)

All this and more is facilitated by the use of entry slips, rather than the books themselves. One can work on them easily at odd moments in the library or at home or elsewhere.

The result is not necessarily a unified main-entry catalog. In many libraries, Kayser observes, separate catalogs are maintained for dissertations, other short items, and certain categories of ephemera. He sympathizes, recommending, however, that the dissertation catalog be limited to items bought for advanced studies. Such special files were indeed to become virtually standard in scholarly libraries all over Europe.

The link to the shelves is the next concern. Kayser does not favor entering location symbols in the alphabetical catalog, just the permanent accession number. Location data are left to the shelflists (procedural details fill pp. 55-58); advantageous are individual *Handbüchelchen* for each bookcase and shelf (pp. 61-62), booklets obviously similar to the *tabulae* which used to be attached to the end of each unit of shelving in late medieval and Renaissance times. Most of this he gladly credits to Daehnert, whose Greifswald catalog, he says, is not so well known as it deserves because it is so expensive.

Subject control brings up the rear of the discussion. And within the very plan to rearrange the aforementioned slips under subject headings is the advice to prepare analytical entries for parts of books before destroying the alphabetical order of the slips.

Very prominent at this point is Kayser's preoccupation with the incompleteness of the subject catalogs known to him. What will the reader do, confronted by such an instrument? Take a good bibliographical guide to the literature of a subject, he urges the librarian, and mark in red or with stars the leading works in the collection; add their permanent numbers as one does in the alphabetical catalog. This idea too was to interest later generations.

Kayser ends his text with a sample worksheet for the *Standortsreperto-rio* (p. 69), or shelflist, complete with location symbols. The balance of his brochure consists of an alphabetical list (pp. 71–99) of the published works of an admired scholar, analytics included, and a subject index to that list which furnishes the accession numbers (pp. 100–123).

Another attack on the systematic catalog was delivered (1808–1810) in the first volume of Schrettinger's textbook, already mentioned. This volume contained his first three *Hefte,* allocated respectively to library organization (purpose, shelving, marking), the alphabetical name-catalog, and the systematic catalog. Schrettinger was well informed and in many respects practical, but seemed to his critics to be eclectic and confusing. That would not do in an introduction for students. In the opinion of Friedrich Adolf Ebert (1791–1834), offered apologetically but firmly at age twenty-four in a letter to Schrettinger, and again more elaborately in his 1820 pioneer treatise on education for librarianship, *Die Bildung des Bibliothekars* (2d rev. ed., Leipzig: Steinacker u. Wagner), the beginner would simply turn to the study of good catalogs. Molbech, author of another important treatise on the subject, contended that Schrettinger never understood the systematic catalog in the first place because he did not understand philosophy.

Ebert himself does not, in *Die Bildung,* explore deeply the problem of subject control, but offers guidelines which keep the fully systematic approach at arm's length. He urges (1) heavy reliance on historical divisions, (2) avoidance of the ideal-theoretical and preference for the practical-homogeneous, and (3) wariness of getting caught in a system rooted in viewpoints of the moment. Mindful of Naudé's touching confidence about complex works, he (4) denounces the failure of the library systems known to him to provide a class for the history of morals and culture and their inclination to dump such works in "miscellany"—that is far too easy. He also (5) recommends that classification be determined by content rather than literary form; travel books ought for instance to be arranged by place, not according to their accidental appearance as journals or something else. (How common was that?) The concluding advice (6) is to be flexible, not evading necessary change but avoiding the arbitrary.

The Ebert brochure does not undertake to deal with any subject at length but is apparently unusual in the explicit note taken of the implications for shelving of the predominance of this or that format among the books in major subject areas as libraries then knew them. He points out that Bibles and authoritative church records are mainly folios, for example, hardly ever octavos. Recent literary scholarship, and certain other materials, are on the contrary so heavily small-format that one section of shelving is usually enough for the folios of that department. Antiquities and the fine arts, nature and architecture, again, need considerable provision for big folios. In some other categories like history, the situation varies with the habits of the country in which the book is produced, the Dutch preferring quartos for classic writers and smaller sizes for others.

This clearly sensible reasoning made a better impression than Schrettinger's because the issue was kept simple. Schrettinger aroused opposition partly because he seemed to give so much emphasis to the aesthetic appeal of shelving in physically homogeneous groups and the role of décor in utilizing various construction features of the building. In sorrow and bitterness he returned to the arena in 1829, with a second volume containing rebuttals of the criticisms of the first three *Hefte* (1808-1810), additions and corrections to them, and at last his fourth *Heft*, devoted among other things to the alphabetical *Realkatalog* and issues of library administration. Among his supplementary remarks to the earlier statements on shelving in *Heft* 1, offered by way of pained rejection of the charge that he was downright eccentric, Schrettinger declares that there is a way to protect sensible subject arrangement from interference by format differences: "the shelves in every class in a library should be movable" (II:35). If that idea had been advanced before, the fact does not seem to have been reported widely.

Class and Subject: Schrettinger   Considerably more important, for all the exaggeration and confusion which limited its impact, was Schrettinger's handling of the systematic versus the alphabetical subject approach. The former, he objects, is so constructed that the operator must know not only that the book in hand concerns "Luxury" but whether the frame of reference is "the National Economy, the Police, theological or philosophical Morality, or History, or even Poetry, etc." (II:49). The *Realkatalog* on the contrary focuses directly on the individual subject. He projects this instrument as the ultimate aggregate of special catalogs listing all the material on one subject or another in books or parts of composite publications, somewhat akin to the vertical and other special files of later times. He further submits that to list only the titles of complete works is but the "first power" of a catalog. Bringing out individual titles by means of analytics raises it to the "second." Adding data on the life of the author and the fate of his work brings it up to the "third," and makes of the *Realkatalog* a tool very useful in other libraries. To devotees of the systematic catalog this was scandalous. Molbech said it was "one of the most monstrous ideas which could ever have emanated from a literary scholar and bibliographer" (p. 233).

But they were missing a point worthy of note, even if Schrettinger had not expressed it very clearly. The contrast he drew was at bottom the difference between the function of a hierarchical subject classification, which relates topics to the larger ones embracing them and to the smaller ones within them, and the specific subject heading, which can bring together material from all manner of larger frameworks. The possibility of applying the same headings in other libraries was one of the reasons he envisaged the *Realkatalog* so broadly. The necessary corollary, standardization via authority files, apparently did not occur to him: he argues that assigning subjects in an alphabetical array is easier than placing them properly in a logical sequence, but admits unhappily that the whole job must be done by one person to minimize inconsistency. If he knew how inconsistent one individual can be, he kept his doubts to himself.

It appears, moreover, that Schrettinger was a trailblazer in the whole area of what came to be known as subject headings. One defines a subject, he explains, by asking four questions:

1 What is the actual subject the work treats?
2 Under what name will one ordinarily look it up?
3 Under what other labels can the same thing also be sought?
4 Is this subject not so closely related to several others that one of them cannot really be treated apart from the rest? (II:143).

He next disposes of the familiar reliance on key words in titles with fresh emphasis on the risks involved. Citing "On the Sale of Goods from a Mortgaged Shop," he points out how useless it would be to draw the reader's attention to any one of the three nouns separately. Check as to common usage, he adds; it is too easy to devise a false heading from ignorance. He does not mention the compound-subject possibility.

Usage also brings up the question of language. Scholars will incline toward Latin, but Schrettinger thinks the mother tongue is a much better choice. After all, "We labor in the first place for our countrymen" (II:149). Besides, while no language has just the right word for every need, the dead languages lack a great many terms required in contemporary life.

He is worried about synonyms, variety in spelling—*Censur* and *Zensur* for instance, and the tendency of terms to change their meaning from one age to another. But the solution already known for centuries, the cross-reference, is not mentioned in this connection. He simply pleads for consistency.

Where subjects overlap, one should use the most exact term, or the one which appears on the title page, or all of them. No more than see-references does he think of the similarly venerable see-also.

On the other hand, where a term has several meanings, Schrettinger advises distinguishing them with parenthetical guides, a solution widely accepted long afterward. He also uses parenthetical modification to create subject subdivisions, such as "Church History (General) and Church History (German) (II:152). Nervous about the opposition, he adds a note that one should be sure this doesn't become an array of systematic subdivisions.

The Systematic Made Practical; Molbech Christian Molbech, a leading organizer of Danish intellectual life, veteran of twenty years' service at the Royal Danish Library, was a vigorous defender of the systematic catalog. His views were published first in 1828 and 1829 in the Danish learned journal he had founded, reissued in book form in 1830, and translated into German in 1833 by Henning Ratjen of Kiel University, who in that very year was promoted from under- to chief librarian. Molbech's starting point in principle is that the systematic catalog is second in importance only to individual entry for every work, whether bound separately or jointly (everything is to be bound). He thinks in fact, not only that the systematic catalog renders a shelflist unnecessary, but even that, with good systematic arrangement, the catalog itself is not necessary either. That idea had been voiced before.

Practically speaking, Molbech begins with careful examination of the title, backed up by subject knowledge; he remarks that even famous librarians have done this part of the work with inexplicable carelessness and indifference. If the title does not really provide enlightenment as to the contents of the book, the main topic or the class or subclass the book belongs in must be added to the description. True, this is a deviation from the strictly bibliographic view of title page transcription and will not please the bibliographic specialists, but it really is necessary, especially when the title page will later be used to classify the work.

While Molbech is certain that "overall alphabetical arrangement is unthinkable" (Molbech, *Über Bibliothekswissenschaft*, p. 51), his confidence in the systematic approach is by no means unqualified. One must ask, he submits, (1) whether a catalog arranged according to the encyclopedia, or logical, system is necessary for a library; (2) whether, if such can be shown, the books can and must be shelved in complete accord with said catalog; (3) whether, if developing such an instrument is very difficult or impossible, the disposition and shelving of books do not matter, or at least are independent of the encyclopedic system and rest on some other basis; (4) whether a different approach, for instance a scientific library system and its catalog, can fill the bill. He answers that on point 1 the necessities of shelving demand a catalog close to the shelving rather than ideal-encyclopedic. As for point 2, complete accord is impossible, if only because so many books are on hand which were written long ago and can now be assigned to any one of several places in a logical structure. On point 3 more challenges: cannot books be shelved by entry, regardless of content, or simply by arbitrary numbers unrelated to entry or anything else? (Some later libraries would indeed take advantage of closed stacks to shelve by accession number.)

Pursuing point 4, he reasons that the objective is a *"Bibliotheksystem,"* which avoids subjecting the "intellectual principle" to the merely "material principles of space and size" (Molbech, p. 62), and tries to guarantee the reverse. Here too Molbech testifies to the influence of the dialectic lately expounded by Hegel.

Although Molbech dismisses Schrettinger's view of the systematic catalog as crippled by ignorance of philosophy, he does not recommend an intimate commitment. The librarian following Hegel's use of Logic and Ethics, he observes, would run into trouble because no one else uses those terms for the same body of material. Likewise, it is not prudent to reclassify all the books about places with each political change. The basic policies ought to be, first, "a middle way between the strictly encyclopedic theory and the disorder of an unregulated mechanical approach" (p. 71); that is, a philosophical base is vital, but one must be able to expand flexibly. Second, a scientific pattern must be modified practically by the three formats so that the shelving may correspond to it. Once all the classes have been worked out, permanent shelving numbers should be assigned to each book. In fact, shelving should correspond to the catalog arrangement except for oversize books and perhaps a few other special categories.

It would be very nice to standardize all this, beyond national boundaries and traditions (as Ebert has suggested), but norms thus widely valid seem unattainable because the character and form of book titles vary so much. No wonder, adds translator Ratjen in a note, that French expert E. G. Peignot has lately concluded that no perfect bibliographic system yet exists and it is perhaps impossible to devise one.

Other Technical Advances   To the foregoing appreciation of Molbech may be added recognition of a few practical advances registered during these years by either librarians or persons close to libraries. Tribute to ingenuity was Reuss' method (1790–1796) of linking the book on the shelf with the badly lagging subject catalog, at Göttingen: he entered in the book not only the subject class but the number of the page in the *Realkatalog* on which it was listed. This was a step closer to the modern call number combining a subject symbol and a book number, ultimately the basis of relative-location shelving; but, nearer though that achievement lay, it was still far off. More immediately significant was the increasing use, generally for preparatory operations but sometimes for permanent parts of the catalog apparatus, of the *Zettel,* or individual sheet, perhaps of octavo dimensions, often held in batches by one means or another. These *Zetteln* were of course much more easily manipulated than pages in a bound volume; they represent a stage in the long evolution toward the card catalog, a level which seems to have been reached in 1834 at the University of Kazan under librarian N. I. Lobachevsky (better known as an inventor of non-Euclidean geometry). Of interest also is the already-mentioned attempt at a union catalog in the days of confiscation and centralization in France. In the realm of cataloging technique it seems to have contributed nothing remarkable. But it may be a significant episode in the development of the art of writing technical instructions for laymen; and one can hardly doubt its importance as an example of the impact of political change on culture.

Toward the end of the period under review, Leyden University librarian J. P. Namur introduced a device destined to be imitated by many after him. Composing in 1839 a systematic catalog for the Royal Athenaeum of the Grand Duchy of Luxembourg, he established an order in which nations and continents were arranged consistently wherever geography or language subdivision seemed to him appropriate; he used it under History, Natural Science, Belles Lettres, and several other main divisions. (Details appear on p. 53 of E. I. Shamurin's invaluable *Geschichte der bibliothekarisch-bibliographischen Klassifikation,* Bd. II, tr. from the Russian; München-Pallach: Verlag Dokumentation, 1968.)

Classification Schemes and Life   Plainly visible in a few of the classification patterns is the Baconian stamp, Memory-Imagination-Reason. Many more accept the century-old "Paris bookseller" or "French systematic" plan, enshrined in 1810 in Jacques-Charles Brunet's *Manuel du Libraire et de l'Amateur de Livres* ("Manual for Booksellers and Booklovers"), wherein all materials are arranged under the five familiar main heads of Theology, Jurisprudence, Sciences and Arts, Belles Lettres, and History, plus Miscellaneous and Encyclopedic. Several French bibliographers and others were skeptical, pretty sure that something better was conceivable; but Brunet long remained enormously influential.

Among his many subdivisions, and unmistakable in other systems with a larger number of main divisions, are new features. One is the standardization of scientific subjects so greatly enhanced by the widely respected labors of the Swedish naturalist Karl von Linné, his French colleagues Georges Buffon and Jean Baptiste de Lamarck, and others. The sequence began sometimes with the lower forms, sometimes with God or man, but the great chain of being was clear.

Expressive on the other hand of changes in daily human life and thought are the new slots for the publications of learned societies and for periodicals, and for the subjects now entering the scene, in offices, markets, and university curricula: Agriculture, Commerce, Statecraft, Pedagogy, Statistics. Breaking away from Philosophy were Philology and Natural Science, the Management of Government, Finance, and Production. The social sciences were emerging from jurisprudence. Indicative of these changes are the appearance of categories for Schoolbooks and Writings for Young People in the Hinrichs trade bibliography of 1821, for Bridge- and Street-Construction, in Namur's 1834 classification, and for collections of government-related statistics in the 1839 subject index to Kayser's *Bücher-Lexikon*. That a Belgian national bibliography of the same year should have places for Bibliography and for *"Revues et Journaux"* is not particularly surprising; perhaps less common was its slot for *"Romans, théâtre, poésie, mémoires"* (in Petzholdt, p. 51).

Furthermore, in several classification systems of the years 1793–1810, reality-focused, use-accented topics are explicitly labeled "positive," in contrast with the "a priori" (based on assumptions or dogma). These were fruits partly of Baconian and scientific seeds, partly of the contemporary thinking called "utilitarianism," and of the idea of progress, associated with Condorcet. The next generation added the Hegelian concept of inevitable unfolding of the Idea, and the revolutionary spirit of Utopians like Saint-Simon. Directly inspired by the latter, Auguste Comte in 1830 gathered the *"sciences positives,"* and much more, in a *"philosophie positive."* Like Bacon, he worked out a pattern in which each segment led to the next logically. Like Bacon and many others, he stressed "Systematic appreciation of what is, renouncing the discovery of the origin and final purpose thereof" (*Discours sur l'esprit positif*, 1844, sec. 13; Fetscher ed., Hamburg: Meiner, 1956, p. 28). Thus did he shed the Aristotelian metaphysics possibly appropriate to the first two stages he discerned in human history, the Theological and the Metaphysical. The Positive phase, the epoch of science and progress, called rather for recognition of how little could be known for sure. One must regard all as "relative to our organization and situation" (*Discours*, p. 28). Clearly, for all Comte's social and political enthusiasm, such language could not have brought much comfort to librarians.

Relativity nevertheless had to be mastered in libraries on practical grounds, regardless of philosophical commitment. A major step toward relative-location call numbers must be credited to the Marquis Paul Antoine de Fortia d'Urban (1756–1843). A prolific scholar concerned with bibliographic guidance, he offered in 1819 a plan to use as classification symbols twenty-five letters of the Latin alphabet (he omitted W). A was assigned to Encyclopedias; B through D to his three divisions of Belles Lettres, and so on. Besides, he recommended that a second letter be used for language and period divisions: AO and AP, for example, for "'Systematic encyclopedias in

Latin,'" AO being for those "'composed before the invention of printing'" (quoted in Shamurin, II:36). On behalf of the patron seeking such help, moreover, he added a third letter to distinguish among different editions of the same title: AOA through AOE were allocated to five editions of Martianus Capella's fifth-century *De Nuptiis* ("Wedding of Mercury and Philology").

Distinctions of this kind had long been made in massive bibliographies, and were to become commonplace in classification systems like that of the Library of Congress. Fortia d'Urban thought of them as an aid to the reader regardless of the size of the collection. That was unusual, and applying letters to them equally so.

In his 1821 edition, the author acknowledged the urging of some critics that he use instead mnemonic symbols. But he declined because he interpreted the proposal as meaning the use of abbreviations like Geom. for Geometry, and anticipated results overlengthy as well as inconveniently tied to one language. Devices independent of language like the number system Melvil Dewey was going to make famous half a century later, it seems, did not occur to him. Since library shelf control was not directly part of the discussion, one can only imagine what he would have thought of the problem of the call number as used almost universally in later days, not only to characterize a book but to locate it even in a closed-stack library.

Germanica Focuses on Library Purposes and the Development of Librarians

In the years under review, the question of public service in the broad sense, and the problems of training professional librarians, were apparently defined more closely than before. The evidence most convenient is the discussion offered by Ebert, Schrettinger, and Molbech.

Purpose, Management, and Personnel The purpose of the library as seen by Ebert, and presumably by most of those managing the substantial libraries everywhere in the Western world, was to place at the disposal of scholars the heritage of the past. Some, like Ebert, were also concerned with the library collections as national patrimony. Schrettinger, speaking of serving one's countrymen, was perhaps a little more conscious of the potential broad audience. Molbech would have no part of that, so far as central or principal libraries were concerned. Their collections ought to exclude the material thought of merely in terms of "popular enlightenment or literary pastimes." Many such items can be bought cheaply anyway. Notions about liberal use, loan of everything to everyone, and so on, "are not just antiquated and unserviceable, but actually contradictory and inconsistent" (Molbech, *Über Bibliothekswissenschaft*, p. 216). He remembers sad experience at a foreign university library, where novels were loaned and circulation rose, where relatives and friends were brought in—until the "blunder was recognized and the practice ended" (p. 217)! That sort of thing belonged only in "circulating libraries" (p. 217). And to tolerate abuses like underlining, ripping out of pages, etc., is certainly not *"Liberalität"* but *"Barbarei"* (p. 221).

Accordingly, it seems that regulations for the use of the library remained restrictive in most of the larger institutions. Freer behavior was probably accepted far less there than in the newer libraries catering directly to the middle class and the working people.

Bearing on these patterns also is the notable role of the state in Germany and France, alluded to at several points in the treatises just mentioned, in contrast with the rather different circumstances obtaining in England and the United States, where so much was sponsored privately. Ebert (1820) calls for more attention to the laws governing libraries. Molbech (in Danish in 1828-1829 and in German in 1833) urges that above all, book choice and buying be handled by the librarian without interference from nonlibrary superiors; he therefore praises the Prussian regulations governing the Royal Library in Berlin, but disapproves of the Munich situation, where the librarian is answerable on too many matters to a commission of the Royal Academy of Science.

Schrettinger, fighting the domination of library administration by university or governmental committees—and he was not the last to have to do so!—projects sharply in 1829 the question of backing by the highest state authority for the powers of the librarian. Whether a university or municipal or other corporate body is involved as sponsor, the national government should determine (1) who is to be the librarian, (2) the policies under which he will spend the money appropriated, (3) the relationships to be maintained among the libraries of a *Land* (county or province), (4) who is to be allowed to use the library, (5) when, and (6) what kinds of books are to be available under what conditions. It is hoped that on all but point 1, the librarian will enjoy "preliminary participation at least for advice" (II: 195). This will give him more confidence to discuss the building, book security, choice of staff, table of organization, and regulations for use. Authority must go with the responsibility in his hands; for him to guard against contrary tendencies among officials on the scene is inescapable. But the state must help too: "for the librarian alone can and must know, what is necessary, useful, and healthful for his institution" (II: 196).

It is probably not a coincidence that the men who penned the thoughts discussed above were associated with large libraries in the Germanic area, in an environment dominated by university scholars and expanding government bureaucracies. Familiar disadvantages included the German university regulations which often stipulated or at least recommended that the librarian be a professor. Professional recognition apart from traditional scholarship therefore required ideological struggle. To be taken seriously in the sense that library posts should not be distributed as charity or political rewards and that pay should be respectable doubtless involved persistent maneuvering as well as argument.

In 1808, in his first *Heft*, Schrettinger defined library science as "'the precepts necessary to the purposeful organization of a library, built systematically on firm principles carried in essence to their highest levels'" (quoted by Molbech, p. 17). He did not however develop his thoughts on education for librarianship until his final *Heft*, published in 1829. Meanwhile, Ebert produced the first substantial statement of the subject, in 1820.

Education for Librarianship: Ebert   Although much impressed by certain predecessors, Friedrich Adolf Ebert did not hesitate, in his late twenties, to call attention to a glaring gap in library literature, the education of the librarian. He had been a junior librarian at the University of Leipzig for three years when he wrote (1815) a letter to Schrettinger—mainly deferential but also barbed here and there, to Schrettinger's known annoyance. When he composed his brochure on the education of librarians, *Die Bildung des Bibliothekars,* Ebert was "secretary" of the Royal Public Library at Dresden.

He begins in the ancient and honorable style, apologizing for appearing in print after only seven years' experience. This is not a text, he insists, merely an essay on method. Why bother? If Solomon complained of the number of books issued long before book fairs, stereotyping, and factories, think of what faces the librarian now. Furthermore, the spirit of study and creativity is now hemmed in by circumstances, "alienated from life and deprived of influence over it" (*Die Bildung,* p. 7). The critical scholar turns to rummaging in archives, interested only in what will support his deductions. But the age is so superficial that this important change is not noticed in the latest work (Schrettinger's first volume) on librarianship as a profession. Key phenomena are grasped at without real thinking, in flight as it were; inevitably, therefore, it has been discovered overnight that library science consists "simply of information about arrangement, and not also about administration" (*Die Bildung,* p. 8). Earlier times paid for that particular foolishness; things are no better now.

Really, the librarian's "traffic with the present is largely just mechanical"; the challenge is to serve posterity, by "mature and untrammeled" choice of what is worth assembling, and organizing it to last (*Die Bildung,* p. 9). Never mind the discouragements; moaning will not help. Let those who wish, go to the rich private collections. Real professionals will tackle the main job with self-sacrifice, not because some government decree demands it but because they know how valuable their contribution will be. (Ebert is probably alluding to statutes like that emanating in 1813 from the Royal Library in Berlin.)

To be qualified, the librarian needs the same knowledge others need; but his equipment must be more comprehensive and varied. If scholars must command Greek and Latin, the librarian requires also French, Italian, and English. In fact, in another half-century he may also have to know Spanish and Portuguese, and be ready to learn the other Western languages. The Oriental tongues are not so necessary, but it is advantageous to understand some Hebrew. Even more vital is history, "the science of sciences, basis and rule of all true study, yes, of life itself" (*Die Bildung,* p. 12). Working for the future, one must bestride the present, unshaken by waves of disorienting opinion in a world full of crisis. (This probably owes something to the attention drawn to history by the 1810 to 1812 lectures of B. G. Niebuhr, and the appeal to history in Fichte's evocation of German national spirit.)

Important also are knowledge of literary history and bibliography beyond the compendia, diplomatics (abbreviations and related devices in manuscripts), and such arts as copper engraving and archaeology. Encyclopedias must be mastered, not for the sake of absorbing all the trivia but to appreciate the variety of human knowledge and avoid becoming one-sided.

Of personal assets the first is a good memory. "For sure . . . pitiable" is the librarian who has to have his catalog at hand to find what he wants (*Die Bildung,* p. 15). Necessary too is the ability to write by hand cleanly, clearly, and fast. The mechanical should not be looked down on. Much time and trouble can be avoided if the librarian can take care of a loose page himself; besides, the book repairer is likely to be working under him and following his directions.

All the education spoken of, all the personal qualities mentioned, are but prerequisites. They do not by themselves fit one to "conduct daily business" (*Die Bildung,* p. 16). If that were only regarded more seriously than it has been to date!

"I have yet to read the biography of a librarian wherein it was not reported that when he took office he found the library entirely or partly disorganized" (*Die Bildung,* p. 16). The new man, if he concerned himself with the mess, always cleaned it up, of course. But when we read the biography of his successor, somehow the story is the same thing all over again. Plainly, goals and plans are needed; juniors must be inspired to prepare soundly for their future responsibilities.

The present texts "should be sedulously avoided" (*Die Bildung,* p. 18). They offer two equally dangerous paths: either coarsely mechanical hit-and-miss shelving at fixed locations, or a superfinely spun systematic arrangement, quite impracticable. Both are presented in the latest text, Schrettinger's *Versuch;* the effort to combine them is hopeless because of the contradiction. (The book is otherwise very useful, adds Ebert in a footnote; one doubts that Schrettinger was mollified thereby). The trouble is that the contradiction perplexes the beginner, who soon turns simply to studying what is done in a good catalog (Ebert names several).

Learning the proper transcription of titles from such guides is indeed an excellent start: Francke's precision is a splendid model. Next, the student should master anonyma and pseudonyma. Afterward he moves on to the systematic catalog, comparing his model with others, first the conventional types, then the more complex examples. (Outstanding catalogs are referred to throughout.) This should enable him to arrive at some judgments about general classifications; then special ones should be examined. By this time he is prepared to try his own hand at cataloging materials in an area known to him, working on features which turn up in all sorts of catalogs. Checking his own product against the styles in use, and against their mode of arranging entries, will be enlightening.

Only up to a point, however: fixed norms are dangerous because there is so much variation, national and otherwise. The French "will never let anyone take away the Sciences and Arts class." The Germans would be so much better off if they at least accepted something standard; right now, though, "every German library has its own setup, sometimes good sometimes bad, and no librarian is at home in another's library" (*Die Bildung,* p. 25). Since each sees itself as working scientifically from a priori principles, agreement will not be reached easily.

Steering a sound course between arbitrariness and too much flexibility is important. In any case, "The managing librarian must consistently follow through on what he himself has recognized as law; otherwise there would be no library science" (*Die Bildung,* p. 31).

Having covered the fundamentals of description and classification, the student is ready to explore specialities like incunabula. The French and English catalogs are fine mentors for physical description; they teach the Germans. (Ebert does not mention another recent French lesson, as it were, the publication which for the first time distinguished between general and specialized bibliography, E. G. Peignot's *Répertoire Bibliographique Universel* issued in 1812. Perhaps that is evidence of absorption with library catalogs rather than with bibliography at large.)

In this connection, as well as otherwise, it must be understood that format variation is always a threat to sound arrangement. By and large, one can succeed with only three such distinctions, each size of book being arranged on the same subject pattern. (Several pages are devoted to advice on notation.)

Altogether the keystone in education for the developing professional is attentive reading of library descriptions and energetic examination of the library he himself serves. He is always on the lookout for the advantages in what he sees, listens to his experienced seniors, and is welcomed into the professional family. Experimentation to improve matters helps a new man to learn the business, but it should be done as little as possible on library time.

Now that the would-be librarian has "graduated" and is ready to make decisions himself, a few tips may be offered. For one thing, establish a plan and keep a diary of everything relating to it; assist successors thereby to avoid waste and blunders. Further, when ready for changes, remember that a library which has had order of some sort dare not be inaccessible for even a single day, no matter how profound the reorganization. It should always be demonstrable, moreover, that the librarian believes in the words "seek, and ye shall find" (*Die Bildung,* p. 51). Like Argus of the hundred eyes, he never comes back to the desk without something relevant, no matter how small his collection may be.

Personal characteristics count heavily. One of the most important, if not the most important, is a strong sense of order and grasp of detail. It may be vital in the event of failure of memory or a sudden death. Another is wisdom regarding the reputation of the library and judicious firmness with readers who want to bend the rules. Dedication! He cannot simply go home when the library is closed—such hours are too precious for posterity. Truly may it be said of him also, "born, not made" (*Die Bildung,* p. 56).

The framework for finding the right sort, for counteracting *"Egoismus"* is badly defective. The most routine, "insignificant" posts in daily life are filled on the basis of examinations or credentials of preparation; "only the office of librarian is so far conferred without any testing" (*Die Bildung,* pp. 58-59). The appointment is often a sinecure for a ward heeler or a refuge for a broken-down pedagogue. No wonder German librarians have produced less than they could. Careful examining could clear away such flaws and make librarianship really honorable.

Of course the pay is too low. When a man has to engage also in alien work, he cannot give his professional duties the required energy and time; he becomes embittered and his judgment is impaired. Even the lower school posts bring more income, although the librarian needs more to pay for correspondence and his own books. Oppressive also is uncertainty as to what will become of his work; an understanding superior is essential.

The laws governing the libraries need a good critical review; too much is obsolete or dependent on oral tradition or whim. New laws are needed, under which the properly qualified librarian will really have authority, on the one hand to perform his work without interference, and on the other to back him up in dealings with the public. Overdetailed regulations are not desirable, particularly when they forbid local readers to use material proudly displayed for utter strangers. As for the careless or unprincipled library user, superior authority must support the librarian in enforcing discipline, or the collections will suffer painful losses.

These words have been spoken, concludes Ebert, although those "more worthy and experienced" than he have been silent (*Die Bildung,* p. 67). He hopes they will reach the ears of those with the necessary understanding and concern.

Recruiting and Schooling: Schrettinger   Discussing the production of personnel under the heading of Administration in his fourth *Heft* (1829), Schrettinger declares that anyone who thinks a literary education is sufficient for librarianship ought to read Ebert. Not even a *Polyhistor* can operate a library without special study and practice; such men are not good prospects. For the librarian has got to embrace the whole realm of science and art with "even-handed love," without favoritism for any particular subject class, a difficult thing for a scholar. To obtain staff with that breadth of view and dedication, individuals who will be "completely librarians" (II: 193), one must recruit youngsters with the necessary knowledge of languages. Furthermore, to assure concentration, such apprentices should enjoy not only congenial working conditions but enough cash so that they need not seek their bread as writers and be led to think of their library tasks only as drudgery.

Schrettinger further recommends that a "Librarian-Nursery" (II: 190) be established at the principal library of a province. It would both produce librarians for the various libraries of the province and contribute to the standardization of library practice.

Librarianship, Library Education, and a Journal: Molbech   Historian Molbech, expressing his views first in a Danish learned journal, then in book form, devotes a section of his treatise to explaining this part of the subject more thoroughly than his predecessors. His starting point is a dual emphasis: librarianship is a matter of theory and practice, and it consists of two principal branches, organization and administration. Organization endures only through proper administration, and sound administration is possible only if the organization is correct to begin with. One must therefore have a staff prepared "to meet the needs of those who read in the library and also those who wish to borrow the books; to exhibit rare and remarkable volumes; and to guide those desiring enlightenment on this or that subject" (Molbech, *Über Bibliothekswissenschaft,* p. 118). An outsider seldom has a complete picture of all the relationships involved; hence the priority of practical experience over scholarship. Although the library is much affected by national and political factors, the key is the librarian's own qualities. "Only in our age" (Molbech, p. 119) has it been widely realized that a librarian must be something more than a learned man who knows how to utilize books and libraries for his own studies. The old habit of appointing to a library directorship a scholar in need of a job is almost a thing of the past.

To master all the pertinent knowledge, to be able to sustain the claim of "all things to all men," seems beyond human capacity, even for a Leibniz (Molbech, p. 121). And can one assume unconditionally that a Leibniz or a Pierre Bayle, a Dr. Johnson or a Kant, would be the best person to manage a library? (Molbech quotes Ebert on the disorder so often accompanying change of administration.) Actually, thanks to national differences, a librarian trained in Germany could operate a library in England or Italy more easily than an English or Italian librarian could serve in Germany, But there simply is no satisfactory curriculum: the administrative and other practical qualities a librarian needs cannot be acquired outside a library.

The details have been covered by Ebert. The task may sound impossible. I'm not so far from that view myself, says Molbech. Where does one find this paragon, equally accomplished in literature, languages, book matters, and manuscripts, a critic of knowledge and taste—with a good head for business? Certainly a serious librarian will have little time for nonlibrary concerns; even manuscript service in the library must be regarded as a second-rank duty. How much there is to know! Brunet's *Manuel* is rich, but does not help when one looks up a book not known in Paris or not sought by French book lovers. The good librarian will keep up with literature internationally and see to it that the growth of his collection is not just quantitative. He will, as Ebert insists, need dedication; but that is no excuse for poor status and pay.

Molbech's next section, on administration, emphasizes the dependence of good service upon proper division of labor, smooth operation, and minimal paper work. He endorses weekly or at least monthly staff conferences, including the top officials, as urged by Ebert in an encyclopedia article.

No less important is the subject of the portion of Molbech's work which follows, collection building. Serving particular patrons or a particular field, is hard enough; universal coverage is an appalling challenge. The archival responsibility must be met, but books are to be judged not for rarity or point of view but for current utility. Don't waste space because a supposed bargain for a large mass of old material turns up; there is too much of that sort of thing in Germany. Equal care is needed regarding the new publications; there are no ready universally applicable rules. Journals must now be thought of too. One cannot receive the entire flood, but each field should have some representation. Since judgment is needed here, indeed, more than anywhere else in the library, it would be a good idea to found "a library journal or a critical-bibliographical periodical with special reference to the needs of libraries" (p. 203).

The Library in the Public Eye

In the Magazines British workingmen were exhorted by the Society for the Diffusion of Useful Knowledge to buy good books and patronize cooperative libraries on the ground that they were not only worthwhile but cheap. Thus spoke the *Penny Magazine* in its third issue, April 14, 1832 (1:21); and again, at greater length, taking note of worker privation and defending the desire of "the humbler classes" for "amusement," on September 28, 1833 (2:373). Comparable material was also disseminated by both secular and church bodies in tracts, in England and the United States. That a substantial portion of the hoped-for audience read these messages is very unlikely. As noted above, response varied with motivation and opportunity and at no time reached a high level, although it was higher in the United States than in England.

Even in the journals read by the respectable, libraries were in those years only beginning to find recognition. The Utilitarians who conducted the *Westminster Review* and favored the prospective University of London took occasion in July 1827 to criticize "public" library service in England. The medium was a so-called review of the 1819 printed catalog of the British Museum, to which in fact the discussion devotes no specific attention whatever. "Wherefore did men make libraries?" (*Westminster Review* VIII:106.) To preserve the books or use them? The "exquisite skill of the English nation in rendering the most noble collections of books unavailing" (VIII:-107) was worth a short survey.

The British Museum merited treatment first, a fine collection with a reading room "well frequented." The staff were "extremely polite and attentive; in this one alone of all our public libraries, are civility and intelligence to be found." But since it was open during the working day, and the professionals using it could best come in the evening, or on holidays, "it is not so useful as it might be, and as it ought to be" (VIII:107).

Several other libraries pass in review. In connection with that of the College of Surgeons, kept inaccessible on the ground that the catalog is not complete, it is observed that "a library with a catalogue is best, but a library without a catalogue is better than no library at all" (VIII:111). At the Pepysian Library, Magdalen College, Cambridge, a stranger may look at a book only in the presence of a fellow; that kills use of the library, since the condition is no more decent than "for a husband to caress his wife in the ungenial presence of an old maid." The Vatican Library is gentler, employing "hypocritical subterfuges" to exclude the studious. Thanks to these customs, "the imposter who publishes a quacking book, finds it much easier to declare in his preface that he has searched through such a library, than to take the trouble to do so in fact; and he may generally be quite sure that no one is in a condition to contradict him" (VIII:113). The Bodleian too wins several stiff paragraphs.

The critic's eye then moves to the "large and valuable libraries in most of our cathedral towns and cities" (VIII:119), generally locked up and often rotting. The "unheeded" books in those libraries and at Oxford would take care of not only the London University requirements but "many noble reading-rooms for the public in different quarters of the metropolis, and in the large towns" (VIII:125).

Librarians, except at "the first-rate libraries," seemed a dubious lot. "The poor low wretch . . . usually placed in this office" gradually "contrives" to throttle the operation. Would-be readers at public libraries are "often of humble rank, the inferiors in the eyes of the world, even of the librarian"; and they certainly know less of the procedures than he. They are accordingly "unable to contend with him" and are "at his mercy." The chief librarian "in public libraries of this class" enjoys as a rule a "large" salary; as a gentleman, he will not give himself any trouble (VIII:119). Indeed, librarians are like any other government official "who neither discharges the duties of the office himself, nor suffers another to do it" (VIII:120).

The need of the hour, finally, was a survey of the state of libraries in England, by "two or three persons, other than priests." They should study the number and kind of books in the collections, the regulations for admission, the times when the libraries were open, and the number actually admitted within a given time. To push for greater use of the presently locked-up book treasure was a "sacred duty" (VIII:125).

These *Westminster Review* comments may well have helped evoke the Parliamentary investigation begun in 1835, which heard numerous worthy reform proposals from future librarian Edward Edwards, at that time an uncommonly observant young reader. His urging easier access to the senior staff of the British Museum led a member to ask whether he would not "'consider it rather below the situation of a gentleman of sufficient eminence to fill the situation of Librarian, if he were compelled to give attendance in the reading room.'" Not at all, replied Edwards: the practice had been routine in the Museum "'formerly'" and was "'frequent . . . on the Continent.'" (Quoted conveniently from the official record on p. 20 of W. A. Munford's *Edward Edwards,* London: The Library Association, 1963.)

Government hearings on libraries did not however attract much attention. Nor, to judge from the entries beginning with "Library" in *Poole's Index,* were there more than a baker's dozen of articles on library matters in English-language periodicals up to 1840. And allusions to contemporary periodical articles (mainly German) in Schrettinger, Ebert, and Molbech are decidedly sparse.

In the Encyclopedias A better indicator of the level of public interest, probably, is the modest expansion accorded library affairs in the general encyclopedias. Much was already more or less standard. As already noted, *Encyclopaedia Britannica's* third through sixth editions added only some new data on English libraries; no article on catalogs was included so far. Abraham Rees continued the same Chambers-dependent "Library" article in his thirty-nine-volume *Cyclopedia* of 1819. But he did contribute apparently for the first time a paragraph on Thomas Bray's parish libraries, and notes on several libraries established in London between 1800 and 1805.

On the other hand, encyclopedia users were believed to be interested in something more about catalogs than the sort of narrative available in the *Encyclopédie.* Thus does Rees seem to pioneer, writing on catalogs of libraries, as well as catalogs of stars. He neatly defines "Catalogue" as "a list or enumeration of the names of several books, men, or other things; disposed according to a certain order." He begins with Willer, the Frankfort Fair catalogs, and Bassé's compendium, furnishing a critical discussion supported by many references to scholarly works in the field, including one title in German as well as several in Latin; the lengthy paragraph ends with a cross-reference to the article "Bookseller." The next portion acknowledges that old libraries were ill-balanced in subject coverage, "agriculture, manufacturers, and trade" being "thought unworthy of the notice of the learned, and of being preserved in large collections." Rees nevertheless feelingly declares that since "perhaps the greater part" of the old catalogs "no longer exist," that "a complete series of them is no where to be found," the labors of Cless and Draud, for all their errors, have proven worth "the attention of those who wish to acquaint themselves with the history of literature."

Now set before the reader is an outline of types of catalogs, with examples. Noted as guiding principles are the following:

> the order of the times when the books were printed . . . form and size, as [in] the common booksellers' catalogues; . . . the alphabetical order of the authors' names . . .; the alphabetical order of matters or subjects which are called real or classical cataloges [i.e., German *Real-*] . . . lastly, . . . mixed method . . . [for example] first divided according to the subjects or sciences, and afterwards the books in each are recited alphabetically.

Rees then appreciates two very well known catalogs of private libraries and goes on to urge the following criteria for such an instrument:

> that it indicate at the same time the order of the authors and of the matters, the form of the book, the number of volumes, the chronological order of the editions, the language in which it is written, and its place in the library [the call number?]; so as that all these circumstances may appear at once, in the shortest, clearest, and exactest manner possible.

From that point of view, he concludes, "all the catalogues yet made will be found to be defective." That statement may have been accurate, but by Rees' own testimony it was not based on enough evidence to be considered scientific.

Probably better entitled to such a rating is the solid and dispassionate, if brief, article on catalogs (*"Bücherkataloge,"* 2:104) in the fifth edition of the Brockhaus product (Leipzig, 1819–1820; 10 vols.), notable bibliographically and market-wise for bearing not only the "French"-style title of the earlier editions, *Conversations-Lexikon,* but a good lengthy German title consonant with contemporary feelings. The catalogs of "significant libraries" are pronounced important historically from both the general literary viewpoint and a special one "which could be called library-related." The reader is guided first through the bibliography of catalogs celebrated for either the total resources registered, notable selection, rarities, or a special concentration like the history of Hungary. Then come similar introductions to catalogs admired respectively for descriptive cataloging, subject classification, or their performance in both departments. Most of those mentioned were already famous, but the article was up to date enough to list one published in 1817.

Still more significant is the entry on libraries *("Bibliotheken,"* 1:750–753). If the earlier encyclopedias dealt rather casually with a large number of libraries and tended to focus on those in the reader's own country, if they treated the subject in the spirit of high-level recreation and a bit of nationalistic boasting, Brockhaus set a new fashion. The survey is merely a single column long, but careful in chronological and geographic balance as well as in the handling of facts. Noteworthy is the opening statement that the supposition about the "earliest library," at Memphis in ancient Egypt, is "probably a misunderstanding." The scientific approach is further evident in such references as those to the ninth-to-eleventh-century libraries on the Greek islands and to Richard de Bury under his true family name, "Augervyle." On library holdings the compiler is probably too trusting of earlier claims; greater rigor was however soon to come.

F. A. Ebert himself wrote in the early 1820s a fifteen-page signed article on *"Bibliotheken"* for the monumental and never-finished *Allgemeine Encyclopädie* of university librarian J. S. Ersch (1766–1828) and collaborator J. G. Gruber. The very first sentence (X:54) declares that much of what is said about ancient libraries is "imaginative." He offers six and a half columns on the story down to the invention of printing, heavily footnoted. The balance of the essay is a documented survey of libraries, country by country, with alleged holdings.

Immediately after this entry is apparently the first encyclopedia article on library science *("Bibliothekswissenschaft"),* offered explicitly as a brief summary of what has already appeared in Ebert's *Die Bildung des Bibliothekars* (discussed above).

The Ersch and Gruber material is frequently cited in Ratjen's translation of Molbech; but who else read it is something not readily ascertainable. It does seem to have influenced the revisions of library articles in the eighth edition of Brockhaus in 1833. Whereas claims about ancient libraries were in the fifth edition disparaged gently, the very first sentence in the eighth edition article speaks of them as having been laid "imaginatively." Many more holdings data are offered than in the fifth edition. The older reference to Biblical "Antiquities," by the way, has been garbed anew as Biblical "Archeology" in the eighth edition (I:872–874). Most significant, an article has been added on "The Librarian," half a column ending with an invitation to read Ebert.

The new status of the library is still more clearly manifest in the seventh edition of *Encyclopaedia Britannica* (1830–1842). Volume XIII, part I, issued in 1836, offers thirty-three pages on "Libraries," displaying in both text and footnotes broad knowledge of contemporary scholarship, including the materials presented by Edward Edwards before the Parliamentary Select Committee on the British Museum (1835). Although the space given British libraries is understandably disproportionate from an international point of view, respectable coverage is accorded not only to ancient but to medieval libraries and the services of the monks, and to most countries of Europe. The weight of the discussion is the traditional description of holdings. Some attention goes to architecture and decoration, some to hours and conditions of reader service. Money spent is mentioned now and then. Distinguished librarians are occasionally named. But librarianship as a profession is dealt with only insofar as it is implied in the reports of collection building, the statement on the Göttingen catalogs, and the vignette of the cataloging routine at the Imperial Library at St. Petersburg. (Perhaps the availability of illustrations of the cataloging slips used there helps account for the apparent novelty of incorporating them in an encyclopedia article.) The article writer himself plainly declares (in his conclusion, p. 318) that "Bibliography. . . .may in fact be said to constitute the Science of those who are intrusted with the formation and superintendence of Libraries."

Whatever imports, especially from England, may have reached North American eyes during this period, immigrant Francis Lieber (1800-1872) began a noteworthy career in education and political science with the *Encyclopaedia Americana* published by Carey & Lea of Philadelphia (1829-1833) in thirteen volumes. Based on the seventh edition of Brockhaus (1827-1829) with revisions during the very years Lieber was turning out his version, it was very popular and reprinted several times. Those exposed to it might have learned not only what Brockhaus offered on library history and holdings but a little more (VII:535-536) about celebrated institutions in France, Italy, and the United States not in the German product. Some of these data were apparently drawn from a work cited by Lieber although not by Brockhaus, Petit-Radel's near-classic *Recherches . . .* of 1819. Reading Lieber's work might also have spread some acquaintance with the book trade, catalogs of books, and censorship (II:189-193).

In the North American Review 1837 A few years afterward, in July 1837, the *North American Review,* voice of the New England intelligentsia, published a review essay of the sort characteristic then but rarely in later times. Young George Washington Greene (1811-1883), Rhode Island teacher-essayist, displayed one advantage of long residence in Europe, discussing libraries on the basis of Balbi's *Essai Statistique* (1835) and two other recent European works. The assertion that access to the great libraries of Europe required "no introduction, no recommendation, no securities" (45:134) may have been an exaggeration. That the institutions referred to were provided with librarians who "under different titles, corresponding to the duties imposed upon them, receive from government regular salaries, proportioned to their rank, and to the services which they perform" (45:134) was substantially true in Germany and France but not very often elsewhere. Yet, to have drawn attention to such personnel and their status was probably surprising as well as enlightening to many readers.

Without undertaking to render a full report, the writer did feel obliged to counteract some curious current impressions (which he did not identify precisely). In the "public libraries of Europe" were two classes of books, "books for study, and books of reference." To the beginner the latter were "useless"; to the intermediate level of interest they were "of more or less value"; to the serious investigator, "indispensable" (45:136-137). Perhaps the works of reference were important "at the present moment" to few "in America," but "every appearance indicates a great and speedy augmentation in their number." Serious research and writing had begun, a "literary class" was emerging; books were needed for every branch of "research and in-quiry," to "leave idleness no excuse for the lightness of its labors, and poverty no obstacles, which industry may not surmount" (45:138).

Could progress be cited? Yes, in Boston, Philadelphia, and New York. So far as the colleges were concerned, their libraries were, with few excep-tions, "restricted to the use of the students, the professors, and the members of the corporation or directors, under whatever name they may be classed; none of these are supposed to study in the library, but call at stated hours for the books they want; and strangers and students, not connected with the institution, can only obtain books by a special concession or through some individual of the privileged body" (45:139–140). Available also were sub-scription libraries.

Much more effort was called for. We were behind Europe but could certainly perform "with equal success" (45:140). The task must be ap-proached in a national spirit, first of all by enlarging the Library of Congress. Building up its collections should not, however, be distorted by bibliomania. For any "public library, . . . good, or in other words, correct editions answer every purpose of rare ones" (45:147). Brunet had furnished an "unerring guide," superior to "every other bibliographical treatise that we have seen." Finally, a good library required "a competent endowment, or appropriation, to be employed according to a carefully formed plan of annual expenditure" (45:148). More could be said, but not in a mere introduction. "The subject is one that may be deferred, but cannot long be neglected. It will go on gaining upon public attention, until seen by all in its true light, and in all its bear-ings" (45:149). Then, at last, would a "rich harvest of glory" be reaped, justifying the investment (45:149).

Richer harvests were indeed ahead, in glory and grain; also in pride, prejudice, and other problems. The eagle's wings were about to stretch out over libraries.

Chapter Eight

THE LATER NINETEENTH CENTURY

In the years between the launching of the first library periodical and the establishment of formal education for librarianship, capitalist society reached its peak of forward motion. This was the era of the railroad and the large factory, the big city, and the division of Africa among imperialist powers; of the corporation, labor organization, and strikes; of working-class ideology, Social Darwinism, social insurance, public education, and public libraries. Particular areas were further marked by characteristics peculiar to them, the United States being notable for changing forms in the subjection of the Negro, a great wave of self-assertion by women, the passage of family farming from an admired way of life to victimization by corporate growth, and the challenge of immigrants who seldom knew much English upon arrival.

Notable in library life was the emergence of new features in high relief, which for that reason exposed a contrast long in the making between them and older characteristics. In those portions of Europe stamped with the library traditions of German scholarship, little new occurred in the learned libraries, and the popular book service initiated after 1840 grew up almost entirely isolated from them; yet the struggles of the academic librarians for recognition advanced the profession mightily. In Great Britain, the fortunes of the scholarly libraries were less significant and the issues of public library service more nearly in balance with them, although contact between the two worlds was very limited; professional progress, apart from the contributions of Antonio Panizzi at the British Museum, was rather dependent upon stimuli from the United States. The last named was the weakest in scholarly library development until the later stages of the period under review, but virtually revolutionized service to the nonscholar through the tax-supported free library which gave a new and distinctive meaning to the adjective "public"; precisely these events nourished and were nourished by the bursting forth in the United States of professional organization and publications, not so profound theoretically as the labors in Germany but probably more widely influential.

Library Service in the Early Days of Tax Support (1840–1875)

The German Scholarly Library   When Robert Naumann (1809–1880), Leipzig schoolteacher and also city librarian, issued a prospectus in September 1839 for his proposed journal, *Serapeum,* he emphasized the need of the scholarly libraries for an organ of their own; he justified the idea not only on general grounds of dignity but on the practical ground that existing catalogs and bibliographies frequently overlooked valuable items in certain libraries. His fortnightly journal was to be devoted to such data, and to new acquisitions and personnel changes; it would review only books on library science or particular libraries. For such coverage the subtitle was indeed fitting: "Journal of Library Science, Manuscript Information, and Older Literature." The supplementary *Intelligenzblatt* was to announce important new literature in German, English, French, Italian, and Dutch.

These plans were carried out. The *Serapeum* articles were devoted overwhelmingly to library holdings of manuscripts; less space was allotted to book reviews and personnel and budgetary data. By the end of the first year, Naumann offered with apologies for its incompleteness a "Directory of German Libraries," listed in alphabetical order of their locations (in Germany, Austria, and Switzerland), each with the name of the librarian (no. 24, Dec. 31, 1840, pp. 385–395). Captioned separately as *Intelligenzblatt zum Serapeum* were a parallel series of fortnightly releases devoted to the new publications. The first issue, January 15, 1840, is a partial register of German books, resumed in the fourth issue. The second and third issues list journals published in 1840 in Germany, England, and France. The fourth issue announces not only German books but those from Holland; the fifth, books from Germany, France, England, and Sweden. Many of these supplements, besides a section for the books, carry a section consisting of book advertising.

Meanwhile, from 1840 until his retirement in 1884, Julius Petzholdt (1812–1891), Saxon Royal Librarian and bibliographer extraordinary, edited an *Anzeiger* ("Herald") specializing in the current bibliography of librarianship. It was an annual for the first ten years, monthly thereafter.

One may suppose that these journals contributed to the growth of the (state-financed) budgets and collections of the German university libraries, the average for which rose from 4,000 or 5,000 *Thaler* in 1850 to 13,000 in 1875 and 30,000 in 1912. Göttingen and Tübingen normally received twice the average; both their book stocks exceeded 200,000 in 1850, and Göttingen in 1875 was one of the three with more than 300,000 volumes. On the other hand, since the man in charge was not a full-time professional librarian (the Göttingen appointee of 1860 was the first), and the customary professor-librarians seldom took a thoroughly professional view of their library responsibilities, care of the holdings and service to readers suffered. Part of the problem was the pattern then predominant of vesting control of the library in a faculty library committee. Several efforts were made to transfer that control to the librarian, conspicuously but vainly at Tübingen, during the years from 1836 to 1844.

The situation was further complicated by the expansion of the seminar system, from philology in the days of Fichte, to history and natural science in the 1820s and 1830s, to German and Romance-English studies afterward. What this came to mean by the time Herbert Baxter Adams saw it in the mid-1870s at Heidelberg (and brought it home to Johns Hopkins University) was not merely subject specialization but physical dispersion of holdings in the respective seminar quarters: many a German university had no central library at all.

Meanwhile, however, professional librarianship advanced at the great territorial libraries historically separate from the universities and unhampered by faculty privileges. Some city libraries like Zürich's had long been also the libraries for the local universities, but that was not the case with court or *Land* libraries theoretically at the service of a whole duchy, for instance. Karl August Barack (1827–1900) not only showed what could be done, at the *Land*-and-university library of Strasbourg in the seventies, but challenged the university's faculty library committee as superfluous. From that moment on their importance declined.

The next generation brought numerous cumulating convictions and changes. One major force was the work of Karl Dziatzko (1842–1903), reorganizing the collections at the University of Breslau, between 1872 and 1878, with the blessing of the Prussian Ministry of Culture; the key contribution was the launching of alphabetical catalogs on individual slips or cards, and the standardized rules of entry devised for the purpose. Another influence was the arrival of news about the expanding collections in the United States and England, especially in the leading public libraries supported by tax revenues. Germany, argued the editor of the new *Centralblatt für Bibliothekswesen* in 1884, needed to benefit from foreign conceptions of library service and the career of librarian. Trained personnel would be in demand; there ought to be an institute to produce them, linked with higher education. The new journal would seek to advance German library life to those objectives; all issues were open to discussion; controversy was bound to help. Likewise vital were the subsidies to pay contributors furnished by the Prussian Ministry of Culture, and the subscriptions bought by numerous German librarians and by the French Ministry of Public Instruction. (Leipzig: Harrassowitz, 1884, 1:1–5, iii–iv.)

Twenty years later, as he looked back, editor Otto Hartwig expressed satisfaction. He had emphasized "the practical in our calling; the techniques" (1903, 20:2). And he had not hesitated to emulate the attractive model of the English journals by supplementing the professional core with miscellany about events and people. (He could have added that his call for formal education in 1884 presumably aided the appointment in 1886 at

Göttingen of Karl Dziatzko as the first professor of "Library Auxiliaries to the Disciplines.") Despite complaints, particularly about the alleged paucity of technical and statistical material, the subscription list had held up. The hoped-for broad scope of *Centralblatt* had, however, suffered an unavoidable restriction. The steadily rising movement for popular libraries and reading halls was so distinct in character that a different organ had proven necessary: thus had been created in 1900 the parallel journal, *Blätter Für Volksbibliotheken und Lesehallen*.

The German Popular Library These agencies, remote from the haunts and habits of scholarship in Germany, had begun as products of two different efforts. The first, initiated by Karl Preusker in the 1830s, has been mentioned. Presumably favorable to its thrust were the rise of the German book trade and press, a self-conscious liberal middle-class audience, the new comforts gained by advancing productivity, political freedom until the turnabout after 1848, and the close relationship between scholarship and life. Nevertheless, the Grossenhain experiment was not emulated elsewhere. Library activity was undertaken instead on a much narrower plan, the uplift designs of the preachers, quite conservative and religious-nationalistic: by 1845 they had established 38 outlets in their own image in Saxony, 34 in Prussia, and a total of 161 in Germany. Once the original impulse was exhausted, however, a lack of real interest among the people was apparently added to the lack of democratic involvement, and the libraries petered out.

A new stimulus was meanwhile on its way from another direction. University of Berlin history professor Friedrich von Raumer (1781–1873) founded in 1841 the Association for Scientific Lectures. He had lately visited England and Italy and in 1843 went to the United States. Riverboat companions who knew Plutarch's *Lives* told him that their information came from libraries and lecturers; he was impressed especially by the school district libraries of New York. In 1846, encouraged by the Association's cash reserves from lecture fees, he proposed loan libraries open to all, blessed by the City of Berlin and supported jointly by it and the Association. The idea was disquieting to those resenting the admission of women to the lectures and the extension of opportunity to any citizen, and fearing the political unrest then blanketing Europe. By 1850, nonetheless, four such libraries welcomed the public, and after eight years' apparent success they won enlarged support from the municipality. The collections stocked primarily history and travel, but neither romances nor contemporary poetry like Heine's, because several poets were politically disapproved. The holdings were controlled through a union catalog in which each of the four units had its Roman number symbol, a technique which does not seem to have been utilized earlier.

Similar popular book collections soon appeared all through German-speaking central Europe. They were progeny of the New York prototype insofar as literate adults were admitted, and in their utter isolation from the scholar-oriented university, city, and *Land* libraries. They were quite different in their dependence upon private fund raising rather than taxation. Sponsors included both religious groups and secular adult education interests. The latter became more active than ever after the military defeat of neighboring countries and the formation of the German Empire in 1871, setting the stage for the victory of the factory and cartel systems. A leading jurist and a leading historian, for example, sponsored a series of popular pamphlets on everything from Catholicism to railroads, the "German Contemporary and Controversial Questions" (1872–1893). Number 67, released in 1876, was "Popular Libraries: Their Tasks and Organization"; its author, Robert Jannasch (1845–1919), a prominent teacher and writer on economic policy. Which fact is the more significant, that the library pamphlet was one of the shortest, thirty-eight pages, or that the subject was included in the series at all? (The data are in C. G. Kayser's *Bücher-Lexikon*, Bd. 20, 1871–1876, L–Z, Leipzig: Weigel, 1877, pp. 765–766.)

Precisely how such efforts were received in various quarters is not altogether clear. It is known, however, that organization was widespread in the eighties, the very epoch in which Otto von Bismarck, the "Iron" Chancellor, was counteracting labor activity with antisocialist laws and state-sponsored social insurance. In 1886, for instance, the Upper Austria Association for Popular Education claimed thirty-two book collections for public use.

Editor Hartwig's above-mentioned sensitivity to the rising activity in the popular sector, especially abroad, was doubtless stimulated by the contrast evident in the list of "new books in the library area" he presented in his first issue (*Centralblatt für Bibliothekswesen*, 1:37–38). The five German-language items are a Luther bibliography, a history of printing, a bibliography of learned society publications, a study of old German illustrated Bibles, and a study of prohibited books. Similar are a Swedish book-trade history, a French history of bookbinding, and three French reports on manuscript inventories. Only two continental publications seem to look to the future, a Dutch national bibliography for the years 1850 to 1882, and a French collection of laws on public libraries. Traditional bibliography remains plain in a catalog of Buddhist Sanskrit manuscripts at England's Cambridge, and a catalog of early prints in the British Museum; even in a bibliography of Ptolemy's "Geography" issued at Harvard. Unmistakably different, however, is the tone of the other three United States contributions recorded: a catalog of books related to fishing whose title refers also to fishing laws, a work on *Libraries and Readers* (W. E. Foster's, New York, 1883), and another on *Libraries and Schools* (S. S. Green's, New York, 1883).

Statutory Provision for the Free Public Library in the United States The half-century under review, as will appear below, witnessed notable advance in United States academic libraries only in its last fifteen years, a little later than in the leading German institutions. The public library scene, however, enjoyed a revolutionary transformation. For the first time in history, it became possible for "any" literate adult to borrow a book without leaving a deposit or paying a direct fee. This occurred somewhat in the United Kingdom at the same time, and its implementation was severely marred in the United States by the handicaps blocking Negroes and children; the expansion of opportunity was nevertheless monumental.

The new epoch, acknowledging as parents the subscription library experience and the precedent of tax support for the school-district library, opened in New Hampshire in 1849. A statute effective July 7 empowered "'any town . . . and the city council of any city'" in the state, to "'raise and appropriate money'" to procure library materials, buy land and erect buildings for their accommodation, and compensate such staff "'as may necessarily be employed in the establishment and management of such library.'" The second section prescribed that a library thus created be open to "'the free use of every inhabitant of the town or city where the same exists.'" The third authorized acceptance and use of gifts on behalf of "'the prosperity and utility'" of the library. And the fourth promised to "'every town or city in which a public library shall be established'" under the act, copies each year of "'the laws, journals, and all other works published by authority of the State, for the use of such library'"; the Secretary of State was responsible for the distribution. (Reproduced in Shera between pp. 192 and 193.)

The access and gifts policies are plainly not new. Novel at the local level, although not at the state level, is the provision for large-scale document distribution. Most important, of course, is the explicit approval of local action to raise money by taxation for library service, just as it had been authorized a decade or so earlier for school support.

Six of the states which passed library laws in the next forty years held to the same pattern, setting no limit on tax support. But it was more common by far (twenty-three states) to impose one: the maximum varied from ⅓ mill to 2.5 mills per dollar of taxable property. Whether or not a library should be supported at all was a matter of popular vote, according to the laws of more than half the states.

The body authorized to collect such revenues and govern the library was most often either a board appointed by the mayor with the advice and consent of the council or the council itself. Actually, the age was one of rapid expansion of responsibility for municipal government, and board government was common for eleemosynary institutions. In some states they operated in the New Hampshire style, under a "short form" law. In others the libraries were regulated with more precision, after the fashion of the Illinois 1872 statute, which mandated the appointment of trustees to three-year terms, spelled out their powers, prescribed support by a separate library tax, and put the levy in the hands of the city council. A special variant of great importance in particular states was the government of libraries by school boards rather than local councils, as in Indiana; the school district played a key role in Michigan and Ohio but failed as a format for library organization nationally. The matching grants to libraries begun by Rhode Island in 1875 were likewise administered by the state board of education.

The 1853 Conference To have enacted such provisions required struggle in many instances, for the record reveals no eagerness of small property owners to tax themselves, and the common man of that epoch is not known to have read much besides the Bible and the newspaper. The Civil War would shortly be introducing farm boys to dime novels, and immigrants and urban slumdwellers would be posing other problems encouraging the improvement of public library service. Meanwhile, an effort was made to stimulate activity before the great battle over slavery.

The New York Conference of 1853 was a weak beginning, a trial run producing little for libraries. The "Call," May 1853, went forth over the signatures of several leading librarians like C. C. Jewett and W. F. Poole, and a number of nonlibrarians known to be sympathetic. Of these, the Worcester, Massachusetts, preacher Edward Everett Hale was to become the best known, thanks to his celebrated tale, "The Man Without a Country." Educator Henry Barnard was also a sponsor. British Museum librarian Antonio Panizzi reportedly found impressive this manifestation of United States activism.

In August, Jewett wrote unhappily that he had "'seen but very few'" interested, and "'some, on whom I had counted,'" unwilling to "'take any active part.'" This he attributed to a reluctance among "'our fraternity'" to any sort of ostentation. He apologized for lacking the time to engage in the prior correspondence known to be a prerequisite for success, but estimated that the meeting "'cannot be a failure unless we raise expectations which we cannot meet.'" (Quotations supplied by G. B. Utley in *The Librarians' Conference of 1853,* Chicago: American Library Association, 1851, pp. 29–30.)

The conference opened on September 15 in the "smaller chapel of the University of the city of New York" (later New York University). Of the eighty-two men (no women) in attendance, thirty were afterward listed in the *Dictionary of American Biography.* They were from every northeastern state except Maine, Vermont, and Delaware, and from communities as far away as San Francisco. Two represented the New Orleans interest, but they were the only ones from the south.

Jewett's opening address as president was a model of caution. The only purpose of the gathering, he said, was exchange of ideas and encouragement. "'Each, when at home,'" he confessed, found little of that except in his own spirit. The gentlemen of the press would, he trusted, appreciate the fact that the participants were too busy to be well prepared and in several instances were unaccustomed to public speaking. Thus should all contribute without fear; it was hoped that "'our meeting will have its influence upon the public.'" (Quoted in Utley, pp. 41–42.)

He made a particular point of the focus of the present meeting upon "'our wishes for the public, not for ourselves.'" He dismissed bibliographical associations, the devotees of the rare and exotic. The time had come for the new emphasis. "'This is the first convention of the kind, not only in this country, but so far as I know, in the world.'" Expanding knowledge of good books and access to them was its business. "'In every village,'" he asserted, it was being asked, how to obtain such books, keep them, and use them. He offered no source for that assurance, however, any more than he did for the remark that "'we are preeminently a reading people.'" His confidence that we were richer than any other country in the general diffusion of small collections of books was probably better grounded in fact. Of concern also were the needs of research. (Quoted in Utley, pp. 42–44.)

The Reverend S. Osgood of New York took the floor on behalf of what he called "popular libraries." By that he meant libraries like the one he had been asked to represent, the Providence Athenaeum, founded on subscriptions in 1836 and currently holding "nearly twenty thousand . . . of the choicest books" (convention record, in Utley, p. 153). The importation of books was welcome, whereas the contemporary immigrants made him nervous. He intended of course good books; the "bad books" in their "stealthy advances" needed to be "tracked to their dens" (Utley, p. 154). He quoted Milton.

Although we were not equipped like Europe with respect to great libraries, we were "probably not much behind, if at all behind, any portion of Europe in the number of books collected in our villages, and available to the community at large." There was indeed "no more cheering view of our Young America" than the tens of thousands of "young men" gathering around popular institutes with their libraries and courses of lectures. To inspire the formation of "one new institution of the kind anywhere in the land" would he thought justify the existence of the convention. Donations should be encouraged. Unsatisfactory, surely, was the state of affairs just reported by President Jewett, wherein "the number of libraries, of a public character, containing 1,000 volumes and upwards" was only 423, and the total number of volumes held, apart from school collections, only 2.2 million. Resolutions emphasized the importance of promoting in towns, institutions, and schools, *popular* libraries" of 1,000 to 10,000 volumes, and a manual to guide their staffs.

Edward Everett Hale warned that school boards had found publishers' rivalries for exclusive contracts too much to handle; also that the desired achievement would be diluted by accepting the other meaning of "popular" in book selection. The very fact that books were now inexpensive meant that there was "really no need now to accumulate" the ephemeral "in a public library." (Utley, pp. 157–158.)

Since action was referred to a committee which was to report "at the next annual meeting" (Utley, p. 158), and there was none, no direct consequence ensued.

Discussed also was the question of distributing public documents to "the principal Public Libraries," not just a few favored ones (Utley, p. 158). The Smithsonian Institution was thought capable of furthering this undertaking discreetly. A committee was appointed to carry the memorial to Congress, but it does not seem to have arrived there. Passed unanimously, albeit without much effect, was a plea for distribution of state and federal "statute laws . . . in their original and unabridged condition," to the "public or incorporated law libraries throughout the United States." Likewise saluted was a resolution cordially recommending "the mutual interchange, so far as may be practicable, of the printed catalogues of all our public libraries." (Utley, p. 160.)

Of the data shared in the how-we-do-it sessions, reporter Utley writes, "one is impressed with the meagre incomes, the small number of volumes, and, for the college libraries, the limited open hours" (p. 61). Service considerably less than forty hours a week suited only occasional needs; research was hardly even on the agenda. Sharp was the contrast with the libraries serving young men off campus, traditionally open all day and many evenings. Of course they did not possess many books—5,000 to 10,000 on the whole.

Hardly more successful were the schemes for collection building through international exchange of documents, set forth in a letter from Alexandre Vattemare of Paris.

Bibliographic control absorbed considerable attention. Outstanding in the light of later events was the exhibition of a "a copy of a new index to the Periodical Literature of England and America" by William F. Poole, of the Mercantile Library of Boston. The conferees unanimously urged similar treatment of "the transactions and memoirs of learned societies." Referred on the other hand to the Business Committee was a plan for a "Catalogue of Standard Works relating to America" (Utley, p. 162). And to "a special committee of the sponsoring New York Historical Society" went encouragement to pursue the idea of an "index and chronology of American newspapers" (Utley, p. 161) in their files, to be supported by 200 subscriptions of 50 dollars each. (While many a library was to prepare partial indexes on cards, it was nearly a century before even a union list of holdings was published, Gregory's of 1937.) The convention also received a letter from France with a classification plan, heard a warning that a classified catalog needed an alphabetical index, and was urged by Jewett to promote centralized cataloging (more below).

That the group did not promptly reconvene was probably the product of many forces. The principal one was the familiar problem of a leadership crisis. Two of the five arrangements committeemen left librarianship; Jewett departed from Washington, the designated location for the projected second meeting, when in 1854 he was obliged to resign from the Smithsonian Institution; a fourth lived in Ohio; and the fifth felt unable to carry the burden alone. Besides, the financial backer suffered reverses and withdrew. Neither the depression of 1857 nor the gathering storm over slavery could have helped.

Service Advances to 1876 in the United States, the United Kingdom and France   Despite these handicaps to organization, the number of library outlets in the United States of America increased greatly during the years between 1850 and 1875, by comparison with the period 1825–1850 (tabulated in the U.S. Bureau of Education's *Public Libraries in the United States of America . . . Special Report, 1876,* pp. 784–787). Of the "public" libraries reported to exist in 1875, the 551 foundings of the earlier quarter-century were rendered quantitatively minor by the 2,240 of the later period. Outstanding in numbers of units established were the "academy and school" libraries, a category including secondary schools, normal schools, business schools, and women's seminaries and institutes; but excluding common or district schools and church and Sunday schools. The count rose from 173 to 628. A sharper upswing, from 81 to 467, was enjoyed by the "social" libraries (athenaeums and young men's and subscription libraries). Foundings of libraries called "public" in this table ("free public" in some others), distinguished by nominal fees or none, inconsequential in the period 1825–1850, rose modestly to 257 in the years 1850–1875. College libraries initiated in the first period numbered 76; in the second, 182. At the same time, the college literary societies added 40 to their number in the earlier period and 128 in the later one; some were larger than the college library, from venerable (1783) Dickinson in Pennsylvania to recent (1865) Kenyon in Ohio.

From a geographic viewpoint, it is noteworthy that New York was the leader in more instances than any other state, Massachusetts usually second, and Pennsylvania and Ohio close behind. Only once does a Southern state rank high enough to merit mention: Virginia's seven college libraries founded between 1825 and 1850. Educational and religious traditions were sufficiently different among the leading states to suggest that other factors played a part perhaps even greater: population density and problems in certain areas, wealth, and leadership. Study of the facts on a per capita basis, by legislative districts, might well improve our understanding.

The record of growth in number of units cannot unfortunately be matched by a record of growth in holdings. Data are assembled (1876 *Report*, pp. 775-777) for a handful of libraries established before 1800, depicting the increase of their respective book stocks from 1776 to 1800 and from 1800 to 1876. But they are far too few and unrepresentative to warrant treatment as a sample of the whole. In that area we are obliged to be content with the figures for 1875. Of the "public" libraries then possessing at least 500 volumes (1876 *Report*, pp. 793-796), it is clear that the majority were tiny: 2,441 of the nearly 3,000 held less than 5,000 volumes. (And those queried by the Bureau of Education did not include the elementary schools.) Only 99 had more than 20,000 volumes; only 17 had more than 50,000. The returns, moreover, were sometimes loose with dates and other facts, tending to give a picture brighter than reality. Whatever the Bureau of Education staff may have thought of that, they limited themselves to such devices as referring to personnel listed (1876 *Report;* pp. 1143-1174) as "librarian or other officer reporting."

How library holdings were affected by the tariff on imported goods is an issue apparently not yet investigated. The law of September 11, 1841, protected materials destined for use by the United States government or institutions of learning. A new omnibus bill of August 30, 1842, likewise carried a general exemption clause for library and artistic materials imported in good faith for literary purposes or academic collections. Later statutes largely maintained the same policies, except that the basis of the duty was changed in 1846 from "per volume" or "per pound" (depending upon the category) to the value of the item imported. In July 1870 a blanket exemption was granted materials printed more than twenty years, and after August 1, 1872, immigrants could bring books in duty-free if they had possessed them less than one year and did not intend them for sale or transfer to others.

Perhaps equally important and little studied is the bearing of the struggle for international copyright. Denmark provided it by law in 1828, Prussia in 1836, and England in 1837, but the reciprocity clauses could not become effective until the Berne Convention of 1886. One major reason for the troubles of the years between was the pirating of English writings by United States publishers and vice verse. When Charles Dickens toured the United States in 1842 his major purpose was the advancement of international copyright; he spoke feelingly about it in public lectures in Boston (February 1) and elsewhere.

Whatever the significance of these and other conditions may be, for library development, few innovations in library service, it seems, were publicized in the United States before the founding convention of the American Library Association. One was the latest wave in the 250-year-old controversy over spending Sunday in any pursuit other than formal worship. Boston liberalism sought Sunday service for working people. The library super-

Artist's sketch of women borrowing books at the New York Mercantile Library, about 1850. (Courtesy of The Bettmann Archive, Inc.)

intendent, religious conservative Charles C. Jewett, was among the resisters, and disagreeable debate was one feature of the years from 1865 to 1867. By 1876, however, it was possible to report that "within the last few years several public libraries in the larger cities have thrown open their rooms for reading on Sundays" (1876 *Report*, p. xx).

A more distinctive advance was the branch library. Successful in England, it soon won advocates among Americans despite early failures under the auspices of the Mercantile Library Association in the New York City area (reported without dates in A. E. Bostwick's *The American Public Library*, New York: Appleton, 1917, p. 15). In Boston in the 1870s, fear was expressed lest establishing branches diminish the use of the main public library. The day was won on the grounds that the edifice had too few seats anyway, that certain sections of the city manifestly accounted for very few of its borrowers, that the poor should not have to pay for transportation to a free library, and that branches were patently the best way to reach special clienteles like industrial workers and non-English-speaking residents.

Railway workers, a recent addition to the scene, were drawing particular attention. First, in the years beginning in 1846, came a number of reading rooms at railway centers organized after the English fashion by the men themselves, just as had already occurred among the skilled ranks in industry. Such installations appeared in 1855 at Northfield, Vermont; in Montreal in 1857; in Altoona, Pennsylvania, in 1858; and at Colón, Canal Zone, in 1860. Jewett mentioned thirteen in 1850; Rhees in 1859 reported thirty-five. The sixties and seventies saw many more, among them several associations with constitutions and bylaws. The library in the Boston station of the Boston & Albany Railroad is said to have had a reference section and to have been tended by a "librarian" two hours each week; were there others like it?

Eventually more numerous and influential were the comparable units begun a few years later by the Young Men's Christian Association. Founded in England in 1844 for the nondenominational spiritual uplift of young tradesmen, it took root in the United States in 1851. The top item on the secular activity list was usually a library or reading room. The years after the Civil War brought quite a few more, backed by local groups of the Women's Christian Temperance Union; little of their contribution has been reported to date.

Equally noteworthy, if not indeed more so, philosophically, was the trailblazing of Samuel S. Green at the Worcester Public Library in 1871. As he later recalled developments, people did not seem to come to the library, and it was hypothesized that they needed help using it. The staff was therefore oriented accordingly:

> "It was made a rule that everybody should be received with courtesy, and made to feel that he is an owner of the library, and that its officers are bound to give a reasonable amount of time to finding answers to his question. . . .It has been a cardinal principle that the officers should manifest a persistent determination not to allow the inquirer to leave the building without getting—if a possible thing to find it—an answer to his question." (Quoted from Green in Robert K. Shaw, *Samuel Swett Green*, Chicago: American Library Association, 1926, p. 27.)

As Green's biographer notes, "in 1871 . . . [that] was pretty radical doctrine" (Shaw, p. 27).

England was no stranger to radical doctrine even in the 1840s, as the Chartist movement testifies. Not very much of it, however, affected libraries, although the suppression of Chartism in 1848 found librarian Edward Edwards (1812–1886) declining to be deputized as a policeman to face the Chartists and indeed signing the call for a new Charter. Actually, the land was full of "libraries." In particular, the Mechanics' Institute movement was on the rise, for various reasons, mainly corollary to advances in technology and concern over labor and political challenge. One was the 1841 law granting a building to an institute maintaining a children's day school; another, the Scientific and Literary Societies Act of 1843 which extended tax exemption to certain institutes. Besides, after initially excluding newspapers (unlike the private subscription libraries), the institutes gradually during the forties admitted them. By 1850 every county in England had at least one mechanics' institute, the density being greatest in the industrialized areas of the north; the total number in the United Kingdom exceeded 700, with a reported book stock of 815,000 and an annual circulation of 2 million. Ironically, this success apparently derived somewhat from the decline of scientific and technical material in the collections and the increase in fiction and other light reading. Nevertheless, the tide began to recede in the sixties; twenty years later several leading institutes were absorbed by the new colleges of technology.

This shrinkage of the institute role obviously owed a good deal to both reading habits and the educational response to new industrial pressures. Even before those influences took effect, however, the fact that the mechanics' institutes were never free was utilized by a few dedicated men as one argument to obtain state authorization for public libraries financed by property taxes. "A Statistical View of Public Libraries in Europe and America," published in the March 1848 issue of the *Journal* of the Statistical Society of London, projected English needs dramatically if in part inaccurately. Edward Edwards, the compiler, found enough encouragement to collect more data from United Kingdom libraries. Already known for his testimony at the earlier hearings on the British Museum catalogs, he brought his public library materials to the new Parliamentary Select Committee appointed in 1848 at the instance of lawyer-reformer William Ewart (1798–1869).

Hearings began in February 1849. Some fear was registered that free reading would stir more of the very unrest the House of Commons wanted to counteract. But the cause was pushed vigorously by Ewart and others on the civic ground that libraries would cost less than jails and the economic ground that England was competing with the industry of a Europe increasingly providing its workers with libraries (Panizzi's attempt to correct this misconception failed). A number of other members of Parliament doubted that many workers would find the energy to patronize libraries, an expectation frequently borne out in the years that followed. Outright objectors proved a minority, however, and August 1850 saw passed The Public Libraries Act, 1850.

Unlike the New Hampshire statute, this law contemplated implementation of the act only in towns of 10,000 population or more in England and Wales, and only upon the request by the town council for a referendum and a two-thirds approving vote by the taxpayers; if such a vote was not forthcoming, another try had to wait two years. (The 1854 act for Scotland authorized instead conducting a poll upon demand of any five qualified voters, within two days of the meeting at which the demand was filed.) Adoption authorized councils to pay for quarters, thanks in part to the disquieting discussions of building costs and debts generated by the 1841 report of the S.D.U.K. Public funds could also be used for furnishings and staff, but not books: donations were taken for granted. Admission was to be free, and the expenses were to be met on the basis of a property tax of one half-penny per pound. Revenue on that basis was plainly going to be inadequate, and few communities expressed any interest. In fact the first one to act on the opportunity, the City of Norwich, while it voted approval in September 1850, enjoyed no library service until 1857.

The desirability of improving the English law was recognized in 1855. The rate was raised to one penny per pound, the scope extended to towns of 5,000 population, and the purchase of library materials legalized, including binding and repairs. Progress was slow nonetheless. By 1860 only twenty-eight libraries had been established under the act; and in the following decade, when the Liverpool Free Library had about 50,000 books, Mudie's famous circulating library (subscription, 21 shillings a year) was increasing its stock at the annual rate of 170,000. Subsequent laws provided some stimulus—also enough complexity to require a consolidating act in 1892.

Meanwhile, help arrived in the 1870s from a series of acts establishing compulsory school attendance.

Improvements in English higher education also featured the years in question. The needs of urban middle-class life had already been reflected in the late twenties in the courses at London University and were now finding further response at many additional new institutions. Workingmen's colleges entered the scene in the fifties and sixties, and reforms were instituted at the older schools like Oxford: in 1858 dissenters were for the first time allowed to study for the B.A., and in 1871 all religious tests were eliminated. Colleges for women arose, but women were not yet admitted to university degrees. What these developments signified for library service has apparently not been placed within convenient reach. On the other hand, it is clear that the collections at Oxford and Cambridge and the other universities enjoying legal deposit privileges benefited from the contemporary tightening of enforcement.

The forces nourishing libraries for the rank and file in the United States and the United Kingdom were also apparent in France, but remained basically private and philanthropic. A Paris venture of 1836 fell victim to a fire, and another of 1850 failed for lack of interest. The Second Empire, however, was soon characterized by a rapid growth of large-scale industry, which drew into town large numbers of peasants. Educating them was favored by the liberal bourgeois and Utopian Socialists, but opposed by conservative empire forces. In 1862, together with reform in the small-town school libraries (see below), the scene was enriched by the Franklin Society for Promoting Peoples' Libraries, comprising mainly middle-class figures, and determinedly nonpolitical and nonsectarian. Between 1868 and 1878 it raised and spent more than half a million francs on propaganda for libraries, a *Catalogue Populaire* for book selection, and a journal of proceedings.

A comparison of the foregoing with circumstances in the rest of Europe during those years apparently remains one of the many tasks of the future.

School Reform and Libraries; Children How much the movement for tax-supported library service to all gained from compulsory school attendance is as yet undetermined. Obligatory schooling presumably means more persons able to read; but the facts are on the record quite diverse. When Prussia set the pace on the Continent in the mid-eighteenth century the motivation was royal nation building in a centralized style; compulsory schooling antedated by approximately a full century both industrialization and the emergence of serious popular challenge to the ruling landowners. Whatever nourishment was thereby supplied to the soil in which the popular libraries were planted is not readily traceable; nor is the school library story.

France, soon after the Revolution, undertook bourgeois nation building also with emphatically centralized schools. Industrialization was anticipated, and indeed materialized in the 1820s, before it occurred in Germany. Small communities began to be equipped with school libraries in 1831; by 1848 they held 2 million francs' worth of state-furnished books. Libraries for teacher were established in 1837, but in the turmoil of 1848 and 1849 were proscribed together with all educational meetings, feared as sources of radical behavior. According to a report rendered in 1879, the school library books disappeared during those days, none being locatable in 1850. By 1860 attention was again being given to the matter, and the following year the Minister of Education urged upon the Emperor the value of the "communal libraries" for school use and a plan to require each school to maintain its own *armoire-bibliothèque* (literally, "closet-library"). A royal decree of 1862 endorsed these recommendations and governed the practice of the next twenty-odd years, supervision being entrusted to an Advisory Commission on School Libraries. State subventions were soon supplemented by municipal grants and private gifts; the institutions thus revived were, like the school district libraries of New York, available not just to pupils but to local adults. Numbering 4,833 in 1865, with some 300,000 volumes, they multiplied by 1889 to 36,326, with well over 5.5 million volumes. The elimination of tuition in the public schools in 1881 strained the funds at hand for books other than textbooks, but the crisis was surmounted with state aid. In the words of *La Grande Encyclopédie* (about 1888), these libraries were "the real popular libraries of France" (V:664).

England had long offered instruction in letters to large numbers of the general populace, first under church auspices, then in secular schools of a more or less public character; industrialization and unrest brought more attention to the question after 1775. One by-product of the early nineteenth-century campaign for the Charter and other improvements was the "Ragged School" movement, which by 1844 had reached the level of a union in London. These agencies of instruction for the poor often included some books available for home reading, and the added financial support attracted from philanthropists in the 1850s doubtless helped; the movement survived until shelved by compulsory schooling under the Act of 1870 and its successors. If the service rendered by the "Ragged Schools" was not really library service, that privilege was first brought to precisely the poorest children of all, thanks to the American Civil War. The shortage of cotton riddled employment in the English mills, and the Manchester Public Library opened the first children's room in 1861 partly to afford the young sufferers a haven.

This may have been the first instance under secular sponsorship in which book service to children was offered on premises whose staff included at least one person regarded as a librarian. Certainly nothing of the sort is plain in the data from Germany and France. The trend in the "librarian" direction soon to rise in the United States helped differentiate the Anglo-American tradition from the established continental tradition.

How many child-serving units were known in English public libraries in the next few years is not clear, but the news did reach the United States. A study of English practice submitted in 1867 to the Boston Public Library was the basis for proposals for a department for the "younger readers." To trace the paths by which that report fertilized more United States thought and action would be enlightening.

There were, meanwhile, numerous native patterns and pressure at work. The long tradition of compulsory basic schooling in the northern jurisdictions of the New World bears witness to the influence of Calvinism. Foundations had been laid in the seventeenth century in both Puritan Massachusetts and Dutch New York. By the 1830s the beginnings of industrialization and the rapid spread of the franchise among white males encouraged attention in Massachusetts, Connecticut, and Rhode Island to both compulsory schooling and child labor restrictions. The first compulsory school attendance law, enacted by Massachusetts in 1852, required for each child aged eight to fourteen at least twelve weeks of schooling annually, of which six must be consecutive. From the end of the Civil War on, as factories multiplied, railroads spread, and immigration rose, similar statutes were passed elsewhere: by 1890, in twenty-seven states and the District of Columbia. Parent and employer resistance had to be dealt with repeatedly. In the South, where the problems did not yet include substantial industry or immigration, such legislation was born and mainly died with the short-lived Reconstruction legislatures (1865–1876).

As for book service to children, the Sunday School activity has already been noted. The "school district" libraries fashioned in New York were emulated in other states rather steadily: twenty altogether are recorded as operating them in 1876. But their adult education aspect was apparently the principal appeal, except where, as in New York, they were regarded as desirable competition for the commercial circulating libraries and the "trash" popular with youth.

A much broader outlook is evident in the organization of library service to the "'96 percent,'" the children of the "'mass of the people'" who needed library opportunity "'as nearly free as possible,'" by Ira Divoll in St. Louis (quotations from Divoll presented in U.S. Bureau of Education, *Public Libraries in the United States . . . Report,* 1876, p. 981). He began his campaign in 1860, three years after becoming St. Louis school superintendent: the key features were a low fee for life membership and an inalienable connection with the public schools, the latter governing book selection. Not until nearly the end of the war was clear progress registered, the birth and incorporation of the Public School Library Society. By November 1865, a little more than $5,700 had accumulated in the till and a librarian had been appointed. Promotion was excellent: the library absorbed one after another of various other libraries in St. Louis, collections being exchanged for memberships; and the librarian publicized his resources by means of school visits. In 1869 the books were transferred to the ownership of the school board; more small libraries were absorbed; in 1872 the Public School Library opened the doors of its own building to the school population. Admission of the general public waited until 1874 and the authority of a special act of the Missouri Legislature.

The episode testifies to the continuing importance of private effort as a catalyst for meeting public responsibility. Similar enterprises apparently had their moments contemporaneously in several other large cities, but the aggregate evidence does not seem to have been studied yet. Such stimulating was soon to be writ large by Andrew Carnegie.

A different element colored the picture when Caroline M. Hewins (1846–1926) became in 1875 the librarian of the Young Men's Institute at Hartford, Connecticut. In this subscription library of 20,000 volumes, some were for children, in the manner of the British mechanics' institutes. Miss Hewins disapproved of the brutality and vulgarity said to have marked certain titles (which ones is not entirely clear) and received permission to discard them, from the institute president. One wonders whether a male librarian would have had to obtain such permission. However that may be, women were entering librarianship just as they were entering many other occupations more rapidly than before, thanks to the changes speeded up by the Civil War. By 1876 there were nearly twice as many women as men in primary school education, a striking harbinger of what could be expected soon in libraries.

The future was further suggested in two other ways. Miss Hewins discerned in the Agassiz Society, at Pittsfield, Massachusetts, an opportunity to awaken children's interest by means of bird lore and bird study; she formed a "children's chapter" of the society in Hartford, developing walks and storytelling as library activities. Meanwhile, Boston Public Library had found the youth avid patrons. Suggested in the 1872 annual report, in connection with proposed changes in the building, was a "'juvenile'" library with its own entrance, to relieve the main entrance "'at certain hours from the crowds of youth of both sexes'" (quoted in G. Rees' valuable *Libraries for Children* . . .; London: Grafton, 1924, p. 90). Precisely what age group was intended does not appear.

Professional Leadership

The Bureau of Education and Its 1876 Report The progress of "public" libraries was next given a tremendous lift by several events, first, the establishment of the federal Bureau of Education and its informational activities. Certain educators had for years been advocating a federal service role in their field. The Morrill Act of 1862 for land grant colleges undercut resistance-on-principle, and by March 2, 1867, former teacher James A. Garfield, representative from Ohio and later President, saw through to enactment the bill establishing "'a department of education, for the purpose of collecting statistics and facts'" and disseminating them; for its "'management'" was provided a Commissioner of Education (quoted in H. Kursh, *The United States Office of Education* . . ., Philadelphia: Chilton, 1865, pp. 11–12). Distinguished educator Henry Barnard, the first commissioner, quickly produced substantial masses of data, and assured the public that they were in demand; partly for that reason the agency survived sharp attack, although it was treated shabbily, Barnard's own salary being cut his very second year. (For the next forty, moreover, the appropriation for its reading resources never exceeded $1,700; most of it was invested in periodicals.) Meanwhile Barnard focused on school conditions, teacher conditions, and school libraries. Opposition remained considerable; he resigned in March 1870.

Barnard's successor, General John Eaton, more supple, achieved more. By the end of his administration (1870–1886), the library had grown to 18,000 books and 47,000 smaller items, and the agency's statistics and reports by specialists were an accepted part of the federal scene. In the 1871 report, libraries appeared distinctively. More information distributed helped produce more to be distributed: the 1872 report carried 67 pages of library statistics, assembled in response to Bureau inquiries; 1,080 "libraries" with 100 volumes or more were thus recognized where only 161 had been in 1870. Pressure for information continued to mount: in 1874 the Commissioner undertook to prepare a large special report for the 1876 Centennial Exhibition in Philadelphia. He later noted that obtaining the data had obliged his staff to communicate, in some 7,000 letters, not only with libraries and schools but with "'postmasters, officers of states and counties, of courts, prisons, reformatories, etc.'" (Quoted in C. A. Elliott, "The United States Bureau of Education . . .," *Proceedings* of Library History Seminar No. 3, 1965, ed. Zachert, Tallahassee: Florida State University, 1968, p. 105). Ainsworth R. Spofford, Librarian of Congress, entered into the labors early, by invitation, and many other non-Bureau experts were added likewise. The document appeared under date of August 31, 1876.

One of the truly historic items in the literature of librarianship and of United States civilization, the Commissioner of Education's special report opens with emphasis on the increase in library activity, the manifest need for information, and the legitimacy of federal interest therein. That legitimacy did have to be established and defended. The constitutional tradition placed responsibility for education in the states, as congressmen and others repeatedly reminded those seeking a larger federal role. General Eaton's tactic was to devote a page and a half of the editors' introduction to an appreciation of federal publications and their distribution. A particular point was made of the fact that "many librarians are unacquainted with the steps they should take to procure these publications for their libraries as issued, and so lose the opportunity of procuring them at all, and many large communities are thus deprived of benefits intended for them. . . .Public libraries are the proper place of deposit for such collections . . . these collections will be begun and regularly increased and maintained in every part of the Union (1876 *Report,* p. xiii). The last phrase was very likely addressed to the Southern politicians and their friends elsewhere who were committed to "states' rights." (It was soon to be revealed that they had enough strength to obtain, in exchange for Rutherford Hayes' election, the removal from the South of the troops which had been protecting the newly free Negro.)

Stressing the same theme again, the "Plan of the Report" draws attention to "the history of the relations of the General and State Governments to public libraries . . . showing the province of each as defined by necessity and experience, and exhibiting in detail the result . . ." (1876 *Report,* p. xiv). Illustrative are the data on expenditures by the "General" government "for libraries and sundry publications, from 1800 to 1874," set forth in a table on pages 832 to 835, not to mention the history of copyright deposit, distribution systems, etc., in Chapter XI. (To these evidences might well be added the publication at government expense of the *Proceedings* of the National Academy of Sciences, from 1863, and the annual reports of the Smithsonian Institution, from 1847 on, noted later in the *Report of the U.S. Commissioner of Education,* for 1892–1893; 1895, I:707.)

The editors also declared that "economy as to time, labor, and expense," as well as "proper presentation of the subject and the exigencies of the case," urged issuing the report as an entity, rather than "a series of Circulars of Information extending over a considerable period," (1876 *Report,* p. xiii). Inasmuch as this reasoning could have been applied to a good many other products of the Bureau's labors, but was not, it seems proper to infer that the Bureau was very anxious indeed to make a big impression with its report. Whether or not it succeeded is a question not yet explored. We do not know how much it was read or heeded in its own day. Nor are we likely ever to learn how much more attention particular portions of it might have attracted, had they been issued individually as circulars of information.

A four-part plan is sketched, the consequence of the Bureau's consultation with "eminent librarians." First, history: as the studies by Jewett and Rhees have demonstrated, note the editors, the whole story of each library would take too much space; this reporting is accordingly limited to "classes" of libraries, with certain exceptions: "the principal libraries of colleges, of theological schools, and of historical societies" and "the public libraries in leading cities of the United States, where the chief depositories of literary treasures are found." The centennial year appears to justify a piece on "American public libraries at the time of the Revolution"; likewise, the library's role as "adjunct" to formal education of every type and level, and to programs of correction and "elevation" of the law breaker. The libraries of "historical societies, of young men's mercantile and young men's Christian associations" deserve notice too. Even "art museums in connection with free public libraries" are to be included. (1876 *Report,* xiii–xiv.)

At a higher level of concern are the college libraries and the free public libraries. The "usefulness" of the former might well be enhanced "by means of professorships of books and reading." (Did the report team know the tradition going back to Morhof in the seventeenth century?) What the colleges do for the "fortunate," the "free public libraries . . . rightly administered" can do for "all": they are "indeed . . . 'the people's colleges.'" (1876 *Report,* p. xiv.)

Plainly inscribed thus is a complex of commitments: to the culture enjoyed primarily by the upper classes, based on respect for meaty books and the time and energy to profit from them; to education as the officially respectable means of advancement, in an epoch of sharp competition and widespread corruption; to the patriotism more meaningful to white Anglo-Saxon largely native-born Protestant elements than to either Blacks or the rising tide of continental Catholic and Jewish immigration; and on the other hand, without any explicit qualification whatever, to the service of "all," with the aid of government, state and national.

The discussion thus generated absorbs twenty-four chapters (1 through 23 and 38) of the thirty-nine in the report, 637 pages of the total of 1,187. (Where "history" ends and "part two" on "present conditions and extent" begins is not clear.) The "third part . . . what may be called the economy and administration of public libraries" comes next: buildings and management, cataloging and indexing, binding, "periodical literature and society publications," reference books, and the literature of libraries and librarianship— thirteen chapters occupying 280 pages. These essays remain remarkable for breadth and depth of thinking, covering a great deal more than can be faithfully portrayed here. The conspicuous weaknesses are the very limited attention to school libraries, fleeting references to the role of women in librarianship, and the dead silence on the Negro. (Service to children is barely mentioned either, but it had not at that time become a major issue.)

Chapters 37 and 39 focused on statistics, filling 257 pages (supplemented by numerous tables in earlier chapters). Chapter 37 is devoted to "the difficulties in the way of instituting a just comparison between different libraries." A foundation is laid with lengthy quotations from Balbi, the European expert cited earlier (p. 309). What he reveals about Europe, it is pointed out, is not necessarily reflected precisely in the United States, "but every student of the subject will at once admit that" European developments "exercise an appreciable influence" (p. 745). Whoever pursued the analysis learned, if he did not already know, a good deal about the great libraries abroad, and the state of statistics internationally; also, that the subject had been dealt with in the United States, "within the past two years . . . in two different works" held to be "standard authority" (p. 758).

Whatever influence may have been exerted by European models, several attempts had been made in the United States and abroad between 1836 and 1876 to estimate the holdings of libraries in the United States. The resulting data were presented in parallel columns (1876 *Report,* pp. 762–773); their full significance would still remain to be assessed nearly a century later. The importance of the question was stressed, in the table of holdings of older libraries in 1776, 1800, and 1876, by leaving the spaces for unknown quantities blank, "in the hope that they may one day be properly filled" (1876 *Report,* p. 774).

As for increments and losses, evidence had been found for nearly $15 million worth of private gifts of "money, land, and buildings," to "public" libraries, at least five-sixths in the thirty-five years just ended. The "real amount" was thought to be nearer $30 million. "In the present state of library statistics," moreover, it was impossible even to estimate the contributions of books. A study of twenty-three libraries' records on losses disclosed a percentage much smaller than the loss "of paper currency in circulation during the same period." Nearly three times as many books, apparently, wore out "in honorable service" as were victims of "carelessness and dishonesty." (1876 *Report,* pp. 814–815.) Public library managers need not worry about their public.

To the truly vital question, what that public was taking from the library and reading, the answer was "'No one knows'" (1876 *Report,* p. 816). It was "rare to find two libraries" classifying books on the same pattern, unless they happened to be organized by the same individual. Several examples were given, enough to demonstrate "the hopelessness of any effort to reconcile the statistics of circulation of different public libraries unless greater uniformity of classification is found practicable by librarians" (1876 *Report,* p. 817). Variations in assignment to a given class were an additional obstacle, too familiar to require discussion.

Less appreciated, on the other hand, was the difficulty of inferring reading trends from even the best statistics presently obtainable. The basic term "volume" was ambiguous, its use unsettled in relation to "editions," especially in fiction. Since "70 to 80 per cent of all the books taken from public libraries comprise works of fiction," this was no simple matter (1876 *Report,* p. 818). Some assembled evidence was at hand and offered, "with much hesitation"; it "must be received with great caution." In particular, it was believed "that the average percentage of fiction read is rather understated than placed too high" (1876 *Report,* p. 819).

The problem of poor basic record keeping was compounded by uneven response to surveyors. W. J. Rhees had been able in 1864 to give *(Manual of Public Libraries)* the names of 2,902 libraries, but the number of volumes for only 1,338 of them; the libraries simply did not respond as asked to. A circular issued in 1871 to "all known public libraries," with only thirteen questions, elicited replies from but 180, and only three answered all thirteen questions. The main obstacle, evidently, was the "quite general neglect or inability to keep statistics" (1876 *Report,* p. 828). A new effort was made in 1872; a seventy-one-question inquiry brought answers from 306 "public" libraries. But on one significant item after another, the "no response" proportion was larger than 25 percent: "average number of readers in the year" (56 percent), "average weekly circulation of books" (39 percent), "Does the library invite readers and borrowers to nominate books for purchase?" (27.4 percent), etc. Besides, high returns were not always high comfort: 86 percent answered the question about fireproofing of their buildings, but only 19 percent of the respondents reported their building fireproof, 1.5 percent regarded them as "nearly" fireproof, and 79.5 percent declared theirs not fireproof.

More libraries submitted returns in 1875 and 1876, those with 300 volumes or more numbering 3,682. Yet, less than half reported on their permanent funds, income and expenditure, growth of book stock, or circulation. This was hardly surprising, in view of the large proportion of very small collections and the "many cases, as in school and academy libraries," in which "no regularly appointed librarian" was provided for (1876 *Report,* p. 1011).

In none of the statistics presented, declared editors S. R. Warren and S. N. Clark, "does a figure or other item appear that is not substantiated by what in our judgment is the most trustworthy evidence procurable" (1876 *Report,* p. xxxv). Yet the total state of affairs, the Commissioner observed, still precluded the long-range trend studies and the international standardization of nomenclature for educational statistics so much needed. The demand for special reports like the present one on libraries was nevertheless "increasing, and will not be long satisfied without them" (1876 *Report,* p. ix). The prognosis was evidently accurate: only two years later, July 1878, the Council of the Library Association (United Kingdom) authorized the collection of library statistics, and in September 1879 a statistical department to assemble public library data.

Internationalism generally was not a major concern in the fashioning of the 1876 report, but it was by no means neglected. For one thing, the editors rounded off their "Introduction" with a few paragraphs about libraries in Canada, Mexico, Brazil, and Japan. Also, there were two pages (133–135) about European institutions in "Public Theological Libraries," by "A Librarian." More significant data about library progress in other countries was furnished in the chapter (XXXVI) on "Library Bibliography" by A. R. Spofford, Librarian of Congress. He begins with a tribute to "the only systematic treatise on the subject in the English language," Edward Edwards' *Memoirs of Libraries,* and Julius Petzholdt's *Katechismus der Bibliothekenlehre* (2d ed., 1871), "undoubtedly the most valuable" work on internal management (1876 *Report,* p. 733). He regrets that a comprehensive bibliography published in Europe in 1840 has not been kept up to date and estimates that its

548 pages of "titles of all publications relating to libraries in all countries" might now be "more than quadrupled. . . .without devoting more than a line or two to each publication" (1876 *Report,* p. 734).

Of the data set before the British Parliamentary committees in 1835 and 1850, concerning the British Museum library, he is impressed especially by the testimony as to "the supply of books, the conveniences to students and to the public, the inconvenience of the absence of printed catalogues, etc." Actually, "the largest libraries in the world are wholly without complete printed catalogues," although there is no lack of writing about cataloging, and there are so many schemes for classifying books that "a classification of the systems themselves has fairly become a desideratum." He denounces "system-mongers" in general and Baconian notions in particular (1876 *Report,* pp. 734–735) but goes on to add information about several important European catalogs (pp. 735–737). The accompanying bibliography (pp. 739–744) includes nearly every book of consequence then known, in English, French, German, Latin, Italian, and Danish; and references to magazines, all but one in English. It does not refer to anything in Russian or Spanish. One small but very helpful contribution is a contents note for the Mader anthology of 1702 to 1705. In the companion chapter (XXXI) on "Periodical Literature and Society Publications," moreover, he salutes (p. 684) Reuss' *Repertorium* and the Royal Society *Catalogue of Scientific Papers.* Spofford's attention to works published abroad expressed a level of capacity and interest seldom equalled in later times.

Library Journal   Allusions to materials published abroad, "in any language," also appeared in the descriptions of the "departments" in the newly created *American Library Journal.* The orientation was nevertheless domestic and pragmatic. The "Prospectus," as reproduced in the "Introduction" to the 1876 *Report* of the Bureau of Education, listed Melvil Dewey of Amherst as managing editor, and as associate editors half the male librarians of distinction in the northeastern states, from John S. Billings of the Surgeon-General's Office to Justin Winsor of the Boston Public Library. It began with an extract from Winsor's annual report for 1869, lamenting the absence of "'schools of bibliographical and bibliothecal training whose graduates can guide the formation of and assume management within the fast increasing libraries of our country.'" They might, however, never be warranted; libraries manifestly could furnish "'inestimable instruction'" to their own novices. The *American Library Journal* was intended to serve "these and like purposes." It would try to be "eminently practical, not antiquarian." (Was that an allusion to *Serapeum,* or Petzholdt's bibliographical organ?) Each "department" was described briefly: included were not only English-scholarship-style "notes and queries," but job opportunities.

The journal was to be issued monthly, "about 32 pages small quarto," from the offices of *Publishers' Weekly,* whose editor and publisher, Frederick Leypoldt, had been offering notes on libraries in those columns from the very first number in 1872, a "Library Number" in October, and since January 1876 a "Library and Bibliographical Notes" department. The editing would however be performed in Boston, to take advantage of "the justly famed libraries and librarians of that vicinity." (Was twenty-five-year-old

Dewey displaying tact? Actually, Boston was the headquarters of his publishers, the Ginn brothers, but that was not mentioned.)

As for timing, the journal's birth followed closely the publication of "the Special Report . . . issued by the United States Bureau of Education"; its "real object," continued the prospectus, was "in fact, to form a periodical supplement to this work." In particular, the journal editors hoped their product would aid in the "early completion" of Poole's index and arrangements for "annual or monthly supplements," the preparation of a guide to special collections and rare works in the United States, and the like. Not only information but samples of all sorts were solicited. A limited audience being anticipated, the subscription price was $5.00 "for the first year," to be sent to F. Leypoldt in New York (pp. xxviii–xxix). To editors Warren and Clark of the Bureau's Special Report, the new journal's prospects seemed very good indeed.

The Dewey-Leypoldt creation did in fact become the official organ of the American Library Association for the thirty years beginning in November 1877, and, having dropped the adjective "American," it was also until June 1882 the official organ of The Library Association (of the United Kingdom). Dewey and Richard R. Bowker were the editors from 1876 to 1879, Dewey and Frederick Leypoldt in 1880. That burden was carried for the next thirteen years mainly by Charles A. Cutter. The deficits were made up, for the first ten years, by Leypoldt and Bowker.

Meanwhile, the 1876 *Report* was hailed in the first (September, 1876) number of the journal, where it was described most carefully (I:7-10), and an editorial praised it for being "so complete" and "so authoritative." General Eaton, and editors Warren and Clark, had surely earned "the respect and gratitude of foreign as well as American librarians." Their labors were bound to be invaluable to "the development of education in America." Happily, 10,000 copies had been printed, for distribution not only to the libraries participating in its preparation, but to leading foreign libraries and other interested parties. Again, on January 31, 1877, an editorial took pleasure in noting that, as predicted, the report had been recognized as a uniquely admirable contribution to educational literature (*American Library Journal,* I:177).

The American Library Association The same active minds, and some others, deserve much of the credit for launching the American Library Association. Inasmuch as a conference had been held in 1853, and many library leaders agreed in principle on the desirability of improved action of a related sort, the question was at bottom simply, when would the time be ripe. The Centennial Exhibition in Philadelphia evidently furnished the occasion. A library conference as part of the festivities was discussed by several parties in the summer of 1875. Next April, Cutter supported the idea in *The Nation,* and Dewey conducted conversations to the same end with Winsor and others in Boston. In May, together with their labors for their new periodical, Leypoldt and Bowker in New York set about organizing a library conference, and Dewey joined forces with them. That sort of strength was necessary, inasmuch as many stood by skeptically, a situation familiar to pioneers. W. F. Poole, one of the deans of the profession, regarded Dewey, half his age, as an upstart, and Spofford viewed conventions in general as "usually mere wordy outlets for impracticables and pretenders." (Spofford to Leypoldt, May 29, 1876, reproduced with much else pertinent in Edward G. Holley, *Raking the Historic Coals: The A.L.A. Scrapbook of 1876,* Beta Phi Mu. 1967, p. 43.) The youthfulness of some others like Charles Evans of Indianapolis gave the debate a flavor of "generation gap"; but, once Justin Winsor decided to back the convention, at Poole's urging, Poole himself and other veterans found the idea acceptable. Enough of them were ready to sign the call in mid-June to assure satisfactory attendance.

The meeting in Philadelphia was apparently contemplated originally for August, but protestations about the heat to be expected led the planning committee, chaired by Winsor, to delay the action until October 4. The 103 who came, including thirteen women (many others were doubtless unable to, the Panic of 1873 having damaged many a budget), were interested in cataloging and classification, indexing magazines, the provision of other bibliographical tools, and what to do about the abuse of library materials. According to *The New York Times* of October 5, the opening day furnished papers on "Some Objections to Public Libraries" by Poole, "The Preservation of Pamphlets" by Cutter, "A Universal Catalogue" by J. G. Barnwell of the Mercantile Library of Philadelphia, and "The Size of Printed Books" by Evans. A follow-up report two days later advised that Spofford had read a paper on copyright and Dewey another one on a new system of cataloging, and that the convention had memorialized Congress to erect a new building for the Library of Congress.

On Friday evening, October 6, a number of the delegates assembled by invitation at the Historical Society and crowned the three days' labors by forming the American Library Association. *The New York Times* (October 7) announced the election of Justin Winsor as president; Henry A. Homes (of the New York State Library), Spofford, and Poole as vice presidents; and Dewey as secretary and treasurer. Dewey had been conference secretary too. It is sobering to note that the reportage in *The New York Times* was rather brief, and that nothing whatever appeared about these developments in Appleton's *Annual Cyclopaedia* for 1876 (New York: 1877; new series, vol. I). More serious, a portent of much larger problems, there was again no participant from the South. And what is one to make of the observation by historian Holley (*Raking the Historic Coals,* p. 114, ftn. 4) that a paper on "The Qualifications of a Librarian . . ." apparently occasioned no discussion?

Possibly for those reasons among others, Dewey's editorial of November 30 in *Library Journal* (1:90) declared that the Philadelphia conference had done well because "it made public expression and confirmation of faith" in the library as an instrument in the development of the people. In the number dated January 31, 1877 (1:178) he accented as "the first great need . . . the proper organization, simple but thorough, of American library interests," and recruitment of librarians for the Association. The objectives were not merely "social benefits and *esprit de corps*" but "labor-saving." Without a flourishing professional organization "Poole's Index will remain uncompleted" and each cataloger would continue to struggle in isolation. Individuals could not accomplish these tasks; only the association could. By March 31, Dewey was contending that "the interest manifested in the proposed library co-operation" in cataloging, indexing, and the like, "is sufficient to satisfy the most sanguine." The first task, still, was to organize the association satisfactorily; the second, to establish a supply committee to promote the saving of time and money through uniformity, standards, and bulk purchase. Then could we move on to the main problem, "the education of the masses through libraries, by securing the best reading for the largest number at the least expense." (1:245–247.)

That laudable objective was very soon to prove further distant than it seemed to be at first. Whether "the best reading" would attract "the largest number," who was to define "the least expense," would be controversial questions for many years to come.

Meanwhile, *Library Journal* asserted on July 31, 1877, that the task of the coming "second" conference of librarians was to study, modify, and seek acceptance for the recommendations of the various association committees. There might be less brilliance than at the founding conference, but the satisfactions would be no fewer. When the gathering opened, on September 4, 1877, in New York, the *Journal* (2:5-7) reported President Winsor as expressing pleasure with the achievements of the first year; they included a new effort to report on United States libraries, the establishment of the journal, and the emulation stimulated in Europe. (There was also a Winsor warning, which seems cryptic a century later, about the danger that the organization could be "used for unworthy purposes.")

The editorial in the same issue (2:14-15) pronounced the meeting as successful as its predecessor of 1876, noted that the New York City press had given friendly and liberal coverage, and set down a few additional points. Uniform cataloging was said to be advancing, thanks to the labors of the Cooperative Committee on a "code of recommendations" and to a publishers' agreement on a schedule; urged now was the issuance by the publishers of uniform title slips agreeable to both the book trade and the librarians. Further, the editor endorsed continuation of Poole's Index, advising that a committee was working on it.

Turning to new business, the editor considered first the question of the government of growing public libraries, observing that "free libraries are vain delusions unless based on the intelligent desire of the local community and reflecting its needs and its appreciation," but criticizing sharply the wastefulness of keeping a library at the mercy of waves of "economy." (These remarks were provoked by the Boston City Council's blundering foray, 1876-1877, into the salary patterns at the Boston Public Library; Winsor's and many others' had been reduced—one reason he accepted the offer to move to the Harvard Library.) Desirable were a minimum tax on the basis of incorporation authorized by the state and support beyond that minimum under the control of local governments, the best way to assure steady effort at cultivating public understanding. Apart from that, it seemed best for a library to be governed by a special board representing the town. Altogether, the writer recommended association promotion of permissive legislation.

Other matters touched editorially were greater care in distribution of public documents, the association's welcome decision to appeal for membership to all interested in its work, and the impressive numbers and quality of the delegation going to the international library conference in London.

The 1877 conference was reported on page 2 of *The New York Times* of September 5, sandwiched between crime news and the delivery-service success story of "Alvin Adams, the Expressman." President Winsor's audience was described as "about 50 gentlemen," many of whom were named. His address, paraphrased by the *Times,* appears to have begun with an expression of concern (not mentioned in *Library Journal*) over the "supreme ignorance of the work of the librarians in the man of culture as in the man of affairs." With the scholar there was at least some point of contact, "whatever the diversity of range." But it was "by no means so easy to impress the mercantile perceptions with what the profession of the librarian calls for . . . [T]he money-makers are apt to think that a knowledge of books precludes of necessity the business habit, which, in fact, is often independent of training." Librarians must and could counterpose "personal acts of kindness" and prevention of "ill-directed labors"; that would enlist on their behalf a sufficient "body of the rising generation."

The *Times* story went on to summarize the contribution of the special committee appointed the year earlier to advance Poole's Index. "Lists of periodicals" proposed for indexing were submitted; also, "rules for indexing" for the new edition and "recommendations as to the manner of doing the work." Cooperative effort was stressed particularly, and the forthcoming international conference in London mentioned as a possible source of wider sharing.

There followed a long paragraph devoted to Poole's speech on "State Legislation in the Matter of Libraries." The district school plan had not worked well. Poole saw important lessons to be learned. The "modern" public library system, a phenomenon of "the last 25 years," had learned from the mistakes which wrecked the district libraries.

> It asks for no appropriation from the State for its support, and hence requires no State supervision. Those communities only which have the population, wealth, and disposition to support a public library can have one. It is a local institution, and the only function of State legislation in the matter is giving these communities the right to levy a local tax for the support of the library, and affording it the same protection given to other municipal institutions.

Poole did not, reportedly, "suggest any specific plan of legislation," or recommend any association commitment. He would only "in a general way" urge promotion of public libraries where they did not exist.

This was followed by a discussion, continued the *Times.* Bowker moved that a committee be appointed to study the role of legal provisions in public library management; it was passed. The remaining time that day was given to cataloging; no details are mentioned.

The lead paragraph in the *Times* story of September 6 stated that nothing had yet been done about booksellers' discounts, that necessary improvements in the documents distribution system were discussed at length, and that rules for uniform cataloging were moving right along. Another long paragraph was given to Poole's paper on library architecture and the discussion around it. Consideration was given also to use of printed slips "in books

. . . which would afford dealers and warehousers a knowledge of the character of the book, and become in a measure a uniform catalogue throughout the country"; to the new binding called "buckram"; and to the question of how to enter noblemen's names (family name was preferred). Authorized to represent the association at the English conference were not only the executive board members but any other member "they might see fit to select."

Of the last day, the *Times* of September 7 reported a comparative examination of European and American libraries, discussion of the most desirable size of books and of abbreviations in catalogs, and the unveiling of two plans: one for uniform statistics and the other for increasing the utility of the association.

U.S. Progress, 1876-1890   Thanks partly to forces long at work, and partly to the stimuli of the seventies, library utility now moved forward in certain respects. The association itself was involved in the gestation during these years of an instrument to help small libraries with book selection. In an article in *Library Journal* for August 31, 1877, the editor deprecated the alleged advantages of a universal catalog and urged a select, annotated list. The association was admirably suited to such a task: it should appoint five experts to draw up guidance to some 10,000 titles appropriate for a general library in an average community. He envisaged currency by way of frequent new editions. The product would be so useful that libraries, he thought, would gladly allow some staff time to those sharing the work of preparing the guide. He sketched some simple marking devices which would readily indicate which books ought to be top priority and which could wait; adding call numbers would be a giant step toward cooperative cataloging; a new library might by using the new tool avoid a consultant's fee.

The divergence between advocates of comprehensive, or even universal, bibliography and those concerned more with critical selective bibliography was at least as old as the late seventeenth century. However much or little of that was known to the debaters of the 1870s, Dewey's proposal faced not only limited support but some very knotty practical obstacles. Its first gain in the hands of the Co-operation Committee of the American Library Association was, by July, 1878, an expression of rather restrained hope for its realization: "attempting" was the key term. The only decisive note was the acceptance of the American Philological Association's advice to spell the principal term "catalog," dropping the familiar "ue." Incidentally, what began as a "general co-operative catalog" was quietly converted by a *Library Journal* caption into an "A.L.A. catalog." (For these and the following data, thanks to R. Bidlack in *Library Quarterly*, 27:137-160, July 1957.)

The committee announced only a month later numerous particulars about the "Coming Catalog," one being the reduction of the anticipated list to 5,000 titles. The proceedings were evidently regarded as teasing by some, for the September *Library Journal* carried an open letter from "F" asking bluntly when the first instalment would appear. Dewey's editorial response was the observation that the project needed only someone's "labor of love" to organize it and enlist libraries in implementing the plan; he was confident that it would be done sooner or later—later, if dependent upon compensation. He had flood-lit the dilemma to be faced often in the days that followed, especially as an individual's standing was increasingly affected by his salary and total income, the dilemma: should librarians insist upon proper financial support for necessary tasks and leave them undone without it, or should they manage somehow through volunteer labor at the cost of undermining the professional stance?

Taking the bull by the horns, the Co-Operation Committee created in November, 1878, a Committee on Preparation. A subscription price in advance was set at $2.50 for a 250-page work. Neither pleas nor ominous warnings about the greater cost of an individual catalog seemed to avail. Hope rose when Frederick Perkins in December 1879 left the Boston Public Library for Dewey's Reader and Writers Economy Company, the idea being to apply Perkins' talents in part to the "Coming Catalog." But the progress actually made on that basis was upset in less than a year by Perkins' going off to an attractive post in the San Francisco Public Library. When Poole complained at the 1883 convention in Buffalo that subscribers were being abused by a four-year delay, Dewey rejoined that the profession had waited thirty years for *Poole's Index,* and was indubitably proud of it. The future seemed to lie with a possibility that the Bureau of Education would print and distribute the the catalog, if the editorial burden were carried by someone else; Dewey accepted the "draft," with the reservation that it must wait until he finished the second edition of his decimal classification.

Between that responsibility, larger than he anticipated, his new career as a library educator at Columbia, and various other activities, the "Coming Catalog" was clearly, in 1886, still "coming." Responding to many pressures for publication activity, the Milwaukee conference of A.L.A. established that year a Publishing Section, whose program was expected to include various bibliographical tools and catalog cards for new books. Financing was reckoned on the basis of dues of $10.00 a year for both individuals and institutions. It proved insufficient promptly in connection with catalog cards; and the 1890 publication of *Reading for the Young,* John F. Sargent's 121-page revision of the earlier work by Caroline Hewins, was a bookkeeping success only because the author received no compensation for the manuscript. The saving power of another world's fair was a few years in the future.

If there were good reasons to assist small libraries with book selection, many librarians perceived that the larger collections created an equally important need for guiding the would-be reader amid riches which might otherwise overwhelm him. Perhaps the first to bring this thesis forward was Samuel Swett Green of Worcester, Massachusetts; and the convenience of his point in winning more money from the city fathers was by his own testimony more than coincidental. Patrons needed individual help, he told the 1876 Conference, in a paper published also in *Library Journal* (1:74–81, October 1876). He stressed cordiality, and its likely influence upon the pursestrings of the local authorities. Since, however, the focus was technique rather than broad policy, it was easy to counter-argue that better catalogs and the like would do just as well.

Formal schooling was contributing both positively and negatively to the preparation of individual service soil. On the negative side was the native pragmatic emphasis on the practical in basic instruction. It was strengthened philosophically by the reasoning of Herbert Spencer ("What knowledge is of most worth?"), and pedagogically by the Pestalozzian "object" teaching, both of which found much favor in the middle of the century. On the positive side was the successful promotion between 1840 and 1880, by their publishers, of anthologies of approved reading (McGuffey's series was the most famous); they formed an admirable foundation for the Herbartian stress of the eighties on teaching the best literature for moral values.

Significant also in the late seventies and eighties was the attention given to relationships between schools and libraries, notably at the 1879 convention of the American Library Association. By 1885 that body was able to examine data on the subject from seventy-five schools, assembled in an official report. Two years later the National Association of Teachers (subsequently renamed the National Education Association) sponsored a program on teaching pupils the use of reference books in the library. Thus was undermined the hallowed tradition of barring from public libraries persons under age fourteen. As for the "public-school" libraries purporting to serve both clienteles, Grand Rapids Public Library chief H. J. Carr, at the A.L.A. 1889 conference, dubbed them "so-called" and declared that "nearly all . . . are quasi-free public libraries . . . doing absolutely or practically the work of such" (A.L.A., *Annual Conference Proceedings, 1889,* Chicago, p. 208).

At the secondary level, the nourishment was apparently still weak. The free high school, in existence officially since 1827 in Massachusetts, did not become a serious rival to the academy before the Civil War; the real increase of the public institution began between 1880 and 1890, when the reported numbers rose from 800 to 2,426. "The special field of the school or academy library" is barely mentioned in the conventional reference works; the weight of the remarks in the *Report of the Commissioner of Education, 1892-1893,* is as much hortatory as descriptive of actuality (I:693-697, 917-919).

In the majority of the colleges, judging from data gathered by the Commissioner for his report for 1888-1889, the state of affairs was not greatly better. As analyzed by Lodilla Ambrose in *Library Journal* (April, 1893), the overwhelming fact was small collections. One had to descend the size ladder to 25,000 to 30,000 volumes before one reached a frequency of more than ten institutions. In fact, the vast majority are recorded (*Library Journal,* 18:113) as having less than 10,000, with 43 percent of the students dependent upon libraries of under 5,000 volumes. Scarcely surprising therefore are the mournful notes that only one-third of the college librarians were exclusively librarians rather than mainly professors and that few libraries offered guidance to readers or were open on Sundays or holidays.

Promising change struggled ahead on some fronts. One sign of the times which proved to be positive was the paucity of printed catalogs and the rise of card catalogs. Another, mentioned in the *Report of the Commissioner of Education, 1892-1893* (I:925), was the dying of the literary activity of the college literary societies and the uniting of their book collections with the college's own "very generally" since the 1876 *Report.* Furthermore, according to the same authority, the proportion of college libraries not open daily was one-seventh in 1877 but a mere one-fortieth "now." In 1877 the books were available in effect only to the faculty; "now, by means of reserved books and long library hours, the privilege is extended to all students" (I:928). Facilities were provided for use on the premises wherever loan was not permitted. Yet, loan to a student for a limited time of a book needed in his work was still not allowed, although it was a faculty privilege as a matter of course; besides, unlimited loan to professors "almost invariably leads to abuse" (I:929). Several institutions had been experimenting with lectures on the library and its use, but no more than a dozen or so were still trying. More successful were the limited devices of complaint books, shelves for displaying new books, and a box for purchase suggestions.

At several larger institutions, vital change was in motion. In 1872 Harvard abolished all requirements for particular subjects for seniors; twenty years later nearly all Harvard education was elective. Library, laboratory, and seminar became in 1876 the matrix at Johns Hopkins for the individual research and related development ever since called "graduate work." In one scholarly field after another, the center of activity and publication was transferring to or being founded at a university. These forces placed great demands upon libraries as servants of specific types of effort, even if assistance to the individual was not yet clearly on the agenda. The central versus the departmental library had been reported in 1876 as "now beginning" to be an issue (U.S. Bureau of Education, *Public Libraries in the United States . . . Special Report,* p. 61). The 1892–1893 *Report* (I:925) remarked on the emergence "in the last ten years" of a pressure for departmental libraries, and counter-pressures notably on grounds of economy, a debate still very familiar nearly a century afterward.

The end of the period saw the establishment by the American Library Association of a college library section (1889) and a trustees' section (1890).

Cataloging and shelving, and the development of classification and subject guidance, will be discussed below.

By 1883, the Buffalo Conference of the American Library Association heard a statement on aids and guides for readers which indicated a new degree of "'personal assistance reported from various libraries all over the country'" (quoted conveniently, with much else pertinent, in S. Rothstein's "Reference Service in American Libraries, 1850–1900," *Library Quarterly,* 23:9, January 1953). The context was still a list of devices, and some librarians thought of it even in 1889 as suitable only for small libraries, as a last resort. On the other hand, Dewey, wrestling with the problems of education for librarianship at Columbia, was justifying instruction in interpreting a collection to its users. In 1886, the work of personal assistance became at Columbia's Library a distinct "reference department." The very next year, the examining committee of the Boston Public Library advised that since the catalog was but one means of linking the inquirer with what he sought, personnel should be on hand who were specialists in such guidance. William Foster of the Providence Public Library recommended creation of a reference department in 1883, and again in 1890, this time as "urgent." A new era was at hand.

Easing the operation of all libraries "which loan books to readers for home use, including both school, free-public, and pay-public, and proprietary or association libraries" were the improvements in charging devices and routines (A.L.A., *Annual Conference Proceedings, 1889,* p. 203). A questionnaire to some 300 libraries, returned by two-thirds, of which 146 were "Free Public," offered enlightenment at the St. Louis conference in 1889.

Reporter H. J. Carr, of the Grand Rapids Public Library, began with some history, noting particularly that the old mercantile ledger had held its own for library loan records until early in the Civil War, thereafter gradually superseded by a charging slip or card of one sort or another.

He then summarized the responses to the sixty-two questions, emphasizing the largest and most homogeneous group of respondents, the 146 free public libraries. The "minimum age at which takers are allowed to draw books for home use in their own name" was most often fourteen; second in frequency, twelve. About half required formal "guarantors for all book-takers" and another thirty-eight "a reference to some responsible party"; twenty-seven free libraries, and seven of the twenty-two fee libraries, required none; the balance were in between. Noteworthy in the matter of formal guarantors are the eleven libraries stipulating a male property owner or freeholder and the five accepting only a male or an unmarried woman; the restriction, "as explained by some" (p. 209), derived from the laws of certain states under which the bond of a married woman was valueless. Most of these libraries asked for a registration signature in some fashion; borrowing privileges in most free public libraries ran indefinitely. Borrowers' cards were common in the free public libraries and customarily carried charging dates; they were not so often used in the other libraries. More than half the respondents were stamping dates on charging cards or slips, and thirty more were writing them; some used different colored inks to distinguish between loans and returns.

The loan periods were strikingly uniform, 132 of the 203 respondents setting it at fourteen days or two weeks. Some libraries made distinctions between "magazines and books, or new books and older ones, or as to number of volumes and size of work, or between juvenile and adult readers, or city and country borrowers." Nearly all libraries allowed renewal, quite a few only once. Assessment of fines for overdues was "a very general custom," the rates fairly similar. (Reporting librarian Carr remarks in this connection, although apparently not in others, that "when such practice originated, or what were the motives that led to it, are matters which do not now especially concern us" [p. 211]; the motivation expressed in current regulations was to deter theft or other abuse.) At ninety-nine libraries, a borrower failing to pay a fine was deprived of his privileges until he made good. Fees were sometimes charged for replacement of a lost library card.

Carr ended his report with a thirty-nine-item annotated bibliography composed almost entirely of materials on the subject published in *Library Journal*.

However their offerings and style may have affected their course, libraries of more than 300 volumes called "public" in 1876, reached in 1884 and 1885 the number 5,338, with aggregate holdings of 20.6 million volumes (U.S. Bureau of Education, *Report of the Commissioner of Education, 1884–1885, 1886*, p. ccxxix). By comparison with the data of 1875 (1876 *Report,* p. 797), those were increases of 45 and 60 percent respectively, far higher than contemporary population growth. The forces producing so marked a quantitative change were also generating a qualitative transformation discerned at the time with varying degrees of sensitivity. Samuel S. Green, capable of "radical doctrine" about pleasing borrowers in 1871, offered principles of book selection in 1892, first to state libraries, then to "a general subscription library with a constituency mainly of people of leisure," and only third, with no apparent emphasis, to "a public library in a great manufacturing town, or a special library for architects and engineers" (1892–1893 Report I:702). Perhaps more aware of the already settled triumph of the tax-supported species, George W. Cole wrote in the same compilation that "founding public libraries" had so many advantages that they were now "springing up in nearly every town and city where they have not heretofore been established." This advance owed much to the work of the American Library Association, he went on; in fact, more than to "all the other causes combined." (1892–1893 Report, I:713–714.)

Notwithstanding this powerful undertow, the railroad reading rooms continued to flourish for the time being. In 1883, there were seventy YMCA railroad branch reading rooms in the United States, sponsored by two-thirds of the railroad companies, which provided $75,000 a year for their support. Paid thus were sixty-one branch secretaries, whose duties included operation of the book collection. So strong a commitment is rather persuasive evidence of corporate concern to counteract the militancy manifested in the national rail strike of 1877. The holdings were mainly "standard" novels, magazines, and religious items. Much the same was true also of the libraries maintained primarily for railwaymen by the WCTU.

The International Conference of 1877 The impulse of the achievement at Philadelphia traveled widely. It found an exceptional response in England, an international conference being organized in London the very next year. The bulk of the 140 libraries and three governments represented were of course in the United Kingdom itself, 43 in London and 69 in other communities, only about one-fourth called "public" or "free." The names of seventeen libraries were registered on behalf of the United States, eight of them public and five academic. Represented also were Belgium, Denmark, France, Greece, Italy, and Australia. German librarianship was saluted in the opening address, especially for contributing the professional term *Bibliothekswissenschaft* ("library science") and much experience with systematic catalogs. German librarians played no part in the deliberations, however; as a nonlibrarian proxy explained, October was the wrong time for them because they were all "closely connected with the schools, colleges, and universities" and absorbed in the just-opened "winter *semester*" (Conference of Librarians, London, 1877, *Transactions and Proceedings*, London: Whittingham, 1878, p. 164).

Conference president John Winter Jones, librarian of the British Museum, began the meeting by crediting "America . . . that country of energy and activity" with the idea. But he went on to remark that the logical preoccupation of the Philadelphia gathering, "their library system," was of only limited relevance in the United Kingdom; the 1876 Report by the Bureau of Education underlined the absence of anything comparable about "the British Colonies." (*Transactions*, pp. 1–2.)

Of the numerous topics touched, from universal bibliography to the damage done to bindings by heat, a few seem worth a few moments attention. Perhaps first in importance, the service rendered the mass of the population was judged inadequate. One of the complaints about recent efforts was that "free" meant "charity" to the English taxpayer and was accordingly annoying; the United States term "public" sounded better. Among the other possibilities mentioned were the large lending libraries "now being" sponsored by "the managers of certain co-operative societies . . . in connexion with their stores." (The impact of the Rochdale movement on libraries deserves study.)

"On the Admission of Fiction in Free Public Libraries" was one of the longer contributions. Speaker Peter Cowell of Liverpool was surprised that the subject was brought up, because fiction seemed to him "virtually settled" as a major component in "free lending libraries." Despite cherished myths to the contrary, it was plain that "younger" readers, women, and mechanics liked novels well enough so that 75 percent of the Liverpool circulation was fiction. He noticed the same of United States libraries; Boston's Perkins was quoted from the 1876 *Report*. After commenting on various aspects of the question, Cowell concluded that "complying with the exact taste of the general public in the matter of fiction" was a vital question for "this first English meeting of librarians." (*Transactions,* pp. 60–67 passim.)

The discussion was substantial. Justin Winsor stated that the Boston librarians were satisfied that the catalog could be made to "correct the normally large percentage" of fiction used in libraries furnishing it. He meant the annotating of "our printed popular catalogues," begun "some years ago," with information about books and authors; it was applied to the subject references first in history, biography, and travel, and others afterward; the results demonstrated that "you need have no apprehension of the engrossing effect of fiction" (*Transactions,* p. 152). Poole rejected the idea that fiction needed any justification. Novels "even questionable" were not circulated. Some that were would not appeal to a person of culture to read at all. The objections came from persons of high culture who had forgotten their earlier and lower stages of development. Calling certain items trash, he thought, was wrong: it was all a question of appropriateness to a particular library's clientele. Everything was worth preserving, "not everywhere, but *somewhere.*" (*Transactions,* pp. 153–154.) Cowell of Liverpool, and a compatriot from a mechanics institute, shook their heads at the hypothesis that readers of novels or "trash" would necessarily rise in their taste; they were committed to "good" fiction in moderation. Cowell did specify that fairy tales were unobjectionable and ought to be circulated freely among children.

The tendency for United States and United Kingdom librarians to differ was perhaps more clearly manifest on the subject of the age of admission. William F. Poole cited what was evidently most unusual then—no restriction whatever "in the libraries of the Western States of America" (*Transactions,* p. 170), adding that the sixteen-year limit in the Eastern states was often nominal because youngsters used their parents' cards to check out books anyway. Winsor endorsed the broad view, offering the firm conviction that the only requirement was "establishment of the borrower's identity." These practices were evidently not acceptable yet in the United Kingdom, but the Plymouth librarian noted that "at Bristol and other Free Public Libraries special rooms and books had been provided for young readers" (*Transactions*, p. 170).

Discussion of technical topics was largely traditional, but some promising notes were sounded. After Charles A. Cutter's new rules for alphabetically arranged catalogs (see below) were praised, Cutter himself defended subject cataloging (whether alphabetical or systematic) against British skepticism as both achievable and desirable. German interlibrary loan was hailed by a librarian from Cincinnati. And Justin Winsor observed, "I think we do not fully comprehend the possible uses of the telephone" (*Transactions*, p. 175).

The problems of finance were skirted gingerly. State aid was mentioned wistfully. But the only practical activity reported was the United States employment of women. Justin Winsor reveled in "our pick of the educated young women . . . with a fair knowledge of Latin and Greek, a good knowledge of French and German, deducible knowledge of Italian and Spanish, and who do not stagger at the acquisition of even Russian"; but conceded that their "high value" was attributable above all to their accepting salaries lower than men's for equivalent work. The only woman present, apparently, was Annie Godfrey, lately librarian of Wellesley College, Melvil Dewey's wife-to-be.

Neither library literature nor library education, it seems, was considered on this occasion.

The Library Association and United Kingdom Achievements to 1890 Somewhat like the conference in Philadelphia the year before, the international meeting in London closed with a session (October 5, 1877) which organized The Library Association of the United Kingdom. It differed noticeably from its United States prototype in limiting nonlibrarians to 40 percent of the membership. But it was sufficiently sympathetic to the precedents of "earnestness . . . frank cordiality . . . freshness and practical adaptability" to accept *Library Journal* as its own organ, for the few years mentioned above. The editorial board became half American and half British. That initial meeting also set up a Metropolitan Free Libraries Committee, to do something about the scandalous absence of public library service in London. (Whatever it did, Thomas Greenwood wrote in 1886 that the "Metropolitan Free Libraries Association" seemed to have existed only in name; *Free Public Libraries*, London: Simkin, Marshall, 1886, p. 259.) The following April saw the appointment of another committee, of the sort already noted in the United States, to develop a prime book selection tool, a General Catalogue of English Literature. In July, the association stepped ahead of its United States counterparts by authorizing the collection of library statistics. A lively interest was meanwhile manifested in the efforts of the association's committee to help with Poole's Index. In 1879 the association sponsored a proposal to consolidate the various Library Acts, assigned a committee to study the question of a journal, and organized a statistical department. On October 15, 1880, the Council of the Library Association named a Committee on the Training of Library Assistants.

Not all was clear sailing. A resolution proposing limitation of fiction in public libraries was passed on September 23, 1879, and a motion to open libraries on Sunday rejected. There was also sharp, unresolved, difference of opinion on certain problems of descriptive cataloging. By 1882, a Training Committee report was accepted, and the first exhibition of library appliances held. In 1884 to 1885 examinations for professional recognition were instituted, and the questions were printed in *The Library Chronicle* for June-July, 1885. Sunday service was still being voted down.

Particularly troublesome was the consolidation of national library laws. One reason was controversy over a proposal for inspection of libraries by the national Education Department. Another was the uneven development of the powers of local government: while municipal corporations were created in 1835, to deal with many urban challenges beyond the capacity of the traditional parish structure, loose ends abounded, and many more statutes were needed to tie them up. The parish remained the key unit in London so far as libraries were concerned at least until the Metropolitan Management Act of 1885 defined "districts." The Act of 1887 then placed library authorities on the same footing as certain other types with respect to ability to borrow money. That undermined the widespread resistance in the London parishes to voting money for an institution which might benefit "outsiders"; many problems nevertheless remained for later solution.

If the Act of 1887 may be regarded as profiting from the euphoria around Queen Victoria's Jubilee, benevolence warmed not only the public libraries but the British Museum, which finally managed to assemble the funds to print catalogs for public use. Contemporary dreams of universal bibliography, however, remained dreams. The effects upon periodical publication are harder to judge. *Library Journal* ceased to be the official organ of the Library Association on July 7, 1882; *Library Chronicle* was launched in January 1884, but lasted only until December 1888. In that month, with more solid business arrangements, *The Library* began a long and useful career.

While these evidences of progress go largely to the credit of The Library Association, certain individual contributions were of key importance. Even before the conference of 1877, Edward Edwards and several others had rendered great service advancing the cause of public library service. Soon after that historic gathering, vital aid was afforded by noted economist W. Stanley Jevons (1835–1882): his "The Rationale of Free Public Libraries" appeared in the reform monthly *The Contemporary Review,* in March 1881 (pp. 385–402), and was reprinted two years later in his collection, *Methods of Social Reform* (London: Macmillan). Free public libraries were known to be inexpensive, declared the protagonist of "utility," but much more should be said; just as Post Office savings were a thrift-teaching device, free libraries were "engines for creating the habit and power of enjoying high-class literature, . . .carrying forward the work of civilisation which is commenced in the primary school" (*Methods,* p. 31). Furthermore, they were among the "many social devices which carry the benefits of wealth to those who have no wealth" (*Methods,* p. 32). Having studied library annual reports, Jevons observed that "too many science lectures, cheap entertainments, and free openings of exhibitions, intended for the genuine working men, are taken advantage of chiefly by people who could well afford to pay; but in the Free

Library the working man and the members of his family put in an unquestionable appearance" (*Methods,* p. 34). He cited from loan records such
occupations as accountants, bedstead makers, bricklayers, chain makers,
clergymen, and commercial travelers. He added that keeping books in the
home required space, an expenditure item of consequence.

In harmony with the contemporary concern for improving local government and extending its benefits to rural areas, Jevons spoke sympathetically
of the problems of library service where "numbers and concentration" were
lacking (*Methods,* p. 37). He urged consideration of joint endeavor by ad-
joining local governmental units, already possible under the 1866 amendment to the libraries acts, but so far as he knew untried. Earlier efforts to
service the countryside were acknowledged but Jevons did not mention that
they had not involved anyone regarded as a librarian.

The labors of British librarians nevertheless drew his praise, and even
such mundane matters as mechanical circulation equipment were accorded
some space in his essay. He called the advances of the preceding twenty
years "surprising" and credited them "greatly" to "the reflex effect of
American activity," but added that the Library Association "has soon become a thoroughly British body" (*Methods,* p. 51). His peroration introduced
a list of practical works on library operation, one of which, W. E. A. Axon's
"Hints on the Formation of Small Libraries Intended for Public Use," he
described as "well-known" (*Methods,* p. 52), a tract prepared originally for
the Co-operative Congress of 1869 and reprinted often. Axon does not seem
to have created any stir in the United States; to learn why not might be
worth while.

Thomas Greenwood   *The Library Association Record* of December 15, 1908,
includes two obituaries of Thomas Greenwood, one by Axon, the other by
the better known James Duff Brown. Greenwood was thus honored because
"his work and influence were regarded as essential elements in the British
library movement" (*The Library Association Record,* X:633). He was also
respected as a self-made man, who not only worked for a few years at the
Manchester Free Library which had given him treasured opportunities for
study, but retained a lively interest in everything about free libraries, from
book selection for boys to state tax subsidies. He does not, however, appear
in the *Dictionary of National Biography,* and the United States librarian who
read only *Library Journal* would not have known of his contributions to
public librarianship.

In 1886 Greenwood published a book, *Free Public Libraries* (London:
Simpkin, Marshall & Co.), because, he said, the acceptance of compulsory
tax-supported schooling had expanded "the intelligence of the public" but
failed to produce "a corresponding increase" in the public library installations authorized since 1852. "Public Libraries and News Rooms," he went
on, "can never be wholly or entirely free any more than can water and gas";
the word was used nevertheless because it had "a prepossessing sound." The
need of the hour was guidance in how to persuade the taxpayers to vote
application of the public libraries act. One favorable sign was "the growing
importance of the Annual Conference of Librarians" and the "clear and

practical papers" read there. He looked forward to more help by way of "a large and comprehensive scheme of Local Government Reform" (a turn of events actually just a few years in the future). (Greenwood, pp. vii–x.)

Greenwood proposed to make his own contribution by commenting on what he had seen or heard about at home and in the United States. Thus he explained how little the penny-in-the-pound would burden thousands of taxpayers, suggested other sources of revenue most libraries could utilize, and urged state aid. He praised much about contemporary service in public libraries to adults, youth, and schools; especially did he emphasize staff hospitality and the role the public library could play in helping teachers choose proper books "instead of being as now, at the mercy of the publishers' travellers" (salesmen) (p. 278). He encouraged well-balanced book selection, citing evidence as to the backgrounds of adults actually using certain libraries.

Of particular importance were his observations on library public relations and library management. His seventh chapter, "The Educating of Public Opinion for the Adoption of the Act," is a manual of public relations, and a very good one. The British taxpayer, Greenwood warns, is "very often a tough customer" (p. 140); make haste slowly. The first battle front is the press; publisher Greenwood lays out some notably shrewd reasoning about the sequence of events to be anticipated. Second are the clergy and others who speak at public gatherings. He stresses volunteers, organization, and "profuse distribution of handbills and circulars" (p. 146).

Then he identifies the enemy order of battle:

I The better-class people, who do not see why they should be taxed for the benefit of other classes.

II Those who say that books are so cheap nowadays that no one need be without them.

III The enemies of education—and there are not a few of these.

IV The burdened (?) ratepayer, who objects on principle to all rates and taxes.

V The working classes, who very often are not particularly anxious for the adoption of Free libraries.

VI The folks who don't care for books, and fail to see why other people should. . . .

VII Those who say that providing Free Libraries out of the rates kills private benevolence in this direction.

VIII Shareholders in subscription libraries, who fear that the movement will depreciate the value of their shares. As a matter of fact, Free Libraries will do nothing of the kind . . . it cannot be made too widely known. . . . (Pp. 146–147.)

Other classes might be added, but those are enough. Specific answers to each are "scarcely necessary" (p. 147). Public meetings are the appropriate means of education. Speakers should be brief and pointed, and go easy on statistics. Nor should a vote of commitment be pressed early; if premature, it may lead to disaster.

No less important is good management. With all due respect to committees and commissioners, they would have "little or no idea of the work they have before them" and must "at any cost secure the services of a man" who did. He would need full authority to succeed. Some committees had, strangely, behaved very differently. Fortunately that was "rare," because the majority were "men of business capabilities" ready to treat the librarian as a "gentleman, and not as some junior clerk in a warehouse, requiring continually to be watched and checked" (Greenwood, pp. 185-186). The "beau-ideal" chief librarian was not a man charging and discharging books at the desk but the book selector and cataloger and guide: "a man keenly in touch with the reading public, a man of infinite tact, a good disciplinarian, with the bump of order prominently developed, of ready resource, and who has the pages of the catalogue printed in his mind's eye" (p. 385). To pay such individuals poorly, on the basis of supply and demand, was really not so logical as it might appear. Greenwood exhorted "Free Library Committees" to think it over.

Greenwood's last chapter is valuable for a list of librarians, few of whom bore clearly female names. Also very helpful is the appendix reproducing the text of the key British statutes from 1855 to 1884.

The book sold for 5 shillings when first published. In May 1887 a smaller format (12mo.) work of the same title was offered for one shilling. By 1892 there was a "4th edition, revised," at 2 shillings sixpence. (The data are in *The English Catalogue of Books* for 1886, 1887, and 1890-1897.) Circulation was probably substantial in the United Kingdom. Its impact should be studied, in comparison with others of its type then being issued in the United States and perhaps elsewhere too.

Social Change, the State, and Libraries

Urbanization and Other Factors for Library Change   When the work of the American Library Association and The Library Association of the United Kingdom is recognized as the vital center of progress, when one adds appreciation of such organizers and stimulators as Dewey and Greenwood, it remains to be explained why their accomplishments mark these particular years, rather than some earlier or later time.

In the first place, urbanization manifestly played an important part. The percentage of the population residing in communities of 100,000 or more rose in the United States from 6 in 1850 to 15.5 in 1890. For England and Wales the corresponding figures are 22.58 in 1851 and 31.82 in 1891; for Scotland, 16.9 and 29.8. Yet they certainly did not outstrip the United States in advancing public library service during those years. Nor did the seven provinces of Australia, whose capital cities had 29.1 percent of the population in 1891; or Uruguay, whose single capital accounted for 30.4 in 1890. How badly was Germany hampered by a mere 4.8 percent in the cities of 100,000 or more in 1871 and 12.1 percent in 1890? (The classic assemblage is Adna F. Weber, *The Growth of Cities in the Nineteenth Century . . .;* New York: Macmillan for Columbia, 1899; see particularly the summary table, CXII, on pp. 144-145.)

If one broadens the discussion, utilizing the percentages of the population in communities of 20,000 or more (same source), the results seem no different:

Country	Date	Percentage
England and Wales	1891	53.58
Scotland	1891	42.4
Australia	1891	38.8
Netherlands	1889	31.3
Uruguay	1890	30.4
Cuba	1887	28.5
Belgium	1890	26.1
Turkey in Europe	1885	24.9
United States	1890	23.8

Evidently the degree of urbanization was not necessarily the decisive factor associated with either the organization of the American Library Association and The Library Association of the United Kingdom or their successes. It is possible, nevertheless, that importance should be attached to the rate of increase of urbanization: roughly 40 percent in England and Wales, between 1851 and 1891, 80 percent in Scotland, and 110 percent in the United States. Unfortunately, the data required for serious pursuit of the point are lacking.

Let us consider next what so many library promoters talked about, either bringing the workingman into the stream of opportunity or trying to shape his thinking and behavior at the ballot box, or both. The workingman was struggling in the French factories of the sixties; and the war with Prussia and the suppression of the Paris Commune set him back in the seventies; the unions became fully legal only in 1884. Not ordinary needs but scholarship, for the most part, was the orientation of the long-established respectable municipal libraries in the principal cities. Their very existence, moreover, helped block the initiation in those cities of Anglo-American style public libraries. The Bibliothèque Nationale responded about 1885 with a nonscholarly collection of 40,000 volumes in a "Public Room," which survived until 1934 for lack of convincing competition. Paris also had by 1890 fourteen lending libraries subsidized modestly by state funds; despite that asset, and organization since 1881 as a *syndicat,* they boasted a mere 2,000 to 5,000 volumes each. Additional lending libraries sprang up in several locations in the 1880s, sponsored for political or religious propaganda advantage. The small towns still enjoyed access to "school libraries," but their clientele were not the masses of urban workers.

Early steps toward organization in Germany were severely obstructed in 1878 by Bismarck's club: an "anti-socialist" law, and in the eighties by his carrot: social insurance. The "popular libraries" might be said to have complemented these measures, but they were far short of true library service.

The United Kingdom too witnessed important events: strikes in the sixties for the reduction of the working day to nine hours, nominal legalization of unions in 1871, and removal of several crippling handicaps in 1875. Socialist propaganda played a modest role. On the other hand, working-class voting was not a large-scale phenomenon until the reform of 1884.

Somewhat in parallel, the workers of the United States developed several craft unions in the fifties and sixties. Despite countermeasures ranging from law to rifle fire, the industrial-type Knights of Labor stepped from secrecy to public life in 1878, and the mideighties were marked by the birth of the American Federation of Labor and the struggle for the eight-hour day. White male workers already could vote; the franchise remained to be won by women and Negroes. Generally speaking, no great interest was manifested in libraries. Although a considerable number of workers registered and borrowed books, for example, from the brand new (1886) Enoch Pratt Free Library in Baltimore, that was partly a consequence of unemployment and hard times; as conditions improved the following year and the library became more familiar, the circulation fell off a little; the rise in 1888 was slight. It was hardly a surprise. The laboring people, a good many women among them, were burdened by nasty working conditions, long hours, and low pay. Child labor was common, and as late as 1890 only one-third of the children entering the first grade in the Baltimore public elementary schools reached the fourth grade. Altogether, not many workers were in a position to read with comfort and pleasure. They were not among the forces urging expansion of library service. As for those who feared them, promotion of library service may have been nourished by confidence that since the workers were not demanding it, it would not be dangerous.

The context in which public library organization made rapid progress in the United States was thus not just urbanization, still less urbanization plus worker pressure for library service, but more likely forebodings about worker activity as an economic and political challenge. To this should be added certain special factors which mark the record in the United States far more plainly than in England and Wales. What was then called "republicanism," or an equal chance for every (white male) "American" to become president, was peculiar to the United States; nothing of the sort existed in Europe, except among a handful of intellectuals. That chance was to be implemented through education. Calvinism indeed was committed to the virtues of education through reading, and the momentum of that commitment far outlasted the declining proportionate strength of enrollment in Calvinist churches. It was at the very heart of the efforts evoked in the mideighties by a "new" immigration conspicuously non-Calvinist. The "Americanization" never thought necessary for the earlier, mainly Protestant, Germans and Scandinavians, probably not held worth the trouble for the English-speaking Irish, became a major concern of those who watched the boom in non-Protestant arrivals from eastern and southern Europe: Slavs, Hungarians, Jews, Italians. "Americanization" became an important facet of many forms of education, particularly in the Atlantic ports and such inland centers as Chicago. Public libraries helped stir the "melting pot." Many an immigrant responded, even though labor would soon react unfavorably to Mr. Carnegie's library philanthropy.

The significance of deep-going currents of change is further revealed by the enlargement of library service in Russia, precisely because the advance of the human condition there lagged considerably behind progress further west. Until 1861 the peasants were shackled by serfdom, and the support of intellectual life remained dependent far more upon nobles than upon the relatively few bourgeois. The emancipation of the serfs signalled a new stage, altering the rural economy in the direction of national and international markets and broadening the governmental process both nationally (the Duma) and locally (the *zemstvo*). City libraries arose at numerous locations, usually open more hours than the venerable state libraries; many other communities benefited from the garrison libraries established under the military reforms of 1862 and accessible to civilians. Not to be discounted either were the circulating libraries organized in the principal cities of western Russia mainly by Jewish bookdealers. Yet the population was still one-third illiterate, and the government was able to obstruct challenge by such measures as the 1882 censorship of journals and newspapers, which ruined many liberal organizations; also the founding in 1884 of religious schools to offset the secular *zemstvo* schools, and in 1891 the forcing of all schools under the control of the Orthodox Church Synod.

What libraries may have meant to the working people and others engaged in struggles of various kinds, during this epoch, has been investigated very little. Neither the renowned *History of Trade Unionism* by Sidney and Beatrice Webb (London: Longmans, Green, 1920; rev. ed. 1935) nor the monumental survey of the late 1880s, Charles Booth's *Life and Labour of the People in London* (London: Macmillan, 1889–1903) makes any reference to libraries. The corresponding materials for other countries should be examined too.

National Libraries; Panizzi   Whatever the relationship of the library movement to the rank and file, considerable vigor was evident in the sphere of national libraries. Several new ones appeared on the crest of revolutionary waves: in 1857 in Mexico as a new constitution was being written under the aegis of the Minister of Justice, Juárez, and in 1879 in Bulgaria as a similar document was being prepared to celebrate the "autonomous principality" status just wrung from the Ottoman Empire with the aid of various European rivals. The great economic and cultural advances in Argentina and Brazil in the sixties and seventies, owing much to the immigration of capital and skilled labor, and the struggles of positivist thought with clericalism, were marked by railroads on the one hand and solid improvements in their respective national libraries on the other. The unification of Italy contributed the reorganization of a number of existing institutions as "national" libraries, in the 1870s. More prominent was the enlargement of the collections (800,000 volumes by 1890) and the development (1845–1881) of a much-admired systematic catalog, at the former Elector's Library in Berlin, known from 1809 to 1918 as the Royal Library.

Size does not necessarily mean influence. The imperial library in St. Petersburg ranked in 1860 second largest in the world, thanks partly to Count M. A. Korf's demand for strict enforcement of legal deposit. Although the director (1849–1862) was also very much aware of the public and turned the library's face outward with new arrangement and catalogs, the example meant little; for the library life of the Slav area (and for that matter publication in the Slav tongues) was from the outset largely unknown to the Germanic-Romance west, as indeed it would remain for many a decade to come. Nor did the more favorably situated Bibliothèque Nationale, the largest of all with well over 1 million volumes in 1860, exert the healthiest of influences. The great Paris institution was badly hobbled for half a century attempting, after a German fashion, to control the vast holdings of printed books by means principally of partial systematic catalogs. They did not meet the need, and only in the mideighties did reform measures (to be noted below) produce tangible benefits to readers.

Outstanding for progress important in itself and respected elsewhere was the British Museum, led to the front rank during this period by Antonio Panizzi (1797–1879). As noted earlier, the British Museum in its youth received a pittance from Parliament, obliged to depend somewhat on deposit copies of current English books but much more on gifts to fill its shelves. By 1843 the parliamentary grant had reached only £3,000, from which were purchased 3,140 "works"; another 2,409 arrived as deposit copies. The corresponding figures for 1845 are £4,500, 7,630 works purchased, and 3,596 depository items. (Cited in Edwards, I:482.)

Panizzi was fully conscious of the numerous weaknesses in the collections. (His command of all aspects of the library's character, indeed, is probably the main reason he advanced to one leading position after another despite his Italian birth and radical youth.) Besides, he enjoyed the advantage of cataloger Thomas Watt's skill and devotion, and the intimate knowledge of the holdings Watts acquired when the books were moved in 1838. With such aid, Panizzi developed between 1843 and 1845 a powerful memoir comparing the British Museum with other national libraries, and asking for £10,000 a year for the next ten years, in addition to the £5,000 then supposedly usual. The plea went through the trustees to the House of Commons, and won a partial victory. The House authorized £10,000 a year for three years (in the event, the last year's grant was cut considerably). Although the shortchanging of cataloging and binding in the allocations forced curtailment of the purchase program, striking progress was registered. In 1843, there were for instance perhaps no more than 1,000 books on the United States. Panizzi noticed young Henry Stevens (1819–1886), expatriate American scouring London for libraries back home. Stevens was soon buying United States books for the British Museum, enough to move the trustees to sponsor a catalog of them in 1856; at Panizzi's retirement in 1865 they exceeded 100,000 and were quite likely the best such collection in existence.

Worth attention also is the unusual relationship between the British Museum Department of Printed Books under Panizzi and copyright deposit. The statute of 1814, requiring that eleven libraries ("corporations") be furnished copies of every work published in the United Kingdom, manifestly pushed the "public" case too far, inasmuch as only one of the eleven, the British Museum, offered its books and premises to anything like "public" use. The arrangements were changed markedly by the act of July 1, 1842. A copy of every book published in London was to be delivered to the British Museum within one month of its issuance; if published elsewhere in the United Kingdom, within three months; if in a British Colony, within one year. Named as depositories also were Oxford, Cambridge, Trinity College in Dublin, and the Advocates Library in Edinburgh.

The enforcement of the new law left much to be desired. Panizzi, asked in 1848 by the Royal Commission why many books requested were not on hand, explained that copyright copies were often not delivered and that as a matter of principle he would not buy them. "'Of the works published in the provinces, I believe we get a certain number, but nothing in comparison to the number which is published; of the works published out of England, I mean in Scotland and Ireland, I believe we get almost none at all; and of the works published in the colonies, to which the Copyright Act extends, we get none at all.'" Our source, copyright assistant Robert Cowtan (*Memories of the British Museum,* London: Bentley, 1872, p. 177), adds that, up to Panizzi's time, "the Welsh publishers scarcely delivered a single work of the large number issued annually."

Cowtan remarks on the other hand that his own country is more severe with authors than many other governments, the requirements for copyright being only two copies in France and Austria and only one in the United States and the leading German states (Prussia, Saxony, and Bavaria).

The upshot of the discussions was that the trustees of the British Museum in 1850 placed their authority to receive copyright deposit copies in the hands of Panizzi. Characteristically, he set about collecting what was due promptly and energetically. By the end of 1852 the number of arrivals had risen decidedly, thanks to his travels to publishing centers as well as his determination. The chorus of abuse swelled louder too; although Panizzi was no stranger to it, his health does seem to have paid a price. In fact, it was already under strain, because in 1850 and 1851 Italian patriot Panizzi gave much to rescue moves on behalf of political prisoners (from 1848) in the jails of oppressive Naples.

Another price, so to speak, was the mounting pressure against the insufficient space for books and readers. As early as 1836 and 1837 a possible solution had been perceived in utilization of the inner quadrangle, an area then devoid of buildings. In 1852, Panizzi himself advanced the idea of converting it into a central reading room, emphasizing that any conceivable alternative would require demolition and take longer. After sharp debates, a temporary halt in buying books, and a providential change of government (new Prime Minister Lord Aberdeen had been a conscientious trustee), action on the Panizzi plan was initiated in September 1853. On May 2, 1857, the new facility was formally opened, an additional triumph for the one-time refugee, since March 1856 principal librarian, or chief executive, of the entire British Museum. In the words of the exulting Prosper Mérimée (1803–1870), writer, official inspector of French monuments for a quarter-century, senator under Napoleon III, long Panizzi's friend and admirer, "For the first time, let's hope not the last, a librarian has been asked to build a library. Panizzi furnished the plan for this edifice, destined henceforth, I think, to serve as model" (*Le Moniteur,* Paris, letter from London dated August 26, 1857, in Mérimée's *Études Anglo-Américaines,* vol. 7 of his *Oeuvres Complètes,* Paris: Champion, 1930, p. 141). For the benefit of his home audience, Mérimée went on to describe the complexity of the governing machinery of the British Museum, and pointed out that its holdings were to be compared to those of the Bibliothèque Nationale plus the great Botanical Gardens plus the Louvre. Twitting the English on being *"grands statisticiens,"* he passed along a note given to him which declared that visitors to the British Museum in 1759 had numbered 5 in the month of July; in 1855,

180 a day; and since the opening of the new reading room, never less than 400 a day.

Traffic at that level presumably made welcome the new call slips introduced by Panizzi somewhat earlier. Prior to his time, a reader at the British Museum customarily wrote down what he wanted, frequently several titles, on a small piece of blank paper. He might have consulted the catalog; he might have consulted only his own memory. The assistant then had to sort out the works desired, supply whatever correctives were needed for identification, and add the call numbers. Panizzi changed all that by establishing a standard procedure based on a printed call slip.

His reading room, a rotunda with 20,000 reference works at hand on the immediate shelves, did not spare librarians of the future the necessity of fighting for a share in planning library buildings. But it certainly did exert influence. The Library of Congress was only one of many great institutions soon to be indebted to it architecturally, and the "at-hand" books gave a special meaning to the German term *Handbuch*, well known in so many reference rooms of later days.

The Library of Congress 1840-1890   Although the idea of a national library continued to hang in the air, the Library of Congress approached that level very slowly and haltingly. The years from 1840 to the Civil War were marked first by a toothless provision for copyright deposit at the Library, in the 1846 statute establishing the Smithsonian Institution. Two years later, the campaign led by Frenchman Alexandre Vattemare (1796-1865) won the passage of an act authorizing the exchange of duplicate library materials with foreign governments and duty-free import of the foreign items to be received, even granting the Library Committee $2,000 to work with. Although progress was presumably served by the opening in 1847 of a steamship line between New York and Le Havre, Congress regarded the cost of transporting printed matter with a jaundiced eye, and was not satisfied with the results of the exchange arrangements: they were terminated in 1852. Vattemare made a valiant effort to revive them, submitting documentation to Congress and the librarians' conference of 1853. The benefits were declared to include 30,655 books and pamphlets arriving in the United States, some 25,000 in France, and so on; but Vattemare's time had not yet come.

More important, a fire destroyed more than half the books in the Library of Congress in 1851. Part of the congressional reaction was to furnish new quarters at the Capitol in 1853. Another part was to grant new authority to the librarian. Even though the incumbent happened to be unqualified to exercise it rewardingly, very important in principle was the transfer (March 3, 1853) of the collection-building responsibility from the Library Committee of Congress to the librarian. Allocated $75,000, a good deal more than some had thought obtainable, he assembled 35,000 works, basically a good reference library for legislators. Most of these works were on the shelves when the library reopened on August 23, 1853. Not very many were copyright deposit copies; contrary to the British, who had recently turned over enforcement to Panizzi, with impressive results, the United States Congress decided in 1859 to repeal the copyright deposit law.

The outstanding event of the war years at the Library of Congress was the 1861 replacement of the librarian, a Democrat allegedly of Southern sympathies, by a deserving Republican from Indiana. The new chief was wise enough or lucky enough to name as his first assistant Ainsworth Rand Spofford, a newspaperman from Cincinnati in Washington about one year. Spofford managed the institution during the war, partly because his superior spent enough time in service to win a citation for bravery; in 1864, Spofford became officially the Librarian of Congress.

Spofford's administration was shaped very much like that of Panizzi at the British Museum. On March 3, 1865, it was again prescribed by Congress that a copy of each work published in the United States should be deposited at the Library of Congress; by the end of the following year, ordinary processes of acquisition had brought there nearly 1 million volumes. Extraordinary were the 1866 decision to transfer to the not-quite-national resource more than 40,000 volumes of learned society publications housed until then at the Smithsonian Institution, and the 1867 assignment to the Library of Congress of the $100,000 Peter Force collection of American historical materials. These events and other similar pressures were almost their own argument for more space, and two new wings were added to the Capitol to provide it in 1866 and 1867. Some of the advantage was cancelled by the landmark Act of 1870, which transferred the entire copyright operation from the Department of Interior to the Library of Congress and directed that both deposit copies of each book be sent there too. Spofford managed meanwhile to resuscitate international exchange, organize periodical reading rooms reserved for members of Congress, and produce an alphabetical subject catalog for the adult public. Furthermore, although patrons under sixteen were now excluded, he initiated a campaign to admit the public to Congress' library during the evening as well as during the day, since "'the very numerous class of persons in the employ of the Government at the Capital'" were otherwise deprived of "'any privilege which this library presents'" (quoted by Lucy Salamanca in *Fortress of Freedom* . . ., Philadelphia: Lippincott, 1942, p. 209). Since the collections were primarily intended for Congress, rather than the general public, the situation differed significantly from Panizzi's in London twenty years earlier. Nevertheless, Spofford took equality of opportunity seriously and spoke up again in 1874. No action resulted along those lines until the new building was opened.

In 1871 he advised the Library Committee that his staff of only twelve was doing wonders with a collection nearing 250,000, but that even those twelve were woefully cramped and that the copyright accessions newly directed to them would simply find no space to be received. He submitted several ideas, among them a new building. Response was low key; by 1875 a desperate Spofford was predicting chaos if a change were not made quickly. A special commission of 1878 unanimously favored a separate building. Another eight years passed before precise authorization was enacted. The cornerstone was laid on August 28, 1890. Spofford cannot be regarded as the directing genius of its design, and his book selection policy was disproportionately antiquarian, but he had a right to be satisfied with the product of devotion and persistence.

Other Governmental Action Affecting Libraries Legislative and executive action obviously played vital parts in a number of instances. In an increasing portion of the West, despite the contrary thrust of ideas like those of enormously influential Herbert Spencer (the "survival of the fittest," for example), government was taking a more prominent role in library life than was private enterprise. Notwithstanding the appeal of Social Darwinism in the age of great corporations, intervention on behalf of public and school book service was accepted in the United States as a state and local function. Although the federal government was involved therein only tangentially through such activities as the distribution of documents, that same federal government operated the Library of Congress and an increasing family of libraries in executive agencies. In the United Kingdom, national authorization and funds were required not only in the comparable operations of the British Museum and government department libraries, but to provide a statutory framework for local option regarding public libraries, and in the regulation of book service in schools.

Similar to United States patterns was the accumulation of laws and regulations by individual German sovereignties, both before and after the unification of 1871 under Kaiser Wilhelm I. Yet the governmental stamp at the German "state" level was in many respects stronger than in the states of the United States, visible not only in legal deposit (not made imperial under Bismarck) but in position classification, pay scales, and provision for library training. Saxony in particular, highly industrialized and the scene of much socialist activity, saw in 1876 an official brochure on establishing and administering libraries and the beginning of annual appropriations for libraries.

More strikingly different from both the United States and the United Kingdom were the governmental-library relationships in Italy and France. Although the politico-literary activity of the second quarter of the century called the *Risorgimento* seems to have meant little for libraries immediately, Italian life did move from the revolutions of 1848 through political unification between 1861 and 1867, and national *regolamenti* came forth one after another, beginning in 1869. These directives affected not only the thirty-two libraries henceforth called "state" (belated secularization of vast ecclesiastical holdings was part of the change), but also somewhat the university libraries. The new moves apparently went beyond general and personnel management (see below): the 1889 law, for instance, created a *vigilanza* council at each university governing the allocation of book purchase funds, of which the university librarian was only one member. Inasmuch as the university library collections had been found in 1870 to be grossly lacking in contemporary publications, the move was not necessarily bad.

In France, the shock of losing a war (1870–1871) toppled the Second Empire, and one feature of the birth of the Third Republic was a variety of educational legislation, likewise bearing upon not only celebrated research libraries in Paris and other large cities but (1878–1886) higher education as well. The French actions centered upon establishing several unified universities and university libraries where only a congeries of "faculties" and scattered libraries existed before. Another important sign of a new spirit was the admonition, in the explanatory *Circulaire* of November 29, 1886, from the Ministry of Education, that the university library "is not there any less for the students than for the professors; it must be regulated and administered solely from the viewpoint of the progress of study" (reproduced in *Zentralblatt für Bibliothekswesen*, 4:66, February 1887). Meanwhile, the various decrees affecting the Bibliothèque Nationale were consolidated in a precise statement about personnel and pay, dated June 17, 1885 (likewise in *Zentralblatt*, 2:416–421, September–October 1885).

To grasp fully the meaning of these alterations, we need a comprehensive comparative analysis of the legislation affecting libraries in the middle and later nineteenth century.

Technical Tasks, Technical Education, and the Library Image

Procurement and Catalog Entries   Whether controlled by governmental fiat or not, whether budgetary support seemed adequate or not, acquisitions and book handling continued to be a fundamental concern. The "world" production of books is estimated as having risen from 27,838 in 1828 to 65,190 in 1858 to 100,000 in 1887 (M. B. Iwinski, "La statistique Internationale des imprimés . . .," p. 6). The number of periodicals published is reckoned at 3,179 in 1826, 14,240 in 1866, and 46,678 in 1892 (Iwinski, p. 58). Noteworthy are two phenomena. First, the periodicals issued in *"Amérique"* (Western Hemisphere) were less than one-third of the total in 1826, but nearly half in 1866 and 1892; 1892, in fact, was the year in which the "American" output almost equalled that of Europe; it fell back again afterward (Iwinski, p. 59). Second, the data for 1880 show North America's 76 million people served with 4.76 million issues of "journals" and 22 million issues of "periodicals," or about one issue per three persons; whereas Europe's 301.3 million people were offered 15.7 million copies of "journals" and almost 34 million issues of "periodicals," or about one issue per six persons (Iwinski, p. 68). It would be enlightening to know how European and North American libraries compared in their selection and holdings of these materials.

Information on current publications was being publicized more widely. Coverage of substantial degree already existed in France, Germany, the Netherlands, Great Britain, and Belgium (founding-date order). In the period 1840–1890 it was added successively in Denmark, Austria, Sweden, the United States, Norway, Italy, and Brazil. Meanwhile, many more retrospective bibliographies became available, most of the specialized variety being German. The rare and out-of-print field was newly served by *Book Prices Current* (London), which began its first volume with a list of auction sales prices from December 1 and 2, 1886.

Enough books and journals, old and new, arrived in the larger libraries to force consideration of bibliographic control and shelf space. The period began with Panizzi's rejection of systematic (or classified) catalogs and demand for a carefully developed author-alphabetical guide, with a subject index, to the holdings of the British Museum. Like Schrettinger, Panizzi thought consistency in cataloging dependent heavily upon having all the decisions made by a single person. For that, much time would be needed, a complete draft being desirable before anything was printed; but the trustees declined to wait, insisting upon the printing of all A entries as soon as that portion of the manuscript draft was "finished." Since the only guidance then available to the catalogers was the very general set of sixteen rules prepared in 1834 by his predecessor, satisfactory only for obvious questions, Panizzi

The periodical stacks at the Bibliothèque Nationale, 1893. (Courtesy of The Bettmann Archive, Inc.)

immediately applied himself and some associates to the production of much more precise instructions.

The celebrated ninety-one rules, approved by the trustees in 1839 and published on July 15, 1841, set several precedents. Owing partly to their complexity and partly to their expected significance, they were not merely the prefatory guide so often seen before within a book catalog like the Bodleian of 1674. Nor were they offered like the French Revolutionary union catalog "code" in the hope of producing uniform cataloging by individuals untrained, widely scattered, and employed at the task temporarily. Panizzi's rules were the first modern code for author and title entry, expected to exert considerable influence; they did. Promptly saluted by many contemporaries, they remained the British Museum code, by and large, until 1887, and were studied by such men as Dziatzko at Breslau in the early seventies, their impact clearly visible in other codes. The year 1841 also witnessed the fulfillment of the order to print letter A of the catalog, but the problems were at least as numerous as Panizzi had predicted, and no more volumes were printed while the handwritten catalog proceeded.

Much debated at the time, and since, was the question of the entry of works having no plainly indicated personal author. Panizzi broke with the Bodleian precedent of 1674. Writings having either obvious collective or composite authorship of familiar character were entered accordingly under such rubrics as "Academies" and "Encyclopedias." Those more literally anonymous Panizzi wanted to enter under the first word of the title, but the trustees overruled him and directed entry under any word in it which seemed to have a guidance potential. This did not satisfy Smithsonian Institution librarian Charles Jewett, and he was not obliged to defer to the British Museum trustees. His 1852 rules rejected the catchword approach and directed the entry of any anonymous work under the first word of its title. The consequences were modified with the scope of "anonymous work," then being narrowed by the emergence of the "corporate author."

Corporate bodies as entries became in this period another factor differentiating Anglo-American from predominant continental practice. Panizzi's code authorized it not only for the publications of learned "Academies" (Rule LXXX) but for documents emanating from a variety of organized bodies (Rule IX) and the laws, etc., promulgated by political units (Rule XLVII). Most such items were to be entered first under place, the exceptions specified in basic Rule IX being "academies, universities, learned societies and religious orders." Charles Jewett accepted Panizzi's concept in substance but in 1853 sharpened it by abandoning place as the prime element and declaring in his own Rule XXII that "the heading is to be the name of the body." He also added government departments to the "corporate." Charles Cutter's *Rules for a Printed Dictionary Catalogue* (Washington: Government Printing Office, 1876) crystallized these developments in the *"General principle:* Bodies of men are to be considered as authors of works published in their name or by their authority" and Rules 27 to 40, occupying most of pages 24 to 27. He nevertheless allowed entry by place as an alternative under numerous circumstances; the problem of choice remained to plague librarianship for many a decade to come.

The evolution of corporate authorship disposed of large portions of the "anonyma" of former days. What remained were principally the anonymous classics and contemporary works by authors not yet identified. Adaptable to the former was the idea of the "form" heading used in Panizzi's code for periodical publications, catalogs, etc. Standardization of variant possibilities of a single literary unit yielded such conventional but distinctive entries as Bible and Mother Goose, a permanent feature since Cutter.

His first edition of eighty-nine pages was issued in 5,000 copies. The second, in 1889, filled 133 pages, and was published in 20,000 copies. The success thus implied was to be felt for a long time.

All this was unacceptable in the Germanic area. Corporate authorship was not recognized in either Dziatzko's rules of 1886 or the "Prussian Instructions" (1899) based on them. Entry of such materials under title continued to prevail.

Cross-references for alternative entries and alternative forms of entry were neither new nor invariably utilized. Panizzi's provision of such assistance in fifteen of his ninety-one rules doubtless gave the question more importance.

Aiding the Subject Search; Cutter With respect to subject access, differences were less marked. To furnish a listing of materials by subject, whether in classified or alphabetical order, was well established on the Continent. Göttingen is said to have had a Latin slogan which may be translated as "what is not in the subject catalog is not in the librarian's world." Whether the alphabetical or the classified approach was the better one continued to be debated. Numerous French provincial libraries were in 1877 reported as either provided with classified catalogs or in the process of producing them. On the other hand, the Bibliothèque Nationale classified catalogs were in critically bad shape, and when Léopold Delisle (1826-1910) became the director in 1874 he soon decided that the only solution was to initiate two alphabetical instruments, an author catalog and a subject catalog; nearly twenty years' labor was required before the staff caught up with the total holdings and started to issue a printed author catalog. The leading British public libraries furnished alphabetical subject printed catalogs in the 1870s, but the issue was seldom discussed, apparently. In the "Rough Subject-Analysis of Papers Read Before the Library Association, 1877-1897" (*The Library Association Record,* I:14-15, January 1899), "Subject" appears only in the entry "Universal Subject Index," being left otherwise to what is implicit in "Classification" and "Indexing."

Beneath the surface was the inadequacy for expeditious location of subject information of either the systematic (or classified) catalog, or the manipulation of titles, or classified or alphabetical subject indexes to author-alphabetical lists. Clarification of the issues was peculiarly the contribution of United States figures, above all Charles Ammi Cutter. Opening his chapter (XXVII) on "Library Catalogues" in the 1876 *Report,* he stressed that he would be talking about the "larger town and city" and college libraries, that his remarks would apply little or not at all to the "great European libraries" and "very small town libraries" (ftn., p. 526).

The upper extreme of library size was of course hardly represented in the United States. Furthermore, a great many United States libraries were oriented toward a public far beyond the scholars. Perhaps for this reason in particular, the systematic catalog, arranging entries in a subject hierarchy presumed to be comprehensible to the reader, alphabetical by author or title only within a subject, found favor in surges but never dominated the scene. (The partial record assembled by Cutter in the 1876 *Report,* pp. 577-622, suggests that the classified catalog was prominent between the late 1820s and the mid-1840s and occasionally afterward; thorough analysis might be very rewarding.) Of the seventy-five libraries Cutter circularized in 1875 as to their recently printed catalogs, fifty-seven replied: only two reported a classified catalog, and three more mentioned a classified index to an author-alphabetical catalog.

If the classified catalog was, as Cutter noted, very advantageous to bring out the resources of a library in a particular area, the attractions of an alphabetical approach were undeniably more powerful. The "dictionary" apparatus customary in 1875, however, had by no means reached the level later library users would take for granted. Not only did they vary in such matters as furnishing contents under authors and imprints under subjects. They sometimes limited titles to what would fit on one line. They occasionally excluded "literature" as a class. Most serious, to make a subject entry only on the basis of words in the title of the book was the practice of "nearly all" (1876 *Report,* p. 533)—as, in fact, recommended by Panizzi and many others. Introducing the list of "printed catalogues of public libraries in the United States, arranged by date of publication" (1876 *Report,* pp. 577–622), drawn from European sources like *Serapeum* as well as domestic reports, Cutter submitted this explanation: "S.W.—Subject Word. (In general, the S.W. catalogues do not go behind the title for a subject-word; but some occasionally, and some often, supply a subject-word for books that have none in the title, and become so far S. catalogues)" (1876 *Report,* p. 576).

The earliest instance in the United States of an "S. catalogue"—that is, a subject list not limited to words from titles—seems to be the 1859 dictionary catalog of the Troy, New York, Young Men's Institute, which controlled a collection of 12, 067 volumes. Alphabetical subject indexes were in use before that, the oldest in a single alphabet apparently being the one furnished in Jewett's author catalog for the Brown University Library in 1843.

The feature which most readily (though not invariably) differentiates the true subject-entry from words borrowed from titles is the cross-reference. Insofar as the data collected by Cutter tell the story, the first instance in a United States library was, again, Jewett's 1843 catalog at Brown University, the "Alph. subj.-index" of which had "cr. refs." (1876 *Report,* p. 587). The next one whose equipment looks similar was issued at the University of Alabama in 1848, for its tiny library of some 4,230 volumes; but the index terms themselves were explicitly drawn only from the title pages of the books. The succeeding years saw the appearance of quite a few more catalogs, including several of the dictionary variety; at most, however, they had but a few cross-references. A change seemed to be in the wind in 1861. Published under Jewett's direction was the dictionary catalog of the Boston Public Library Upper Hall: tapping a collection of 55,000 it offered authors, titles, subject words, and cross-references; also analytics "for whatever fills a whole vol" (1876 *Report,* p. 597). In the same year Lowell City library in Massachusetts produced a very similar catalog, although for a collection of only 12,000. Most catalogs thus including author, title, and subject entries nevertheless continued to be prepared without cross-references.

One important reason for the slow pace of these developments was the conviction of some librarians that most readers came to the library with known items in mind. So thought Jewett in the 1850s at the Smithsonian Institution, and so did Joseph G. Cogswell at the Astor Library in New York, introducing the "authors and books" Part I of his catalog published between 1857 and 1861. Cutter on the other hand was, at least by 1877, confident that, "leaving desultory readers out of the question, half the people who go to libraries" were on subject searches with no specific source in mind. He rejected printed bibliographies as substitutes for subject entries in library catalogs, and added the following about the "subject catalog":

> It is costly, but it is cheaper than men and women intelligent and learned enough to be its substitutes, and it does not die or get married as men and women do; it is never tired and forgetful; it requires no vacations, and is never sick. But more than all this is the fact that these male and female attendants, however bright they may be, find that when resort is made to them by readers they absolutely need its assistance to enable them to give information satisfactory either to themselves or to the questioners. (Letter to *The Nation,* 24:87, February 8, 1877.)

More particularly, speaking to his peers in the landmark *Rules for a Printed Dictionary Catalogue,* Cutter analyzed with classic clarity the principles and practical consequences of classed and alphabetical arrangements. He pointed out that "classes" are "subjects" and "general subjects" are "classes" but that "individual subjects" are "never" classes (p. 12). ("Never" would hold up better philosophically than practically.) And in four definitions he contrasted, to the three types of entry dependent upon words in titles, the virtually new fourth type, "*Subject-entry,* registry under the name selected by the cataloguer to indicate the subject" (p. 14). This he buttressed with the contention that *"Subject"* meant "the theme or themes of the book, whether stated in the title or not" (p. 15). The climax was the celebrated rule of "*Specific entry,* registering a book under a heading which expresses its special subject as distinguished from entering it in a class which includes that subject" (p. 15). Rejecting the hitherto customary "class" name and title-catchwords, Cutter had opened a new era in cataloging, although not everyone knew it (not even Dewey, as will be noted shortly).

Cutter's logic won more adherents as his great dictionary catalog of the Boston Athenaeum was issued, between 1874 and 1882. It opens with several "explanations" about authors, subjects, type, and abbreviations. The rules of entry are very similar to Cutter's own, although there are differences attributable mainly to his taking on a task already begun by others. The remarks on type are clear but not extraordinary. The terms abbreviated are interesting in that a list of only eighteen (plus "etc.") includes German *herausgegeben* ("issued") and *und* ("and"), and Italian *intorno* ("about"), none of them translated. Under subject, Cutter illustrates specificity by noting that "a book on the dog, for instance, will be found under Dog, not under Zoology." "But it must be remembered," he adds immediately, "that there are often important, and sometimes the best, treatises on special subjects in general works," referring to the material on Aragon in works listed under Spain. See-also references have not "in general" been furnished from specific headings to more general headings, because "the inquirer can usually see without difficulty what the including subject would be"; but they have been made "very freely" from "general subjects to the various subordinate headings . . . as well as to co-ordinate and to illustrative subjects." Thus the entry for Agriculture is followed by a five-part list of see-also references: subdivisions proper like Clay lands; particular crops; particular animals and insects; related subjects like Chemistry; and "the names of various countries which have published reports of their 'Agriculture Departments' . . ." (I: 32). Such was the state of the art nearly two centuries after Maunsell's beginnings.

No less important in Cutter's view were the elaborate contents notes and analytical entries. The papers in the *Proceedings* of the American Association for the Advancement of Science occupy nearly fifteen columns (I:67–74), and the individual items appear as analytics as well. At the end of the last volume (1882) Cutter observes that when he assumed responsibility for the catalog in 1872 it was equipped with minute analysis of the publications of American historical societies but little more. He feels bound to add in a footnote his conviction that analytics are vital assets, without which many expensive works would "stand upon the shelves untouched." Valuable indeed are the "bibliographical helps which it is becoming the excellent custom to annex to treatises of all sorts," but they are too few and in any case inadequate. He does not understand how any person familiar with "the difficulties of research" can oppose preparation of analytics, and "in fact" does not know anyone so benighted (V:3400). What would he have thought a century later?

A spirit much like Cutter's was meanwhile at work in the library of the U.S. Surgeon-General's Office, where John Shaw Billings (1838–1913) was organizing a card catalog soon famous. From the slips prepared as the basis a printed author catalog was assembled in 1873; then the slips were distributed anew, by subject, alphabetically, much as urged in the 1790s by A. Kayser, whose brochure is listed in the 1876 *Report* (p. 741). Beginning on January 1, 1874, this subject file was enriched with entries for the original papers in current foreign medical journals and transactions, which were reportedly indexed as soon as received. The supposition that an American physician was doing the same thing for United States publications of the same kind proved to be a misunderstanding, and after January 1, 1875, those materials also were sent through the new subject indexing procedure; the hope was expressed that the near future would see like action retrospectively too. (The retrospective listings in the Royal Society of London's *Catalogue of Scientific Papers,* which began to reach the public in 1867, were unfortunately by main entry alone.) Billings' masterpieces were launched in printed form in 1879 (monthly *Index Medicus*) and 1880 (*Index-Catalogue of the Surgeon-General's Office,* vol. 1).

New Devices to Meet Expansion Printed catalogs were becoming larger and larger, sometimes multivolume. The Boston Athenaeum catalog, with five volumes, was unusual but not solitary. Sometimes the major reason was the greatly enlarged role of subjects in the new model dictionary catalog, sometimes the inclusion of analytics and entries for magazine articles, sometimes both. The 1875 catalog of the Public Library of Quincy, Massachusetts, for instance, listed 7,000 books and 4,000 items from periodicals. Thus developed a crisis. A printed catalog had always been out of date when published, even if it was complete, a condition by no means common in the larger libraries of Europe. Now, the rate of appearance of new works quickly made the incompleteness serious.

Furthermore, the expense was intolerable partly because the sales were poor, editions of perhaps 1,000 failing to be fully disposed of. The Boston Athenaeum catalog is classic not only for its professional achievement but because it cost $100,000, three times the sum the library spent on other matters the year (1874–1875) the catalog began to issue from the press.

Altogether, the card catalog, familar since the mid-1850s for current acquisitions, whether printed or handwritten or mixed, was steadily elbowing aside the printed book catalog as a complete library record for the public. Cataloging copy printed either directly on cards or on slips pasted on cards appeared at the Cambridge University library in 1861, at Harvard in 1862, at the Leyden University library in 1871, and soon afterward in France and Germany. In the United States, an 1885 survey disclosed that, of 108 responding libraries, 36 were using cards only, 47 both book and cards, and only 25 the printed book catalog alone.

Another relief device was the "finding list" of a library's holdings on a particular subject, or even encompassing the entire collection, in shelf order. Poole resorted to it when the Chicago Public Library opened in 1874 before conventional cataloging was available. Such lists were sometimes sold to patrons, and when kept limited in scope, were far less expensive than a book catalog. They were not always so limited: the sixth edition of Poole's in 1884 added an alphabetical index and thus invited comparison with some traditional systematic catalogs.

This type of aid to subject searches, governed by classification symbols rather than words capable of alphabetical arrangement, was not to attain the high status in United States libraries of the dictionary catalog (with its subject cards). It was destined to be regarded, especially if complete, as the location and inventory record properly reserved as a rule for staff use, the "shelflist." Although no investigation seems to have been undertaken as to the ability of the general public to cope with classification symbols, it is probably reasonable to assume that the names of subjects were easier to handle. The democratic expansion of public library service in the United States thus seems to account in good part for the downgrading of the shelflist and systematic catalog as assets to library use. Oddly enough, the expression "finding list" was to remain in the United States library vocabulary, not however to continue to denote a portion of a shelflist, but to characterize the function of the dictionary catalog as seen by one of two contending schools of thought.

To prepare cataloging copy once, for all libraries, seemed an obvious advantage to Charles Jewett as early as 1850, and he evoked considerable enthusiasm at the 1853 convention with his six-point program for standardization via Smithsonian Institution rules, a union catalog for participating libraries, and his own brand of stereotyping of cataloging copy for mass distribution. Unfortunately, the clay blocks vital to his scheme proved too responsive to environmental change to fit metal machines reliably; the other ideas were also set aside for the moment. The next generation witnessed the kindred propagandizing of the American Library Association Committee on Title Slips, the 1887 effort by *Publishers' Weekly* which failed to attract more than twenty subscriptions, and actual provision (1889) of sets of slips with at least two of their publications by the learned Selden Society of

England; but such acts were still premature. Also in the future was the overall acceptability for libraries of the typewriter, which had so far achieved only parts of it, a standard keyboard (1874) and lowercase as well as capital letters (1878).

A Standardized and Flexible Class Mark, Notably Dewey's

If the description, which constituted most of a catalog entry, seemed to many librarians incapable of standardized handling, the half-century under review did see some progress in that direction in shelving and classification. Fixed location was customary, and determined in varying degrees by subject, format, and date of arrival of the item being processed. The new university regulations in France of the mid-1880s, for example, insisted upon registering all acquisitions in three categories according to size. Classification schemes abounded, but few if any were utilized at more than one library, thanks to centuries of multiple sovereignties in the German-speaking area and institutional particularism nearly everywhere. Hundreds of thousands of handwritten markings on books and entries in library records discouraged change, just as they would continue to in later generations. Professional thinking as reflected in the *Zentralblatt für Bibliothekswesen* (1884–) focused on rules of entry and types of catalogs, but not classification as such.

The conditions prerequisite to a call for change existed primarily in the United States. Collections were growing ever more rapidly, and the library's public was enlarging. A major consequence of the first development was movable location: "this great improvement," wrote Dewey in May 1879, "has been gaining ground rapidly and steadily for the last three years" (*Library Journal,* 4:193). A major aspect of the second was increasing access of readers to the shelves: urging subject classification in the same article, Dewey contended that it would save time in fetching books for readers "if" they were "not admitted to the shelves" (*Library Journal,* 4:192).

The Decimal Classification, indeed, was the outstanding public response of the epoch to the conditions indicated. As Dewey defined the issue in "Arrangement on the Shelves," (*Library Journal,* 4:117–120, 191–194, March and May, 1879), one could easily forget one overall author-alphabet or chronological listing or title listing or order of accession; variation by size had to be respected, and the main sequence should have dummies to represent what was shelved elsewhere because exceptionally large or small. On the other hand, Dewey said, "I believe there are no two opinions among us as to the necessity of adopting the subject-order as the basis of all arrangements. The only question that arises is where to stop dividing by subject." (*Library Journal,* 4:192.) Further, fixed location was unfriendly to updating subject groupings because materials on the same subject often had to be scattered for lack of space: it became logical to classify by rough, broad categories. But "the relative location, with a full alphabetical index to the classification used," would soon assemble significant homogeneous groups as new titles were added, rendering logical "quite minute classing by subjects" (*Library Journal,* 4:194).

Dewey was not of course the first to classify by subjects or to do so minutely. Yet the symbols he used so facilitated shelving (much on his mind thanks to his Amherst experience) that the attraction of fixed location was seriously undermined. Besides, the markedly mnemonic character of the notation seemed likely to benefit both librarian and reader. He declared, moreover, on the opening page of the preface to *A Classification and Subject Index for Cataloguing and Arranging the Books and Pamphlets of a Library* (Amherst, Mass., 1876), that his scheme had been created at Amherst College, after a study of library literature and "over fifty personal visits to various American libraries" convinced him that their usefulness "might be greatly increased without additional expenditures." Usefulness, he repeated, had taken precedence over "philosophical theory and accuracy" (*Classification,* p. 4).

On the related question of what he owed to earlier contributors, Dewey acknowledged as "perhaps the most fruitful source of ideas" an 1871 plan adopted by several Italian publishers; the St. Louis Public School Library scheme had been used "in filling the nine classes of the scheme," but his own basic pattern had been settled before it came to his notice. He closed with the assurance that he had "no desire to claim original invention" for any part of his work which someone else had thought of before him, and the hope that it would prove "as useful to others as . . . to himself" (*Classification,* p. 10).

The last page of his first edition furnished very important supplementary information about the "Subject Catalogue on large cards" which was dependent upon either the classification or the index. The cards in this instrument bore very precise classification numbers like 942 (7). 14, and were arranged accordingly. But the numbers in parentheses were ignored in shelving, in the "Shelf Catalogue," and in "calling for and charging books." Dewey's conception of a "subject" catalog was therefore not at all like Cutter's, but rather what had often been called a systematic or classified catalog with subjects coded into numerals; subject words were utilized only in the index to his classification scheme. The Decimal Classification would over the next hundred years generate longer and longer class marks consistent with its ignoring of subject headings; librarians, mainly unaware of that presupposition, would pragmatically use subject headings and use or not use long Decimal Classification numbers according to mood and circumstance.

As for shelving, the shelf catalog, and the scheme he was offering to serve them, he declared in the Bureau of Education's 1876 compendium that "three figures seemed best." "In smaller libraries," he went on, "two figures would do very well until the growth required further division," although he suspected that to avoid a possible second handling of books three figures might well be assigned at the outset. Larger libraries would conceivably want "four or even more" (1876 *Report,* pp. 625–626). Accordingly, the first edition of his product comprised 1,000 class marks, none with more than three numbers.

If one adds to all the foregoing Dewey's directed energy and persistence, and business talent, it is not surprising that the Decimal Classification "for Cataloguing and Arranging" library materials evoked interest quickly among United States librarians and somewhat in the United Kingdom as well. His first edition (1876) was printed in 1,000 copies; the second (1885) and third (1888) were issued in 500 copies each; the fourth, 1891, was again in 1,000. Nothing of the sort had ever happened before.

In the light of twelve years' reported experience, at the Amherst 30,000-volume library and elsewhere, Dewey carried the class marks of the second edition to one number beyond the decimal in at least one decade of every main division, conspicuously in the ranges 511–599 (Pure Sciences) and 808–890 (Literature). At many points therein, in fact, the notation provided already reached the second position beyond the decimal. The third edition, 1888, added not only new classes but more scope notes, cross-references, and changes in terminology.

By 1891, Dewey was satisfied that the adoption of his Decimal Classification in more than 200 libraries rendered further alteration "impracticable except for very weighty reasons" (Dewey to the owners of the Dewey Decimal Classification, notice preceding the tables of the fourth edition). Thus began the career of the "integrity of numbers" concept. It probably deserves credit for the success of the Dewey Decimal Classification together with features mentioned by Charles Martel, chief classifier of the Library of Congress: "For many years it [the DDC] remained the only general scheme in print, complete and fully indexed. In this availability more than in anything else lies its practical usefulness which is the cause of its popularity. It is easily applied and may be worked even by persons with little or no experience in classification." (*Library Journal,* 36:412, August 1911.)

To those familiar with the ideas of Francis Bacon, and the "inversion" of his plan (Science first and History last) in William Torrey Harris' classification for the St. Louis Public School Library, Dewey seemed indebted to the Lord Chancellor. Dewey apparently thought so himself. The hierarchical relationships in each of what he called the "special libraries" (Philosophy, Theology, etc.) certainly implied a theoretical factor in his operation. But he himself declared unequivocally in the 1876 *Report* that "theoretically, the division of every subject into just nine heads is absurd." Further: "The impossibility of making a satisfactory classification of all knowledge as preserved in books, has been appreciated from the first, and nothing of the kind attempted. Theoretical harmony and exactness have been repeatedly sacrificed to the practical requirements of the library or to the convenience of the department in the college." (1876 *Report,* p. 625.)

Thus did Dewey demonstrate pragmatism more than a generation before William James won unusual attention to the term with *Pragmatism, A New Name for Old Ways of Thinking* (1907). That it was in fact an old way of thinking is plain if one looks back at the long lineage of library-practical classification, modifying the classification of knowledge for the practical handling of particular bodies of material which did not neatly fit philosophical categories. It is doubtful, nevertheless, whether any scheme prior to Dewey's had been as promising as his in providing, for example, 050 for general periodicals, and the subdivision 05 under a subject for periodicals of that subject; indeed the very concept of the standard subdivision was a most helpful innovation. Supporting a hierarchical book classification by a mnemonic notation drawn from the decimal principle (then much discussed), rendering maximally usable by ordinary minds what had been fashioned by heavily abstract thinking, was of the essence of the Franklin-Jefferson outlook.

The far more sophisticated Hegelian tradition, as processed by Harris

(1835–1909) for the St. Louis Public School Library, enjoyed no comparable influence but did leave significant marks. School Superintendent Harris provided a section (70) for "JUVENILE LITERATURE (unclassified)" for which college librarian Dewey offered no direct parallel. In the spirit of Francis Bacon, moreover, form as the guide "in the principal divisions" was explicit in the consistent gathering of literary materials first under form and only second under nationality (sections 66–69, 71–76); Dewey followed the opposite policy. More important than those contrasts, and several others (Harris, "Book Classification," *Journal of Speculative Philosophy*, 4:114–129; 1870) is the emphasis by Hegelian Harris upon the dialectical interplay of the several aspects of nature and thought: "The *content*—or what books treat of—is not a sufficient basis of distinction to ground a classification on. For any class of books may treat of two or more phases of the content at once. Since Nature and Mind never exist isolatedly, but always in some degree of synthesis, it follows that books which treat thereof will always prove hybrids in such classification." (*Journal of Speculative Philosophy*, 4:115.) Illustrating his view of these hybrids, he pointed out that books on architecture could be classified under either Mechanic Arts or Fine Arts, "according to the point of view taken by the author in composing his work." And while some works on Natural history were "merely descriptive . . . since their object is scientific, they all fall under Science" (*Journal of Speculative Philosophy*, 4:121). Thus did Harris establish the basis for the cardinal distinction between subject headings and classification, both being concerned with content but only the latter, usually, with intent.

The only other pattern of consequence issued during those years in the United States was Charles Cutter's Expansive Classification. Devised in 1873 and first published in 1876, it eventually impressed some observers much more than his rules for a printed dictionary catalog. Like Dewey's it was suited to collections of any size—the expansive notation providing the necessary flexibility—and offered several mnemonic devices such as country numbers. Cutter emphasized the obvious fact that using the twenty-six letters for the first two elements in his notation would give more scope than the mere tens of the purely numerical decimal plan; in fact he expected that advantage to outweigh easily the recognized disadvantage of mixed notation (letters and numbers). Whether he was right or wrong anticipating rapid user adjustment to that or any other regular feature, his scheme was to make its mark on the new schedules created at the Library of Congress but otherwise to fall far short of the Dewey product in library adoptions.

Also apparently well known at the time was the classification developed for the Halle University library *Realkatalog* (systematic) by Otto Hartwig, who published it in 1888 as a supplement (Beiheft III) to *Zentralblatt*. The letter-and-number scheme, nonmnemonic, filled more than 200 pages, with a table of contents but no index. Offered to academic libraries, mainly closed-stack, it enjoyed some influence in Germanica; like many others it was also examined at the Library of Congress as reorganization approached, but rejected as unsuitable.

Building Design and Materials   The library building, the site of all the foregoing, was also undergoing change. Long familiar wall shelving still charac-

The central stacks (magasin) *at the Bibliothèque Nationale about 1890. (Courtesy of The Bettmann Archive, Inc.)*

terized numerous well-known institutions like the Bavarian Royal Library at Munich, and was hardly challenged in central and southern Europe until the 1870s. Meanwhile, however, stacks at right angles to the walls and detached from them became a prominent feature at the British Museum and Bibliothèque Nationale (*magasin* system) in the 1850s and began soon thereafter to appear in German libraries. By the time architect Martin Gropius (1824–1880) showed, with plans (1879) for Greifswald University, that the stack plan was a great space saver, the Germanic culture area clearly needed many new library buildings and the new arrangement was often adopted. Also much admired in the British Museum style were the stacks just eight feet high, placing all books within reach from a three- or four-step ladder rather than the familiar long one from which Ebert had fallen fatally.

Space saving was further encouraged by the realization of Schrettinger's proposal of 1829, the brackets devised by Panizzi to facilitate the vertical adjustment of shelves. While installing them in existing libraries with wall shelving may have entailed more expense than was worthwhile, their use widened as more libraries acquired at least new stacks if not new buildings.

To make brackets of iron rather than wood was clearly advantageous, and iron was utilized for the new-style columns supporting the roof of the rectangular central reading room opened at the Bibliothèque Nationale in 1868. The desirability of using iron instead of wood for shelves too was underlined by the disastrous fire of January 11, 1879, which ruined the important Birmingham, England, Free Library; the subject was first discussed at an American Library Association convention in 1882. Ten years later, an essay included in the U.S. Commissioner of Education's report for 1892–1893 (I: 728) cited the allegation that the fire losses of 1887 had included 126 United States college buildings and libraries. (According to the source, *Century Magazine,* 37:568, February 1889, its authority, the New York *Chronicle,* reported as victims also 146 churches and 515 hotels. The Commissioner's contribution did not quote the *Century's* observation that combustible architecture still prevailed partly from "distrust of theory".)

The better libraries were as a rule well protected and regarded by insurers as good risks; the poorer ones were not. What the experts considered properly protected were libraries " 'kept on iron racks, or in iron cases, in fireproof buildings' " (quoted from an Aetna Insurance Company statement in the *Report of the Commissioner of Education, 1892–1893,* I:728). Noted was the news that the British Museum had a fire brigade composed of staff members, and a code of regulations for its activity. Noted also, in the review of celebrated conflagrations, were the damage to the Mercantile Library of Philadelphia in 1877 not by fire but by the water poured on a burning building next door, and the $42,000 insurance recovered: "the books . . . could still be read, though stained" (*Report, 1892–1893,* I:726). More recently, the 1888 fire at the Peoria (Illinois) Public Library occasioned injury because of both water and mishandling.

Another kind of mishandling was beginning to be counteracted, in the provision of separate quarters for library staff not dealing with the public—notably catalogers and binders, and the administrators. Placement of circulation operations apart from reading rooms also began to gain acceptance, but only after 1875.

Lighting by means of electricity entered libraries in the eighties. The beginning was slow, thanks to the initial cost, but there seems to have been little doubt that the future lay with the new invention. How sharply all the implications were perceived is one of the numerous questions which cannot be answered without study of contemporary thought about libraries. As for heat and ventilation, discussion at library conferences testifies not simply to their importance in temperate zones but their heightened importance as collections grew and public use of the premises increased.

Personnel and Training   The readily available data on library positions and pay, examinations, and training, underline the differentiation between Anglo-American and continental European library traditions. Elaborate schedules of positions and salaries evolved for the various royal, *Land,* and university libraries of Germany during the course of the nineteenth century, but the qualifications were enforced flexibly enough to admit substantial numbers of university candidates unsuccessful in other efforts, volunteers, and so on. When the great educational reforms of the seventies were initiated in Prussia under Friedrich Althoff it was speedily recognized that personnel practices must be overhauled to put library management on a proper basis; indeed it was partly for that reason that the *Zentralblatt für Bibliothekswesen* was founded in 1884. The next year marked another vital step, the raising of librarians' pay to the level of a teacher's at a *Gymnasium* (secondary school–junior college).

Tables of organization and compensation were likewise familiar in France in leading "national" libraries in Paris and many outstanding municipal institutions at provincial capitals. The great reforms of 1878 extended the coverage to additional provincial libraries, public and academic. Meanwhile, Italy entered a new stage as the unified kingdom was established. The *rego-lamenti* of 1876 and 1885 in particular were very precise, perhaps uniquely, setting forth at least on paper a hierarchy from the *prefetto* in charge of each of the two principal "national" libraries down through *bibliotecarii* and *sot-tobibliotecarii* (and manuscript *conservatorii*), then the more or less skilled nonprofessional personnel, to the unskilled helpers at the bottom.

The stated pay ratio between top and bottom categories in Italy (*Zen-tralblatt, 7*:227–229, June 1890) was about 6 to 1, not greatly different from practice in large modern libraries in many lands. A greater spread is evident in the 1885 data for the Bibliothèque Nationale (*Zentralblatt, 2*:420–421, September–October 1885): from 15,000 francs for the *Administrateur-Gén-éral*, to 2,400 francs for the lowest category of *Sous-Bibliothécaires* ("Under-librarians," required to have had an internal apprenticeship at a still lower level); female caretakers and cleaning women were paid as little as 500 francs.

For professional posts, France recognized graduates of the École des Chartes (founded 1821) with responsible appointments to archives and li-braries beginning in 1839; library-bibliographical courses were installed in 1847. State examinations became part of the pattern in 1879 along with the other reforms of the early Third Republic. Librarianship examinations were half a century old as an idea in Germany when they were actually tried at the Munich State Library in 1864; they may have been a part of the instruc-tion inaugurated in 1887 at Göttingen by Karl Dziatzko, but government examinations awaited the nineties. They were introduced in Italy in 1870–1871.

Those approved by the Council of the Library Association of the United Kingdom in December 1884 and administered the following July were novel in their completely nongovernmental sponsorship. They were for "library assistants" who were "certificated" if they passed, not for library directors. Judging from an advertisement to fill a vacancy, published as a letter in *The Library* in April (?) 1889 (Ser. 1, 1:183), such certificate holders were pre-ferred for professional positions by at least some employers.

The extreme of decentralization, the United States library world was slow in adopting the examination as an administrative device, let alone as an instrument common to a large area. Thanks partly to the public discussion of political pressure and other forms of corruption in the seventies and eighties, and the rise of civil service, the Buffalo conference of the American Library Association (1883) resolved that appointments should be made for fitness "'definitely'" and promotions based on merit; correspondingly, that "'in large public libraries, subordinate employees'" should be chosen on the basis of "'competitive examination, followed by a probationary term'" (quoted in *Report of the Commissioner of Education, 1892–1893*, p. 752). The Chicago gathering of 1893 heard that only 17 of the 229 libraries re-sponding had adopted written examinations; consensus among the attend-ants reportedly favored them (*Report, 1892–1893*, p. 751). Meanwhile, the desired assurance about competence in candidates was forthcoming from the conventional examination and degree system now applied to students of librarianship at Columbia (1887), Pratt Institute (1890), and the others which soon afterwards swelled the stream of formal training. Salary data remained to be assembled.

Education for Library Positions   The appearance of Dziatzko's professorship and lectures in rather solitary glory at Göttingen and of Dewey's faculty and school at Columbia helped bring into better focus than before the preparation aspect of professional library service. Many were the questions before the international audience. Whom would a trained person be serving under what circumstances, and what sort of training did he need? How different was service in a scholarly library from service in a popular library? How should instruction be divided between mastery of daily routines and grappling with the higher knowledge normally offered only in universities? How many of which kinds of librarians would need university education? How many would need just library skills on top of classical secondary education? How many would need just the skills that could be obtained in vocational courses or at a vocational school? How was one to approach the training, utilizing, and paying of the increasing number of women entering library work?

In Continental Europe, training, offered by librarians on their own premises, generally led to work in those very scholarly institutions. Whether the books were used largely off the premises (as in Germany) or almost entirely on the premises (Italy), popular library service was not involved, and the persons who provided the latter inhabited a different world, touched by the foregoing measures rarely if at all. The scholarly impulse also carried over into the training and perhaps the expectations of the Germans who managed library service in the classically oriented secondary schools, the *Gymnasien.*

In Germany and the other areas sharing its scholarly traditions, however, the learned atmosphere created a serious problem, defined since early in the century and debated more and more as university libraries expanded both collections and clientele, and drew nearer to full-time library service (far from common). At the head of the staff, whose qualifications were already under discussion, was a director still pressed to be a scholar. To guide that staff and improve service, thought more and more analysts, he had better specialize in precisely librarianship and ease off on academic scholarship if not indeed abandoning it altogether. Significant publications touching on this theme pro and con had appeared earlier; an even more notable contribution was issued in 1871 by the Jena University librarian, Anton Klette (b. 1834), anonymously. Pleading for "The Independence of the Librarian's Calling in Germany as the Basis for a General Library Reform" (*Die Selbstaendigkeit des Bibliothekarischen Berufes . . .*, Marburg: Elwert'sche Verlagsbuchhandlung), he contended that to forget about an academic specialty was necessary not only to enable the director to do his own work properly, but "to attract as associates capable persons who would find satisfaction in the relationship" (1897 ed., p. 16).

If Klette's reasoning neither swept European scholarly librarianship nor relieved it of management headaches, the situation in Anglo-America had not yet reached that level of sophistication. At least one new factor in the United States, the seminar system, tended to tie book use ever more closely to a teaching area; and in 1888, whatever the structure was, two of every three academic librarians were still employed to teach subjects as well as to operate libraries. The American Library Association authorized in 1889 a section called the "College Library Association" for university, college, and secondary school librarians; but most of the distinguished academic librarians were also scholars, and there was apparently no Klette-like voice among them at that stage.

United States campus librarians were in several instances important figures in the leadership of library life, more than can be said of their colleagues in the academic libraries of the United Kingdom. Nevertheless, the arena of professional activity in Anglo-America was clearly dominated by public librarians. The major reason, in all likelihood, is the United States environment, demanding of public libraries immediately and other libraries by implication the servicing of equality of opportunity. Although the tax-supported public libraries were with few exceptions the only ones legally at the disposal of all men, the thrust affected a great many others, as witnessed by the vast scope of the 1876 *Report* on "public" libraries in the United States.

This state of affairs had by no means emerged inevitably. When Ralph Waldo Emerson wrote in "Books" (1870) that colleges badly needed a "professor of books," he was not talking about the versatile scholarly guide projected 200 years earlier by Daniel Morhof. Persuaded from occasional visits to the Harvard Library that "the best of it is already within the four walls of my study at home," he meant apparently no more than that the "professor of books" should identify for the neophyte the few really good titles. (The essay is in *Society and Solitude,* vol. 7 of his *Complete Works,* new and rev. ed., Boston: Houghton Mifflin, 1886; see especially pp. 183, 185.)

Such negativism was of a piece with the views of Erasmus, Descartes, and Hobbes, among others, a tradition of considerable weight. It had to be counteracted. At least two participants in the 1876 compendium issued by the Bureau of Education tried to strike a blow in the cause. William Mathews observed that *"how* to read" was the first task before a student, and urged that instruction be provided "in the leading colleges" by endowing a chair, and elsewhere "by the professor of English literature, or by an accomplished librarian" (1876 *Report,* p. 251). F. B. Perkins submitted a more complex view, defining the mission of a professor of books and reading as teaching "a method for investigating any subject in the printed records of human thought, . . . a means of following up swiftly and thoroughly the best researches in any direction and of then pushing them further . . . a calculus of applied literature" (1876 *Report,* p. 231). It had been possible when printing was invented to be acquainted with all that was known, he thought, but any such idea now was irrational. The mass of reading matter available was "simply enormous" and justified "a technical professional guidance in examining it and selecting from it" (1876 *Report,* p. 234). Many topics would deserve serious consideration, such as reading in other languages, "the use of reference books," and "the proper mode" of reading periodicals and newspapers (1876 *Report,* pp. 238–239). The instructor must enjoy teaching.

More important, the editors themselves furnished in their "Introduction" a section on "The Study of Library Science" (1876 *Report,* pp. xxiii–xxvi) consisting largely of a long quotation from a pamphlet just published (1874) by Dr. F. Rullmann, librarian at Freiburg University, Germany. Addressed to German librarians, it posed the question, should library science become a distinctive field of study at universities? Rullmann had no doubt about the special training necessary to produce a librarian. He mentioned Schrettinger's reflections half a century earlier, respectfully, but contended that the instruction given at a library would not suffice: it had to be a university course, complete with examinations and a formal certificate, the latter to be required for appointment to the post of librarian. Rullman expected two principal benefits, better understanding of balance in book selection, and rapid enrichment of the literature of libraries.

These issues were not discussed at the first meetings of the American Library Association, absorbed as it was with organization and library operational tasks. Some founders were nevertheless thinking about them, either on their own initiative or, perhaps, because they were stimulated by Rullman's remarks or by the 1877 international conference news about courses lately established in Italy. Much opposition as well as indifference had to be overcome.

The Columbia School of Library Economy "We hear a great deal of the importance of having trained librarians," wrote Dewey in *Library Journal* of May 31, 1879; we know how many are deficient, but "forget" why. There were no special schools such as those provided for lawyers and schoolmistresses, "not even a system of apprenticeship." The librarian "must learn his trade by his own experiments and experience." Some professional literature was available, thanks to Edward Edwards, the Bureau of Education, and *Library Journal* itself; much more was needed. Dewey proposed to establish a library school, in association with "some considerable library." (*Library Journal,* 4:147–148; reproduced with many other pertinent contemporary materials in *School of Library Economy of Columbia College, 1887–1889: Documents for a History,* ed. E. J. Reece, New York: School of Library Service, Columbia University, 1937.)

By May 7, 1883, he was pushing his plan before the Columbia Board of Trustees, alleging rather loosely that "universal" support was available ("Original Plan," in Reece, p. 37). Next, encouraged by the backing of Columbia President F. A. P. Barnard (1809–1889), who had just persuaded (June 1883) the Columbia Trustees to allow girls limited access to Columbia instruction, Dewey took the offensive at the Buffalo (1883) convention of the American Library Association. He offered a sketch of the proposed curriculum and emphasized "that potent influence which we call 'the modern library spirit'" (*Library Journal,* 8:288; Reece, p. 6).

From the floor came varied response. W. F. Poole thought that much of what Dewey urged was already being done in many outstanding libraries. He added that practical work could not be taught by lectures, and that experts in those skills had no time to lecture anyway. He conceded that trained personnel were in short supply and averred that he did not "wish to throw cold water on the scheme." [This moved another person present to rejoin audibly that "the gentleman has thrown a whole pool," and is followed in the record by "(Laughter)."] Poole wanted to see some results before the association endorsed the plan. (*Library Journal* 8:289; Reece, p. 7.)

The advantages of training in school over training on the job were doubted by many. But Cutter, who himself offered instruction at the Boston Athenaeum, observed that the apprenticeship route could easily, in a large library, lead to a candidate's knowing well the small part of the institution he worked in but little about anything else. Library school was more desirable because "no one is thoroughly fit to have charge of a library who has not pursued some comparative study, and learned to reason about what he does." (*Library Journal*, 8:290; Reece, p. 8).

The convention asked a committee to study the matter of endorsing Dewey's plan. Later in the proceedings it rendered two reports, the majority favoring thanks to Columbia for its readiness to try an experiment. This view prevailed. The following May (1884), perhaps taking it into account, Columbia established the proposed school and styled Chief Librarian Dewey also Professor of Library Economy ("Original Plan" in Reece, pp. 40–41).

When the American Library Association convened in Milwaukee in July 1886, Chairman Cutter reported for his committee that Columbia's program as embodied in the new Circular of Information was so appealing that he was reminded of a story about a merchant hiring a paragon beginner. "The young men" exposed "to all the influences of the School of Library Economy" would be fit for a better world "and allowed to find employment there." The young women, "judging by those who are already in the profession," would not need such training because "they are angels already." Dewey's response was prosaic and humble. He ended his brief remarks with the assurance, "We wish the A.L.A. to feel that this school is its school" (*Library Journal*, 11: 376, August–September, 1886; Reece, p. 57).

Columbia issued a new circular of information for the school year 1886–1887, cautioning the students that despite the school's conventional name it differed "widely from other schools in its objects and methods." First, it would deal only with "its peculiar work"; it would neither offer "general culture" nor "make up the deficiencies of earlier education." It was not "like an agricultural college, which gives a general literary and scientific course with more or less agriculture included." Second, subjects would be approached in the spirit of "systematic apprenticeship" for speedy learning rather than stretching it out to keep the learner "without salary as long as possible." "Almost nothing of the usual text-book, and recitation" was to be expected. Third, to save time and money, Columbia would "condense the instruction into a single quarter" on the theory that "twelve weeks of earnest work" ought to do "till the need of something more" was evident. For candidates feeling that need and able to give the time, "a two-year apprenticeship" would be provided. (Circular, pp. 26–27; Reece, pp. 86–87.)

Attendance was anticipated "perhaps as much" from working librarians seeking enriched capability as from "young men and women just out of college." Thus the "lectures and direct instruction" were all available "within three months." That was about as long a time as many candidates could be away from the job, and such persons would probably not need the laboratory exercise anyway. "A proper apprenticeship" really called for "two or three years actual experience." Librarians were to be preparing like the young lawyers and doctors, who after graduating spend a few months in offices or hospitals before setting up their own practices. (Circular, p. 27; Reece, p. 87.)

Classes would absorb five mornings a week. Afternoons were reserved for "the bibliographical and extra library lectures, seminars, and club meetings, problems, and the visits to other libraries, binderies, book-houses, etc." and miscellaneous. What would not fit in those afternoons would be arranged on Saturday. (Circular, p. 28; Reece, p. 88.)

Admission was not contingent upon possession of a college degree, because that might exclude some fine prospects. The candidate did have to satisfy the director of his potential, and deficiencies of background would have to be filled in "after entrance."

Expenses comprised first the tuition of $50. Board and room near school would cost $6.50 to $10.00 a week. Notebooks, catalog cards, etc., would run at most $10. Another $5 should be reckoned for "car-fares for class excursions." Important reference books and other aids should also be acquired; "most" were available at school "at greatly reduced prices, conceded to our library students by publishers and manufacturers." (Circular, p. 29; Reece, p. 89.)

Each student would receive on completing his work a certificate "of the time spent, the character of work done, and the success with which the various examinations" had been passed; also commendations if appropriate. The "form of degree to be conferred" afterward, upon those measuring up on the job, had not yet been determined. The school would maintain a placement registry for those desiring such assistance. (Circular, pp. 29–30; Reece, pp. 89–90.)

Instruction was to consist not only of formal lectures but of "conferences or conversations" with busy experts. The course in library economy would be conducted by the director and regular faculty. Bibliography would be presented, subject by subject, by "professors and specialists"; the schedule would have to remain fluid until those gentlemen could advise the library school when they would be available. Supplementary guest lectures would be furnished by "experienced binders, printers, publishers, booksellers, and others" with allied interests. "Entirely independent" of the foregoing were the lectures by leading practitioners on any topic they chose, "a series of favors from friends of the school," to be delivered at their convenience. Finally, the students would have free access to the addresses presented before the various learned societies meeting at Columbia. Named were "the New York Academy of Science, the New York Shakspere Society, the Chemical Society, the Engineering Society, Torrey Botanical Club, the New York Library Club, the Academy of Political Science." (Circular, pp. 31–32; Reece, pp. 91–92.)

In addition, students would be expected to learn by reading, to which end "the school has collected a special library" and would provide duplicate copies as necessary. Conferences and clubs would bring together "teachers and students" for discussion of many types, "with all the greatest freedom of inquiry and criticism." Participation was invited in the deliberations of the Columbia Library Club, a semimonthly gathering of library staff members. By means of the "problem" format, each student would act as though faced with a challenge on the job, working out a solution and presenting it to the class. More of that sort would be learned from visiting "the public and private libraries of New York and vicinity." And from publishers' headquarters would be gained some acquaintance with bookmaking and bookselling, auctions, and the second-hand trade. Work in the library, the most valuable experience of all, would be part of the daily routine; and those taking the full course (beyond the three months) would be assigned to regular duties four hours daily in the library; all such efforts would be supervised. Labor in the library would be regarded as fair exchange for the balance of full-course tuition. (Circular, pp. 33–39 passim; Reece, pp. 93–99.)

The advantages of location in New York City included the practice of the Grolier Club of sending to the library school tickets for students who wanted to visit the club's "series of exhibitions of printing, binding, etchings, etc., which cannot be duplicated elsewhere." The New York Library Club brought together regularly at the Columbia College Library some fifty of the seventy members—all librarians in New York and its vicinity. And the American Library Association had "formally deposited" there "its entire collection of library catalogues, reports, appliances, blanks, and models"; the collection had been enlarged steadily over the past three years especially for the use of the school. The association of the school with Columbia University hardly needed emphasis. (Circular, pp. 43–44; Reece, pp. 103–104.)

After setting forth the details of the curriculum (Circular, pp. 39–42; Reece, pp. 99–102), the Circular of Information recommended that a person able to command the time take the regular college course first, then the three-month library science lecture course, next "one or two years' actual experience," and finally the three-month lecture course "again in review." Two years spent thus (beyond the college foundation) should fit "the faithful student . . . to begin a successful career in the library profession." (Circular, pp. 44–45; Reece, pp. 104–105.) In the matter of general education, "the most important" acquisition was "working" knowledge of German, French, and Latin. In fact, German and French, "if known, will be in daily use." Other tongues could be assimilated later. (Library Notes, 1:268, March 1887; Reece, p. 115.)

Instruction began on January 5, 1887. There were sixteen women and three men paying the fees, and several members of the Columbia staff were admitted to the course without paying fees. New York was represented by six, Massachusetts by five; the balance were widely spread, including George Catlin from Birmingham, England. One of the Saturday attractions was Nicholas Murray Butler, later president of Columbia College, lecturing on the "Relation of Psychology to Pedagogy." Among the "extra lectures" were the following: Ellen M. Coe of the New York Free Circulating Library on "what and how the public read"; Caroline M. Hewins of the Hartford Library on three aspects of service to children; Reuben Guild of Brown University on his forty years' experience; C.E. Sprague of the Union Dime Savings Bank on "Bookkeeping in Librarianship"; Gustav E. Stechert, New York merchant, on book importing; and Ernest C. Richardson of Hartford Theological Seminary on several topics mainly historical. (Reece, pp. 120–121.)

The September 1887 conference of the American Library Association was told by its Committee on the School of Library Economy that the first year had proven on balance very good. Hannah James testified to the breadth of the instruction and the prodding to do one's own thinking. "The Dewey System was taught as a matter of course, but all other systems had a fair and candid hearing." (*Library Journal*, 12:426–428; Reece, pp. 124–126.) In *Library Notes* for December 1887 (2:234–235), Dewey responded with informative comment, and vowed in the stimulating new language of Herbert Spencer, "We classify our Library School under dynamics, not statics" (Reece, pp. 189–190).

Although the enterprise flourished to the satisfaction of Columbia President Barnard and was wrestling with calls for summer sessions and other elaborations, Dewey's commitment to women, and very likely his determined manner about most of what he undertook, won him numerous enemies. In March 1889 the school moved to the New York State Library, at Albany, depriving the students of the Columbia matrix and gaining for them the advantages of direct association with the Regents, who governed all public education in New York. The enrollees spent half their time working in the state library, and the courses were apparently weighted more toward technical operations than to reference service.

Testifying to the same preoccupations were Dewey's supporting publications, on cataloging rules (1886) and on accessioning and shelflisting (1890), and the fact that nearly half the lectures were delivered by visiting practitioners. In librarianship as in so many other occupations at that time, apprenticeship to crafts was steadily being replaced by "technical education": thus did Samuel S. Green describe the Dewey library school in May 1889 (*Library Journal*, 14:269, May–June 1889; Reece, p. 268).

Library Literature Dewey's texts added a mite to an already impressive body of publication. From the epoch preceding library organizations came a long line of printed library catalogs and cognate records, but their design was indicated in a preface only occasionally. Policy debate was a long-established genre, at least since Naudé, although works presenting practical details may have been novel in the late eighteenth century. By the early nineteenth century, political change, library problems, and classification theory combined to produce several library manuals for librarians (which cannot be analyzed here). By the late 1830s the impulse to create periodicals was mature, the first ventures bearing unmistakable signs of their parentage in the attention given to antiquarian interests. They also gathered some library data; but that function was increasingly performed in surveys like Jewett's *Notices of Public Libraries in the United States of America*, the celebrated "Appendix" to his 1851 report as librarian of the Smithsonian Institution. Five years later appeared the first edition of Julius Petzholdt's 217-page *Katechismus des Bibliothekenlehre* ("Catechism of Library Instruction"; Leipzig), number 27 in Weber's "Illustrated Catechisms in the Sciences and Arts" (Kayser, *Bücher-Lexikon*, 14:518–519). This work was noticed widely, influencing the men who launched libraries in Bulgaria, and included (2d ed., 1871) by A. R. Spofford in his guidance essay in the Bureau of Education's 1876 *Report* (p. 733), as "undoubtedly the most valuable" item available. The scene was further enriched by monuments of scholarship, Edward

Edwards' *Memoirs of Libraries* (1859), Petzholdt's *Bibliotheca Bibliographica* (1866), and Alfred Franklin's *Anciennes Bibliothèques de Paris* (1867-1873).

The literature thus accumulated by 1876 was probably known to serious librarians and supporters of librarianship internationally. That many of the works mentioned appear in the catalog of the Boston Athenaeum, that many more are on Spofford's list, is strongly suggestive. United States observers were aware of writings in German and the Romance tongues, but seem not to have been posted on publications in Russian or other Slav languages. Familiarity with United States titles in England is plain enough from such evidence as the discussions at the 1877 conference. What was known of Anglo-American library literature on the Continent is worth an investigation apparently not yet made.

The age of organizations, opening in 1876, would soon produce published transactions and monographic works, but the first phase was an invasion of the periodicals area with striking effects upon their content. *Library Journal* (1876-) and *Library Notes* (1886-1898) in the United States were almost entirely practical, *Library Chronicle* (1884-1888) in England likewise. The German *Zentralblatt für Bibliothekswesen* (1884-) found a middle course between the old and the new, combining bibliographical and other scholarly essays with theoretical discussions ranging from classification to state regulations; library news was a regular feature. *The Library,* in England, experimented (1889) with an alliance of bibliophily and library news, an interim success but destined to yield in part to the Library Association's own *Library Association Record.* The contemporary cognate journals in Hungary (*Magyar Könyvszemle,* 1876-), France, and Italy should be studied, and the whole compared.

Women None of the books mentioned was written by a woman. Women had, however, prepared a few of the printed catalogs in United States libraries, partly perhaps because those expensive instruments were most common in the public and "social" libraries of less than 40,000 volumes, where a woman was most likely to be charged with responsibility. Quite a few in such libraries were probably submitting regular annual reports to their trustees; and the age of conventions and monthly journalism gave women's contributions much wider acknowledgment than before.

Women had long been employed on farms, in textile mills, and even in mines. The Crimean and Civil Wars precipitated women into the rapidly enlarging field of nursing, and they soon afterward became predominant in school teaching. Their entry into librarianship followed as the night the day the rise of the library supported from public funds, especially in the United Kingdom and the United States, and the ease of paying women less than men for any given task.

The first generally known instance of women's employment in a public library seems to have been the experiment tried in Manchester, England, in 1871. Faced with a situation in which young men remained only long enough to find better-paid jobs in commerce and industry, the library advertised successfully for young women. Three were tried at 6 shillings a week, found satisfactory, and given raises (unspecified). Their supervisors, the branch librarians, were not enthusiastic at first but came to favor the idea.

By 1879, when the chairman of the trustees submitted the story to The Library Association conference, there were thirty-one in service, four in "the reference library" and the others in the branches, at wages varying from 10 to 18 shillings a week. Few had left, except for bad health or getting married; the advertisement had never had to be repeated. Hopeful candidates even worked half-time from 5 P.M. to 9 P.M., awaiting regular appointment. Certain "qualities" were mentioned, in which females were "scarcely equal to" males: the only tasks spoken of were "rough work . . . such as opening and shutting windows, going errands, also in reaching books from the higher shelves." At least one youth was wanted also "in case of disorder in the reading-rooms, though this is of very infrequent occurence." For "attendance on readers and applicants for books," the librarians decidedly preferred the girls. (Library Association. *Transactions and Proceedings of the Second Annual Meeting,* London: Whittingham, 1880, pp. 32–33.)

Whether F. B. Perkins or any other United States librarian knew of the Manchester experience in 1876 is not readily ascertainable, but Perkins advanced the same reasoning in his paper "How to Make Town Libraries Successful," in the 1876 *Report* of the Bureau of Education. In a paragraph (p. 430) on the "excessive proportion" of administrative overhead in the annual cost of operating a library, he recommended counteracting it by means of "mechanical appliances . . . better arrangement of book rooms, and . . . other sufficient contrivances of . . . American ingenuity"; also the employment of women "as librarians and assistants as far as possible." They were not suited to "heavy" work. "Precautions" would "sometimes be needed against" the friction arising more often among women "in such places" than among men, but an able supervisor or board of trustees would solve the problem with "admonition, or, if necessary, by a change in the service." Getting along with others, as well as "formal good behavior," would be required to hold the job.

Ten years afterward, women outnumbered men in the Columbia School student body and went on to responsible posts. From the Columbia annual report for 1888 the editor of *The Library* inferred that "librarianship is becoming an occupation for women in America" (1:115, February 1889). He was not however persuaded that the ladies were equal to men in total capacity, even though several had already attained distinction. Several months later, commenting on the proposal of a Polish woman to establish an International Library of Women's Works, he asked why "those enthusiastic ladies who are constantly asserting their mental equality with male man" did not see that "to affirm a positive is to raise a question" (*The Library,* 1:345). It was to be a matter of just a few more years before discriminatory treatment and attitudes led the ladies in librarianship to take counsel together, in public organized assemblages.

The Library as Seen by the Reading Public If the ladies were acknowledged as infusing library service with appealing elements, library activity as a whole obtained public scrutiny most unevenly. The twenty-four-volume ninth edition of *Encyclopaedia Britannica,* issued orginally, volume by volume, between 1875 and 1888, presented to the curious a virtual booklet on "Libraries" (XIV:509–551, 1883?). To "History and Description" it accorded some twenty-seven pages encompassing even contemporary Latin America and the Orient; to "Library Management," five and one-half pages, ending with annotated references to the leading guides: Edwards, Petzholdt, the 1876 *Report* and "the six volumes of *Library Journal*" then available. The remaining nine pages were given to a remarkable table of libraries in the United Kingdom large and small, plus those of 30,000 volumes and upward in other countries. For each was furnished the date of foundation, the printed and manuscript holdings, to whom it was accessible, and such "Special Character and Remarks" as "For use of Students" and "Sci., Engin., cat[alog] pr[inted]."

That the more popular audience was thought to want at least some historical and descriptive information about libraries is evident from the two and a half columns in volume V of *Chambers's Encyclopaedia* (1888–1892) issued originally in London and Edinburgh by W. and R. Chambers and in New York by Collier. The "Libraries" article was followed by a single-paragraph entry on the British "Libraries' Acts" of 1850 to 1871, presumably repeated without updating from the 1874 edition of the encyclopedia. The sole reference was to the current publications of The Library Association.

The interest of the literate outside the profession's own ranks is further documented by the rise of periodical articles in English. *Poole's Index* for 1802 through 1881 lists four and a half columns of entries (many multiple) from "Librarian, Profession of" to "Library Wants." Almost as many are then listed for just six years, four columns in the *Index* for 1882 to 1887, from "Librarian and his Constituents" to "Library Statistics of Europe." The rate then drops: the *Index* for 1887 to 1892 records only two and a half columns of articles, from "Librarian as Educator" to "Library Work—in Schools." Appleton's *Annual Cyclopedia* was meanwhile silent on libraries, although its annual essays on "Literature" included considerable data on publishing trends.

Those who consulted *La Grande Encyclopédie,* which began to appear in Paris in 1886, could profit from a survey of *"Bibliothèques"* (6:647–668; published between April and September 1888) much like that in *Britannica*—first historico-descriptive, then analytical. Under section "V. *Bibliothèques populaires*" it is observed that most cities in the United States have the genuine article, and statistics are cited from the 1876 *Report* of the Bureau of Education. It is also noted that school libraries have not prospered despite the taxes levied to support them; their function is actually performed by the public libraries. The article is illustrated, and supplemented with an up-to-date classified bibliography, dominated by French writings and referring to Petzholdt's directory of German libraries and the *Zentralblatt* but listing nothing in English. A separate piece (6:669–682) sets forth the story of the Bibliothèque Nationale.

Libraries were well established in the German encyclopedia tradition. A study of the five Brockhaus editions issued during these years, and the other comparable works, might prove enlightening.

Noteworthy amid the considerable literature of librarianship available by 1890 is the fact that growing attention to library personnel, on the part of the librarians themselves, was by no means matched by public discussion. An expanding portion of the general populace in the West was turning to public libraries particularly, for practical aid and recreation, but it was going to require a lengthy struggle to obtain recognition of library professionalism. For that the first prerequisite was clear definition of what a librarian ought to be and do. The process was to be shaped in subsequent years by the herding of millions into slums, the deterioration of agriculture and the environment generally, and the challenge to war-torn capitalism from a new society devoted to building socialism.

Chapter Nine

CONTRADICTION AND CHALLENGE

The years between 1890 and the midtwentieth century were marked fundamentally by successive outthrusts of the internal contradictions of capitalist
society, and on the heels of the first one involving it as a whole, the appearance of the first socialist state. Among the principal secondary phenomena
were the penetration by capitalism and its culture of the bulk of the inhabited world, the dominance of the United States of America, and numerous
challenges to both. Characteristic peculiarly of the United States itself were
on the one hand the continued subjection of most Negroes, the domestication of labor union leadership, sporadic struggles over the corporate conquest of the farm, and the congealing of new patterns of subordinate status
for women; and on the other hand the spread of both literacy and better
living on a scale widely noticed.

Where service was already developed, the library scene witnessed few
novelties besides the rise of school and public library children's service in
the United States, predominantly in urban and suburban areas and predominantly for whites. Library life in the Russia of the Tsars bore markings
both common and uncommon; the Bolshevik Revolution's library facet was
an outstanding innovation, not only at the practical level domestically but
ideologically wherever men thought about libraries and librarianship. Technological advance, moreover, confronted both worlds, capitalist and socialist,
with challenges to bibliographical control. The library profession dealt with
manifold problems with varying results, enlarging its numbers and institu-

tional apparatus, but unable to head off competition from documentalists and not achieving equality of standing with the professions long recognized.

Thanks to the richness of the record on some points and the virtual absence of sober consideration of others, the discussion below will be far more selective than what has gone before.

Libraries and Librarianship, 1890 to 1919

Increasing Density of Research Information, 1890–1914   The age of bank-dominated syndicates and cartels, of rivalries preparing for World War I, devoted a modest portion of accumulated capital to research information, partly in enlarged academic libraries and partly in newer repositories. By 1900 Harvard was in a class with the leading European university libraries, having passed the half-million mark in holdings. That was true of hardly any other familiar United States institution, but the future could be read in the tenfold mutiplication of the Indiana University Library budget between 1875 and 1900, and the endowment by private wealth of the Newberry (1887) and John Crerar (1895) libraries in Chicago.

If these establishments were oriented heavily to the past, preoccupation with the present plainly marked the special libraries appearing in business and industry as well as government departments, especially in the United States and Germany. The larger public libraries also hearkened to the new call: the first known technical division opened in 1889 in the Carnegie Library in Pittsburgh and the pioneer public library service to business at Newark in 1904. By 1909 there were enough "special librarians" in various kinds of institutions to form a Special Libraries Association separate from the American Library Association; in fact, the Association of Law Librarians was already three years old.

Information about books available was plentiful. A major gap was filled in 1912 when, at the suggestion of Prussian Education Minister Althoff, an agreement was worked out between Saxony, the City of Leipzig, and the German Book-Dealers' Marketing Association to receive and publicly list deposit copies of new titles.

The rapid increase of book and journal stock demanded ever greater sensitivity to the problems of space and bibliographic control. Where subject classification had for a century or so rivaled format as a basis for shelving, and often gained ascendancy therein, the efficiency of arrangement by size found new supporters like President C. W. Eliot of Harvard (1902). They were not able, however, to counteract the appeal of subject arrangement, for it was greatly enhanced in the United States by the rising popularity of open stacks in public libraries, even though the large academic installations usually continued to keep their own stacks closed. More acceptable than shelving irrespective of the character of the book was the exiling of the newspaper files: the British Museum began to house them in separate quarters as early as 1905, a precedent followed by other great libraries in later days.

As more materials filled more shelves, the need mounted sharply for means which would tell the staff and the readers quickly where a given item means which would tell the staff and the readers quickly where a given item was to be found. The bibliographical armory was enriched not only by such traditional contributions as the massive printed catalogs of manuscripts and incunabula produced notably in France and Germany, but by the maturing of vital new approaches to information. In 1901 the H. W. Wilson Company launched *Reader's Guide,* the first of several indexing periodicals in dictionary catalog style, illustrating successfully what United States production and marketing talent could do. Six years later, the American Chemical Society applied similar resources to the first modern abstracting journal, *Chemical Abstracts.*

Less efficient but equally significant was the organization in 1892 of the International Institute of Bibliography. Thousands of information references were assembled in its Brussels files, and for their control (published in 1905) was developed a complex modification of the Dewey scheme, later called the Universal Decimal Classification. Well suited to bibliographic uses, although not to marking book spines or to shelving, were such UDC devices as linking two class marks (like 311 and 378) with a colon and announcing the presence of material so classified (Statistics of Higher Education) at both locations in the file, 311:378 and 378:311. This procedure, known as "permutation," had the advantage of displaying a relationship between two facets wherever the record appeared, something less easily managed with subject headings and usually not achievable at all unless the full subject tracing appeared on each subject card. (The Library of Congress enters material under STATISTICS and under headings like EDUCATION—STATISTICS but does not divide STATISTICS by fields of application.)

Standardization and centralization advanced only erratically. The Prussian Ministry of Culture sponsored printed catalog cards for Berlin scholarly libraries in 1892 (extended to Prussian universities in 1898), and in 1901 the Library of Congress laid revolutionary foundations by offering its printed cards for sale to any buyer. Yet the "Prussian Instructions" of 1899 preserved the title as the main entry for materials treated in the Anglo-American Code of 1908 as corporate entries, the twin rigidities assuring decades of competition and confusion. Furthermore, although the American Library Association furnished in 1895 a standard *List of Subject Headings for Use in Dictionary Catalogs* and the Library of Congress printed-card tracings exerted standardizing influence, local custom persisted vigorously.

Insignificant by comparison was the difference between the unitary dictionary catalog overwhelmingly preferred in the United States, and the combination long common in continental Europe: an author catalog with few or no added entries by title, subject catalogs either systematic or alphabetical or both (separately), and special catalogs for periodicals, doctoral dissertations, etc. Perhaps unique as basic instruments very similar in nearly every library were their shelflists, the most common means of recording the locations of all items.

Nor could the research-library user count on stability and consistency concerning the kind of literary unit entered in a catalog. The degree to which analytical entries were made for journal articles, essays in collections, monographs in series, and portions of learned society transactions was governed at least partly by binding policies and partly by cost. That the situation was marked by great variation can hardly be doubted, but the subject does not seem to have been investigated.

A new type of response to such stimuli was the unit specializing in both information and guidance as to manipulating existing approaches to it. The pioneer, apparently, was the Information Bureau organized in 1905 by the libraries of Berlin; in 1914 it began issuing its union list of German periodicals in German libraries *(Gesamt-Zeitschriften-Verzeichnis).*

The White Nonscholar in the United States, 1890-1914 If the information desired by the nonscholar using the public library was not notably increasing in density, the urban population clearly was. The years which saw the rise of trade unionism, sharp class struggles, social settlements, and social insurance included also the rapid advance of the public library, absorbing many earlier forms of open-door service. Germany and France, leaders in social insurance legislation, did very little in the public library sector. But where there was no social insurance, in the United States and the United Kingdom (until Lloyd George's 1911 reforms), the public library aided by the philanthropy of steel tycoon Andrew Carnegie assumed a prominent role.

In the United States, Carnegie at first (1886-1896) gave to six Pennsylvania communities fourteen library buildings of a broad community-center character—designed to accommodate art and recreation as well as library service. This investment totalled $1,860,869, and was accompanied by endowments. The six were all towns with Carnegie steel plants, one being Homestead, scene of the bloody riot of 1892 against strikebreakers and employer undercover agents; the library gift to Homestead arrived in 1896. In the second stage (1898-1919), the celebrated donor presented 1,406 communities with building grants aggregating $39,172,981. The main bases were approval of the site and commitment by the recipients to allocate annually a maintenance sum equal to 10 percent of the Carnegie gift. The gift was rarely less than $1,000. Although many beneficiaries were towns as small as the original six, most of the public thereby served were in large cities. On the whole they welcomed the new asset; yet labor long regarded it as a sop or even an antimilitancy bribe. (These and other relevant library data are in G. Bobinski's *Carnegie Libraries,* Chicago: A.L.A., 1969; especially pp. 13-15.)

Carnegie aid was also lavished on other libraries in what he thought of as Anglo-Saxon, therefore superior-potential, areas. Actually, the first grants had been made to towns in the Scotch enterpriser's native land; those to his adopted country came next, and his plan thereafter expanded to include England, Ireland, and Canada. The 125 buildings received mainly by public libraries and partly by college libraries in Canada between 1901 and 1917 were a considerable boon. That was less true of the benefactions in England, where too often the building was far grander than the collections housed, and the penny per pound limit on library tax support actually burdened many with debts they might not have contracted otherwise. By 1919 there were some 3,000 Carnegie libraries altogether; Carnegie had spent 45 million dollars on those in the United States, and another 15 million on those abroad.

His personal interest need not be questioned. It is striking, nevertheless, that his operation was soon institutionalized like so much else of the epoch. Activities in the United States were handled after 1911 by the Carnegie Corporation; those in the United Kingdom, after 1913, by the Carnegie United Kingdom Trust.

Other institutionalized efforts were affected variously. The libraries and reading rooms organized to serve railwaymen, first by railway personnel and later by the YMCA and the WCTU, remained consequential in the United States and Canada for the first few years of the twentieth century. In fact a World's Railway Commerce Congress held in 1893 in connection with the Chicago Columbian Exposition heard a plea for company officials to visit the reading rooms and hobnob with the men. Gradually, nevertheless, the special interest in counteracting the workers' class consciousness was swallowed up in the more generalized format of the public library. Perhaps symptomatic was the organization of such a library in 1898 in suburban Painesville, Ohio (near Cleveland), after twenty-four years' domination of that activity by temperance and YMCA and railroad-linked library units. By no means has all the story been made known.

The efforts of the women's clubs, in high gear after the formation of the National Federation in 1890, differed in that they served no special interest and expressed the noblesse oblige impulse on a small scale according to local circumstances. If what has been extracted from the mainly unprobed records discloses representative trends, it appears that the women's clubs either helped convert quasi-public libraries into fully public institutions or shared in founding brand-new ones.

Another datum bearing investigation is the sensitivity of the expanding public library world to the complexities of "Americanization." It is a matter of record that by 1907 the American Library Association Publishing Board was issuing lists of recommended books in German and Hungarian. Was that a response to requests from the East Coast ports, from coal and steel towns, from elsewhere? What sort of library materials were wanted, and how were they used? What might be learned from a comparison of language-request patterns with population composition?

Better known, thanks to familiarity with the "child-centered" thrust and other new currents in education, reflected notably in John Dewey's *School and Society* (1899), is the rapid advance in the later nineties of library service to children, especially in urban areas. When in 1896 the National Education Association established a Library Section, public libraries were increasingly loaning books to elementary schools, and at least Evanston, Illinois, was maintaining classroom collections in the elementary schools furthest from the public library. Rivalry and debate became fierce in the United States over the comparative merits of the two organizational structures: what looked like double taxation for a single purpose upset the taxpayers, as indeed it would for many years to come. After 1900, however, public library service to children seemed to be a going concern, and the school library movement was able—partly for that reason perhaps—to pick up momentum. New York City's Erasmus Hall High School boasted a trained librarian in 1900, and many libraries in such institutions were soon providing audio-visual aids as well as books. In 1914 the American Library Association authorized creation of a School Library Section.

As service to the urban population forged ahead, devoted labors were exerted also on behalf of rural library service. The soil had been prepared by the farmers' increasing annoyance with lower prices for what they sold and higher prices for what they bought, and the rapid introduction in the eighties of rural adult education, university extension, courses in agriculture in the high schools, and the location near farming areas of experiment stations sponsored by the national purse. Notable from the library viewpoint was the university extension movement in Wisconsin: starting in 1885, it reached in 1906 and 1907 a stage at which "loan package library service" was a prominent activity, an alternative to the correspondence courses promoted by the University of Chicago. Although the National Association of State Libraries, organized in 1898, apparently gave little attention to these activities, the later League of Library Commissions (1904) seems to have tried with some success to fill the gap, thanks in part to the help of the state federations of women's clubs.

The obstacles were many and diverse, to judge from the assessment at the 1907 A.L.A. convention by Mary Eileen Ahern, editor of *Public Libraries.* The women's committee members were new every two years and had to be educated to library needs. The superintendents of public instruction "in many states" were reluctant to lodge in librarian hands "any part of the work which heretofore they have claimed as their own, however ineffectively" they had performed it; greater cooperation was hoped for. "Most of the commissions" had not been able to accomplish "much" for school libraries, and except in Oregon those agencies seemed to be "just about as poorly off as they always have been." Furthermore, bringing public libraries to communities too small to support them or indifferent to them was a problem. Nor could solutions be expected quickly as long as the duly authorized commissions were financed so shabbily by insensitive state legislatures. Some state librarians themselves were obstructive: if a commission established a lending library outside the traveling library system, they asked, "What is left for the general state library?" Many thought state aid to local units better. ("Papers and Proceedings of the Asheville Conference," *A.L.A. Bulletin,* 1:231–234, 1907.)

Despite the handicaps, several devices continued to be used in bringing library service to rural districts. The traveling library, familiar in New York State since 1892 (begun during Melvil Dewey's service, 1888 to 1899, as secretary to the Board of Regents), was now known also in Wisconsin, Maryland, and Saskatchewan, if not elsewhere as well. The loan package system was adopted in 1910 as a principal activity of the new Bureau of General Information in the University of Kansas Extension Division, designed deliberately to reach areas not served by public or school libraries. The federal government, moreover, was authorized under the Smith-Lever Act of 1914 to support an extension teaching program based on cooperation between the state agricultural colleges and the federal Department of Agriculture. How that framework would accommodate library service concerned the American Library Association's Agricultural Libraries Section, established in 1911. By 1914 the Department of Agriculture Library was furnishing through interlibrary loan 896 books to institutions in forty-six states and territories, distributing many duplicates gratis, and expanding the dissemination of bibliographic information.

Further enlightenment might be obtained by examining the record of the innovative (1907–) visits by A.L.A. presidents to the meetings of state library associations.

The Non-White in the United States, 1890–1914   If a civilization is tested by the degree to which its benefits reach the lowliest, the United States had much to explain. Library service to the American Indian was virtually nil. Ultimately a far more serious matter, conditions were not much better for the Negroes, especially in the South, where most of them lived. The end of chattel slavery and demands of political and economic struggle produced strenuous efforts on their part to rise and on the part of others to hold them down. The years 1880–1900 were marked by a flood of literary caricaturing of the free Negro, a plethora of suppressive legislation in the Southern states, much unpunished discrimination and lynching, the 1896 decision of the United States Supreme Court, in *Plessy v. Ferguson,* that "separate but equal" was a proper guide for public behavior. On the plus side, Tuskegee Institute was established in 1881, and by 1900 more than 2,000 Negroes had graduated from institutions of higher learning; numerous black writers and inventors had made their marks. Blacks were now 27.7 percent urban. Opportunity was nevertheless so limited as to evoke first the Niagara Movement in 1905, and—after the horrible 1908 riot at Springfield, Illinois, built around the familiar false "rape" charges—the National Association for the Advancement of Colored People, founded in 1910.

Of particular importance to library life was Negro illiteracy. Whereas illiteracy among the whites ten years old or older had declined from 23 percent in 1870 to 15 percent in 1890, among the "colored" of the same two census divisions (South Atlantic and South Central) the corresponding percentages were 85 and 60. The Commissioner of Education observed that it was not known whether this "remarkable progress" was due "more to the aid of the whites who pay the school taxes than to the efforts of the negroes [sic] themselves" (*Report, 1892–1893,* p. 153). In any case, the massive illiteracy traditionally imposed upon the Black population, and the by no means negligible illiteracy also hampering the white working people of the same area, pulled the national average down noticeably. In 1890 the illiteracy percentages of Germany and Scandinavia were reported at less than 1.7, those of England and France around 7; the United States figure was 13, halfway to the Irish level of 19.4 (*Report, 1892–1893,* pp. 125, 144).

The conquest of illiteracy continued to move with differences reflecting social conditions. Immigrants were reported a mere 13 percent illiterate all the way to 1920; the percentage among the Blacks dropped steadily, but the obstacle was 79.9 percent in 1870, 56.8 in 1890, and still 30.5 in 1910. (U.S. Bureau of the Census, *Historical Statistics of the United States,* 1960, p. 214.)

That library service to Negroes was miserably limited comes as no surprise. The public libraries of the leading cities, early in the twentieth century, admitted Black citizens reportedly without distinction in the Northern and border states but in the South provided library service to them separately or not at all. The first city library for Negroes was built in 1906 in Charlotte, North Carolina, from municipal funds, $5,000 for site and building and $400 a year for maintenance, against a $25,000 Carnegie building for the white community; the Black library relied for book stock largely on gift discards. More respectable efforts mark the record of Louisville (Kentucky) Free Public Library, established in 1905. The first of its seven branches was led from the outset by a Negro librarian, Thomas F. Blue, whose administration of his unit and development of Black personnel were soon widely enough admired to persuade the directors of many Southern public libraries to send Negro prospects to him for training.

The relationship with white activity was in general marginal, and collections in general weak. In Memphis an agreement was made in 1903 between the white library and a Negro-serving normal school. Houston, Texas, opened a branch for Black readers in 1912, mainly on account of the initiative of Booker T. Washington's secretary, who sold the idea personally to Andrew Carnegie, obtaining a grant of $15,000 after Houston's Negro community raised $1,500 for the site. The Memphis library held some 8,000 books, the Houston branch, 5,000. Not strikingly different were the Negro school and college holdings reported by the Commissioner of Education in 1910: two had about 27,000 volumes, nine more between 5,000 and 20,000, but the other 150-odd had less.

As in other aspects of life, this special abuse of Black citizens unmistakably affected for the worse their white neighbors too. Whether one examines the data for Carnegie grants for buildings, by region, or for communities receiving them, it is plain that the South was behind the rest of the nation. Likewise, although state library associations and state library commissions were organized in numerous states shortly before 1900, only one of them, Georgia, was a Southern state. (Assembled in Bobinski, pp. 20–21.)

Attitudes supportive of this state of affairs were deeply rooted. William F. Yust, librarian of the forward-looking Louisville institution during the days of Thomas F. Blue's pioneering, placed before the American Library Association conference of June 1913, at Kaaterskill, New York, most of what has been stated here about library service to Negroes in the early years of the twentieth century. He also drew attention to Negro preference for non-fiction, speculating that the reasons might be a small leisure group among them, or that the users were students and professional persons with serious purposes, or "that the novel does not appeal so strongly to the negro [sic] mind" (the last left unexplained). The conclusions of this white observer, whose record clearly testifies to the best of intentions, include the following:

> (9) That in the South any arrangement which aims to serve the two races in the same room or in the same building is detrimental to the greatest good of both. Complete segregation is essential to the best work for all.... (12) That the best solution of the problem is a separate branch in charge of colored assistants under the supervision and control of the white authorities. ("Papers and Proceedings of the Kaaterskill Conference," *A.L.A. Bulletin*, 7:167, 1913.)

The Nonscholar in Europe, 1890–1914 Library service to the nonscholar in Europe bore features similar to those in the United States only in minor measure. Conspicuous was the chain of events affecting Norway. Hans T. Lyche (1860–1898) acquired some education and other experience in the

United States in the eighties, began writing articles for home publication, then returned home and pursued the publicizing of the world's best writers in translation on all manner of subjects, including libraries. This harmonized well with the Norwegian literary renaissance of the last quarter of the century, and Norway's becoming independent of Sweden in 1905. By that time Haakon Nyhuus (1866–1913) had worked for several years at the celebrated Newberry Library in Chicago, in outstanding professional company, and was also back home in Oslo ready to introduce (1898) United States cataloging practices and library equipment. His focus on public libraries, in a country largely lacking the scholarly library atmosphere dominant in German tradition, facilitated the infusion of such United States ideas as open shelves, the traveling library, and service to children just a few years after their acceptance in the United States itself.

These impulses were soon evident in Sweden and Denmark too. Children's service was introduced in the Stockholm Public Library in 1914 largely at the instance of a library scholar who had lately continued her studies in the United States; the basis, however, was voluntary contributions. State support and central control, as in France, had long shaped the Swedish secondary schools, whose collections, incidentally, had like many such institutions elsewhere in Europe inherited scholarly works from the days of secularization and confiscation. What this meant to young readers, what impact was exerted by the Library Act of 1912, needs clarification. Denmark seems to have offered service to children through the schools alone.

In the branch system developed around the Budapest Public Library, also, spoke United States influence, explicitly. The hundreds of book collections installed in villages between 1900 and 1914, by the Ministry of Rural Economy, seem more of the French or Swedish sort. The contemporaneously established popular libraries in the towns were indebted to both public and private effort.

The United Kingdom, with a long tradition of voluntary library financial support, was accordingly somewhat further from the United States model. Although, as noted earlier (p. 407), it was favored with Carnegie grants, tax-supported public library development was eased only moderately by the financial and other local-government reforms of the mid-eighties; real progress awaited removal of the limitation of the penny per pound tax rate. What sort of library service was furnished at the numerous settlement houses and workingmen's colleges launched between the establishment of Toynbee Hall (1884) and the outbreak of war in 1914, how much library interest was registered in the plans and actions of the Fabian Society (1883) or the Labour Party (1900), are matters remaining to be explored. Rural service was still heavily dependent upon volunteers, and about as scattered and feeble as in the United States. Libraries were in respectable condition in the ancient and honorable private "grammar" schools, but not yet on firm foundations in the tax-aided secondary schools appearing in the eighties and nineties. Nor were book collections regarded as necessary in public elementary education (1870–), oriented primarily toward terminal schooling introductory to work; the administrative and curricular improvements of 1902 and 1904 did not alter that neglect.

At several places in the Netherlands, public libraries were firmly rooted and loaned books for use in the schools. Children's service was more often organized by independent societies; sometimes their collections were given a home in a public library. Notable in the Belgian record in that area is the coincidence of a French museum director's speech in praise of United States pedagogy and library service to children, and the talents of the Ghent Women's Union. On behalf of opportunity for workers' children, the ladies organized in 1909 a Society for Libraries for Children which succeeded within one year in opening Belgium's first public library for children. Municipal revenue bought the books but did not extend to buying or renting space: the collection was housed in a disused classroom, but that seems to have been the sole involvement of the schools at that stage.

Striking also, on the Belgian scene first, was the phenomenon of the circulating library maintained as part of the offerings of a workers' club run by a workers' party. In Belgium such libraries appeared in Socialist Party clubs; when is not clear. But they were well enough established by 1905 to impress a leader of the Spanish Radicals, who launched comparable Casas del Pueblo in Barcelona partly with a view to advancing bourgeois republicanism and repulsing Catalan nationalism throughout Spain. The Casas and their book service may have helped produce the circumstances in which was born in 1915 (see below) the first publicly supported library school in Europe.

Largely untouched by United States influence were the library services to nonscholars in France, the German-speaking areas, and Russia. In France, public library service of the Anglo-American sort hardly existed. A survey of conditions in 1902 reported more than 3,000 *bibliothèques populaires* and more than 40,000 *bibliothèques scolaires*. The former, dependent largely on private backing, rarely consisted of more than an office without a reading area. The latter, controlled by the Ministry of Education decree of 1862, were designed primarily for pupils, although accessible also to their families. In neither type were the collections up to date or serviced by trained personnel. Energetic efforts were made at reform, publicizing the greater progress in the United States and the United Kingdom; but social distance was surely just as great in France and apparently not counteracted by the "public library idea," possibly because French centralization allowed so little play to local initiative. Probably important also was the contradiction between the valuable library service long furnished by rival church agencies and the intense anticlericalism of most liberals and radicals.

Even more distinctive were the multiple jurisdictions in Switzerland, Austria, and what was now Germany. Very powerful were the influence of the long-standing religious traditions and the newer preoccupation with the challenge of trade unionism and Marxist thinking among the workers. Many popular libraries and reading rooms were supported by church organizations; many others by the popular education associations, the Ethical Culture Society, and the Comenius Society. Striking nonetheless are the sponsorship of reading rooms in Jena (1895) by the Zeiss optical fortune and in Essen (1899) by the Krupp munitions leadership. (Had they heard anything of the railroad reading rooms in England and the United States?) These institutions offered the attraction of open-shelf browsing, but seldom furnished reference service and rarely enjoyed tax support.

The United States example stirred several observers to promote tax-supported public library service, particularly Constantin Nörrenberg and the others who developed the Book Hall Movement in the mid-nineties. Directed against the sharp class differentiation then customary in library facilities in most of Europe, and the low standing of the popular library, it urged with some success the attractions of service to anyone, offered over many more hours weekly, managed by professional librarians, organized in systems, and financed by public revenue. Collections, buildings, and librarians in Germany improved somewhat, but tax support won no clear victory. Besides, the ranks of the interested were split about 1910 between those who wished to serve all as they chose to be served, and those who believed that librarians should choose only the best for them and indeed should accordingly hold down both the collections and their use. The latter won much approval from educators, but the former was more appealing to the librarians and tended to keep the upper hand. Library opportunity for children meanwhile remained almost exclusively in the care of popular education associations, welfare organizations, and above all religious societies; the moral accent was pronounced.

Morality of one sort was also an abiding concern of the Russian Orthodox Church, expressed in the schools and their book collections. The revolutionary students and intellectuals were pursuing another, with the aid of libraries and library tactics possibly unique. They were appreciative users of the familiar municipal libraries, if Lenin's testimony about those in Samara (550 miles southeast of Moscow) and Krasnoyarsk (Siberia) is a good indicator. They may have known too the modest rural school collections, available to adults apparently in the manner of New York and France; these reportedly numbered some 5,000 in 1905. They were assuredly glad to take advantage of certain large private libraries like educator A. P. Skliarenko's in Samara, comprising both legal and illegal holdings, and others like that of Maxim Gorky's merchant friend A. Derenkov in Kazan (middle Volga), altogether illegal. Besides, at a number of locations, the revolutionaries maintained their own illegal libraries.

The outbreak of 1905 revealed workers as well as intellectuals and peasants as forces for revolution. The Bolsheviks, who regarded the workers indeed as the leading force, and had just (1904) defined their own commitment to disciplined activity, undertook by 1908 among other things to campaign for the democratizing of the public libraries. One renowned salvo was the laudatory attention drawn by Lenin to the annual reports of the New York Public Library which he read in Polish exile. Arguments contrary to liberal loan policies emanated not only from church and secular conservatives but from a number of individualistic admirers of Nietzsche, who thought any group-serving instrument evil; such hindrances were to prove minor.

Librarianship, 1890–1914 As Europe approached the cataclysm which invited the revolutionaries to undertake their profoundly influential actions, library service was characterized at large by a number of principal patterns.

The library open to all and usually tax-supported, with a dictionary catalog and reference service, often with shelves accessible to any patron, dominated the United States scene, was prominent in Scandinavia, and played a significant role in the United Kingdom. Most of Europe, on the other hand, was marked by a sharp division between the world of the scholarly library and the world of the popular book collection. In the former, whatever the source of income, reference service was available and shelves usually closed; alphabetical arrangement was taken as normal for an author file but regarded as no more than a legitimate competitor with systematic arrangement in subject files; titles as added entries were scarcely thought of. Popular circulating libraries were decidedly open but had no reference service, at times no professional staff, and were seldom regarded as really "libraries" at all (the word *Bibliothek* was still not applied to them in 1970).

Staff development was shaped in part by these forces. When the pioneering James Duff Brown (1862–1914) first published his *Manual of Library Economy* in 1903 (London: Scott, Greenwood), one of his observations was the contrast between the 300 women (12 percent) among the 2,500 professionals in the municipal libraries of the United Kingdom—25 women being chief librarians—and the condition in the public libraries of the United States, where the proportion of "women librarians and assistants" was nearer 95 percent (*Manual*, 1st ed., p. 87). The lag in the United Kingdom, he believed, originated in prejudice, less money to offer, and the absence of any means of acquiring training comparable to the library schools of the United States (six were then in operation). Brown himself, although he advised against "a mixed staff" and recommended employing only women if one employed any, nevertheless contended that those employed in libraries "should be paid at the same rate as men or lads performing similar duties" (*Manual*, 1st ed., p. 88). These views were repeated in the next two editions (1907 by Brown and 1920 by W. C. B. Sayers). Indeed, struggle was necessary, since employing women was commonly recommended in Anglo-America as an economy device, a standard deduction from the principles of business management.

That the United Kingdom was nearer to Europe than to the United States was further evidenced in the very fact that a separate organization, the Library Assistants Association, was formed in 1895 and began to give its own examinations.

Although hardly any women worked in university or other scholarly libraries in the United Kingdom, it was precisely in that sector, in Germany, that debates arose over their employment, their training, and what should be expected of them. Many pages of the early *Zentralblatt* were thus occupied. Examinations for librarians had been instituted in 1893, first in Prussia and then Bavaria and Saxony, but they concerned only full-scale professionals with university degrees, men nearly always if not always. As the growth of scholarly collections pressed hard upon this limited cadre for procurement accounting, cataloging and classifying, efforts were made to turn over the less demanding tasks to non-university-trained personnel, including many women. In 1909 Prussia began to examine and certify the "middle service." The regulations of 1912 brought the two a little closer together by obliging the assistants to attend lectures and practice sessions at either Göttingen or the Royal Library in Berlin. By that time the middle-rank individuals actually outnumbered the full professionals in several German scholarly libraries. The Austrians, who had held off hitherto, now conformed.

The Third Republic followed a rather different course, in which women played little or no part. Professional employment at the major libraries in Paris was controlled by a special regulation of 1885, and in 1897 a similar regulation affected the other leading public libraries and the university libraries. Dominant was the diploma of the École des Chartes. However, enforcement of the rules was sufficiently lax to permit many scholars unfamiliar with library routines to acquire professional posts in libraries, and to allow many appointments of persons not professionals at all. In 1906 appeared the Association of French Librarians, which undertook among other things to fight the École des Chartes monopolistic insistence on its seventy-year-old archivist-palaeographer examination; little headway was made by 1914. At that stage middle-rank personnel were a handful.

In the numerous state-regulated scholarly libraries of Italy the contrast between elaborate educational requirements and low pay and slow promotion was severe. Hope for improvements was nourished in 1896 with the formation of the Italian Bibliographical Society and its *Rivista delle Biblioteche*—bringing together librarians, bookdealers, bibliophiles, and university professors.

Interest emerged in Russia from two directions. A bibliographical society was organized in Petrograd in 1899, and within a few years had a libraries section. In 1908 the latter was reorganized as the Libraries Society; next year it reported ninety-four members, all but four in Petrograd; in 1910 it launched *Bibliotekar'*, or "The Librarian." The first issue included the results of a questionnaire survey of people's libraries: only 439 responded of 3,975 queried, but evidence was thus publicized concerning library operations in five provinces (Bessarabia, Vladimir, Vologda, Voronezh, and Vyatka). *Bibliotekar'*'s initial issue also included a review of Russian handbooks on librarianship: several of pamphlet size had appeared since 1859; the only full-length treatment was L. B. Khavkina's of 1904 (of whom more below). In 1911 the journal sponsored an all-Russian conference, which attracted 177 persons from Petrograd itself, 148 from Moscow, and 115 from other places in Russia. They represented 150 people's libraries, 97 scholarly libraries, 24 rural libraries, and 15 private establishments. The gathering divided accordingly into a section for people's libraries, a section for scholarly libraries, and many subsections, but their very proceeding in concert was less like the French and German practice than like the American Library Association model. The accompanying exhibits were standard internationally.

A few of the sixty-two addresses at the 1911 conference were delivered by women, another characteristic still noteworthy in Europe. One of them, Liubov Borisovna Khavkina (1871–1949), had been a librarian and scholar in Kharkov for nearly fifteen years when she appeared (1904) at the Third All-Russian Conference on Technical and Professional Education with proposals for library science education; as noted, she was the author of a major treatise. Four years later, with funds left by liberal industrialist Alfons Leonovich Shaniavskii (1837–1905), a people's university was founded in Moscow, and in 1913 Miss Khavkina installed among its courses a few in library science. They proved more durable than the library conference, which apparently failed to reconvene in 1912, or *Bibliotekar'*, which ceased publication in 1915. Shaniavskii University was to be reorganized in 1918 as Sverdlov University, the Higher Party School of the Bolshevik Party, but a valuable precedent had been set.

Even more influential, in due course, was the commitment of the revolutionaries. Writing for *Rabochaia Pravda* ("Workers' Truth") on July 18, 1913, from exile in Cracow, Poland, V. I. Lenin enthusiastically cited statistics from the 1911 report of the New York Public Library. Such hospitality to all books and all readers, regardless of age or language, he emphasized, was one challenge of "western civilization" Russia should welcome.

Whatever degree of dignity or satisfaction then attached to their work, librarians' pay was not yet likely to attract large numbers of able individuals. The nearest thing to a comprehensive comparative analysis, apparently, is the sketch of "Salaries" in John MacFarlane's *Library Administration* (London: G. Allen, 1898, pp. 34–39), recommended as the best survey in the contemporary German guide (Arnim Graesel, *Handbuch der Bibliothekslehre*, Leipzig: Weber, 1902; a revision of Petzholdt's classic *Katechismus*; p. 176, ftn. 1). It is thus reported that the top personnel in the leading libraries—the Library of Congress, the British Museum, and so on—by and large were paid $5,000 at the turn of the century.

For the compensation of the bulk of librarians, however, indicated by MacFarlane in scattered fashion for Germany, only generally for the United Kingdom, and otherwise hardly at all, one must turn to the 1892 data in the *Report of the U.S. Commissioner of Education 1892–1893* (pp. 46–47, 754–763), the U.S. Bureau of Labor Statistics' *History of Wages in the United States from Colonial Times to 1928* (1934, Bulletin 604; pp. 295, 412, 439, 451 and passim), and the figures presumably from the nineties used in J. D. Brown's *Manual* of 1903 (especially p. 83). The chief librarians in the 170 reporting libraries in the United States, mainly but not all public, were receiving an average of $1,364. Those in British public libraries may have averaged £400 (Brown), equal to a little less than $2,000 (or $1,250 if the remarks at the International Library Conference of 1897 are more accurate; *Transactions and Proceedings*, London, 1898, p. 45). United States locomotive engineers earned on the average about $4.15 a day, which for 300 days' work would bring in $1,245. First assistants in the 170 United States libraries mentioned were averaging annually $642, while their British counterparts were paid close to $525. "General assistants" in the same United States libraries drew an average of $375 annually; most of their British colleagues were paid, apparently, still less; for comparison, United States spinners of woolens and worsteds were then averaging around $300 annually.

The ratio of top library pay to the bottom, insofar as these data permit an approximate calculation, was between 5 to 1 and 4 to 1. If we ignore that spread for the moment, we may compare to the resulting inflated United States "average" of nearly $800 for librarians an equally artificial "average" of $600 paid in 1892 to the teachers and supervisors in public schools in United States cities of population over 8,000. (Reckoned very roughly from the figures for the academic years 1891–1892 and 1892–1893.) In both instances the more significant measure, the median, would without doubt be lower.

While it is possible to assemble additional data for the balance of the period between 1890 and 1914, comparability and trends would be most difficult to establish, except in one respect, the effect of professional training on library salaries in the United States. In 1914, Josephine Adams Rathbone reported (*Library Journal,* 39:188–190) of the graduates of the Pratt Institute School of Library Science, that their average pay in 1896 (the first six classes) was $607, that the average in 1908 was $773, and that the average in 1913 was $1,138. This information had been obtained from 262 alumni in library posts, of whom 160 worked in public libraries, 48 in government and other special libraries, and 39 in "college and school" libraries. A survey of cognate facts about Indiana libraries meanwhile brought forth from ninety-two respondents evidence that librarians generally earned much less: the only institution paying as much as $2,160 annually to the head librarian had an income of $14,464, while seventy-one with incomes up to $3,275 paid $600 or less; assistants were of course worse off; libraries were urged to apply to salaries 40 to 50 percent of their income (*Library Journal,* 39: 196–197).

As perceived in 1897 by the librarians able to attend the International Conference in London, poor pay was unquestionably a stumbling block, but the future beckoned winningly nonetheless. Most of the 641 hailed from the United Kingdom and the United States, several from Commonwealth countries, a few from Europe. Of the last, Léopold Delisle was in the audience but only Karl Dziatzko read a paper (on early state aid to printing). Major attention was given to public library service, administration, architecture, and history; bibliography, cataloging, and classification; and education for librarianship. Also touched on were service to young readers, opportunities for women, the progress of libraries in various parts of the British Empire, and museum librarianship. Several were cast historically, a few philosophically. As was now customary, the participants had at their disposal an exhibit of library appliances.

More equipment featured the International Exposition of the Book Industry and Graphic Arts, held at Leipzig in May 1914. Although the United States government was not represented, the American Library Association shared the proceedings officially. Among the United States products creating favorable impressions were a wall chart displaying statistically the growth of libraries in the United States between 1875 and 1913, a model of a "typical small branch library," Library of Congress printed cards and card trays, the Library of Congress classification, and the books and furnishings designed for use by children. "We caught one man in the act of removing a book from the children's section," reported delegate Theodore W. Koch to the A.L.A. Leipzig Exhibit Committee (*Library Journal,* 39:595; 1914), but were less fortunate with at least one other.

Contrariwise, Koch's description brought to the readers of *Library Journal* an appreciation for German devotion to the practical, awareness of "interesting books" in German public and university libraries, and a reminder of the distinctive workingmen's libraries and reading rooms. Both Germans in general, and certain groups of workingmen, were shortly to set patterns evoking far less satisfaction.

War, 1914-1919 On June 28, 1914, the Austro-Hungarian emperor's nephew and presumptive heir was assassinated at a town in one of the imperial subject territories. On August 4, German armies crossed the Belgian border. Cartel rivalries had broken out into war.

The *Library Association Record* for August 15–September 15, 1914, announced (p. 409) that the Oxford convention scheduled for August 31 to September 4 would be postponed; the October 15 issue announced that a roll of honor would be maintained, to preserve the names of librarians serving in uniform (p. 512). The December 15 number carried a call for contributions for "novels and magazines" for "a large lending library" to be organized on behalf of the troops from the colonies, encamped on Salisbury Plain awaiting assignment (p. 550). Conviction that public libraries had a great role to play in the war was expressed promptly, one of the earliest occasions apparently being the North Midland Library Association meeting on November 19, 1914.

The tone was different in *Zentralblatt für Bibliothekswesen*. In the combined issues 9 through 11, dated September–November 1914, emphatic reference was made to "the battle for our national existence, which nasty neighbors have forced upon us" (31:473), and pride was expressed in the librarians among those already honored with the Iron Cross. Library service to scholarship was going to suffer from lack of staff, but it was worth bearing. The next issue printed greetings to the Association of German Librarians from the Austrian Association for Library Affairs, stressing "brotherhood in arms and culture in battle against a whole world of hate, envy, meanness, and utterly unscrupulous desire to crush us" (31:509). Also reproduced was the response of heartfelt thanks. Readers of *Zentralblatt* nonetheless found in each issue the usual news of librarianship abroad, including data credited to *Library Journal* and various British and Unites States library annual reports. One wonders how many of them shared the sentiments expressed at official levels.

The mustering of men to the colors was felt promptly in Germany in all walks of life: the scholarly libraries were afflicted by staff shortages throughout the war years. The official spirit, at least, did not flag. When the French occupied Strasbourg (November 24, 1918), *Zentralblatt* published a call for assistance to the German librarians driven from their jobs and homes (35:-288). There was also a determined reference to "fatherland culture," the loss to it of numerous writers and scholars on account of the fighting, and a projected Hall of Fame honoring them (35:205). As Anna Seghers would write afterward, the dead were to stay young.

In the United Kingdom the personal impact may have been very similar, but the verbalizing seems to have been lower key, as so often in English behavior. Distress was evidenced a good deal more just after the war, when amid the omnipresent inflation such obligations as soldiers' and veterans' welfare absorbed huge sums of money which might have been applied in part to library development. Within these discouragements, however, emerged a strong positive note: it was in 1919 that the penny per pound limitation on the tax rate was removed, substantial attention given to rural library service, and a library school founded in a university context, at University College, London. Thus matured many earlier efforts, including the recommendations prepared by W. G. S. Adams in 1915 for the Carnegie United Kingdom Trust.

During the first half of the war the United States was officially neutral. *Library Journal*'s September 1914 editorial anticipated the wreck of the Leipzig Book Exhibit and mourned a bevy of professional meetings "postponed" indefinitely. It noted the plea from Paul Otlet, the director of the Brussels Institute, for the protection of the "enormous bibliographic and scientific collections" in his care. "To suppose that the librarians of France are in any sense the 'enemies' of their fellow librarians in Germany" was "monstrous." The editor's "professional friendships" were "as sincere north of the Rhine as south of it," appreciative equally of German thoroughness, French brilliance in analysis, and English "sanity in things political." Sympathy was offered to "each and all of the contestants," with hope for an early peace. (*Library Journal*, 39:657.)

The next issue's editorial deplored the disruption of international efforts at Berne, Switzerland, the warlike surroundings now afflicting the Brussels Institute, and the death in an early battle of the contemporary Carl Baedeker of the travel-guide dynasty. The Leipzig Exposition was for all practical purposes finished, although "the contracts of the exhibitors require continuance until the end of October." Library progress in Europe had come to a "sudden stop," as indeed augured earlier by the retarding effects in Germany and Russia of the enormous military budgets. Hope lay "above all" in the fact that "this is not a people's war but a war of the general staffs, in which the people suffer"; human bonds of affection would survive "national prejudice." Further, the library progress rising just before the hostilities began made it clear that "if the people could have voted by plebiscite there would scarcely have been war." Control of governments by peoples would aid international good feeling, and the library profession might be "foremost" in this achievement. Meanwhile, there was no reason not to extend help to such individuals as the Belgian librarians now without libraries or jobs (*Library Journal*, 39:737–738).

The same number of *Library Journal* recorded the destruction by the German army of the city of Louvain, the University library included. The atrocity occurred August 27, the Library Association denounced it on September 4, and restoration efforts were reported being organized under Dutch leadership.

At the 1915 convention of the American Library Association normal concerns absorbed the usual time, and the principal reference to the war was an address on the implications for libraries of peace propaganda and the peace movement. Two years later the United States was deeply involved in the conflict. Libraries felt it not so much through individual sacrifice, because women were a large part of the profession and were in uniform only as nurses, as through the shift of energies and funds to War Library Service. Working closely with more prestigious organizations like the Red Cross and YMCA, the librarians were not confident about their own standing with the public, and were apparently satisfied for the sake of fund raising to have the Library War Council composed entirely of nonlibrarians. By November 11, 1918, several million books had been processed for use in more than 300 military encampments and such other locations as 300 vessels; 1.5 million books had been shipped overseas. Instrumental in this labor were close to

300 librarians on leave from their posts. At least one observer, speaking at the 1917 session of the League of Library Commissions (*A.L.A. Bulletin*, 11:361), warned that the civilian commitments of library service might suffer. That view of priorities may have helped win from Congress, also in 1917, a broad exemption for libraries from the restrictions of the Trading with the Enemy Act.

In one vital respect United States library service was indeed lagging. "How Shall We Interest and Induce Our Faculty and Students to More General Cultural Reading?" had been probed in 1915 by Montana State College librarian Elizabeth Forrest. She had sent a questionnaire to forty-two "technical institutions of collegiate rank," on the basis of the federal lists of agricultural and mechanic arts colleges. She had not asked the "large university libraries" because their work was so different from that of "more limited colleges." And she had not asked the Black-serving institutions, because "work with representatives of a race recently in slavery must present far greater difficulties than our own" (*A.L.A. Bulletin*, 9:159). Although contrary sentiment existed in both the Black and the white ranks, none seems to have been expressed on that occasion.

Highlighting the want of progress during the war years is the January 1919 *Library Journal* (44:40–41) feature reproducing a German war library service leaflet and discussing it with an air of wonder. The enemy had obviously been behaving much like the Allies. Interest was expressed in knowing "some day" how the German people compared with "our own" in contributing to the book drive, and how the German servicemen reacted to their camp library service. But there was no comment on the discriminatory treatment of Black United States servicemen by their own government, which awarded them no Medals of Honor and a mere handful of Distinguished Service Crosses, whereas the French conferred Croix de Guerre on entire Black regiments. Nor apparently does the record for 1919 reveal any reaction to the contrast between the energy expended in seventy lynchings and twenty-five riots directed at returning Black servicemen and the continued neglect of library service to the Negro population at large.

Meager progress in sensitivity may be discerned. The Spanish-American War seems to have been reflected in United States librarianship by nothing more than the production of book lists about Cuba and Spain. The First World War aroused feeling mainly because libraries were destroyed and the conduct of international library business inconvenienced . The habit of distinguishing between one's self as a librarian and as a human being was to become deeply rooted.

A contrary view was held by a tiny minority of librarians, the half-dozen women of certain New York City library staffs who, according to July 1917 *Library Journal* (42:530), established the first library local in the American Federation of Labor. What sort of headway they made is a topic apparently not yet investigated.

Proletarian Challenger and Established Bourgeois: Some Library Successes and Failures

Revolution and Adult Education   The innovations of 1917, in Russia, are much better known. On March 12 the Tsar was overthrown by a reform movement of aristocrats and bourgeois. The provisional government they organized did not meet the mass desire either for withdrawal from the war (Russia lost more men than any other belligerent) or for land unencumbered by "redemption dues" (imposed as the serfs were emancipated in 1863) or similar burdens. Accordingly, power was transferred on November 7 to the worker-soldier-peasant council ("soviet") movement led by the Russian So-cial-Democratic Labor Party (Bolsheviks), separate since 1904 from the Men-sheviks or "minority" of the R.S.D.L.P., and soon to rename themselves the Communist Party of the Soviet Union.

Libraries, internationally recognized as an instrument of popular educa-tion, were given prompt attention by the new government. Before the vic-tory month was out, applying his earlier views, Lenin urged benefiting from the best Western models, especially those in Switzerland and the United States, by establishing international interlibrary loan, transporting books post-free, and keeping reading rooms open from 8 A.M. to 11 P.M. every day including Sundays and holidays. He strengthened the great public (formerly imperial) library at Petrograd by ordering shifted to its staff numerous per-sonnel then performing at the Ministry of Public Information what he con-sidered far less useful services. The importance of books and libraries in educating the people was reiterated with frequency, and book abuse became a penal offense.

If preserving and developing the best of capitalist products and tech-niques seemed to the Bolsheviks consistent with their philosophy of dialec-tical materialism, no less important was the question of organization and follow-up. In April 1918, Education Commissar A. V. Lunacharskii was di-rected to work out designs for archives administration and national library service; in June the Council of People's Commissars rebuked the Education Ministry for insufficient concern and demanded a report on progress twice a month. On July 17 a Council decree declared that most libraries were under the supervision of the Libraries Department of the Commissariat for Educa-tion at the national level (at that time the Russian Soviet Federated Socialist Republic, i.e., most of European Russia other than the Ukraine), and stipu-lated consultation as necessary with other commissariats with reference to their own libraries; every institution and organization possessing a library was to report the fact by August 15. Another decree, dated November 26, 1918, reiterated that the Commissariat of Education was in charge of all requisitioning and confiscation of libraries and books. A monthly statistical report of library activities was called for in a decree of February 1, 1919. Under a resolution of January 17, 1920, enemy (White Guard) literature was to be shipped to the Commissariat "for preservation and public use in state libraries." In April, another decree pronounced national property all collec-tions of printed matter other than those being produced by the literary and educational presses sponsored by the Commissariat itself. It also charged three-man committees with implementation at the local level; one member of each committee was to be a representative from the Workers' and Peas-ants' Inspectorate. (Conveniently assembled in translation, in *Lenin, Krups-kaia, and Libraries*, ed. S. Simsova, London: Bingley, 1968.)

A number of related steps were being taken in other sectors. Legal deposit, shaken severely by war, revolution, and civil strife, was reestablished in June 1920 on more elaborate foundations. An official Book Chamber was organized in each Union Republic, charged with bibliographic as well as storage duties. A State Publishing House was founded in November, the first of what became in time a sizable group, and apparently the first in history.

Meanwhile, in October 1919, the first of several moves was made to enlist the aid of friends abroad in furnishing Russia with the recent Western books and journals in which, thanks to geography and cultural and political factors, it was rather weakly stocked. June 1921 saw an exchange agreement with the University of Illinois, and the creation of a special governmental unit to obtain for each major Russian library copies of the latest foreign scientific and technical publications. Soon afterward much thought was given to preparing subject-and-location indexes to these materials.

In harmony with those activities and their stated principles, the Bolshevik negotiators at the Peach of Riga (preliminary in October 1920 and signed the following March) undertook by Article 10 to restore to Poland the archives, libraries, and other cultural property stolen after the eighteenth-century partitions. Thus returned home the Zaluski collection, to become in 1928 a major component of the reincarnated Polish National Library.

By November 1920 the Council of People's Commissars was able to announce a plan for a single network embracing all the libraries in the R.S.F.S.R., including children's reading, and providing for "staffs of instructors" (in Simsova, p. 41). Like the earlier revolutionary steps in library service in the United States—tax-supported universal access, the widely marketed Dewey Decimal Classification, and the similarly standardizing mass-produced Library of Congress printed catalog cards—the Bolshevik national plan raised the concept of library service to a still higher level.

Characteristic was the comprehensive view. Having examined a critical analysis by a librarian, Lenin noted in *Pravda* (February 7, 1921) that about one-fourth of the listed "libraries" did not actually exist yet and that of those that did, about half were "reading huts." He urged not simply more assiduous labor with these institutions but, in direct connection with them, taking advantage of the capitalist techniques of publishing books in serial form in newspapers, printing books cheaply in magazine format, and integrating the whole. Abolition of newspaper subscriptions had already proven impractical despite its appeal; "We must ensure that, generally speaking, books and newspapers are distributed free only to libraries and reading rooms which provide a full service to the whole country and to all the masses of workers, soldiers, and peasants. This will accelerate, intensify and increase the effectiveness of the people's search for literacy, enlightenment and learning. Only then will education advance in seven league boots." Part of the "second step from capitalism to communism," he went on, was to "discover how to give the people through each of the 50,000 libraries and reading rooms two separate newspapers, all necessary textbooks and world classics, and books on modern science and engineering." (Simsova, pp. 32–33.)

More explicit arrangements for the distribution of reading matter were prescribed by the Council of Commissars on November 28, 1921. There was to be guaranteed "in the first place a service to the system of state schools, libraries, agitation centers, reading huts and workers clubs, and the provision of reading matter for the workers." The Revolutionary Military Council was responsible for supplying literature to military organizations, including Red Army units. Likewise, agitational and informational literature distribution fell to the departments and institutions concerned. Book prices would be controlled by the sponsors, based on cost of publication. Domestic distribution required a license under the regulations of the Commissariats of Internal Affairs and Education; foreign sales were to be governed by the Commissariats of Education and External Trade. The dissemination of printed matter through the "educational institutions . . . to the working masses" was to be guided by instructions from the Commissariat of Education, said instructions being due "within a fortnight." (Simsova, pp. 41–42.)

When Lenin died, in 1924, the 1.5 million prerevolutionary patronage of the public libraries had expanded to the neighborhood of 5 million. Foundations had been laid for service not only in urban areas inhabited overwhelmingly by Russians, Ukrainians, White Russians, and the Baltic peoples, but in the farming districts—even those with Asiatic populations just coming out of illiteracy, whose culture Marxist theory projected as "national in form, socialist in content."

Adult Urban Service in the Capitalist World since 1919 If the Bolsheviks were putting into practice the idea of the library as the people's university on a scale not yet seen in the land of its origin, the latter did give the question continuing attention. In 1916 library educator Mary Wright Plummer (1856–1916) tried to shore up uncertain spirits by furnishing philosophical premises. Touching on basic concepts seldom discussed at library meetings, she contended that, whatever credit was due determinism, civilization had been built by the exercise of free will. It had thus "worked" and thereby met the test for truth and value devised by "our great pragmatist." The challenge of rising classes and awakening peoples, of "the call of women of all civilized countries to be pressed into service," demanded new choices. Wise choices required knowledge and free access to information. The churches admitted their failure "to trust the truth and the people," and higher education was suspect. Much therefore devolved upon the free library. It must be defended against not only obvious assault but "insidious and gradual changes in its personnel, or in its rules, or in its guiding factors." (*A.L.A. Bulletin,* 10:111–114, 1916.)

One could accept that view and still adopt any number of specific programmatic positions, some of which decidedly conflicted with each other. Two main schools of thought were readily observable: those who were ready to sally forth into community concerns and those who drew the line around strictly library functions and declined "welfare" responsibilities. This division was to be writ large in the decades to come.

At the 1919 convention of the American Library Association, John H. Leete of the Carnegie Library in Pittsburgh submitted that "new relations must be established between capital and labor, between employer and employed, between government and the governed." He saw a great mediatory role for the library, "a public institution free from religious prejudices and class interests." (*A.L.A. Bulletin,* 13:115.) Only a few months later the nation was embroiled in a steel strike. How the United States library world reacted to it is a subject awaiting study.

Although restlessness in the United States and elsewhere was attributed by many publicists and politicians to the events in Russia, the latter seem to have had no such impact upon librarians in the United States. In the absence of a comprehensive analysis, one must for the present be content with fleeting glimpses. The March 1919 number of *Library Journal* reprinted several educational documents from March 1918, as reproduced in translation by *The Nation*. Applying to libraries in the city of Smolensk (200 miles west of Moscow), they revealed in precise microcosm the revolutionary inventory then being conducted all over Russia; references were made to quantities of books, lists of periodicals in reading rooms, statistics of use, etc. A "Note" stipulated that the order "does not affect persons who have libraries consisting of less than 500 volumes, if these libraries are not intended for public readers." (*Library Journal*, 44:184.) The November issue used as a filler (p. 724) a passage from a contemporary report indicating marked expansion in the number of library service outlets both urban and rural. Nothing appeared in the 1920 issues. On April 15, 1921, an obituary for Semen A. Vengerov (1855-1920), a leading bibliographer cut down by typhus, paid tribute to the book chambers established by the Soviet government to carry on the work organized by Vengerov, and expressed pleasure over the public protection of his "literary treasures" (*Library Journal*, 46:350).

Meanwhile, the Asbury Park Conference issue of the *A.L.A. Bulletin*, June 1919, included a report (13:221-223) from the A.L.A. representative in Vladivostok. The service rendered to the troops secretly sent to Siberia to help the counterrevolutionary forces fight the Bolsheviks was of course bolstering their morale. There was no comment on the reprehensible nature of the mission.

The preparation of a new stage in public library activity in Anglo-America seems thus to have owed little directly to either controversy at home or revolution abroad. Rather, the forty-year-old orientation toward the rank and file was sharpened by wartime experience. On the one hand the low cultural level of the troops was startling to many educators. In 1918 Albert Mansbridge (1876-1952), dean of British worker education through university extension, organized the World Association for Adult Education; 1921 saw the appearance of both the related British Institute of Adult Education and a Marxist rival, the National Council of Labour College. On the other hand, battle-area service had exposed many librarians to individual readers' needs for the first time. One major consequence was intensified interest in the United States in work with the foreign-born, adult self-education, work with the blind, library service in institutions like hospitals, and library extension generally. The "Enlarged Program" considered by the American Library Association in 1919 and 1920 would have been addressed to those areas. But its individual welfare characteristics seemed to many librarians beyond their charge, revision of the A.L.A. constitution to permit more centralized management aroused great suspicion, and under a shower of accusations including financial malfeasance the proposed program died aborning.

Yet the needs were real. By 1922 new units in several large public libraries were organizing informal service to individuals and small groups, information and reading guidance as well as the lectures known to an earlier age. The following year marked the publication of two influential books emphasizing among other things readability, Oliver Stanley's collection of essays from the British Institute of Adult Education (*The Way Out,* London: Oxford University Press) and James Harvey Robinson's *The Humanizing of Knowledge* (New York: Doran). The ground was ready for William S. Learned's creative synthesis, *The American Public Library and the Diffusion of Knowledge* (New York: Harcourt, Brace, 1924): reader's advisors seemed a prominent device, but the message was rather to integrate their function with the work of all public service librarians.

For the Carnegie Corporation to have sponsored the Learned study and report was in line with earlier Carnegie contributions, and in harmony with the wave toward adult education, manifested in the organization in 1926 of the American Association for Adult Education. The United States library leaders responded with a bulletin called *Adult Education and the Library* (1924–1930) and authorization for their own study, published in 1926 as *Libraries and Adult Education;* the recommendation for a permanent Board on the Library and Adult Education was accepted. Meanwhile, beginning in 1925, more than sixty "Reading with a Purpose" programs were issued for the benefit of out-of-school adults. Reading, indeed, remained the principal concern of many librarians, to the disadvantage of the broader program elements encouraged by Learned. Between that philosophical difference and perennial library budget limitations, library adult education programs were destined by and large to display vigor only when subsidized. The foundation gifts were no less welcome because they derived from wealth sweated out of two generations of the work force and since seeking shelter against progressive income taxation.

Foundations played a key role in the United Kingdom too. The removal of the penny limit on property taxation in 1919 was accompanied by an important grant of powers to county councils. In 1925 the Carnegie United Kingdom Trust stepped forward with supplements to tax revenue. But a nation transformed by the war from a creditor into a debtor, and beset by inflation and several major strikes, needed more. The grim truth about austerity in library budgets—the disastrous results in collections, personnel, buildings and outlook—was unveiled in the Kenyon report of 1927, and again in a five-year study by a team under the leadership of Lionel McColvin, financed by the Rockefeller Foundation and published in 1938.

Neither the Russian challenge nor the Anglo-American adult education movement had much influence on central European practice. The "popular library" and "reading room" genre acquired some additional respectability in 1914 when two new ventures were launched in Leipzig, long the home of the leading book fair. One was the Institute on Readers and Writing; apparently the first of its type, it was to be matched some ten years later by the labors of Douglas Waples and other celebrated scholars at the University of Chicago and Columbia University. The other Leipzig unit was a school to prepare women for librarianship in popular libraries. Sponsored by the Central Institute for Books for the People, it utilized premises furnished by the Women's University and was led by librarian Walter Hofmann (1879–1952), internationally known for his promoting of popular library service. Among those present at the inaugural ceremonies was the distinguished librarian-bibliographer Adelaide Hasse (1868-1953) of the New York Public Library, not, however, to discuss service to adults in the style of the United States but simply to represent the United States delegation to the book fair.

Owing something perhaps to the labors for which Hofmann was conspicuous, German library life was also being enriched by the movement toward unified libraries. Beginning before the war and lasting beyond it, a series of organizations and reorganizations brought certain scholarly and popular libraries together under one roof, as a rule continuing their separate existences intramurally, to be sure. How much interpenetration of ideas and spirit resulted is a question not answered easily. It does seem clear, however, that these combined institutions were rather quickly adjusted to the uses of Hitler's National Socialists in the 1930s; conquest of the popular library was to be expected, and it is possible that the very combination facilitated an intrusion into the scholarly library which would otherwise have taken longer.

Rural Library Service since 1919　The nationalistic component in the popular libraries and the unified libraries found intense expression in the postwar years wherever an Allied Occupation plebiscite was arranged to settle the political fate of a German border area. Directed at the voters on behalf of a victory for German sovereignty was, among other activities, a Border Book Service. It would be very interesting to learn what degree of success was attained.

Another investigation yet to be made would tell us whether rural library service had by that time advanced as far in Anglo-America as in the U.S.S.R. and the border areas of Germany. Scientific agriculture was sufficiently vigorous in the United States to have evoked *Agricultural Index* in 1916 and a readiness of libraries to pay a higher subscription price to the businesslike H. W. Wilson Company six years later; university extension played a notable role in several states in serving country dwellers' reading and informational needs generally. But the strain on university library resources was acknowledged at the 1923 American Library Association by W. W. Bishop of the University of Michigan (*A.L.A. Bulletin,* 17:268-270). The wave of the future lay with the county library, then coming to prominence in California, prominence observed in Russia, which borrowed for advice expert Harriet G. Eddy.

In 1922, a County Libraries Round Table appeared at the American Library Association annual conference, and in 1923 the Association was asked to endorse the policy proposition "that the county is a logical unit of library service for most parts of the United States, and that the county library system is the solution of the library problem for county districts" (*A.L.A. Bulletin,*17:229). This message reached many quarters; in November an endorsement was obtained from the National Grange ("Patrons of Husbandry"), and the 1924 convention heard that the International Harvester Company was friendly because educated farmers bought more equipment. Taking stock in 1925 revealed a curious contradiction: "the very thing of which we were so proud" in the East, a library in every town, was proving to be the "worst stumbling block" (*A.L.A. Bulletin*, 19:298–300) in shaping county library service. In the West, on the contrary, the greater distances and thinner population were generating county service before town libraries had time enough to become significant obstacles.

The obstacles were challenged in that year, 1925, with *County Library Service*, not the first work on the subject but the first substantial contribution sponsored by the American Library Association. Well-versed Harriet Long opened it by referring to the commitments by the A.L.A. Council and the National Grange. She then confronted her reader with the dismal facts that county library service was then enjoyed by residents in only 200 of the nearly 3,000 counties in the United States, and 42 of the 200 were in California. She alluded to Theodore Roosevelt's appreciation of rural values, the Commission on Country Life which he appointed, and the subsequent concern in many circles with the farmer's isolation. She cited a product of that concern published in 1922 by the Nebraska Experiment Station, J. O. Rankin's *Reading Matter in Nebraska,* a survey of 1,338 farm and 188 town homes. General and farm newspapers were widely read. But nearly three farm homes in every four lacked women's magazines, only one in five had a family or household magazine, and less than one in thirty-three received periodicals prepared primarily for the younger members of the household. It seemed plain enough that the words spoken originally at the 1921 A.L.A. convention were still pertinent: "It is not enough to reach the leaders; it is not enough to reach the educated; it is not enough to reach those who are graduated from colleges or agricultural schools. The problem is that of reaching the whole crowd!" (Long, pp. 7–14 passim.)

The Fiftieth Anniversary Conference of 1926 found the county activists petitioning to be recognized as a section in the association. Discussions continued to reveal, however, that less than 10 percent of students at an institution like Iowa State College (Ames) had ever used a public library, that their home towns also lacked high school libraries, and that there was many a "strictly rural center where no club or American Legion Post exists, nor on account of the consolidation of schools, even a school where books might be housed" (*A.L.A. Bulletin,* 20:474–476, 505–509; 1926). No great difference was made by the experiment in Louisiana financed by the Carnegie Corporation, or the devoted labors elsewhere of county and extension librarians, or the A.L.A. *Rural Library Service Handbook* (1927), or the brochure on *Rural Libraries* issued by the Department of Agriculture in 1928 as Farmers' Bulletin No. 1559. As the last item noted, deprivation of library service afflicted 6 percent of the urban population but 80 percent of the rural; "the deficiency in library service to negroes [sic] is even more impressive" (p. 4).

The problem was not simply the values in the civilization of the United States, where, continued the brochure, for every dollar spent by the public on public library support eleven went for soft drinks and twenty-eight for candy. Farm dwellers did not feel at home in city libraries, and insufficient money could be found to develop what they might have preferred. A national conference in Chicago in March 1929 focused on these questions the thinking of the American Farm Bureau Federation, the National Congress of Parents and Teachers, the General Federation of Women's Clubs, and Rockefeller-supported General Education Board and the Rosenwald Fund.

The American Federation of Labor was not represented. Proposals were made for "state and federal aid," a plainer phraseology than what had long been applied to public aid to business, "tariffs" and "land-grants" for instance. A year later, introducing Volume VI No. 7 of *The Reference Shelf,* "County Libraries," Julia E. Johnsen observed that the principal obstacles were apparently conservatism, apathy, and ignorance and that a million dollar endowment was being sought for a new attack upon them.

The stock market crisis of October 1929 introduced to the nation at large the economic ills already familiar to a large proportion of the rural populace, the mines, and the textile industry. The number of persons living on farms, which had been declining while the total population rose, actually increased between 1930 and 1935, thanks to urban suffering, but the normal tendency soon reasserted itself. The census reported a population of 123 million in 1930 and nearly 133 million in 1940; the farm component, despite the temporary rise in the mid-thirties, numbered in 1940 the same 30.5 million as in 1930. (U.S. Census Bureau, *Historical Statistics,* pp. 7 and 47.) A leader of the Wisconsin Free Library Commission could note that "the small villages and hamlets" were "disappearing" (*A.L.A. Bulletin,* 24:365; 1930), but neither he nor any of the other interested librarians could halt the inexorable transformation of most of farming into "factories in the field" with a shrinking labor force. The scene apparently included no stimulus for library service comparable to the German urge to keep border populations or the Russian determination to remake all men.

Nor did anything of that sort emerge in the United Kingdom, where rural prospects were markedly poor.

The Library and the Negro in the United States since 1919 Little benefited by any library activity in the rural South, or in the Northern ghettos, were the Negroes, still 16.4 percent illiterate as late as 1930. Their own struggles for equal opportunity, and the slowly spreading disquiet among librarians about both them and the South generally produced some useful exposure at the Swampscott (Massachusetts) conference of 1921. It was pointed out that the public and association libraries of nearby Salem placed more volumes at the disposal of its 43,000 population than did all the public libraries of North Carolina's Asheville, Charlotte, Winston-Salem, Greensboro, Durham, Raleigh, Goldsboro, and Wilmington and that the book and pamphlet holdings of the University of North Carolina were exceeded by those of Salem's Essex Institute.

Concern now gathered momentum, and the Detroit conference in June, 1922, witnessed the first annual meeting of the new Work with Negroes Round Table. The 100 librarians in attendance were given a report on the results of a questionnaire sent to 122 libraries by the two-year-old 135th Street Branch (in the heart of the Negro ghetto) of the New York Public Library. The first of the five questions asked what percentage of the local population was Negro and second, whether they had free access to the library. The 98 respondents indicated that free access was almost entirely limited to the Northern and Western states having few Negroes. Familiar service devices in the South included separate branches, and "stations" or classroom collections or both, in Negro schools. Specialized attention in the better sense was a feature of the public library service to the Negro populace of New York, Cleveland, and Cincinnati.

Black "assistants" were common in segregated branches, according to the replies to the third question, and occasional in the nonsegregated systems with few Negro patrons. The 135th Street Branch of the New York Public Library itself had "tried the experiment of a mixed white and colored staff to serve better a Negro public" (*A.L.A. Bulletin,* 16:363; 1922). No indication of success or failure was reported.

As to the training of Negro assistants, the replies to the fourth question made clear that none then working in a public library had received library school instruction. The nearest approach, apparently, was the summer school of the Indiana Library Commission, to which had been sent the "colored assistants" of two Indiana libraries. For the most part, library chiefs dispatched their prospects to Louisville or furnished on-the-job training themselves. The New York Public Library expected to have a Black candidate in a library school next year, and the Public Library of Washington, D.C., planned to enroll one at Howard University, the District's college for Blacks.

In the matter of Negro participation in library government, the fifth issue, an answer from a Northern city, "characteristic" then and afterward was, "'We make no distinctions of race or color, and no question has ever arisen. There are no "special classes" represented on the board.'" Indeed, Negro board members were reported only from segregated institutions in the South. Probably not unique, moreover, was the view from Atlanta: "'We tried having an advisory committee from the colored people, but as they did not confine their activities to advice, we disposed of them.'" At any rate, a questionnaire to fifteen Southern libraries had elicited consensus that "a mixed board of control is impossible, a white board with an advisory Negro board impracticable, a Negro board unsuccessful." (*A.L.A. Bulletin,* 16:363–364.)

The Birmingham librarian who contributed this information thought Negro needs different from white needs, and therefore requiring particular study. He was also convinced that adequate service to the Negro was 25 percent cheaper than to the white. Discussion then revealed that one reason for the lower cost was the price of the books purchased, "cheaper because more elementary." Both Louisville and Evansville declared their service to Negroes on the contrary more expensive than service to whites. The former emphasized its attempts through selection of the better fiction "to cultivate the social imagination as distinct from folk imagination"; more books were read there per capita than in any white community in the South. Mary U. Rothrock of Knoxville urged equal opportunity and "generous consideration"; she advised those who would work with Negroes to "think and listen and say little." (*A.L.A. Bulletin,* 16:364.)

There was no doubt about the challenge among those committed to progress through education and the library as one instrument thereof. The hustings awaited pioneer spirits. Tommie Dora Barker of Atlanta, who opened a branch in the largest Negro area of the city in July 1921, reportedly considered the school and the library "important restraining influences for Negroes" (*A.L.A. Bulletin,* 16:365). That was good orthodox doctrine; was it a representative judgment? An effort to convert the Round Table into a permanent A.L.A. section evoked a majority opinion that the question was too sectional, and that another Round Table next year should suffice. Perhaps Ernestine Rose had not been understood well enough when she reflected on New York's experience with the 135th Street branch, the fact that no other branch yet had any Negro assistants, and her expectation that the segregation question would rapidly face the North.

For the time being, indeed, the spotlight continued to be trained on the South. The American Library Association's Committee on Library Extension, reporting in 1926 on *Library Extension . . . Public Library Conditions and Needs* (Chicago: A.L.A., p. 75), although recognizing that "the problem is no longer entirely sectional," believed that library service to the "Southern Negro . . . warrants separate consideration" and gave the matter its Chapter 6. That 55 public libraries out of 720 (in the fourteen Southern states other than Delaware, West Virginia, and Missouri) were now attending to Negro needs where only 14 so reported in 1913, was plainly a gain; but 89 percent of the Black population of the South still had no access to libraries. Particularly deprived were the 75 percent of the Negroes who lived in rural areas. Nor were libraries in educational institutions in a position to fill the gap. Budgets were inadequate, trained librarians lacking. The best that could be said was that book selection and administration in Negro city high schools varied over "a wide range" (*Library Extension*, p. 77). Hope was discerned in the consequences of state educational surveys, the improvement of the training of Negro teachers, the raising of the standard of living through agricultural extension work, and "the new Negro library school at Hampton, Va." (*Library Extension*, p. 78).

By 1928, reported Louis Shores, librarian at Fisk University, he was urged on the one hand to establish a library school for Black professionals, and on the other cautioned that existing training facilities would suffice for some time to come. He therefore undertook a market survey, obtaining a 90 percent return, replies from seventy-four cities with substantial Negro populations. Some thirty, all Southern except Evansville, Indiana, offered segregated service to Blacks. Another seventeen offered none, the largest being Charleston, South Carolina. Limited service, provided under plainly demeaning conditions, was common in the smaller Southern communities and occasional in larger ones. Twelve Northern and border state libraries alone, mainly in major cities, received Negro readers both in branches intended exclusively or primarily for them, and also freely in the rest of the system's units.

Training opportunities were not reportable with the desired clarity. From the New York and Los Angeles responses it appeared that Black librarians were obtaining training without obstruction in the library's own facilities. A few other major city libraries declared that library education was open to Negroes just as to whites, but the data do not give unmistakable evidence that any Blacks were in fact so enrolled. In a number of instances the prognostication was frankly exclusionary: either "no need" was discerned, or meeting a need seemed unlikely to occur soon. Shores concluded that the South would need "trained assistants to take charge of the colored branches" and that the demand would "in the next few years" exceed the supply furnished by the existing facilities. Although there were at the moment more library schools than jobs for the graduates, in general, "the Negro community is still untouched" by the stimulation given other citizens. Equal opportunity meant "more than giving the Negro a building and some books and blaming him because he does not take advantage of them . . . It means that the Negro must be subjected to the same proselytism that has characterized the spread of library service to other non-using groups." (*Library Journal,* 55:154, 1930.) Without a doubt, more trained Black librarians were needed.

Emphasis upon the rural aspect of the problem was borne out by the 1935 data showing that only one-sixth of the Southern Negroes resided in places having public library service. It was hardly a surprise that, of the 565 public libraries in thirteen Southern states, only 83 were open to Blacks. Eleven counties in seven Southern states had been favored with demonstration programs, mainly branch libraries in schools, between 1929 and 1935, financed by a grant from the Julius Rosenwald Fund. The experience helped prepare the local mind for acceptance of Works Progress Administration projects, but the library service offered to the Negroes was actually much less satisfactory than that the whites enjoyed in the same communities, and even the latter undertaking was in dire need of more money. The record was the best in West Virginia and Texas.

This gloomy picture was clearly described in a staff study for the U.S. Advisory Committee on Education by Doxey Wilkerson, Negro scholar at Howard University, published in 1938. The preceding year, the committee's own recommendations ranged widely enough to include school libraries. Throughout the depressing recital runs the refrain that state plans for libraries should stipulate "avoidance of any discrimination between races in the services provided by Federal funds" (*Report,* p. 212, for example). Projecting the critical situation once more with a review of all previous investigations was one of the contributions of another distinguished Black, Eliza Atkins Gleason, granted a doctorate by the University of Chicago in 1941 for her *Southern Negro and the Public Library* (University of Chicago Press). Her warning that millions of Blacks still lacked library service and that what they got was "generally" poor, seemed worth brief mention as Carlton B. Joeckel addressed the Library Extension conference at the University of Chicago in August 1944 (*Library Extension,* University of Chicago Press, 1946, p. 17).

By this time, the international struggle against fascism, and the increasing activity for equal opportunity in the United States on the part of the Negroes themselves and many sympathetic whites, was reflected in the erosion of "separate but equal" as the legal standards. In 1938 the Supreme Court held that a state providing within its own borders legal education for whites must furnish it likewise for Blacks. In 1950 the doctrine was advanced in one case to bar a separate law school for Negroes which was demonstrably not the equal of the white law school sponsored by the same state, and in another case to require that a Black admitted to graduate instruction be treated precisely the same as a white. The climax of the epoch was reached in 1954, when the court ruled on five basically similar cases, embracing schooling for Black students in one Northern and four Southern jurisdictions, including the District of Columbia, where equal protection of the law had to be invoked under the fifth rather than the fourteenth Amendment. *Plessy v. Ferguson* was explicitly rejected as a guide for behavior in public education. There, "'separate but equal' has no place," wrote a unanimous bench, in *Brown v. Board of Education of Topeka, Kansas* (347 U.S. 483).

Worthy of particular note is the doctrine cited repeatedly in the briefs of the complainants, that "education" comprehends the entire process of developing and training the mental, physical, and moral powers of human beings. Clearly, there would be no more constitutional than ethical warrant for any sort of discrimination in libraries. How far the nation had to go was indicated by the position of the most advanced libraries organized to serve Blacks. The median book collection of the eleven Southern universities for Negroes was in the school year 1951–1952 40 percent below the median for the collections in fifty somewhat smaller white institutions. Library expenditures per student for books at eleven selected white institutions varied around a median of $13.06, while the nine Negro universities other than long-established Howard and Tuskegee had a median of $8.85. (Dorothy M. McAllister's data in "Library Resources for Graduate Study in Southern Universities for Negroes," *Journal of Negro Education,* 23:58–59, 1954.) Not many years afterward, it would be revealed that access for Blacks to leading public library collections still suffered considerably more restriction than had been generally supposed. That Black librarians felt similarly limited professionally was to be made clear in the late sixties by the formation within the American Library Association of a Black Caucus.

The Library in Formal Education since 1919   If working class challenge drew more energy to "adult education," if the requirements of capitalism undermined traditional agriculture and in the United States gave the Negro just enough to keep rebellion below the surface, formal education and the libraries serving it were also affected by their own particular pressures.

Technological and political change urged more dissemination of skills, and the traditional liberal arts defended themselves against threatening neglect with counterattacks. The twenties and thirties were accordingly featured by stepped up allocation of social wealth to college support through both public and private channels, and a rapid spread of variety in course offerings. In 1918 the British Parliament created a University Grants Committee, eighteen men not on university payrolls whose task was to guide the distribution of public subventions to higher education. The initial emphasis was on the provinces: the institutions thus favored received in 1920 no less than 20 percent of their revenue from the national purse. In 1925 the percentage swelled to 30 percent, the grantees now including Oxford and Cambridge. By 1946 the hand of society was unmistakable: the national subsidy accounted for 55 percent of the incomes of the campuses involved. Library holdings mounted steadily, housed often in new buildings, usually arranged in the open-access stacks so prominent in the United States, and very soon crowding badly the space available.

Except for the rare items possessed by the older institutions, the libraries of the British universities were considerably less impressive than those of the leading institutions in the United States, principally because the latter's service style was affected powerfully by the pleasingly generous public library model. Yet, apart from those leading institutions the situation was shabby in the United States too. As the "aspirin age" approached its apotheosis in 1929, the Carnegie Corporation was moved to examine the hundreds of colleges the world had never heard of. Over the next ten years its teams surveyed the private liberal arts colleges for whites in the United States and Canada, and the increasingly important junior colleges. In the early thirties it granted for book purchase somewhat more than $1 million to domestic colleges, $213,300 to the Canadian institutions, and $300,000 to domestic junior colleges.

In parallel were developed two celebrated book selection guides, Charles B. Shaw's for college libraries and Foster Mohrhardt's for junior college libraries, underwritten by the Carnegie Corporation and published by the American Library Association. Although the institutions aided with grants chose their books, the procurement was facilitated by a Central Purchasing Office at the University of Michigan, an impressive demonstration of what might be done. Issued likewise, in 1932, were W. M. Randall's *The College Library* and J. T. Gerould's *The College Library Building,* part of a desperately needed attack on the absence of standards and meaningful statistics.

In the years between 1938 and 1943 the same foundation looked at the libraries of teacher-training institutions, the colleges catering to Negroes, and the land-grant installations. Thirty-odd among the first group were granted nearly $200,000 for books late in 1938. A sum half as large was allocated from 1940 to 1942 to twenty-eight Black college libraries, together with praise for the Hampton Institute Library School and reproof for widely noted indifference among administration and faculties. The twenty-three land-grant schools visited were reported to have libraries suffering less from lack of money than from lack of interest; no grant was made.

The academic libraries of Europe and Latin America maintained smaller staffs than those in the United States, and rarely provided open-shelf service. Not easily compared with any United States institution is the German-style "technical university," another topic deserving investigation.

Commitment had never been lacking among those concerned with school libraries. *Standard Library Organization and Equipment for Secondary Schools of Different Sizes* was issued in 1920 by the A.L.A. with the endorsements of the National Education Association and the North Central Association of Colleges and Secondary Schools. In 1922 the A.L.A. Committee on Education declared that it proposed to bring into cooperation for library service and instruction in library use "the two public educational systems, the schools . . . represented by the National Education Association and the libraries represented by the American Library Association" (*A.L.A. Bulletin,* 16:176). Two years afterward the *Third Yearbook* of the Department of Elementary School Principals carried a few articles on school libraries, and in 1925 the principals' and librarians' Joint Committee on Elementary School Library Standards published an influential *Report.* The 1925 *Yearbook* of the department also offered material on pupil reading interests outside school.

When in 1926 the larger city schools in the United States were checked for library service, librarians were reported universal in high schools, common in junior high schools, and rare in elementary schools. Those employed by the boards of education were paid like teachers, but those on public library payrolls fared worse. The more interested superintendents among those responding were eager to have school librarians step out of the characteristic caretaker role and share school life. On October 5, the editor of the National Education Association *Journal* told the American Library Association fiftieth anniversary conference that the school library lay "at the very root of the new pedagogy of individual differences." He thought five steps necessary to implement that understanding: explaining the school library to "school people" not yet enlightened; establishing "a federal bureau of library research"; disposing of "obscene, trashy and worthless literature"; relating library service to "education and life"; and above all, producing "trained school librarians." This message was reproduced as the headpiece in the first *School Library Yearbook,* published in 1927 by the Education Committee of the A.L.A.

Specific objectives detailed in that same *Yearbook* included a conference of A.L.A. and National Education Association executive boards, a committee on education in each state library association, school library advisors or supervisors in each school system, on each state staff, and at A.L.A. headquarters, training facilities on a state or regional scale—backed up by certification specifically in librarianship, equipment qualitatively equal to that in laboratories, appropriate funds—"if possible through state grants, based on state and local survey," and instruction in library use and appreciation from elementary school through university (pp. 9–11). Suggested syllabi for the last-mentioned constituted the bulk of the first *Yearbook.*

The second *Yearbook* (1928) announced nothing spectacular in progress toward the stated goals but did disseminate a challenging essay by Dean William F. Russell of Teachers College, Columbia. He noted new school libraries, new appointments of school librarians, and the approval of new courses for their training; but "nowhere . . . the agreement usually found as to educational procedures" on the part of either the school authorities or the librarians," as to the proper function of the library in the life and operation of the school." Four types of school serving were identified: the public library branch, in or near a school; the branch specifically designed to serve children, in or near a school; a "service station" in a school, wherein the librarian performed library duties but essentially "guards the books"; and the emerging "school library as an integral part of the school" (*Yearbook,* pp. 49–50, 1928). Concerning this last, Russell explained the advantages of individual instruction over class instruction, trained teaching over recitation, and interpenetration of subjects over rigid compartmentalization. He hoped to see the day when both "libraries in schools" for children and "schools in libraries" for adults would be superseded by "a new educational institution . . . which combines the best features of both" (*Yearbook,* 1928, p. 53).

Furnished also were the curricula for school librarianship prepared by the A.L.A. Board of Education for Librarianship and adopted by the association. "Minimum standards" were set forth.

The *Yearbook* for 1929 led off with a discussion relating the school library to each of the NEA "Seven Objectives of Education." The 1931 *Yearbook* assembled "School Library Standards and Departmental Rulings" in fifteen states, the standards issued by the six regional associations and the National Catholic Education Association, and the certification provisions in fifteen states. The 1932 *Yearbook* emphasized the "standards" then on record, and studies intended to "aid individual librarians in setting up standards for their own libraries." Tribute was paid to earlier landmarks, the school principal identified as "probably the most important factor in planning the school library program," and wise money handling stressed as "doubly imperative" in "the present economic situation" (pp. v–vi).

The periodical, convention, and special report literature documenting educational discussion and activity had by 1929 developed to the point where the Wilson Company launched *Education Index*. One of the numerous phenomena its entries helped spotlight was differentiation: by geographic region, population density, or level of school administration. Despite the apparent absence of comprehensive analysis, it may be noted that school library service advanced more rapidly at the secondary than at the elementary level. The *Standard Catalog for High School Libraries* was the first (1928) designed by the Wilson Company for educational institutions, whereas *Fiction Catalog* had been issued first in 1908, *Children's Catalog* in 1909, and several sections of the *Standard Catalog for Public Libraries* since 1919.

Progress was nevertheless decidedly uneven. Data for 1929 about small high schools revealed a predominantly dreary picture of poor collections, poor quarters, and responsibility in the hands of a teacher with too many duties and too little training. Even the stronger school systems tended to assign the library to a teacher with several classes and little or no preparation in library science. When the Office of Education sponsored a study in 1932 (Bulletin no. 17, 1932, Monograph no. 17, 1933) of secondary schools regarded by competent authority as "the best," the returns from 390 indicated that inadequate facilities were regarded as the main obstacle to good service, and inadequate staff next. The median collection held 2,540 books, the number of books per pupil being highest (11.0) in the schools with the smallest enrollment. Where library and study hall were combined, the books were used more than where they were separate; the principals and teachers were pleased but the librarians were not. Before too many more years rolled by, the problem of student motivation would raise the question of discipline to critical heights and the study hall library would be recognized almost universally as a farce.

Library service in elementary schools was moving forward more slowly. The later twenties saw almost nothing about them in the yearbooks of the Department of Elementary School Principals, but by 1932 the question concerned enough planners to devote to that subject the 1933 volume. As declared by the Editorial Committee in the preface, "the single textbook, the recitation" and cognate devices had given way to the flexible "enriched activity program," requiring "more books, handier books, better books." Ideas on solving these problems were therefore gathered from library and school personnel and set before the school principals. The department president declared that every "up-to-date elementary school" had "at least the beginnings of a library," but added for the benefit of the others that libraries and techniques for using them soundly were "the most far-reaching and important movement in elementary education today" (*The National Elementary Principal*, 12:117–119, June 1933). However true that may have been, the balance of the volume (pp. 121–518, the "Twelfth Yearbook") remains a classic assemblage worthy of more serious analysis than has been placed in the public record.

Out-of-School Service to Children Potentially competitive as well as supportive was the children's part of the public library. Expansion beyond the prewar scale was promoted by the establishment in 1919 of National Children's Book Week. In October 1924 appeared *The Horn Book Magazine*, published by the Bookshop for Boys and Girls in Boston under the nominal sponsorship of the Women's Educational and Industrial Union. The purpose was "to blow the horn for fine books for boys and girls—their authors, their illustrators, and their publishers" (*Horn Book*, 1:1). Actually, the output was already impressive at least quantitatively: in 1925 the Wilson Company issued two versions of the third edition of *Children's Catalog*, one of 4,100 titles and the other of 1,200.

Furthermore, the very thrust of educational effort so significant for school libraries brought enough educators' questions to the children's librarians for the latter to be described at the 1928 American Library Association conference as "quite agitated by the importance of the matter" and the risk of upsetting some educators with their answers (remarks of Effie L. Powers, *A.L.A. Bulletin*, 22:376). The impact of the children's demands upon publishing, lately conspicuous, and the call for professional library guidance in all manner of institutions serving children, made clear a pressing need for more trained personnel. Remaining unclear at that juncture, and long afterwards, was the relationship with school libraries and their trained personnel.

To the semiofficial observers in Britain, this continuing state of affairs seemed, by 1949, attributable "largely" to "an excess of zeal" (*The Year's Work in Librarianship, 1939–1945*, London: The Library Association, p. 162). That the public libraries might be concerned about their patronage, and that difference of opinion should mark the discussion of the proper role of the school library, were understandable for the United States but rather less than the prime concern in the United Kingdom. There, despite the enlarged share of public support under successive statutes and regulations between the reforms of 1918 and the Butler Education Act of 1944, the issue was still who should have mainly training for employment in ordinary occupations and who should go on to university study. Subsidiary struggles centered on the age to which school attendance was compulsory, administrative forms, science versus the humanities, and even religious commitment. The Butler Act prescribed a library in each tax-aided secondary school. Opportunity for all, however, tended strongly in the direction of job preparation, and the term "libraries" is conspicuously lacking from the indexes to the leading monographs on the subject. Happily, service to children in public libraries attracted increasing attention from the thirties onward, the only untoward note being the difficulties of book supply when the Hitlerite bombings of the early forties necessitated temporarily evacuating children from big cities to country areas.

Public library children's service advanced more rapidly in Scandinavia, thanks partly to the United States influence, and in the principal cities of the Low Countries. As early as 1928 it was possible to publicize some twenty years of similar, even more elaborate development in Germany, in a brochure on children's reading rooms and a breezy little article in *Library Journal* (53:307–308, 1928). Likewise reported in the first *Year's Work in Librarianship* (1929) were a 106-page section of a Soviet manual and eight magazine articles devoted to service to children; a decade later, the same medium mentioned the organization of a traveling library for children by the Leningrad Metal Workers Union.

"The future relationship between the public and school library service," wrote *The Year's Work in Librarianship* in 1929, "is a subject which is occupying the minds of the leading librarians in America, Britain, and the Continent" (p. 138). The average librarian was not familiar with the curriculum, and the average teacher unacquainted with the nature of library work. Debate was prominent over how to produce professionals soundly prepared on both counts; also, on the question of whether or not to supervise what a child reads. Note was taken of the fact that "in some of the Latin countries there are few available children's books with which to stock a library" (*Year's Work, 1929*, p. 146). A generation later, service to children in Europe and the United States was still mired in the same philosophical and administrative contradictions, and in Latin America it remained a very minor enterprise awaiting sharp social and political change to obtain serious consideration.

Librarianship Almost a Profession

The Proliferation of Structures Beset by mounting demands for service and the urge to provide it, library leaders established more organizations, midwifed—if not actually creating—new bibliographic controls, gave slowly increasing attention to the possibilities of mechanical and electronic devices in library operation, expanded professional education more rapidly than standardized evaluation and recognition of the product, and created a professional literature abundant but weakly represented at the level of solid self-criticism.

National library associations were fairly common in 1919. In fact, a number of subnational associations were on the scene too, the Ontario Library Association for instance, founded in 1900. The American Library Association had set two attractive precedents not quickly emulated elsewhere: the 1908 president was Canadian university librarian C. G. Gould, and the 1911 president was Buffalo Public Library Assistant Director Theresa Hubbell Elmendorf. Notable in the twenties was the emergence of the Association of Special Libraries and Information Bureaux (1924) and the International Federation of Library Associations (1927), which by 1936 had eased considerably international library loan. More particular interests and obligations found such expression as the Dutch Institute for Documentation and Bibliographic Control (1921), the Association of Research Libraries and Music Library Association organized in the United States in 1931, and the world Congress for Documentation in Paris in 1937, which brought together delegates governmental and nongovernmental from forty-five countries. Differentiation of function and point of view, a hallmark of any major enterprise, appeared in A.L.A.'s Committee on Classification of Library Personnel in 1923, the Staff Organizations Round Table in the New Deal and CIO days of 1936, and the Library Unions Round Table two years later.

Organized support for bibliographic control met with success in several areas, especially when the war fronts ceased to exist. The German Book began in 1921 to issue a series of trade bibliographies at three levels of frequency. The International Institute of Bibliography, relocated in the mid-twenties from Brussels to Deventer (Holland) and finally to The Hague, invested major effort in a second, French, edition of the Universal Decimal Classification, issued between 1927 and 1933. In 1937 the Institute became the International Federation for Documentation. Subsequent labors progressed most rapidly with a complete German edition and abridged editions in several other languages. Assessment of the impact internationally of the Federation and the Universal Decimal Classification, and indeed of the rich body of ideas emanating from founder Paul Otlet, is a remaining responsibility helpfully identified by W. Boyd Rayward (*Library Quarterly,* 37:259–278, 1967).

In the United States, meanwhile the *Subject Headings Used in the Dictionary Catalogs of the Library of Congress,* originally released in parts between 1909 and 1917, attained a "second edition" in 1919 with three supplements during the twenties. The third edition appeared in 1928, and in 1931 was introduced the first cumulative supplement, which intercalated several quick-frequency interim supplements. Notable in the fourth edition, 1943, was the inclusion of the "see from" references until then recorded only in the Library of Congress' own manuscript records. The manifest unsuitability of this powerful equipment for small general libraries was long since recognized, the Sears list having been born in 1923. The equally manifest absence of a theory for constructing subject headings and subject-heading lists in English, let alone in general, was acknowledged periodically, like Banquo's ghost. More easily satisfied, by the Library of Congress in 1930, was the demand for Dewey Decimal Classification numbers on the catalog cards it offered for sale. Like approval greeted the succession of new reference tools. In 1927 appeared that monument of largely volunteer labor, the *Union List of Serials of the United States and Canada.* The somewhat similar guide to German holdings of foreign journals, *Gesamtverzeichnis der ausländischen Zeitschriften 1914–24,* arrived between 1927 and 1929. The early thirties greeted several celebrated United States commercial products, *Essay and General Literature Index* (1931), *Vertical File Service* (1932), and *Ulrich's Periodical Directory* (1932). The League of Nations began the *Index Translationum* in 1932, later continued by UNESCO. A Rockefeller Foundation grant of a quarter of a million dollars meanwhile (1927–1932) permitted laying bases for a National Union Catalog at the Library of Congress; but lack of comparable resources, among other things, interrupted the *Gesamtkatalog der Wiegendrucke* ("Union Catalog of Incunabula" in German libraries) when in 1939 it had barely made a dent in the letter B.

Book searches and other information coordination were already familiar in Europe, thanks to the Berlin Information Bureau and the cognate institutions rising in several other centers after the First World War. The problem was faced seriously in the United States later, partly because it seemed like so much else a private concern, until the public purse was enlisted because it was not profitable. In the Depression of the thirties, theories of regionalism were in vogue, and some librarians thought them better adapted to information handling than the national-center approach. The first unit designed thus, the Bibliographic Center for Research, Rocky Mountain Region, was organized in 1934-1935 by public and academic libraries and housed at the Denver Public Library. It began with sets of cards from the Library of Congress, the Folger Shakespeare Library (Washington, D.C.), the John Crerar science library of Chicago, and the Concilium Bibliographicum (Zürich); its services comprised not only numerous research activities but cooperative purchasing. A few more were organized in subsequent years, no two identical, and none widely emulated.

One reason, beyond doubt, was the nearly complete lack of participation by business and industry, committed not to advancing society's knowledge but to private profit. Of importance also, probably, were the geographic size of the United States, the great diversity of even nonprofit institutional types and interests, and the still powerful tradition of preferring nongovernmental auspices and financing wherever possible. The contrary thrust was to be largely a byproduct of two more wars and the steadily growing pattern of assuring equipment sales by obtaining huge federal contracts in the name of public commitment.

The more limited devices known since the Middle Ages, union catalogs and union lists, presented fewer obstacles, and were produced multifariously in both the United States and Europe.

The problems of a multiplying number of items and operations were dramatized in part by Fremont Rider's challenge in 1944 (*The Scholar and the Future of the Research Library,* New York: Hadham Press) that library holdings would double every ten to twenty years and outpace the available resources. One response was new attention to compact storage of conventional books; another was greater experimentation with microforms. For the latter there was a long-developed base in microreproduction of several kinds, microfilm having been widely accepted in 1928. Xerography was developed in 1937 but needed almost a generation to mature as the premier library copying instrument. Libraries also gained from contemporary improvements in building design and materials, and heating and ventilation, although architects did not always listen enough to those who were to use their product and fell short of fully satisfactory library buildings oftener than necessary.

Developing more slowly but fundamentally much more significant was the calculating device. By the 1930s it had the benefits of electrically energized automatic relays, the Second World War brought semiconductors and other key advances in electronics, and 1950 saw the first commercial computer marketed. Meanwhile, fifty-year-old scientific management had generated vast paper work; punched-card technology emerged to cope with it and helped in the major task of opening library minds to the possibilities of mechanical and electronic aids to information handling.

Schooling and Thinking As the twentieth century opened, the proliferation of structures in the library world and outside it shaped several patterns of education for librarianship. Involved were the familiar questions of purpose, framework, operation, and consequences.

In the pre-Dewey pre-Dziatzko stage, so to speak, the continental librarian was expected to be a devoted technician worthy of his humanist scholar chief, who was usually a university graduate but seldom equipped with schooling in librarianship; underlings in scholarly libraries learned their trade on the job. Libraries oriented toward a broad public, predominant in Anglo-America, provided no specific library training for the chief either, book learning by whatever means acquired being thought adequate preparation; his subordinates picked up what they needed to know by doing it. The main difference was that the continental leadership absorbed classical languages and such related skills as paleography; these assets were not valued highly in the United States, largely for lack of books in those languages or need to read them. Skill in personnel management was not yet prominent on the agenda for schooling because it was remote from the scholarly traditions of the Continent and the practical United States leaders did not yet have more than a handful of large libraries to operate.

The epoch begun by Dewey's school at Columbia and Dziatzko's largely isolated lectures at Göttingen drew increasing attention to organized schooling at an institution other than the employing library itself. Advance was for many years paltry on the Continent: the Dziatzko lectures did not become a full curriculum, and the "middle service" personnel, developed partly from Italian models to relieve the scholars of administrative routines and formally acknowledged in Prussia in 1909, were not required to have even a secondary education diploma. In 1915 the Commonwealth of Catalunya went further with its "higher school for librarians" in Barcelona, training women for service not only at the sponsoring scholarly Biblioteca de Catalunya but in the "Popular Libraries" in both Barcelona and various other towns. The faculty may have included university professors from the start; it unquestionably did later (1932–1933 brochure). Also awaiting clarification is the question of its financing, whether a direct allocation from the Commonwealth budget or a suballocation through the public library or the university, as in the United States. The survival of this enterprise through sharp political changes (1924, 1925, 1930), and ultimate transfer in the 1930s from Catalan to the Spanish-language mainstream, is a story of minority politico-cultural experience which ought to be studied.

In the United States, curricula multiplied steadily under a variety of auspices, but an organized education context was plainly the wave of the future, partly because apprenticeship was giving way to vocational training in most production other than the building trades, and partly because political conditions favored the rise of state universities. The American Library Association had blessed Dewey's original models, but preferred to encourage and criticize from the sidelines through its Professional Training Section rather than accept the financial and other burdens of direct sponsorship of education and certification for librarianship. When in 1915 ten schools (several connected with universities) formed the Association of American Library Schools, it remained for seven years independent of the

A.L.A. Contrariwise, the United Kingdom contributed the unique stimulation of the examinations by The Library Association itself and the modes of preparation they led to, mainly independent of formal schooling.

In both the United Kingdom and the United States, the several levels of professional responsibility tended toward merger into a career ladder, the upper end of which, at least in public libraries, was the directorship itself.

By 1919, as the war ended, more thought was lavished on the university context for producing professional librarians of all kinds. The Carnegie United Kingdom Trust granted £1,500 ($7,500) a year for five years to launch the London School of Librarianship at University College, a challenge to the prevailing Library Association arrangements pleasing some and annoying others. In the school year 1920–1921 the Göttingen chair was transferred to Berlin and a full curriculum pushed; formal recognition in Prussian regulations came in 1922; not until 1928, however, was library leader Fritz Milkau able to find the time and cooperation from others to establish an institute for training non-university-graduate supportive staff. Similar "institute" training for professionals was then already in operation in Scandinavia, but the graduates were acceptable only in public libraries; the university libraries preferred to take university graduates and give them on-the-job instruction.

Overall integration seemed to be left for the United States. In 1919 the Carnegie Corporation commissioned Charles C. Williamson to examine library education, and in 1923 he strongly recommended (*Training for Library Service*, New York: Updike) a university setting, a university-type faculty, sharp differentiation between professional and clerical tasks, and a national board for examination and certification of graduates. Although the last, long established in Europe, was no more congenial than before to the American Library Association, it did favor the other proposals, on the whole. In 1924 it formalized the Board of Education for Librarianship, which tried to develop standards among the congeries of "library science" offerings under a great variety of auspices, worked closely with the virtually indispensable Carnegie Corporation and other foundations, and developed numerous other programs of its own. Visiting and accrediting library schools were inevitably delicate: the first crisis loomed in 1930 but was surmounted; the future held many more.

Meanwhile, considerable Carnegie money found its way into higher education for librarianship, the most conspicuous expression being the Graduate Library School organized in 1927 at the University of Chicago. The first Ph.D. in librarianship was conferred there one year later, but Williamson's valid emphasis on theory as one hallmark of a profession, and the inevitable downgrading of nonprofessional duties, fed a predictable reaction. Not only were occasional tactless graduates a problem in relationships with library clerical staffs, but the purely graduate-professional curriculum was itself challenged. If a candidate lacked practical experience, his academic preparation was not always welcomed by employers. Yet, if the period of enrollment included any of the practical, it strengthened the conviction of many campus administrators that librarianship was not truly graduate study. Indeed, for some fifteen years beginning in 1926, the Association of American Universities influenced acceptance of the baccalaureate rather than the master's degree as the right one. Celebrated philosopher Abraham Flexner even denied in 1930 that "pharmacy, library science, town-planning, social service, etc." belonged in a university at all (*Universities . . .*, New York: Oxford University Press, p. 172).

The complexities of life, however, were inexorably pushing more and more service professions toward joining theology, law, and medicine in the university framework. The future was to bring the United States sharp debate, rather, as to what education for librarianship should be offered at, respectively, the undergraduate level, the master's level, and the doctoral level. Competition for status and pay favored emphasis on the graduate levels even when the content did not necessarily justify it. While the same factors gradually intruded on British practice as well, continental Europe, both capitalist and socialist, long retained the older distinctions between education for scholarly library service and education for popular library service.

In 1925, when an A.L.A. questionnaire extracted data from "1,243 public or semi-public libraries and 261 college and university libraries" with more than 5,000 volumes (*A Survey of Libraries in the United States,* Chicago, 1926, I:10), it was evident that school-trained personnel were not yet preponderant in public library staffing, more than half of the respondents' "librarian" employees having had less than six months' training, even in libraries of more than 100,000 volumes. On the other hand, there were in each size category a few (2.65 to 4.20 percent) graduates of a two-year library school course and several (11.35 to 21.97 percent) from one-year courses; roughly one full-time staff member in every five was a college graduate (*Survey,* I:136). In the responding academic libraries the proportion of "librarian" personnel with less than six months' training was distinctly smaller, exceeding 50 percent only in those of more than 100,000 volumes. The percentage of individuals with two-year credentials from a library school ranged from 8.2 to 16.1; those with one-year training ranged from 26 to 34 percent; two-thirds were college graduates (*Survey,* I:264). Comparable data about school librarians were not furnished.

The proportion of college graduates on these staffs bears comparison with the proportion in other occupations (except for teaching itself). What will such a study reveal about opportunity for women?

Instruction was available in the United States in 1928 at the accredited level in sixteen library schools out of a total of at least 140 programs of some sort, in thirty-seven states, the District of Columbia, and Hawaii. That may go far to explain why the half-dozen or so states "certifying" public or school librarians or both did so on the basis of academic credentials, but did not administer the examinations long established for scholarly library posts in France, Italy, and Germany, and for public libraries in the United Kingdom. The staff of the last-mentioned in 1928 had passed Library Association examinations but were graduates of library science courses far less often than in the United States.

The value attached to schooling and experience in the United States is reflected in the ratios between the top and bottom salaries for 1925. The A.L.A. *Survey* data indicate (I:137, 265) a ratio of about 4 to 1 in public libraries of more than 100,000 volumes, and about 3 to 1 in academic libraries of that size; the ratios were of course smaller in the smaller libraries. The average annual salary reported for a nonsupervisory professional was generally a little short of $1,500 in public libraries and exceeded that figure only in the largest academic libraries. Compare the average annual earnings of 1925 in some other occupations (U.S. Bureau of the Census, *Historical Statistics of the United States,* p. 91):

Clerical workers, manufacturing	
and steam railroads	*$2,239*
Postal employees	*2,051*
Ministers	*1,769*
Street-railway employees	*1,565*
Gas and electric employees	*1,448*
Public school teachers	*1,263*

Unevenness and uncertainties of data preclude exact comparison, but one may note that special librarians reportedly earned in 1947 a median salary of $3,300, while the entrance salary for professionals in other kinds of libraries ran about $600 less. The American Library Association urged in January 1948 a minimum starting salary for a professional of $2,800 (*Library Journal,* 73:641,1687 and passim; 1948). That figure was exceeded by the average annual earnings in 1947 of all full-time employees in transportation, mining, and contract construction (*Historical Statistics,* p. 95).

These material circumstances both derived from and encouraged the continued preponderance of women in United States libraries. Altogether, only a handful of librarians had both the opportunity and desire to demonstrate high intellectual capacity through publication. In any case, the literature soon became notably "practical." Manuals of internal management had in fact been almost commonplace by the middle of the nineteenth century, and may well have overshadowed quickly the polemics conspicuous then and afterward.

The last quarter of the century saw the beginnings of a broader literature giving prominence to the relationships between the library and its public; there were many such titles in the years just before the outbreak of war in 1914, nearly every nation being represented. Neither group of works, apparently, has yet been subjected to critical historical analysis in English.

The philosophies of librarianship expressed in these and other publications seldom testified to grounding in general philosophy or social theory. Perhaps as significant an example as any is the long drawn out debate over public library service to adults: the library as an educator who will uplift, preferably although not necessarily with the client's agreement, versus the library as the salesman whose customer is always right. A Mary Wright Plummer was able to deal with the theoretical questions as posed by pragmatism, but the impact of that philosophy upon library adult education remains one of many fundamental phenomena in library history not yet probed.

What has been probed with notable vigor is what the "public," campus or noncampus, "gets" for its money. The surveying prior to the foundation of the American Library Association and The Library Association (of the United Kingdom) was usually fact gathering with critical intelligence, but the facts gathered were not evaluated systematically. It was precisely for that purpose, among others, that professional library organizations were formed. Some of what their numerous committees produced, from the late 1870s on, may be followed in the contemporary library periodicals; other material would have to be exhumed from unpublished archives. In any case, the aggregate quality of this output remains to be judged.

How seriously such library efforts were taken by scholars in other fields has not been studied either, but it seems likely that, in Anglo-America at least, the librarians themselves thought advantageous for impact as well as for financial support the sponsorship of major investigations by outside agencies, a role to which history called in the first place the Carnegie Corporation. Again, the University of Chicago Graduate Library School was established with a faculty largely nonlibrarian in background, and its curriculum emphasized the psychology and sociology of reading and library service rather than the old "library economy" routines the candidates were supposed to know all about before they arrived. Many of the graduates became library administrators or teachers and some became creative thinkers; more library school programs acquired similar characteristics. Librarianship even produced in 1940 E. W. McDiarmid's *The Library Survey* (Chicago: A.L.A.). Nevertheless, the Public Library Inquiry of 1949 to 1952 was conducted by the Social Science Research Council with a sociologist in charge, and after twenty years (1930–1950) of surveys of individual institutions by their own staffs or peers from other institutions, libraries which could afford the luxury turned to management firms. It might be enlightening to examine by comparison the proportion of critical reviewing thus assigned to outsiders in the other institution-based professions.

Calling on management specialists for guidance in what involved the use of money was probably advantageous for many United States libraries both operationally and in terms of their image in a business-minded culture. Beneficial to the librarians' professional concerns and their self-image was the establishment in the United States and the United Kingdom of several journals of a substantially new type, neither focused mainly on current news and practical problems nor devoted to the everyday affairs of a particular geographic area or a particular type of library.

The first, *Library Quarterly,* was launched in 1931 with a $25,000 grant from the Carnegie Corporation and supporting assurances from the University of Chicago concerning the editors' salaries, etc. The inaugural article by C. C. Williamson challenged the library to rise "to its opportunity as a social institution and education force" (I:3) and underlined the absence from library science of the investment in research characteristic of numerous other fields of endeavor. The "little sporadic work here and there by individuals that may possibly be classified as research" (I:5) was intolerable. Librarians dared not go on being "empirical" in their thinking "rather than scientific" (I:8), because "the mere executive librarian, not recognizing the complexity of the problems he has to deal with, will not know when to call in the outside expert" (I:12–13). Checking the files of the existing journals for serious "original research" had been a "startling" experience (I:5). Would there be enough now to fill the columns of the proposed medium for scientific thought in librarianship?

This bold and largely successful move amid economic depression was soon followed by a partly similar one at the instance of those concerned with librarianship in higher education. By 1938 the College and Reference Section of the American Library Association had become the Association of College and Reference Libraries, and *College and Research Libraries* appeared a year later. It was among other things a response to the discovery by Harvie Branscomb (*Teaching with Books . . .* Chicago: A.L.A., 1940) that most college students did not use their college libraries and that there seemed to be no correlation between that use and grades received. Number seven of the new periodical's stated purposes was the stimulation of "research and experimentation for the improvement of the service" (I:9) and publication of the results. But its other seven purposes were no more specifically focused on the problem as defined by Branscomb, and the next thirty years would make very little progress toward solving it, perhaps because the social and political roots of the matter were regarded, characteristically, as not the business of librarians as such. The general narrowness of focus of *College and Research Libraries* is further evidenced by the far fewer articles than in *Library Quarterly* which drew upon librarianship outside the United States, and by the near-absence of substantial contributions by women, a handicap inherent in United States higher education but counteracted somewhat by *Library Quarterly*.

The next important entrant on the scene testifies to the greater international consciousness in Europe than in the United States, and also to the fact that opportunity for women in the Old World was beginning to rival the limited progress in the United States. The Association of Special Libraries and Information Bureaux (Aslib), organized during the twenties with much Carnegie help, bravely unveiled at the war's end in June 1945 the *Journal of Documentation,* "devoted to the ways and means by which problems of the dissemination of contributions to knowledge may be studied, and sources of information made accessible" (I:4). Soon clear was a great sweep of concern both geographically and technically. Women contributors shared the front rank from the outset.

In another act of faith, almost simultaneous, the All-Union Book Chamber of the severely battered U.S.S.R. issued in 1946 the first number of *Sovetskaia bibliografiia.* Reflecting a society in which not only libraries and schools but the production and distribution of book materials were public enterprises and subject to direction as parts of community planning, it offered in combination scholarly writings on the book trade, the book arts, librarianship, and bibliography in each of its several meanings.

Whether based on the comprehensive planning of a totally nonprofit society, or the limited planning of a nonprofit island in a profit-based society, librarianship continued to be a profession characterized by contradictions. Thoroughgoing assessment of the literature had been contributed long since, as noted, by Julius Petzholdt, and noteworthy select guidance was published from time to time, from the United States 1876 *Report* to Margaret Burton and Marion E. Vosburgh's *A Bibliography of Librarianship,* sponsored in 1934 by the University of London's School of Librarianship. If the latter excluded Slavonic and Oriental language materials, it did at least draw on Western European tongues, an important step beyond the much larger but strictly Anglo-American *Bibliography of Library Economy . . . 1876 to 1920,* compiled in 1927 by H. G. T. Cannons (Chicago: A.L.A.). Happily, multinational sources were utilized as *Library Literature,* issued in the United States from 1934 on, continued by and large what Cannons had begun; and in 1950 *Library Science Abstracts* commenced an English-based service, covering fewer library science periodicals than *Library Literature* but several in neighboring departments like industrial research and education.

Yet studies in depth entered the record in lopsided proportion. The continental professionals had always been attentive to historic holdings and problems of bibliographic control, a good deal less to their respective publics; they seldom had responsibility for school libraries. The British public librarians and documentalists produced numerous thought-provoking contributions but communicated with each other very little.

The United States and the socialist world were different in their own unique ways. Thanks to the late development in the United States of a connection between university education and librarianship, the dominance of public library service to all, and the role of women therein, the Ph.D. did not even arrive on the scene until nearly 1930; it never became a requirement for full professional recognition because it was not designed to train for the key functions—management of personnel, money, and public relations. When doctoral dissertations were written, hardly any were produced by women, and very few dealt with precisely the service areas least known to men, school libraries and service to children. The new assessment journal, *Library Trends,* noted in its third issue (January 1953) that school librarianship had attracted so far virtually no research beyond the master's essay level. It would be many years before notable change could be reported.

The socialist world, heavily influenced by Soviet Russian example, tended to be featured by two partly contradictory patterns. On the one hand, the prerevolutionary separation between the scholarly and the popular (and juvenile) was still clear after 1945 in the separate training arrangements, eligibility standards, and status. On the other hand, a linkage had been developing since the early twenties, peculiar to the socialist world. The Lenin Library in Moscow was not only a center of scholarship but in charge of field help and supervision, exercised through the "methodists," over hundreds of public ("mass") libraries. This role, apparently much broader than that of any Western library, was emulated as more nations adopted socialism, and subjected to adaptation according to circumstance. Thus the "methodist section" at Komensky University Library in Bratislava (Slovakia) was by the sixties responsible for aiding and in some respects supervising the libraries in several secondary schools in the Bratislava area. If this type of enterprise has been favored with research and evaluation, the documents have not been publicized in the West; how successfully it has nourished cross-fertilization cannot readily be judged.

Full professional recognition seemed in the middle decades of the twentieth century to call in the first place for more evidences of rigorous research and hard thinking than had been vouchsafed so far. That in turn brought up the question of values: what level of mental capacity did society choose to assign to such efforts; could it rely traditionally on the attractions of the marketplace, or would it have to organize a deeper commitment, a commitment engaging the social structure from bottom to top?

BIBLIOGRAPHY
OF WORKS QUOTED

Adams, Henry: *History of the United States of America,* New York: Scribner, 1889.

A.L.A. Bulletin, 1(1907) to date.

American Journal of Education, 3(June 1828):357 ("Intelligence"); 4(September–October 1829):464–471 (University of London data).

American Library Association: *Annual Conference Proceedings, 1889,* Chicago.

————: *Annual Conference Proceedings, 1907–1948,* in *A.L.A. Bulletin.*

————: *Libraries and Adult Education,* Chicago: American Library Association, 1926.

————: *Rural Library Service Handbook,* Chicago: American Library Association, 1927.

————: *A Survey of Libraries in the United States,* vol. 1, Chicago: American Library Association, 1926–1927.

————: Committee on Library Extension: *Library Extension . . . Public Library Conditions and Needs,* Chicago: American Library Association, 1926.

American Philosophical Society: *Early Proceedings . . . ,* compiled by one of the secretaries, from the manuscript minutes of its meetings from 1774 to 1838, Philadelphia: McCalla & Stavely, 1884.

Ammianus Marcellinus: "History," in *Ammianus Marcellinus,* translated by John C. Rolfe, Cambridge, Mass.: Harvard University Press; London: Heinemann, 1935–1939.

The Ante-Nicene Fathers . . . , edited by Alexander Roberts and James Donaldson, revised by A. C. Coxe, New York: Scribner, 1885–1897.

Appleton's Annual Cyclopedia, 1876, new series, vol. I, New York, 1877.

Apuleius Madaurensis: *Works* . . . , London: G. Bell, 1910.

Aristotle: *The Basic Works,* edited by Richard McKeon, New York: Random House, 1941.

———: "Topica," in *Works,* edited by W. D. Ross, vol. 1, London: Oxford University Press, 1928.

Athenaeus: *The Deipnosophists,* translated by Charles B. Gulick, London: Heinemann; New York: Putnam, 1927–1943.

Augustine, Aurelius, St: *The Works of Aurelius Augustine,* edited by M. Dods, vols. I–II, "City of God," vol. IX, "On Christian Doctrine," Edinburgh: T. & T. Clark, 1871, 1873.

Bacon, Francis: "Advancement of Learning," and "New Atlantis," in *Selected Writings,* edited by H. G. Dick, New York: The Modern Library, 1955.

Balbi, Adrien: *Essai Statistique sur les Bibliothèques de Vienne,* Vienne, 1835. Quoted and translated in *Public Libraries in the U.S.A.;* reviewed with some quotation and translation by G. W. Greene, "Libraries," *North American Review,* 45(1837):116–147.

Barwick, George Frederick: *The Reading Room of the British Museum,* London: E. Benn, 1929.

Becker, Gustavus (comp.): *Catalogi Bibliothecarum Antiqui,* Bonn: Cohen, 1885; Bardi reprint.

Beda Venerabilis: *Baedea Opera historica,* translated by J. E. King, "The Ecclesiastical History of the English Nation," vol. I, vol. II, pp. 1–389; "Lives of the Abbots," vol. II, pp. 392–445, London: Heinemann, 1930.

Bernard of Clairvaux, St.: *The Steps of Humility,* translated by George Bosworth Burch, Cambridge, Mass.: Harvard University Press, 1942.

Bidlack, Russell: "The 'Coming Catalog' . . . (1877–1904)," *Library Quarterly,* 27(1957):137–160.

Bishop, W. W.: "Some Responsibilities of University Extension Service," *A.L.A. Bulletin,* 17(1923):268–270.

Blakey, Dorothy: *The Minerva Press, 1790–1820,* London: Printed for the Bibliographical Society at the University Press, Oxford, 1939.

Blum Rudolf: *Vor-und Frühgeschichte der nationalen Allgemeinbibliographie,* Frankfort am Main: Buchhändler-Vereiningung, GMBH, 1959; also in *Archiv für Geschichte des Buchwesens,* 2(1960):233–303.

Bobinski, George S.: *Carnegie Libraries,* Chicago: American Library Association, 1969.

Bodley, Thomas: *Letters to Thomas James, First Keeper of the Bodleian Library,* edited by G. W. Wheeler, Oxford: Clarendon Press, 1926.

———: *The Life of Sir Thomas Bodley, written by himself,* in *Literature of Libraries in the Seventeenth and Eighteenth Centuries* (see below).

Booth, Charles: *Life and Labour of the People in London,* London: Macmillan, 1889–1903.

Boston Athenaeum: *Catalog of the Library of the Boston Athenaeum*, Boston, 1874–1882; Hall reprint.

Bostwick, Arthur E.: *The American Public Library*, New York: Appleton, 1917.

Brant, Sebastian: *Narrenschiff*. Berlin: Spemann, n.d.

————: *The Ship of Fools*, translated by Alexander Barclay, New York: Appleton, 1874.

Bridenbaugh, Carl: *Cities in Revolt*, New York: Knopf, 1955.

Brockhaus' Konversations-Lexicon, 5th ed., Leipzig: F. A. Brockhaus, 1819–1820.

Brockhaus' Konversations-Lexikon, 8th ed., Leipzig: F. A. Brockhaus, 1833.

Brodrick, James: *St. Peter Canisius, S.J., 1521–1597*, Chicago: Loyola University Press, 1962.

Brown, Charles H.: "Some Objectives for Agricultural Libraries," *A.L.A. Bulletin*, 20(1926):474–476.

Brown, James Duff: *Manual of Library Economy*, London: Scott, Greenwood, 1903.

————: *Manual of Library Economy*, 2nd ed., London: Scott, Greenwood, 1907.

————: *Manual of Library Economy*, 3rd ed., revised and rewritten by W. C. Berwick Sayers, London: Grafton & Co.; New York: H. W. Wilson, 1929.

Brown v. Board of Education of Topeka, Kansas, 347 U.S. 483 (1954).

Burton, Margaret, and M. E. Vosburgh: *A Bibliography of Librarianship*, London: The Library Association, 1934. Franklin reprint, 1970.

Burton, Robert: *The Anatomy of Melancholy*, edited by Rev. A. R. Shilleto, London: G. Bell, 1903.

Butterworth, Charles C.: *The Literary Lineage of the King James Bible, 1340–1611*, Philadelphia: University of Pennsylvania Press, 1941.

Byrd, William: *The Secret Diary of William Byrd of Westover, 1709–1712*, edited by Louis B. Wright and Marion Tinling, Richmond, Va.: The Dietz Press, 1941.

Calvin, Jean: *Institutes of the Christian Religion*, edited by John T. McNeill, translated by F. L. Battles, Philadelphia: Westminster Press, 1960.

Cannons, H. G. T. (ed.): *A Bibliography of Library Economy . . . 1876 to 1920*, Chicago: American Library Association, 1927.

Cassiodorus Senator: *Cassiodori Senatoris Institutiones*, edited by R. A. B. Mynors, Oxford: Clarendon Press, 1961.

Chambers, Ephraim: *Cyclopaedia*, London, 1728.

Chicago. University Graduate Library School. Library Institute: *Library Extension*, Chicago: University of Chicago Press, 1946.

Codex Theodosianus: *The Theodosian Code and Novels, and the Sirmondian Constitutions*, translated by Clyde Pharr, in collaboration with T. S. Davidson, and M. B. Pharr, Princeton, N.J.: Princeton University Press, 1952.

College and Research Libraries, 1(1939).

Comte, Auguste: *Discours sur l'esprit positif*, 1844, Fetscher ed., Hamburg: Meiner, 1956.

Conference of Librarians, London, 1877: *Transactions and Proceedings,* London: Whittingham, 1878.

Council in Trullo: "Canons," in *A Select Library of Nicene and Post-Nicene Fathers of the Christian Church,* 2nd ser., vol. 16, p. 396 (see below).

Cowtan, Robert: *Memories of the British Museum,* London: Bentley, 1872.

Culver, Raymond B.: *Horace Mann and Religion in the Massachusetts Public Schools,* New Haven, Conn.: Yale University Press; London: H. Milford, Oxford University Press, 1929.

Cutler, William Parker: *Life, Journals and Correspondence of Rev. Manasseh Cutler, LL.D.,* edited by W. P. Cutler and J. P. Cutler, Cincinnati: R. Clarke & Co., 1888.

Cutter, Charles Ammi: Letter to *The Nation,* 24(February 1877):87.

————: *Rules for a Printed Dictionary Catalog,* Washington: Government Printing Office, 1876. [c75]

De Bury, Richard: *The Philobiblon,* edited by E. C. Thomas, London: K. Paul, Trench, 1888.

Deetjen, Werner: "Eine Bibliothekarprüfung des achtzehnten Jahrhunderts," *Zentralblatt für Bibliothekswesen,* 45(1928):303–305.

Descartes, René: *Philosophical Works,* translated by E. S. Haldane and G. R. T. Ross, London: Cambridge University Press, 1931.

Dewey, Melvil: *Classification and Subject Index for Arranging the Books and Pamphlets of a Library,* Amherst, Mass., 1876.

Diodorus Siculus: "Library of History" in *Diodorus of Sicily,* translated by C. H. Oldfather, London: Heinemann; New York: Putnam, 1933–1948.

Diogenes Laërtius: *Lives of the Eminent Philosophers,* translated by R. C. Hicks, London: W. Heinemann; New York: Putnam, 1925.

Ditzion, Sidney: "The District-School Library, 1835–1855," *Library Quarterly,* 10(1940):545–577.

Dougnac, M. T., and M. Guilband: "Le Dépôt Légal . . . ," *Bulletin des Bibliothèques de France,* 5(1960):283–284.

Drolet, A.: *Les Bibliothèques Canadiennes, 1604–1960,* Ottawa: Le Cercle du Livre de France, 1965.

Durie, John: *The Reformed Librarie-Keeper,* in *Literature of Libraries in the Seventeenth and Eighteenth Centuries* (see below).

Ebert, Friedrich Adolph: *Die Bildung des Bibliothekars,* 2nd rev. ed., Leipzig: Steinacker u. Wagner, 1820.

————: "Bibliotheken," "Bibliothekswissenschaft," in *Allgemeine Encyclopädie,* edited by G. S. Ersch and J. G. Gruber, Leipzig: Gleditsch, 1818–1889.

Edwards, Edward: *Memoirs of Libraries,* London: Truebner & Co., 1859.

Ehrle, Franz, Cardinal: *Historica Bibliothecae Romanorum Pontificum,* Rome: Typis Vaticanis, 1890.

Elliott, Clark A.: "The United States Bureau of Education . . . ," *Proceedings* of Library History Seminar No. 3, 1965, edited by Martha J. K. Zachert, Tallahassee, Fla.: Florida State University, 1968, pp. 98–111.

Emerson, Ralph Waldo: "Books," in *Society and Solitude*, vol. 7, *Complete Works*, new and rev. ed., Boston: Houghton Mifflin, 1886, pp. 179-210.

Encyclopaedia Americana (1829-1833), edited by Francis Lieber, Philadelphia: Carey, Lea & Carey, vol. 11, pp. 189-193.

Encyclopaedia Britannica. Photocopies and other data courtesy of Encyclopaedia Britannica, Chicago. 1st ed., 1768; 2nd ed., 1776-1784; 3rd ed., 1797; 6th ed., 1820-1823; 7th ed., 1830-1842, vol. XIII, pt. 1 (1836); 9th ed., 1875-1888, vol. XIV, pp. 509-551.

Encyclopédie, nouv. éd., Génève: Pellet, 1777-1779.

Epistolae obscurorum virorum, the Latin text with an English rendering, notes, and an historical introduction, translated by Francis Griffin Stokes, London: Chatto & Windus, 1925.

Erasmus, Desiderius: *Essential Works,* edited by W. T. H. Jackson, New York: Bantam, 1965.

Escher, Hermann: "Die Bibliotheca Universalis Konrad Gessner's," *Viertelsjahrschrift der Naturf. Gesellschaft in Zürich,* 79(1934):174-194.

————: "Der Bibliothecarius Quadripartitus des J. H. Hottinger," *Zentralblatt für Bibliothekswesen,* 51(1934):505-522.

Esdaile, Arundell James K.: *The British Museum Library: A Short History and Survey,* London: G. Allen, 1946.

Europa: Chronik der Gebildeten Welt, 3(1838):181-183, "Ueber Volksbibliotheken," signed "H . . . K."

Evelyn, John: *Diary,* edited by E. S. DeBeer, Oxford: Clarendon Press, 1955.

Flexner, Abraham: *Universities: American, English, German,* New York: Oxford University Press, 1930.

Fontaine, Jacques: *Isidore de Séville et la Culture Classique dans L'Espagne Wisigothique,* Paris: Études Augustiniennes, 1959.

Forrest, Elizabeth: "How Shall We Interest and Induce Our Faculty and Students to More General Cultural Reading?" *A.L.A. Bulletin,* 9(1915):159.

Franklin, Alfred Louis Auguste: *Les Anciennes Bibliothèques de Paris,* Paris: Imprimérie imperiale, 1867-1870; Imprimérie nationale, 1873.

————: *La Sorbonne,* 2.éd., corr. et augm., Amsterdam: Gerard Th. van Heusden, 1968.

Franklin, Benjamin: *Autobiography,* edited by Leonard W. Larabee [and others]. New Haven, Conn.: Yale University Press, 1964.

Franklin, Benjamin: *The Papers of Benjamin Franklin,* edited by L. W. Larabee, New Haven, Conn.: Yale University Press, 1959— . [still in process]

————: *Writings,* edited by Albert Henry Smyth, New York: Macmillan, 1907.

Funaioli, G.: *Grammaticae Romanae Fragmenta,* Leipzig: Teubner, 1907.

Gassendi, Pierre: *Epistolae,* Lugduni: Anisson, 1667.

Gellius, Aulus: *The Attic Nights of Aulus Gellius,* translated by John C. Rolfe, London: Heinemann; New York: Putnam, 1927.

Gennadius: [Supplement to] St. Jerome's "Lives of Illustrious Men," in *A Select Library of the Nicene and Post-Nicene Fathers of the Christian Church,* 2nd ser. vol. 3, pp. 385-402 (see below).

Gesner, Konrad: *Appendix Bibliothecae . . . ; Epitome . . . per Josiam Simlerum . . . ,* Tiguri and Christophervm Froschoverum, MDLV.

Gleason, Eliza Atkins: *The Southern Negro and the Public Library,* Chicago: The University of Chicago Press, 1941.

Goethe, Johann Wolfgang von: *Dichtung und Warheit,* Stuttgart: Cotta, 1902-1907, vol. II.

————: *Lexikon der Goethe-Zitate,* edited by Richard Dobel, Zürich: Artemis, 1968.

Gottlieb, Theodor: *Ueber Mittelalterliche Bibliotheken,* Leipzig: Harassowitz, 1890.

Graesel, Arnim: *Handbuch der Bibliotheks Lehre,* Leipzig: J. J. Weber, 1902.

La Grande Encyclopédie, Paris: Lamirault, 1886-1902, 5:664; 6:647-689.

Gray, Austin K.: *Benjamin Franklin's Library,* New York: Macmillan, 1937.

Greene, Evarts B., and Virginia D. Harrington: *American Population before the Federal Census of 1790,* New York: Columbia University Press, 1932.

Greenwood, Thomas: *Free Public Libraries,* London: Simpkin, Marshall, 1886.

Hadamowsky, Franz: "Eine Bibliothekarprüfung im Jahre 1701," *Biblos,* 2(1953): 11-14.

Haines, C. R.: "The Library of Dover Priory . . . ," *The Library,* 4th ser., 8(1927-1928):73-118.

Harris, John: *Lexicon Technicum,* London, 1725.

Henning, Hans: "Aus dem Leben und Werken Johann Michael Franckes," *Zentralblatt für Bibliothekswesen,* 72(1958):273-298.

Herodotus: *Histories,* translated by Aubrey de Selincourt, Baltimore, Md.: Penguin, 1964.

Hobbes, Thomas: *Leviathan,* reprinted from the edition of 1651, with an essay by W. G. Pogson Smith, Oxford: Clarendon Press, 1909.

Holley, Edward G.: *Raking the Historic Coals: The A.L.A. Scrapbook of 1876,* Beta Phi Mu, 1967.

Hoole, Charles: *A New Discovery of the Old Art of Teaching School . . . ,* London: Crook, 1659-1660. Scholar Press facsimile reprint, 1969.

The Horn Book Magazine, 1(October 1924).

Huarte de San Juan, Juan: *Examen de ingenios. The Examination of Men's Wits,* English version by R. Carew, 1594, Gainesville, Fla.: Scholars' Facsimiles and Reprints, 1959.

Hugh of St. Victor: *Didascalicon: A Medieval Guide to the Arts,* translated by Jerome Taylor, New York: Columbia University Press, 1961.

International Library Conference, London, 1897: *Transactions and Proceedings,* London, 1898.

Isidor of Seville: *Origines,* as *Etymologiarum libri XX* in Migne, J. P., ed., *Patrologiae . . . Series latina . . . ,* Paris: Migne, 1844–1882, vol. 82, cols. 9–728.

Iwinski, M. B.: "La statistique internationale des imprimés; . . . ," *Bulletin de l'Institut International de Bibliographie,* 16(1911):1–139.

Jacob, Louis: *Traicté des Plus Belles Bibliothèques Publiques et Particulières . . . ,* Paris: Chez Rolet le Duc, 1644, avec privilege du Roy.

Jerome, St.: "Apology in Answer to Rufinus," in *A Select Library of the Nicene and Post-Nicene Fathers of the Christian Church,* 2nd ser., vol. III, pp. 482–540 (see below).

————: "Lives of Illustrious Men," in *A Select Library of the Nicene and Post-Nicene Fathers of the Christian Church,* 2nd ser., vol. III, pp. 359–384 (see below).

Jevons, W. Stanley: "The Rationale of Free Public Libraries," *The Contemporary Review,* March 1881, pp. 385–402; reprinted in *Methods of Social Reform,* London: Macmillan, 1883.

Jewett, Charles C.: *Fourth Annual Report of the Smithsonian Institution Board of Regents,* Washington, 1850.

John of Salisbury: *The Metalogicon,* translated by Daniel D. McGarry, Berkeley: University of California Press, 1955.

Johnson, Julia E.: "County Libraries," *The Reference Shelf,* vol. 6, no. 7 (1930). New York: H. W. Wilson Co.

Johnston, William Dawson: *History of the Library of Congress,* vol. 1, 1800–1864, Washington, Government Printing Office, 1904.

Jordan, W. K.: *Philanthropy in England, 1480–1660 . . . ,* New York: Russell Sage Foundation, 1959.

Journal of Documentation, 1(1945–1946).

Kalm, Peter: *America of 1750. Peter Kalm's Travels in North America,* translated and edited by Adolph B. Benson, New York: Wilson-Erickson, 1937.

Kaufman, Paul: *Libraries and Their Users: Collected Papers in Library History,* London: The Library Association, 1969.

Kayser, Albrecht Christoph: *Über die Manipulation . . . ,* Bayreuth, im Verlag der Zeitungsdrückerei, 1790.

Kayser, Christian Gottlob: *Bücher-Lexikon,* Bd. 20, 1871–1876, L–Z, Leipzig: Weigel, 1877.

Kirkland, John T.: "Literary Institutions—University—Library," *North American Review,* 8(December 1818): 191–200.

Klette, Anton: *Die Selbstaendigkeit des Bibliothekarischen Berufes . . . ,* Marburg: Elwert'sche Verlagsbuchhandlung, 1897.

Koch, Theodore W.: "Opening of the A.L.A. Exhibit at Leipzig," *Library Journal,* 39(August 1914):595.

Korty, Margaret B.: *Benjamin Franklin and Eighteenth Century Libraries,* Philadelphia, 1965. (American Philosophical Society Transactions, new ser., vol. 55, pt. 9).

Kraus, Joe Walker: *Book Collections of Five Colonial Libraries: A Subject Analysis,* Urbana, 1960; Ann Arbor, Mich.: University Microfilms, 1964.

Kulischer, Josef: *Allgemeine Wirtschaftsgeschichte des Mittelalters und der Neuzeit. Bd. II: Die Neuzeit,* München: Oldenbourg, 1928; 1965 ed. unaltered.

Kursh, H.: *The United States Office of Education . . . ,* Philadelphia: Chilton, 1965.

Learned, William S.: *The American Public Library and the Diffusion of Knowledge,* New York: Harcourt, Brace, 1924.

Leete, John H.: "Reaching All Classes of the Community," *A.L.A. Bulletin,* 13(1919):111–1170

Leland, John: *The Itinerary of John Leland in or about the Years 1535–1543,* edited by Lucy T. Smith. Carbondale, Ill.: Southern Illinois University Press, 1965.

Letters of Obscure Men, see *Epistolae obscurorum virorum.*

Leyh, Georg: "Die Gesetze der Universitätsbibliothek zu Göttingen vom 28 Oktober, 1761," *Zentralblatt für Bibliothekswesen,* 37(1920):1–30.

"Libraries," *North American Review,* 45(1837):134–149.

The Library, 1st ser., 1(1889), 115, 183, 345.

Library Association: *Transactions and Proceedings of the Second Annual Meeting,* London: Whittingham, 1880.

Library Association Record, 1(1899), 14–15; 10(1908), 633.

Library Journal, 1 (1876) to date.

Library Trends, 1(1953).

Lipsius, Justus: *De Bibliothecis Syntagma,* in *Literature of Libraries in the Seventeenth and Eighteenth Centuries* (see below).

Literature of Libraries in the Seventeenth and Eighteenth Centuries, edited by John Cotton Dana and Henry W. Kent, Chicago: A. C. McClurg, 1906–1907; reprint, Metuchen, N.J.: Scarecrow, 1967.

Lomeier, Johannes: *A Seventeenth-Century View of European Libraries; Lomeier's De Bibliothecis, Chapter X,* translated by John W. Montgomery, Berkeley: University of California Press, 1962.

Long, Harriet: *County Library Service,* Chicago: American Library Association, 1925.

Luther, Martin: *Reformation Writings,* translated from the Weimar ed. by B. L. Woolf, New York: Philosophical Library, vol. II, 1956.

————: "To The Councilmen," *Works,* American ed., vol. 45, edited by W. I. Brandt, Philadelphia: Muhlenberg Press, 1962, pp. 339–378.

McAllister, Dorothy M.: "Library Resources for Graduate Study in Southern Universities for Negroes," *Journal of Negro Education,* 23(1954):51–59.

MacFarlane, John: *Library Administration,* London: G. Allen, 1898.

Macray, W. D.: *Annals of the Bodleian Library,* 2nd ed., enlarged, Oxford: Clarendon Press, 1890.

Mader, J. J.: *De Bibliothecis* . . . , Helmstadt: Mueller, 1666.

Massow, Julius von: "Ideen zur Verbesserung . . . ," *Annalen des preussischen Schul-und Kirchwesens,* 1(1800):76–143, 181–260, 361–395. Extracts in Mirbt, pp. 27–34.

Mather, Cotton: *Magnalia Christi Americana,* London: Parkhurst, 1702.

Maunsell, Andrew: *Catalogue of English Printed Bookes,* London: A. Maunsell, 1595; photoreproduction, London: Gregg Press, 1965.

Merimeé, Prosper: *Études Anglo-Américaines,* vol. 7 of *Oeuvres Complètes,* Paris: Champion, 1930.

Mersenne, Marin: *Correspondence,* . . . editée et annotée par Cornelius de Waard . . . Paris, 1933– .

Milton, John: *Areopagitica and Other Tracts,* Boston: Beacon Press, 1951.

Mirbt, Karl-Wolfgang: *Pioniere des öffentlichen Bibliothekswesens,* Wiesbaden: Harrassowitz, 1969.

Molbech, Christian: *Über Bibliothekswissenschaft,* Leipzig: Hinrichs, 1833.

Montaigne, Michel de: *Oeuvres Complètes.* Textes établis par A. Thibaudet and M. Rat, Paris: Gallimard, 1962.

———: *Selected Essays,* translated by C. Cotton and W. C. Hazlitt, edited by Blanchard Bates, New York: Modern Library, 1949.

Montesquieu, Charles Louis de Secondat: *Oeuvres Complètes,* Paris: Gallimard, 1949–1951.

More, Thomas: *Utopia,* in *Famous Utopias,* edited by Charles M. Andrews, New York: Tudor Publishing Co., 1937.

Moréri, Louis: *Grand Dictionnaire Historique,* nouv. éd, Paris: Libraires Associés, 1759.

Morhof, D. G.: *Polyhistor.* Lübeck, 1747.

Muhlenfeld, Johanna: "A Children's Library in Berlin," *Library Journal,* 53(1928):307–308.

The National Elementary Principal, vol. 12, no. 5 (June 1933).

Naudé, Gabriel: *Advice on Establishing a Library,* edited by Archer Taylor, Berkeley: University of California Press, 1950.

———: "Lettres inédites de Gabriel Naudé à Peiresc," *Bulletin du Bibliophile,* 1886, (Paris), 115–160, 337–359, 481–505.

———: *Surrender of the Library of Cardinal Mazarin,* in *Literature of Libraries in the Seventeenth and Eighteenth Centuries* (see above).

Die Neu-eröffnete Bibliothek . . . , Hamburg, 1711, described in *Neue Anzeiger,* 25(1864):2–3.

Neue Anzeiger . . . , *25(1864):2–3.*

The New York Times, October 5–7, 1876; September 5–7, 1877.

Nicholas V, Pope: *Canone Bibliografico,* appendix A, pp. 359–381, to Giovanni Sforza's *La Patria, la Famiglia e la Giovinezza de Papa Niccolo V,* pp. 1–400 of *Atti delle R. Acc. Lucchesa di Scienze, Lettere ed Arti,* t. XXIII, 1884.

Norris, Dorothy M.: *A History of Cataloguing Methods* (London: Grafton, 1948).

Norton, Andrews: "Intelligence and Remarks," *North American Review,* 5(September 1817):430–438.

Oldenburg, Henry: *Correspondence,* edited and translated by A. Rupert Hall and Marie Boas Hall, Madison: University of Wisconsin Press, 1965—   . [in process]

Pennington, Edgar L.: "The Beginnings of the Library in Charles Town, South Carolina," American Antiquarian Society *Proceedings,* new ser., 44(1934): 159–187.

Penny Magazine, 1(Apr. 14, 1832):21 ("Library"); 2(Sept. 28, 1833):373 ("Libraries for Working Men").

Petit-Radel, Louis-Charles-François: *Recherches sur les Bibliothèques Anciennes et Modernes . . . ,* Paris: Rey et Gravier, 1819.

Petzholdt, Julius: *Bibliotheca Bibliographica,* Leipzig: Englemann, 1866; reprinted, Nieuwkoop: B. DeGraaf, 1961.

Philo Judaeus of Alexandria: "Preliminary Studies," in *Philo, with an English Translation,* translated by F. H. Colson and G. H. Whitaker, London: Heinemann; New York: Putnam, 1929–1962.

Plinius, Secundus, C.: *Natural History,* Cambridge, Mass.: Harvard University Press. n.d.

Poole's Index . . . , 1802–1906.

Pope, Alexander: *Poems,* edited by J. Butt, New Haven, Conn.: Yale University Press, 1963.

Power, Effie L.: "The Children's Library in a Changing World," *A.L.A. Bulletin,* 22(1928):376.

Prideaux, W.: "Library Economy in the Sixteenth Century," *Library Association Record,* 11(1909):161.

Plummer, Mary Wright: "The Public Library and the Pursuit of Truth," *A.L.A. Bulletin,* 10(1916):111–114.

Quincy, Josiah: *The History of the Boston Athenaeum,* Cambridge, Mass.: Metcalf & Co., 1851.

Quintilian: *Institutio Oratoria,* translated by H. E. Butler, London: Heinemann; New York: Putnam, 1920–1922.

Rabelais, François: *The Five Books of Gargantua and Pantagruel,* in the modern translation of Jacques Le Clercq, New York: Modern Library, 1944.

Rathbone, Josephine Adams: "Salaries of Library School Graduates," *Library Journal,* 39(March 1914):188–190.

Reece, Ernest J., (ed.): *School of Library Economy of Columbia College, 1887–1889: Documents for a History,* New York: Columbia University, School of Library Service, 1937.

Rees, Gwendolyn: *Libraries for Children . . . ,* London: Grafton, 1924.

Reinhard, Marcel R.: *Histoire de la Population Mondiale de 1700 à 1948,* Paris: Éditions Domat-Mont-Chrestien, 1949.

Reusch, Heinrich (ed.): *Die Indices Librorum Prohibitorum des Sechzehnten Jahrhunderts,* Niewkoop, de Graaf, 1866; 1961 reprint.

Rider, Fremont: *The Scholar and the Future of the Research Library*, New York: Hadham Press, 1944.

Roberts, William: *The Earlier History of English Bookselling*, London: Low [etc.], 1889; Gale reprint, 1967.

Robinson, James Harvey: *Petrarch*, New York: Putnam, 1914.

Rogers, James E. T.: *A History of Agriculture and Prices in England . . .* , Oxford: Clarendon Press, 1866–1902; Kraus reprint, 1963.

Rothstein, S.: "The Destiny of the Concept of Reference Service in American Libraries, 1850–1900," *Library Quarterly*, 23(January 1953):9.

Royal Society of London: *Philosophical Transactions*, 1(1665) to date.

Sainte-Beuve, Charles-Augustin: "Gabriel Naudé," in his *Oeuvres*, Paris: Gallimard, 1960, vol. II, pp. 466–509.

Salamanca, Lucy: *Fortress of Freedom*, Philadelphia: Lippincott, 1942.

Sarton, George: *A History of Science*, Cambridge, Mass.: Harvard University Press, 1952–1959.

———: *Introduction to the History of Science*, Baltimore: Williams and Wilkins for the Carnegie Institution of Washington, 1927–1948.

School Library Yearbook, nos. 1, 2, 5 (1927, 1928, 1932), Chicago: American Library Association.

Schrettinger, Martin: *Versuch eines vollständigen Lehrbuchs des Bibliothekswissenschaft*, Munich: Lindau, 1808–1829.

Schroll, M. Alfred: *Benedictine Monasticism as Reflected in the Warnefrid-Hildemar Commentaries on the Rule*, New York: Columbia University Press, 1941; AMS Press reprint, 1967.

A Select Library of the Nicene and Post-Nicene Fathers of the Christian Church, 2nd ser., translated and edited by Philip Schaff and Henry Wace, New York: The Christian Literature Co., 1890–1900; Grand Rapids, Mich.: William B. Eerdmans, 1952–1957.

Seneca, Lucius Annaeus: *Ad Lucilium epistolae morales*, translated by Richard M. Gummere, London: Heinemann; New York: Putnam, 1930.

Serapeum, 1(1840); 2(1841).

Shamurin, E. I.: *Geschichte der bibliothekarisch-bibliographischen Klassifikation*, Bd. II [translated from the Russian] München-Pallach: Verlag Dokumentation, 1968.

Shaw, Robert K.: *Samuel Swett Green*, Chicago: American Library Association, 1926.

Shera, Jesse H.: *Foundations of the Public Library . . .* , Chicago: University of Chicago Press, 1949.

Shores, Louis: *Origins of the American College Library, 1638–1800*, Nashville, Tenn.: George Peabody College for Teachers, 1934.

———: "Public Library Service to Negroes," *Library Journal*, 55(Feb. 15, 1930): 154.

Simsova, Siva (ed.): *Lenin, Krupskaia, and Libraries*, London: Bingley, 1968.

Steiner, B. C.: "Rev. Thomas Bray and his American Libraries," *American Historical Review*, 2(1896-1897):59-75.

Stephani, Heinrich: *Grundriss der Staatserziehungs-Wissenschaft*, Leipzig: Severin, 1797; extracts in Mirbt, pp. 24-25.

———: *System der öffentlichen Erziehung*, Berlin: Froelich, 1805; extracts in Mirbt, pp. 36-43.

Strabo: *The Geography*, translated by Horace Leonard Jones, London: Heinemann; New York: Putnam, 1923-1931.

Streeter, Burton Hillman: *The Chained Library: A Survey of Four Centuries in the Evolution of the English Library*, London: Macmillan, 1931.

Swift, Jonathan: "The Tale of a Tub," in his *Prose Works*, edited by Temple Scott, London: G. Bell, 1900-1914, vol. I.

Taylor, Archer: *General Subject Indexes since 1548*, Philadelphia: University of Pennsylvania Press, 1966.

Ticknor, George: *Life and Letters*, 6th ed., Boston: Osgood, 1817.

U.S. Advisory Committee on Education: *Report*, 1938.

U.S. Bureau of Education: *Public Libraries in the United States of America . . . Special Report . . .* , part I, 1876.

———: *Report of the Commissioner of Education, 1884-1885*, 1886.

———: *Report of the Commissioner of Education, 1892-1893*, 1895.

U.S. Bureau of the Census: *Historical Statistics of the United States, Colonial Times to 1957*, 1960.

U.S. Bureau of Labor Statistics: *History of Wages in the United States from Colonial Times to 1928*, 1934 (Bulletin 604).

U.S. Department of Agriculture: *Rural Libraries*, 1928 (Farmers' Bulletin 1559).

U.S. Office of Education: *The Secondary-School Library*, 1933 (Bulletin, 1932, no. 17, Monograph 17).

Utley, George B.: *The Librarians' Conference of 1853*, Chicago: American Library Association, 1951.

Voltaire, François Marie Arouet de: *Correspondence*. Texte établi et annoté par Theodor Besterman, Paris: Gallimard, 1963, vol. I.

———: *Oeuvres complètes*, nouv. éd., Paris: Garnier Frères, 1877-1885, t. 44.

Watt, Robert: *Bibliotheca Britannica*, Edinburgh: Constable, 1824.

Webb, Sidney, and Beatrice Webb: *History of Trade Unionism*, London: Longmans, Green, 1920; rev. ed., 1935.

Weber, Adna F.: *The Growth of Cities in the Nineteenth Century . . .* , New York: Macmillan for Columbia, 1899.

Weld, Isaac: *Travels through the States of North America*, 1807 ed., New York: Johnson Reprint Corp., 1968.

Westminster Review, 8(July 1827):105-127 (review).

Wheeler, G. W.: *The Earliest Catalogues of the Bodleian Library*, Oxford: Oxford University Press, 1928.

————: "Readers in the Bodleian, Nov. 8, 1602–Nov. 7, 1603," *Bodleian Quarterly Record,* 3(1922):214–217.

Wilkins, Ernest H.: *Petrarch's Later Years,* Cambridge, Mass.: Medieval Academy of America, 1959.

Willard, Sidney: "State of Learning in the United States," *North American Review,* 9(1819):240–259.

William of Malmesbury: *Willelmi Malmesbiriensis Monachi De Gestis Regum Anglorum . . . ,* edited by William Stubbs, London: Printed for H.M.S.O. by Eyre and Spottiswoode, 1887–1889 (Rolls series, no. 90, 2 vols.; Kraus reprint, 1964).

Williamson, C. C.: "The Place of Research in Library Service," *Library Quarterly,* 1(January 1931):1–17.

————: *Training for Library Service,* New York: Updike, 1923.

The Year's Work in Librarianship, vol. II, 1929; vol. XII, 1939–1945, London: The Library Association, 1930 and 1949.

Zentralblatt für Bibliothekswesen, 1(1884), 2(1885), 4(1887), 6(1890), 20(1903), 31(1914), 35(1918), 45(1928).

ADDITIONAL REFERENCES

The references listed here represent key resources which have not been acknowledged in the text. Although they are subdivided by chapter of initial relevance, many of these titles are applicable to other chapters as well.

CHAPTER ONE

Besterman, T.: *The Beginning of Systematic Bibliography,* 2d ed. (Oxford University Press, 1936).

Irwin, R.: *The English Library* (London: Allen & Unwin, 1966); *The Heritage of the English Library* (New York: Hafner, 1964); *Origins of the English Library* (London: Allen & Unwin, 1958).

Pauly, August F. von: *Real-Encyclopädie der Classischen Altertumswissenschaft,* neue bearb. . . . .hrsg. von Georg Wissowa (Stuttgart: Metzlerscher Verlag, 1894-   ): "Bibliotheken," "Buch," "Buchhandel" (III); "Collegium" (IV); "M. Terentius Varro" (Supplementband VI, 1935, cols. 1173–1277).

Reichmann, F.: "The Book Trade at the Time of the Roman Empire," *Library Quarterly,* 8:40–76, 1938.

Shamurin, Evgenii I.: *Geschichte der Bibliothekarisch-bibliographischen Klassifikation,* Bd. I (Leipzig: VEB Bibl. Inst., 1964; tr. from the Russian).

Stahl, William H.: *Roman Science* (Madison: University of Wisconsin Press, 1962).

CHAPTER TWO

Bolgar, R. R.: *The Classical Heritage* (Cambridge University Press, 1954; Harper Torchbook 1125, 1964).

Curtius, Ernst R.: *European Literature and the Latin Middle Ages* (New York: Bollingen Foundation, 1953; Harper Torchbook 2015, 1963).

Ghellinck, J. de: *L'Essor de la Littérature Latine au XIIe Siècle,* 2d ed. (Brussels: Brouwer, 1955).

Grabmann, M.: *Die Geschichte der Scholastischen Methode* (Freiburg: Herder, 1911); II:54–91, "Die Bibliothek der Scholastiker des 12. Jahrhunderts."

Hardy, Thomas D.: *Descriptive Catalogue of Materials Relating to the History of Great Britain and Ireland to the End of the Reign of Henry VII* (London: Longmans, 1862–1871; Rolls Series no. 26); Introduction.

Haskins, Charles H.: *The Renaissance of the Twelfth Century* (Cambridge: Harvard University Press, 1927).

Laistner, Max L. W.: *Intellectual Heritage of the Middle Ages* (Ithaca: Cornell University Press, 1937); pp. 93–116, "Bede as a Classical and a Patristic Scholar."

Lesne, E.: *Les Livres, "Scriptoria," et Bibliothèques du Commencement du VIIIe à la Fin du XIe Siècle* (Lille: Facultés Catholiques, 1938; his *Histoire de la Propriété Ecclésiastique en France,* t. IV).

Randall, Lillian M. C.: *Images in the Margins of Gothic Manuscripts* (Berkeley: University of California Press, 1966).

Thompson, James W.: *The Literacy of the Laity in the Middle Ages* (Berkeley: University of California Press, 1939); *The Medieval Library* (University of Chicago Press, 1939; with supplement, Hafner, 1957).

Walzer, Richard: *Greek into Arabic* (Cambridge: Harvard University Press, 1962).

Wormald, F., and C. E. Wright, eds.: *The English Library before 1700* (University of London, 1958); chap. VII (Knowles). "The Preservation of the Classics."

CHAPTER THREE

Buddensieg, Tilmann: "Gregory the Great, the Destroyer of Pagan Idols; the History of a Medieval Legend Concerning the Decline of Ancient Art and Literature," *Journal of the Warburg and Courtauld Institutes,* 28:44–65, 1965.

Callus, Daniel A.: "The Contribution to the Study of the Fathers Made by the Thirteenth-Century Oxford Schools," *Journal of Ecclesiastical History,* 5:139–148, 1954.

Faucon, Maurice: *La Librairie des Papes d'Avignon* (Paris: Thorin, 1886–1887).

Franciscan Educational Conference: *Librarianship and the Franciscan Library* (Washington, 1944).

Garrod, H. W.: "The Library Regulations of a Medieval College," *The Library,* 4th ser., 8:312–335, 1927.

Ghellinck, J. de: "Le Catalogue des Bibliothèques Anglaises en 1410," Congrès International des Bibliothécaires et des Bibliophiles tenu à Paris, 3–9 avril 1923. *Procès-verbaux et Mémoires* (Paris: Jouve, 1925), 454–455.

Grabmann, M.: *Mittelalterliches Geistesleben* (Munich: Heuber, 1936); II:424–489, "Hilfsmittel des Thomasstudiums aus alter Zeit."

Haskins, Charles H.: *Studies in Medieval Culture* (Oxford: Clarendon Press, 1929); pp. 36–71, "University of Paris in the Sermons of the Thirteenth Century."

Humphreys, K. W.: *The Book Provisions of the Medieval Friars* (Amsterdam: Erasmus, 1964).

Legge, Mary D.: *Anglo-Norman Literature and Its Background* (Oxford: Clarendon Press, 1963).

Marigo, Aristide: "Cultura letteraria e preumanistica nelle maggiori enciclopedie del dugento: lo 'Speculum' ed il 'Tresors'," *Giornale storico della letteratura italiana,* 68:1–42, 289–326, 1916. (In a complete but unpublished English translation on file at Kent State University's School of Library Science.)

Rouse, Richard A.: "Bostonus Buriensis and the Author of the *Catalogus Scriptorum Ecclesiae,*" *Speculum,* 41:471–499, 1966.

Savage, Ernest A.: *Special Librarianship in General Libraries, and other papers* (London: Grafton, 1939); pp. 285–310, "Cooperative Bibliography in the 13th and 15th Centuries."

Se Boyar, G. E.: "Bartholomaeus Anglicus and His Encyclopaedia," *Journal of English and Germanic Philology,* 19:168–189, 1920.

Smalley, Beryl: *The Study of the Bible in the Middle Ages,* 2d ed. (Oxford: Blackwell, 1952).

CHAPTER FOUR

Bay, J. C.: "Conrad Gesner, the Father of Bibliography," Bibliographical Society of America *Papers,* 10:53–88, 1916.

Cassirer, Ernst: *The Individual and the Cosmos in Renaissance Philosophy* (tr. from the German of 1927; Harper, 1953; Torchbook 1097, 1964).

Chappell, A. F.: "Rabelais and the Authority of the Ancients," *Modern Language Review,* 18:29–36; 1923.

Csapodi, Csaba, "Die Bibliotheca Corviniana und die Ergebnisse der neueren Forschungen," *Zentralblatt für Bibliothekswesen,* 85:577–588, 1971.

Connolly, B.: "Jesuit Library Beginnings," *Library Quarterly,* 32:133–147, 1962.

Davis, Charles T.: "The Early Collection of Books of S. Croce in Florence," American Philosophical Society *Proceedings,* 107:399–414, 1963.

Escher, Hermann: "Konrad Gessner über Aufstellung und Katalogisierung von Bibliotheken," *Mélanges Offerts à Marcel Godet* (Neuchâtel: Attinger, 1937), pp. 119–127.

Febvre, Lucien [et al.]: *L'Apparition du Livre* (Paris: Michel, 1958).

Fischer, Hans: "Conrad Gesner (1516–1565) as Bibliographer and Encyclopedist," *The Library,* 5th ser., 21:269–281, 1966.

Goldfriedrich, Johann: *Geschichte des Deutschen Buchhandels* (Leipzig: Verlag des B.D.B., 1886–1913).

Hill, Christopher: *Intellectual Origins of the English Revolution* (Oxford: Clarendon Press, 1965).

Hirsch, Rudolph: *Printing, Selling, and Reading, 1450–1550* (Wiesbaden: Harrassowitz, 1967).

Jayne, Sears: *Library Catalogues of the English Renaissance* (Berkeley: University of California Press, 1956).

Karl, Louis: "Le Roi Matthias de Hunyad, Mécène et Bibliophile," *La Bibliofilia,* 36:370–382, 1934.

Keller, Abraham C.: "The Idea of Progress in Rabelais," *Publications of the Modern Language Association,* 66:235–243, 1951.

Kristeller, Paul: *Renaissance Thought* (New York: Harper Torchbook 1048, 1961).

Malclès, L.-N.: *La Bibliographie* (Paris: Presses Universitaires de France, 1962).

Montgomery, John W.: "Luther and Libraries," *Library Quarterly,* 32:133–147, 1962.

Ong, Walter: *Ramus: Method, and the Decay of Dialogue* (Cambridge: Harvard University Press, 1958).

Phillips, Margaret M.: *The "Adages" of Erasmus* (Cambridge University Press, 1964).

Randall, John H.: *The School of Padua and the Emergence of Modern Science* (Padova: Editrice Antenore, 1961).

Réthi, Charlotte: "Das ungarische Bibliothekswesen . . . ," *Bibliothek und Wissenschaft,* 4:120–124, 1967.

Robb, Nesca A.: *Neoplatonism of the Italian Renaissance* (London: Allen & Unwin, 1935).

Schutz, Alexander H.: "Why Did Rabelais Satirize the Library of St. Victor?" *Modern Language Notes,* 70:39–41, 1955.

Seton-Watson, R. W.: "The Abbot Trithemius," *Tudor Studies Presented . . . to Albert Frederick Pollard* (London: Longmans, 1924), pp. 75–89.

Taylor, Archer: *A History of Bibliographies of Bibliographies* (New Brunswick, N.J.: Scarecrow Press, 1955); *Renaissance Guides to Books* (Berkeley: University of California Press, 1945).

Ullman, Berthold L.: "Some Aspects of the Origin of Italian Humanism," *Philological Quarterly,* 20:212–223, 1941; "Renaissance—the Word and the Underlying Concept," *Studies in Philology,* 49:105–118, 1952.

Weiss, Roberto: *Humanism in England during the Fifteenth Century* (Oxford: Blackwell, 1957).

Witty, Francis J.: "Early Indexing Techniques . . . ," *Library Quarterly,* 35:141–148, 1965.

Woodward, William H.: *Studies in Education during the Age of the Renaissance, 1400–1600* (Cambridge University Press, 1906).

Yates, Frances: *Giordano Bruno and the Hermetic Tradition* (University of Chicago Press, 1964).

CHAPTER FIVE

Aston, Trevor H., ed.: *Crisis in Europe, 1560–1660* (New York: Basic Books, 1965), pp. 195–222 (M. Roberts), "Queen Christina and the General Crisis of the Seventeenth Century."

Blum, Rudolf: "Bibliotheca Memmiana, Untersuchungen zu Gabriel Naudés 'Avis . . . '," *Bibliotheca Docet: Festgabe für Carl Wehmer* (Amsterdam: Erasmus, 1963), pp. 209–232.

Boer, Josephine de: "Men's Literary Circles in Paris, 1610–1660," *Publications of the Modern Language Association,* 53:730–780, 1938.

Brown, Harcourt: *Scientific Organizations in Seventeenth Century France (1620–1680)* (New York: Russell & Russell, 1967 reprint of 1934 publication).

Conley, C. H.: *The First English Translators of the Classics* (New Haven: Yale University Press, 1927).

Davidson, Allan: "Catholics and Bodley," *Bodleian Library Record,* 8:252–257, 1971.

Estienne, Henri: *The Frankfort Book Fair . . . ;* edited . . . by James W. Thompson (1911; reprinted New York: B. Franklin, 1968).

La Grande Encyclopédie (Paris: Lamirault, 1886–1902): "Naudé" (24).

Jones, Richard F., and others: *The Seventeenth Century . . .* (Stanford University Press, 1951); especially pp. 264–290 (George B. Parks), "Travel as Education."

Lawler, John: *Book Auctions in England in the Seventeenth Century* (London: Stock, 1898).

Leyh, Georg: "Grundsätzliches aus der Geschichte der Bibliotheken," *Zentralblatt für Bibliothekswesen,* 57:337–351, 1940.

Loemker, Leroy, E.: "Leibniz and the Herborn Encyclopedists," *Journal of the History of Ideas,* 22:323–338, 1961.

Malclès, L.-N.: "Le Fondateur de la Bibliographie Nationale en France . . .: Louis-Jacob . . . (1608–1670)," *Mélanges d'Histoire du Livre et des Bibliothèques offerts à M. Frantz Calot* (Paris: D'Argences, 1960), pp. 245–256.

Masirovits, Susan: "The Jesuit Libraries in Spanish America, 1573–1767," unpublished M.L.S. research paper, Kent State University School of Library Science, 1972.

Naudé, Gabriel: *Lettres Inédites d'Italie à Peiresc, 1632–1636,* ed. P. Tamizey de Larroque (Paris: Techenez, 1887).

Pollard, Graham, and A. Ehrman: *The Distribution of Books by Catalogue from the Invention of Printing to A.D. 1800 . . .* (Cambridge: Roxburghe Club, 1965).

Rice, James V.: *Gabriel Naudé* (Baltimore: Johns Hopkins Press, 1939).

Rossi, Paolo: *Francis Bacon . . .* (University of Chicago Press, 1968).

Schunke, Ilse: "Die Systematischen Ordnunugen und ihre Entwicklung . . . ," *Zentralblatt für Bibliothekswesen,* 44:377–400, 1927.

Seaborne, Malcolm: *The English School: Its architecture and organization, 1370–1870* (London: Routledge and Paul, 1971).

Thorndike, Lynn: *History of Magic and Experimental Science* (New York: Macmillan, 1923–1938); vols. VII–VIII: "The Seventeenth Century."

Yates, Frances A.: *The Art of Memory* (University of Chicago Press, 1966).

CHAPTER SIX

Ariès, Philippe: *Centuries of Childhood* (New York: Knopf, 1962).

Bock, Friedrich: "Zur Geschichte des Schlagwortskatalog in Praxis und Theorie," *Zentralblatt f. B.,* 40:494–502, 1923.

Clarke, Jack A.: "Librarians to the King, the Bignons, 1642–1784," *Library Quarterly,* 36:293–298, 1966.

Concha, Carlos: "The Oldest University in South America," *Hispanic American Historical Review,* 9:107–114, 1929.

English Bibliographical Sources: Series I: Periodical Lists of New Publications (1699–1766) (London: Gregg [reprints] 1964–1966).

Fisher, Lillian E.: "Teodoro de Croix," *Hispanic American Historical Review,* 9:488–504, 1929.

Guhrauer, Edward G.: "Bibliothekarisches aus Leibnizes Lebens und Schriften," *Serapeum,* 12:1–30, 1851.

Kaufman, Paul: "English Book Clubs and Their Role in Social History," *Libri,* 14:1–31, 1964–1965.

Keogh, Andrew: "Bishop Berkeley's Gift of Books to Yale in 1733," *Overbibliotekar Wilhelm Munthe* . . . (Oslo: Grøndahl, 1933), pp. 128–147.

Kern, Marie: *Daniel Georg Morhof* (Leipzig: Harrassowitz, 1928).

König, Helmut: *Zur Geschichte der Nationalerziehung in Deutschland im Letzten Drittel des 18. Jahrhunderts* (Berlin: Akademie Verlag, 1960).

Lanning, John T.: *The University of the Kingdom of Guatemala* (Ithaca, N.Y.: Cornell University Press, 1955).

Leonard, Irving A.: "On the Mexican Book Trade, 1683," *Hispanic American Historical Review,* 27:403–435, 1947.

McGill, Esther: "The Evergreen Tree of Diabolical Knowledge," *Bookman,* 73: 267–272, 1939.

Morison, Samuel Eliot: *Founding of Harvard College* (Cambridge: Harvard University Press, 1935); *Harvard College in the Seventeenth Century* (Cambridge: Harvard University Press, 1936); *The Intellectual Life of Colonial New England,* 2d ed, (New York: New York University Press, 1956).

Paulsen, Friedrich: *Geschichte des Gelehrten Unterrichts auf den Deutschen Schulen und Universitäten* . . . (3.Aufl.; Leipzig: Veit, 1919–1921).

Pivec-Stelè, Melitta: "Mittelalterliche Bibliotheken in Slowenien," *Orbis mediaevalis: Festgabe für Anton Blaschka* . . . (Weimar: H. Bühlaus Nachfolger, 1970), pp. 174–191.

Predeek, Albert: "Bibliotheksbesuche eines Gelehrten Reisenden in Anfangs des 18. Jahrhunderts," *Zentralblatt f. B.,* 45:393–407, 1928.

Ranz, Jim: *The Printed Book Catalogue in American Libraries, 1723-1900* (Chicago: American Library Association, 1964).

Sutherland, Stella H.: *Population Distribution in Colonial America* (New York: AMS Press, 1966c36).

Townsend, Henry: *The Claims of the Free Churches* (London: Hodder and Stoughton, 1949).

Verner, Mathilde: "Adrien Baillet . . . ," *Library Quarterly,* 38:217-230, 1968.

Verona, Eva: "Die Aufhebung der kroatischen Klosterbibliotheken unter Josef II," *Festschrift Josef Stummvoll* . . . (Wien: Hollinek, 1970), pp. 439-452.

Wilson, Arthur M.: *Diderot . . . 1713-1759* (New York: Oxford University Press, 1957).

Also Recommended (available too late for proper use here)

Kaufman, Paul: "Community Libraries in 18th Century Europe," *Libri,* 22:1-57, 1972.

Prüsener, Marlies: "Lesegesellschaften im 18. Jahrhundert," *Archiv für Geschichte des Buchwesens,* 13-1/2:189-301, February 1972.

CHAPTER SEVEN

Butts, Robert F.: *The College Charts Its Course* . . . (New York: McGraw-Hill, 1939).

Clayton, Howard: "The American College Library, 1800-1860," *Journal of Library History,* 3:120-137, 1968.

Ditzion, Sidney: "The Anglo-American Library Scene . . . ," *Library Quarterly,* 16:281-301, 1946; and "Mechanics and Mercantile Libraries," *L.Q.,* 10:192-219, 1940.

Jackson, Sidney L.: *America's Struggle for Free Schools . . . 1827-1842* (Washington: American Council on Public Affairs, 1941).

Marwinski, Felicitas: "Karl Benjamin Preuskers Bibliothekspropagandistisches Wirken zur Hebung der Volksbildung . . . ," *Z. f. B.* 85:449-452, 518-529, 1971.

McMullen, Haynes: "College Libraries in Ante-Bellum Kentucky," *The Register of the Kentucky Historical Society,* 60:106-133, April 1962; *The Founding of Social and Public Libraries in Ohio, Indiana and Illinois through 1850* (University of Illinois Library School Occasional Papers, no. 51, March 1958); "Social Libraries in Ante-Bellum Kentucky," *The Register of the Kentucky Historical Society,* 58:97-128, April 1960; "Special Libraries in Ante-Bellum Kentucky," *The Register of the Kentucky Historical Society,* 59:29-46, January 1961.

Munford, W. A.: "George Birkbeck and Mechanics Institutes," *English Libraries, 1800-1850* (London: University College, 1958), pp. 33-58.

Peckham, Howard H.: "Books and Reading on the Ohio Valley Frontier," *Mississippi Valley Historical Review*, 44:649-663, 1957-1958.

Reisner, Edward H.: *Nationalism and Education since 1789* (New York: Macmillan, 1922).

Also Recommended (available too late for proper use here)

Ellis, Alec: *Library Services for Young People in England and Wales, 1830-1970* (Oxford: Pergamon, 1971).

Hassenforder, Jean, *Développement comparé des bibliothèques publiques en France, en Grande-Bretagne et aux États-Unis dans la seconde moitié du XIXe siècle (1850-1914)* (Paris: Cercle de la Librairie, 1967).

Le Livre et la Lecture en France (Paris: les Éditions Ouvrières, 1968).

Riberette, Pierre: *Les Bibliothèques Françaises pendant la Révolution (1789-1795)* (Paris: Bibliothèque Nationale, 1970).

CHAPTER EIGHT

Bestor, Arthur E.: "The Transformation of American Scholarship, 1875-1917," *Library Quarterly*, 23:164-179, 1953.

Cecil, H. L. and W. Heaps, *School Library Service in the United States* (New York: H. W. Wilson, 1940).

Csapodi, Csaba: "Geschichte der ungarischen Bibliotheken," *Biblos*, 19:276-285, 1970.

Ditzion, Sidney: *Arsenals of a Democratic Culture* (Chicago: American Library Association, 1947).

Esdaile, Arundell: *National Libraries of the World . . . ,* 2d. ed. rev. by Hill (London: The Library Association, 1957).

Feyl, Othmar: "Bücher, Bibliotheken und Leser in der russischen Gesellschaft des 19. Jahrhunderts," *Festschrift zum 60. Geburtstag von Hans Lülfing am 24. November 1966* (Leipzig: VEB Bib. Inst., 1966; 83. *Beiheft zum Zentralblatt für Bibliothekswesen*), pp. 97-133.

Gottlieb, Fritz: "Die deutsche Bibliotheksbewegung der vierziger Jahre," *Zentralblatt für Bibliothekswesen*, 31:489-501, 1914.

Jaeschke, Emil: *Volksbibliotheken (Bücher- und Lesehallen) . . .* (Leipzig: Göschen, 1907).

Joeckel, Carleton B.: *The Government of the American Public Library* (Chicago: University of Chicago Press, 1935).

Kalisch, Philip A.: *The Enoch Pratt Free Library . . .* (Metuchen, N.J.: Scarecrow, 1969).

Long, Harriet G.: *Public Library Service to Children . . .* (Metuchen, N.J.: Scarecrow, 1969).

Monroe, Paul, ed.: *A Cyclopedia of Education* (New York: Macmillan, 1911-1913).

Munford, W. A.: *Penny Rate* . . . (London: The Library Association, 1951).

Murison, William J.: *The Public Library* . . . (London: Harrap, 1955).

Richie, Joan F.: "Railroad Reading Rooms and Libraries in Ohio, 1865–1900," unpublished M.L.S. thesis, Kent State University School of Library Science, 1964.

Rowland, Arthur R., comp.: *The Catalog and Cataloging* (Hamden, Conn.: Shoestring Press, 1969).

Thurber, Evangeline: "American Agricultural College Libraries, 1862–1900," *College and Research Libraries*, 6:346–352, 1944–1945.

Trichaud, Lucien: *L'Education Populaire en Europe. 1 . . . Grand-Bretagne* (Paris: Les Éditions Ouvrières, 1968).

Also Recommended (available too late for proper use here)

Allred, John R.: "The Purpose of the Public Library: The Historical View," *Library History*, 2(5):185–204, Spring 1972.

CHAPTER NINE

Barcus, Thomas R.: *The Carnegie Corporation and College Libraries, 1938–1943* (New York: Carnegie Corporation, 1943).

Bishop, William W.: *The Carnegie Corporation and College Libraries, 1928–1938* (New York: Carnegie Corporation, 1938).

Bol'shaîâ Sovetskaîâ Entsiklopediîâ, 2.izd. (Moskva, 1957): "Khavkina, L. B." (46:20), "Shaniavskii, A. L." (47:524), "Shaniavskogo Universitet" (47:524).

Dangotte-Limbosch, R. C.: "Les Bibliothèques pour Enfants à Gand," *Revue des Bibliothèques et Archives de Belgique*, 7:263–275, 1909.

Fonotov, G. P.: "Lenin and Libraries," *UNESCO Bulletin for Libraries*, 24:118–125, 1970.

Generalitat de Catalunya. *Escola de Bibliotecàries, 1932–33* (Barcelona, 1933).

Kildal, Arne: "American Influence on European Librarianship," *Library Quarterly*, 7:196–210, 1937.

Also Recommended (available too late for proper use here)

Bloomfield,Mark A.: "Between the Acts," *Library Review*, 22:359–362, 1969–1970.

Ellis, Alec: "Public Library Services for Children in England and Wales, 1928–1942," *Journal of Librarianship*, 3:41–59, 1971.

NAME INDEX

SUBJECT INDEX